this
business of
MUSIC

the definitive guide to the music industry

8th edition

M. William Krasilovsky and Sidney Shemel

Contributions by John M. Gross

Billboard Books
an imprint of Watson-Guptill Publications,
New York

Senior editor: Bob Nirkind
Production manager: Ellen Greene
Book and jacket design: Eric Baker Design Associates

First published by Billboard Books, an imprint of Watson-Guptill Publications,
a division of VNU Business Media, Inc.
770 Broadway
New York, NY 10003
www.watsonguptill.com

Library of Congress Cataloging-in-Publication Data

Krasilovsky, M. William
   This business of music: the definitive guide to the music industry/ M.
   William Krasilovsky and Sidney Shemel; contributions by John Gross.--8th ed.
      p. cm.
   Includes index.
   ISBN 0-8230-7757-8
      1. Music trade--United states. 2. Music--Economic aspects. 3. Copyright--
   Music. 4. Popular music--Writing and publishing. I. Shemel, Sidney, II. Title.

ML3790 .S5 2000
338.4'778'0973--dc21   00-032495

This book was printed using the Scala family of fonts and the Helvetica family of
fonts.

Manufactured in the United States

First printing, 2000

5 6 7 8 9 / 07 06 05 04 03 02

Dedication

In the memory of William Dawson, friend, client, teacher, music educator, arranger, composer, and conductor

Acknowledgments

We wish to acknowledge our special indebtedness for this revision to our research assistants, Tayo Kurzman and Tom Silis, as well as to the following persons: Lewis Bachman, Dr. Peter M. Boyle, Sue Collins, Ed Cramer, David Grossberg, Carol Hernandez, Ronald S. Kadden, Mike Kissel, Amy LaCour, Maxyne Lang, David Leibowitz, Ellen Meltzer-Zahn, Sverre Sundman Olofsson, Kenneth C. Pohlmann, Gary Roth, Dr. Ecke Schnabel, Gerald Schoenfeld, Jim Steinblatt, Sandy Thomas, William Velez, and Laurie Woog. Appreciation and gratitude are due to Charles J. Sanders of the National Music Publishers Association and to Steven J. D'Onofrio and Associates, Washington, D.C.

The outstanding assistance of the Billboard Books staff on all editions is gratefully acknowledged. Special appreciation is due to our editors, Bob Nirkind, Sylvia Warren, and Martha Cameron for their patience and care.

Table of Contents

Part Three Music Publisher and Writer Agreements and Practices

Part Four Other Aspects of the Music Business

Documents included on accompanying CD-ROM

Copyright Act of 1976

Sonny Bono Term Extension Act

Copyright Regulation 201: General Provisions

Copyright Regulation 202: Registration of Claims to
    Copyright

Copyright Office Information Circular 7B: "Best Edition"

Copyright Registration Forms:
    CA, PA, RE, SR, TX, VA, Document Cover Sheet

American Federation of Television and Radio Artists
    AFTRA Sound Recordings Code
    AFTRA Standard Exclusive Agency Contract Under Rule 12-B

American Federation of Musicians
    Exclusive Agent-Musician Agreement
    Contract Form L-2 (Local Engagement)
    Single-Engagement Collective Bargaining Agreement
    Contract T-2 (Traveling Engagements)

American Society of Composers, Authors & Publishers
    Writer Application
    Publisher Application
    Membership Agreement
    Digital Audio Royalty Form and Fact Sheet
    Request for Publishing Company Name Reservation
    ASCAP Credit Weighting Formula
    ASCAP Payment System Explained (*Playback* Magazine: April–May 1999;
    Aug.–Sept. 1999; Oct.–Nov. 1999; Jan. 2000)

Broadcast Music Inc.
BMI Writer Application
BMI Publisher Application
BMI Writer Affiliation Agreement
BMI Publisher Affiliation Agreement
BMI Work Registration Form
BMI Royalty Information Booklet

SESAC
Publisher Affiliation Agreement
Writer Affiliation Agreement

Songwriters Guild of America
Ten Basic Points Your Contract Should Include
Overview of the SGA Popular Songwriters Contract
Popular Songwriters Contract

Sample Agreements
Artist Inducement Letter
Certificate of Authorship
Commercial Jingle License
Copyright Assignment (Short Form)
Cue Sheet Sample (Television Film)
Demo Shopping Agreement (Producer/Artist)
Estimated Recording Budget
Foreign Subpublication Agreement (Short Form)
Grant of Terminated Rights
Joint Ownership of Copyright (Copublishing)
Licensing Recording for Film
Master License
Mechanical License (United States)
Notice of Termination Under Section 304(c) of P.L. 94-553 (90 STAT. 2541)
Personal Management Agreement
Photography Agreement
Popular Songwriter Contract—Single Song
Producer/Artist Agreement
Recording Artist Agreement (Exclusive)
Sale of Copyright
Songwriter Exclusive Copublishing Agreement
Synchronization and U.S. Theatrical Performing Rights License
Tour Agreement

Introduction

In the first edition of *This Business of Music*, published in 1964, we stated our goal as follows:

> This book has been written with a view towards assisting participants in the music and recording industries to understand the workings of the business and their rights and obligations. It is meant to present the economic facts for day-to-day decisions and actions and to act as a simplified guide to common legal concepts underlying business determinations. ... It is hoped that the participants in the music business may use this volume to increase their understanding of its practices both here and overseas.

We have maintained this goal throughout the book's various updates. Even a casual review of the revisions made in each edition shows the dramatic cultural, technological, and international changes that the music industry has had to respond to over the years. Some of the changes that we have highlighted in previous editions include:

- Copyright revision under the Copyright Act of 1976
- U.S. participation in the Berne Convention
- The rise of cable television
- The introduction of compact discs
- Changes in record distribution patterns
- The dominance of the major labels and music publishers

To some it might seem that this volatile industry has gone about as far as it can go. On the contrary, in this eighth edition we highlight major new challenges:

- The new technology of music on the Internet

- ▸ Digital record performance rights for record companies and artists
- ▸ New treaty agreements that aggressively enforce copyright protection
- ▸ Reduced record distribution by independents and a new reliance on the majors
- ▸ Revised markets in Europe as a result of the European Union (EU) and the introduction of the euro and other consolidated marketing practices
- ▸ New problems and opportunities resulting from major increases in film and stage investments in music
- ▸ Conformance with an international copyright duration at life plus 70 years

In the first edition of *This Business of Music*, we bravely estimated that record sales in the United States would reach $1 billion dollars by the year 1970. In the seventh edition, we reported that retail sales figures had grown to $10 billion as of 1993. By 1997, retail sales had reached $12.24 billion, almost one-third of the $38 billion world market. In this eighth edition we confidently forecast that, as a result of music sales through the Internet and downloading, digital audio broadcasting, and do-it-yourself custom-made compilation albums, unit sales will continue to increase, but the bottom line is impossible to predict.

In the seventh edition of *This Business of Music* we put forward a number of questions regarding the challenges posed by data banks, encoding, satellite broadcasting, video, and digital audio broadcasting ("streaming"). In this edition we devote a new chapter—Chapter 41—to these and other technological issues that have developed since the last publication.

In the late 1960s Marshal McCluhan stated: "The medium is the message." In the new millennium print, broadcast, and other performance or mechanical forms of reproduction are no longer discrete entities: the message is dominant and all media have converged. Print is now presented on a personal computer monitor in the same manner as film; records can be heard and downloaded via the same home computer. Music has become the essential ingredient in this mass convergence. Our goal in this edition, therefore, is not only to educate our readers about the customs and practices of the music business but also to give them useful tools for survival in this new world of media convergence.

Indeed, the new technology has become a dominant concern in the music industry. Lawyers question whether existing copyright and criminal laws are up to the challenge and, where necessary, focus on the need for new legislation to protect the industry in domestic and international commerce. We think it is likely that new forms of financial compensation will develop, but it is imperative that they remain consistent with the copyright clause of the Constitution: "To promote the progress of science and useful arts, by securing for limited times to authors the exclusive right to their writings and discoveries."

BE SURE TO VISIT OUR WEBSITE: *www.thisbusinessofmusic.org*

Part One

Music Business Trends
and Transformations

1

The Music Industry in the 1990s

This business of music is a dynamic and ever-changing field. Its consumers include amateur and professional performers as well as listeners. By the mid-1990s, 45 percent of American households included at least one member who played a musical instrument, the piano and the guitar being the two most popular. But according to a U.S. Department of Labor report, there were only 274,000 music-related jobs in 1996, and significant numbers of musicians were "between engagements." "Musicians often must supplement their income with earnings from other sources because they can find only part-time or sporadic employment," the report stated.

On the other hand, the category of "listener" encompasses practically the entire population. The average American 12 years old and older listens to about 25 hours of radio per week, much of it as background music in restaurants, hotel lobbies, elevators, and factories. People listen to music in airplanes, while playing video games or jogging, or while driving. Car radios alone reach four out of five adults.

Music is big business in the United States. There are about 10,300 commercial radio and 1,550 television stations in operation and an estimated 533 million radios and 175 million television sets in use. Ninety-nine percent of American homes have radios—an average of five or more—and 98 percent have at least one television set, which is on almost 7 hours a day.

In 1997, cable advertising alone reached $7.86 billion. By 1999, 67.2 percent of American homes with television had cable TV; over 66 million subscribers to some 10,700 cable systems generated more than $22 billion in total cable revenue. An estimated 85 percent of American households had videocassette recorders (VCRs), which were in use about 5 hours per week.

Finally, between 1997 and 1998 unit sales of prerecorded home music video programming rose 45.9 percent, from 18.6 million units to 27.2 million units, with a dollar value of $508 million. In 1998, digital versatile disc (DVD) music video shipments rose to 485,000 units, with a dollar value of $12.2 billion.

New technology has always had a dramatic effect on the music business, ever since the day Al Jolson sang "Mammy" in the first public demonstration of the "talkies" (motion pictures with sound). The industry has progressed from Edison's cylinder recordings to shellac 78 rpms, long-play 45 rpms and 33 1/3s, to 8-track tapes and cassettes, to compact discs (CDs), and DVD. Recording studios are relying more and more on synthesizers, drum machines, and digital equipment for recording, engineering, and mixing. And just as bar coding has made retail inventory control much more efficient, new methods are being developed to identify performance and mechanical rights with greater accuracy. In the late 1960s Marshal McCluhan stated: "The medium is the message." In the new millennium, the message is dominant and all media has converged.

Industry Growth

For 25 years, beginning in the mid-1950s, sales of sound recordings grew an average of 20 percent a year. The most dramatic growth came in the 1970s when sales (based on manufacturers' suggested list prices) rose from less than $2 billion at the beginning of the decade to over $4 billion in 1978; that year, however, sales began to fall sharply, reflecting in part the American economy as well as the effect of home taping.

But this situation changed in 1984. When compact discs (CDs) entered the consumer market, sales once again exceeded $4 billion. By 1988, the combined dollar volume of record, tape, and compact disc shipments rose to $6.25 billion, according to the Recording Industry Association of America (RIAA). By 1998 sales figures for combined audio and music video product had risen to $13.7 billion.

Between 1997 and 1998, CDs grew 15.1 percent, while cassette sales decreased 6.8 percent. Sales of CD singles dropped 21.8 percent. Vinyl LPs and singles continued to decline to relatively insignificant sales.

In 1994 the RIAA reported that rock, country, and pop registered as clear favorites among consumers. Country more than doubled in size over the previous five years, rock's share of the market came down from a high of 41.7 to a still impressive 35.1 percent, while rap decreased slightly from the prior year, to 7.9 percent. By 1998 the situation had changed: rock was now at 25.7 percent, country at 14.1 percent, R&B at 12.8 percent, and rap, at 9.7 percent, was slightly below pop, at 10 percent (see Table 1-1).

RIAA statistics show that by 1998 record stores were still the primary retail outlets for records and tapes, with 50.8 percent of the market, down from 56.2 percent in 1993 and 71.7 percent in 1989. Other retail outlets such as department stores, electronic stores, and mass merchant stores (K-Mart, Target, etc.) had captured 34.4 percent of the total market, a sizable increase from 15.6 percent in 1989. Nonretail outlets such as record clubs had their worst showing since 1990, with only 9 percent of the market, while other mail-order outlets achieved a slight increase to 2.9 percent. Finally, on-line sales grew to 1.1 percent of the market, tripling their 1997 market share and equaling television mail-order sales.

In other areas, aggregate annual sales of sheet music increased steadily from $309 million in 1988 to $433.5 million in 1997. According to the American Music Conference, the combined sales of musical instruments and accessories totaled $2.4 billion in 1998.

Collections by performing rights organizations have also climbed in this period. In 1998 the American Society of Composers, Authors, and Publishers (ASCAP), which included over 40,242 writers and 18,727 publishers, collected $508 million on behalf of its members, about 25 percent from foreign sources. In 1994 ASCAP collected $422.7 million, and in 1983 it collected $198 million.

Broadcast Music Inc. (BMI), which represents about 140,000 writers and 60,000 publishers, collected $455 million at the end of fiscal 1998. Foreign sources accounted for about 23 percent of total receipts in 1997. BMI reported collections of $242 million in 1989, $124.6 in 1984, and $34 million in 1970. The third U.S. performing rights organization, SESAC, would not make recent figures available; in 1983 it collected $5 million. According to SESAC, its membership includes some 2,000 writers and publishers and has a catalog of more than 200,000 compositions.

Factors Relating to Growth

New technology has been responsible for much of the industry's growth. In 1948 the LP was introduced; stereo dominated toward the close of the 1960s.

Table 1-1

Percent of Market for All Music Genres, 1989, 1993, and 1998

	1989	1993	1998
Rock	41.7%	30.2%	25.7%
Country	7.3	18.7	14.1
R&B	9.5	10.6	12.8
Rap	6.4	9.2	9.7
Pop	15.0	11.9	10.0
Gospel	3.1	3.2	6.3
Classical	3.6	3.3	3.3
Jazz	4.9	3.1	1.9
Oldies	0.9	1.0	0.7
Soundtracks	0.7	0.7	1.7
New Age	1.4	1.0	0.6
Children's	0.3	0.4	0.4
Other (includes Latin)	4.0	4.6	7.9

Source: Recording Industry Association of America, 1998 Consumer Profile.

Prerecorded cartridges and cassettes, which were introduced in the mid-1960s, opened an entirely new market for record manufacturers. In 1983, cassettes became the configuration of choice, but by 1993 CDs dominated unit sales, with cassettes constituting only about 35 percent of unit sales and vinyl less than 1 percent.

Today's technology includes digital audio tape (DAT), the tape counterpart to the CD. DAT tapes are smaller than the standard cassette and permit up to 2 hours of programming—more than twice as much as a CD. However, unlike the practically indestructible CD, DAT tape deteriorates. DVD audio may render DAT obsolete as this technology promises even greater programming capacity and carries no threat of deterioration.

Videocassettes and videocassette recorders (VCRs) have also accounted for considerable growth. VCR sales passed the $1 billion mark by 1981 and increased rapidly to over $5 billion by 1986. By 1998, 85 percent of all American households were equipped with VCRs. In 1993 videocassette rentals and purchases totaled $133.2 billion. Whether the videocassettes were full-length films with background or incidental music or musical motion pictures or concerts, the music industry gained substantially from this market. Although for a while laser discs did cut into the audiovisual market, the prevailing trend indicates that DVDs are the wave of the future, offering superior home viewing.

Industry growth over the last few decades can also be attributed to new marketing methods: rack jobbing, mail-order and record clubs, and, most recently, the Internet. Rack jobbing was introduced in the mid-1950s; record companies set up and maintained large-scale displays of records and tapes in supermarkets, variety stores, department and discount stores, drugstores, and other retail outlets.

In the 1950s record companies set up clubs to target older consumers. CBS created the Columbia House Club in 1955; since 1991 it has been jointly owned by Sony (CBS's successor) and Time Warner. The RCA Record Club, which was first created in 1958, is now known as BMG Direct Marketing and is an affiliate of Bertelsmann Music Group. As of 1998, record club sales had declined to 9 percent of the total U.S. market, supplemented by other direct marketing of another 2.9 percent. Germany, the United Kingdom, and the Netherlands have an even higher percentage of total sales through clubs. Market research suggests that aging baby boomers prefer the convenience of record clubs to the noise and hassle of shopping malls and large retail outlets.

By the end of the 1990s, on-line record stores and chains such as CDNow, Music Boulevard, Tower, and Sam Goody, as well as on-line bookstores such as amazon.com and barnesandnoble.com, were targeting both the older home shopper and the young, college-aged computer browser through the Internet, offering an immense selection of mail-order CDs, DVDs, videocassettes, and tapes.

It is widely believed that there is a long-term benefit to the music industry in the expansion of leisure time in United States. Older persons have more income upon retirement , and those who continue in the current workforce have larger entertainment budgets. In 1998, consumers 45 years and older accounted for 18.1 percent of the record-buying market; this was an increase of 1.6 percent over the previous year and almost double the market share of 1988. However, experts predict that market share in this age group will decline considerably over the next 10 years as the number of Americans age 35 and 40 years is expected to decrease by roughly 13 percent by 2008. The most active buyers in the music industry, the under-30 group, will be a proportionately larger part of the market, and we can expect merchandising and advertising strategies to shift accordingly.

Demographic shifts have opened up new domestic markets. According to SoundScan, Latin music sales for the first 6 months of 1998 were 6.941 million units; this represents an 11 percent increase from the same point in 1997. The U.S. Hispanic market has been steadily increasing since 1993, except for a temporary 12 percent decrease in sales for 1997. Figures for 1999 are even more promising. They show a substantial increase in audio and video unit sales, as well as higher dollar sales due to increased sales of CDs over lower-priced cassettes and a 16 percent increase in dollar sales from 1993, to $570.8 million.

In 1999, 454 U.S. radio stations were broadcasting full-time in Spanish, up from 365 in 1993. Audience share was 6 percent of total U.S. radio listeners, up from 5 percent in 1996. Unfortunately, most of the advertisers are local, and therefore less profitable than national advertisers, which have been slow to buy time on Latin stations. Nevertheless, ad expenditures for Spanish language radio amounted to $15 billion in 1998, representing a significant market for Latin music.

The countries that now form the European Union have lowered their trade barriers. This is having profound effects on the music business. It has led to both consolidation and competition among the various European subpublishers, record companies, and performance and mechanical collection societies. In the open-border world of Europe, the legality of exclusivity within any area of the European Union must be called into question. Some "social and cultural" national favoritism is allowed, but with international broadcast programming, deregulation of broadcasting, and joint film production and marketing, the goal of having a consolidated European market that nearly matches the North American seems to be viable.

Factors Inhibiting Growth

The RIAA estimates that lost sales due to counterfeiting, piracy, and bootleg-ging amount to over $1 million *every day* in North America. According to an RIAA study, home taping has resulted in lost sales of records and prerecorded tapes equal to 325 million albums annually, or about $1.5 billion a year.

Recently, the music industry has been concerned about DAT technology. Initially, it opposed the introduction of DAT into the United States because it was afraid that DAT would stunt the CD market and result in mass home duplication of high-quality recordings, with an attendant loss of compensation to record companies, artists, and music publishers. Ultimately, the copyright industries and the manufacturers of DAT equipment reached an agreement, which was officially legislated in the Audio Home Recording Act (AHRA) of 1992. (See Chapter 7, "Copyright Sound Recordings.") As of 1999, neither the expectations nor the fears of the interested parties had been fully realized. Nevertheless, growth trends of all digital devices as a form of broadcast entertainment are being closely observed.

Another industry concern involves compressed digital-format files, most commonly known as MP3 files, which can easily be downloaded from the Web free of charge. In 1999, the RIAA sent a mass notification to pressing plants warning them against making bootleg records from such downloaded MP3 files. Subsequently, it successfully litigated a number of cases, including one in which over 1.5 million illegal CDs were impounded. In 1988, the RIAA sent educational material to over 200 colleges in an effort to reduce large-scale MP3 downloading practices on campus. In 1999, several major universities cooperated with the RIAA in denying university Internet facilities to students posting unlicensed CDs on MP3 files. Its more traditional campaigns against flea market vendors resulted in seizures of over 300,000 pirated cassettes in 1998, with guilty pleas and convictions rising to 204 for the year.

Chaotic distribution and intense competition have also inhibited growth in the record industry. Rising business costs and uncertain conditions in the music industry have made it difficult for small record companies to continue independently. As a result, many have made manufacturing and distribution arrangements with major record companies. Independent record distributors, who used to rely for hits on these larger independent record companies, have lost considerable ground, and many have gone bankrupt.

Proposed Legislative Changes

When he was presiding over of the U.S. Patent Office, Thomas Jefferson stated: "Laws and institutions must go hand in hand with the progress of the human mind. As that becomes more developed, more enlightened, as new discoveries are made...institutions must advance also to keep pace with the times. We might as well require a man to wear still the coat which fitted him when a boy." Technological advancements necessitate legislative review and changes. Since 1994, significant and timely legislative changes have occurred in rapid succession, largely in response to new requirements under the Berne Convention and the General Agreement on Tariffs and Trade (GATT) and to the need for artist digital performance rights. The new statutes are as follows:

- 1994: Uruguay Round Agreements Act passed by the World Trade Organization.
- 1995: Digital Performance Right in Sound Recordings
- 1997: No Electronics Theft Act, which defined criminal acts in digital recording.
- 1998: Technical correction to 1976 Copyright Act, which amended the definition of *publication* to include pre-1978 sound recordings.
- 1998: Digital Millennium Copyright Act, in compliance with the World Intellectual Property Organization (WIPO) treaty to prohibit the falsification, alteration, or removal of copyright management data on digital copies
- 1998: Sonny Bono Term Extension Act, to conform to copyright duration in other major nations
- 1999: Fairness in Music Licensing Act, which exempts small restaurants and shops from performance licensing

Each of these is reviewed in the various chapters concerning nature of copyright, sound recording copyright, duration of copyright, and international copyright.

Part Two

Record Industry Agreements and Practices

2

Recording Artist Contracts

A lot of kids dream of becoming recording stars, of being the next Bruce Springsteen or Lauryn Hill, Ricky Martin or Shania Twain. But it's often a long, tough road between the dream and the recording contract. Would-be stars must first make contact with a record producer or an A&R (artists and repertoire) executive, usually through a recommendation from a friend, an agent, another artist, or a music publisher. Or they may put a demonstration record into a producer's hands or get a break simply by haunting the offices of the record companies. Assuming that their talent has been recognized and they have been offered a recording contract, artists must then negotiate a fair and reasonable agreement. For this, they need an understanding of the basic elements of a standard recording contract and, preferably, the aid and advice of a knowledgeable representative, such as a manager or an attorney.

The Standard Agreement

Under the standard agreement, the artist is engaged to render his or her personal services as a recording artist on an exclusive basis for the purpose of making recordings from which phonograph records can be manufactured. (The accompanying CD-ROM contains a sample exclusive "Recording Artist Agreement.") The term *phonograph records* encompasses compact discs, cassettes, and any and all other devices, including audiovisual devices (i.e., videos) that contain the artist's recorded performances. A *device* includes all technology, whether presently known or invented in the future, that is capable of transmitting music through cyberspace, with the possible exception of digital audio broadcasting.

The artist is required to appear at times and places designated by the record company to perform for recordings. Although the standard agreement states that the musical selections to be recorded will be selected by the record company, in practice the company will give the artist a voice in this decision. (This is discussed in more detail under "The Selection of Material," page 18.)

When dealing with any union-affiliated label, the artist is required to be a union member, or become one within 30 days, and must be paid no less than union scale as established in agreements with the applicable union, either the American Federation of Television and Radio Artists (AFTRA) or the American Federation of Musicians (AFM). Most artists receive an advance that is in excess of union scale. Each of the major labels is union-affiliated.

The record company agrees to pay all recording costs, including artist's advances; fees to the producer-arranger, the copyist, and the musicians; studio and equipment rental charges; and mixing and editing costs. These recording costs are deemed to be advances against, and recoupable out of, royalties that might otherwise be paid to the artist.

Duration of the Contract

The standard contract runs for a term based on the delivery of a minimum number of recordings (usually enough to constitute one album) plus a period of time thereafter (usually 9 months). The record company may have an option to extend the agreement for one or more successive albums. Even when the contract period is stated in years, a contract year is invariably connected with the delivery of a product, since the passage of time without the delivery of recordings is of no interest to a record company.

Most recording contracts are signed in or otherwise made subject to the laws of New York State or California. Under California law a personal service contract that runs more than 7 years cannot be specifically enforced. New York does not have a maximum term for such contracts; only a court of law can decide whether the length of an exceptionally long-term commitment violates public policy. Contracts with minors are special situations that may require shorter contract terms. (See Chapter 3, "Contracts with Minors.")

If an artist fails to perform, most recording contracts permit a suspension of the contract and a corresponding extension of the period during which the record company has the exclusive right to the artist's recording services. Theoretically, if the artist continues to fail to perform, he or she could be bound indefinitely. However, courts have generally tended to grant relief to the artist. For example, in *Vanguard Recording Society, Inc. v. V. Kweskin,* 276 F. Supp. 563 (S.D.N.Y. 1967), a New York federal court refused to enjoin the artist Jim Kweskin from performing for a different record company where enforcement of a suspension clause for an indefinite period would make the contract "harsh and unreasonable."

MCA Records brought an action in California state court to prevent the recording artist Olivia Newton-John from recording for another label after an alleged breach by the artist in the delivery of recordings. The court of appeals stated that the artist could not be prevented from recording for another company for a period longer than the one in which her commitments to MCA could have been fully performed. This was considered to be 5 years: an initial period of 2 years plus three 1-year options. MCA unsuccessfully contended that the term could be extended for up to 7 years by reason of contractual language permitting suspension until the delivery of recordings was completed. As a consequence, record companies usually define the duration of a recording contract in terms of delivery of a stipulated number of albums, not in terms of a stated number of years. (See *MCA Records, Inc. v. Newton-John*, 90 Cal. App. 3d 18 [1979])

Under section 3423 of the California Labor Code, record companies must pay a guaranteed minimum amount per year before they can obtain an injunction against an artist attempting to leave a label while still under exclusive contract. The minimum payment schedule is as follows:

> Year 1: $9,000
> Year 2: $12,000
> Years 3–7: $15,000

Recording budgets and tour support payments are not part of this guaranteed minimum amount.

It is essential to note that this California statute relates to obtaining a court order barring recording for another company, but does not affect the continuing right to sue for monetary damages for any such forbidden recording. However, no injunction can be obtained in a California court without the applicable minimum compensation. These sums must be guaranteed payment obligations and not merely contingent amounts paid under a royalty deal without advance or guarantee. However, the "contingent" factor of earned royalties can be used to pay the additional sums required in years 4 and 5 ($15,000) and in years 6 and 7 ($30,000) as long as such sums are actually paid. Any amounts earned in excess of statutory minimums in any particular year can be carried forward as a credit for the next or subsequent years' minimums.

A fail-safe clause in the California law provides that an artist can still be prevented from terminating an agreement that is not in conformity with the requirements of the law if the record company makes a lump-sum payment to the artist that is 10 times the required minimums. For example, if the first year guarantee of $9,000 were missing, a record company could still make a $90,000 late payment to prevent an artist from terminating by reason of the omission. This is appropriately called the "superstar insurance provision."

All major-label or other union-affiliated recording contracts with instrumentalists must be approved by the American Federation of Musicians. If a contract is not rejected within 30 working days of submission, it is deemed approved. The AFM's standard recording contract favors agreements that do not extend beyond 5 years.

Group Artists

A recording contract may cover two or more artists who perform together as a group. In addition to acquiring the exclusive right to the group's recording services, the record company acquires the exclusive right to use the group's name on records during the term of the agreement. If the group has recorded previously on another label, the contract may include a provision recognizing the right of the first record company to continue using the group name on its recordings.

The time may come when, for various reasons, the group members' paths diverge. When a group member drops out, a satisfactory replacement must be found. This may cause problems between the record company and the remaining group members. The record company may wish to select or approve the replacement so as to ensure the continuation of the group's special sound or quality, but the group may fight for the right to select its own replacement.

The record company may also contend that it is entitled to continue to record the dropout artist as a solo artist, especially if the departing member is a standout performer in the group. The terms of an agreement covering a potential solo artist entail separate negotiations when the group is first signed. The provisions ordinarily run the gamut of those commonly contained in a solo artist agreement, including the initial period of the recording contract, renewal options, royalties, advances, and recording and release commitments.

In some instances, an A&R person may propose that two artists under separate agreements perform together on one or more records. A combined recording made by well-known artists, for example, Julio Iglesias and Willie Nelson, may achieve greater sales than records featuring each artist separately. Record contracts anticipate the royalty problems created in such cases by providing that the royalties and the joint recording costs be apportioned among the artists according to a formula specified in the contract.

Exclusivity

Record companies customarily acquire the exclusive right to record an artist during the term of the recording agreement. Without exclusivity, different companies could issue competing versions of an artist's recordings, with resultant confusion. Furthermore, a record company would probably be unwilling to spend time and money developing and promoting an artist if the artist were also recording for other labels at the same time.

Exceptions to exclusivity do exist, especially in classical music and jazz. An artist with sufficient clout may also negotiate separate distribution agreements for different geographical territories; in such cases the artist is in effect exclusive to different record companies in different territories. In these instances, record companies will seek appropriate contractual assurances that new recordings will be made available to every company at the same time. Otherwise buyers might purchase records imported from outside the territory, thus undermining the company that has exclusive distribution rights in that territory.

Many performers make a livelihood performing as *sidemen*. They are not the featured performers on recordings, and they are not prominently highlighted on the album cover, packaging, or advertising. Most exclusive recording artist contracts cover any and all recording services except where waived specially. Accordingly, it is desirable to specify the terms and conditions under which sideman services can be performed for other record companies. Typical negotiated terms require credit to the artist's regular record company, such as "courtesy of ..."; limitation of name credit as sideman other than on the front of the album cover; a maximum of two or threes songs on which the sideman services can be used in any one album; and sometimes a limitation to no-royalty status.

Artists may wish to be part of a movie soundtrack album distributed by another record company. The artist's own record company may feel that this exception to its exclusivity is worthwhile, since it promotes the exposure of the artist. Much depends on the bargaining position of the parties as well as the concessions made by the distributor of the soundtrack album. These concessions may include proper credit to the artist's label and royalty payments to the artist's record label. Generally, the artist's record company will reserve the right to distribute its artist's recording as a "single" or to include it in the artist's own albums, possibly with the right to refer to the movie itself for added promotional effect.

The recording contract usually forbids recording the same selection for another company for a minimum period of time. This is known as the *re-recording restriction*. In most contracts the restrictive period is 5 years from the date of delivery of the recording to the record label or 2 years from the expiration of the term of the recording contract, whichever is later. During this period the record company cannot be faced with competition by the same artist performing the same material.

Recording and Release Requirements

A recording agreement sets forth the minimum number of sides to be recorded during each contract year. A *side* customarily consists of a single composition with a minimum duration of 2 ½ minutes. The minimum number of sides for an album is usually 10 to 12. The agreement may also state that the artist will make additional recordings at the company's request. Sometimes the parties agree that an excess over a certain maximum number of recordings must be mutually approved. The agreement may also contain a provision that if the artist exceeds the minimum recording requirement in any one period, at the company's discretion the excess will be credited against the minimum recording requirements in the succeeding period.

Although a recording agreement signifies the company's intention to produce recordings by that artist, this intention is rarely expressed as a contractual commitment. After the initial recordings are made, the record company may become disillusioned and try to avoid further recording obligations to the artist. Thus, recording agreements sometimes state that the artist shall be paid union scale, or another amount reflecting the cost of prior albums, for the agreed-upon minimum number of sides that remain unrecorded.

Artists quickly sense when companies have cooled toward them, and they may request a release from their contract, which the companies may be willing to grant. But where the parties are unable to agree on a release, the artist faces the prospect of sitting out the balance of the current contractual period. To avoid this situation, artists have negotiated a provision in the recording agreement that releases them if the company allows 6 months or an alternative negotiated period to lapse between a prior U.S. release date and the next scheduled recording session.

From the artist's point of view, recordings are meaningless unless they are released commercially. A company will naturally oppose being forced to release a recording in which it has no confidence. Its position is that it has already made a sizable investment in the recording, but if the recording has no commercial potential, its release would amount to throwing good money after bad.

So as not to be at the mercy of an arbitrary judgment on the part of the company, artists should try to have a release requirement inserted in the contract. For example, a contract may state that the company must release a minimum of one album plus two singles during each 18-month period. If the company fails to comply, and assuming that new recordings have been made, the artist may end the agreement. Even if a record company is forced to release a record, it may still not give it adequate promotional and marketing support, thus virtually guaranteeing the release's failure.

Most record companies have several labels, including a so-called "top-line" label, a midprice label, a budget label, and possibly other specialty labels. In addition to price points, different labels within the same price category at a major record company may have different marketing and promotion teams. An artist with sufficient negotiating power may request that his or her recordings be initially released only on a top-line label. The record company may grant the request for the United States, where it has sole control, but may refuse the request for other countries where licensees are used and where flexibility in pricing is necessary. The record company may also reserve the right to distribute recordings that were initially released as top-line product on midprice or budget labels after a period of time, in order to stimulate additional sales through lower prices.

The Selection of Material

Obviously, choosing the right material—music that is most likely to make the artist a success—is in the best interests of all parties. The companies recognized that experienced artists could be very helpful in finding worthwhile material. In the past, record companies often permitted the artist to exercise creative control, but that attitude changed in the late 1970s with the onset of economic difficulties in the business. Record companies now generally insist on being involved in all creative aspects of recordings and employ A&R people or independent producers to select the material. New artists often have no choice but to allow the record company to select the compositions.

More seasoned artists may be allowed to choose, or at least approve, material that they are to record. Many have been notably successful in composing their own hits, and some top artists, for example, Paul McCartney, Michael Jackson, and Hank Williams Jr., have formed their own music publishing companies. Independent producers such as Jimmy Jam, DeVante, Dallas Austin, Teddy Riley, and Barry Eastmond have a vital role in song selection, and they may also be involved in the writing and publishing of the songs. In order to be assured of a recording by a top artist, publishers will sometimes offer to assign an interest in the copyright to the artist's publishing company. Co-ownership in the copyright gives the artist an incentive to record the material.

Artist Royalties

A typical recording contract provides that the artist is to be paid a royalty that is calculated either as a percentage of the suggested retail list price of records sold, less excise taxes and duties, or as a percentage of the wholesale price of records sold (usually at least double the royalty rate applied to the suggested retail list price). New artists usually receive 7 to 12 percent of the suggested retail list price for domestic sales and a lesser percent for sales outside the United States. Established artists usually get a higher royalty rate. In the case of a superstar, the royalty on domestic sales may start at 15 percent or more of the suggested retail price (or its wholesale equivalent).

In negotiating royalties for foreign sales, artists should try to get not less than 85 percent of the U.S. royalty rate for sales in Canada, 75 percent for Europe, Japan, and Australia, and 50 percent for the "rest of the world". If the American record company owns and operates foreign subsidiaries, the rate may be higher. If the U.S. company owns its Canadian distributor or ships records directly to customers in Canada, the artist royalty rate for Canadian sales should be the same as those for U.S. sales.

With rare exceptions, American record companies do not derive substantial business from exporting records abroad. They license their masters to foreign companies, which manufacture from the masters. Most foreign record companies use the "published price to dealers" (PPD) as the basis for calculating royalties to their licensors. The PPD is comparable to the wholesale price. The royalty paid to its U.S. licensor on full-price sales may range from 17 to over 25 percent of PPD, with reduced royalty rates for midprice or budget product. The percentage that ultimately goes to the artist will depend on the artist's bargaining power.

Domestic royalty rates frequently escalate in increments known as "bumps" based on the quantity of sales. For example, there may be a 1 percent increment for U.S. sales of albums over 500,000 and a further 1 percent increment for sales over 1 million units. Bumps are limited to sales of the albums that have attained the requisite plateaus. Also, royalty rates are often, though not always, increased when a company decides to exercise its option to extend the term of a recording agreement. Such increases apply only to recordings made in the option period, not to recordings made in earlier contract periods. These two forms of escalation are not mutually exclusive; both may be applicable in an appropriate instance.

Record companies pay a lower royalty rate for singles than for albums, because singles are usually less profitable than albums. For example, an artist may receive a 13 percent album royalty but only 10 percent on singles. In the field of dance music, however, single sales can be much more significant than album sales, although compilation albums containing various dance tracks can be quite successful.

Formerly, royalties were based on 90 percent of records sold. This practice originated years ago, when vinyl discs were the main format and the record companies assumed a 10 percent breakage allowance in shipping and handling. Although breakage of CDs and tapes is minimal, this anachronistic practice still continues, but it is increasingly rare.

For most of the 1990s the suggested retail list price in the United States was $6.98 for singles, $11.98 for cassettes, and 14.98 to $16.98 for compact discs. The suggested retail list prices are either published by the manufacturer or extrapolated from the wholesale prices charged to dealers. Retailers are constantly offering records for sale at a discount from the suggested retail list price. If these discounts are subsidized by the manufacturer through a reduction in wholesale prices, the artist whose royalties are calculated on the basis of wholesale prices will suffer a reduction in royalties. However, even artists on a retail price royalty basis usually have a clause allowing pro rata reduction when special higher discounts are applicable.

The cost of packaging is also deducted from the base amount for computing royalties. Packaging costs are usually calculated as follows: 10 to 15 percent of the retail price for vinyl disc albums, 15 to 20 percent for cassettes, and 25 percent for CDs and other "new media" devices. The packaging deduction is predicated on the theory that the artist should receive a royalty based solely on the recording itself, not on the artwork, wrapping, or sales appeal added on by the packaging ingenuity of the record label. In this regard, it should be noted that the record company generally absorbs the entire cost of creating the artwork and other elements of the album packaging. Unlike recording costs, these costs, which can be substantial, are generally not charged back to the artist.

Record companies do not pay artist royalties on records that are given away to distributors for promotional purposes as "free goods," which are, despite the name, intended to be sold to consumers. The amount of these "free goods" (not to be confused with bona fide promotional copies distributed free of charge to reviewers, radio stations, etc.) is generally 15 percent of records sold, and more in the case of special promotions. The artist should try to negotiate a maximum on the amount of free goods that is consistent with actual practice.

Under generally accepted industry practice, retail record stores have the right to return any unsold records to the distributor, who then returns them to the record company. Since artists are not paid royalties on returned (i.e., unsold) records, record companies hold back a portion of an artist's royalties as a reserve against these returns. The artist should negotiate a maximum limit on the amount of reserves, such as 35 percent of album sales during a particular accounting period, and a reasonable time limit for liquidation of the reserve, such as payment within 2 years in equal installments over four semiannual accounting periods, rather than as one lump sum liquidated at the very last moment.

Although CDs are no longer new technology and now make up almost three-quarters of all sales in all formats, record companies frequently reduce the royalty rate payable on CDs by 15 to 20 percent, claiming that they need to be reimbursed for their research and development costs as well as for higher costs of manufacture. In fairness to those record companies that base royalties on a wholesale price, it should be noted that the wholesale price for CDs is generally 75 percent or less than the suggested retail price. For the same reasons, most record companies will pay only 75 percent or less of the otherwise applicable royalty rate for new technologies and formats. For their own protection, artists may endeavor to limit the royalty rate concessions for new technologies to a stipulated period, such as 2 years, or to a stipulated sales levels; Alternatively, artists may try to get a so-called favored nation clause stating that if in the future the record company changes to a more favorable royalty computation formula, this formula will also be applied to the calculation of the artist's royalty.

An artist may have an *all-in* royalty agreement; this means that the artist must pay the independent producer's royalty, typically 3 percent, out of his or her own royalties. For example, if the artist's royalty is 12 percent of the suggested retail list price, the producer gets 3 percent, leaving a 9 percent net artist royalty.

Here is a typical all-in royalty calculation on a $14.98 CD where the artist's base royalty is 12 percent:

12 percent – 3 percent (producer's royalty) = 9 percent

9 percent X .75 (25 percent reduction for packaging) = 6.75 percent

6.75 percent X .85 (15 percent for "free goods") = 5.74 percent

5.74 percent X .80 (20 percent reduction for CDs) = 4.59 percent

4.59 percent X .65 (35 percent reduction for reserves) = 2.98 percent

2.98 percent of $14.98 = $0.447

The artist's royalty account will therefore only be credited initially with less than 50 cents for each $14.98 CD distributed by the record company (subject to an increase if the reserve turns out to be greater than the units actually returned). This is a far cry from $1.79 (12 percent of $14.98) per CD.

Note that the calculation of royalties does not take into account items charged against an artist's royalty account, such as a portion (or all) of video production costs or a portion (or all) of independent promotion costs. The cost of the promotion of records by independent parties hired by the record company to obtain radio airplay of records can be substantial, up to $100,000 or more for a release. This should be an important issue during negotiations. Artists should not have to pay such costs out of their royalties; at most, half of such costs should be a charge against artist royalties.

Lest it be believed that the lower royalty payable to new artists generally indicates high profits to record companies, bear in mind that most albums fail to recoup their recording costs and represent a loss. The RIAA reports that 85 percent of album releases do not recover their costs. On the other hand, the status of recoupment of an artist's royalty account bears no mathematical relationship to a record company's actual profit on any given release.

In the United States three large record companies own their own record clubs. One is Columbia House and the other is BMG Direct Marketing. As well as handling records from their parent company catalogs, the record clubs distribute products of other companies. Usually, they obtain a license for the masters and pay a royalty that is either a flat sum per selection per record sold or a percentage of the club's regular price to members, less a packaging deduction. The current royalty paid by Columbia is 9.5 percent of the regular club price based on 85 percent of records sold and not returned. No royalties are computed on the substantial shipping and handling charges of the record clubs.

A common provision in artists' contracts is that the royalty payable to the artist for record club sales will be 50 percent of the royalty rate for retail sales. The clause may further state that no royalty will be payable for "bonus" or "free" records given away to club members.

Popular recording artists may fear that a record club will flood club members with free or bonus records of their performances, for which royalties will not be payable. To meet this objection, the recording contract can provide that the number of records of the artist given away by a club cannot exceed the number sold. The record company can achieve similar protection in its agreement with a club.

Record clubs contend that, at least in the United States, many club purchases represent sales that would not otherwise have been. With the rapid increase in sales via the Internet, this argument has decreasing merit. The record clubs also argue that they make it possible for smaller record companies to compete with the majors, at least in this distribution channel, thereby making them more effective in retaining and acquiring artists.

Recording Costs

Artists generally do not receive any royalties until the record company has recovered all of its recording costs incurred for the artist's records. The cost of making a record depends on many factors, including the size of the project, the cost of bringing in an outside producer, the complexity of the recordings, and the level of perfection desired. Recording costs for relatively new artists can range from $80,000 to $150,000 or more for one album. Established artists have been known to run up costs in excess of $500,000 for an album. Original-cast albums of Broadway shows may cost as much as $100,000 or more, depending on the size of the cast. On the other hand, "greatest hits" albums entail little or no additional recording costs, since they are assembled from existing recordings—although the addition of one or more new recordings is not unusual and can run up costs.

The record company will recover its costs for *all* recordings made by the artist from *all* artist royalties. Thus, if three of an artist's albums are released and only the last one is successful, no royalties will be payable to the artist until the recording costs for all three albums have been recouped from the royalties earned on the successful record. Obviously, it will take longer to recoup recording costs at a lower royalty rate than at a higher one.

Record companies may liken the system of recoupment of recording costs from royalties to a joint venture in which the production costs and overhead must be repaid before the partners divide any profits. Record companies contend that they are justified in recouping all their costs first because they are the ones taking the large financial risk while the artists invest only their time. They also point out that many artists derive major income from songwriting and personal appearances—income in which the record company does not share, even though the company's recordings may have been essential in building the artist's popularity and generating such income.

Recording Funds

In some instances recording artists are their own producers; more frequently the artist hires an independent producer. It is increasingly common for record companies to provide artists with a recording fund. The artist is then responsible for paying all third parties out of the fund, which is customarily disbursed in three segments: the first upon commencement of recording, the second upon completion of basic tracks, and the balance upon delivery of finished master to the record company. The artist can retain the difference (if any) between the recording fund and the actual recording costs; this gives the artist an incentive to keep within the budget. Recording funds, like recording costs paid directly by the record company, are always treated as advances against artist royalties.

The contract may contain a formula for computing recording funds. This formula may set forth the fund for the first recording and contain parameters for funds for subsequent recordings, generally based on two-thirds of the average royalty earnings on U.S. sales through normal retail channels for the artist's most recent two albums, with stipulated minimum and maximum amounts. (This subject is dealt with at greater length in Chapter 4, in the section entitled "Recording Funds.")

Publishing Rights

Many artists are also successful composers and many record companies are affiliated with music publishing firms. A publishing interest in a composition reduces the risk of the recording company in investing in and exploiting a record of the composition. For this reason, a record company may argue strongly for contract language giving the company the right to acquire through its affiliate a publishing interest in compositions written by the artist and recorded under the recording agreement.

Record companies may claim that, except for a publisher's distribution of printed copies and attempts to secure cover records of the same composition, it is difficult to differentiate between what a record company and a publishing firm will do to exploit a musical composition. A record company sends promotional copies of records to radio and television stations and has its promotional staff call on disc jockeys to encourage the playing of records. It may also advertise its records on the radio and in trade publications. All of these activities will result in publishing income, since there will be broadcasting performances for which the performing rights organization will pay royalties, sales of records for which the record company will remit mechanical license fees, and sales of sheet music if the composition becomes popular.

In some cases, the artist may agree, believing that the additional interest of the record company, through its affiliated publishing firm, may lead the record company to make greater efforts on the artist's behalf. Alternatively, the artist may be willing to compromise by granting an interest in publishing income only from the particular record issued by that company, or by entering into a copublishing arrangement with the record company's publishing affiliate rather than assigning all of the publishing rights to the record company's publishing affiliate.

Artists who own their own publishing firms are most likely to resist assigning their interest in the copyright or publishing income. Some artists argue that the record company's publishing enterprise is a mere shell and does not offer any publishing services over and above the activities of the record company. A recognized publisher has the staff and budget to supplement that of the record company, and thus effectively promote the artist's work. The artist may be acting in a self-defeating manner, however, if the independent publisher obtains and promotes a cover version of the same composition by a competing recording artist. This is less likely to happen when the publisher is an affiliate of the artist's record company.

If the record company does become the artist's publisher, it will most likely attempt to recoup the artist's recording costs from publishing royalties that would otherwise be payable to the artist. Artists should negotiate vigorously to disallow this practice, known as *cross-collateralization*, as it can substantially diminish the artist's publishing income.

Controlled Compositions

A *controlled composition* refers to any composition written, owned, or controlled, in whole or in part, by the artist. The record company may seek a reduced royalty rate for a mechanical license for controlled compositions, commonly 75 percent of the minimum *compulsory* rate (also known as the *statutory* rate) under the 1976 Copyright Act. In the year 2000 the full rate would be 7.55 cents per composition, so the bargain rate on controlled compositions would be only 5.66 cents.

In addition, although CDs today often contain more than 10 compositions, record companies usually stipulate that they will pay only 10 times the minimum rate for the CD, no matter how many compositions are included. Further, the contracts with the artists may provide that to the extent mechanical license fees for controlled and noncontrolled compositions exceed the maximum rate the company has agreed to pay, the excess is deductible from monies otherwise payable on controlled compositions and (if not sufficient) from artist royalties or advances. In effect, this places the responsibility on the artist to negotiate favorable mechanical license rates with outside publishers for compositions that the artist proposes to record.

The record company does not usually pay artist royalties on free goods and similarly seeks not to pay mechanical royalties for controlled compositions. The artist will contend that such royalties should be paid because free goods are merely a form of discount that the record company should absorb. Often a compromise is reached, with the record company agreeing to pay mechanical royalties on 50 percent of the albums distributed as free goods.

Under a controlled-composition clause, the record company will fix the reduced mechanical license fee as of a particular date; the applicable rate on that date remains in effect forever and does not change regardless of increases in the compulsory license rate. The artist will attempt to provide for the latest possible date, such as the date of record release, in order to take advantage of any increases in the compulsory license rate. For the same reason, the company will insist on an earlier date, such as the recording or delivery date of the master.

Packaging

A potent sales factor is the packaging of an album. Eye appeal is very important in attracting buyer interest. Included in eye appeal will be pictures of scenes or of the artists, designs, and various types of printing for the album title and the names of the artists. The company will claim to be the best judge of packaging, but an important artist may achieve the right to approve the packaging or even to prepare and furnish it subject to the company's approval. The contract may provide that the artist may not unreasonably withhold approval, in order to avoid an impasse that would bar the release of an album. Approval of packaging may be limited to the domestic area; the company may claim that it cannot supervise packaging by its foreign licensees.

Tour Support

Touring is an excellent means of promoting an artist's album, as sales consistently increase in areas in which the artist performs. However, for most newer artists, the costs of touring exceed the income derived from the engagements.

Record companies sometimes subsidize tours on the theory that the tour will promote sales of the record, which in the long run will provide more income than is disbursed for the tour. But some recording agreements may provide that tour support is recoupable against future artist royalties. The artist should negotiate to make tour support nonrecoupable or only partially recoupable. The development of video as a promotional tool has reduced the importance of conventional tour support. (A sample "Tour Agreement" is listed in the accompanying CD-ROM.)

Video Rights

In most contracts the definition of "records" includes audiovisual devices as well as more traditional types of records. Record companies will negotiate for the right to control the use of recordings in audiovisual form and to restrict the artist from performing in such media, such as in feature films, for other companies.

A key area in contract negotiations between artists and record companies concerns music videos. Videos are usually visualizations of songs performed by the artist. They are a significant promotional tool, and recording artists will try to get their record companies to produce at least one video for each of their albums. Because videos can be expensive and difficult to place on the various video channels, such as MTV, record companies resist making any firm commitments.

Most recording contracts provide that artist royalties are not payable on videos that are distributed to promote record sales. Royalties should be payable on videos that are distributed commercially. Although the commercial market for videos is still quite limited, this may change in the future with the increased use of alternative distribution modes, such as DVDs and the Internet.

Generally, 50 percent of the video production costs are recoupable out of artist royalties from the sale of records (which they are supposed to promote) and 100 percent are recoupable out of artist royalties from the commercial sale of the videos.

Under copyright law, a video producer must obtain from a copyright proprietor or its agent a synchronization license to record protected music in synchronization with or timed relation to the pictures in a video. Permission is also necessary to publicly perform, make copies of, and distribute the music as a part of the music videos. With "controlled compositions", record companies will demand that the artist provide free video licenses. While artists may agree to this if the video is for promotional purposes, they may balk if the video is being exploited commercially. (See also Chapter 35, "Music Videos.")

Assignment

In certain circumstances, for example, in the event of a sale or merger, a record company may wish to assign its rights to a recording agreement to another entity. In most contracts there is no prohibition against the assignment of the agreement. This unfettered freedom of assignment can be injurious to an artist, particularly when the new owner lacks the same interest in the artist as the original record company.

New artists may not be in a position to quibble about the assignability of their contract, although successful performers will seek to limit such assignability. Sometimes a contract includes a "key man clause," referring to an individual who has been important in getting an artist to sign on with a particular company. Such a clause may give the artist the right to terminate the agreement if the "key man" (or woman) leaves the company for any reason. Given the volatile nature of employment in the industry, record companies are understandably reluctant to include key man clauses in their contracts.

Some record companies will agree to limit the possibility of assignment to "successors in interest," that is, to successors who acquire all or substantially all of the assigning record company's stock or assets. This is a way of assuring the artist of the continuing financial viability of the successor, which would be at least as big as the original company. A small company may be financially unsound and unable to invest sufficiently in good personnel and quality recordings.

An artist may grant consent in advance to an assignment to a company with equal or better standing in the industry in terms of gross receipts and credit rating. An artist may be willing to authorize assignment if the original record company continues to be liable for the fulfillment of all obligations, or if the assignee is an entity owned or controlled by the original company or any company distributed by one of the major labels.

Artists may wish to authorize assignments of all the recording company's artists and masters, as in the case of sale of the entire business or in the event of a merger. In such instances there is a good likelihood of a stronger company emerging, with resulting benefits to the artist.

Ownership and Use of Masters

A recording agreement is usually written as an employment contract, and unless otherwise stated, the record company will claim that the results and proceeds of the artist's services belong to the record company as a "work-for-hire." This means that the artist retains no interest in the physical tapes or masters or the copyright in the sound recordings and is restricted to a claim for contractual compensation and royalties. Exclusive rights under the copyright in sound recordings are limited to reproduction, the preparation of derivative works, and distribution; the right of public performance is not included.

Determining whether the artist is an employee producing a work for hire or an independent contractor is a complicated subject that is treated in depth in Chapter 17, "Works for Hire." The answer affects copyright ownership, the duration of copyright, and copyright termination rights.

A record company will jealously guard its ownership rights in masters and copyrights. However, in rare cases with certain highly successful artists, record companies have agreed that the ownership of the masters and copyrights will revert to the artists after a period of years. Artists who desire to transfer to another record company find that the reversion of their recordings is a valuable right that enhances their worth to a new company. Where a reversion right is not granted, artists and their new company have been known to bid substantial sums to acquire ownership of the old masters and copyrights.

A record company can usually use a recording as it sees fit. It may issue the recording on any label it desires, and it may couple the recording with the recordings of other artists. Established artists will try to restrict a record company's unlimited discretion, especially seeking to limit the time within which a record company may (without artist's consent) release the artist's records at less than full price, the use of artist's recordings in motion picture scores or in advertising, or the number of artist's recordings that can be used in any compilation.

Coupling

It is common for record companies to issue recordings that couple the performances of various artists into a compilation album. Although marketed successfully in the past, today such albums are used mostly for promotional purposes. However, "do-it-yourself" compilations are growing, thanks to kiosks and such Internet services as musicmaker.com; these enable the consumer to create a custom compilation of personal favorites. Fearing that they may be cheapened and damaged by association with artists of lesser stature, artists will try to negotiate the right to approve such couplings of their recordings. If the artist is of sufficient stature to merit the granting of this type of request, the record company will want contractual protection that the artist's approval will not be unreasonably withheld.

Accountings and Defaults

Artist recording agreements usually provide that the recording company will account to the artist semiannually and that if the artist fails to complain within a certain period, such as within 1 or 2 years from the date the statement is rendered, the artist will be deemed to have waived any objections to any royalty accountings. This is known as the "account stated clause." The artist should not overlook this clause, which is designed to safeguard the company from disputes arising long after the facts are made known to the artist, since the courts will uphold a provision that appears reasonable. In the absence of a contractual right to audit the record company's books, an artist will have to sue in court in order to obtain the right to audit. The record company will not otherwise be obliged to open its books for inspection.

If a company fails to account for or pay royalties when due, artists may commence legal proceedings against the company. Artists may wish to treat the breach as an excuse for terminating the agreement, freeing them from all obligations and services to the company. However, unless the agreement specifically authorizes such termination, a court will have to determine whether the breach is a material one that justifies the cancellation. A slight delay in rendering accounts and payments would not be regarded as material, whereas long delays after many demands might be.

Other defaults may occur. For example, the company may refuse to allow an inspection of books and records, even though the artist has a contractual right to do so. The company may fail to release recordings which they have committed to release or record the artist at given periods as provided by the agreement. Here again artists run a risk that a court will not recognize such defaults as sufficient grounds for termination unless the agreement specifically authorizes cancellation in such events.

The record company will strongly oppose a default clause that does not require a written notice of defaults and a sufficient opportunity to remedy them. It may completely refuse to accept a unilateral right of termination by the artist, although it may be willing to agree to an arbitration clause. Many recording contracts specifically state that the artist's only remedy for nonpayment of royalties is monetary damages and that the artist does not have the right to terminate the contract in the event of nonpayment of royalties.

Bankruptcy

A normal recording contract, consisting of an initial contract period and subsequent option periods, will potentially continue for an extended period of time. Recordings made during the exclusive term of the agreement will be owned by the record company and will potentially continue to be sold indefinitely, thereby giving rise to an ongoing royalty payment obligation. These relationships between the artist and the record company may, however, be interrupted or revised by a bankruptcy proceeding involving either party.

Several independent record labels—Stax, General Recorded Tapes (Chess), All Platinum, Springboard—filed for bankruptcy in the 1980s. In each instance the debtor's master recordings were sold and the net proceeds were distributed among the debtor's creditors. Delinquent artist royalties are ordinarily general debts with no priority in bankruptcy. Future artist royalties constitute a continuing obligation that is assumed by the party that acquires the master recordings. That party also takes over any unrecouped balance in the artist's royalty account.

In some record contracts there is an attempt to treat bankruptcy as cause for returning the record masters to the artist. Such a reversion of valuable rights would be contrary to the principles of bankruptcy, as it would give an unlawful preferential treatment to the artist at the expense of other legitimate creditors.

At times, recording artists have resorted to the bankruptcy courts to free them from onerous exclusive recording contracts. Robert Noonan (professionally known as Willie Nile), an Arista Records recording artist, had accumulated a deficit royalty recoupment account that required the sale of a large number of records before it would become positive. He also had significant financial obligations for prebankruptcy legal expenses and his manager's $60,000 arbitration award. He had a limited cash flow and insubstantial assets. Arista Records, despite low sales, exercised its options to extend the agreement for 18 months, during which Nile would have been obligated to record two albums, in addition to two already made. Arista refused to give Nile any further advances to help him pay his financial obligations. Nile commenced a Chapter 11 proceeding and sought to terminate all future contractual obligations to Arista as part of a financial reorganization plan. Nile subsequently exercised his right to convert the case to a Chapter 7 ("straight") bankruptcy proceeding, which Arista resisted strongly, since it would have deprived the court of the possibility of affirming Nile's recording contract. In the matter of Noonan (17 Bankr. 793 [S.D.N.Y. 1982]), the U.S. district court ruled against Arista, thereby giving Nile the fresh start which he sought.

Record companies may argue that artists who file for bankruptcy do so "in bad faith" for the sole purpose of breaking their recording contract or pressing the record company to renegotiate the agreement. This contention is of dubious merit when a performing artist is in actual financial distress and is evidencing a need for the protection of the Bankruptcy Code.

In a case involving the artist George Jones, then under contract to CBS Records, a bankruptcy court held that the trustee in bankruptcy was vested with the artist's right to receive record royalties on prebankruptcy recordings. The court also decided that CBS could continue to recoup its advances in respect of such recordings from royalties on sales generated by the recordings. It is of interest that Jones's discharge in bankruptcy was ultimately denied for his failure to produce records of his financial status and business transactions for the year preceding the filing of his petition.

3

Contracts with Minors

Historically, the age of legal maturity was 21, but there has been a marked statutory trend in the majority of states to lower the legal age to 18. Prior to reaching the age of legal maturity, an individual is regarded as an "infant" or a "minor." While still legally considered infants when their professional careers skyrocketed, Elvis Presley, Stevie Wonder, and Bob Dylan earned large amounts of money and had considerable sums invested in them by record companies, managers, and the like in the music business. Today growing numbers of singers, rappers, and musicians like Brandy, Usher, Leann Rimes, and Britney Spears are breaking into the music industry before the age of legal maturity. The success stories of many teenage celebrities tend to obscure the legal difficulties originating from their status as minors.

Generally, the common law has regarded minors as not having the maturity of mind or judgment required to make legally binding agreements. Unless a contract involves the necessities of life—food, clothing, housing—a minor can void an agreement within a reasonable period of time after reaching the age of maturity. The other party to the agreement cannot avoid its contractual obligations to the minor.

Contracts with minors contain a financial risk: the minor may disaffirm (i.e., repudiate) their agreement. Even if a minor fraudulently misrepresented his or her age—a common occurrence in the search for employment and a career—this is not sufficient legal ground to enforce a contract or collect damages from the minor for breach of contract. The sole risk in dealing with the minor is placed on the other party. This has greatly discouraged investment in training and promoting young artists.

The statutory age of majority in the key music industry states—California, New York, Tennessee, and Illinois—is now 18 years: a contract signed by a person 18 years or older cannot be disaffirmed on the ground of infancy. This has significantly eased the problems of the entertainment industry in dealing with artists ages 18 to 21.

In recognition of the difficulties involved in contracting with minors, many states have established procedures for the court approval of such agreements. This formal approval has the effect of preventing disaffirmance.

Disaffirmance of an Agreement

A minor's act to disaffirm or void an agreement does not have to follow any particular pattern. Typically, written notice of disaffirmance on the ground of minor status is sufficient. Other such acts include making contracts that are inconsistent with the agreement in question or pleading infancy as a defense in an action brought under the contract.

Ratification of an Agreement

An agreement that is entered into by a minor becomes fully enforceable if it is ratified after the minor reaches the age of majority. Ratification does not need to be in written form. Silence for a certain period of time after reaching the age of maturity is considered sufficient ratification of a completed transaction. A contract can be deemed legally ratified if the artist performs certain acts indicating an intent to continue with the agreement after reaching the age of majority: for example, coming to a recording session or accepting compensation for future performances.

Statutory Provisions of Contracts with Minors

In many states, statutes deal with the enforceability of contracts with minors. Since New York and California are centers of the music industry, our focus will be on the statutes in those states.

New York

For contracts involving the services of persons under 18 in the fields of entertainment or professional sports, New York has provided a statutory method of ensuring that the agreements cannot be disaffirmed on the grounds of infancy. A procedure has been established for court review and approval of contracts as well as agreements for managerial and agency services. It does not cover music publishing agreements, such as an exclusive writer's contract or a minor's approval of his or her parents transferring their renewal rights in the copyrights of songs. There are three basic requirements for court approval: (1) the contract must be fair to the minor, (2) the contract may not extend beyond a term of 3 years, and (3) the minor's parents must consent.

A contract cannot be approved if its term of service, including any extensions by option or otherwise, goes beyond 3 years from the date of the agreement; however, it may contain any covenants or conditions binding on the minor beyond 3 years if they are found by the court to be reasonable. For example, the New York Law Revision Commission has gone on record as being in favor of permitting an agent's commissions to continue beyond 3 years on royalty-producing property created during the original 3 years of the agreement. It has also recommended that a minor who is a recording artist should be allowed to agree not to re-record a song for a competitor for a period longer than 3 years; the normal clause in the record business restricts such re-recordings for at least 5 years from the date of recording of the record.

The first step for obtaining judicial approval is to file a petition. The petition must include a copy of the agreement, a schedule of estimated earnings, and the consent of the parents.

The next step is a court hearing, at which the minor must be present. The court appoints a legal guardian, usually a parent of the minor, whose function is to collect and save the earnings on behalf of the minor. The court may also appoint a guardian *ad litem* ("for the suit" or "for the action"), who is usually an attorney knowledgeable on the subject matter of the contract. This guardian reviews the agreement and advocates fairness for the minor, at the expense of the petitioner. Complicated and unfair contracts (ones requiring much negotiation) are the primary reasons for delays in the whole procedure.

If there is a claim that the well-being of the minor is being impaired by performance of the contract, the court may either revoke the approval or suspend approval until an appropriate modification of the contract has been made.

CALIFORNIA

Under California statutes, court approval can be sought for agreements with minors under 18 that cover the employment of a minor in the entertainment field as an actor, a recording artist, or a writer; the purchase, sale, or licensing of literary, musical, or dramatic properties for entertainment purposes; and service contracts between duly licensed managers or agencies and minors in the entertainment field. Employment or other agreements cannot be disaffirmed by a minor after court approval.

Unlike New York statutes, California law does not contain a 3-year limit on an agreement; a term of employment of up to 7 years may be approved. As in New York, a California court may require earnings to be set aside for the benefit of the minor.

Since most new artists disappear from the public eye after one or two recordings are released and since the procedure for seeking approval usually involves attorneys' fees and expenses as well as court appearances of the minor, guardians, and other parties to the agreement, applications for approval of contracts with minors are rarely filed.

THE PARENT'S GUARANTEE OF CONTRACT PERFORMANCE

Those drafting contracts with minors have sometimes insisted that the parents or guardians become a party to or a guarantor of the contract for the minor's

performance. This may have strong psychologi~~ ~
ance by the minor, although it does not prevent
the agreement. Unless protected by statute, pare.
such contracts become potentially liable for large
for breach of contract by a minor.

Pursuant to New York statute, unless the contr.
a parent or guardian is *not* liable for the services of a
entertainment. There is no similar provision in Califo

4

Independent Record Producers

In the 1950s and 1960s, A&R executives reigned supreme at record companies. They selected the artists, taught, encouraged, and supervised them, and got the credit for nurturing the hits. They were so highly regarded that their substantial salaries were sometimes augmented by special bonuses or small royalties that were rarely charged to the artist royalty accounts.

In the late 1970s and early 1980s, the independent producer came to the fore, assuming more and more of the A&R function. Entire recording budgets are now delivered into the hands of a producer with a good track record, who is given carte blanche in supervising recording sessions and handling the postproduction editing of tapes.

In his autobiography *Rhythm and Blues: A Life in American Music,* Jerry Wexler, renowned producer and former co-owner of Atlantic Records, noted that there are three kinds of producer.

> The first is the documentarian, like Leonard Chess, who took Muddy Waters' Delta blues and recorded them just as Muddy played them—raw, unadorned and real ... replicated in a studio what he heard in a bar. ...The second category—the producer as servant of the project ... an impassioned fan [who] ... somehow finds himself in charge of the sessions with no special cachet. His job is to enhance: meaning find the right song, the right arranger, the right band, the right studio—in short, do whatever it takes to get the best out of the artist ... The third category—producer as star, as artist, as unifying force ... every item in a record—the rhythm track, strings, background vocal, lead vocal, instrumental solo—was a tile in a mosaic. The design was solely of his making, not the singer's or the songwriter's.

Whether documentarian, project leader, or studio superstar, increasingly the producer is relied on by the music industry to deliver hits, remain within budget, and stimulate the artist's productivity.

There have been some noteworthy pairings of artists and independent producers.

Producer	Artist
Robert John "Mutt" Lange	Shania Twain, Backstreet Boys, Bryan Adams
Jermaine Dupri	Jay-Z, Mariah Carey, Usher, 'Lil Kim
Dave Lillywhite	Dave Matthews Band, Morrissey, Phish
Craig Street	Cassandra Wilson, Me'shell Ndegeocello, k.d. lang
Byron Gallimore	Faith Hill, Tom McGraw, Randy Travis

Artists themselves often become independent record producers. They start out producing or coproducing their own recording sessions, and then, once they have achieved a certain track record as producers, they carry on parallel careers as producer and artist. For example, The Artist Formerly Known as Prince has produced Madonna, Chaka Kahn, and Mavis Staples, while singer-rapper Lauryn Hill has produced songs for both Aretha Franklin and Whitney Houston.

The growth of the role of the independent producer has largely paralleled the record industry's increasing emphasis on albums rather than singles. Since the latter part of the 1970s, most singles have failed to achieve sufficient sales to recoup production and marketing costs. They are now used primarily as promotional aids for the sales of albums. For the last decades of the twentieth century, the market has been largely an album market, and the potential for successful albums by an artist is what justifies the substantial investments made by record companies. This may change with the abilities to download individual tracks via the Internet. In any event, while the artist remains the most important part of the mix, employing an independent producer with a good track record is considered to be a good business decision, especially where large recording budgets are involved.

The Role of the Independent Record Producer

Independent record producers perform a number of important functions. They serve as talent scouts; they often choose appropriate musical material and select and supervise arrangers, accompanists, studios, and engineers; and they are critical to keeping recording costs within budget. At times an executive producer may be appointed to assist the independent producer, particularly with regard to business affairs.

By the mid-1990s, the independent producer often assumed the role of arranger as well. This happened primarily when tracks were laid down at an early session and the words and melody were added later, often at a different recording studio. Whether the producer-arranger should be listed as coauthor of the music is unclear under these circumstances, and a potential source of copyright confusion. In current practice, the strong role and bargaining position of producers like Sean "Puffy" Combs, who often writes, arranges, and performs on a song, ensures that the producer is credited as a writer and that his music publisher may claim copublishing status as well.

Today, the producer may also have control over the different textures used in a song, such as layered keyboard or harmony vocals. Further, with the increased use of sampling in mainstream music, the producer's role as arranger frequently involves integrating a sample into a new song. However, to the extent that a recording is a "cover" of an existing copyright, the producer-arranger has no legal right to intrude on existing writer or publisher credits.

Label Deals and Pressing-and-Distribution Deals

Independent producers with particularly desirable artists under contract may be able to negotiate a *label deal* with a major record label. A label deal may provide that records will be released under the trade name and label of the producer. Producers claim that a label deal helps them attract artists to their fold. Such deals may also be advantageous to producers who wish to develop their own recording and manufacturing operations in the future.

When negotiating label deals with record companies, producers will seek both fixed and royalty compensation. *Fixed compensation* may be in the form of a weekly overhead payment, other periodic payments, a fee for each recorded master, or a combination of these elements. *Royalty compensation* will be a percentage of the wholesale or retail list price of records sold. The percentage will depend on the bargaining power of the producer, who is usually responsible for paying royalties to recording artists. Where this is the case, the "all-in" royalty payable to the producer's label must be sufficiently high to cover both the artist royalty and an override to the producer.

The record company may seek the contractual right to apply the royalties or profits from the hits of one artist to recoup the recording costs of another less successful artist. This practice, an example of *cross-collateralization*, is a major issue in most label deals. A production company may find itself in financial difficulties if it has to pay royalties to its successful artists at a time when its ready cash has been consumed by the overhead and unrecouped recording costs of less successful artists. An independent producer may negotiate an agreement with the record company to provide that artist royalties payable through the producer's label are excluded from cross-collateralization.

In "pressing-and-distribution" arrangements, the production company relies on profits from distributing the product rather than on royalties. Under such an arrangement, the record company deducts pressing charges, mechanical royalties, and other specified expenses, including a negotiated distribution fee, which is akin to a royalty, as payment for its services. Distribution fees of 20 to 30 percent of gross dealer prices are common.

Royalty Agreements

If an independent producer is hired to supervise an artist already under contract to a record company, the producer's royalty in the United States is usually 3 percent of album sales. A highly successful producer may get a royalty rate of 4 percent, with escalations on volume, usually an additional 0.5 percent on each additional 500,000 units, up to a specified maximum. Packaging deductions, "free goods" exclusions, and royalty reductions for record club, foreign, and other sales are generally calculated in the same manner as the artist's royalties.

A record company usually does not have to pay this royalty until recording costs have been recouped out of the net artist royalty (i.e., gross royalties less the royalties payable to the producer). On rare occasions, recording costs are recouped from the combined artist and producer royalties; this results in faster recoupment and both artist and producer receive royalties sooner. Even when a producer produces less than an entire album and has no control over recording costs incurred by others, costs for the *entire* album are recouped before a record company begins to pay any royalties. Although this practice seems unfair, it works two ways: the producer may benefit from the sales of a single produced by someone else—sales that contribute to the recoupment of the entire album's recording costs.

Upon full artist recoupment, the producer is paid royalties retroactively to the first record sold. However, royalties are subject to further recoupment on any producer advances made at the time of recording. Where both artist and producer royalties are used for recoupment, there is usually no retroactive producer royalty. Rather, royalties are granted only on records sold from the date of full recoupment.

In a producer-artist royalty package, where the producer pays the artist's royalty, gross royalty rates may range from about 10 to 14 percent of the retail list price (or the equivalent royalty based on wholesale); of this, the artist's royalty rate is generally 7 to 10 percent and the producer's rate is 3 to 4 percent, with the usual royalty deductions for packaging, foreign sales, etc. All monies paid by a record company to obtain a recording, whether as payments to the producer or as expenditures for recording costs, are deemed advances against and recoupable from the total royalties payable by the record company.

The recording fund for an important artist or an established producer may be several hundred thousand dollars per album, with a royalty package (based on retail) of 18 percent or higher.

If the independent producer acts as arranger, he or she is entitled to be listed as arranger for union-scale purposes. Arranger's fees are not deducted from producer royalties, but are an additional recording cost ultimately absorbed by the artist.

Recording Funds

When independent producers are hired to make a recording, either by the record company or by the artist (see discussion in Chapter 2 under "Recording Funds"), the company will frequently agree to provide a stated recording fund for each project. This fund is in lieu of a recording budget supervised by the record company and is treated as an advance against royalties. The producer and the artist retain whatever is not spent on recording costs as compensation for their services. Thus, if the recording fund is $150,000 and the actual studio, engineering, musician scale, and other recording costs equal $100,000, the balance of $50,000 is available as compensation for the producer and the artist. This balance is separate and apart from any royalties payable after the record company has recouped the recording fund, although a portion of the fund may be allocated to a producer fee, which will be treated as an advance against producer royalties.

Determining the amount of the recording fund in the first instance is a matter of negotiation between the producer, the artist, and the record company. A balance must be struck between expected sales on the one hand and adequate compensation for the producer and the artist on the other hand. A $100,000 fund for a recording with limited sales potential might be excessive, whereas a $250,000 recording fund for a potential blockbuster album might be too little if insufficient funds were to remain for marketing and promotion costs. From the standpoint of the producer and the artist, an extremely low recording fund can result in little or no compensation, as all monies will be absorbed in actual recording costs.

Sometimes recording funds are based on two-thirds of the preceding album's gross royalties (i.e., producer and artist royalties combined, before recoupment charges) calculated on the basis of U.S. sales during a fixed period, typically 6 to 9 months from the release date. When this formula is used, record club, foreign, or other types of sales are customarily not included in the calculation. The resultant calculation is then subject to a so-called minimum-maximum amount. A record company may be unwilling to write a blank check for $1 million dollars simply because the previous album was a blockbuster, so it will fix a maximum amount of the recording fund in order to reduce its future risks. On the other hand, the producer or artist will demand a minimum recording fund even if the preceding album is a failure. Typically, minimums are about one-half of maximums.

The risk of the producer or artist incurring costs in excess of the agreed fund can sometimes be alleviated by the provision of an "over-budget allowance" of, say, 10 percent. This protects against unforeseen expenditures such as delays in the arrival of a major guest artist. Alternatively, the budget is simply "reforecast" by the record company to accommodate cost overruns. (A sample estimated recording budget is on the accompanying CD-Rom.)

Production and Development Deals

Often independent producers and new artists establish a working relationship before either party has a commitment from a record company. In such a situation, they may enter into a joint venture, which delineates their respective rights and obligations, including the sharing of advances and royalties, in the event that they obtain a record contract. (A sample "Producer-Artist Agreement" is listed in the accompanying CD-ROM.)

In a development deal, the division of income between a producer and an artist will vary. In a simple arrangement, the producer and the artist may agree to share all receipts on a fixed-ratio basis, for example, a 50-50 split. It may be in a producer's interests to agree to pay a fixed royalty to the artist. For example, a development deal may provide that the artist will be paid a base royalty of 7 percent, calculated in the same manner as the distribution agreement that the producer hopes to enter. If the record company grants the producer a better base royalty than 14 percent, the producer may do better under a fixed artist royalty arrangement.

If the artist and producer agree to make a demonstration recording, the producer may have to furnish or procure studio facilities and musicians. A producer with a successful track record may be able to obtain a modest demonstration record budget from a record company or music publisher. This is referred to as a *demo deal*. In return, the subsidizing party may acquire the right of first refusal, that is, a first option on signing the artist. Whether or not the artist is signed, the subsidizing party is guaranteed the right to recoup the recording funds out of the first receipts.

In the absence of a demo deal, the producer may obtain other types of financing. For example, in order to persuade a studio to defer or reduce its charges, the producer may offer the studio a small royalty participation in the resultant recording. This agreement is often referred to as a *spec deal*. The producer and the artist may also seek to have musicians defer or reduce their charges. Thus, payment to a studio or to musicians may be structured as off-the-top deductions from any advances or royalties that are received. The contract may call for certain minimum payments to the artist and the producer as the next off-the-top deductions prior to an ultimate profit sharing between the artist and the producer.

Under a typical development deal, the parties agree to cooperate in obtaining a recording contract that contains specified minimum terms. Over and above an understanding that the record will be produced or distributed by a major company, the parties may stipulate that the contract must contain a minimum album recording commitment by the record company and that the net artist royalty, after deducting the producer's royalty, must not be less than a certain percentage.

While the producer may assume responsibility for negotiating with the record company, the artist may retain a right of consultation or approval. The artist may also insist on the right to replace the producer or to appoint a coproducer if the resulting recordings do not achieve specified chart action. The producer may have the right to approve the new producer or coproducer, assuming such approval is not unreasonably withheld. Under the contract, the costs of the new producer or coproducer are deductible from the share other-wise due to the first producer. If a record company does not exercise its contract options, the artist-producer contract may grant the producer 3 to 6 months to obtain a new record contract.

Often such contracts have a *pass-through arrangement*. This means that the artist receives the same benefits as the producer from any provisions negoti-ated by the producer on such complex matters as record club rates, foreign sale rates, premium and budget record rates, rights of audit, and royalty escalations. Often the contract will contain a clause to the effect that if the terms of the master purchase-distribution agreement (between the record company and the producer) differ with the artist-producer agreement, then the terms of the purchase-distribution agreement shall take precedence and be incorporated into the production agreement.

Producer Fees

Independent record producers will rarely produce recordings for an artist under contract to a label without cash fees. These fees are usually in the form of advances recoupable from the producer royalties, although occasionally they are deemed to be nonrecoupable bonuses. Advance payments to independent producers for work with artists on minor labels may be as low as $1,000 a song. Producer advances of $20,000 to $60,000 per album that includes 8 to 10 songs are not unusual.

Producer advances and royalties are accounted separately from mechanical royalties payable to songwriters or publishers. When mechanical license fees are payable to the artist or producer in their capacity as songwriter or publisher, the contract should be scrutinized for cross-collateralization clauses that would make all advances chargeable against payments of *any kind* that may be due to them.

Music Publishing and Follow-up Rights

Producers often control the music publishing rights for original recorded material. They thereby derive additional compensation from performance fees when the record is played and mechanical royalties when records are sold. In some instances, the record company may bargain to acquire some or all of the music publishing rights controlled by the producer. Alternatively, the company may be willing to settle for a "controlled-composition" rate, which is custom-arily 75 percent of the statutory rate (the minimum compulsory mechanical license rate under the 1976 Copyright Act; see Chapter 2).

When acquiring a new artist's master recordings from a producer, a record company will usually insist on obtaining rights to subsequent recordings by the artist. It will be the company's position that, having expended time and money in establishing an artist, the company is entitled to continue with an artist.

An independent producer who is engaged to work with an artist under contract to a record company may negotiate the right to continue as the producer of future recordings. Under such a clause, the record company may not use other producers for the artist unless and until the initial producer declines to produce additional recordings. For example, the producer may request a contractual clause stating that if a certain level of sales is achieved within a specified time period, he or she will be given the right to produce future recordings on the basis of the same or higher fee and royalty. For purposes of calculating the sales plateau, there may be a provision limiting "free goods" and providing that records in a reserve for returns must be counted. The time period should be short enough to be within the normal production period for a follow-up record and yet long enough for the sales plateau to be achieved. Often the time period is from 6 to 9 months or to the date of commencement of the next studio session, whichever comes earlier.

A record company may be content to have the producer produce and supply further recordings, but usually it will want a recording contract with the artist and a separate agreement with the producer regarding future recordings, fixed compensation, and royalties. Or the record company may take an option to enter into a recording contract with the producer, the artist, or both within a given period of time, for instance, within 120 days of the acquisition of the initial master. Assuming that the record is issued within 30 days after its purchase, the company then has 90 days in which to evaluate the market acceptance of the record before exercising its option. For convenience, the company may execute a record agreement with the artist at the same time that it makes a master purchase agreement with the producer. However, the artist agreement will not become effective unless and until the option is exercised.

Contractual Safeguards

If the independent producer wishes to preserve his contractual relationship with the artist and therefore refuses to consent to a recording agreement between the artist and the record company, the record company may still safeguard its own interest in the artist through an *artist inducement letter,* which states that:

1. The artist is familiar with the agreement between the producer and the company, including any right of first refusal regarding subsequent recordings by the artist.
2. The artist will abide by the producer agreement insofar as it pertains to his or her personal recording services.
3. The artist will look solely to the producer for royalty statements and payments.
4. A breach of the agreement between the producer and the artist will not excuse performance by the artist in accordance with the agreement between the producer and the record company.

A copy of an artist inducement letter is available on the accompanying CD-ROM.

The record company must protect itself against the possibility that the producer may become unavailable, for any reason, to produce further recordings for the artist. Accordingly, the company may insist that if this happens, the recording contract between the producer and the artist will be assigned to the record company. As a safeguard against the producer's unwillingness to execute a formal written assignment, most contracts provide that the record company may sign such an assignment on the producer's behalf.

In addition, the record company may insist that the agreement between the artist and producer be in a form satisfactory to the company. In particular, the company may require that the recording contract may be enforced by the company; that the company shall receive notice of any alleged defaults by the producer; that the company shall be given an opportunity to cure such defaults; and that if the producer's defaults are incurable, the company has the right to take over the producer's recording agreement with the artist with no responsibility for past defaults by the producer.

For recordings of artists under contract to the producer, the record company will require the producer to make appropriate warranties that the material is original and the recordings do not infringe on any rights of third parties. The company will also look to the producer for warranties that all recording costs have been paid so that no claims will be made against the company for unpaid bills.

Under its agreements with the AFM and AFTRA, the company must procure a warranty from the producer that the musicians and vocalists who made the master were paid union scale for their services. This warranty must appear in the master purchase agreement and, in accordance with the union agreements, state that it is for the benefit of the unions. Unless the producer is a signatory to the agreement with the unions, the company guarantees the accuracy of the representation as to musicians and the vocalists. Finally, in order to insure that the company is not faced with future competition by its own artist, the company will require the producer to agree not to permit the artist to re-record the same material for a certain period, which is customarily 5 years from date of delivery of the recordings or 2 years from the expiration of the exclusive artist agreement, whichever is longer.

Because the producer is an intermediary between the artist and the company, the company must obtain from the producer the contractual safeguards that the company would include in agreements with the artist. The company will also seek from the producer additional provisions to protect the company from the effects of default or misunderstanding in the relations between the producer and the artist.

Producers, on the other hand, must realize that they stand to some extent in the position of the artist and that they must attempt to secure the contractual clauses that would be required by artists. Thus, producers should watch for appropriate provisions relating to accountings, audits, renewal of the agreement, prohibitions against re-recordings, guarantees of release of records pressed from the master recordings, and so on.

Furthermore, producers must bulwark their special position as producers with clauses ensuring their control of the artist and the material. The company may try to limit such control in order to maintain a voice in future recording projects by the artist.

5

Foreign Distribution Agreements

American record companies use various methods to distribute their recordings outside of the United States. Multinational companies such as Universal Music Group (resulting from a merger of the PolyGram group of labels and the MCA group of labels), Sony, BMG (which includes Arista), and the WEA/EMI group own and operate their own subsidiaries in most major territories and distribute through licensees in others. Smaller U.S. companies generally use licensees for foreign distribution, either a local affiliate of one of the major multinational companies or a local independent record company. There are advantages and disadvantages to either method.

It is simpler to have one large multinational company handle the contractual and servicing aspects of foreign distribution. The power of a major multinational concern in distributing product cannot be overlooked; a major corporation may be in a better position to pay large advances to acquire product. On the other hand, a small U.S. company may get more individualized attention in the catalog of an independent local representative, whereas its product may get lost among the many releases in a large multinational company's catalog.

A major U.S. company may set up a hybrid arrangement. It may use local record companies for pressing and distribution as well as independent promotion, and set up branch offices as well. When a branch office handles distribution the American company has better control over the release and promotion of its own catalog. The branch office can also contract with local artists to make recordings. If a recording is a success, the profits can be considerably greater than the royalties received under a licensing agreement. On the other hand, the American company is likely to have to forgo the advances or guarantees of monies that might otherwise be available under a licensing agreement. There may be losses due to overhead, unsold product, and other factors in a branch setup, in contrast to the more certain royalties from a success under a licensing agreement. (A sample "Master License" agreement can be found on the accompanying CD-ROM.)

Royalty Provisions

In the past, foreign licensees customarily paid royalties based on the suggested retail list price in the country of manufacture or sale . Today, most foreign licensees base royalty payments on the wholesale price or on the published price to dealers (PPD) fixed by the mechanical rights societies for the computation of copyright royalties. Royalty rates used to range from 8 to 17 percent, based on 90 percent of net sales. Today, royalty rates range from 12 to 26 percent or more and are based on 100 percent of net sales. (Net sales are gross sales less disc jockey and other promotional records, as well as returns and other credits.) There is a reduced rate for midprice and budget product, usually half the rate of the top-line product. With the growing importance of lower-priced product in foreign markets, the reduced rate is vital to most foreign licensees.

If the American licensor has to pay artist royalties that are higher than usual, the licensee may be required to pay a supplemental royalty. Otherwise, the licensor would realize little or no profit. This would occur in the case of superstars who command royalties in excess of customary artist royalties. Albums made with the original Broadway musical cast and certain motion picture soundtrack albums, especially if the motion picture is based on a popular Broadway musical, may also command higher royalties. For these special recordings, licensing royalties may rise to 28 percent or more of the PPD, or be governed by a formula that is equivalent to 3 to 5 percent higher than the artist royalties payable by the American licensor.

The price used for the royalty base will exclude both a packaging allowance and excise taxes and purchase taxes such as the value-added tax that is common in many countries other than the United States. Packaging allowances in license agreements is usually lower than those used in the United States, as little as 6.5 percent of the retail list price (or its wholesale or PPD equivalent), and may be eliminated entirely. The foreign licensee's royalty payments must also cover any royalty obligations that the American licensor has to the AFM's the Music Performance Trust Fund and the Special Payments Fund. (Chapter 6, "Labor Agreements," contains a full discussion of these two funds.)

Term of Advances and Guarantees

The American licensor will try to negotiate monetary advances and royalty guarantees from the licensee, not only for the immediate financial reward, but also to ensure vigorous action by the licensee in promoting and exploiting the licensor's records.

The minimum term of a licensing agreement is usually 3 years. Where distribution agreements cover an entire catalog, most licensees will insist on a 1-year minimum period to manufacture and exploit recordings that are delivered during the last half-year of the agreement.

As a bargaining point and an incentive to greater efforts by the licensee, licensors may only agree to an extension of the term if royalty earnings have exceeded the guarantee for the original term. They may also require an increase in the royalty guarantees.

If the licensee has made substantial guarantees of royalties or releases and the licensor's catalog has failed to meet expectations, the licensee may reserve the right to cancel the agreement at an anniversary date prior to normal expiration of the agreement or to extend the term for an additional period. And as a defense against the licensee's incompetence or lack of effort, the licensor may reserve the right to cancel the agreement if the licensee fails to achieve stated minimum royalty earnings within a certain period.

The licensor will want the licensee to release a minimum amount of product during the term of the agreement. A fairly common clause states that if a licensor's release attains a listing on the *Billboard* Top 100 charts it must be released in the licensed territory. Record companies that are affiliated with motion picture companies may insist on the release of all soundtrack albums when the film is shown in the licensed territory. American record companies with original Broadway cast albums may demand the release of such albums at least in the English-speaking countries as soon as they are available for release outside the United States; but the licensee may negotiate to prevent such a requirement if an album featuring a local cast has been made in the licensed territory.

Recording contracts with top artists sometimes stipulate that the artist's recording be released not only in the United States but in certain other territories as well. In this case, the licensee may be required to release these artists' recordings in its local territory.

When artists go on a foreign promotional tour and appear on local radio and television and in concert halls, auditoriums, and nightclubs, it is important that release of their recordings coincides with their appearances in a given territory. Distribution agreements may contractually require a licensee to make such releases and to cooperate in promoting an artist on tour. They may also require the licensee to order copies of the artist's videos and to arrange for them to be given appropriate exposure in the territory.

Centralized Manufacture and Exclusivity

A common complaint by licensees is that the anticipated sale of an American recording does not warrant the expense of manufacturing it locally, while the cost of importing the finished product at regular export prices is prohibitive. To reduce the cost of importation to manageable proportions, the licensor sometimes agrees to export records at cost, relying on the sales royalties for its profits. In effect, the American licensor acts as the manufacturing plant for the licensee. This procedure has the advantage of promoting the exposure of the licensor's records in a particular territory until they become popular enough to merit local manufacture.

In some instances, a licensee working under this arrangement may agree to purchase a minimum number of records from a selected group in the licensor's catalog. Such an agreement should cover the following issues:

- A minimum purchase of any releases that have achieved American chart action
- A limited time to designate a minimum order for any other recordings which the licensee wishes to acquire rights to for the territory; if the licensee fails to act within the time frame, exclusive right to other such recordings will be waived
- A discount for volume purchases
- An advance against purchase orders
- The duration of the agreement
- An option to terminate
- Advertising and promotional guarantees
- Cooperative guarantees
- The responsibility of importer for mechanical royalties
- The applicable law governing disputes

At this writing the European Union (EU) includes Austria, Belgium, Denmark, England, Finland, France, Germany, Greece, Ireland, Italy, Luxembourg, the Netherlands, Portugal, Spain, and Sweden. Together, these countries created a common market allowing people, goods, and services to move more easily among them. Other countries have expressed interest in joining or developing closer ties with the European Union. It has over 370 million consumers and is expected to have 400 million some time in 2000.

Import duties no longer exist within the European Union. It is now possible for records and jackets manufactured in one EU country to be shipped to another at no additional expense aside from freight charges. Licensees of the same American licensor can make contractual arrangements to purchase the licensor's product from each other. The result has been centralized manufacturing, which cuts costs and potentially increases the number of items that are released from a licensor's catalog. Centralized manufacturing has also been encouraged by the increasing acceptance of the original packaging, in the language of the country of origin (usually English). The abolition of tariff barriers has accelerated the trend toward licensing arrangements with a single licensee for the entire EU. Centralized manufacturing tends to occur most often where the licensees are affiliated with each other as subsidiaries of a large multinational record company.

By January 1, 2002, all continental European currencies will be replaced by a single currency known as the euro. This new currency was first introduced on January 1, 1999, at a time when divergent currency valuations made the unified marketing of recordings within the EU countries complex and inefficient. Prices for CDs varied from an equivalent low of US$17.55 in Portugal to an equivalent high of US$23.30 for the same album in Finland. Not a single

European country approached the suggested U.S. retail list price of $14.98 to $16.98. In addition, the American practice of widespread discounting was unheard of in Europe. If the euro succeeds, the volume of mass marketing within the EU will increase substantially, since aberrations and disincentives caused by varying prices will have been eliminated. At the same time, there will be more incentive to make arrangements within the EU that encompass all member countries.

Licensees desire exclusivity for their particular territory, especially when they have made substantial guarantees of royalties and releases. Within the EU exclusivity is severely restricted by the regulations that mandate free competition, the unrestricted transshipment of goods across borders, nondiscrimination, and market unity. In fact, records first sold anywhere within the EU under the authority of the copyright holder or its licensee may be imported into or exported out of any member country. Consequently, if an American record company licenses its Dutch subsidiary to manufacture and sell certain records, a British company may buy them in bulk and export them to England, in contravention of the so-called exclusive rights granted by the licensor to another British company.

Another development that is rapidly bringing an end to traditional exclusivity arrangements is digital distribution. Digital distribution simply ignores national boundaries. While this may speed up and increase the efficiency of distribution, it does raise serious economic problems for record companies attempting to maintain their tradition "bottom-line" profits based on the distribution of "hard" copies of phonorecords.

Broadcast Performance Fees

Under the International Convention for the Protection of Performers, Producers, Phonograms, and Broadcasting Organizations—the so-called Rome Convention, signed in 1961 by several foreign countries but not the United States—when a record is used for broadcasting or any communication to the public, the user is required to pay a fee to the performers, the producers, or both, depending on local law. The principal European broadcasting systems, whether owned by the state or privately, pay broadcast fees to the representatives of record companies. Fees are also collected from jukebox proprietors, dance halls, nightclubs, and other users of recordings.

These fees are also collectible for broadcasts and performances of American records released in a foreign territory. In agreements with licensees, licensors are frequently granted an interest in the fees, usually 50 percent. But major licensees may insist on retaining broadcast performance fees until such time as the United States passes legislation providing that American broadcasters pay similar performance fees. Where fees paid to the licensee are not allocated in direct relation to the broadcasts of particular records, the agreement with the licensee may provide for an allocation to the licensor in the ratio of the licensee's sales of the licensor's records to the total sales of records by the licensee. Although it seems fair that the licensor receive a share of these fees, many licensees are unwilling to take the time and effort to extrapolate them, except in the case of major licensors and commercial users of recordings.

Music Publishing Clearances

The licensee customarily assumes the obligation to obtain licenses to reproduce copyrighted musical material that is contained in the licensor's recordings, as well as in audiovisual devices such as promotional videos, which embody such material. This involves the payment of so-called mechanical royalties which are based on the number of copies that are sold. (See Chapter 21, "Foreign Publishing.")

Labels

Major multinational firms usually have no problem requiring licensees to use the licensor's own label, but relatively unknown independent companies may have a harder time getting licensees to agree to this. Licensors want to use their own labels in order to gain prestige, name recognition, and acceptance by local dealers and the public. Such recognition makes it easier for a licensor to switch to another licensee, set up its own local enterprise (assuming it is not already part of a multinational structure), and promote its product through unified multinational advertising and other methods. For all these reasons foreign licensees may resist a request for the use of a specific label. They do not wish to build up a potential competitor. They may claim that valuable sales will be lost because the public will not purchase records on unknown labels. As a compromise, a licensor may propose the use of a split label, composed of the licensor's and the licensee's labels.

For their own protection, American companies should register their labels promptly as trademarks in foreign countries. Companies that delay doing so may find that their right to use their labels has been preempted by local registrants.

First Refusal

A foreign licensee may pick and choose from among a licensor's recordings. Many recordings may never be released by the licensee, either because they are unsuitable to the local market or because the licensee is granting priority to other product. Needless to say, just because a recording is not released in a given territory does not mean that it wouldn't sell there.

Under the circumstances, a licensor may be unwilling to commit its entire catalog exclusively to a single licensee. Instead, the licensee may have priority in selecting recordings from the catalog for local release; the licensor then has the right to place any recordings that are not selected within a stated period with other licensees. This arrangement is often referred to as a *right of first refusal.* In order to prevent confusion about the licensor's representative in the area, the primary licensee may require that releases by other licensees not give prominent credit to the licensor.

A licensee being asked to commit to substantial release guarantees or advances may well balk at receiving merely a right of first refusal. It will demand an exclusive right to all the licensor's recordings whether or not they are released locally, claiming that some recordings may become appropriate for release in the future and that confusion will result if recordings by the same artist are released on different record labels. The licensor may agree, concluding that such releases will skim the cream off its catalog and provide little gain from releases by other licensees.

Record Clubs

There are record clubs in most of the principal territories of the world. Foreign licensees with their own record clubs or arrangements with third-party record clubs will seek the right to release a licensor's recordings through such channels.

Some licensors may refuse to permit sales through record clubs without prior approval. Licensees frequently request the right to pay reduced royalty rates on club sales, contending that they themselves receive a limited licensing royalty from clubs owned and operated by third parties. If the licensee operates its own record club, it will assert that the high cost of advertising and large amounts of uncollectable monies mandate a reduced royalty rate on club sales. The rates will be the subject of bargaining and are usually one-half of the rates applicable to regular retail sales.

Coupling

The licensee may wish to have the right to couple the performances of various of the licensor's artists, or of the same artist drawn from different releases, into a single package commonly known as a *compilation.* Compilations are quite popular in Europe, particularly in the dance field.

In some countries, especially where the singles market is insignificant, coupling is essential if recordings are to reach the consumer. However, the licensor may fear that its image or the image of its artists will be downgraded by this procedure and may therefore prohibit any coupling without its consent. The licensor may permit coupling from among its own recordings but not with the recordings of other labels. Where the licensor's recordings are released locally on its own label, it is unusual for a licensee to propose the coupling of such recordings with those of other labels.

Reciprocal Arrangements

In negotiating the foreign release of their record catalogs, American licensors must consider the possibility of reciprocal licensing agreements. Americans have become more receptive to foreign artists, and many foreign recordings are released in the United States. Some reach the top of the record charts—for example, the British group the Rolling Stones and the Italian opera singer Andrea Bocelli.

In return for an exclusive license for its American recordings, the American licensor may negotiate for either an exclusive right—or a right of first refusal—to distribute the foreign licensee's recordings in the United States and Canada. The terms for the distribution tend to be similar to those in the arrangement between the foreign licensee and the American licensor.

A reciprocal arrangement is usually not possible when the licensee is a member of one of the large multinational record combines. As may be expected, the foreign recordings of Sony, BMG, WEA/EMI, and the Universal groups are channeled to their respective affiliates in the United States. However, on occasion foreign recordings not absorbed by the American affiliates are placed with unaffiliated American record companies.

Cover Recordings

A *cover record* is a competing version of the same song made after the original recording has been issued. Cover records may be a great source of friction between a licensor and a licensee. Obviously, a licensor will be hostile to its licensee releasing a cover record and may insist on a clause prohibiting cover records made by the licensee.

If the licensed recording is suitable for the local market, a licensee may be willing to exclude a cover version. This is especially true for instrumental recordings. But if the lyrics of a licensed recording are in English, its release in an area in which English is not the indigenous language may be meaningless. In these instances the licensee may be unwilling to preclude a local-language cover record, pointing out that otherwise its competitors may obtain a great advantage. Some artists record in various foreign languages and are thereby able to head off cover records.

The two parties may compromise by agreeing that the licensee will not release a local cover version earlier than an agreed-upon interval—for example, 2 to 3 months—after the release of the licensed recording.

As a matter of good relations with their licensors, the major multinational record companies with affiliates in many countries generally avoid cover versions.

Publishing Rights

All the major record companies in the United States have affiliated music publishing companies. This is true outside the United States as well. The American licensor who controls music publishing on its recordings may be faced with a request that the licensee's publishing affiliate be appointed as the exclusive subpublisher for the American publisher in the licensed territories. In the smaller record markets, such as Scandinavia, it is argued that the economics of the record business require the additional income that can be derived from music publishing in order to support maximum promotion of a record catalog. This is clearly a bargaining point, and the American firm has to evaluate many aspects of its proposed agreement before reaching a decision on the matter. Considerations include the strength of the local publisher, existing commitments or prospects of the licensor's publisher affiliate, and the possibilities of increased guarantees.

Samples and Materials

Licensors send out samples of old and new recordings to licensees so they can decide which recordings they wish to release in their territory. These samples are usually shipped via express mail or digitally so that the licensee may review them quickly. Although there may be no charge for the samples, it is not uncommon to require the licensee to pay for packing and for freight and other transportation costs.

It is usually more cost-effective to manufacture recordings locally than to import finished records from the United States. For the purpose of manufacture, the licensee orders digital audio tapes (DATs)—master tapes from which CDs, cassettes, and vinyl albums can be made locally. For the production of album covers, the licensee may request cover images, either as negatives or in digitized form, or order copies of printed front covers or back liners. The licensee usually pays at the licensor's cost price for orders of DATs, negatives, and printed covers or liners, as well as the costs of packing and shipping.

Accountings and Auditing

In any dealings with foreign licensees it is important to appoint companies that are reputable and financially responsible. Otherwise the licensor may be faced with disputes over many items, including accountings and royalty payments.

The agreement between the licensee and licensor may require quarterly or semiannual accountings: licensors prefer quarterly accountings; licensees prefer semiannual accountings. The accountings should set forth in detail the computation of the amounts due, including the number of records sold from each recording, broken down by configuration, as well as the royalty rate and all deductions and other charges.

The American licensor should obtain the right to audit the licensee's books as to records manufactured and records sold. Licensees usually require that the cost of the inspection and audit be borne by the licensor and be conducted by a certified or chartered public accountant. The licensee should also agree to produce its accountings to the mechanical rights society in the licensed territory. This should serve as a simple check on the accuracy of the licensee's royalty reports to the licensor.

Termination Procedure

At the end of a licensing agreement, the licensee will have on hand DATs and an inventory of finished records. To protect its interests and those of a successor licensee, the licensor will want to control the licensee's disposition of such items.

It is common to provide for a 6-month period after the final date of the agreement so that the licensee can sell off the inventory of finished records. Without such a sell-off period, the licensee would have to stop releasing any new product months before the final date of the agreement. This could operate to the detriment of licensee and licensor. To protect itself, the licensor may provide that all sales in the sell-off period shall be in the normal course of business and at regular prices; otherwise the product may be downgraded by severe discounting and other practices.

The licensor may require a written list of the inventory, to be supplied within a short period after the expiration of the licensing agreement. The list provides information useful to the licensor and any new licensee regarding the state of the prior licensee's inventory. The licensor may also have the right at any time after the expiration of the licensing agreement to purchase from the licensee, at the licensee's cost (and perhaps a small additional percentage), all or part of the unsold inventory. The new licensee may be interested in purchasing this inventory. Where the old licensee is not trusted, the licensor may wish to acquire the inventory so as to avoid the risk of new pressings continuing to be sold under the guise of inventory.

The licensee is usually required to dispose of materials other than finished records in one of four ways:

1. Deliver them to the licensor in the United States or the licensed territory
2. Transfer them to a new licensee
3. Destroy them under the licensor's supervision
4. Destroy them and supply an appropriate affidavit to that effect

The licensee and the licensor may also determine whether the costs of delivery are to be borne by the licensee or the licensor, as well as whether the licensee is entitled to reimbursement for the cost of the materials to be delivered.

Variations in Currency Values

Licensors should be aware that changes in the exchange rate can have an impact on the amount of royalties earned in U.S. dollars. Where exchange rates are volatile (as they have been in the past in Brazil, Mexico, and Southeast Asia), the time when royalties are computed and paid can be vital. Contractual negotiations should specify whether royalty conversions to U.S. dollars will be computed (1) at the time records are sold, (2) at the time of licensee's receipt of payment for records sold, (3) at the close of the royalty accounting period, or (4) at the close of the royalty accounting period when the licensee is contractually required to account to the licensor.

Currency fluctuations can work to the detriment of the licensee, who pays advances to the licensor in U.S. dollars at the time a license agreement is signed but then recoups those advances at later dates when the exchange rate may be less favorable.

Transmittal of Funds

Even the routine transfer of funds from a licensee to a licensor requires international bank transfers. If these transactions are by wire, additional charges may be involved. Some international licensee firms maintain U.S. bank accounts for the convenience of all parties.

For the few areas in the world where governmental regulations impede the free flow of local funds to the United States for the payment of record royalties and guarantees, the licensing agreement may stipulate that the licensor may direct the licensee to deposit the requisite funds to the credit of the licensor in a local depository designated by the licensor. The money then becomes available for local use by the licensor.

Jurisdiction over Disputes

Disputes may occur between the licensor and the licensee regarding the interpretation of the licensing agreement, royalty statements, or other matters in the agreement. The American licensor will seek to have U.S. courts or arbitration designated as the exclusive forum for the determination of controversies; this avoids the great expense of litigation in a foreign tribunal. Naturally, the foreign licensee will assert that the forum should be local because the facts are local.

To determine whether the dispute will be adjudicated on American or foreign soil, negotiations are necessary. To avoid an impasse, some negotiators compromise by requiring the claimant to accept the jurisdiction of the responding party, thereby increasing the incentive to settle disputes. Given the cost and unpredictability of litigation, alternative dispute resolution procedures, such as mediation and arbitration, are increasingly used in agreements. There may, however, be legal questions about the enforceability of adjudicated disputes if they do not conform to the due process requirements of the licensee's country, where enforcement is being sought. Legal counsel should be consulted in this area.

Default Clauses

It is advisable that the licensing agreement between the American licensor and the foreign licensee contain a complete, detailed clause setting forth the rights and obligations of the parties in the event of a default.

A default is deemed to be material if the licensee fails to (1) pay guarantees and royalties when due, (2) render complete accountings when due, or (3) comply with contractual requirements as to minimum releases of the licensor's records. The licensor should also provide that the bankruptcy or insolvency of the licensee constitutes a material default. The licensee will strive for a provision under which it is entitled to a notice of default and a period in which to remedy it.

Ordinarily, where there is a material default, the American licensor has the right to cancel the agreement. When there is such a cancellation the licensee may not have the right, usually granted at the end of an agreement, to sell off any inventory of finished goods.

The default clause should reserve to the licensor all rights to seek damages, accountings, or other relief, in addition to canceling the agreement.

6

Labor Agreements

Two unions exist for performers in the record industry, the American Federation of Musicians (AFM) and the American Federation of Television and Radio Artists (AFTRA). Musicians, leaders, contractors, copyists, orchestrators, and arrangers of instrumental music are covered by the AFM; vocalists, actors, announcers, narrators, and sound effects artists are represented by AFTRA. Under the employers' agreements with both unions, employees must either be members of the union or become members by the 30th day of their employment.

Membership dues for the AFM consist of a one-time national fee of $65 plus local fees varying from a nominal $1 to $35; annual national dues of $46 and local dues of lesser amounts; and "work dues" of 1 to 5 percent of union-scale wages; of which 1 percent goes to the national union. For detailed information about membership, benefits, payment schedules, etc., contact the AFM at 1501 Broadway, Suite 600, New York, NY 10036; telephone: 212-869-1330; fax: 212-764-6134; Web site: http://www.afm.org. See also the accompanying CD-ROM for copies of the following AFM forms: "Exclusive Agent-Musician Agreement," "Contract Form L-2 (Local Union)," "Collective Bargaining Agreement," and "Contract T-2 (Traveling Engagements)." Some AFM rates are listed in Appendix F.

AFTRA has a uniform initiation fee of $1,000 covering both national and local membership, plus initial work dues of $442.50; additional work dues are billed annually on May 1 and November 1. These additional dues are based on the member's AFTRA earnings during previous year; rates range from 1 to 5 percent, as determined by each local unit. During the year 2000, AFTRA plans to implement a uniform national schedule in stages. For information regarding current dues, benefits, payment schedules, and membership rates, contact AFTRA at 260 Madison Avenue, New York, NY 10016; telephone: 212-532-0800; fax: 212-545-1238; Web site: http://www.aftra.org. The accompanying CD-ROM also contains a copy of "Standard AFTRA Exclusive Agency Contract."

Key Labor Agreements

The main agreements between the two labor unions and the recording industry are the "AFTRA Code of Fair Practice for Phonograph Recordings" and the AFM "Phonograph Record Labor Agreement."

Both agreements cover the essential negotiated points for members' services within the record industry, including minimum scale payments; residual payments; health and retirement provisions; vacation, overtime, and holiday pay provisions; union contractor requirements; and instrumental cartage for musicians. The recording industry also has certain obligations to the AFTRA Health and Retirement Funds and to the AFM's Special Payments Funds and the Phonograph Record Trust Fund.

Arbitration

Under the AFTRA Code of Fair Practice for Phonograph Recordings, any dispute between a record company and AFTRA, or between a record company and a member of AFTRA arising out of the AFTRA agreement or out of any contract made on or after April 1, 1987, must be submitted to arbitration.

If there is an exclusive recording agreement with an artist, and "the Company has reason to believe that the artist has recorded or contemplates recording in violation of the contract," the company may apply to any court having jurisdiction over the artist for an injunction and other relief arising out of the particular act.

An arbitration panel consists of three arbitrators. The initiating party—AFTRA, the record company, or the artist (with the written consent of AFTRA)—appoints the first arbitrator. The responding party must then name its arbitrator within 3 days. The two arbitrators then have 5 days to choose a third arbitrator from a panel submitted by the American Arbitration Association. In the event that the parties are unable to make a choice within the allotted time, the AAA decides for them. The award granted by a majority of the arbitrators is final and binding on the parties, and an official, binding judgment consistent with the terms of the arbitrators' award may be entered by any party in the highest court of the forum, state or federal, having jurisdiction.

As of this writing, AFM agreements do not provide for arbitration.

AFTRA and AFM Scale Payments

The AFTRA rates vary according to specific job classifications: soloists and duos; group singers; actors and comedians; narrators and announcers; and sound effects artists. There are also special rates for performers in original-cast albums and for vocalists "stepping out" of groups in recording sessions.

AFTRA scale payments for TV commercials vary according to on- or off-camera appearance, the duration of the commercial, and factors such as regional or national airing, cable use, Spanish-language versions, and "wild spots" (broadcast times designated at the discretion of the station at a discounted rate). Basic payments are supplemented as and when the on-air use occurs. AFTRA scale payments for radio commercials have complex formulas and involve factors such as single, duo, or larger groups; national or regional use; and, if regional, major cities included or excluded.

Under the AFTRA code, *nonroyalty* singers are entitled to additional union-scale payments, depending on the number of recordings sold in the United States on or after December 15, 1974. (A recording ceases to be considered a basis for additional payments 10 years after the date of its first release to the public as a single or as a part of an album.) Only sales in normal retail channels are counted. Record club, mail-order, and premium sales are excluded, but CD sales through the Internet are included, and sales from digital distribution are under discussion.

A recorded side that has been previously released in album form does not earn contingent-scale payments from further release in any other album. If released as a single, it does not accrue contingent-scale monies for release in any other single. If a single is incorporated into an album, it is then eligible for contingent-scale payments.

For albums other than cast albums, there are incremental fees of 50 percent of minimum scale per plateau to be paid if sales reach specified levels. As of 1999, these levels were (a) 157,500, (b) 250,000, (c) 375,000, (d) 500,000, (e) 650,000, (f) 825,000, and (g) 1,000,000, (h) 1,500,000, (i) 2,000,000, (j) 2,5000,000, (k) 3,000,000. As for single sales, there are contingent scale payments of 33 ⅓ percent per plateau to be paid. As of 1999, these plateaus were (a) 500,000, (b) 600,000, (c) 750,000, (d) 850,000, (e) 1,000,000 and (f) 1,500,000 are achieved.

Contingent-scale payments to nonroyalty AFTRA artists may not ordinarily be recouped or charged against royalties or other payments due to AFTRA royalty artists. But the record company may, subject to the consent of the covered artist, credit overscale payments in excess of 2.5 times the minimum scale against contingent payments. All contingent-scale payments are subject to contributions to the AFTRA Health and Retirement Funds.

The AFM agreement makes provisions for minimum wages and other working conditions for instrumentalists, leaders, contractors, arrangers, orchestrators, and copyists. The provisions are detailed and extensive. The union should be consulted for specific terms.

As of February 1, 2000, a musician on nonclassical recordings became entitled to $302.85 as a basic session rate for a 3-hour session. This rises to $313.45 as of February 1, 2001. There are also premium rates for recording sessions held on Saturdays after 1:00 p.m., as well as on Sundays, listed holidays, and during certain late night hours. Leaders and contractors receive not less than double the applicable sideman musician's scale. A musician who plays more than one instrument during a recording session (arbitrarily called "doubling") is paid an additional 20 percent of the base rate and the regular overtime payment. An additional 15 percent is paid for each subsequent instrument played during the session.

AFM Special Payments and Trust Funds

When employers sign the AFM Phonograph Record Labor Agreement, they also agree to contribute a percentage of their profits to the AFM Phonograph Record Special Payments Fund, the Phonograph Record Trust Fund, and the Motion Picture Special Payments Fund agreements. Motion picture collections have substantially increased because sales to video, TV, and cable have raised both record sales and royalty collections. Compilation albums and licensing to clubs and film companies have also resulted in increased payments.

These funds are a major benefit of union membership. After deduction of expenses, the monies in the SPFs are disbursed as a continuing royalty to members of the AFM who have participated in the recordings on a nonroyalty basis. Payments are made yearly to those musicians who performed as union musicians at one or more sessions within the past 5 years. The amount of each recording musician's payment is determined by how many union recording sessions he or she has participated in. Participation is not limited to hit recordings or even to the actual commercial release of a recording once the session has been completed, and once qualified, the payments continue for 5 years.

The monies collected in the Phonograph Record Trust Fund are used to arrange and organize "the presentation of personal performances by instrumental musicians in the areas throughout the United States, and its territories, possessions and dependencies, and the Dominion of Canada ... on such occasions and at such times and places as in the judgment of the Trustee will contribute to the public knowledge and appreciation of music." The performances are to be organized for live audiences, and may be broadcast, when no admissions fees are charged, "in connection with activities of patriotic, charitable, educational, civic, and general public nature." The activities must be without profit to the Trust Fund.

Each agreement applies only to records containing music "which was performed or conducted by musicians covered by, or required to be paid pursuant to ... [the] Phonograph Record Labor Agreement." If the services of union members on a particular record consist solely of arrangements, orchestrations, or copying, then that record is not subject to either agreement.

The record companies' payments to the Phonograph Record SPF is based on record, tape, and CD sales. The schedule for payments is based on the manufacturer's suggested retail price, as follows: for records and tapes to $3.79, the rate is 0.54 percent; for records and tapes to $8.98, the rate is 0.52 percent; for compact discs to $10.98, the rate is 0.52 percent.

In computing payments, the record company must report 100 percent of net sales. There are certain allowances in connection with the computation of payments. First, there is a packaging deduction from the suggested retail list price in the country of manufacture or sale: 20 percent for phonograph records and 30 percent for tapes, cartridges, and compact discs. Second, there is an exemption for singles of the first 100,000 sold of each title. Third, excepting record clubs, there is an exemption of up to 25 percent of the total records, tapes, cartridges, and compact discs distributed, representing "free" records, tapes, cartridges, and compact discs actually distributed. And fourth, for record clubs there is an exemption for "free" and "bonus" records, tapes, cartridges, and compact discs actually distributed up to 50 percent of total distribution, with the record manufacturer paying the full rate on half of the excess of the "free" and "bonus" records, tapes, cartridges, and compact discs over the 50 percent, in addition to full-rate payments for all records actually sold by clubs.

Suggested retail list prices must be computed exclusive of any sales or excise taxes on sales of records and tapes. If a record company does not use the manufacturer's suggested retail price, it must negotiate a new equivalent basis for computing payments.

For each record subject to the Special Payments Fund Agreement, there is a 10-year limitation, from the year of release, on the sales for which payments must be made.

Record manufacturers pay lesser amounts to the Phonograph Record Trust Agreement. Payments are calculated on record sales at the rate of 0.23625 percent of the manufacturer's suggested retail list price, up to a maximum of $8.98, for each record and tape sold, whether singles, albums, or extended-play records. For compact discs, the maximum suggested retail price is $10.98. The allowances and exemptions are similar to those used to calculate payments to the Phonograph Record SPF, with some exceptions; the exemption for singles is the first 150,000 sold of each title. There is also an exemption for the first 25,000 units of a title, whether albums, tapes, compact discs, or other devices. There is a 5-year limitation for payments to the Phonograph Record Trust Agreement.

The Motion Picture Special Payments Fund is structured differently because revenues are generated differently in the motion picture industry. Payments are based on a musician's actual works in scoring a specific theatrical or television move. Each union signatory producer contributes a percentage of the revenues for that specific project. Those payments are then divided among the musicians who performed the actual services. Musicians on that project receive SPF payments for that specific movie as long as the picture continues to be profitable for the union signatory company.

Finally, all sales, assignments, leases, licenses, or other transfers of master recordings are subject to the provisions in the Special Payments Fund Agreement and the Phonograph Record Trust Agreement. This applies to any person or company doing business in the United States, Canada, or Puerto Rico. Those who are licensed to do business outside the domestic area must agree to make the necessary payments to the licensor, who is responsible for remitting them to the appropriate funds.

AFTRA Health and Retirement Funds

The AFTRA Health and Retirement Funds provide medical coverage and retirement benefits for eligible AFTRA members. The record companies are required to pay to the funds an amount equal to 10 percent of the gross compensation paid to the performer by the company. Included in the "gross compensation" are all forms of payment, including "salaries, earnings, royalties, fees, advances, guarantees, deferred compensation, proceeds, bonuses, profit-participation, shares of stock, bonds, options and property of any kind or nature whatsoever paid to the artist directly or indirectly." The 10 percent payment is limited to the first $100,000 of gross compensation paid to the artist in any calendar year.

Royalty Performers

The AFM basic agreement makes a distinction between a musician who is a phonograph record "royalty artist" and one who is not. A *royalty artist* is one who "records pursuant to a phonograph record contract which provides for a royalty payable to such musician at a basic rate of at least 3 percent of the suggested retail list price of records sold (less deductions usual and customary in the trade) … or a substantially equivalent royalty," or "plays as a member of (and not as a sideman with) a recognized self-contained group." A *recognized self-contained group* consists of "two or more persons who perform together in fields other than phonograph records under a group name" and record under a phonograph record contract providing for a royalty "at a basic rate of at least 3 percent of the suggested retail list price of records sold (less deductions usual and customary in the trade) or a substantially equivalent royalty." Furthermore, all musicians in the group must be members of the AFM.

At the first session for a single record side a royalty artist receives only the basic session rate and related overtime rate regardless of whether he or she plays multiple parts, doubles, overdubs, or "sweetens" (e.g., adds strings, horns, or woodwinds to a previously recorded basic rhythm track).

The AFM agreement states that recording contracts must contain a covenant that the contract "shall become effective unless it is disapproved by the International Executive Board of the American Federation of Musicians of the United States and Canada, or a duly authorized agent thereof, within 30 working days after it is submitted to the International Executive Board. The parties acknowledge that this provision is not intended to provide a device for the parties hereto to avoid their obligations."

For recordings of the same side, the AFTRA code stipulates that a royalty artist shall receive minimum union scale, with a maximum payment of three times scale regardless of the length and number of sessions. The record company must state in the production memorandum that is filed after a recording session whether or not the performer is a royalty artist. The record company must also furnish the artist "at least semiannually and to AFTRA upon request, ... so long as there shall be sales, a full and proper accounting in order to correctly ascertain the amount of royalty ... due artist."

Contractors

Under the AFTRA code *contractors* are "those artists who perform any additional services, such as contacting singers, pre-rehearsing, coaching, or conducting singers, arranging for sessions or rehearsals, or any other similar or supervisory duties, including assisting and preparation of production memorandum." The contractor's duties include acting as liaison between the performers and producer, seeing that all AFTRA provisions are enforced, and completing and filing all appropriate forms with AFTRA within 48 hours. At each recording session, the contractor must fill out the pertinent information on the AFTRA Phonograph Record Sessions Report Form and deliver a copy of the form to the record company representatives. The record company initials the form, indicating that a recording session has been held, and the contractor files the report with AFTRA. This report is over and above Schedule A, a production memorandum, which the record company must furnish to AFTRA within 21 calendar days after the recording session. The production memorandum should provide sufficient information to permit a computation of the appropriate performing fee, as well as setting forth the gross fee paid.

A contractor is required for all engagements of nonroyalty group singers consisting of three or more persons. The contractor must be one of the singers unless the group is all-female or all-male. A contractor is also required for all original-cast albums employing a singing group of three or more; the contractor does not have to be a member of the singing group.

The contractor is to be present at all times during the recording session and receives, in addition to the regular union-scale payment for vocalists, an additional scale payment for services as a contractor. The AFTRA scale payment for contractors is the same as for additional vocalists.

The functions of a contractor are not generally defined in the AFM basic agreement. In practice, however, the contractor hires the necessary musicians for the recording session and often hires the AFTRA contractor, who in turn hires the required singers. An AFM contractor must be used if 12 or more sidemen are employed for any session. The contractor, who may or may not be one of the sidemen, must attend the entire session. The contractor is paid not less than double the applicable sideman's scale, with no extra payment for his or her services as sideman. It is the duty of the contractor to supply completed W-4 forms as well as B report forms to the record company for each recording session. The forms are due within 15 working days of the performance and are the basis for the payment of union scale by the record company.

Dubbing

Dubbing, also called *overdubbing*, is the addition of vocal or instrumental performances to music already recorded. The AFM basic agreement prohibits dubbing except as specifically permitted by other provisions of the agreement. Dubbing is allowed only if the record company gives prior notice to the union and pays union scale and fringe benefits for the new use. Both during and after a recording session, the record company may add live vocal and instrumental performances to a recording without additional compensation to the musicians who made the original recording.

Under the AFTRA agreement, dubbing also means converting or transferring a performance made in a medium other than phonograph records (e.g., radio, television, or motion pictures) for use as phonograph recordings. This is sanctioned by AFTRA provided that the record company meets certain conditions: providing a notice to AFTRA, paying AFTRA scale to the performers, obtaining the consent of the "star or featured or overscale artist," if any, and acquiring the consent of the artist who has performed the vocal soundtrack, if any, for the "star or featured or overscale artist." The provisions for payment are comparable to AFM reuse fees.

The AFTRA agreement does not prohibit overdubbing. It provides that if the "artist participates in multiple tracking (i.e., sings again to the original track at the same session), he shall be paid for the session as if each overtracking were an additional [record] side."

AFM Interactive Department

In 1997, the AFM Electronic and Media Services Division organized an interactive department to cover special projects, including wages, pension, and health and welfare benefits. The AFM has an experimental and multimedia agreement that addresses requests for scales in all current existing interactive and new media areas. This agreement is renewed and updated every year. It outlines the new recording scales and guidelines for musicians' performances on CD-ROM, DVD, and dedicated console platform productions, for Web site and Web link menu music, and for live streaming performances on the Internet. It also contains the scales for virtual reality rides and kiosks and the guidelines for new use of existing music on the Internet or as interactive product. This information may be obtained by contacting the AFM West Coast office at 800-237-0988, ext. 202.

Protections against Illicit Practices

Purchases or leases of master recordings by record companies are an accepted part of the music business. There are well-established and well-financed independent producers who sell or lease master recordings to record companies. There are also young musicians who make master recordings on spec, inspired by faith in their own talents; lacking the capital to operate under union standards, these young entrepreneurs may record in makeshift studios with nonunion musicians or with union musicians who are willing to accept less than scale.

AFTRA and the AFM are fully aware of the illicit practices in the field and recognize them as threats to the employment of union members and to the maintenance of minimum union pay rates. For this reason the unions have included certain provisions in their agreements that appear designed to make the record companies assist in policing the field.

Paragraph 17 of the AFM agreement prohibits a record company from acquiring recordings that were recorded in the domestic area or by a resident of the domestic area unless the musicians were paid wages and fringe benefits at least equal to the union scale in effect at the time the recorded music was produced. To satisfy its obligations, the record company may include certain stipulated clauses in its agreement to acquire the master recordings:

1. A representation and warranty by the seller or licensor that the recorded music does not come within the terms of Paragraph 17 or that the requirements of Paragraph 17 are satisfied
2. A statement that the representation and warranty were included for the benefit of the union and may be enforced by the union or by the person it may designate

The record company guarantees the representation and warranty if the seller or licensor was not a party to an AFM agreement when the recording was made.

To satisfy the provisions of the AFTRA agreement the record company must obtain from the seller or lessor the following warranty and representation for the direct benefit of AFTRA and the performing artists:

That all artists whose performances embodied thereon were recorded in the recording territory, have been paid the minimum rates specified in the 1990–1993 AFTRA code of Fair Practice for Phonograph Recordings or the applicable Code then in effect at the time the recording was made, and that all payments due to the AFTRA Health and Retirement Funds have been made.

The record label must submit this warranty to AFTRA on Schedule D. Alternatively, the record company may file a Schedule A, which lists the performers and payments made by the company. If the warranty is false and the seller or lessor was not a signatory to the AFTRA code when the recording was made or acquired by the record company, then the company must pay the performers minimum scale and make any applicable contributions to the AFTRA Health and Retirement Funds.

Attorneys are occasionally asked to advise a potential purchaser about future royalty obligations to the artists on the recordings. Unless the seller specifically agrees to continue paying royalties to the artist, a legal obligation is created between the artist and the purchaser even in the absence of a specific assumption. This is called a *lien,* which attaches to the property, which, in this situation, is the master. The union rights to the royalties are the same as those of the artist's.

The AFTRA Code of Fair Practice for Phonograph Recordings clearly attempts to solve this problem. It refers to any transfer of title to or rights in a master recording by "sale, assignment, pledge, hypothecation, or other transfer, or by attachment, levy, lien, garnishment, voluntary bankruptcy, involuntary bankruptcy, arrangement, reorganization, assignment for benefit of creditors, probate, or any other legal proceeding." Under the AFTRA code the transferee is responsible to the artist for royalties due under the artist contract for sales of phonograph records made by the transferee or its licensees. Such responsibility accrues after a default by the producer of the records in the payment of artist royalties and receipt by the transferee of written notice by the artist specifying the default, together with due proof of the artist's royalty arrangements. The transferee's responsibility is only in respect of sales after receipt of such notice.

The AFTRA agreement also requires that any transferee of title or rights to a master recording who is not a signatory to the AFTRA code shall sign an agreement with AFTRA assuming the obligations referred to in the previous paragraph. The transferer continues to have the same responsibility to the artist and to the AFTRA trust fund for all sales by the transferer's successor in interest, unless the successor is a Code signatory.

In agreements transferring an interest in a master recording, every record producer must include provisions incorporating the aforementioned royalty responsibility to the artist on the part of the transferee, as well as a covenant requiring the same undertaking in all subsequent transfers.

Domestic and Foreign Territory

The AFTRA agreement states that it applies to the making of phonograph recordings in the United States, its territories, and its possessions, all of which is referred to as the "recording territory." No clause regulates recordings made outside the recording territory.

The AFM agreement is not so restricted. It covers recordings made in both Canada and the United States, or in a present territory or possession of either country, all of which is called the "domestic area." The agreement also encompasses any residents of the domestic area who are engaged to perform as instrumental musicians, leaders, contractors, copyists, orchestrators, or arrangers of instrumental music in the recording of phonograph records outside the domestic area.

According to AFM bylaws, its members are prohibited from rendering services outside the domestic area unless they have written authorization from the union to do so. Penalties for a violation include a fine not exceeding $10,000, or expulsion from the union, or both.

New Rights for Performing Artists

Under the Rome Convention of 1961 (discussed in Chapter 5), broadcasters in signatory countries must pay a fee for the right to broadcast a recording to the public. The AFTRA agreement stipulates that if the fee is paid to the record company, within 30 days of a written request by either party the record company and the union will bargain in good faith about the portion payable to the performers. If a separate payment is made to the performers, no negotiation is necessary.

In recent years the AFM has been pressing Japan to pay American musicians a fair portion of record rental collections. The initial benefit to American artists was $2.3 million for the period 1996–1997. The Alliance of Artists and Recording Companies (AARC), which represents 130 recording companies and 1,400 featured artists, distributes the funds to royalty artists (discussed in section below). AFTRA and AFM will make payments to background singers and musicians.

Promotional Videotapes

Master recordings are often used in promotional videotapes. The AFM agreement stipulates that for video promo selections produced on or after February 1, 1995, each nonroyalty musician who performs "on camera" is to be paid $188.04 per 12-hour day for each such selection. Pension and welfare payments are to be made at the rates set by the AFM. For every half-hour of work performed in excess of 12 hours, the musicians must receive time and a half.

If a promotional videotape is marketed to consumers as a videocassette or videodisc, if worldwide revenues reach $5,000, the record company is obligated to pay to the AFM the sum of $500 for distribution to the musicians whose services were employed in the production of the video's master recording. If worldwide revenues exceed $75,000 for a tape produced on or after February 1, 1987, the record company must pay the AFM 1 percent of any excess, less the $500 previously paid, for distribution to the same musicians. If a royalty artist's contract provides for participation in revenues and if the contract so allows, then the payments to the AFM based on revenues may be reduced to the extent the payments would otherwise be due to the royalty artist. These payments constitute the only ones owed to the AFM and the musicians arising out of the production and exploitation of promotional videotapes.

The general structure of the AFTRA code provisions regarding video promos tends to resemble the AFM structure. In the 1997–2001 Sound Recording Code, parties agreed to a side letter calling for negotiations at a later date for the terms of a new music video agreement to govern the performers on all videos produced by or at the direction of a signatory record company. The parties also agreed to a "move-over" fee (assigned when a recording is transferred to an audiovisual format, i.e., TV or film) of $550.00 effective January 1, 1999, to be shared by all signers whose song is used in the music video.

The appropriate unions must be considered in planning any video production: the Screen Actors Guild, the Writers Guild of America, the Directors Guild of America, the Producers Guild of America, and the International Association of Theatrical and Stage Employees. This goes beyond the scope of this publication.

7

Copyright in Sound Recordings

Section 101 of the U.S. Copyright Act of 1976 clearly distinguishes phonorecords from sound recordings, as follows:

> "Phonorecords" are material objects in which sounds, other than those accompanying a motion picture or other audiovisual work, are fixed by any method now known or later developed, and from which the sounds can be perceived, reproduced, or otherwise communicated, either directly or with the aid of a machine or device. The term "phonorecords" includes the material object in which the sounds are first fixed... .
>
> "Sound recordings" are works that result from the fixation of a series of musical, spoken, or other sounds, but not including the sounds accompanying a motion picture or other audiovisual work, regardless of the nature of the material objects, such as disks, tapes, or other phonorecords, in which they are embodied.

Copyright Protection for Published and Unpublished Works

The 1976 Copyright Act defines *publication* as distribution "to the public by sale or other transfer of ownership, or by rental, lease or lending," as well as the offering to distribute "phonorecords to a group of persons for purposes of further distribution." A recording is considered published if it is sold to the public or offered to wholesalers or retailers for ultimate sale to the public.

Federal copyright protection went into effect for all sound recordings fixed and published on or after February 15, 1972. However, unpublished sound recordings could not be registered for federal copyright until January 1, 1978. Sound recordings published before February 15, 1972, are not eligible for federal copyright protection, but they may be protected under common law or state antipiracy statutes. (See Chapter 8, "Bootlegging, Piracy, and Counterfeiting.") The 1976 Copyright Act limits this protection to 75 years, however; after February 15, 2047, sound recordings published on or before February 15, 2047, will fall into the public domain, notwithstanding any protection under state law.

But in 1998 it took an act of Congress to protect the many thousands of sound recordings published prior to February 15, 1972, from being stripped of even this modest common law state copyright protection. In *La Cienega Music Co. v. ZZ Top*, 53 F.3d 950 (9th Cir. 1995), the appellate court ruled that La Cienega had forfeited all copyright protection to the 1960 ZZ Top recording of "La Grange" because it had failed to print a copyright notice on the recording. The record and music industry rallied behind La Cienega and appealed to Congress to confirm that the 1976 Copyright Act's definition of a published work was not retroactive to an era when sound recordings were barred from being copyrighted. They further argued that forfeiture for failure to affix a copyright notice, or to register a renewal claim 28 years later, should not apply to such early sound recordings even though they were commercially and publicly sold to a wide public. Congress agreed and amended the Copyright Act accordingly.

Authorship

The 1976 Copyright Act states that the copyright of a sound recording rests initially with the "author" or "authors" of that recording. However, the act does not establish who the author is. At times this may be difficult to determine, inasmuch as the final recording reflects the contributions of various persons involved in the recording process. It is usual for the copyrightable elements in a sound recording to involve authorship both by the performers on the recording and by the record producer in charge of planning the recording session, recording and electronically processing the sounds, and assembling and editing them into the final sound recording. In some cases the record producer contributes very little and the performance is the only copyrightable element. In other cases, such as recordings of bird calls and airplane motors, the record producer's contribution is the sole copyrightable aspect.

Authorship, and ultimately ownership, of the recordings is a matter of bargaining between the parties involved. If there is no employment relationship or agreement by performers to assign the copyright to the record company, the copyright in the sound recording is owned by the performing artists and/or the producer. If the work is prepared by an employee in the course of his or her employment, it is a work-for-hire and the employer is the author. Virtually every recording agreement between a record company and an artist provides that the sound recordings are created for the company as works-for-hire. But just because it says so in the agreement does not necessarily make it so: this is an issue that has yet to be determined. (For a full discussion of this issue, see Chapter 17, "Works for Hire." See also a sample "Certificate of Authorship" on the accompanying CD-ROM.)

Rights of the Copyright Owner

The copyright gives the owner of a sound recording the exclusive rights to reproduce it, to distribute the records to the public, and to make derivative works based thereon. The copyright does not include cover or sound-alike records, i.e., sound recordings that imitate or simulate the original copyrighted sound recording; therefore the owner does not have the ability to prevent such recordings from being made and copyrighted by others.

There is no domestic provision for broadcast performance fees, the copyright owner is not entitled to license or receive royalties for the public performance and broadcasting of nondigital recordings. Since the United States is not a signatory to the Rome Convention, discussed in Chapter 5, other signatories generally do not pay American record companies, artists, or producers any share of that country's sound recording performance royalty pool. As a result, American record companies, artists, and producers have lost an estimated $600 million or more of these royalties over the past several years. Limited performance fees are assessed for digital recordings. (See "Digital Performance Rights," page 79.)

The practice of renting a lawfully purchased copy of a record was barred by a special act of Congress in 1984 and extended for the life of the copyright in 1993. This restriction does not apply to the lending of records for nonprofit purposes by public libraries or to the rental of motion picture soundtracks and videos, which are classified as audiovisual works.

For a full discussion of the duration of copyright, see Chapter 11, "The Duration of Copyright Protection and the Limitation of Grants.")

Notice of Copyright

Generally speaking, a sound recording is not deemed to be a "copy" of the musical composition or other material contained in the recording. As a consequence, it is unnecessary to place a copyright notice such as "©1990 M.B.Y. Music Publishing Co. Inc." on a sound recording in order to protect the underlying musical work. Furthermore, since March 1, 1989, the effective date of the Berne Convention Implementation Act of 1988, copyright notice on published copies of works, including recordings, is no longer required to maintain the copyright. However, it is still advisable to use a copyright notice for various reasons. For example, a copyright notice is necessary for protection in those relatively few countries that impose such formalities and are members of the Universal Copyright Convention but not members of Berne (e.g., Colombia and Venezuela). A copyright notice may also deter infringement by providing a clear warning that copyright is asserted. Moreover, under the copyright laws it serves to defeat a defense of "innocent infringement." It also helps prospective users to locate copyright owners in order to secure appropriate licenses.

Under the copyright statute, the copyright notice on a sound recording should appear on the surface of the copies or on the label or container in such manner and location as to give reasonable notice of the claim of copyright. The notice is to comprise the symbol ℗, the year of the first public distribution of the sound recording, and the name of the copyright owner of the sound recording.

Deposit for the Library of Congress

The 1976 Copyright Act requires that within 3 months from the date of publication of a phonorecord in the United States, the copyright owner or the owner of the exclusive right of publication shall deposit in the Copyright Office, for the use or disposition of the Library of Congress, two complete phonorecords of the best edition, together with any printed or visually perceptible material published with such phonorecords. The deposit should include the entire container or package as well as the disc or tape inserted therein. The deposit is not a condition of copyright protection.

Copyright Registration

There is no requirement for copyright registration under the 1976 Copyright Act, and registration is not a condition of copyright protection. Registration of any published or unpublished work is permissible at any time during the existence of copyright in the work.

For registration the applicant must file an application on a form prescribed by the Register of Copyrights, together with a $30 fee and the following deposits:

1. For an unpublished sound recording, one phonorecord
2. For a published sound recording, two complete phonorecords of the best edition
3. For a sound recording first published outside the United States, one complete phonorecord as so published

A deposit of phonorecords for the Library of Congress referred to above will satisfy the deposit provisions for registration if the phonorecords deposited are accompanied by the application and fee described in this section and by any additional identifying material that the Register of Copyrights may require by regulation. (For a further discussion of copyright deposits and registration, see Chapter 10, "Copyright Law in the United States.")

Copyrightable Works

Albums

Although an album consists of several separate recordings, notice of copyright is not a complicated matter. Where there is only one copyright owner, one notice will suffice, and the album may be registered for copyright as a collective work in one application. In that event, only the overall title of the collective work will be indexed and cataloged in the records of the Copyright Office. For the separate indexing and cataloging of individual selections, the copyright owner may file a different application for registration together with a separate fee for each selection. If the album has been the subject of a registration, the application for registration of an individual title should indicate that the single is from the album.

Derivative Works

With respect to derivative works, sound recordings are treated like other works under the copyright law. If it is a new version of a public-domain work or a new version of a copyrighted work produced with the consent of the copyright proprietor, the new version is regarded as a "derivative work" and is copyrightable as such. Insofar as a sound recording contains recordings reissued with substantial new recorded material, or recordings republished with materially edited abridgments or revisions of the basic recording, the sound recording is considered a copyrightable derivative work. Many new recordings that use licensed samples of an earlier copyrighted recording fall within this derivative copyright status. If an original recording is rearranged, remixed, or otherwise altered in so substantially creative a manner as to constitute "authorship," it is worthy of derivative copyright. So is a remix of a 3-minute recording into a 5-minute version that emphasizes rhythm tracks and de-emphasizes vocals in a manner more suited to the demands of dance clubs. Of course, a remix and the use of instrumental loops in an authorized sample would eminently qualify for a new sound recording copyright in the resulting version. The copyright in the derivative work applies only to the new material or to the changes or revisions in the underlying work. Where there are only minor additions to or variations from the original recording, it is not an original work of authorship able to be registered as a derivative work. The issuance of a tape of a sound recording previously released only in disc form would not qualify for a new registration.

If a notice of copyright is used for derivative works incorporating previously published material, the year of first publication of the derivative work suffices; there is no need to show the year of the earlier published material.

Compilations

Under the 1976 Copyright Act, a *compilation* is defined as "a work formed by the collection and assembling of pre-existing materials" or one that consists of "data that are selected, coordinated or arranged." The resulting work must be such that it "constitutes an original work of authorship" as a whole.

It is common for sound recordings to appear in compiled albums, which are very salable. "Greatest hits" series are released by many record companies. Each compilation is afforded statutory protection as such, without adding to or diminishing from the protection under the copyright law for individual selections. If the compilation contains selections that have had a substantial remixing or alteration or addition of sounds, these selections, in respect of the new matter or changes, are entitled to protection as new works.

If a notice of copyright is used for a compilation, it may contain only the year of the first publication of the compilation, not the earlier years of publication of the component selections or the names of the different owners of the individual selections. Unless there is an express transfer of the copyright, in whole or in part, the copyright owner of the compiled work is presumed to have acquired only the privilege of reproducing and distributing the separate editorial or other compiler's contribution.

AUDIOVISUAL RECORDINGS

As previously noted, sound recordings do not include sounds "accompanying a motion picture or other audiovisual work." But when a soundtrack album is released *before* the motion picture in which the soundtrack is contained, the recording is generally deemed eligible for the ℗ copyright notice and for copyright protection as a separate sound recording. The earlier release removes the recording from the category of "accompanying" the film.

Even if a soundtrack album comes out after the release of the motion picture, it is common for record companies to use the ℗ copyright notice and to file an application for copyright registration of the album as a sound recording. This is justified on the ground that the soundtrack album usually contains edited, assembled, or rearranged versions of the basic motion picture soundtrack music or dialogue and may be construed as a compilation or derivative work.

Foreign Sound Recordings

Many sound recordings originate outside the United States. If they are unpublished they are subject to copyright protection in the United States without regard to the nationality or domicile of the authors. If they are published they may also be entitled to U.S. copyright protection, on condition that:

1. The author is a national or a resident of, or if the work if initially or simultaneously published in, a Berne Convention country
2. The author is a national or a resident of, or if the work if initially or simultaneously published in, a foreign country with which the United States has copyright relations pursuant to a treaty
3. The work is within the scope of a presidential proclamation extending protection to works of nationals or residents of a foreign nation that protects works of U.S. citizens or residents or works first published in the United States on substantially the same basis as the foreign country protects works of its own citizens or works first published there.

Often, in foreign countries, sound recordings are considered a neighboring right and are not afforded a full term of copyright protection. For example, in England a sound recording is entitled to only 50 years of protection; other copyrighted works, such as books, receive protection for the life of the author plus 70 years.

Most commercially viable foreign recordings are now protected under provisions of the Berne Convention Implementation Act of 1988. This protects not only residents and citizens of Berne Convention countries but also recordings that were first or simultaneously published in any of the Berne countries as of the date of U.S. accession. There is broad coverage of foreign sound recordings dating back to at least February 15, 1972. As to foreign recordings predating 1972, there is clearly a common law status the same as that for sound recording protection that does not apply to U.S.-originated recordings. (See also Chapter 8, "Bootlegging, Piracy, and Counterfeiting.")

Sampling

Sampling is the process of dubbing portions of previously recorded music into new recordings. These musical quotations are either duly licensed on a prior basis or they may be unauthorized copyright infringements waiting for claims to be presented.

There is no such thing as a "fair use" privilege for sampling music in a conventional commercial recording. In *Grand Upright Music v. Warner Bros. Records,* 780 F. Supp. 182 (S.D.N.Y. 1991) a U.S. district court held that rapper Biz Markie's use of the song "Alone Again Naturally" by Gilbert O'Sullivan was copyright infringement and imposed damages and attorney's fees. Moreover, the court referred the case to the U.S. attorney for possible prosecution as willful criminal infringement.

Samplings differ from conventional infringements in that they use not only the song's music and lyrics but the sound recording itself. Thus, there are two parties for any permissions, claims, or litigation: the song copyright proprietor (usually the music publisher) for a mechanical license and the sound recording copyright proprietor (usually the record company) for a master use license.

A sampling can be a musical insert within the body of an original song and recording, ranging from a few seconds to more extensive quotations. Or it can be the use of an earlier recorded segment in a recorded loop fashion, so that a short segment becomes an extended accompaniment, as in the accompaniment to a rap artist.

With the advent of digital technology, sampling has become quite prevalent. Issues yet to be addressed are whether a sampling that is otherwise substantial enough to be an infringement should be subject to injunctive relief or merely judicial awards of profits and/or damages. (See also "Sampling and Copyright Infringement" in Chapter 19.)

Master Licensing

What may appear to be merely a nondubbing right of the sound recording copyright proprietor also covers the important role of master licensing for motion picture, television, or film and for sampling into other record derivative uses. Thus, a use of a post–February 15, 1972, master recording in a motion picture soundtrack for background or other purposes requires a license from the sound recording copyright owner. This derivative use into other media is subject to open negotiation and has no compulsory license except in limited instances.

One example of such negotiations is full exemption for educational broadcasters. Another is the inclusion of public broadcasting stations and networks within blanket compulsory licenses. However, in both instances, further negotiation is required before there can be a sale of any such programming to the public or for foreign or other uses outside of the specified permitted uses. Even commercial broadcasters can use protected sound recordings for what is known as "ephemeral" use where a copy is made for inclusion in a program for a single use and without repeated programming. For example, copying the sound recording into a TV show tape is permitted provided that it is limited to one showing.

Audio Home Recording Act

The 1992 Audio Home Recording Act (AHRA) has been a great disappointment to the music industry. It has produced negligible financial returns, and its stated intention of easing the road toward equitable entry of DAT equipment into marketing has not been reached.

The AHRA attempts to shield the consumer against copyright infringement liability for home copying for noncommercial use and protects hardware manufacturers, sellers of digital equipment, and blank-tape marketers from infringement liability on payment of a statutory blanket license fee: a 3 percent surcharge, collected as if it were a tax. One-third of the fee is split evenly between the music publishers and writers, and the remaining two-thirds is divided as follows: 60 percent to the record companies, 36 percent to the featured artist, and 4 percent to nonfeatured musicians and vocalists.

The complexities of appointing agents for this collection and distribution has brought traditional groups, such as ASCAP, BMI, and Songwriters Guild of America, into action. A newly formed not-for-profit group called the Alliance of Artists and Recording Companies (AARC) formed by the Recording Industry Association of America (RIAA) has assumed responsibility for collections. In 1997, AARC reported collections of $878,000. The expenses of operations have made the collections to the date of this writing seem uneconomical, but at least the groundwork is in place. However, these blanket license fees do not obviate the need for negotiation for mechanical and synchronization licenses for customary commercial uses, whether analog or digital.

The Digital Performance Right in Sound Recordings Act of 1995

The Digital Performance Right in Sound Recordings Act of 1995 is similar to AHRA in that it attempts to fill the void in legislation for the protection of copyrighted works that are digitally transmitted over the Internet. The act deals with both the digital performance and the digital distribution of sound recordings.

DIGITAL PERFORMANCE RIGHTS

Until now, the United States, which has never signed the Rome Convention, has not recognized any broadcast performance rights; only public performances of a musical composition have been eligible for performance royalties. The Digital Performance Right in Sound Recordings Act changes that by creating a performance right in digital sound recordings.

Digital transmissions are classified according to whether they are nonsubscription, interactive, or subscription services. *Nonsubscription services* are free, noninteractive digital transmissions, sometimes known as "Internet radio." Like nondigital broadcast services (e.g., AM and FM radio), these services are not subject to a licensing fee under the act. *Interactive services* transmit digital sound recordings at the user's request. The service is free and often takes the form of a 45-second promotional music sample. *Subscription services* also transmit digital sound recordings at the user's request, but for a fee. Interactive transmissions are subject to a license that is voluntarily negotiated between the service and the record company, whereas subscription transmissions are subject to a statutory licensing fee.

The statutory licensing requirements mainly affect three subscription music services: Muzak's DishCD (part of Echostar's satellite-based Dish network); Digital Music Express (music subscription service owned by TCI Music); and Digital Cable Radio Associates, a jointly owned service of EMI, Sony, and Warner together with cable firms Cox, Time Warner, Continental, Comcast, and Adelphia. The statutory digital performance licensing fee that went into effect on June 1, 1998, is 6.5 percent of gross revenues from transmissions to residences by means other than conventional FCC-licensed broadcast, audiovisual cable, or television. (It is interesting to note that the RIAA originally sought a much higher rate, 41.5 percent, arguing that a music service ought to pay the same percentage for recorded music as cable firms have to pay for motion picture programming. The rate that was finally agreed upon, 6.5 percent, is more analogous to the public performance rate.)

The receipts from statutory or voluntarily negotiated licenses (including mechanical royalties) are collected by the record companies (not by ASCAP, BMI, and SESAC, the traditional performance rights societies) and divided among the companies themselves, the featured musicians and vocalists, and the nonfeatured musicians and vocalists, as follows: 50 percent goes to the record companies, 45 percent goes to the featured musicians or vocalists, and 5 percent is set aside in two equal escrow funds for distribution to nonfeatured musicians and vocalists. The escrow funds are managed jointly by the record companies and the unions. Recipients do not have to be union members.

When the collection of receipts is pursuant to a voluntary negotiated license, performers get paid in accordance with their individual contracts or collective bargaining agreements. In many instances, the artist contracts establish a percentage of net miscellaneous receipts and the collective bargaining agreements have their own provisions for miscellaneous revenues (or provisions for reuse or new media).

DIGITAL DISTRIBUTION RIGHTS

The Digital Performance Right in Sound Recordings Act also establishes a statutory digital mechanical license rate that differs from the conventional statutory rate for analog records. When a digital record is transmitted for duplication over telephone lines, by cable, or by satellite, the act provides for a digital reproduction rate that is either voluntarily negotiated or statutory. This parallels the procedure used to set digital performance rates.

The legislation provides that artist-songwriters who have negotiated a controlled-composition rate in their contract will not get any additional benefit from the statutory mechanical license fees if:

1. The contract is dated on or before June 22, 1995
2. The contracts, regardless of date, is entered into after the song has been recorded and the artist continues to act as his or her own publisher

Instead, the controlled-composition rate in the contract will continue in effect.

Digital Millennium Copyright Act of 1998

The Digital Millennium Copyright Act of 1998 implements provisions from two World Intellectual Property Organization treaties. It requires performance fees be paid to artists and labels for recordings played on digital radio. However, various issues regarding licensing and monetary rates remain to be settled. (The Digital Millennium Copyright Act is discussed in more detail in Chapter 41. Selected excerpts from the act can be found in Appendix D.)

8

Bootlegging, Piracy, and Counterfeiting

In the record business, the bootlegger, the pirate, and the counterfeiter are all part of the same nefarious clan. They each misappropriate the services of the artist and the product owned and paid for by a legitimate manufacturer and benefit at the expense of record companies, performing artists, music publishers, unions, and the federal and local governments.

Bootlegging is the unauthorized recording of a live or broadcast performance. *Piracy* is the unauthorized duplication of the actual sound recording—the CD, tape, or record. *Counterfeiting* is the duplication of the packaging, artwork, and label as well as the sound recording.

For example, a college student downloads an album from the Internet and e-mails it to a friend as a "gift"; this is bootlegging. The Brigand Record Company makes copies of a Decca recording of the Rolling Stones, slaps the Brigand label on the packaging, and sells the recording at a greatly reduced price; this is piracy. A guitarist on the roster of Universal Records records the theme for a television show that is a significant commercial success. The Brigand Record Company manufactures copies of the record, slaps on a duplicate of the Universal Records label, and markets them as the original product; this is counterfeiting.

The counterfeiter and the pirate can afford to charge substantially less than the legitimate manufacturer and still make a profit because their only costs are pressing and duplication charges, covers and labels, and distribution expenses. They only copy successful records, and therefore don't have to carry the burden of the 85 percent of recordings released in the United States annually that, according to the RIAA, fail to make a profit. The record company incurs the recording costs, while the pirate and the counterfeiter steal the profits. The recordings are often of inferior quality, artists lose out on royalties, music publishers lose out on mechanical license fees, union members lose payments to the trust funds, and the government is cheated of income tax payments. In the end, we all lose.

According to information supplied by the RIAA, in 1998 the record industry worldwide lost about $5 billion annually due to piracy. The United States alone was said to lose nearly $1 million a day. Over 338,000 counterfeit or pirated CDs and over 359,000 illegally produced tapes were confiscated in 1998. The number of cassette tapes confiscated dropped 12.8 percent from 1997, whereas the number of CDs confiscated increased 163 percent from 1997. This dramatic rise may be due, in part, to the considerable antipiracy efforts of the RIAA; however, the growing ease and decreasing cost of CD duplication are undoubtedly dominant factors.

Federal Legislation

Prior to 1982

Until 1962 it was not a federal crime to transport or sell phonorecords with counterfeit labels, and state laws were either nonexistent or ineffectual. In 1962, Congress passed an anticounterfeiting label law, but it was difficult to enforce because the prosecution had to prove both knowledge and fraudulent intent on the offender's part in transporting, receiving, selling, or offering for sale records to which the counterfeit labels were stamped, pasted, or affixed. Moreover, the penalties were relatively modest.

Federal copyright protection was finally granted to sound recordings published on and after February 15, 1972, and to all sound recordings, published or unpublished after January 1, 1978. (See Chapter 7.) A violation of the exclusive rights of the copyright owner of a sound recording now became a copyright infringement subject to civil action. The court could order an injunction, the impounding and destruction or other reasonable disposition of the infringing articles, and certain financial penalties: either (1) the copyright owner's actual damages and any additional profits of the infringer, or (2) statutory damages for any one work of $500 to $20,000, or (3) in the case of willful infringement, damages of $500 to $100,000, at the court's discretion. The court may also award court costs and reasonable attorney's fees to the prevailing party and order the destruction of all matrices, masters, tapes, film negatives, or other articles by which the records and tapes may be reproduced.

Piracy and Counterfeiting Amendments Act of 1982

Until 1982 a first-time charge of copyright infringement was merely a misdemeanor charge; federal prosecutors were unlikely to pursue criminal copyright infringers, and offenders were subject to relatively small penalties—a small risk for the enormous profits they stood to make. However, with the passage of the Piracy and Counterfeiting Amendments Act in 1982, infringement of the copyright in a sound recording involving willful action for purposes of commercial advantage or private financial gain is now punishable as a felony. Federal prosecutors are now more willing to pursue these crimes, and possible offenders are more effectively deterred.

Under the section "Trafficking in Counterfeit Labels for Phonorecords and Copies of Motion Pictures or Other Audiovisual Works" (18 U.S.C. 2318), any person who knowingly traffics in a counterfeit label affixed or designed to be affixed to a copyrighted phonorecord or a copy of a copyrighted motion picture or other audiovisual work may be fined up to $250,000 and/or imprisoned for up to 5 years. The prosecution no longer has to prove "fraudulent intent," merely that the offense of trafficking in counterfeit labels was knowingly committed. In addition, the penalty under this statute requires that all counterfeit labels be forfeited and destroyed or otherwise disposed of by the court.

Suppliers of equipment may also be liable under the section "Trafficking in Counterfeiting Goods or Services" (18 U.S.C. 2320). For example, in 1997 a supplier was found guilty of contributory infringement because he knew of the intended use of his duplicating equipment and proceeded to supply it nonetheless. Judgment of $7 million was granted the 26 record companies that acted in this infringement case. The computation was $1,000 for each of 56 recordings plus $7 million dollars in trademark damages—three times the estimated profits of the defendant over a 2-year period.

URUGUAY ROUND AGREEMENTS ACT OF 1994

The Uruguay Round Agreements Act (URAA), which created new protection against international bootlegging, added a new Chapter 11 to the U.S. Copyright Act, making it unlawful for anyone without permission "to fix, in copies or phonograms, sounds and/or images of a live musical performance or to reproduce copies or phonograms from such unauthorized fixations; to transmit or communicate to the public the sounds and/or images of a live musical performance; or to distribute, rent, sell, or traffic in copies of phonograms of live musical performances without consent of the performer."

Anyone who violates Chapter 11 of the Copyright Act is subject to the copyright infringement remedies set forth in the Copyright Act (injunctive relief, impounding, statutory or actual damages and profits, and costs and attorney's fees), and on conviction, courts are authorized to require the forfeiture and destruction of the illegal copies or phonograms, as well as, in the court's discretion, "any other equipment by means of which such copies or phonorecords may be reproduced, taking into account the nature, scope, and proportionality of the use of the equipment in the offense." The new law also provides that copies or phonorecords of live musical performances "fixed" outside the United States without authorization will be subject to seizure and forfeiture "in the same manner as property imported in violation of the customs laws." The U.S. Customs Service is authorized to seize "bootleg" material fixed abroad.

The URAA also added a new section to the U.S. Code providing criminal penalties for the "unauthorized fixation of and trafficking in sound recordings and music videos of live musical performances" when done "knowingly and for purposes of commercial advantage or private financial gain" (18 U.S.C. 2319). Penalties include fines and/or imprisonment.

As discussed in Chapter 7, not all sound recordings are covered by federal copyright. Prior to 1972, the record industry was forced to rely largely on lawsuits in state courts, under theories of unfair competition, to prohibit the piracy of recordings. This was not very effective. Apart from different interpretations of law in the 50 separate states, an injunction in one state did not bar a pirate from renewing his or her operations in another state. A pirate enjoined by one record company from duplicating its product could simply switch to copying records and tapes manufactured by another record company.

Under the 1976 Copyright Act, sound recordings that predate federal copyright protection will continue to be covered by state law until February 15, 2047, after which they will fall into public domain. Record companies can still seek redress against piracy in state court, but civil lawsuits have little deterrent effect on record pirates. As a result, the recording industry has been successful in convincing practically all the states in the United States to pass criminal legislation prohibiting the unauthorized reproduction and sale of recordings. These laws have proved very effective in limiting record piracy. For example, the antipiracy law of California provides for a graduated system of penalties of up to 5 years in prison and up to $250,000 in fines for those who manufacture, distribute, or sell recordings that do not bear the true name and address of the manufacturer.

Compulsory License for Sound Recordings

At one time it was possible for pirates to obtain a compulsory license to mechanically reproduce songs contained in sound recordings, and were thus shielded from possible lawsuits by or on behalf of the music publishers. Under the 1976 Copyright Act, they can no longer obtain the necessary compulsory license without the consent of the copyright owner. This represents a statutory enactment of the decisions of the federal courts interpreting the provisions of the prior Copyright Act. These decisions were the outcome of protracted litigation brought primarily by publishers affiliated with the Harry Fox Agency, the mechanical licensing agency for most U.S. publishers, which has been active in these lawsuits. Music publishers can now readily sue counterfeiters on these grounds.

The pirating of recordings without the consent of the copyright owner constitutes a willful infringement of the music copyright. The pirate is subject to civil actions for such infringement under the 1976 Copyright Act; the remedies include injunctions, the impounding and destruction of infringing materials, and money awards for damages, the infringer's profits, court costs, and attorney's fees. For willful infringements of the music copyright there are also criminal penalties: a fine of up to $25,000, imprisonment of up to 1 year, or both. It is the announced decision of the U.S. Department of Justice to prosecute those who pirate pre-February 15, 1972, sound recordings on the grounds of infringement of the copyrights in the musical compositions contained in the recordings.

Because many record companies are associated with music publishers who publish original music, music publishers are strongly motivated to pursue civil and criminal actions against pirates of the recordings issued by their affiliated record companies.

International Treaties Regarding Piracy

In 1971, representatives from approximately 50 nations, including the United States, met in Paris and drafted the Geneva Convention for the Protection of Producers of Phonograms against Unauthorized Duplication (Geneva Convention of 1971) to protect sound recordings against piracy. The United States ratified the treaty on March 10, 1974. Other signatories include Argentina, Australia, Austria, Barbados, Brazil, Chile, Costa Rica, Czechoslovakia, Denmark, Ecuador, Egypt, El Salvador, Fiji, Finland, France, Germany, Guatemala, Holy See, Hungary, India, Israel, Italy, Japan, Kenya, Luxembourg, Mexico, Monaco, New Zealand, Norway, Panama, Paraguay, Peru, Spain, Sweden, United Kingdom, Uruguay, Venezuela, and Zaire. Signatories agree to protect the nationals of other states against the making or importation of unauthorized duplications of sound recordings if the intent is to distribute them to the public. National legislatures are permitted to implement their treaty obligations by means of copyright law or other specific right or in other specifically enumerated manners. (See also Chapter 20, "International Copyright Protection.")

The United States has long recognized the need for cooperation among foreign governments in order to achieve anticounterfeiting goals; local statutes must be passed and also enforced. Each year the U.S. Trade Representative publishes a Priority Watch List of countries deemed to be in violation of international trade laws controlling piracy and counterfeiting. This annual review examines the protection of U.S.-owned intellectual property in over 70 countries. The 1999 report listed the Dominican Republic, Egypt, Greece, Guatemala, India, Indonesia, Israel, Italy, Kuwait, Macao, Peru, Russia, Turkey, and Ukraine and detailed how each country had impacted American entertainment companies.

9

Record Covers, Labels, and Liner Notes

Album packaging is one of the most effective advertising tools for records. An eye-catching illustration can attract consumers who may not be familiar with a new recording artist. Extensive liner notes, often featured on special reissues or boxed sets, may entice the devoted fan or music scholar to purchase recordings that they already own in order to learn more about their favorite artists or recordings.

The cost of packaging production, including design fees, photographer's fees, and preparation of artwork, can range from $3,500 to $10,000. Most record companies absorb these expenses as a cost of production but deduct 10 to 25 percent from the artist's royalty base for these packaging expenses. For example, a CD may sell for $17.00, but the packaging deduction of 25 percent will reduce the artist's royalty base to $12.75. The substantial $4.25 difference enables the record company to recover both creative and manufacturing costs for the album packaging.

Traditionally, album packaging includes the album title and attached labels, which may contain descriptive information, including the names of the songs, the artists, and the record company; illustrations; liner notes; and the names of the producer, the engineer, and the songwriter. Since 1958, the National Academy of Recording Arts and Sciences (NARAS) has given annual awards to art directors for Best Album Packaging. These awards are based on the illustrations (photographs and artwork) and the liner notes.

Album Titles

Albums feature various types of titles. Some albums are simply titled with the name of the performer; for example, *Ricky Martin* was the title of Latin star Ricky Martin's 1999 hit album. Other titles describe the album's musical content, for example, *Songs of the West, Love Songs,* or *Golden Hits of the Sixties.* Most titles, however, are arbitrary creative titles chosen by the artists, such as

Alanis Morissette's 1998 release, *Supposed Former Infatuation Junkie,* or *I Am ... The Autobiography* by Nas.

On Broadway cast albums, the name of the show is the title, and the phrase "original cast album" is featured. Motion picture soundtrack albums name the film in the title and prominently display the phrase "original sound-track album" or, in the case of a re-recorded score, "original motion picture score."

Illustrations

Typically, illustrations—either photographs or artwork—grace the covers of many record albums. Photographers who supply pictures for album covers require their models to sign releases granting the right to use the photographs for commercial purposes. Without such releases, models may claim an invasion of their rights to privacy and publicity. They may further claim a violation of specific statutes that forbid the use of photographs for commercial endeavors unless the model consents in writing.

Under the 1976 Copyright Act, "pictorial, graphic, and sculptural works" are all eligible for copyright. These works are defined to include "fine, graphic, and applied art, photographs, prints, and art reproductions." The copyright in the artwork may be registered in the artist's name unless it was specifically created as a work-for-hire. For example, in the case of *Johannsen v. Brown,* 797 F. Supp. 835 (D. Ore. 1992), the court ruled that an artist who created an illustration on his own time and with his own tools and materials, who had absolute control over the project and was under no duty to furnish the illustration, was an independent contractor, and accordingly his illustration used for a cover design was not a work-for-hire.

Under the Berne Convention, a copyright notice is not needed in order to protect a work. However, the 1976 Copyright Act, as amended, grants record companies the option of attaching a notice of copyright to each record publicly distributed. The form of the notice should include the word "copyright," the abbreviation "copr.," or the symbol ©, accompanied by the name of the copyright proprietor, an abbreviation by which the name can be recognized, or a generally known alternative designation of the proprietor. For photographs, works of art, and reproductions of works of art, the 1976 Copyright Act does not require the year date in the optional notice. However, failure to include such date forfeits the benefit of protection by the Universal Copyright Convention outside the United States.

In further compliance with the Berne Convention, record covers may be registered for copyright on Form VA for published or unpublished works of the visual arts. (See Chapter 10.)

In the case of soundtrack albums, the artwork is often the same as the artwork used to advertise the film and the copyright notice on the packaging should be consistent with the copyright notices employed by the motion picture company for the protection of the artwork and the photographs. Thus, if the name of the motion picture company and a particular year and date appear in its notice, caution prescribes that the same name and date be contained in the record packaging copyright notice placed in proximity to the artwork or photos. The copyright notice in the name of the motion picture company will also apply to the recording insofar as it is derived from the film soundtrack. If a record company elects to use a notice of copyright for a soundtrack recording, it is likely to employ a notice of copyright in its own name on the packaging in addition to that of the motion picture company. (A sample "Photography Agreement" can be found on the accompanying CD-ROM.)

Liner Notes

Liner notes encompass the descriptive material on CD or cassette inserts or on the back of an album. This material may include the names of the songs on the recording, biographical information about the performers, comments on the contents of the album, the names of the producer, engineer, songwriters, and the like.

Liner notes are protected by copyright under U.S. copyright law. However, in accordance with artwork regulations, copyright notice is optional. Although such a notice on the back cover of an album may also serve to encompass the artwork on the front cover, several authorities on the subject have recommended a cautious approach and suggest placing two copyright notices on the album, one on the front and one on the back. Placement of the copyright notice on the spine of an album cover is not recommended.

Liner notes of substantial length are registered for copyright on Form TX for published or unpublished nondramatic literary works. (See Chapter 10.)

Recording Identification

With the coming of compact discs, three-letter codes were developed to identify the nature of the original recording technology. These codes frequently appear on the back of the packaging. DDD indicates that a digital tape recorder was used for the recording session, the mixing and editing, and the mastering. ADD indicates that an analog tape recorder was used for the original recording session, but a digital recorder was employed for subsequent steps. AAD indicates that an analog tape recorder was used during the recording session and for subsequent mixing and editing, but a digital tape recorder was used for the mastering or transcription.

Many of the old monaural recordings are of interest to the present generation of record buyers who have only stereophonic record players. As a result, record companies have altered the monaural masters so that they can be played on stereophonic equipment. However, the Federal Trade Commission received complaints that the record companies were selling these altered recordings as if they were originally recorded for multichannel stereophonic reproduction, so it published a standard legend that must be printed prominently over the title of such recordings, as follows: "This Recording Altered To Simulate Stereophonic Reproduction."

Trademarks

Under the Lanham Act of 1946 the words "Registered in U.S. Patent and Trademark Office," or "Reg. U.S. Pat. and TM Off.," or the symbol [r] should be printed close to the trademark on album covers.

On occasion, a cover will include an unregistered trademark. Until a registration certificate is issued by the Patent Office, it is improper to use the notices referred to in the preceding paragraph. However, it is common to use the word "trademark" or the abbreviation "TM" in conjunction with a mark for the purpose of giving actual notice to the public of a claim to the mark. (See Chapter 31 for a full discussion of trademarks.)

Anticounterfeit Practices

To combat the counterfeiting of records, Polaroid and 3M make special labels for record jackets that resist photo-offset duplication by presenting a three-dimensional effect that uses the logo, signature, or seal of the manufacturer. CBS, MCA, and other record manufacturers use custom-made cassette boxes that have the company logo embedded in the plastic.

Bar coding uses imprinted variant lines and numbers as an aid to inventory and sales control of records. The bar codes are usually printed on the jackets or on the back of inserts for CDs and cassettes, but they are also sometimes included in affixed stickers. Through computer readers, the retailer, wholesaler, and manufacturer can keep track of sales and inventory by categories such as record label, artist, title, and release number.

The latest technology in packaging was developed by Avery, a leading manufacturer of spine labels. The spine label, which is used to prevent tampering and theft, now includes both bar code and SoundScan digital data. The resulting technology combines shoplifting prevention and accurate sales reports in a convenient manner. In addition, the labels may now carry a record company's hologram in order to protect against counterfeiting.

In its 1994 annual report, the RIAA stated that its "legal arsenal against pirates includes state laws requiring recorded music to display the 'true name and address' of the manufacturer." In 28 states, the name and address of the record company must appear on each record distributed in the state. In California, failure to comply may result in fines of as much as $250,000 and jail sentences up to 5 years. Similar penalties exist in other states; some are more stringent, some more lenient. These initiatives have been especially effective because they empower state and local authorities to respond quickly to counterfeit activity without (literally) making a federal case out of it. In 1993 the "true name and address" statute in Washington state was upheld following a constitutional challenge by a convicted cassette counterfeiter.

By virtue of the statutes, record companies or artists aggrieved by the misleading practices of other companies are better able to institute appropriate action to protect their rights by suits for injunction or damages or by complaints to federal, state, and local authorities.

Warning Stickers and Censorship Issues

In 1985 the Parents Music Resource Center (PMRC) initiated a movement to promote the labeling of albums that contained sexually explicit or perverse lyrics, or lyrics that promoted violence, rape, or the use of illegal drugs or alcohol. A number of states proposed legislation that would have required parental advisory warning labels on certain albums and held retailers liable for selling nonstickered records. Encouraged by the retail and wholesale segments of the record industry, in 1990 the RIAA created a uniform label to be affixed to CD and cassette packaging in certain situations. The approved label, which reads "Explicit Lyrics—Parental Advisory," is now used by the 55 members of the association where the issuing company considers it appropriate. This voluntary practice was adopted as a practical means of heading off legislative action.

In fact, the proposed legislation caused much concern among music business participants and was actively opposed by the National Association of Record Merchandisers, the Recording Industry Association of America, the National Academy of Recording Arts and Sciences, the American Civil Liberties Union, People for the American Way, the Country Music Association, and various artist and writer groups and representatives.

Opposition to the use of warning labels focused on the issue of free speech. Even a voluntary labeling supervised by the record industry trade association is perceived as a response to pressure from certain advocates imposing moral standards on the public at large. Making stickering a statutory requirement is a potentially complex and confusing procedure. Often vague and indefinite guidelines can jeopardize unsuspecting retailers, who have little time or inclination to monitor recorded product, or put them in the position of having to act as censors.

The problem of stickering is to some extent part of the broader problem of attempting to define and restrict obscenity. Prosecutions for obscenity depend on an exception to the First Amendment constitutional right of free speech. In 1989, a U.S. district court judge in Florida held an album by the rap group 2 Live Crew to be obscene, making it the first recording to be declared obscene by a federal court. A record store owner who continued to sell the album was arrested. Two members of the group were also arrested for performing one of the album's songs before an adult-only audience.

The ruling of obscenity by the U.S. district court was based on a finding of guilt under a three-part judicial standard set forth in a 1973 U.S. Supreme Court case:

1. Whether the average person applying contemporary community standards would find that the work, taken as a whole, appeals to the prurient interest
2. Whether the work depicts or describes, in a patently offensive way, sexual conduct specifically defined by the applicable state law
3. Whether the work, taken as a whole, lacks serious literary, artistic, political, or scientific value

All three standards must be satisfied to make a finding of obscenity.

Obscenity cases represent a conflict between the First Amendment and the enforcement of community moral standards, including the need to protect the community young. According to one jurist, this necessarily presents a "penumbra," a shady region somewhere between black and white. There is no clear consensus as to what constitutes obscenity. In a 1964 opinion, Justice Stewart of the U.S. Supreme Court frankly stated that he could not define obscenity, but he knew it when he saw it. Many obscenity decisions are reached by divided courts with learned dissenting opinions, indicating the unknown and dangerous waters that may have to be traversed by record industry participants. Even community standards may vary from locality to locality.

The danger of criminal prosecution and fines for violations of state and local obscenity laws must be heeded by record industry participants, especially in connection with those albums that may emphasize sexual or violent themes.

Part Three

Music Publisher and Writer Agreements and Practices

10

Copyright Law in the United States

Copyright literally means "the right to copy." The term, which refers to that body of exclusive rights granted by law to authors for the protection of their writings, includes the exclusive right to reproduce, publish, and sell copies of the copyrighted work, to make other versions of the work, and, with certain limitations, to make recordings of and perform the work in public.

Copyright is an intangible property right, best understood by distinguishing it from the physical property itself. In the words of the Copyright Act of 1976:

> Ownership of a copyright, or of any of the exclusive rights under a copyright, is distinct from ownership of any material object in which the work is embodied. Transfer of ownership of any material object, including the copy or phonorecord in which the work is first fixed, does not of itself convey any rights in the copyrighted work embodied in the object.

For example, someone who purchases a collection of letters written by a famous person owns the letters but not the right to publish copies of the letters; that right belongs to the person who owns the copyright. The right to copyright is based on authorship and exists separate and apart from its physical expression.

Copyright protects the expression of ideas, not the ideas themselves. The films *Star Wars* and *Star Trek* are both based on the idea of space travel. The films *Interview with a Vampire* and *Dracula* are both based on the idea of vampires. Similarly, the musical compositions "The Twist," "Twist and Shout," and "Let's Twist" all relate to the dance craze of the 1960s. None is a copyright infringement of another since each constitutes an original expression of the idea.

Copyright Revision, 1790 to 1976

Article 1 of the U.S. Constitution states that the purpose of copyright is "To promote the Progress of Science and useful Arts, by securing for limited Times to Authors and Inventors, the exclusive Right to their respective Writings and Discoveries." These words are embodied in the Copyright Act of 1790, which provided protection against the copying of certain printed materials. Performance rights were granted statutory protection in 1889. The right of mechanical reproduction presently applicable to phonograph records was added in 1909, when piano rolls were prominent. (See page 192 for a discussion of mechanical rights.)

By the mid-1950s the Copyright Act of 1909 was completely antiquated. Supreme Court Justice Abe Fortas observed that administering the statute called "not for the judgment of Solomon but for the dexterity of Houdini." The act provided the courts with little guidance in coping with the vast technological changes that had taken place in the intervening years—innovations such as television, cable television, transcriptions, synchronization with film, offset printing, Xerox reprography, and long-playing records.

In 1955, the U.S. Copyright Office initiated a number of valuable studies in preparation for a general revision of the copyright act and circulated 34 reports on a multitude of problems to a panel of consultants and to the general public. It then prepared and circulated for review preliminary drafts of a new copyright statute and, in 1964, submitted a general revision of the 1909 copyright statute to Congress. A number of interested groups were opposed to particular provisions relating to cable television and jukebox performance fees and performers' rights in sound recordings, but finally, after 12 years of hearings and industry compromises, Congress passed the Copyright Act of 1976. (The Copyright Act of 1976 and related amendments are available on the accompanying CD-ROM.)

The Copyright Status of Sound Recordings

The 1976 Copyright Act defines *sound recordings* as "original works of authorship comprising an aggregate of musical, spoken, or other sounds that have been fixed in tangible form." *Phonorecords* are "physical objects in which sounds are fixed"—records, tapes, CDs, and so forth. Two factors affect the copyright status of a sound recording: when and whether it is published. *Publication* is "the distribution of copies of phonorecords of a work to the public by sale or other transfer of ownership, or by rental, lease or lending"; the offer "to distribute copies or phonorecords to a group of persons for purposes of further distribution, public performance, or public display, constitutes publication." (Public performance is not a publication.)

Sound recordings published on or after February 15, 1972, and all sound recordings published or unpublished on or after January 1, 1978 (the effective date of the Copyright Act of 1976), are covered by federal copyright. Sound recordings published prior to February 15, 1972, or unpublished prior to January 1, 1978, are covered by state common law until February 15, 2047, at which time they fall into the public domain. (For a full discussion of sound recording copyright, see Chapter 7.)

Common Law Copyright

Works that are *not* fixed in sheet music, song folios, phonorecords, or other tangible medium of expression—for example, a musical composition improvised or developed from memory but not recorded or written down—do not qualify for statutory copyright. They are protected by a parallel system of *common law copyright*, which exists under individual state law. Common law copyright springs into being without any formality, registration, or notice. It offers an author, composer, or artist complete protection against the unauthorized commercialization of his or her work as long as it is not fixed in a tangible form sufficiently permanent or stable to permit it to be perceived, heard, or otherwise communicated for a period of more than transitory duration. Even a widely viewed "live" television or radio presentation of a song can be protected under common law if it is not recorded simultaneously with its transmission.

Until passage of the 1976 Copyright Act, common law copyright was perpetual and not limited to any number of years. At that time all common law works were brought under federal statutory provisions (called "preemption"), effective January 1, 1978, and measured in duration in the same manner as a new work created after that date. But where the author was already dead for the full period of copyright, the former common law copyright was given a statutory minimum further duration. The original minimum was until December 31, 2002, with a further extension of 20 years, to December 31, 2027, if the work was put into published form before the original 2002 deadline. The original deadline is still in force as December 31, 2002, but the Sonny Bono Term Extension Act extends the deadline to December 31, 2047, when the work is published before December 31, 2002.

Prior to January 1, 1978, common law protection covered works not "published," commonly used to refer to printed versions but, in the music industry, a term subject to confusion and varied interpretation especially with regard to phonograph records. With the exception of sound recordings first fixed before February 15, 1972 (for which preemption is delayed until February 15, 2047), the revision law has preempted any state common law or statutory protection for any of such works fixed in tangible form. It has legislated, with the exceptions noted below, the same duration of protection for previously existing common law works as is granted for new works created on or after January 1, 1978. For a discussion of duration see Chapter 11 under the section entitled "Pre-1978 Works Not Previously Published or Copyrighted."

Statutory Copyright

Under the 1976 Copyright Act musical compositions may be copyrighted if they have been "fixed" in some visible or recorded form only under the federal copyright law, except for sound recordings first fixed before February 15, 1972. The federal statutory copyright applies to both unpublished and published works. The 1976 Copyright Act defines publication as "the distribution of copies of phonorecords of a work to the public by sale or other transfer of ownership, or by rental, lease or lending." It goes on to provide that the offer "to distribute copies or phonorecords to a group of persons for purposes of further distribution, public performance, or public display, constitutes publication." (Public performance is not a publication, regardless of the size of audience.)

In a 1995 decision involving the song "La Grange" recorded by the band ZZ Top, the court of appeals ruled that a widely sold recording issued prior to 1978 was sufficient "publication" to have required a timely renewal of copyright registration under the then-applicable law, thus forcing a song into public domain for failure to register and renew. The decision caused major concern in the music industry, and the trade associations, together with other music interests such as ASCAP and BMI, successfully petitioned Congress for a clarification of the 1976 Copyright Act. This resulted in a Congressional declaration in 1998 that a pre-1978 record release was not deemed a basis of forfeiture for the absence of the then-required copyright notice or 28-year renewal of the song.

Copyright Registration

It is relatively simple to register a copyright claim with the Copyright Office. The copyright owner may register a work at any time during the copyright protection period. This basic registration secures the statutory benefits of registration to all authors and other owners of rights in the work. A qualifying "deposit" (in the form of a compact disc, cassette tape, printed copy, or unpublished manuscript) must be delivered to the Copyright Office at the time of registration. The U.S. Copyright Office reported registrations of works in the performing arts, including musical works, dramatic works, choreography, pantomimes, and motion pictures and filmstrips, for fiscal year 1998 as follows:

	Published Works	Unpublished Works	Total
Registrations, all performing arts	49,622	92,848	142,470
Registrations, sound recordings	14,590	17,092	31,682

For purposes of registration, the United States is considered the country of origin if:

- Publication occurred first in the United States.
- Publication occurred simultaneously in the United States and a non-Berne nation. ("Simultaneous publication" means within the first 30 days of publication.)
- Publication occurred simultaneously in the United States and another Berne nation that provides the same term of protection as, or a longer term of protection than, the United States.
- The work is unpublished, and all of the authors are U.S. nationals, domiciliaries, or habitual residents.
- The work is first published in a non-Berne nation and all of the authors are U.S. nationals, domiciliaries, or habitual residents.

It is prudent for a copyright owner to promptly register and deposit both published and unpublished works and thereby place the public on notice of his or her claims to copyright. In the case of a work of U.S. origin or a foreign work originating in a non-Berne nation, the copyright owner cannot commence an action for copyright infringement until copies of the work have been duly registered and deposited. Once this is done, legal action can proceed promptly, even if registration is late and the infringement predates registration. For all works regardless of origin, including Berne works not of U.S. origin, the possibility of recovering statutory damages and attorneys' fees is not available for infringements of unpublished, unregistered works unless the work is registered within 3 months after first publication.

The Copyright Act of 1976 provides that in a judicial proceeding a registration certificate for a "registration made before or within five years after first publication of the work shall constitute prima facie evidence of the validity of the copyright and of the facts stated in the certificate." For subsequent registrations, the evidentiary weight of a registration certificate is within the court's discretion. Therefore, the statutory presumption is not available to late registrants who wait more than 5 years from the initial publication of their song. The 5-year registration deadline for the statutory presumption is not applicable to unpublished songs.

As a result, it appears prudent for a copyright owner to register and deposit promptly both published and unpublished works and thereby place the public on notice of his or her claims to copyright. As indicated above, except for Berne Convention works whose origin is not the United States, the absence of registration impedes the right to sue promptly for infringement. For all works, the failure to register eliminates the remedies of statutory damages, the possible awards of attorney's fees, and the right to use the evidentiary presumptions with regard to copyright validity and the facts stated in the certificate.

There is another benefit to registering a copyright: a claimant who wants to replace lost or mislaid certificates or deposits can apply for copies. Unpublished manuscripts or facsimile reproductions are kept for the entire period of copyright protection. Published manuscripts are retained for the longest period deemed practicable and desirable by the Register of Copyrights and the Library of Congress. Under their most recent determination, published copies delivered with the registration claim are not retained for more than 5 years from the date of such deposit except for visual arts works (pictorial, graphic, or sculptural works), which are kept for 10 or more years. However, the depositor or the copyright owner may request that the deposited material be retained for a period of 75 years from the date of publication of a work.

Some songwriters try to circumvent the need for registration of an unpublished song by sending a copy of their manuscript to themselves by registered mail and then leaving the sealed envelope unopened. They believe that the date on the envelope and the contents of the envelope, when shown in a court proceeding, conclusively demonstrates the priority of their authorship in suits against third parties for infringement. While there may be some merit to their position, copyright registration is likely to be immeasurably better than a self-addressed sealed envelope in proving that the work deposited with the registration was in existence on the date of the application and was not fraudulently concocted or modified just prior to the initiation of an infringement action in order to be similar to the defendant's song.

The Copyright Office has a liberal policy with regard to accepting applications for copyright registration. It has stated: "We will register material which we feel a court *might* reasonably hold to be copyrightable, even though personally we feel that it is not subject to copyright." For example, if a claimant unearths an original version of Scott Joplin's "The Entertainer" in an attic and attempts to register it, the Copyright Office might reject the claim on the grounds that the composition is in the public domain. However, a brief melodic variation of a segment of the same work might be registered as an arrangement of a public domain work, even if there is some doubt as to the substantiality of the new material.

For many years, the United States was the only country that insisted on copyright formalities as a condition to the preservation or assertion of legal rights in copyrights. These formalities consist of:

- ► Copyright registration
- ► Copyright notice
- ► Deposit of copyrighted works with the appropriate government agency

Other countries, notably signatories of the Berne Convention, refused to require these copyright formalities for protection under their appropriate copyright laws, while the United States refused to waive such formalities as to foreign works. However, desirous of joining the Berne Union, the United States made certain changes in its copyright law by enacting the Berne Convention Implementation Act of 1988. One modification was the abolition of the mandatory notice of copyright for works published for the first time on and after March 1, 1989, the effective date of the Berne Convention Implementation Act. Another change made non-U.S. Berne Convention works exempt from the requirement that the work be registered before a copyright infringement suit could be commenced. Another change was the elimination of the requirement that a "transfer of copyright ownership" be registered in the Copyright Office before a transferee could institute a lawsuit in its name. Although these formalities often served valuable functions as a public record of ownership and transfers of ownership, it is now recognized that international copyright relations are more important.

Foreign copyrights originating with members of the Berne Convention have a unique ability to be revived from the public domain. Under the Berne Act, a foreign copyright which was in the public domain in the United States because of failure to comply with the formalities of copyright notice or renewal registration could be restored to full copyright status provided that the copyright would not otherwise have expired by reason of the passage of time. (See Chapter 11, "The Duration of Copyright Protection and the Limitation of Grants," and Chapter 12, "The Uses of Public Domain.")

Copyright notice remains a required formality under the Universal Copyright Convention, which became effective in 1955 and to which the United States and many other countries still adhere. However, the UCC is now only a factor in the case of those few countries that adhere to it and not to the Berne Convention. (The Universal Copyright Convention is considered further in Chapter 20, "International Copyright Protection.")

Registration of Published and Unpublished Works

It is not necessary to register an unpublished work in order to register it when it is published. It is not necessary to reregister a previously registered unpublished work when it is published. However, if a published version of a previously registered unpublished work contains sufficient new matter to constitute a derivative work, a second registration of the derivative published work is appropriate to protect the added material. ("Derivative works" are those created subsequent to the original work and based on a variation: for example, the Beach Boys' "Surfin' U.S.A." is a variation of Chuck Berry's prior "Sweet Little 16.")

To register a copyright claim for a published work, send the following to the U.S. Copyright Office, Library of Congress, 101 Independence Avenue S.E., Washington, DC 20559-6000:

- *Unpublished works:* One complete copy or phonorecord of the work, whichever best represents it. (Retain a duplicate. Manuscripts and phonorecords are not returned.)
- *Works first published in the United States:* two copies of the best edition of the work.
- *Works first published outside the United States:* one copy (as first published) of the work.

- *Works published only in phonorecords:* two complete phonorecords of the best edition.
- *A contribution to a collective work:* one complete copy of the best edition of the collective work. (For a definition of "best edition," see page 104.)
- A completed application form (available through the Copyright Office).
- A registration fee of $30 payable by check, money order, or bank draft to the Register of Copyrights. Cash is sent at the remitter's risk.

The Copyright Office makes available, without charge, the following copyright application forms used in the music business:

- *Form PA* (for works in the performing arts): This form is used for published or unpublished musical works, including any accompanying works; dramatic works, including any accompanying music; pantomimes and choreographic works; and motion pictures and other audiovisual works. It is used for most applications for copyright registration of musical compositions prepared for the purpose of being "performed" directly before an audience or indirectly "by means of any device or process." Form PA does not cover sound recordings.
- *Form SR* (for sound recordings): This form is used for published or unpublished sound recordings. This is the only form that needs to be filed if the copyright claimant for both the musical or dramatic work and the sound recording are one and the same and if the claimant is seeking a single registration to cover both aspects of these works.
- *Form TX* (for nondramatic literary works): This form is used for all types of published and unpublished works written in words (or other verbal or numerical symbols) except for dramatic works, periodicals, and serials. The form includes lyric books as well as poems that may be used as lyrics.
- *Form VA* (for works of the visual arts): This form is used for published and unpublished "pictorial, graphic, or sculptural works," including two-dimensional and three-dimensional works of fine, graphic, and applied art; photographs, prints, and art reproductions; and maps, globes, charts, technical drawings, diagrams, and models. It covers pictorial or graphic labels and advertisements.
- *Form RE* (for renewal registrations).

In addition to these basic application forms, the following forms are used in the music business:

- *Form CA* (for supplementary registration): This is used to apply for a supplementary registration under Section 408(d) of the Copyright Act of 1976 in order to correct an error in a copyright registration or to amplify the information given in a registration.
- *Document cover sheet:* This form is required when U.S. citizens file assignments and transfers of copyright and other papers for official registration. It requires submission in duplicate, with a separate cover sheet for each document submitted. The required information includes the identification of the

parties, the nature of the document, and the title of the work. If a photostat of an original signed document is submitted, it must be accompanied by a certification under oath that it is a true copy of the original document. This information should be sent to Document Unit LM-462, Catalog Division, Copyright Office, Library of Congress, Washington, DC 20559.

Each of the above forms contains simple instructions for its completion and filing. Copies of all of these forms can be found on the accompanying CD-ROM or downloaded from the U.S. Copyright Office Web site (http://www.loc.gov/copyright/forms). Once a work is registered, a copyright registration number is issued, preceded by the initials of the form used in the application: PA for performing arts, RE for renewal, VA for visual arts, and so on. Unpublished works are further identified by the letter U: for example, PAU for an unpublished work in the performing arts. All registrations prior to 1978 are recorded on index cards. Entries from January 1, 1978, to the present are recorded electronically. Entries are published in the *Catalog of Copyright Entries* and available for inspection on microfiche in the Search Room of the Copyright Office and in the Library of Congress. Entries from January 1, 1978 to the present are also published on the Internet.

Because the duration of copyrights originating in and after 1978 is now generally measured from date of death of the author, except for work-for-hire works, filers should provide the following information in compliance with Section 409 of the 1976 Copyright Act:

- ► The date of any author's birth and death
- ► A statement of whether the work was made for hire
- ► A statement of how the claimant obtained ownership of the copyright if the claimant is not the author
- ► Previous or alternative titles under which the work can be identified
- ► The year in which creation of the work was completed

If a compilation or derivative work is based on or incorporates a preexisting work, that work must be identified in the registration application, together with a description of the new material. (See Chapter 12, page 139.)

The Copyright Notice

As originally enacted, the 1976 Copyright Act required that all publicly distributed copies of published compositions bear a notice of copyright, but under the Berne Convention Implementation Act of 1988, this requirement no longer applies. Nonetheless, it is still highly recommended, especially for reprints of works first published with a notice before March 1, 1989. A copyright notice makes it easy to find the copyright holder who can provide the requisite permission or license.

Paragraph 401 of the Copyright Act of 1976 states that the notice shall consist of either the word "copyright," the abbreviation, "copr.," or the symbol ©, accompanied by the name of the copyright owner, or an abbreviation by which the name can be recognized, or a generally known alternative designation of the owner. In the case of printed literary, musical, or dramatic works, the notice must also include the year of initial publication. A copyright notice usually looks like this: "© 1995 John Doe" or "Copyright 1995 by Jane Doe." The copyright notice for phonorecords uses a ℗ instead of the ©. (See page 74.)

The 1909 copyright statute specified where the notice should appear for certain categories of work. This is still significant for works published before 1989 because an earlier failure to comply could be fatal to a copyright claim. For musical works, for instance, the notice had to be placed on either the title page or the first page of the music. Under the Copyright Act of 1976, the copyright notice is to be placed on "copies in such manner and location as to give reasonable notice of the claim of copyright." The Register of Copyrights may prescribe by regulation, as examples, specific notice positions to satisfy this requirement, although these specifications are not "exhaustive" of what may be otherwise "reasonable" notices.

The Universal Copyright Convention requires that each copy of a published work bear the symbol © accompanied by the name of the copyright proprietor and the year of first publication. The symbol should be placed in such manner and location as to give reasonable notice of claim of copyright. Other formalities, such as the registration and deposit of copies, are waived, but each country can require formalities pertaining to its own nationals and to works first published there. The U.S. standard for the placement of the optional notice is the same as under the Universal Copyright Convention. However, incentive for compliance under this convention is now substantially diminished because there are relatively few countries that are members of the Universal Copyright Convention but not of the more liberal, and more effective, Berne Convention.

The Deposit of Copyrighted Works

Under the Copyright Act of 1976, as amended by the Berne Convention Implementation Act of 1988, the copyright owner or the owner of the exclusive right of publication must deposit in the Copyright Office, for the use or disposition of the Library of Congress, two copies of the best edition of the work within 3 months of publication in the United States with or without notice of copyright. This is irrespective of whether there is an application for copyright registration. If the work is a sound recording, two complete phonorecords of the best edition must be deposited, together with any printed or visually perceptible material published with the phonorecords; the deposit includes the entire container or package as well as the disc or tape itself.

Best edition is defined as the one published in the United States before the date of deposit that the Library of Congress deems most suitable for its purpose. The Register of Copyrights may exempt such a deposit or require the deposit of only one copy. Literary, dramatic, and musical compositions published only in the form of phonorecords are exempt from deposit. ("Copyright Regulation 201: General Provisions" and "Copyright Regulation 202: Registration of Claims to Copyright" discuss deposits for the Library of Congress and for copyright registration. Regulations 201 and 202 and "Copyright Office Information Circular 7B: Best Edition" are available on the accompanying CD-ROM.)

At any time after publication, the Register of Copyrights may demand the required deposit in writing. If the registrant fails to comply within 3 months, he or she will be liable to (1) a fine of not more than $250 for each work, (2) a payment to the Library of Congress of the total retail price of the copies or phonorecords demanded, and (3) an additional fine of $2,500 for willful or repeated failure or refusal to comply.

Deposit is not a condition of copyright protection. It serves two purposes: it identifies the work in connection with copyright registration and it provides copies for the use of the Library of Congress. The deposit of copies has been an integral part of the U.S. copyright system from its beginning in 1790. The administration of the registry system was placed in the Library of Congress in 1870; since that time, a single deposit has served both purposes.

A deposit as evidence of the copyrighted work must be viewed with some caution. While unpublished manuscripts or facsimile reproductions are kept on file for the life of the copyright, the Register of Copyrights and the Librarian of Congress may, at their discretion, dispose of published works after their retention for the longest period deemed practicable and desirable. This period for most works has been fixed at 5 years from the date of deposit. Under the Copyright Act of 1976 a request may be made for retention of deposited material for the full term of copyright.

In 1939, music deposits received prior to 1928 and then retained were transferred to the Library of Congress's music division, where they are preserved and available for consultation. Additional musical compositions deemed appropriate for such preservation have been regularly transferred to the music division since that time.

Transfers of Copyright Ownership

Under the Copyright Act of 1976, there may be a "transfer of copyright ownership" in a copyright or in any of the exclusive rights included in a copyright. The transfer may be by means of a conveyance or by operation of law. The copyright or exclusive rights may also be transferred by will or by intestate succession. Transfer includes an assignment, mortgage, exclusive license, or any other conveyance, whether or not limited in time or place. It does not include a nonexclusive license.

The transfer, other than by operation of law, must be in writing and signed by the owner of the rights conveyed or an authorized agent. If the transfer is acknowledged before a notary public or other person authorized to administer oaths in the United States, the certificate or acknowledgment becomes prima facie evidence of the execution of the transfer.

The transfer of copyright ownership may be recorded in the Copyright Office. The recording fee is $65 for any document relating to a single title, plus an additional $15 for each group of up to 10 titles. When the ownership is recorded, the Register of Copyrights returns the documents together with a certificate of recordation.

Under the 1976 Copyright Act, following the recordation, all persons are on constructive notice of the facts in the document recorded; in other words, all members of the general public are presumed to be fully aware of the facts of ownership. This is on condition that the work has been registered for copyright and that the document recorded specifically identifies the work involved so that a reasonable search under the title or registration number of the work reveals the document. Under the 1976 Copyright Act, the transferee could not begin an infringement action until the transfer had been recorded. This had the effect of encouraging the recordation of transfer of ownership. The Berne act eliminated this requirement. Recording a transfer is still encouraged by a provision of the 1976 Copyright Act, which states that in the event of conflicting transfers, the prior one prevails if it is recorded so as to give constructive notice (1) within 1 month after execution in the United States, or (2) within 2 months after execution abroad, or (3) at any time before recordation of the later transfer. Without such a recording, the later transfer prevails if recorded first in the manner required to give constructive notice, provided that the later transfer is made in good faith for a valuable consideration, or on the basis of an agreement to pay royalties, without notice of the prior transfer.

Nonexclusive licenses in writing, signed by the owner of the rights licensed or the owner's agent, whether recorded or not, are valid against later transfers. Such licenses also prevail against a prior unrecorded transfer if taken in good faith and without notice of the transfer. A transfer is always valid between the transferee and the transferer, with or without its recording, since both parties are on notice of their own acts.

Regardless of the transfer, the optional copyright notice may continue to contain the name of the prior owner. The new owner may substitute his or her name in the copyright notice. This change of name need not be preceded by recording the transfer in the Copyright Office. (The short-form assignment of copyright is available on the Copyright Office's Web site and on the accompanying CD-ROM.)

Errors in the Copyright Notice

Under the Copyright Law of 1909, the omission of a copyright notice would generally invalidate the copyright. A distinction should be drawn, however, between the absence of notice on copies or phonorecords published or distributed *before* March 1, 1989, the effective date of the Berne act, and *on or after* March 1, 1989. On copies published or distributed on or after March 1, 1989, the absence of a copyright notice no longer divests a work of copyright protection. On copies published or distributed before March 1, 1989, the absence of a copyright notice is to be treated under the Copyright Act of 1976 (effective January 1, 1978) as it existed before the effective date of the Berne Act. Under the 1976 Copyright Act, omission of a copyright notice does not cause the automatic forfeiture of copyright protection or throw the work into the public domain. If notice is omitted from "no more than a relatively small number of copies" of phonorecords distributed publicly, the copyright is not invalidated. Even the omission from more than a relatively small number of copies does not affect the copyright's benefits where registration of the work has already been made or is made within 5 years after the publication without notice and where there are reasonable efforts to add the notice to copies of records publicly distributed in the United States after discovery of the omission. Similarly, there is continued copyright protection if the omission violated a written requirement by the copyright owner that authorized copies or records were to bear a prescribed notice.

Before the Copyright Act of 1976, a postdated copyright notice or a notice without a name or without a date would ordinarily constitute a fatal defect in the copyright. Under the 1976 Copyright Act, if a name or a date is omitted in the notice or if a notice is postdated more than 1 year from the date of first publication, the work is treated as if it had been published without any notice.

Since the Berne Act is not retroactive insofar as works of U.S. origin are concerned, the copyright owner should take the necessary curative steps under the Copyright Act of 1976 to remedy any defect in order to avoid forfeiture of copyright.

Under some circumstances, innocence is a defense to an infringer. In that regard there is a difference between infringements before March 1, 1989 and infringements on or after that date. For copies of a work published on or after March 1, 1989, the absence of a copyright notice does not divest a work of copyright protection, but the presence of a proper copyright notice invalidates a defense of innocent infringement. If the defense is successful, this may result in the reduction of the actual or statutory damages awarded by a court to the copyright holder.

For copies of a work published prior to March 1, 1989, the Copyright Act of 1976 governs. That tended to liberalize the effect of omissions or defects in copyright notices. Curative steps could be taken to avoid forfeiture of the copyright. These include registering the work within 5 years after the publication without notice and adding notice to copies distributed in the United States after discovery of the omission. Under the 1976 Copyright Act an error in the name of the copyright owner in the copyright notice does not affect the validity or ownership of the copyright.

There are a number of results from omissions of, or defects in, copyright notices under the 1976 Copyright Act. If the infringer was misled, he or she would not be liable for actual or statutory damages prior to his or her receiving notice of a copyright registration. In that situation the court, in its discretion might still allow claims for the infringer's profits, prohibit future infringement, or require the infringer to pay the copyright owner a reasonable license fee determined in order to continue the venture. In cases of an incorrect name in a copyright notice, where the infringer acted in good faith on the authority of the person in the notice and the Copyright Office records did not show the real owner in a copyright registration or in a document executed by the person named in the notice, then the infringer has a complete defense to an action for infringement. Where there are relatively minor infringements by teachers, librarians, journalists, and the like completed before actual notice of registration, a court may disallow statutory damages and restrict the liability, if any, to the innocent infringer's profits. (For a further discussion of infringement, see Chapter 19.)

Due diligence in searching for copyright claims and history of the copyright can be shown by paying the Copyright Office $65 per hour to conduct a search. (See Chapter 40 for search procedures conducted by the Copyright Office, as well as alternative search facilities.)

The Correction of Errors

Under the Copyright Act of 1976, the Register of Copyrights may establish procedures whereby an earlier copyright registration may be corrected or amplified, but not superseded, by a supplementary registration. Consequently, if a registration has been made with an incorrect name of the owner or an inaccurate date of publication, the error can be indicated in an application for a supplementary registration. This application identifies the earlier registration and is accompanied by a $30 registration fee, the same amount required for the prior registration. The Copyright Office has published Form CA for such supplementary registrations.

Titles of works are not subjects of copyright but merely a means of identifying a work. A change of title does not require a new copyright registration. It is the practice of the Copyright Office, when receiving a request in writing, to prepare without charge a cross-reference entry under the new title, to appear in the general indexes. If a permanent official record is desired, a formal signed statement outlining the pertinent facts can be submitted for recording the title change in the same manner as an assignment of copyright; the fee is $65, the same as for recording an assignment.

Fair Use

It is surprising how frequently songwriters and others in the music business think that copying four bars or less of someone's music is permissible despite copyright protection. This error may stem from a misinterpretation of the doctrine of *fair use,* which recognizes the right of the public to make a reasonable use of copyrighted material in special instances without the copyright owner's consent. For instance, a book reviewer may quote lines from the book reviewed to illustrate his critical appraisal. Similarly, musicologists and other researchers may use reasonable extracts of copyrighted works in preparing a new scholarly text or commentary. These are clear examples of fair use.

Fair use has been applied for many years as a judicial exception to the exclusive rights of a copyright owner to print, publish, copy, and vend a copyrighted work. In the Copyright Act of 1976, the doctrine of fair use has been included in the statute itself. The provisions of the fair use section are generally consistent with what had been the treatment under case law prior to the statute.

It may be difficult to determine in advance what will be held to be a fair use, however, because the language of the statute is illustrative rather than absolute. It recognizes that the fair use of a copyrighted work may be used "for purposes such as criticism, comment, news reporting, teaching (including multiple copies for classroom use), scholarship, or research." The factors to be considered in determining fair use include:

1. The purpose and character of the use including whether such use is of a commercial nature or is for nonprofit educational purposes;
2. The nature of the copyrighted work;
3. The amount and substantiality of the portion used in relation to the copyrighted work as a whole; and
4. The effect of the use upon the potential market for or value of the copyrighted work.

The Music Publishers Association of the United States, the National Music Publishers Association, the Music Teachers National Association, the Music Educators National Conference, the National Association of Schools of Music, and the Ad Hoc Committee on Copyright Law Revision have prepared a set of guidelines for the fair use of music for educational purposes. These guidelines set forth the extent of permissible copying of music for educational purposes, with a caveat that conditions may change in the future, so the guidelines may have to be restricted or enlarged. It is important to note that the guidelines are not intended to limit the types of copying permissible under fair use as defined in the Copyright Act of 1976.

The guidelines permit emergency copying for a performance, making a single copy of a sound recording of copyrighted music for aural exercises or examinations, editing or simplification of printed copies, and making multiple copies (not more than one per pupil) of partial excerpts not comprising a performable unit, and not exceeding 10 percent of a whole work. There is a general prohibition, except as specifically exempted, against copying for performances, the copying of workbooks, exercises, and tests, and copying to substitute for the purchase of music.

The criteria for fair use set forth in the 1976 Copyright Act codified earlier fair use standards reflected in case law. For example, in a 1972 case (*Robert Stigwood Group Ltd. v. John T. O'Reilly et al.*), one court, faced with the defense of fair use by Catholic priests who had presented their revised version of *Jesus Christ Superstar,* ruled that the defendants' production could not qualify as "literary and religious criticism of the plaintiffs' work." The court stated that the defendants' presentation "(1) is obviously a substitute for plaintiffs' work; (2) copies almost all of the plaintiffs' lyrics, score, and sequence of songs; (3) undoubtedly has and will injure plaintiffs financially; (4) is definitely in competition with plaintiffs' performances; and (5) does not serve or advance the greater public interest in the development of news, art, science or industry."

Another court has held that the reproduction of "some more or less disconnected 'snatches' or quotations from the words of ... [a] song" was fair use. On the other hand, another court decided that the use in a commercial of a short extract of the basic melody of a work was not fair use. All factors in respect to fair use must be considered, and the *quality* of the use—not only the *quantity* used—is important.

In 1994, the U.S. Supreme Court ruled unanimously that a parody can qualify as a fair use exception to the copyright laws and that courts should decide on a case-by-case basis whether a particular work qualifies or infringes on a copyright. The case concerned a parody of the song "Oh, Pretty Woman" by the rap group 2 Live Crew. The court determined that a parody qualifies for exemption even if it is in relatively bad taste and that no royalties are required if the parody qualifies as fair use.

An especially controversial area of copyright law is the taping of a copyrighted work that is broadcast on radio or television. In general, taping a copyrighted work off the air for commercial purposes constitutes copyright infringement. However, off-the-air videotaping in the home for private use has been held by the U.S. Supreme Court to be permissible as fair use. The practice largely involved time shifting—the taping of a program for delayed viewing at home.

Litigation has not as yet settled the propriety of home audio recording of a broadcast or phonorecord for private use. However, in connection with the passage of the Sound Recording Amendment Act of 1971 creating a limited copyright in sound recordings, the House Judiciary Committee commented that "it is not the intention of the Committee to restrain the home recording, from broadcasts or from tapes or records, of recorded performances where the home recording is for private use and with no purpose of reproducing or otherwise capitalizing commercially on it."

In cases involving fair use, where there is doubt regarding its applicability, it is prudent to apply for a license from a copyright proprietor. The existence of the fair use exception tends to strengthen the bargaining position of the applicant for the license.

Copyright Protection of Song Titles

Copyright protection does not extend to the titles of songs or to other copyrighted materials insofar as they are titles. Indirectly, copyright may become involved if the words in the title are an important segment of the song lyric. However, while court decisions have tended to cloud the matter, titles that achieve a secondary meaning in the minds of the public by becoming associated with a particular work have traditionally been safeguarded by the doctrine of unfair competition. The courts invoke this doctrine to prevent the public from being deceived or defrauded as the result of a product being passed off as if it were the product of the plaintiff.

Record albums frequently use an individual song title as the featured title for the album itself. Use of the titles of popular songs helps to set the mood of the album, identifies the type of music contained, and attracts album buyers. No extra payment to the music publisher over usual mechanical royalties is customary. It is common for the publisher to insist on the full statutory mechanical rates when the title of its song is used in this manner, even though the songs in the remainder of the recording are licensed at lower rates customary for budget line albums.

Property rights in titles can be extremely valuable. Motion picture producers regularly pay large sums for the use of song titles such as "Ode to Billy Joe" or "Alexander's Ragtime Band." Not all titles are sufficiently unique for the assertion of legal rights against a motion picture use of the title, though. For example, Walt Disney issued a movie using the title *The Love Bug* without a license from the publisher of the musical composition, "The Love Bug Will Bite You (If You Don't Watch Out)." Disney was able to show that the film involved a "Volkswagen automobile with human attributes" and was not based on or related to the musical composition of the plaintiff. The court found that the "Love Bug" phrase was "oft used" and that the plaintiff had failed to establish the requisite secondary meaning and likelihood of confusion to support relief.

Compulsory Mechanical License for Recordings

Under section 115 of the Copyright Act of 1976, when the copyright owner authorizes a person or entity to distribute recordings of a musical composition, other than one originating in a dramatic show, to the public, any other person may also record and distribute recordings of the work after giving written notice consistent with the regulations of the Copyright Office and paying a statutory royalty rate on each record made and distributed. A record is considered to have been distributed if possession has been "voluntarily and permanently parted with." The written notice and the statutory rate together constitute a *compulsory license*. While author and music publishing groups have argued vehemently against the continuation of the compulsory mechanical license, record industry representatives have fought strongly and successfully for its retention.

The statutory rate of 2 cents was first established in the Copyright Act of 1909. The first review of statutory mechanical royalty rates occurred in 1987, and they are subject to periodic review. The 1997 rate was jointly proposed by the National Music Publishers Association, the Songwriters Guild of America, and the Recording Industry Association of America and accepted by the Librarian of Congress at the recommendation of the Copyright Office. The rate as of January 1, 2000, is 7.55 cents per composition up to 5 minutes' duration, or 1.45 cents per minute or fraction thereof, whichever is larger.

The compulsory mechanical license fee was originally subject to review by the Copyright Royalty Tribunal (CRT) established under the Copyright Act of 1976. However, the tribunal was replaced in 1992 by a three-person ad hoc arbitration panel called the Copyright Arbitration Royalty Panel (CARP). The Register of Copyrights chooses two members from a panel of more than 100 available experts in the field, and those two choose the third member, who serves as the chairperson. The CARP panel is only called into session if industry negotiators do not resolve the issue voluntarily.

The compulsory mechanical license for recordings allows the making of an "arrangement of the work to the extent necessary to conform it to the style or manner of interpretation of the performance." Even a "sound-alike" recording, with an arrangement similar to that of a prior recording, is permitted; however, a licensee must avoid changing the basic melody or fundamental character of the work. There can be no claim made to an arrangement as a derivative copyright unless consented to by the copyright owner.

The Copyright Act of 1976 eliminated a prior statutory requirement of a formal "notice of use" by the copyright proprietor. It provides instead that "to be entitled to receive royalties under a compulsory license, the copyright owner must be identified in the registration or other public records of the Copyright Office." The copyright owner cannot require royalty payments for records made and distributed before being so identified, although the copyright owner can recover damages for records made and distributed after such identification. Accordingly, it is prudent for a copyright owner to register his or her copyright before records are made and distributed.

The copyright owner may negotiate the terms of a mechanical license instead of following the procedure for a compulsory license. A negotiated mechanical license ordinarily permits quarterly accountings and payments, instead of the monthly ones under oath required under a compulsory license by the 1976 statute, and usually dispenses with the requirement of cumulative annual statements made by a certified public accountant. (See Chapter 15 for a full discussion of mechanical licenses.)

Record Rentals

Although there can be no legal objection to the well-established practice of selling and trading used CDs and cassettes, the rental of records has been a matter of major industry concern. After successful lobbying for statutory protection, a special restrictive amendment was passed in 1984. Under this Record Rental Act of 1984, regarding copies of sound recordings acquired on or after October 4, 1984, there can be no commercial rental, lease, or lending by the owners of the copies unless authorized by the copyright proprietors of the recordings and of the underlying musical works. A record company desiring to sanction such activities can negotiate a license from the music copyright proprietor or may obtain a compulsory license of the musical works in accordance with the established system applicable to the making and distribution of recordings.

However, for rentals, leasing, and lending, a compulsory license requires the payment of a royalty to the music copyright owner over and above that payable for the sale of records. The compulsory licensee must share its rental, lease, or lending revenues with the music copyright owner in the proportion that revenues from the sale of recordings are allocated between the copyright proprietors of the sound recording and the underlying music. (For a further discussion, see Chapter 15, "Mechanical Rights.")

Jukebox Public Performance Fees

The first jukebox, called a Nickel-in-a-Slot, was a modified version of Edison's phonograph. This coin-operated phonograph first appeared in the Palais Royale Saloon, San Francisco, on November 23, 1889. Jukeboxes reached their peak in the 1960s, with an estimated 300,000 in service. Usage declined from the late 1960s through the mid-1980s. However, with the advent of new CD and digital technologies, there has been a resurgence in usage; jukebox music now reaches an estimated 75 to 80 million Americans each week.

The 1976 statute defines a *jukebox* as "a coin-operated phonorecord player" that meets the following criteria:

- It performs nondramatic musical works and is activated by insertion of a coin.
- It is located in an establishment making no direct or indirect admission charge.
- It offers patrons a choice of works from a readily available list of titles.

Under the Copyright Act of 1909, owners of jukeboxes were generally exempted from paying public performance fees. The only direct benefits to copyright owners from jukebox use were mechanical license fees paid by record manufacturers who sold records to the jukebox industry. During studies preliminary to copyright revision, the Register of Copyrights termed the exemption a "historical anomaly." Finally, after heated legislative hearings, the exemption was eliminated.

Under the Copyright Act of 1976, jukebox owners must obtain a compulsory public performance license for nondramatic works by filing an application with the Copyright Office and paying to the Register of Copyrights a yearly fee for each jukebox. However, the Berne Convention Implementation Act of 1988 amended the 1976 law to provide for negotiated public performance licenses between the jukebox operator and the copyright owner. The parties are encouraged to submit to arbitration if necessary to facilitate negotiated licenses. These licenses take precedence over the compulsory license, but compulsory licenses remain in effect if private agreements are not negotiated or if they are terminated.

The statutory fee was initially set at $8 per box, subject to later determinations first by the Copyright Royalty Tribunal and now by CARP. The fee was increased to $25 in 1982 and $50 in 1984. Provision was made by the tribunal for later cost-of-living adjustments in the fee, as indicated by the consumer price index. As a result, the fee was set at $63 per jukebox in 1989.

In 1990, the Jukebox License Agreement, a 10-year licensing agreement, was negotiated between the Amusement and Music Operators Association and the three U.S. performing rights organizations, ASCAP, BMI, and SESAC. This agreement authorizes the jukebox performance of all the music handled by the three performing rights organizations. The agreement led to the formation of the Jukebox License Office, which administers the agreement, currently under SESAC's supervision. After administration costs, revenues are split by private agreement between the three participants. The license must be renewed yearly, and the annual rates, as of this writing, are $323 for the first jukebox, $61 per box for the next nine jukeboxes, and $50 each for all subsequent jukeboxes. To qualify for the reduced per-box license in such groups, the licensee must be a single entity regardless of where the licensed jukebox is located, including across state lines.

Licensing information can be obtained from the Jukebox License Office, 1700 Hayes Street, Suite 201, Nashville, TN 37203-3014; telephone: 800-955 5853, fax: 615-320-4004; e-mail: jukebox@edge.net.

Copyright and Cable Television Transmission

Television broadcasting is technically limited to the geographic area covered by the initial transmission, and unless there is a network extension of a broadcast area or syndicated use of videotaped programs, the audience of an originating television broadcast is necessarily confined. Nevertheless, signals from distant metropolitan stations are brought to more rural environs by means of sophisticated community antenna television (CATV) facilities, thereby extending the audience beyond the area originally anticipated by copyright owners that licensed the broadcaster.

Cable television systems may be described as commercial subscription services that pick up television broadcasts of programs initiated by others and retransmit them to paying subscribers. In a typical system there is a central antenna for the receipt and amplification of television signals and a network of cables for transmitting signals to subscribers' receivers. In some cases, CATV systems initiate their own programming.

In a 1968 ruling concerning claims by copyright owners against CATV facilities, the U.S. Supreme Court held that cable television systems were not liable to copyright owners for the retransmission of copyrighted material. According to the Court, the cable systems were not active "performers" but merely retransmitters of already licensed material—extensions of the passive viewers whom they serviced.

The Copyright Act of 1976 changed preexisting law, requiring cable television systems to obtain a license from copyright owners for the retransmission of distant non-network programming. A cable television system can get a compulsory license on compliance with various formalities, including the recording of certain information by applying to the Copyright Office. Semiannual accounts must be submitted to the Register of Copyrights showing the number of channels used, the stations carried, the total number of subscribers, and the gross receipts from providing secondary transmission of primary broadcast transmitters. Section 111 of the 1976 statute sets royalty rates, to be paid semiannually by the cable systems and computed on the basis of specified percentages of the gross receipts. Receipts from subscribers for other services such as pay cable or installation charges are not included. Separate reduced-fee schedules are provided for smaller cable systems.

After deducting administrative costs, the Register of Copyright deposits the balance with the U.S. Treasury. After a further deduction for new administrative costs, CARP distributes the monies among the copyright owners or to their designated agents once a year. CARP also settles controversies among claimants and reviews cable television royalty rates periodically on the basis of standards and conditions set forth in the Copyright Act of 1976. The first basic review was made in 1980; further reviews have been made every fifth calendar year. CARP has the authority to revise the royalty rates.

Licensing for Noncommercial Broadcasting

The Copyright Act of 1976 grants noncommercial public broadcasting a compulsory license for the use of published nondramatic literary and musical works as well as published pictorial, graphic, and sculptural works. The license is subject to the payment of reasonable royalty fees, as established by CARP. With regard to music, public broadcasters are allowed to synchronize nondramatic musical works with their programs as well as to perform the programs. They are not allowed to broadcast an unauthorized dramatization of a nondramatic musical work or an unauthorized use of any portion of an audiovisual work.

The act encourages negotiated private agreements between copyright owners and public broadcasters. Voluntary agreements between such parties that are negotiated before, during, or after the determination of terms and rates by CARP supersede such terms and rates.

Satellite Carrier Compulsory License

Effective January 1, 1989, satellite carriers were authorized under section 119 of the Copyright Act of 1976 to retransmit the signals of television broadcast stations for the private home viewing of satellite dish owners. The compulsory license was extended in October 1994.

A statutory rate was established at 12 cents per subscriber per month for each retransmitted independent broadcast station and 3 cents per subscriber per month for each retransmitted network-affiliated station. These rates are subject to voluntary negotiations, which can now be referred to arbitration before a CARP panel appointed by the Copyright Office if unsuccessful. The Register of Copyrights receives the fees paid and, after deducting reasonable administrative costs, deposits the fees with the U.S. Treasury for later distribution by CARP to copyright owners who have filed claims.

11

The Duration of Copyright Protection and the Limitation of Grants

The U.S. Constitution grants exclusive rights to the copyright holder "for limited times." The extent and duration of the limited period of protection is a matter of statutory definition, which has varied throughout the history of copyright in the United States. When the copyright expires, the works become part of the public domain, "free as the air." (Public domain is discussed in Chapter 12.)

Terms of Copyright Protection

The Copyright Act of 1909 provided for a possible copyright term of 56 years: an original copyright term of 28 years and a renewal term of another 28 years. The Copyright Act of 1976 increased the total period of protection to 75 years. The Sonny Bono Term Extension Act of 1998 added a further 20 years of copyright protection. (See also the accompanying CD-ROM for a copy of the act.)

Under the Copyright Act of 1976, effective January 1, 1978, there are four main categories of copyright protection:

- Pre-1978 works in their original 28-year term of copyright
- Pre-1978 works in their renewal 28-year term of copyright
- New works created on or after January 1, 1978
- Pre-1978 works not previously published or copyrighted

A fifth category of copyright protection was created under the Sonny Bono Term Extension Act of 1998 to cover those relatively rare situations of a work in extended-renewal term (after the 56th year) where no actions have been taken under the 1976 Copyright Act's rights of termination. The act allowed only specified family members to take action of termination, not executors, administrators, or trustees, as permitted under the Sonny Bono Term Extension Act. (See page 134–135 for a fuller discussion.)

Pre-1978 Works in Their Original Term of Copyright

For pre-1978 works in their original 28 year term of copyright, the Copyright Act of 1976 made provision for the term to continue for the full 28 years specified in the 1909 copyright statute; it also preserved the 28-year renewal term of copyright and extended it by an additional 19 years, for a total protection period of 75 years. Subsequent amendments further extended the renewal term to 67 years, bringing the full duration of copyright to 95 years.

Pre-1978 Works in Their Renewal Term of Copyright

For pre-1978 works already in or registered for their renewal term, the Copyright Act of 1976 extends the renewal period so that copyright protection lasts for 75 years from the date the copyright was originally secured: the original 28-year term plus the 28-year renewal term plus the 19-year extension. The 20-year extension stipulated by the Sonny Bono Term Extension Act of 1998 increased the total protection to 95 years.

New Works

For new works created on or after January 1, 1978, the duration of copyright protection is the life of the author plus 70 years. Where there is a joint work, the 70 years are measured from the death of the last surviving coauthor.

However, where the identity of the author remains unrevealed in anonymous or pseudonymous works or in the case of works made by an employee for hire, the duration of protection is 95 years from the year of first publication or 120 years from creation, whichever expires first. If the author of an anonymous or pseudonymous work is later officially identified in the records of the Copyright Office, the copyright endures for the life of the identified author plus 70 years.

If records maintained by the Copyright Office do not disclose a date of death of an identifiable author after a period of 95 years from first publication or 120 years from creation, whichever is earlier, it is presumed that the author has been dead for at least 70 years. Reliance on this presumption in good faith is a complete defense to an infringement action.

Pre-1978 Works Not Previously Published or Copyrighted

Prior to the Copyright Act of 1976, a work not under statutory copyright or in the public domain was covered by common law copyright under applicable state law. The 1976 Copyright Act provided federal copyright protection for such works on the same basis as new works—in other words, for the life of the author plus 70 years. If the works are anonymous, pseudonymous, or works made for hire, the copyright now endures for 95 years from first publication or 120 years from creation, whichever first expires. In all cases, the copyright endures until at least December 31, 2002. If the work is published before

December 31, 2002, the copyright endures until at least December 31, 2047.

The Terminal Date of Copyright Protection

Under the Copyright Act of 1909, an application for renewal had to be filed within 1 year of the expiration of the original term (day and month) of copyright. The Copyright Renewal Act of 1992 made renewal and extension automatic; inaction does not result in a lapse of copyright protection. Furthermore, the Copyright Act of 1976 extends copyright dates to the end of the calendar year in which they would otherwise terminate. This may result in a slight prolongation of a term that might otherwise expire earlier in of the year. However, it facilitates the computation of dates.

For example, under the 1909 Copyright Act, the first 28-year term of copyright obtained on July 1, 1972, would have ended on June 30, 2000; now it ends on December 31, 2000. Because renewal and extension are automatic, copyright protection is assured until December 31, 2067 (not June 30, 1967). For a new work fixed on July 1, 1978, the term of copyright protection is the life of the author plus 70 years. If the author died on February 15, 1980, the 70-year period would expire on December 31, 2050, not on February 14, 2030.

It is worth noting that, with respect to 1950 copyrights and later copyrights now in their first term of copyright, the principle of year-end termination of copyright terms has affected the computation of duration, although in some cases the recapture of copyright under renewal concept has been delayed to end of year. Under the Copyright Act of 1909 the 1-year period would have run from one anniversary date to another: for instance, from April 30 to April 30. But by reason of the year-end termination of the term of copyrights, the 1-year period is a calendar year: that is, from January 1 to December 31.

The Duration of Copyright Protection for Joint Works

A *joint work* is defined in the 1976 Copyright Act as one "prepared by two or more authors with the intention that their contributions be merged into inseparable or interdependent parts of a unitary whole." A song can qualify as a joint work where authors write words and music together or where one or more authors write words and other authors separately write the music. For joint works fixed on or after January 1, 1978, the statutory term of protection is 70 years from the death of the last surviving author. This is beneficial to the heirs of the earlier-deceased coauthors because the heirs of the first author get the advantage of a longer term based on the later death date of the surviving collaborator.

The Determination of Date of Death

The computations of copyright terms under the Copyright Act of 1976 present practical problems with respect to determining the dates of death of obscure or unknown authors. The Register of Copyrights is obligated to maintain current records of author deaths. Any person having a copyright interest may record in the Copyright Office statements of the death or living status of an author, in compliance with the regulations of the Register of Copyrights.

After a period of 95 years from the publication of a work or 120 years from its creation, whichever expires first, any person may obtain a certification from the Copyright Office that its records disclose nothing to indicate that the author is living or has been dead for less than 70 years. In that case, the person may rely on a presumption that the author has been dead for more than 70 years. Such reliance in good faith is a complete defense to an infringement action.

Copyright Renewal Registrations

As noted previously, copyright renewal applies only to pre-1978 works in their original term of copyright as of January 1, 1978. The passage of the Copyright Renewal Act of 1992 alleviates the need to renew in nearly all cases. If there has been a valid assignment of renewal rights, the automatic renewal benefits the prior assignee, whereas if there has been a death of the author or a failure of a surviving author to assign his or her rights of renewal, the automatic benefits as to new uses accrue to the author or the statutory successors without further notification to the Copyright Office, although notice should be sent to the performing rights society and mechanical or other licensing agents.

If the copyright is not affirmatively renewed, certain rights commonly known as the "Who's Sorry Now" benefits remain with the prior publisher. These rights, which include all continuing royalties that are based on a derivative copyright (including old copyrightable arrangements), will continue to flow to the prior publisher even into the renewal term, unless a renewal claim is registered. (See page 122 for a further discussion.)

A further change in the renewal procedure, to be used only in the rare instance of a work that was not previously registered within its original 28-year term of copyright and where a combined basic registration is essential at or before the renewal registration, is found in the Copyright Office Addendum to Form RE. Where a work was published in printed form during the original term between January 1, 1964, and December 31, 1977, the addendum form is to be used. (The reason for the cutoff date of 1977 is that subsequent works are no longer subject to renewal provisions in any respect.)

When considering renewal rights, in all applicable instances, if the renewal right was originally the author's, the appropriate renewal claimants are:

- ▸ The author, if still living
- ▸ *If the author is dead,* the widow, widower, or children of the author
- ▸ *If there is no surviving widow, widower, or child,* the executor named in the author's will

> ▸ *If there is no surviving widow, widower, or child, and the author left no will*, the next of kin of the deceased author

In the case of certain works that were originally copyrighted by a proprietor, the right to renew rests with that proprietor. This includes posthumous works and periodical, encyclopedic, or other composite works, or works copyrighted by an employer or corporation that hired someone to create the work. Where there is a collaborator on a song, the benefits of renewal accrue to each writer if they survive into renewal or to their statutory beneficiaries as noted above. A renewal copyright is a new and independent right, and not merely a prolongation of the first term. While the courts uphold assignments of the renewal right, the fulfillment of the assignment depends on the survival of the author into the renewal year. In the event that the author does not survive, the assignee's rights are defeated by the beneficiaries designated in the Copyright Acts of 1909 and 1976, such as the widow, widower, children, executor, or next of kin.

In 1990 the U.S. Supreme Court considered a case involving Alfred Hitchcock's motion picture *Rear Window,* which is a derivative work based on a published story. The license to the film company purported to cover the original copyright period and the renewal period of the story. However, the author of the story died before the expiration of the original 28-year copyright period, and the renewal copyright owner or its assignees had not authorized the exploitation of the movie within the copyright renewal period. In a 6-to-3 decision, the Court ruled that without such authorization, the continued exhibition of the film or its exploitation in the form of videocassettes during the copyright renewal period constituted an infringement. This precedent would appear to apply also to derivative works based on music, where the author of the music dies before the copyright can be renewed. The *Rear Window* ruling is only applicable to renewal copyrights that are officially registered and does not occur if automatic renewal is relied on. This situation does not concern 39-year termination situations (19-year extension plus 20-year extension) where the 1976 and 1998 statutes specifically protect continued derivative uses.

It is important to recognize that U.S. renewal recapture rights do not normally affect foreign continuance of the granting of rights. However, in a 1997 decision, a British court ruled that the copyright to the song "To Know Him Is to Love Him" reverted back to legendary producer-songwriter Phil Spector 28 years after publication because of a provision in the AGAC (presently Songwriters Guild) contract that provided for the reversion of world rights at the end of the original term of copyright.

Limitations of Old Transfers and Licenses

The *right of termination* represents a resolution of the basic question of whether there should be any limitation on the term of a new assignment or license of rights by authors in order to protect them against transfers of their rights for an inadequate remuneration. The Copyright Act of 1909, as amended, sought to accomplish this by providing for the renewal copyright to vest in the author or the author's heirs. It was the conclusion of the Register of Copyrights that this concept should be eliminated "because it has largely failed to accomplish the purpose of protecting authors and their heirs against improvident transfers, and has been the source of much confusion and litigation." The Register recommended that some other provision be made to protect the authors and their successors.

The right of termination is in contrast to the old right of renewal. Whereas the original concept of renewal as a means to safeguard the author and his or her successors from improvident full transfers of copyright, the failure to fulfill the renewal technicalities resulted in early public domain status. The termination provision is aptly summarized as "The squeaky wheel gets the grease," inasmuch as the copyright is not forfeited for failure to terminate; the original publisher simply continues as owner of a continuing extended copyright term.

For existing copyrights in their first or renewal terms as of the end of 1977, exclusive or nonexclusive transfers or licenses of the renewal copyright or of any right under it made prior to 1978, covering the extended renewal period under the Copyright Act of 1976, can be terminated at any time during the 5-year period beginning at the end of 56 years from the date the copyright was originally secured or from January 1, 1978, whichever is later. This termination, which applies only to the 19-year extension period under the 1976 Copyright Act, can be put into effect by a written notice served at least 2 years and not more than 10 years in advance of the termination date within the 5-year period.

For the purpose of the termination of grants, the principle of the year-end expiration of terms of copyright, enacted under the Copyright Act of 1976, is inapplicable. The measurement of 56 years from the date a copyright was first secured is from the actual date, and there is no prolongation to December 31. The 5-year period and the 2- to 10-year notice periods are also measured without reference to the year-end expiration of copyright terms.

An example of typical computations involved in the termination of a grant follows. Assuming that a copyright in a musical work was secured on April 30, 1946, its 56th year would thus be completed on April 29, 2002; its termination might be made effective in the 5-year period from April 30, 2002, to April 30, 2007. Assuming that the author is alive and decides to terminate on April 30, 2002 (the earliest possible date), the advance notice must be served between April 30, 1992, and April 30, 2000.

In the case of an author who made the transfer or license, the termination notice has to be authorized by the author or, if the author is dead, by the surviving spouse and children (or the children of a deceased child). A surviving spouse with no children, or a surviving child with no parents, owns the entire termination interest. If a surviving spouse has children, the spouse receives 50 percent and the children as a group possess the other 50 percent. Rights of children are exercised by majority rule *per stirpes:* the children of a dead child succeed to the interest of their parent, which interest is computed as if the parent were alive. Children of a dead child are bound by a majority action among themselves in voting the share of their parent. If a surviving spouse opposes termination, no action by the children can effect a termination because neither the spouse nor any number of children has more than a 50 percent interest to constitute a majority.

Where there are joint authors, there can be a termination of a particular author's share by that author or, if the author is dead, by the surviving spouse and children who own more than 50 percent of the author's termination interest. There need not be a termination of the whole work, nor does a majority of all the authors have to consent to the termination of a partial interest. Consequently, it is possible to recapture the lyrics of a song alone or the music alone or an undivided interest in the whole song. This is only applicable to songs originating before 1978 because later songs are governed by a different termination provision. (See next section, "Limitations of New Transfers and Licenses.")

There may also sometimes be grants of rights in renewal copyrights made by persons other than an author. A widow, widower, or children or others entitled to renewal copyright, such as the next of kin, may have assigned their interests in renewal copyrights. Under the 1976 Copyright Act, a pre-1978 grant by a person or persons other than an author covering the extended renewal period is subject to termination by the surviving person or persons who executed the grant at any time during the 5 years after the 56th year from the date the copyright was originally secured.

A termination is effective regardless of any prior agreement to the contrary by any person, whether an author or an heir. The form of such a prior agreement, including an agreement to make a will or to make a future grant, is immaterial. The termination does not affect derivative works, such as motion pictures, made before termination under authority of a transfer or license. Works made for hire or bequeathed by will by statutory renewal beneficiaries are also excluded from any right of termination.

Notices of termination must comply in form, content, and manner of service as prescribed by the Register of Copyrights. (See "Notice of Termination Under Section 304(c) of PL 94-553" on the accompanying CD-ROM.) A copy must be recorded in the Copyright Office before the effective date of termination, as a condition to its effectiveness.

Limitations of New Transfers and Licenses

The right of termination of past grants involves only pre-1978 works and those persons who would benefit from the earlier 19-year extension—now 39-year extension—of the prior overall 56-year copyright period applicable to pre-1978 works. A right of termination also applies to new exclusive or nonexclusive grants of a transfer or license of copyright or of any right under a copyright made by the author, other than by will, on or after January 1, 1978. There is no right of termination regarding grants made by the author's successors in interest—for example, members of the family—or by the author's own bequests. It is immaterial whether the new grant is in respect of old or new works.

Under the 1976 Copyright Act, new grants made in or after 1978 of a transfer or license executed by the author may be terminated at any time during a period of 5 years beginning at the end of 35 years from the date of the execution of the grant. However, if the grant covers the right of publication of the work, as do most songwriter and recording artist agreements, the termination may become effective during a period of 5 years beginning at the end of the 35 years from the date of publication or 40 years from the date of the execution of the grant, whichever is earlier. Termination is put in effect by written notice served not less than 2 or more than 10 years before the desired date of termination within the stated 5-year period.

Publication under the 1976 Copyright Act includes the distribution of copies or phonorecords to the public. It is likely that an initial song publication in the form of printed editions or recordings occurs close to the date of execution of a songwriter contract. Consequently, 35 years from the publication date ordinarily marks the beginning of the 5-year period of termination, rather than 40 years from the date of the execution of the agreement. The significance of the publication date makes it essential that publishers and writers keep careful records of that date.

For example, if the date of the execution of the songwriter agreement is April 10, 1980, and the date of publication is June 10, 1980, the 5-year period of termination would begin on June 10, 2015 (35 years from publication), rather than April 10, 2020 (40 years from execution). For a termination date of, say, June 10, 2015, the notice of termination must be served between June 10, 2005, and June 10, 2013.

In another example, a songwriter contract with a music publisher granting the publisher all rights in a song, including the right of publication, is executed on April 10, 1980, and the song is published on August 23, 1987. Inasmuch as the contract covers the right of publication, the 5-year period of termination would begin on April 10, 2020 (40 years from execution), rather than August 23, 2022 (35 years from publication). If the author wishes to put the termination into effect on January 1, 2023, he or she has to serve advance notice of the termination between January 1, 2013 and January 1, 2021.

The notice of termination of new grants made in or after 1978 must be authorized by the surviving author who executed the grant or, if the author had collaborators, by the majority of all collaborators who signed the grant. If the author or any collaborator is dead at the time of notice of termination, the rights of the deceased author may be exercised by the surviving spouse and children (or the children of a deceased child), who under the 1976 Copyright

Act would own more than one-half of the deceased author's termination interest. As a result, in the case of new grants made in or after 1978 of a transfer or license, as distinguished from old grants of interests in renewal copyrights, the failure or refusal of any coauthor of a joint work who executed the grant to join in a notice of termination may defeat the notice and benefit the then-publisher because a majority of the collaborators who signed the grant are essential for effective termination of such 1978 and subsequent grants.

As with old grants of renewal interests, the right of termination does not apply to works made for hire and to grants made under the author's will. Derivative works, such as motion pictures, prepared before the termination under authority of the original transferee may continue to be used under the terms of the transfer. In all other respects, the right to terminate a new grant exists regardless of any agreement or contract to the contrary.

When a majority of collaborators concur, a surviving author who has contracted away all rights in a new grant is in a better position under the Copyright Act of 1976 than under the 1909 statute. This is because the grant of a renewal copyright interest was enforceable without a time restriction against an author under the 1909 Copyright Act if the author survived. However, under the 1976 Copyright Act a living author cannot waive his or her right to terminate a new grant after the 35th (or 40th) year, regardless of any agreement to the contrary, unless it is within the limited time period of 10 years before the intended date of termination.

An author who did not grant away renewal rights under the 1909 Copyright Act could recapture them at the end of 28 years, instead of at the close of 35 years under the 1976 Copyright Act. Also, in the case of an author who died before the copyright renewal period, under the Copyright Act of 1909 rights reverted to his or her heirs at the end of the initial 28 years regardless of the assignment of renewal rights by the author.

The Copyright Act of 1976 requires that a notice of termination involving new grants comply in form, content, and manner with regulations of the Register of Copyrights. To be effective, a copy of a notice must be recorded in the Copyright Office before the effective date of termination. In the rare instance wherein termination rights were not asserted under the 1976 Copyright Act, possibly because of failure to act within the required period or because there was no widow, widower, child, or grandchild, there is a further right of termination under the 1998 Sonny Bono Term Extension Act. This right can be asserted by the surviving members of the immediate family or, in their absence, by the original author's executor, administrator, trustee, or other representative.

Termination of Old Grants by Authors

Pre-1978 grants of a transfer or license covering the extended renewal term of copyright can be made by the author or by the author's surviving spouse, children, executor, or next of kin. When old grants by authors are terminated, the rights revert at the effective date of termination to all persons who own the termination interest on the date of service of the notice of termination. This includes owners who did not join in the notice of termination. The reversion is in the same proportions as the ownership of the termination interest.

For example, if an author dies and is survived by his widow and two children, the widow will own 50 percent of the reverted interest and each child will own 25 percent. If there are also two grandchildren by a deceased child, the share would be apportioned as follows: the widow owns 50 percent, each live child owns 16.67 percent, and each grandchild owns 8.33 percent.

If rights under a grant by the author have reverted to the surviving spouse, to the children, or to both, only those who own more than one-half of the author's termination interest may grant further transfers or licenses, and their grant binds the owners of the reverted interest. For the purpose of further grants, the deceased holder of a reverted interest is represented by the author's legal representatives, legatees, or heirs at law.

Termination of Old Grants by Nonauthors

As noted previously, old grants of a transfer or license can be made by persons other than an author. These would be among statutory beneficiaries entitled to claim renewal rights under the Copyright Act of 1909 on the death of an author before the renewal term of copyright. Such beneficiaries are his or her widow or widower, children, executors, or next of kin.

Termination may be made only by the unanimous action of the survivors of those persons who executed the grant. From the appropriately notified date of termination on, the rights revert to all survivors who were qualified to participate in the election to terminate, even if they were in the minority group who did not join the notice. Each such party is a co-owner of rights and is entitled to a proportionate share of all earnings. For purposes of a new sale, transfer, or license, a majority vote is again required, and even a party who refused to join in a previous majority is entitled to share not only monetarily but also in the vote constituting a new and additional majority for making such sale, transfer, or license.

Termination of New Grants

There is a right to terminate new exclusive or nonexclusive grants or licenses of copyright or any right under copyright made by the author, other than by will, on or after January 1, 1978. New grants made by others cannot be terminated.

On termination, rights revert, as in the case of old grants by authors, at the effective date to the persons owning the termination interest as of the date of service of the notice of termination. Those owners who did not join in the notice of termination are also included. The reversion is in the proportion of the owners' share of the termination interest. As in the earlier example, the widow will own 50 percent of the reverted rights and each child will own 25 percent. If there are also two grandchildren by a deceased third child, the proportions are as follows: the widow owns 50 percent, each living child owns 16.67 percent, and each grandchild owns 8.33 percent.

Further grants of terminated rights may be made by a majority of the new owners of the terminated rights, whether or not they are the same parties who took the initial action to terminate the rights.

Time Period for Making Further Grants

Further grants, or agreements to make a further grant, of rights terminated in old or new grants are valid only if made after the effective date of termination. There is an exception in favor of the grantees or their successors whose rights were terminated. An agreement made with them in the interim between service of the notice of termination and the date of termination is valid. This is particularly beneficial to music publishers, who after receipt of a termination notice may enter into new agreements with the owners of the termination interest before any other publishers can. (A sample "Grant of Terminated Rights" can be found on the accompanying CD-ROM.)

Music Publishers' Rights after Termination

Notwithstanding termination, a derivative work made under the authority of a grant before termination can continue to be used. In a case involving the termination of the song "Who's Sorry Now"—the former music publisher contended that under the "derivative works exception" it had the right to collect and share in mechanical royalties from the sale of old recordings. In 1985 the U.S. Supreme Court upheld this contention on appeal in a 5-to-4 decision. (See *Mills v. Snyder*, 469 U.S. 153 [1985].)

What this means is that, notwithstanding the termination of the right to grant new licenses such as for motion pictures or new recordings, the former publisher continues as before termination in its collections on old records, and so on, subject, of course, to continued royalty obligations under the old contract to the author or the author's estate.

In 1995, the Second Circuit Court of Appeals further reviewed the "Who's Sorry Now" benefits in a case involving the song "When the Red Red Robin Comes Bob-Bob-Bobbin' Along," first recorded in 1926. The 1995 decision concerned a claim by a terminating party that ASCAP performance rights also had to be allocated according to whether the record or TV film being performed on the air was a pre-termination or post-termination recording or score. The court ruling was mixed: After termination, ASCAP publisher performance earnings from pre-termination movies and television programs would continue to go to the former publisher who granted the original synchronization license. However, with respect to royalties attributable to radio performances of pre-termination sound recordings as well as to a commercial jingle performed on television in the post-termination period and for all unidentified television and radio performances and to printed-use royalties, regardless of continued uses of standard arrangements originating in the pre-termination period, the new publisher-designee of the terminating writers' successors would prevail. (See *Woods v. Bourne Co.*, 60 F.3d 978 [2d Cir. 1995].)

The decision relied on the legislative purpose of exempting old licensed uses and retention of terms of the prior license. This legislative purpose was to protect the derivative licensee's substantial investment against having to rene-gotiate with the new owner. It treated the contested flow of royalties as a mere incident to that purpose. Accordingly, to allow interference with the right of television broadcasts of earlier films would create a state of bargaining and litigation that the legislators wished to avoid, whereas the continued use of records was of a different technical and market character.

In a 1998 litigation concerning the soundtrack to the film *Sleepless in Seattle*, a court of appeals ruled that the terminating heirs of the lyricist of the song "Bye Bye Blackbird" were entitled to 50 percent of all U.S. mechanical royalties even though the track was a pretermination Joe Cocker recording. The reason for the ruling was that the license for the soundtrack recording was different from the prior license: it was a CD configuration, not an LP or 45 rpm recording; furthermore, it was a different recording than in its former presen-tation—a soundtrack rather than being coupled with other songs—and under a different license identification number than appeared on the original Joe Cocker record label. Consequently, the film synchronization license as well as the soundtrack mechanical royalties accrued to the benefit of the terminating parties.

Aspects of the Termination of Grants

Publishers and writers should keep in mind the following aspects of the termi-nation of *old grants* of renewal rights made before 1978:

- ▸ There can be a statutory termination under the 1976 Copyright Act of the music publisher's rights in respect to only the extended 39-year term. The rights regarding the original and renewal terms, a 56-year period in total under the 1909 Copyright Act, remain unchanged.
- ▸ Since the publisher's rights to the new 39-year extension can be termi-nated, its domestic administration and printing agreements should be expressly subject to the possible termination.
- ▸ The termination of old grants by the author of renewal rights can be put into effect under the 39-year extension by the author or, if the author is deceased, by the surviving spouse and children (or children of a deceased child). if the executor or next of kin owned the renewal right, they can also terminate the grant under the 39-year extension.
- ▸ The termination by widows, widowers, and children (or the children of a dead child) of old grants of renewal rights by the author, under the 39-year extension is ineffective unless a majority in the termination interest agree;

a surviving spouse cannot act without the approval of one or more of the children, and vice versa. If persons other than the author make a grant, the termination must be made unanimously by the survivors who executed it. If there are several writers, each writer's share is treated separately for termination purposes.

- Only the old publisher can enter into a valid new agreement for continuing rights between the date of the termination notice and the effective date of termination; valid agreements with other publishers of reverting rights can be made only after the effective date of termination.
- If there is no timely termination notice, the rights of the prior publisher extend for the period in the old grant to the publisher, including the extended 39-year term subject to a second chance of later termination under the Sonny Bono Term Extension Act of 1998.
- A termination does not affect the right to use derivative works, such as motion pictures, made before the effective date of termination under the authority of an old grant of a transfer or license, subject to continuance of the original royalty payments to the original recipients and not necessarily identical to the terminating parties. This is because the author's will may have bequeathed such royalties to other parties.

Publishers and writers should keep in mind the following aspects of the termination of *new grants* made after 1977:

- The music publisher's rights can generally be terminated effective 35 years from publication or 40 years from execution of the grant, whichever is earlier.
- The termination of new grants can be made only by the surviving spouse and children (or the children of a dead child) of a deceased author. If there are no such blood relatives, the termination will be ineffective.
- There can be no termination of new grants unless those entitled to a majority of the termination interest are in favor of it. Thus, for example, a widow cannot act without her children and vice versa. If there are several writers, a majority of the collaborators must concur; dead writers are represented by their surviving spouses and children (or the children of a dead child).
- Only the prior publisher can make a new agreement for continued rights between the date of notice of termination and the effective date of termination; assignments by the terminating parties to the reverting rights can be made only after the effective date of termination.
- In the absence of a termination notice, the post-1977 grant continues to be effective and the old publisher will keep its rights. However, under the Sonny Bono Term Extension Act of 1998 there is a further right of termination that affects the final 20 years of copyright if the first right of termination was not acted on.
- A termination does not affect the continuing right to use derivative works, such as motion pictures, made before the effective date of termination under the authority of the original publisher.

Foreign Duration of Copyright and Protection Outside of the United States

U.S. law regarding the duration of copyright protection does not normally govern the period of protection in foreign countries. Although the copyright in works may have expired in the United States, these works may still be protected in other countries.

The international copyright norm of life of the author plus 50 years is generally expanding. Effective July 1995, the European Union extended copyright protection to life of the author plus 70 years, and as a result the United States added an additional 20 years' copyright protection in 1998. This extension was necessary because it is important that the term of protection for the works of an American author in a foreign country should not exceed that offered under the domestic copyright law of the country of origin, depriving American authors and publishers of full international protection for the extended term.

For the international protection of American works under the law of a particular foreign country, American publishers and authors can rely on the Berne Convention, the Universal Copyright Convention, or on certain special laws and treaties discussed in Chapter 20, "International Copyright Protection." The United States joined the Berne Union on March 1, 1989, and it has been an adherent of the Universal Copyright Convention since September 16, 1955. The Berne Convention and the UCC do not ordinarily protect the works of an American author published in the United States before the date of adherence to the particular convention. However, compositions that were first or simultaneously published in Canada, England, or another Berne country qualify for Berne protection under the so-called back-door approach.

The UCC provides for an "elective rule of the shorter term." A work first published in the United States or an unpublished work of an American national is protected in a foreign country for (1) a period equal to the U.S. copyright term or (2) the copyright term in the foreign country, whichever is shorter.

Under the Berne Convention, the United States and the 128 other Berne Union members have agreed to apply the minimum life-plus-50-years standard to works that qualify for Berne protection. Since Berne members agree to treat nationals of other member countries like their own nationals for purposes of copyright, American authors often receive higher levels of protection than the guaranteed minimum. It should be noted that although the Berne Convention does not cover minimum terms for sound recording copyrights, the U.S. extension to 70 years from death or 95 years from fixation date for work-for-hire compositions applies, notwithstanding shorter terms for sound recordings in Europe.

12

The Uses of Public Domain

When the famed Hollywood composer Dimitri Tiomkin was called to the stage to receive one of his four Oscars for an outstanding motion picture score, he gave credit to his "collaborators," Bach, Beethoven, and Brahms. A number of years later composer Marvin Hamlisch, in accepting the Oscar for his contribution to *The Sting,* acknowledged his debt to the original composer of many of its tunes, Scott Joplin. In each of these cases, what was being acknowledged was music that was in the *public domain*—music unprotected by copyright. Reliance on music in the public domain may also be noted in the sheet music of such popular songs as "Our Love," "'Til the End of Time," and "Suddenly." Indeed, three of Elvis Presley's number one hits were based in part on music acknowledged to be in the public domain: "Love Me Tender" (based on "Aura Lee"), "It's Now or Never" (based on "O Sole Mio"), and "Surrender" (based on "Come Back to Sorrento"). In addition, experts can point out many thousands of songs based on undisclosed public domain sources.

Unsophisticated members of the music industry may think there is something unethical or shameful about reliance on music in the public domain, but certainly a great composer such as Dimitri Tiomkin was no less creative for his recognition of a cultural debt to the ages. As Goethe once correctly stated, "The most original modern authors are not so because they advance what is new, but simply because they know how to put what they have to say as if it had never been said before."

On the other hand, the frequent claim of full originality when a work in actuality is based partly on music in the public domain has been a source of confusion and even unfair business practices. In the 1960s, for instance, the British *Performing Right Yearbook* noted that a growing problem in the distribution of performance fees was the false claim of full originality for works that deserve only partial credit; it went on to say that the majority of such false claims came from overseas (meaning the United States).

Music in the public domain is useful to a number of different people and groups.

- Music publishers use songs in the public domain in many folios and instructional series for reasons of budget economy and free adaptability.
- Record companies include varying numbers of songs in the public domain in albums, especially in budget albums, to avoid mechanical royalty payments.
- Artists who are composers obtain copyrights on arrangements of songs in the public domain presented in their repertoire.
- Television film scores and advertising jingles and announcements frequently use music in the public domain in order to avoid high synchronization fees and to have full freedom to adapt in any form.

Works in the Public Domain

Public domain is the opposite of copyright: it lacks the element of private property granted to copyright; anyone can make full, unrestricted use of the material. It is literally "free as the air."

Copyright is granted for a limited time; once a work is published, it does not stay protected permanently. Find any sheet music published in the United States before 1923 , and you can be certain that the song is in the public domain. Most works in the public domain are so categorized because their term of copyright protection has expired or because they reached their 28th year of copyright protection and were not registered for U.S. renewal copyright. (Under the Copyright Renewal Act of 1992, renewal is now made automatically by the Copyright Office; failure to renew no longer places the work in the public domain; see Chapter 11.)

Other works fall into the public domain much earlier or may join the public domain from the time of their creation. Generally, anything written and published for the U.S. government is in the public domain from the outset. With limited exceptions, prior to October 27, 1923 , the generally effective date of the Copyright Act of 1976, anything published without a copyright notice fell into the public domain regardless of later attempts to correct this situation. As famous a song as "The Caissons Go Rolling Along" became public domain material because of a defective copyright notice.

The omission of copyright notices for works first published between January 1, 1978, and March 1, 1989, the effective date of the Berne Convention Implementation Act of 1988, may invalidate a copyright under the Copyright Act of 1976, but there is greater flexibility and the omission may be forgiven. (See pages 100–101.) For works published for the first time on or after March 1, 1989, mandatory notice of copyright has been abolished, although voluntary use is encouraged by certain benefits that accrue from the use of notice.

Catalogs of American music publishers suggest that there is an apparent enthusiasm among educators for the works of the Russian composer Kabalevsky. While this enthusiasm is undoubtedly merited, it is also convenient that American publishers can use these and other Soviet works without having to obtain a copyright license. The Soviet Union didn't join the Universal

Copyright Convention until May 27, 1973. Works published before that date are still in the public domain for U.S. purposes, although works published subsequently are subject to U.S. copyright protection. (Russia has not joined the Berne Convention, which would provide retroactive protection for works previously in the public domain.)

The difficulty of determining public domain or copyright status in the international field is increased by the fact that most foreign countries respect copyright in a work for 50 years after the death of the author, whereas under U.S. copyright law, concerning works first fixed before January 1, 1978, protection is measured in terms of specific years. This results in a lack of uniformity when a specific work enters public domain status throughout the world. Accordingly, U.S. users who are relying on public domain status to compile a printed folio of songs, make a budget album, or synchronize the score of a film must investigate the foreign copyright status thoroughly before allowing the work to be exported. U.S. users should also be very cautious in determining whether the work is actually in the public domain.

The Uruguay Round Agreements Act (URAA), effective December 8, 1994, which implements the GATT agreement on trade-related aspects of intellectual property rights (TRIPs), restores copyright protection to foreign works that are in the public domain in the United States but still under copyright protection in their source country, if that country is a member of the Berne Convention. To qualify for automatic restoration, the work must be in the public domain as a result of failure to comply with statutory formalities, lack of subject matter protection, or lack of national eligibility and must originate in a Berne Convention source country. Use of the restored work after constructive or actual notice of the intention to enforce restored copyright rights is an infringement, and full statutory remedies are available.

The Purposes of Public Domain

The U.S. Constitution authorizes copyright only "for limited times." Thus, the policy against perpetual private rights in writings is set forth in the highest law of the land. A study issued by the Copyright Office prior to the passage of the Copyright Act of 1976 stated the following reasons for this policy:

> It is generally believed to be to the benefit of the public that once the work has been created, and the author protected for a sufficient time to have produced the original incentive, the work should become available to be freely used by all. There is believed to be a greater probability of more varied editions of works of lasting value, and a wider opportunity to distribute existing works competitively, and use them as a basis for new creation, if they are freely available. It is basic to our economic system that profits in this area should be gained by more efficient manufacture, better distribution and the like, rather than by perpetual protection, once the purpose of the protection for a limited time has been achieved.

In the words of Judge Learned Hand, one of the most respected federal appellate judges, "Congress has created the monopoly in exchange for a dedication, and when the monopoly expires the dedication must be complete."

The composer or music publisher, naturally enough, may object to not being able to pass on property to grandchildren as easily as a neighbor who creates a shoe factory. However, consideration should be given to a policy that favors limited restraints on uses of what is thought to be the national cultural heritage. Imagine the block on cultural development if each of the heirs of Beethoven, Bach, or Brahms had to be located in order to grant a license for a Moog synthesizer or a New York Philharmonic performance of the classics.

Prior to the enactment of the Copyright Act of 1976, arguments were advanced for a longer term of copyright and a more delayed entry into the public domain. A renowned German music industry leader, Dr. Erich Schulze of GEMA, the German performance and mechanical rights society, stated: "If the term were unlimited, arrangements would have to be made to ensure that the rights can be exercised even though a great number of heirs might be involved. If, at some later date, all of the heirs should have died, the copyright would have to pass to the state." Dr. Schulze pointed out that life expectancy in the United States had changed since the passage of the Copyright Act of 1909, which gave a maximum 56 years of copyright protection: "At the turn of the century, [life expectancy was] 48.23 years for newborn males and 51.01 for newborn females; in 1960, 67.4 for newborn males and 74.1 for newborn females." In 1987, life expectancy in the United States had increased to 71.5 years for males and 78.3 years for females. Since medical science had achieved the extension of life expectancy, Dr. Schulze contended, the term of copyright should be similarly extended to cover the lifetime of the author and his or her immediate family. This was the standard adopted by the Copyright Act of 1976—the life of the author plus 50 years and, for existing works, an extra 19 years equaling a total of 75 years. This standard had been adopted previously by a majority of the world's countries. (Duration of copyright is discussed in Chapter 11.)

Initially there was opposition to the Sonny Bono Term Extension Act, which provides for a further 20-year extension of copyright. Writing in the December 21, 1998, issue of *The Wall Street Journal,* Professor Richard A. Epstein of the University of Chicago stated: "Removing these works from the public domain works a huge uncompensated wealth transfer from ordinary citizens to ... holders, corporate and individual, of preexisting copyrighted material. It also produces a net social loss by restricting overall level of use of this material." In a lead editorial dated February 21, 1998, *The New York Times* actively opposed a 20-year extension of copyright, arguing that "the tendency when thinking about copyright, is to vest the notion of creativity in the owners of copyright. But, artists ... always emerge from the undifferentiated public, and the works in the public domain ... are an essential part of every artist's sustenance."

The true reason for the 20-year Sonny Bono Term Extension Act was the need for U.S. authors and other copyright parties to participate on an equal basis with their trading partners in the European Union and with other Berne Convention countries that had extended their copyrights to author's life plus 70 years. American corporations were afraid that other countries would fail to honor U.S. copyrights for the enlarged period if Americans did not have reciprocal extensions.

In some countries there is a unique *public domain payant*. This is a state fund which collects royalties on public domain material for distribution not to heirs of the creator but to new and deserving artists and writers. This practice tends to reduce users' incentive to favor public domain at the expense of copyrighted works. It also encourages deserving new writers whose works may someday themselves be a part of a national cultural heritage.

Determining the Public Domain Status of Works

The public domain is like a vast national park with no guards to stop wanton looting, with no guides for lost travelers, with no clearly defined fences or borders to stop the innocent wayfarer from being sued for trespass. Much of the music material in the public domain is tainted by vague and indefinite claims of copyright in minimal or obscure "new versions." Even more of the musical public domain is lost to the public by oblivion resulting from the failure to maintain complete public archives. There are, however, various sources of information to help one determine whether copyright claims exist on a given work. These sources include the U.S. Copyright Office, the Library of Congress, editions of old songs, catalogs of performing rights societies, the Harry Fox Agency, and various reference materials.

U.S. COPYRIGHT OFFICE

The Copyright Office is exclusively concerned with works protected by copyright and has no jurisdiction over public domain. It keeps no separate record of works in the public domain. And because it does not list works in its *Catalog of Copyright Entries* that have not been registered for the renewal period of copyright, it is the potential user of public domain material who must determine whether the renewal copyright has been forfeited. Moreover, if a faulty claim to copyright has been presented to the Copyright Office, there is no public notice of rejection by the Copyright Office.

However, the Copyright Office does perform some very valuable services in an investigation of copyright status. On request, its staff will search its records for a fee—at this writing, $30 for each hour or fraction of an hour consumed. Based on the information furnished to it by the requesting party, the Copyright Office will provide an estimate of the total search fee. Anyone requesting a search should include the Copyright Office's estimate in the letter. The office will then proceed with the search and provide a report either in writing or by telephone, at the option of the requesting party. The report will cover copyright registrations and claims. It will not certify the public domain status but it will give essential information as to whether there is another claimant to the copyright, whether the copyright has been renewed, and whether the initial claim for copyright is of such a date that public domain status, by reason of expiration of the period of protection or failure to renew, has occurred.

It is the basic policy under the Copyright Act of 1976 that copyright deposits are to be kept as long as possible. However, the Register of Copyrights and the Librarian of Congress jointly have the power to dispose of them at their discretion when they no longer consider it practical or desirable to retain them. During the term of copyright, unpublished works may not be destroyed or otherwise disposed of unless a facsimile copy is made for Copyright Office records. The depositor of copies or the copyright owner of record may request retention of deposited material under Copyright Office control for a period of 75 years from the date of publication of a work, including fees. There is a charge of $135 per copyright deposit.

Once a copyright expires, the Copyright Office does *not* keep previously deposited manuscripts of unpublished or published music. Consequently, it is up to the potential user to locate a copy of the public domain manuscript unless, by chance, the Library of Congress chose in its discretion to keep a copy. Accordingly, a search for and inspection of copies of published or unpublished works registered for copyright should be made *in advance* of the expiration of copyright. The nature of copyright is such that the Copyright Office itself does not ordinarily make a copy of a published or unpublished work on deposit with it. Therefore, unless written permission of the owner is obtained to make a copy, in the absence of a certified need for litigation purposes, an on-the-spot inspection of a manuscript is required.

Other search services are available through the office of Thomson & Thomson Copyright Research Group, 500 E Street SW, Washington, DC 20024. Some major users of material in the public domain, rather than risk a judgment involving substantial investment on the basis of only one such report, rely on two or more reports requested simultaneously.

LIBRARY OF CONGRESS

Not all copyrighted works are destroyed or lost when they are no longer within the copyright term of protection. The purpose of requiring a deposit of "two complete copies of the best edition" with the registration of claim to copyright is to offer the Library of Congress an opportunity, in its discretion, to keep a reference copy. Of course, even the more than 630 miles of shelves in the Library of Congress, holding over 88 million items, do not make it a universal archive of all previous publications. The Library of Congress has the right to transfer to its permanent and reserve collections one or both of the domestic editions registered for copyright and the one copy deposited for foreign works.

In practice, the Librarian of Congress determines which published deposits of the Copyright Office are to be transferred to the Library of Congress or other government libraries or used for exchanges or transfer to any other library. As for unpublished works, the Library of Congress may select any deposits for its collection or for transfer to the National Archives of the United States or to a federal records center.

EDITIONS OF OLD SONGS

If a copy of sheet music or other printed version bears a date earlier than 75 years ago, the music and lyrics may be assumed to be in the public domain in the United States.

The Lincoln Center Library of the Performing Arts in New York City maintains an extensive collection of old-time popular songs ; an inspection of this collection is desirable for determining information on actual early editions. Sheet music and other published copies of old songs can often be obtained from private collections or dealers. It is important to have access to early editions so as to avoid copying a new version or new arrangement of a work that is otherwise in the public domain.

Some users of works in the public domain use a system of "most common denominator" as a means of determining true public domain. This is a method of gathering together many versions of a known public domain work and copying only those portions of words or music that appear in several different sources. The services of an expert musicologist are sometimes helpful here, especially in instances such as uses in motion pictures, where great financial inconvenience would occur if a valid claim were to be presented after initial use.

In many cases where the underlying melodic source for a popular composition is in the public domain, the musical contributions made to the original source by a copyright claimant may be of a minor and limited nature. For example, a songwriter may write a song entitled "Darling, I Love You" based on a Bach sonata. Another songwriter would be entitled to write a new instrumental work on the same sonata or put new lyrics to it. In either case, the later songwriter has a valid claim to copyright on his or her version, provided that the songwriter has not copied any of the earlier writer's musical or lyric additions to the underlying sonata. The later writer is well advised, however, to use a different title for the new version to avoid confusion in the collection of mechanical and performance fees.

CATALOGS OF PERFORMING RIGHTS SOCIETIES

The ASCAP and BMI catalogs of songs in their repertoires provide convenient lists of copyright claimants and, by a special notation such as an asterisk in the ASCAP book, indicate the public domain status of the basic underlying work. SESAC also has an extensive catalog of its works that frequently shows underlying public domain status by reference to "arranger" instead of "composer." In certain instances the SESAC catalog has many listings of the same musical work under different SESAC publishers, making it evident that the underlying work is in the public domain.

The failure of ASCAP, BMI, or SESAC to list a work as public domain does not necessarily determine the issue, however. Some works filed as completely original may be based on a public domain composition, and the societies may not look behind the filing.

HARRY FOX AGENCY

The Harry Fox Agency, which administers mechanical and synchronization rights on behalf of publishers in the United States, maintains voluminous files that contain significant information regarding public domain status of compositions. This is required for the licensing functions of the agency. Inquiry may be made of the agency as to whether a composition is in the public domain. Harry Fox Agency is located at 711 Third Avenue, New York, NY 10017.

OTHER REFERENCE SOURCES

Finally, a number of print-based reference sources offer information regarding copyrighted material or public domain works. In 1993, a new subscription newsletter called the *Public Domain Report* was introduced. This publication offers reliable information on public domain status for U.S. purposes and includes an offer to deliver on request the original sheet music. The newsletter is of particular interest to advertising agencies and film companies that may wish to have assured sources of such materials.

To date, PDR has reported nearly 13,500 public domain works to its readership. Although originally available by mail order, the *Public Domain Report* is now only available on-line to subscribers. This publisher also offers the *PDR Music Bible,* a two-volume series that includes more than 7,000 listings and reviews of public domain music. An extensive public domain sheet music library and custom copyright research services are available to all PDR clients. Contact Public Domain Research at PO Box 3102, Margate, NJ 08402; telephone: 609-822-9401; fax: 609-822-1638; e-mail: info@pubdomain.com; Web site: http://www.pubdomain.com.

BZ/Rights also offers accurate public domain listings in their publication, *The Mini-Encyclopedia of Public Domain Songs,* which lists the 800 best-known works in the public domain as well as information on composers to help determine copyright status of music throughout the world. BZ/Rights & Permissions may be contacted at 121 West 27th Street, Suite 901, New York, NY 10001; telephone: 212-924-3000; fax: 212-924-2525; e-mail: info@bzrights.com; Web site: http://www.bzrights.com.

Record Research has put out *Pop Memories, 1895–1951: The History of American Popular Music.* This study presents in chronological order a detailed list of hit recordings of each year. For public domain purposes, the simple arithmetic of subtracting 75 years should suffice. Record Research Inc. may be contacted at PO Box 200, Menomonee Falls, WI 53052-0200; telephone: 414-251-5408; fax: 414-251-9452; e-mail: record@execpc.com; Web site: http://www.recordresearch.com.

A similar source based on song titles is found in a handy listing of a limited number of public domain songs in the ASCAP booklet *ASCAP Hit Songs*. The hit songs are listed by year, beginning in 1892. Among the well-known songs included are such classics as "Sidewalks of New York," "Sweet Rosie O'Grady," "Gypsy Love Song," "St. Louis Blues," "There's a Long, Long Trail," and "Alexander's Ragtime Band," plus such recent additions as "Down by the O-Hi-O," "The Japanese Sandman," and "Avalon" (all from 1920), Gershwin's "Swanee of 1919," and Irving Berlin's "A Pretty Girl Is Like a Melody."

Copyright Registration of New Versions and Arrangements of Works

When filing for registration of a new version of copyright material, a copyright claimant must designate the new matter on which the claim is based; however, this designation rarely appears on printed copies of the music. For instance, a new arrangement of "The Star Spangled Banner" may show a copyright notice for the year 1981 in the same manner and form as would appear on a new and original composition. Therefore, it may be necessary to look up the application for registration in the Copyright Office to determine the new matter for which protection is claimed. (See Chapter 13 for a discussion of arrangements and new versions of public domain works.)

The Copyright Act of 1976 dictates that applications for copyright registration of a compilation or derivative work include "an identification of any preexisting work or works that it is based on or incorporates, and a brief general statement of the additional material covered by the copyright claim being registered." The Committee on the Judiciary of the House of Representatives has stated Congress's intent that the "application covering a collection such as a songbook or hymnal would clearly reveal any works in the collection that are in the public domain, and the copyright status of all other previously published compositions. This information will be readily available in the Copyright Office."

As discussed in Chapter 10, application for copyright registration of works of the performing arts, including musical compositions, is made on Form PA. Item 5 of the form contains questions designed to determine whether an earlier registration has been made for the work and, if so, whether there is any basis for a new registration. Item 6 of the form calls for information on compilations or derivative works and requests the identification of any preexisting work that the current work is based on or incorporates: for example, "Compilation of 19th-Century Military Songs." It also asks that the applicant give a brief general statement of the additional new material covered by the copyright claim for which registration is sought.

The Copyright Office has stated previously that "new matter may consist of musical arrangement, compilation, editorial revision, and the like, as well as additional words and music." Thus, if a new folio of public domain works is published, a claim of copyright may be based on a "new compilation" if nothing else has been added to the public domain works. Another possible description of added material might be "new compilation, fingering, stress marks, and introductory material." Claims premised on new lyrics should show where the new lyrics occur, such as "new first and third verses." Most claims based on a new music arrangement merely designate in what lines the changed arrangement occurs, if limited to specified lines; if there is a new musical version arranged for soprano, alto, bass, etc., a statement to that effect may be made.

It is unfortunate for users that the designation of new material occurs only on official applications and is not available for inspection except in the files of the Copyright Office in Washington. However, it is only the deposited copy of the work that may not be copied; copies of applications may be ordered, with or without the consent of the claimant. A copy of the application can be obtained by supplying the details of the registration number from a search report and paying a fee in accordance with the form supplied by the Copyright Office.

In the case of an application for copyright registration by a composer who has based a work on a public domain source there may not be an entry under item 6 of Form PA. The composer, in failing to complete the item, may in effect be claiming that the work is completely original, although this claim is incorrect. Therefore, inspection of applications will not always reveal the extent of public domain material, if any, embodied in a particular composition.

The Copyright Status of Sound Recordings

Statutory federal copyright was initially extended to sound recordings first fixed and published in the United States on or after February 15, 1972. Recordings published before this date, and unpublished recordings fixed before January 1, 1978, are protected in a number of states under common law copyright and antipiracy statutes, as discussed in Chapters 7 and 8. The Copyright Act of 1976 contains a limitation on the duration of protection under state law of sound recordings fixed before February 15, 1972. It is provided that state law protection will no longer apply on and after February 15, 2047, and that federal protection will not ever apply. Therefore, on February 15, 2047, which is 75 years from the effective date of the statute that initially extended federal protection to recordings, sound recordings fixed before February 15, 1972, will be in the public domain. This 75-year duration for sound recordings is not extended to 95 years by the Sonny Bono Term Extension Act.

13

Arrangements and Adaptations

The public does not hear songs or see them in written form until arrangements of the songs have been made. Songs usually require some development by arrangers, whose efforts may vary from mere transposition of keys and elaboration of chord structures to more creative work. Foreign-language songs are rarely presented to the American public with foreign lyrics; foreign lyrics must be substantially revised, and not just translated, in view of the necessary adaptation of rhyme and accents.

Arrangers have often been lauded as being more important to the success of a popular record than the original writers. Linda Ronstadt's work with arranger Nelson Riddle on her 1987 album *What's New* prompted her to make the following tribute: "To be able to sing Nelson's arrangements was like floating in pure musical ecstasy and emotion. It was so heavenly I hated for it to end." Unfortunately, when another of Riddle's arrangements was used for the historic "duet" of Natalie Cole with her deceased father, Nat King Cole, for the Grammy Award–winning recording "Unforgettable," Riddle was not credited as arranger on the resulting 1992 release. Riddle's widow sued for false labeling.

Jazz performers commonly make such substantial revisions to the basic song that it would take an expert musicologist to identify the source of the melodic material. Many rock and roll singers make their own impromptu arrangements of songs while performing, sometimes due to their inability to read music as well as to their desire for spontaneity.

The vital impact of rock music on the role of the arranger is well described in Milt Okun's *Great Songs of the Sixties:*

> What basically happened was that the rhythm section, consisting of bass, guitar, drums and piano, which formerly gave the underpinning to a band, stepped to the front and became the whole band.... Since most of the excitement comes from rhythmic development, plus improvisation, the trained arranger is not needed. Now there is arranging by group. One

by-product of rock thus has been the unemployment of arrangers. ...
Music ... has been stripped down to pure rhythm, or rhythms, categorized
... with beat-specific names like hard house, techstep, jungle and speed
garage. ... On a hip-hop radio station ... all that matters is the beat, the lyric
and the grain of a voice.

Head Arrangements of Compositions

The traditional order of creative services goes from composer, to arranger,
orchestrator, and copyist, to finished music fit for performance or recording.
However, confusion has been created by the many forms of popular music
such as reggae, rap, dance, world, rhythm and blues, and country where there
is more spontaneous development of music by "head arrangements," or
layered recordings resulting in the absence of copying entirely and merging of
the functions. When musicians do not read music, they develop alternative
means to the end of arrangement and orchestration. When producers have a
strong influence on a record session, they often perform the orchestrator and
arranger role.

When tracks are laid down before the addition of words and melody, the
arrangement actually precedes the composing and there is confusion as to
whether the underlying track is merely an arrangement of the resulting song
or is a musical portion of the resulting song. This is even more confusing if the
same track is used for successive competitive versions under different titles.
When sampling of existing recorded music is used, the sample is sometimes
the underlying track and thus is an arrangement in fully orchestrated form
waiting for retroactive permission to be granted for inclusion.

The Copyrighting of Arrangements

Under both the 1909 and the 1976 Copyright Acts, arrangements may be copyrighted only if they are made by the copyright owner of the original work or with
the owner's consent. Arrangements used on popular records rarely qualify for
copyrighting under either of these conditions. The copyright owner, whether
publisher or writer, ordinarily does not prepare the record arrangement and
makes no claim for copyright in the arrangement. Moreover, the music publisher
rarely gives consent to copyrighting the arrangement prepared for a recording of
the song, and thus no copyright is taken by anyone in the arrangement used. The
copyright owner issues a more or less standard mechanical license to record,
which in practice is considered to indicate that no objection will be made to the
arrangements required for purposes of recording. The license in this instance
amounts to an agreement not to object rather than a consent or grant of rights.
However, arrangements of works in the public domain may qualify for copyrighting without the consent of the former copyright owner.

There can be no question that in popular music the English version of a foreign song is truly a new version that requires creative effort over and beyond mechanical translation. English versions are nearly always undertaken on assignment from the music publisher controlling the basic copyright; unlike arrangements for purposes of record company sessions, the publisher will claim a further copyright in the new lyric version and the author of the new version will be given credit and royalties.

Arrangers for record company sessions rarely have any relationship to the music publisher and achieve no copyright status; they receive compensation solely from the record company or artists. Some arrangers do work directly for or with music publishers and printed music licensees, and the employer may obtain copyrights on their arrangements. These arrangers are the musically knowledgeable and trained persons who prepare songs for printing in sheet music, orchestration, or folio form. Frequently the songs have already been recorded. Separate arrangements may be required for single instruments and voice and for the diverse parts for different instruments in bands and orchestras. These arrangers are customarily employed on a weekly salary or assignment basis, with no right to royalties, and although their names may sometimes appear on the printed edition, as employees for hire they acquire no rights in the copyright or in renewal copyrights. The employer is considered the author of the work and the initial copyright owner.

The Statutory Treatment of Arrangements

In the past there were disputes as to whether the person preparing musical arrangements was an employee acting within the scope of his or her employment or an independent contractor. The Copyright Act of 1976 clarifies the status of works prepared on special order or commission for use "as a supplementary work." Under the act, if the parties expressly agree in writing that a supplementary work shall be considered to be "a work made for hire," the agreement is binding and the employer is regarded as the author and initial owner of the copyright. The act specifically defines "musical arrangements" as supplementary works for which such an agreement can be made.

The Copyright Act of 1976 sets certain standards for permissible arrangements in sound recordings in connection with provisions for compulsory licenses. Under Section 115 of the act there can be a compulsory license for making and distributing phonorecords of a work once they have been distributed to the public in the United States under authority of the copyright owner. A compulsory license permits the "making of a musical arrangement of the work to the extent necessary to conform it to the style or manner of interpretation of the performance." But the compulsory licensee cannot "change the basic melody or fundamental character of the work." The arrangement is not "subject to protection as a derivative work ... except with the express consent of the copyright owner." (For a further discussion of compulsory licenses, see Chapter 15, "Mechanical Rights.")

No Effect on Duration of Basic Work

The nature of musical arrangements or English-lyric versions assumes the prior existence of the basic work. A question arises as to whether the "derivative work," founded as it is on an earlier composition, has the effect of prolonging the term of copyright in the basic work. The Copyright Office has stated simply that the "protection for a copyrighted work cannot be lengthened by republishing the work with new matter." The Copyright Act of 1976 provides that the copyright in the derivative work "is independent of, and does not affect or enlarge the scope, duration, ownership, or subsistence of, any copyright protection in the pre-existing material."

In practical effect, however, copyrighted new versions created during the copyright term of the basic work may cause the public to accept the new version in place of the basic work, and the publisher may thereby obtain the benefit of the longer copyright term for the new version. Under the Copyright Act of 1976, the term of copyright runs until the 75th year following publication or the 100th year following creation, whichever is earlier, for new versions of a work created by an arranger who is an employee for hire. In the case of an arranger who is an independent contractor, copyright will exist for the creator's life plus 70 years.

Standards of Originality

Not all arrangements are capable of copyright protection, even if they are prepared with the consent of the copyright owner or if the basic work is in the public domain. An element of creative authorship must be involved, but how much is a matter of qualitative judgment that may eventually require judicial determination in case of conflict. The Copyright Office does not claim to compare the new arrangement with the basic work; it does require the copyright claimant to state what new material has been added. Its position is that "when only a few slight variations or minor additions of no substance have been made, or when the revisions or added material consist solely of uncopyrightable elements, registration is not possible."

There are no maximum boundaries on the extent of originality and creativity that can be contributed by arrangements. Béla Bartók once commented that it often takes more skill to make a qualified orchestral arrangement of a folk tune, while being loyal to its origins, than to write an entirely original work. The melodic basis of Brahms's "Academic Festival Overture" is found in the student songs of his day; similarly, Beethoven's "Country Dances" were developed from contemporary folk dances. Bach used already existing hymns in most of his chorales; for this reason he is considered one of the greatest arrangers in history. The great originality and creativity of each of these masterpieces lie in the development of the material.

The minimum requirements of originality and creativity for copyrightable arrangements are indefinite. Courts have made analogies to the rejection of patents for improvements "which a good mechanic could make." In 1850, in *Jollie v. Jaques* (13 Fed. Cas. 910), the Circuit Court for the Southern District of New York stated:

> The composition of a new air or melody is entitled to protection. ... If the new air be substantially the same as the old, it is no doubt a piracy. ... The musical composition contemplated by the statute must, doubtless, be substantially a new and original work, and not a copy of a piece already produced, with additions and variations, which a writer of music with experience and skill might readily make.

Applying these requirements, a later court rejected a claim of copyright infringement on an arrangement of public domain music even in the face of clear proof of copying. The new material in the arrangement, as copied by the defendant, involved adding an alto part and a few notes and rhythmical beats to smooth the transposition from Russian to English lyrics; the English words were not copied. Another court held that a student's piano collection of songs in the public domain could be protected as having "at least a modicum of creative work." This included editorial ingenuity in "fingering, dynamic marks, tempo indications, slurs and phrasing." The court also recognized some value in an original editorial grouping of a series of public domain works, together with original titles. (See *Lindsay Norden v. Oliver Ditson Co. Inc.*, 28 U.S. Pata. Q. 183 [D. Mass. 1936].)

The determination of a "modicum of creative work" may be difficult. In one case a Sicilian sailor was fortunate to have a bad memory and insufficient musical training, since his necessary improvisations of folk songs were deemed to warrant a copyright. In another instance a respected teacher of music theory who was a choirmaster was found to have followed an original melody too faithfully to qualify for an arrangement copyright.

The decision by a leading California copyright jurist, the late Judge Leon R. Yankwich, sheds some light on the rationale for denying copyright to changes that could be developed by any experienced writer. Judge Yankwich said that too broad a basis of copyright in arrangements would lead to restricting the use of many works. It would result in permitting a Charles Laughton to forbid other actors from portraying Henry VIII in the same creative manner as that which he employed or in a Sir Laurence Olivier monopolizing the innovations in his portrayal of Hamlet. Judge Yankwich felt that a basic copyrighted work should not be subject to division into segments to the detriment of the original author or, in the case of works in the public domain, to the detriment of the public.

An important practical consideration in determining the extent of originality or creativity to be required by a court is the reluctance of members of the judiciary to qualify themselves as art or music experts. In *Bleistein v. Donaldson*, 188 U.S. 239, 250 (1903), Justice Oliver Wendell Holmes stated the prevalent judicial position, which is equally applicable to music and art:

It would be a dangerous undertaking for persons trained only to the law to constitute themselves final judges of the worth of pictorial illustrations, outside of the narrowest and most obvious limits. At the one extreme some works of genius would be sure to miss appreciation. Their very novelty would make them repulsive until the public had learned the new language in which their author spoke. It may be more than doubted, for instance, whether the etchings of Goya or the paintings of Manet would have been sure of protection when seen for the first time. At the other end, copyright would be denied to pictures which appealed to a public less educated than the judge.

This refusal to become a critic of art and music is not just an expression of judicial modesty; it is essential for the orderly and efficient operation of the courts. The judge who passes on the minimum standards of originality or creativity of an arrangement (standards that are equally applicable to a completely new composition) does not have to put a stamp of cultural approval on the piece. In the words of the late Judge Sylvester Ryan of the U.S. District Court for the Southern District of New York, a judge must merely find sufficient "fingerprints of the composition" in the arrangement or succession of musical notes that can "establish its identity."

Derivative Works

The Copyright Act of 1976 categorizes a *derivative work* as one that involves the recasting, transformation, or adaptation of a prior work. Among the examples given are musical arrangements and lyric versions of formerly instrumental works.

Musical arrangements are rarely categorized as derivative works because there are generally no major changes to the original. But an immediate practical effect of adding lyrics to instrumental works is the sharing of writer royalties and performance society credits. If the previous work is relatively dormant and can only achieve commercial value through the suggested change, the original composer is unlikely to object to the sharing of his or her income. But the composer of an established and popular work may resent the new writer who "horns in" on the original material, except where it is used in conjunction with the lyric, the new title of the lyric version, or other new arrangement.

The original writer and the publisher will be concerned with the selection of the new writer, the authorship credit, the publishing rights to be acquired from the writer, whether the writer will be credited with future earnings on the instrumental version as well as the new lyric version, and whether there will be a contractual limitation on obtaining still another lyric version.

Since the music publisher usually selects and engages the lyricist or arranger, the publisher may protect itself and the original writer contractually from some of the problems arising with derivative works. The Copyright Act of

1976 makes special provisions for an arranger, by express agreement in writing, to be treated as an employee for hire, with all rights under copyright in the publisher as author. In the absence of such an agreement, the arranger or the new lyricist may still be an employee for hire acting in the course of his or her employment. Where there is an employment for hire, all rights under copyright for the new versions reside in the publisher, subject only to agreed-upon accounting and credit obligations. No right to terminate the grant of rights to the publisher at any time will vest in the new writer or his or her statutory heirs or successors. For the protection of the original writer, the agreement with the lyricist or arranger can provide that the first writer will continue to receive all writer royalties for the use of the earlier material in its original form.

As for works originating on or after January 1, 1978, the Copyright Act of 1976 states that the owner of a lawful derivative work can continue to use and license uses of that work despite the exercise by an author of his or her right of termination. In the case of relatively simple musical arrangements of pre-existing works, questions arise as to whether the resultant works are the derivative works contemplated by the statute. It may be assumed that only arrangements with sufficient originality to be copyrightable will result in derivative works envisaged by the act.

As an example, the legislative history refers to motion pictures, which may continue to be used despite termination by authors. Congress recognized that the continuing use of a multimillion-dollar investment in creating a motion picture version based on a prior published story or novel should not be jeopardized by the statutory heirs of the author of the prior literary work. Likewise, the continuing ownership of substantial new lyrics in an otherwise terminated song may well qualify the publisher-owner of such revised lyrics to continue to exercise rights in the entire song when such lyrics are used, notwithstanding termination of the earlier version.

Arranger credits were involved in the case of "When the Red Red Robin Comes Bob-Bob-Bobbin' Along" (*Woods v. Bourne Co.*, 60 F.3d 978 [2d Cir. 1995]). This was a test action supported by the Songwriters Guild of America to contest the claim of the former publisher that, notwithstanding a valid termination of publishing grants, the old publisher continued to be the owner of all arrangements of ASCAP publisher credits when old records were performed.

After a full trial, the district court ruled that although musical arrangements are recognized as a possible derivative use to be protected against termination, the words should not be read in a vacuum. The court ruled that a mere cocktail piano arrangement or preparation of arrangement for sheet music or folio use does not qualify for a claim to all recorded renditions of the song involved. It is well known that most commercial recordings rely on the recording artist's own arrangement and not the standard sheet music form. In addition, the court recognized that it is likely that the arrangement as presented in the published sheet music might very well be substantially based on the original composer's demonstration version even though a simple lead sheet may have been the only registered version.

The court considered numerous versions of the one song and concluded that, except for a major choral version such as that by Fred Waring's Pennsylvanians, there was not sufficient showing that the publisher contributed copyrightable derivative material sufficient to stand on its own. The court required "unusual" new material rather than routine arrangement. In this respect, the *Bourne* case states that derivative works must have more than trivial variations to rely on new harmonies to qualify for continuing rights of the former owner in the arranged version notwithstanding a termination by the original creator's heirs of the original music.

Prior to the *Bourne* case, there was an important Supreme Court decision concerning the 1923 song "Who's Sorry Now" and the effects of termination by the statutory heirs. The original publisher, while acknowledging that termination had effectively taken place, relied upon the same specific exception of the statute allowing the former publisher to continue to collect royalties where a derivative work had been created prior to the termination. The publisher successfully asserted that a sound recording is a derivative work and that, although the recording artist is unlikely to have used standard sheet music arrangements prepared by that publisher, the statutory exception nevertheless accrues to the benefit of the original publisher. Thus, any flow of continuing mechanical royalties on such earlier recording under its original license from the former publisher would accrue to the original licensing publisher and not to the statutory heirs who attempted to terminate such status. (See also pages 120 and 122 for a discussion of such benefits.)

Sound Recording Sound-Alikes

Under the Copyright Act of 1976, the copyright owner of a sound recording cannot prevent the making or duplication of another sound recording that uses sounds (for example, an artist recording another version of a previously recorded song), even though the later recording imitates or simulates the earlier copyrighted recording. In effect, the copyright owner cannot prohibit cover records or sound-alike records that imitate the earlier recording. In this sense there is no protection of arrangements made for record company sessions.

Renewals of Arrangements or Abridgments

When must the renewal right be exercised for a copyrighted arrangement or adaptation or other new version of a composition under the Copyright Act of 1909? A case involving the work "12th-Street Rag" contended that the new version as a joint work under that act must be renewed in the 28th year of the original work. (See *Shapiro Bernstein & Co. v. Jerry Vogel Music Co.*, 221 F.2d 569 [2d Cir. 1955].) While this contention has been criticized as being in contradiction to the fundamental nature of new versions as separately copy-rightable works, prudent advisers have advocated the filing of renewal applications in both the 28th year of the original work and the 28th year of the new version.

The Arrangement of Works in the Public Domain

The contracts of many record companies state that the recording artist grants to the label a free mechanical right license for copyrighted arrangements of songs in the public domain that are recorded and controlled by the artist. This results in greater profits to the record company since there are no mechanical royalties to be paid. Where special provision is not made, normal mechanical license fees are charged for the use of copyrighted arrangements of public domain compositions.

ASCAP and BMI pay substantial performance monies to writers and publishers of copyrighted arrangements of works in the public domain. ASCAP has various categories calling for payment of 2 to 100 percent of the credit available for an original song:

- For nonreligious works copyrighted only in a printed folio: 2 percent
- For songs separately copyrighted and published or, lacking publication, for songs that are primarily instrumental works and available on a rental basis: 10 percent
- For new lyrics: 35 percent
- For new lyrics and a new title: 50 percent
- For changes in the music: 10 to 50 percent
- For transferring a primarily instrumental work from one medium to another: 35 percent

BMI pays performance monies for copyrighted arrangements of works in the public domain at a rate based on administrative valuation of the new material, up to 100 percent of the rate applicable to original songs.

Some folk artists and folk music publishers engage in unethical practices by changing song titles without modifying the lyrics or melody. They may claim full originality when they are really only "finders" of songs in the public domain. They register copyrights to such songs, claiming they are "original" works, and fail to set forth accurately the limited amount of any new material, thereby falsely and unfairly obtaining the benefit of the Copyright Act of 1976 provision that places the burden of proof of the invalidity of a certificate of copyright registration on an unauthorized user. This burden may be extremely difficult to sustain because the copyright claimant, as the true finder of songs in the public domain, may be the only witness who can describe the source of the particular song and may be unwilling to admit the public domain origin. The finder of such a song who wishes to legally protect his or her discovery may embellish it with new copyrightable material.

An additional category of new copyrightable versions of songs in the public domain is based on the compilation of parts of different compositions. While copyright cannot be obtained on a segment of a public domain work, the linking of various segments may require such an editorial creative endeavor, aside from original bridge music, that copyright will subsist in the collection as such. The "folk process" of developing folk songs by endless passage from person to person tends to add compilation material. The end product, a song in the hands of a finder, may still be a public domain work. However, the fashioning of a compilation composition by combining, say, a prison folk song with a riverboat work song and perhaps adding another bit or piece from other sources, may result in a copyrightable work.

Foreign Treatment of Arrangements and Adaptations

England, France, and some other major nations differ from the United States in their treatment of writers of arrangements, adaptations, translations, and other new versions. They do not require consent for the second copyright to arise. However, they insist on consent of *both* the original-version proprietor and the second-version owner before use. This results in a parallel set of protective rights that, without prejudice to the original owner, safeguards the creator of the second version.

In the past, the local performing rights societies in France and other European countries recognized the rights of arrangers of copyrighted published vocal works and generally allocated to them two-twelfths of the total performance royalties payable to writers and publishers. This was deductible from the total writer royalties, which for works of European origin usually equal eight-twelfths of the entire performance royalties payable to writers and publishers. If a subpublished work had both a local lyric writer and an arranger, the continental society would ordinarily allocate the two-twelfths between them. This practice was, in effect, an unfair "cut-in" of a local member, who would thus be paid at the expense of American and British songwriters whose original songs were recorded by U.S. or British recording artists without any French or other foreign arrangements. The excuse for what appears to be an injustice was that it was too difficult to distinguish a Frank Sinatra recording of a song from a local recorded cover version. The same situation occurred with regard to lyric adopters of English-language songs into local-language versions. However, in 1991 CISAC, the umbrella organization for various national collection societies, put forward the Amalfi resolution, whereby deductions for new works are made only when the local version is actually performed. Unfortunately, many societies have not altered their databases with respect to the old catalogs and apply the Amalfi resolution only prospectively, from January 1, 1992.

Concerning noncopyrighted works, foreign continental societies normally have plans for grading arrangements in accordance with the amount of original work done by the arranger, and the arranger's share of performance royalties is determined by this grading.

14

Performing Rights Organizations

One of the greatest sources of revenue in the music industry comes from public performance payments collected and distributed by the major performing rights organizations. Yet the basis of operation of each of these organizations was nonexistent until 1897 because Congress had failed to include public performance rights within the copyright statute prior to that date. Even after its inclusion in the statute, there was no practical way to collect substantial monies, since only less important sources such as concerts, dance halls, and cabarets were available before the development of broadcasting, and the numerous copyright owners were not sufficiently organized to license and collect.

Today there are three performing rights organizations in the United States, and they perform valuable services for their members. All three have Web sites that offer services to both member and nonmember users looking to learn more about the often complex world of performance rights societies. They also collect substantial sums of money on behalf of their membership. In 1998, ASCAP announced that for the first time in its history that its receipts had exceeded half a billion dollars, up from $422.7 million in 1994. The 1998 gross for BMI was $455 million compared with $340 million in 1994. SESAC, a privately held licensing organization, does not release its financial report; in 1983 it did report receipts of $5 million. Here is the breakdown of revenue sources for each of the three organizations.

	Television	Radio	Other Domestic	Other Foreign
ASCAP	33%	40%	—	26%
BMI	47	40	13	
SESAC	32	55	13	

Clearing Functions

Despite frequent grumbling by radio broadcasters at the necessity for paying sums akin to a gross receipts tax to performing rights organizations for the right to play music, it is generally conceded that without such organizations inordinate expense and chaos would result. There would be endless searches and bargaining for performing rights involving the owners of both established and obscure songs. Each station would require copyright clearance experts and would undergo programming delays while contacting the owners for each performance. The concept of a general clearance agency for a large group of music rights, undertaking a uniform system of collection and payment is necessary for the orderly supply of music to radio stations. If it were not so, the government might close all performing rights organizations on the ground of violation of antitrust laws.

A Solicitor General's brief, submitted to the U.S. Supreme Court in 1967, supported a lower court finding.

> A central licensing agency such as ASCAP is the only practical way that copyright proprietors may enjoy their rights under the federal copyright laws and that broadcasters and others may conveniently obtain licenses for the performance of copyrighted music. [The lower court] found that single copyright owners cannot deal individually with all users or individually police the use of their songs; and that a single radio station may broadcast as many as 60,000 performances of musical compositions involving as many as 6,000 separate compositions.

In a late-1970s lawsuit in federal court, CBS sought to require the U.S. performing rights organizations to offer for network television programming a per-use license price list that would be available in the case of no direct licensing by copyright owners. A federal court of appeals held in favor of ASCAP and BMI and stressed that CBS had sufficient economic bargaining power and strength to avoid the antitrust factors alleged by CBS. The U.S. Supreme Court upheld the decision.

In the 1983 Buffalo Broadcasting case (*Buffalo Broadcasting Co. Inc. v. ASCAP*, 78 Civ. 5670 [S.D.N.Y. 1983]), an appellate federal court held that antitrust laws do not prohibit ASCAP and BMI from offering blanket licenses to non-network local television broadcasters. In 1985, the U.S. Supreme Court refused to review the decision. The plaintiffs, who were non-network local television broadcasters, had sought per-program licenses limited to music in programs produced by the stations themselves; this was designed to reduce the stations' costs of licensing music in television programs. Under a local federal court determination following the U.S. Supreme Court action, interim license fees were set in connection with local television stations electing to pay ASCAP fees on an interim blanket or per-program basis. The latter allowed some stations to pay less than they would pay on the interim blanket basis and to do so retroactively after April 1, 1985.

While per-program licensing of both ASCAP and BMI affects the total amount of fees collected by either organization, history to date indicates that there is not a material impact on the total amount of fees collected or the amounts available for distributions. The costs and delays involved in processing per-program licenses, applicable in programming such as sports programs and news programs using minimum music spots or background, have created new service firms. These firms report on the specific music requiring per-program licenses and make provision for meeting payment requirements as well as reporting requirements.

After many years of lobbying, the performing rights organizations and their author and publisher members and affiliates were able to engineer the repeal of the statutory exemption of jukeboxes in the Copyright Act of 1976, resulting in modest new sources of revenue. Additional licensing sources established under the Copyright Act of 1976 are retransmissions by cable broadcasters and by public and educational broadcasters. (These issues are discussed in detail in Chapter 10.)

Finally, the burgeoning area of college concert dates is a continuing source of revenues for performing right organizations. It was formerly assumed that college concerts were to be specially treated as low-budget nonprofit events largely in the field of serious music. However, rock and roll and other popular artists regularly appear at stadiums and halls before large audiences on a highly profitable tour basis having little or no relationship to nonprofit educational ventures. Higher performing right music fees have been required for college concerts in recent years.

American Society of Composers, Authors, and Publishers

Founded in 1914, ASCAP is a membership organization. As on November 1999, it had 56,885 writers and 31,150 publishers, with new members being elected every month. ASCAP claims to have the oldest and largest repertoire in the United States, adding approximately 100,000 new titles annually. It gets its money by issuing a *blanket license* for its entire catalog to radio and television stations; the fee is based not on the extent of music use but on gross receipts of the station minus certain adjustments, such as agency commissions and wire charges. Its basic rate is just under 2 percent of the stations' adjusted gross receipts.

ASCAP pays an equal amount to publishers as a group and to writers as a group after an actual overhead deduction. The overhead expense in 1998 was about 16 percent of total ASCAP receipts, compared to 19 percent in 1994. Formerly, ASCAP absorbed the costs of distributing royalties received from foreign societies, but in 1976 a charge was initiated equal to actual costs; this charge has averaged between 3 and 4 percent in recent years.

Two of the most noteworthy services on the ASCAP Web site (www.ascap.com) are ASCAP's Ace on the Web and RateCalc. The Ace on the Web feature is a song database that allows the user to search for songs in the ASCAP repertory. The service, updated weekly, states whether a work is copublished with a non-ASCAP entity and gives the affiliated performance rights society of the non-ASCAP publisher. ASCAP also issues license forms through its EZ-Eagle technology. This is a patent-pending licensing-and-tracking device. It uses Web crawlers combined with high-tech tools to locate sites using ASCAP music in audio and video formats on the Internet, assisting in the identification of the ASCAP songs used, and then qualifying licensees and issuing the license.

In 1998, ASCAP proudly announced that it was the first performance rights organization to make a distribution for licensed Internet performances. The amount was $100,000. It has since multiplied several times annually. (See the accompanying CD-ROM for more information about ASCAP, including copies of the "Digital Audio Royalty Form and Fact Sheet" for writers and for publishers.)

Broadcast Music Inc.

BMI, a competitor of ASCAP, was established in 1940 in a move to increase competition and, according to BMI, to give an alternative to writers and publishers not represented by ASCAP. As of April 1, 1999, BMI represented about 140,000 writers and some 60,000 publishers. Its catalog consists of 3 million works, with an average increase of 11,000 new compositions a month. Like ASCAP, BMI operates primarily under blanket licenses and charges broadcasters a fee based on formulas applied to adjusted gross receipts. The rate is somewhat under 2 percent, but the adjustments are such that the same licensees who use the music of both societies pay somewhat less to BMI than to ASCAP. BMI operates as a not-for-profit organization.

BMI currently operates in three distinct administrative territories; Nashville, which covers the Southeast to Texas; Los Angeles, which handles everything west of the Rocky Mountains; and New York City, which handles the rest.

For many years BMI encouraged Canadian publishers and writers to join a wholly owned subsidiary, BMI/Canada. In 1976 all ownership was transferred to a Canadian trust in order to constitute PRO/Canada, a wholly Canadian performing rights organization that operated in the same way as the ASCAP affiliate, CAPAC. In 1990, the two Canadian societies merged their operations to form the Society of Composers, Authors & Music Publishers of Canada (SOCAN). Board members are composed of equal numbers of Canadian publishers and composers.

The BMI Web site (www.bmi.com) offers a number of innovative services such as: HyperRepertoire, the Songwriter's Toolbox, and the Licensing Toolbox. The HyperRepertoire service is an Internet song database in which the user can search for information on writers or publishers. The database allows the user to search by song title or by writer's name. The Songwriter's Toolbox is a unique educational service that provides information intended to assist songwriters to better understand what BMI does by providing an overview of performance rights, songwriting, music publishing, and copyright. Another part of BMI's educational services, the Licensing Toolbox, gives potential licensees a crash course on how to license music for public performance via radio, TV cable, and the Internet. (See the accompanying CD-ROM for copies of BMI's "Work Registration Form" and "Royalty Information Booklet.")

SESAC

It is generally accepted that SESAC is by far the smallest of the three performing rights organizations in the United States. SESAC is a private licensing company founded in 1930 and presently owned by Stephen Swid, Ira Smith, Freddie Gershon, and the investment banking firm of Allen and Company. The organization represents 1,000 active publishers and 1,000 active writers and has a catalog of more than 200,000 compositions. It differs from BMI and ASCAP in that it allocates negotiated shares to its publisher and writer affiliates, after first deducting overhead expenses, with SESAC retaining the balance as its profits.

Fees charged by SESAC to licensees differ from those charged by ASCAP and BMI inasmuch as they are based on fixed determinants, such as market population served by the station and the station's standard advertising rates, rather than on a percent of gross receipts. SESAC uses a national rate card, applicable to all its broadcast licensees, which gives consideration to the factors of market classification (population) and spot rate. Fees for a full-time AM radio station range from $330 to $7,200 per year. A typical AM station, with an average market population of 300,000 and a maximum 1-minute advertising spot rate of $30, pays an annual fee of $1,020. Like ASCAP and BMI, SESAC licenses virtually the entire broadcasting industry. License fees for other users are also determined by relevant market factors. For instance, cable fees are based on subscriber audience numbers; college and university fees on student enrollment; and hotel fees on room rates, live or mechanical music use, and the number of rooms.

SESAC's Web site (www.sesac.com) offers many similar services as BMI and ASCAP. SESAC's version of the on-line song database is called, simply, SESAC Repertory On-line. The database allows the user to perform a song title search, writer search, and publisher search. SESAC's Web site also offers a service called Internet New Media License, which gives the user information on broadcast licensing and general licensing. In addition, the site gives the user instructions on how to download a SESAC Internet license and how to e-mail specific questions to SESAC.

SESAC has recently made an agreement with Liquid Audio in order to protect copyright owners' performance rights over the Internet. The agreement intends to "simplify music rights licensing and reporting via the World Wide Web" and calls for Liquid Audio to promote SESAC's Internet/New Media License to Web sites that use Liquid Audio's music downloading technology by distributing license agreements and supporting material to Web site operators. Liquid Audio also provides SESAC with information about sites engaging in downloading music in the hope of aiding SESAC to better gauge and collect for performances over the Internet. According to John Stone, Liquid Audio's business development manager, "By partnering with SESAC, we are enabling our customers who offer music on the Internet to handle rights reporting seamlessly so that SESAC affiliates receive payment without hassle." (See the accompanying CD-ROM for SESAC's "Publisher Affiliation Agreement" and "Writer Affiliation Agreement.")

Title Registration

When new members join one of the organizations, they cannot sit back and expect works to be recognized for surveying and distribution purposes without registering the titles. Titles may be registered on paper forms, PC disks, or Macintosh disks. All three formats are available from ASCAP. As of 1995, ASCAP reported that 62 percent of its new titles were registered electronically. Bilingual Spanish-English registration is also possible.

ASCAP's Title Registration Information Center will, on request, supply computer-generated lists of all the member's registered works by title, along with a summary count of total titles.

When a song is administered by an ASCAP publisher, the writer does not need to register it. However, when a song has *not* been placed with an ASCAP publisher, it is essential that the writer register the work if it is expected to generate any broadcast, concert, or other ASCAP-logged performances. Furthermore, ASCAP does not independently record transfers, renewals, and terminations from the Copyright Office. When a song is transferred or subject to recapture by way of copyright renewal or termination, the writer should qualify as a publisher member and register the transferred composition. Failure to do this may result in payments being misdirected to the benefit of the former registrant. It is essential to trigger the new registration by complying with registration rules.

BMI uses the standard paper clearance form and the Automated Title System for registration of new works. When a work is assigned, even if recorded for assignment at the U.S. Copyright Office, BMI does not pick up the information unless specifically informed by the interested parties. BMI requires written documentation from both parties to change their records and further requests the effective date of the assignment.

SESAC uses both the newly created Common Works Registration electronic format and paper clearance.

International Information Collection System

The essential clerical tasks of receiving data on newly registered songs and informing affiliated foreign societies is a matter of major concern. In 1999, ASCAP and two other performing rights societies, Britain's PRS/MCPS and Holland's BUMA/STEMRA, formed the International Music Joint Venture, with an anticipated budget of some $20 million and a goal of saving significant administration costs. John LoFrumento of ASCAP reported, "What we are creating is a platform for the music rights society of the future. We realized that none of us, by ourselves, can afford to develop the complex computing power necessary to handle the millions of transactions expected in the digital age. We are pooling our expertise and resources ... for processing music rights in a world where everything is watermarked and traceable." All other societies, including BMI, have been invited to participate in this joint venture. However, for the present, BMI is continuing its own Internet song title database Hyper-Repertoire, which is searchable by song title or writer and furnishes writer and publisher information.

The International Music Joint Venture is consistent with the goals set by the Confédération Internationale des Societé d'Auteurs et Compositeurs (CISAC), the international federation of authors societies constituting a central physical database that could be expanded with future entries. Here's how it works. A new title, "I Love You, John," by Joan Doe and Richard Roe could originate in the United States and yet be adapted through the efforts of foreign subpublishers into Greek, Japanese, German, and French versions where other writers, and sometimes other arrangers would be entitled to participate in their versions. The database would be confronted not only with language changes but with author credit changes, publisher changes, and even alphabet changes into the Greek and Japanese languages. The joint venture recognizes that music is truly an international industry and that it is at the forefront of technology both in sources of future income and in the background functions of identifying, tracking, and distributing the performance, mechanical, and other expected flows of earnings.

John Hutchinson of PRS/MCPS observed that "we have to collaborate with the service providers to ensure that proper electronic copyright management systems are in place. That means devising a common systems architecture that will allow royalty information and royalties to flow easily into societies, in a readily digestible form." He further remarked that the performing rights societies must expedite distributions consistent with digital-era facilities or else be "left with the difficult stuff like collecting license fees from hairdressers." Hutchinson also said the joint venture's goal for the year 2002 was an overhead cost of about 10 percent for the performing right and less than 3 percent for mechanical digital transactions, and remarked that a true digital transaction should allow international distribution within a matter of days.

The Relative Importance of Performance Monies

In 1997, music publishing revenues worldwide amounted to nearly $6.3 billion. Tables 14-1 and 14-2 show that performance revenues vary from country to country and catalog to catalog, but they are a significant part of the economy. (Synchronization is discussed in Chapter 18.)

Table 14-1

Revenues from Music Performance and Reproduction for Select Countries in 1996 ($ millions)

Reproduction-Based Income

Country	Performance-Based Income*	Phonomechanical	Synchronization
United States	$628.03	$493.00	$79.56
Germany	363.86	263.29	191.27
Japan	250.67	375.78	86.82
United Kingdom	191.08	190.90	34.62
Worldwide	2,722.66	2,004.09	700.72

*Includes radio, television, cable, satellite, and live and recorded performances.
Source: NMPA International Survey.

Table 14-2

Breakdowns for Publishers' Incomes, 1998

Publisher	Mechanical	Performance	Synchronization	Print*
EMI Music	54%	36%	10%	
Warner/Chappell	47%	33%	8%	12%
Peer Music	63%	25%	12%	

*Warner/Chappell is a prominent independent printer; other publishers do not provide separate figures but include it in their mechanical license revenues.
Source: MBI, February 1999, p. ix.

Surveying Procedures

ASCAP and BMI both employ extensive systems of surveying and statistical sampling of actual broadcasts to determine monies to be paid to writers and publishers. Each television network performance is surveyed and credited for payment purposes by both organizations on the basis of an actual arithmetic count, without resort to sampling. This is possible because the networks and the program producers supply program logs and music cue sheets to the performing right organizations. ASCAP and BMI also make tapes of network television performances to verify the accuracy of the information furnished by the networks and program producers.

Tabulating performances on local radio stations necessarily involves statistical sampling; samples are multiplied by formulas established by leading statisticians who are selected separately by each organization. The formulas are used in order to have the sample represent most fairly total national performances without undertaking the inordinate expense of a universal count. Although BMI alleges that it samples more radio hours per annum than ASCAP, ASCAP asserts that its approach is sufficient to achieve fairness and equity.

The sampling methods used by ASCAP and BMI are also applied to local television performances. ASCAP supplements its sampling techniques by reference to cue sheets and to *TV Guide* program listings (which include some 95 regional editions). In addition to references to cue sheets, since 1991 BMI has used television broadcast information compiled by a company called TV Data, which BMI claims offers more comprehensive coverage than *TV Guide*.

BMI also claims that it logs more total television hours than ASCAP. ASCAP has countered with the assertion that its approach achieves both accuracy and fairness. In addition to its samples, logs, cue sheets, and *TV Guide* information, ASCAP uses tape recordings of local television performances made throughout the United States that are analyzed and identified regardless of whether the songs are in the ASCAP repertory. Tapes are made of approximately one-third of its sample (10,000 hours), and ASCAP states that under its independently controlled sampling system the stations and ASCAP management have no prior knowledge of which stations are being taped.

As of 1995, ASCAP expanded its survey, as follows:

- It makes a complete count of all 950 local TV stations concerning music contained in feature films and syndicated TV series that appear on the 100 largest local stations currently in the ASCAP census.
- It covers 100 percent of the performances on Country Music TV and the Nashville Network.
- It has increased college station sampling from 500 hours per year to 7,000 and relies on logs submitted by the stations whenever possible. This will be used for a separate allocation of the college station revenues of $1.25 million per year.
- It has expanded coverage of live popular concerts from 50 to the 200 largest tours (as measured by box office receipts) and accelerated surveying reports by one quarter (3 months) for more timely payment
- It includes 2,500 educational concert programs, giving full census reports on symphonic and recital concerts as well as Disney on Ice, Ringling Brothers Circus, Music Springs, 3M Platinum Service, and AEI background music.

The ASCAP survey includes a sample of approximately 70,000 hours of local programs, syndicated programs, and films. Its cable payout is based on a full census of available cue sheets, logs, tapes, and supplied computer tapes for 30 major cable programming networks.

In 1998, ASCAP reported that it had broadened its television survey to cover more than 5 million performances; this was 10 times more than 5 years ago. Its survey uses three sources: radio, TV, and live concerts. ASCAP's radio survey uses radio station logs, Broadcast Data Services (BDS), electronic data, and listeners in the field. These listeners are in 26 locations throughout the country; they tape programs and send them to New York headquarters for analysis by 24 professional listeners who identify, compare with BDS, and log station data for accuracy.

BMI requires its broadcast licensees to supply, approximately once every 18 months, a station-prepared log of music used in a particular period. BMI uses a private accounting firm to select the stations and takes pains to keep the surveying stations secret from its publishers and writers. It states that it does a substantial amount of taping of both local stations and cable operations to verify their surveys. All surveys requested are used except for the few that are illegible or must be discarded for some similar reason; the number so discarded in any quarter is reported to be well under 1 percent of the total stations surveyed.

The ASCAP system of surveying through taping, especially in local radio play, is more costly than the BMI procedure and results in fewer stations actually being surveyed. ASCAP claims that the secrecy factor involved in taping avoids any possibility of fictional entries or favoritism. BMI points out that its taping acts to verify the surveys supplied to it and that the payment per station, even when multiplied by the applicable factors, is relatively low and the influence of any manipulation would be very small. BMI contends that, especially in the fields of country, R&B, jazz, and Latin music, its access to more logs from small cooperating station licensees offers a broader basis for judging nationwide performance of songs that are less likely to be programmed as frequently on big-city stations.

Both ASCAP and BMI statistically weight the samples received in accordance with the size and importance of the surveyed station and, for network television programs, the time of day of the program. ASCAP's procedure attempts to weight their samples relative to the percentage of dollar receipts from the station involved. BMI also adjusts (in a less exact manner) for the economic importance of the station-licensee by paying more for a network station television performance than for a local television station performance and by compensating more for a Radio 1 network station performance than for a Radio 2 radio performance. Under BMI standards, a Radio 1 station is one that, in the year before the performance, paid a BMI license fee in the top 25 percent of all BMI radio station license fees. A Radio 2 station on a comparable basis paid a license fee in the bottom 75 percent of all BMI radio station license fees. The formula for BMI distribution to its affiliates is published on their Web page under Songwriter's Toolbox. Amounts payable are equal between writers and publishers of each applicable song except where there is an agreement to pay the publisher less than 50 percent, in which case the extra amount is automatically credited to the writer's account.

In 1993, SESAC formed a division called SESAC Latina, which was dedicated to representing Spanish-language music. SESAC Latina formed an alliance with Broadcast Data Systems (BDS) to employ its monitoring system to track performances and distributes royalties based on BDS data. Two years later, SESAC expanded its BDS usage to track affiliates' music across all major radio formats.

For radio formats not monitored by BDS, such as jazz and contemporary Christian, SESAC uses its chart payment system, which makes royalty payments based on chart positions in major trade publications, such as *Billboard, Gavin, Radio and Records* and *College Music Journal*. Although SESAC does not use a weighting system as such, it uses the peak position reached by a song in those publications' charts to determine the song's compensation. Distributions are made quarterly, with a goal of creating a 3-month gap between actual performance and payment.

SESAC uses TV data and cue sheets to track television and cable performances for its affiliates. In 1998, SESAC signed an agreement with Aris Technologies to use its MusiCode digital watermarking system for broadcast monitoring and royalty distribution. With MusiCode, segments of music as short as 3 seconds can be identified. SESAC reviews and analyzes all national network logs, pay-TV logs, and PBS/NPR cue sheets. It also spot-checks the programming of local radio and television stations and reviews regional editions of *TV Guide*, as well as *OnSat*, a guide to programming available by satellite. In addition, SESAC receives extensive information on syndicated television programming through cue sheets supplied by affiliates and producers and the *Nielsen Report on Syndicated Programming*.

Grievance Procedures

It is prudent for writers and publishers to recognize that the surveying and tabulation techniques of ASCAP and BMI are subject to interpretation, and that the reports by the organizations should be carefully reviewed. The late Billy Rose once observed that ASCAP's performance reports on certain of his songs showed in the column "Share" a lesser percentage for his participation vis-à-vis his collaborators than appeared on royalty statements rendered by his publishers. Where there were two other writers involved, he had been credited with one-third of the writer's share of performance fees. He pointed out in an informal ASCAP committee proceeding that he had written the words alone and that therefore his share was 50 percent and the other two collaborators should receive 25 percent apiece instead of one-third. Rose prevailed in his contentions, but ASCAP was careful to stress, in informing other members of the decision, that the writer has the burden of proving unusual divisions of performance fees.

Based on the ASCAP consent decree, the court appoints special distribution advisers to periodically examine the design and conduct of the ASCAP survey of performances, which establishes the basis of its distribution of revenues to members. They report to the court, to ASCAP, and to the U.S. government, making recommendations as to modifications of the ASCAP procedures and practices. Recognized functions of these special distribution advisers include making themselves available in person or by correspondence to ASCAP members who have questions concerning or problems with the ASCAP distribution system. Distribution adviser inquiries have been made into such matters as the credits for music performed at football games, the reduction of credits for qualifying works used as feature songs in films, and the basis for distribution of money received from unsurveyed background wired-music licensees.

Grievance procedures for publisher and writer members of ASCAP were formalized in the Article of Association of the Society based on the 1960 consent decree. A board of review, elected in the same manner as the ASCAP board of directors, was established to have jurisdiction over every complaint by a member relating to the distribution of ASCAP's revenues or to any rule or regulation of ASCAP directly affecting the distribution of revenues to the member. Each complaint must be filed within 9 months from the receipt of the annual statement or of the rule or regulations on which the complaint is founded.

The relief that may be granted by the board of review in terms of monetary payment may not extend back beyond the time covered by the annual statement, except if the alleged injustice is such that the aggrieved party would not reasonably be put on notice of it by his or her annual statement; in that case, the relief given may reach back as far as, in the opinion of the board, is required to do justice. The board of review is obligated to set forth in detail the facts and grounds underlying its decision. There is a right to appeal any decision of the board of review before an impartial panel of the American Arbitration Association.

The BMI grievance procedure, as set out in its 1966 consent decree, requires that "all disputes of any kind, nature or description" between BMI and any writer, publisher, or music user be brought to arbitration in the City of New York under the prevailing rules of the American Arbitration Association.

SESAC is not subject to a court consent decree and has no established grievance procedure covering its relations with its affiliates.

Membership

ASCAP operates under a 1960 court-administered consent decree with the U.S. Department of Justice with respect to the antitrust laws; the decree guides nearly every aspect of its operations. It requires ASCAP to accept for membership any applicant who is (1) a writer with at least one song regularly published or commercially recorded or (2) a music publisher actively engaged in the business with publications that have been "used or distributed on a commercial scale for at least one year." ASCAP actively solicits writers and publishers to join through its full-time staff members located in New York, California, Tennessee, London, and Puerto Rico, as well as through regularly placed trade paper advertisements. In fact, ASCAP acts promptly to accept publisher applications by active publishers, without any prerequisite period of operations. Under the consent decree, ASCAP must also permit members to resign and have procedures clearly in place; members may resign at the end of any calendar year by giving 3 months' advance notice in writing. (ASCAP writer and publisher applications and the ASCAP membership agreement can be found on the accompanying CD-ROM.)

Since 1966 BMI has also operated under a consent decree with the Justice Department. Under the decree, BMI must accept as an affiliate any writer who has had at least one composition commercially published or recorded and any publisher actively engaged in the business and whose compositions "have been commercially published or recorded and publicly promoted and distributed for at least one year." The decree prohibits contracts of more than 5 years' duration. In practice, the term of the publisher agreement is 5 years, and the term of the writer agreement is 2 years, with the following exception: BMI may continue to license compositions in existence at the date of termination until advances to the particular writer or publisher have been earned or repaid. In November 1994 the decree was revised to match ASCAP's. Throughout its history, BMI has been aggressive in soliciting and attracting new affiliates. (BMI writer and publisher applications and membership agreements can be found on the accompanying CD-ROM.)

ASCAP collects an annual membership fee of $50 from publishers and $10 from writers. The dues, according to ASCAP, are used to aid elderly indigent members. BMI has a one-time $250 application fee for new corporate publisher affiliates and a $150 fee for an individual seeking status as a publisher, with no comparable fee for writers. There are no annual BMI charges for either publishers or writers.

SESAC is not bound by a consent decree in any of its operations. However, it actively solicits new publisher and writer members. The basic term of its publisher agreement is 5 years and the term of its writer agreement is 3 years. Such terms are automatically extended for similar periods unless canceled on 3 months' prior notice.

No writer or publisher can collect from more than one performing rights organization for the same songs at the same time, as dual membership or affiliation is not permitted. However, a writer or publisher can resign from an organization and still retain collection rights to songs that have been previously registered with, and continue to be licensed by, that organization.

Although ASCAP and BMI speak of release at the end of the license period of all rights to past songs of members or affiliates who resign, it rarely happens. The difficulty arises when a song is placed with a performing rights organization by both the writer and the publisher. This split origin of rights is rarely matched by joint resignations, and it has been judicially held that either the writer or the publisher can insist on maintaining the status quo with the first organization to which the performing right was jointly entrusted. There are, nevertheless, cases of split licensing. For example, BMI claims the right to license a former ASCAP writer's share while ASCAP continues to license the publisher's or cowriter's share. Or BMI recognizes the right of a BMI affiliate who resigns and joins ASCAP to take his or her share of the rights with him while BMI continues to license the rights of the publisher or cowriter who continues as a BMI affiliate.

Where an ASCAP writer collaborates with a BMI writer and the song is licensed by both societies, both will pay only their own publishers and writers. In the case of a collaboration between an ASCAP writer and a writer not affiliated with a performing rights organization, ASCAP will pay both writers if the unaffiliated writer's contribution is published by an ASCAP publisher and the unaffiliated writer does not give licensing rights to another performing rights organization. When a BMI writer collaborates with a writer not affiliated with a performing rights organization, BMI will not pay the unaffiliated writer.

The Fairness in Music Licensing Act of 1998

The Sonny Bono Term Extension Act of 1998 contained a compromise plan that was supported by the National Restaurant Association. Under the controversial Fairness in Music Licensing Act of 1998, bars and restaurants of less than 3700 square feet and retail stores of less than 2000 square feet that play music via radio or television sets are exempt from paying performance royalty fees. ASCAP and BMI were angered by the loss of revenue, but the compromise was politically expedient in winning passage of the 20-year extension. There is some dispute as to whether the exemption violates the Berne Convention and treaty requirements. If it is determined to do so, the Fairness in Music Licensing Act may be repealed.

The ASCAP Payment System

For over 25 years, all new ASCAP writer members elected to be paid in the same way as the publishers: on the *Current-Performance Plan*. This is a relatively simple calculation based on the number of performance credits recorded by the ASCAP logging system during the most recent available fiscal survey annual year multiplied by the monetary value of a credit for that period. This monetary value is arithmetically determined by the simple division of total credits into total available net earnings to be split among the total group of writers in the plan. For example, the credit value in the year 1999 was over $4.95. In 1989 there were substantially fewer available dollars and thus less credit value—somewhere between $2.62 and $2.98 for the applicable total annual collections.

Effective July 1999, ASCAP writers have the choice of one of two methods of payment: the *current performance plan* and the *averaged performance plan*. All publishers are enrolled in the current performance plan. New writers are automatically enrolled in the current performance plan, but writers can switch from one plan to the other at the end of any 12-month period. Under either plan, payments are calculated using a formula based on the dollar value of an ASCAP *credit*. The number of credits allocated for each performance of a work depends on a number of factors, including:

- Type of performance
- "Hookup" factor—e.g., with network television, the number of stations carrying a broadcast
- "Follow the dollar" factor—the money that ASCAP receives from any medium is paid to writers and publishers for performances in that medium
- Time of day—e.g., prime-time performance of a work is worth more than early morning performance of the same work

In addition, "premium" credits are allocated to songs that earn a predetermined number of radio feature credits during a particular quarter. The dollar value of an individual credit is determined by dividing the total number of performance credits recorded by the ASCAP logging system during a 12-month period—for all writers and publishers—by the total number of dollars (net earnings) available for distribution. In 1998, a credit was worth $4.95.

The quarterly royalties for writers who choose the current performance plan are calculated by multiplying the number of credits earned during that quarter by the current dollar value of a credit. For example, a writer with 475 credits in the fourth quarter of 1998 would have been owed royalties of $2351.25.

The averaged performance plan replaces an unwieldy system, the four-fund plan, which calculated payments using a system of "redeemable credits" rather than dollars earned and taking into account such factors as length of ASCAP membership and whether a song was a "recognized" work. Like the current performance plan, the averaged performance plan pays quarterly royalties on the basis of the monetary values of members' credits. However, 20 percent of each distribution is based on current performance dollars, 60 percent on a 5-year average, and 20 percent on a 10-year average, providing a steadier stream of income.

The dollar value of a credit will fluctuate with the amount of ASCAP receipts and the total number of ASCAP performance credits. In the follow-the-dollar policy of valuation of surveyed performances, ASCAP recognizes that a network TV sponsor pays more on weekends and during prime hours. Performances on Monday through Friday receive 50 percent, 75 percent, and 100 percent of full credits, depending on the time of day, whether morning, midday, or after 7 P.M. For weekends, the midday credits are eliminated in place of a full-payment prime time commencing at 1 P.M. Similar follow-the-dollar formulas are applicable to revenues from radio stations and networks.

One of the most novel concepts in the ASCAP system of credits is the "qualified work" designation. Under this part of the system, a song with a history of 20,000 feature performances, of which the most recent 5 years contributed a total of at least 5,000 feature performances a year, is given higher credits when used in nonfeature roles such as background, cue, bridge, or theme; not more than 1,500 feature performances are to be counted in any one of the 5 years to meet the 5,000 requirement. For purposes of jingle payments, there is also a form of qualified work dealing with works that show 150 feature performances logged by ASCAP in its radio and television surveys within the 5 prior years.

The justification for higher credits lies in the fact that when a background strain or a theme is based on a well-known old standard, such as "Raindrops Keep Fallin' on My Head," the user is getting more value from the use and accordingly recognizes that ASCAP's bargaining power for general license fees is greater than if the tune were a new song previously unknown to the public and commissioned by the user especially for that purpose. Background uses of well-known songs are also considered to advance the plot by public identification with special moods or images associated with the song.

This simplified explanation leaves aside the more difficult issue of describing or justifying the different rates of payment. A "qualified work" used as a theme is accorded half a feature credit, while an unqualified work in the same form receives one-quarter of a feature credit. A background use of even 5 seconds of a qualified work gets half a feature credit, but an unqualified work requires a 3-minute total use for 42 percent of a feature credit, with a proportionate reduction for lesser use, measured by each second of timing, with a minimum payment of 1 percent per use. (The ASCAP credit weighting formula and an explanation of the ASCAP payment system can be found on the accompanying CD-ROM.)

The BMI Payment System

The BMI standard forms of writer contract and publisher contracts do not mention payment rates. Each states in effect that payments will be made in accordance with the current practices and rates of BMI. The regular rates of payment for writers and publishers are the same. Actual payments to writers or publishers distinguish between radio and television performances and between network and local performances. In the case of a network performance, the rate allotted is multiplied by the number of interconnected stations carrying the broadcast. The rate allocated to a local station performance is multiplied by a statistical multiplier based on the ratio of stations logged to stations licensed in each station classification.

BMI has a payment schedule that is distributed to all its affiliates. This specifies the minimum payments that BMI will pay until a new payment schedule is issued. The actual payments made—all monies other than those needed for overhead and reserve—may be and have been higher than the minimum rates. Each payment rate under the schedule covers combined writer and publisher compensation and should ordinarily be divided in half to arrive at the separate payments to a writer and a publisher. In the absence of a publisher, the rate stipulated in the payment schedule is payable entirely to the writer.

In addition, if the publisher and writer agree, the writer may receive more than 50 percent of the total payments; however, the publisher's share can never exceed 50 percent. Under this system, a writer does not need to form a publishing firm in order to collect more than 50 percent of the total performance fees paid, and the number of prospective BMI music publishing firms is reduced. BMI states that its system is "similar to that of other performing rights organizations throughout the world."

On the assumption that there is a publisher and that the writer and publisher share equally in the payment rate, their respective shares under the BMI payment schedule are as follows: There is a payment of 12 cents for a feature radio performance of a popular song on each radio network station and on each Radio 1 station (a station whose BMI license fee is in the top 25 percent of all BMI radio station license fees in the year prior to the performance). There is a payment of 6 cents for a feature radio performance on each Radio 2 station (a station whose BMI license fees are in the bottom 75 percent of all BMI radio station license fees in the year before the performance). A local television feature performance is allocated a rate of $1.50. Network television feature performances in prime time, between 7 P.M. and 1 A.M., earn $9 per station, and in other than prime time, $5. There is no distinction made between AM and FM feature performances on radio. Concert works on radio receive substantially higher payments than performances of a popular song.

Under this system, an individual song receives the base rate in the BMI payment schedule discussed above until a certain plateau of U.S. feature broadcast performances of the song is reached. At this plateau, a higher payment rate ensues under what is called a "bonus level." Works receive bonus station credit for all feature broadcast performances from January 1, 1960, and after.

An *entry-level* bonus payment at 1.5 times the base rate is made for those songs with a cumulative history of at least 25,000 U.S. feature broadcast performances. For those songs with the next higher cumulative history and whose current quarter's performances constitute 25 percent of the current quarter's radio and television performances of all BMI songs, there is a *midlevel* bonus payment of 2.5 times the base rate. An *upper-level* bonus payment of 2.5 times the base rate applies to those songs with the next higher cumulative history whose current quarter's performances constitute 15 percent of the current quarter's radio and television performances of all songs. A *super-bonus* payment of 4 times the base rate is given to those songs with the highest cumulative history whose current quarter's performances make up 10 percent of the current quarter's radio and television performances of all BMI songs. Bonus payments are instead of, and not in addition to, the base rate.

Super-bonus status has been heralded in the past by a special BMI awards ceremony. Some of the songs in this category are "Amapola," "Bye Bye Love," "Don't Be Cruel," "Killing Me Softly with His Song," "Never on Sunday," "Sounds of Silence," "Sunrise, Sunset," and "Up, Up and Away."

Regardless of its prior cumulative history, any song that has 150,000 or more U.S. radio and local television performances in one quarter will be awarded, for all such performances in that quarter, the next higher level of bonus payment than it would ordinarily be entitled to receive.

BMI provides for immediate entry to a super-bonus level for songs identified originally as "show music." These songs originate in (1) a first-class Broadway show or (2) an off-Broadway show that opened after October 1, 1966, and released an original-cast album.

Special credit is also stipulated for a "movie work." This is described as a complete musical work originating in and performed for not less than 40 consecutive seconds as a feature work or theme in a full-length theatrical or television motion picture lasting 90 minutes or more that is released in the United States after October 1, 1966. Such a work is awarded not less than the midlevel bonus payment.

While U.S. network television and public broadcasting station feature performances are counted in computing the cumulative history of a song for bonus purposes, such performances themselves are not eligible for bonus payments.

Advances to Writers and Publishers

From its inception in 1940, BMI followed a policy of granting advances of monies to publishers and writers who negotiated for them. In 1966, ASCAP followed suit. In each case the advances were recoupable and payable only out of earnings that would otherwise be payable to the recipient of the advance. Soon after the 1983 antitrust decision against ASCAP and BMI in the Buffalo Broadcasting case discussed earlier in this chapter, both ASCAP and BMI ceased making advances.

Despite the reversal on appeal and the refusal of the U.S. Supreme Court in 1985 to review the decision, the societies have not reinstated the general policy of making advances. BMI, however, encourages certain significant musical theater, concert, and jazz composers and publishers by agreements for guaranteed annual payments. Some emergency advances are also available from BMI and ASCAP for such contingencies as disability and death.

Loan Assistance

With the cessation of ordinary advances by ASCAP and BMI there has arisen a greater need on the part of some writers and publishers for bank loans or loans from other third parties.

BMI currently has excellent relations with Bank of America, which is headquartered in Nashville, Tennessee. When the bank makes a BMI member writer a loan of 70 percent of average 3-year earnings, BMI transfers 100 percent of the writer's or publisher's account, foreign and domestic. The member writer's royalties are assigned directly to the bank. The bank offers a preferred interest rate, historically as low as 1 point above prime. The bank runs a normal credit check on the applicant and is provided with information from BMI about the affiliate's royalty income stream. Mere affiliation with BMI alone is not sufficient to secure such a low-interest loan; such loans are only possible if the writer can show a reliable past and continuing flow of performance royalties. Because of the process of funneling funds directly to the bank, in some cases where the writer or publisher has a particularly strong catalog, BMI has been able to influence the acceptance of its affiliates.

The Bank of America has a similar arrangement with ASCAP for member loans. ASCAP and BMI use the same procedure with any bank nominated by its affiliate or member, but many banks are unfamiliar with the system and Bank of America thus has a preferred status.

ASCAP maintains two separate and distinct loan services to its members. While offering bank services similar to BMI, ASCAP also offers its members a credit union membership through USAlliance Federal Credit Union. USAlliance offers ASCAP members a variety of services, including low-interest loans, 24-hour customer service, 24-hour worldwide ATM service, and retirement plans. USAlliance also offers services exclusively to ASCAP members such as direct deposit of performance royalties, loans based upon the value of the member's catalog, interest-only payments for royalty-secured loans, and a member services staff specifically trained to deal with the unique needs of ASCAP members.

Insurance Plans

ASCAP and BMI both offer insurance coverage for health and musical instruments. ASCAP arranges health coverage through CNA Insurance Company and dental insurance through CIGNA Insurance. ASCAP has made an agreement with Sterling & Sterling to provide insurance coverage against theft, loss, and other insurable damage for instruments, equipment, computers, and software. This coverage is intended to supplement other types of insurance, such as homeowner, which usually do not cover this type of material. As part of its musical instrument insurance, ASCAP also arranges studio liability insurance to protect studio owners from suits involving bodily injury and property damage.

BMI arranges medical, dental, life, and musical instrument insurance to its members through 10 distinct coverage options. The musical instrument insurance, administered by J&H Marsh & McLennan covers loss for any type of musical instrument or electronic equipment; it also covers sheet music from theft, fire, vandalism, and natural disasters all over the globe.

SESAC has insurance coverage available to its affiliates around the country through Near North Insurance Brokerage of New York. Group medical insurance, excess major medical insurance, Medicare supplemental insurance, accidental death and dismemberment (AD&D) insurance, group term life insurance, and equipment insurance are all available.

Writer Awards

ASCAP has a system of "awards to writers whose works have a unique prestige value for which adequate compensation would not otherwise be received by such writers, and to writers whose works are performed substantially in media not surveyed by the society." There is a two-part special awards panel composed of people of standing who are not ASCAP members: the Popular Production Panel makes special monetary awards to popular music composers, and the Standard Awards Panel allocates such awards to composers of symphonic and concert music. In 1998 a total of $1.8 million was awarded. For popular music awards, applications must be filed by December 1 and May 1 of each year for writer members receiving $15,000 or less a year from regular ASCAP distributions.

For more than 40 years, BMI has presented annual cash awards to student composers of serious music. Six of the recipients of these awards have subsequently received Pulitzer Prizes. The awards, aggregating $15,000 annually, are available to students under the age of 27 who reside in the Western Hemisphere. Awards recipients are selected by a panel of distinguished composers, musicians, and publishers.

SESAC honors its top songs and songwriters throughout the year with various awards ceremonies. Awards are based on cumulative broadcast performances for a 12-month period.

Foreign Collections

Both ASCAP and BMI play a valuable international role for publishers, writers, and users of music. They collect from abroad for their members or affiliates and collect from users in the United States on behalf of foreign societies. Foreign collections are made through affiliated societies in each country and remitted through the domestic organization. It would be a most difficult task for each writer or publisher to supervise the licensing of rights in every country of the world where American music is used. ASCAP has more than 40 foreign affiliates, and BMI has substantially the same; most often the same foreign society represents both organizations, for the United States is unusual in having more than one performing right organization.

BMI charges 3.6 percent of foreign collections as a service fee, which is deducted from remittances to its affiliated writers and publishers. Revenues received by ASCAP from foreign sources are distributed to writer and publisher members on a current-performance basis. ASCAP makes an overhead charge of about 3.5 percent for its foreign collection services. ASCAP distributes foreign revenues to members on the basis of performances reported by the foreign society if the revenue from the society exceeds $200,000 a year. The reports furnished to ASCAP allocate credit in reasonably identifiable form separately by compositions performed and indicate the members in interest.

ASCAP distributes foreign income to its members based on reports received from local societies, even when the fees remitted are under $200,000, as long as the reports identify the works performed and the ASCAP members in interest. ASCAP receives more than $200,000 per year from Australia, Austria, Belgium, Canada, Denmark, England, France, Germany, Holland, Italy, Japan, Spain, Sweden, and Switzerland. With the exception of Canada, a member's credits in these countries are used as the basis of proportional distribution of all other foreign income that is not received in accordance with surveying reports. A similar procedure is used for the distribution of foreign film and television income when it is also not distributed in accordance with surveying reports.

A great majority of American music publishers, despite the convenience of collecting through ASCAP or BMI, have their share of foreign collections in important countries paid to foreign subpublishers or agents. They explain that a local subpublisher will expedite collections and will be more vigilant in claiming rights; some publishers desire to have foreign revenue collected abroad and retained there for capital acquisitions or other local expenditures. Another purpose is to maximize the advances to be paid to the American publisher.

ASCAP and BMI have achieved a major correction of expediting delayed foreign receipts, thus benefiting their writer members and those publisher members who elect to have their foreign performance earnings collected other than through subpublishers. Examples of expedited payments were shown in the ASCAP February 1999 distribution, which covered Sweden, Switzerland, Japan, and Germany through December 1997 and an even more expedited distribution from France and Britain through June 1998. BMI was able to make similar accelerated distributions.

A major cause of alarm for American publishers and writers is the large sum of foreign performance collections not accounted for because of claimed difficulties in identifying American songs under translated or new local titles. Such so-called unclaimed monies go into general funds that are distributed by the foreign performing rights society among its membership, without participation by American writers or publishers. This "black box" distribution can be increased by the failure of the American publisher to appoint a local representative to identify and claim a song in its varied forms. On the other hand, the advantage of having a local subpublisher or agent tends to be offset by the participation of the local representative in the publisher receipts.

Often a subpublication agreement allows the subpublisher to designate a local translator or adapter of the song lyric, who is entitled, among other things, to 25 percent of the total writer's share of performance royalties in the territory. In a number of countries, the translator or adapter is paid 25 percent of the monies that would normally belong to the original writers, regardless of whether the performance was of the original lyric or of the translated or adapted lyric. This is true even when the two versions have different titles and there is no problem identifying which version was performed. To protect their writers, American publishers may prohibit translations or adaptations without their consent, especially where the original lyric version is likely to have significant usage. (For a further discussion of subpublishing, see Chapter 21, "Foreign Publishing.")

Dramatic Performance Rights

Dramatic performance rights, frequently called "grand rights," are to be distinguished from nondramatic performance rights, or "small rights," by the type of use involved and in the practical manner of who administers the rights.

Both the 1909 and the 1976 Copyright Acts grant the exclusive right to perform or represent a copyrighted work publicly if it is a dramatic work. A dramatic work includes material dramatic in character such as plays, dramatic scripts designed for radio or television broadcast, pantomimes, ballets, musical comedies, and operas. In contrast to a nondramatic work such as a musical composition, compulsory licenses under the Copyright Act of 1976 for phonograph recordings, jukebox performances, and performances on public broadcasting systems do not apply to dramatic works. Consequently, the copyright owner of the dramatic work *My Fair Lady* has the absolute exclusive right to authorize or to withhold authorization of the recording or performance in public of the musical play.

A dramatic performance does not make the material a dramatic work. An example of a dramatic performance might be the portrayal of the storyline of the song "Moonlight Cocktail" in a dramatic fashion, such as for a television show using background scenery, props, and character action to depict the plot of the composition.

In practice, however, it is not simple to define a dramatic performance. A leading negotiator on behalf of broadcasters, the late Joseph A. McDonald, said in connection with ASCAP negotiations: "What constitutes a dramatic rendition is a very difficult thing to define ... even though we undertook to be as specific as possible in defining what would constitute a dramatic performance, it still leaves room—wide room—for interpretation."

The ASCAP television license represents the music industry and broadcasting industry representatives' best effort to reach a definition of dramatic performance rights. The effort is necessary because ASCAP obtains from members only nondramatic public performance rights, not dramatic performance rights. Concerning the dramatization on television of a single musical composition that does not necessarily stem from a musical play or other dramatic production, the latest television license states:

> Any performance of a separate musical composition which is not a dramatic performance, as defined herein, shall be deemed to be a nondramatic performance. For the purposes of this agreement, a dramatic performance shall mean a performance of a musical composition on a television program in which there is a definite plot depicted by action and where the performance of the musical composition is woven into and carries forward the plot and its accompanying action. The use of dialogue to establish a mere program format or the use of any nondramatic device merely to introduce a performance of a composition shall not be deemed to make such performance dramatic.

The television license defines the dramatic performance of dramatic musical works such as musical plays as follows:

> This license does not extend to or include the public performance by television broadcasting or otherwise of any rendition or performance of (a) any opera, operetta, musical comedy, play or like production, as such, in whole or in part, or (b) any composition from any opera, operetta, musical comedy, play or like production (whether or not such opera, operetta, musical comedy, play or like production was presented on the stage or in motion picture form) in a manner which recreates the performance of such composition with substantially such distinctive scenery or costumes as was used in a presentation of such opera, operetta, musical comedy, play or like production (whether or not such opera, operetta, musical comedy, play or like production was presented on the stage or in motion picture form).

Radio stations must also take care not to make dramatic uses of music in sequence from the show without specific authorization over and above their regular ASCAP or BMI license. Most radio station problems in this field relate to playing original-cast albums in the same sequence as the dramatic presentation. Under industry practice, no objection is ordinarily made by the copyright owners to the unlimited playing in sequence of instrumentals from cast albums or to the playing in sequence of up to two vocals and an instrumental. Some record companies and publishers obtain clearances for the unrestricted sequential playing of tunes from cast albums and so notify the broadcasting stations.

The standard BMI contract with affiliated writers and publishers gives BMI the right to license dramatic performances, but these rights are restricted. As a result, BMI is not authorized to license the performances of more than one song or aria from an opera, operetta, or musical comedy, or more than 5 minutes from a ballet if the performance is accompanied by the dramatic action, costumes, or scenery of that opera, operetta, musical comedy, or ballet. The writers and publishers of a work may jointly, by written notice to BMI, exclude from the grant of rights to BMI any performances of more than 30 minutes' duration of a work that is an opera, operetta, or musical comedy; exceptions are (1) the score of a theatrical film when performed with the film and (2) the score written for a radio or television program when performed with the program.

The standard SESAC license excludes grand rights, which it states includes "the right to perform in whole or in part dramatico-musical and dramatic works in a dramatic setting." These rights are licensed separately by SESAC.

Where a performance is found to be dramatic, the presentation of the whole or part of a musical play will usually be administered by the writers, based on rights reserved to them by Dramatists Guild contracts. In the case of most music publishers who publish show music, copyright is maintained in the name of the writer, and, accordingly, publishers do not acquire dramatic rights. In many instances, shows previously produced on the Broadway stage are licensed by writers' agents such as Tams-Witmark Music Library and Rodgers & Hammerstein Repertory to amateur and stock groups and to television for dramatic performances.

For music not originating in plays, operas, and the like, the copyright is normally held by the music publisher, who obtains the dramatization rights, although some writer contracts, such as those of the Songwriters Guild, require consent of the writer for the dramatization of a composition. There are also some contracts, especially older ones, where the writer specifically reserved all dramatic rights.

15

Mechanical Rights

The copyright owner owns the exclusive right to reproduce and distribute to the public copyrighted musical compositions on phonorecords, which include compact discs, tapes, and any other material object in which sounds other than those accompanying motion pictures and other audiovisual works are fixed. This right is commonly called a *mechanical right* and the authority to exercise this right is called a *mechanical license*. These terms date from the days when records were reproduced mechanically, rather than electronically. Mechanical rights are an important and lucrative aspect of copyright, different from other rights protected under copyright, such as synchronization rights used in motion pictures, video, and television; print rights; and public performance rights.

Until 1909, anyone could, freely and without compensation to the copyright owner, reproduce copyrighted music by mechanical means. Under the Copyright Act of 1909, Congress recognized for the first time the copyright owner's exclusive ownership of recording and mechanical reproduction rights in musical works. Congress's reason for doing so was twofold. Not only did it want to protect the composer's rights of mechanical reproduction, it also sought to prevent the creation of a monopoly in this area. At the time, millions of piano rolls (the ancestor of records) were being sold every year. The Aeolian Company, a leading manufacturer of piano rolls, had made exclusive contracts with most of the major music publishers to reproduce all the compositions that they owned or controlled. Section 1 (e) of the 1909 Copyright Act changed that. It provided that if the copyright owner used or permitted the use of a copyrighted composition for mechanical reproduction, then anyone else might also mechanically reproduce the composition on payment to the copyright proprietor of a royalty originally set at 2 cents "on each such part manufactured." This is usually referred to as a *compulsory license* and the license rate is referred to as the *statutory rate*. (See also "Compulsory Mechanical License for Recordings" in Chapter 10.)

Although the compulsory license provision called for the payment of the statutory rate "on each such part manufactured," the music industry has interpreted this provision to mean that payment is required for each composition on a record, that is, for each song. (Note that, except for soundtrack records, the motion picture and television industries derive no benefit from the statutory rate; they must seek negotiated synchronization licenses from copyright owners for each use.)

Under the Copyright Act of 1976, the concept of a compulsory mechanical license was continued and clarified. If phonorecords of a nondramatic composition have been distributed to the public with the authorization of the copyright owner, any other person may record and distribute phonorecords of the work by giving a specified notice and paying a statutory royalty. A record is considered distributed if possession has been "voluntarily and permanently parted with."

In 1987, the National Music Publishers Association, the Songwriters Guild of America, and the Recording Industry Association of America negotiated a joint 10-year mechanical royalty rate with the Copyright Royalty Tribunal, which had jurisdiction over determining rates. (The CRT was established under the Copyright Act of 1976 and replaced in 1992 by a three-person ad hoc panel called the Copyright Arbitration Royalty Panel, CARP; see Chapter 10.) Under the joint proposal, effective January 1, 1988, the statutory mechanical royalty rate was set at 5.25 cents per composition up to 5 minutes' duration, or 1 cent per minute or fraction thereof, whichever was higher. This royalty rate increase was based on changes in the U.S. Consumer Price Index (CPI) between January 1, 1986, and September 30, 1987. Future rate adjustments were also stipulated, as follows:

- Rates were to be based on changes in the CPI measured from September to September every 2 years.
- Adjusted royalty rates would become effective on January 1 of the following year, starting in January 1990, and every 2 years thereafter.
- Rate could not decline below 5 cents per composition up to 5 minutes' duration or rise more than 25 percent within any 2-year span, regardless of changes in the CPI.

As of January 1, 1994, the statutory royalty rate was increased to 6.6 cents per composition/1.25 cents per minute. On January 1,1998, the statutory rate became 7.1 cents per composition/1.35 cents per minute, and on January 1, 2000, it increased to 7.55 cents per composition/1.45 cents per minute.

The compulsory license provisions of the Copyright Act of 1976 expressly permit the making of an "arrangement of the work to the extent necessary to conform it to the style or manner of interpretation of the performance." Even a sound-alike recording, with an arrangement similar to that of a prior recording, is permitted. However, a compulsory licensee must avoid changing the basic melody or fundamental character of the work. The author of an arrangement cannot claim a derivative copyright in the arrangement without the consent of the copyright owner.

Compulsory mechanical licenses under the Copyright Act of 1976 apply solely to audio recordings primarily intended for distribution to the public for private use. They are not available for purposes of background music services, broadcast transcriptions, or commercial motion picture synchronization. A compulsory license applies only to the use of musical compositions in new recordings. There can be no compulsory license for compositions used in the duplication ("dubbing") of a prior sound recording, unless consent has been obtained from the owner of the prior recording, which itself was fixed lawfully. This acts as a significant restriction on the pirating of recordings.

Parting with Possession and Returns

Under the Copyright Act of 1976 a record is not considered distributed (and no statutory mechanical royalty is due) unless its possession has been "voluntarily and permanently parted with." In 1976, the 1976 House Committee on the Judiciary stated:

> The concept of "distribution" comprises any act by which the person exercising the compulsory license voluntarily relinquishes possession of a phonorecord (considered as a fungible unit), regardless of whether the distribution is to the public, passes title, constitutes a gift, or is sold, rented, leased, or loaned, unless it is actually returned and the transaction canceled. (H.R. Rep. No. 1476, 94th Cong., 2d Sess. 106)

In the legislative history preceding the Copyright Act of 1976, there is recognition of a record industry practice of distributing records with return privileges.

> Phonorecords are distributed to wholesalers and retailers with the privilege of returning unsold copies for credit or exchange. As a result, the number of recordings that have been "permanently" distributed will not usually be known until some time—six or seven months on the average—after the initial distribution. In recognition of this problem, it has become a well-established industry practice, under negotiated licenses, for record companies to maintain reasonable reserves of the mechanical royalties due the copyright owners, against which royalties on the returns can be offset. The Committee recognizes that this practice may be consistent with the statutory requirements for monthly compulsory license accounting reports, but recognizes the possibility that, without proper safeguards, the maintenance of such reserves could be manipulated to avoid making payments of the full amounts owing to copyright owners.

The committee recommended that the regulations to be published by the Register of Copyrights should

> Contain detailed provisions ensuring that the ultimate disposition of every phonorecord made under a compulsory license is accounted for, and that payment is made for every phonorecord "voluntarily and permanently" distributed. In particular the Register should prescribe a point in time when ... a phonorecord will be considered "permanently distributed," and should prescribe the situation in which a compulsory licensee is barred from maintaining reserves (e.g., situations in which the compulsory licensee has frequently failed to make payments in the past).

The Register of Copyrights has prescribed regulations that, in effect, give a compulsory licensee 9 months at the most, from the month in which the records are relinquished from possession, to hold mechanical royalties in a reserve fund. However, the regulations deny the privilege of holding reserve to a habitual nonpayer of mechanical royalties. Such a licensee is one who, within 3 years from when a phonorecord was parted from possession, has had final judgment rendered against it for failing to pay mechanical royalties on phonorecords, or within such period has been found in any proceeding involving bankruptcy, insolvency, receivership, assignment for the benefit of creditors, or similar action to have failed to pay such royalties.

The Register of Copyrights did not establish any specific criteria for what a reasonable reserve would be. This is governed by general accounting principles.

Notice of Intention

Anyone who proposes to invoke the benefit of compulsory licensing provisions under the Copyright Act of 1976 must serve a "notice of intention" in a form and manner prescribed by the Register of Copyrights. The notice is similar to the "notice of intention to use" under the prior 1909 law. Pursuant to Section 115 of the 1976 Copyright Act, the notice must be sent to the copyright owner either before any records are distributed or within 30 days after distribution. If the records of the Copyright Office fail to identify the copyright owner and his or her address, then the notice requirements can be met by sending the notice to the Copyright Office along with a $12 fee.

Failure to timely serve a compulsory license notice "forecloses the possibility of a compulsory license." In other words, the making and distribution of phonorecords is copyright infringement and the copyright owner has various remedies available (See Chapter 19, Copyright Infringement).

Compulsory License Accountings

Under the Copyright Act of 1976, a compulsory licensee must make monthly royalty payments on or before the 20th of each month for records made and distributed during the preceding month. Accompanying each payment must be a detailed accounting statement made under oath. The copyright owner is also entitled to cumulative annual statements certified by a certified public accountant.

Under the 1976 Copyright Act there is an automatic termination of a compulsory license for failure to render monthly payments and the appropriate accountings when due if the default is not cured within 30 days after written notice by the copyright owner. If a default continues beyond this period, there is an automatic termination of the compulsory license. In addition, once a license has been terminated, parties can be sued for copyright infringement if they continue to make and distribute phonorecords for which royalties are unpaid.

Copyright Owner Identification

There is no obligation under the Copyright Act of 1976 to pay compulsory license royalties to a copyright owner unless the owner is identified in the registration or other records of the Copyright Office. A copyright owner is entitled to receive compulsory license royalties for phonorecords made and distributed after this identification is made, but the owner cannot collect royalties for phonorecords made and distributed before the identification. This provides a strong incentive for early copyright registration by an owner.

Negotiated Licenses

The procedure for monthly accountings and payments under the Copyright Act of 1976 is a strong deterrent to resorting to compulsory licenses. In the music industry it is standard practice for a record manufacturer to account for and pay mechanical royalties quarterly, not monthly, and statements are not usually made under oath. In addition, it is unnecessary to serve a notice of intention to obtain a compulsory license if the publisher issues a negotiated license. (A sample mechanical license form is shown in the accompanying CD-ROM.)

A compulsory license is inapplicable to the first recording of a copyrighted composition. The copyright owner has complete control over his or her decision to make the first recording as well as over the terms and conditions with respect to that recording of the composition. Thus, the copyright owner may insist that higher mechanical royalties be paid, or that the record couple two compositions controlled by the copyright owner, or that the next recording by the same artist include a copyrighted composition from the catalog of the copyright proprietor.

Finally, and most importantly, the possibility of obtaining a mechanical royalty rate of less than the statutory rate militates in favor of a negotiated license. By reason of the compulsory license provisions of the 1976 Copyright Act, the statutory rate has the effect of serving as a ceiling on negotiated mechanical license rates for records distributed in the United States. In practice, however, publishers usually grant initial licenses at the prevailing statutory rate and without additional restriction. It is rare that the maximum statutory rate is exceeded. Indeed, record companies, by the use of "controlled composition" clauses, usually provide for mechanical licenses to be issued at the "minimum statutory rate," such as 75 percent of the statutory rate. By doing this, record companies mean to make applicable the per-song statutory rate when the per-minute statutory rate would be higher.

The Harry Fox Agency

The National Music Publishers Association (NMPA) is a trade association of music publishers. It represents the interests of more than 700 of the leading U.S. music publishers in all pertinent national and international copyright issues, including legislation and U.S. intellectual trade policy. NMPA's far-ranging activities are supported in large part by commissions earned by its wholly owned subsidiary, the Harry Fox Agency, which is located at 711 Third Avenue, New York, NY 10017; telephone: 212-834-0100; e-mail: clientserve@harryfox.com; Web site: www.nmpa.org/hfa.html.

The Harry Fox Agency was established in 1927 to administer mechanical and synchronization rights in the United States for publishers who wished to use its services on a commission basis. The agency represents more than 20,000 music publishers, many of whom are unaffiliated with NMPA. The agency's annual gross collections exceeded $400 million in 1997, reflecting a steady yearly increase. Collections have grown an average of 26 percent annually in the last decade. This was largely due to an increase in mechanical license income from compact discs, during a period when the penetration of CD hardware in the United States rose from 37 to 52 percent in a 3-year period.

The agency's services include the issuance of mechanical and synchronization licenses and the supervision of collections from record companies. It employs auditing firms to regularly check the books of record companies and other licensees in order to ensure proper accountings of mechanical license fees. On behalf of publishers that it represents, the Harry Fox Agency has instituted litigation to pursue delinquent record firms and record pirates, as well as to settle disputes stemming from differing interpretations of the Copyright Act. For its mechanical license services, the agency charges up to 4.5 percent commission on a collection. For its motion picture synchronization licensing services, the agency charges a 10 percent commission, with a maximum of $250 per song. For all other synchronization licensing (including broadcast and standard cable TV, home video, and commercials) and electrical transcription licensing (including syndicated radio, background music, and in-flight music), the agency charges a 5 percent commission, with a maximum of approximately $2,200 per television transaction. The agency issued more than 226,000 mechanical licenses in 1997.

Under the basic mechanical license issued by the Harry Fox Agency on behalf of the publishers it represents, the record company must account and pay for all records manufactured and distributed. The license calls for quarterly accountings and payments and provides that failure to make accountings and payments constitutes grounds for the revocation of the license. It also states that service of a notice of intention to obtain a compulsory license is waived.

The license further states that the record company has requested a license under the compulsory license provision of the Copyright Act. It provides that the licensees have all the rights granted to and all the obligations imposed on users of copyrighted works under the compulsory license provision, with certain exceptions relating to quarterly instead of monthly or annual accountings and a waiver of the notice requirements.

The courts have held that the Harry Fox license form is a modification of the compulsory license provisions of the Copyright Act and is not a separate, private contract. This preserves the statutory remedies afforded by the Copyright Act as well as federal jurisdiction. The Harry Fox license is generally nonassignable, and a separate license is required for each type of phonorecord configuration the licensee desires to manufacture or distribute, (i.e., CDs, cassettes, and singles).

In 1987, in the case of *T. B. Harms Co. v. Jem Records* (655 F. Supp. 1575), a federal district court in New Jersey ruled that according to the U.S. Copyright Act of 1976, the importation of phonorecords into the United States (regardless of whether such records were legally manufactured abroad and were subject to royalties at the place of manufacture) still requires a license from the owner of the U.S. copyright in the songs contained in the imported record. Although this case was never appealed to the Third Circuit Court of Appeals and is not technically binding in other judicial circuits, since that time the Harry Fox Agency has required that import licenses be issued to record importers for the mechanical use of copyrighted music. Under this type of mechanical license, royalties are payable on all goods imported, whether or not they are ultimately sold.

Other U.S. Mechanical Rights Organizations

A number of other agencies handle the licensing of mechanical rights in the United States. The American Mechanical Rights Agency (AMRA) was organized in 1961. AMRA licenses mechanical and synchronization rights for music publishers and writers, charging a fee of 5 percent of the gross collections. AMRA also represents a number of foreign mechanical rights societies. AMRA is located at 1888 Century Park E., Suite 222, Los Angeles, CA 90067; telephone: 310-785-1800; e-mail: amracalif@aol.com.

Other firms offering services to publishers and writers include Copyright Management and Publisher's Licensing Corporation. Copyright Management is located at 209 10th Avenue S., Suite 507, Nashville, TN 37203; telephone: 615-321-0652. Publisher's Licensing Corporation is located at PO Box 1648, FDR Station, New York, NY 10150-1648; telephone: 212-228-0660. The annual receipts of these other U.S. mechanical rights organizations are estimated to be very small in comparison with those of the Harry Fox Agency.

The Songwriters Guild of America (SGA) has a catalog administration plan for its songwriter members who retain publishing rights. The Harry Fox Agency reports to and through the SGA for those writer-publisher members who use its services. (See Chapter 22, "The Writer as Publisher.")

The Canadian Mechanical Rights Organization

In 1976, the Canadian Musical Reproduction Rights Agency Limited (CMRRA) assumed the functions previously carried out by the Harry Fox Agency in Canada. CMRRA charges a fee of 5 percent of the collections made for any publishers. American music publishers deal mainly with CMRRA, which is located at 56 Wellesley Street W, Toronto, Ontario M5S 2S3; telephone: 416-926-1966; fax: 416-926-7521; e-mail: www.cmra.ca. Other Canadian mechanical and synchronization licensing agents deal with French-language recordings in Quebec, as well as with works originating in certain European countries such as Italy, Spain, and France. The main alternative agency is Société du Droit de Reproduction des Auteurs (SODRAC), located at 759 Victoria Square, Suite 420, Montreal, PQ H2Y 2J7; telephone: 514-845-3268; fax: 514-845-3401; e-mail: sodrac@login.net.

International Mechanical Rights Societies

In 1993, the Harry Fox Agency established the Fox Agency International (FAI) as a special-purpose subsidiary with offices in Singapore, Taiwan, and other locations in Asia. Through its agreement with the Audio Publishing Commercial Association of the Republic of China (APAROC), which represents more than 100 Pacific Rim record companies, the FAI is able to protect and promote authors' and publishers' rights throughout the Pacific Rim.

In addition, the Harry Fox Agency has affiliations with various territorial mechanical right societies and can make arrangements for them to act as agents to collect local mechanical license fees on behalf of U.S. publishers in more than 60 countries other than Canada. The fees charged by the local societies tend to average 15 percent, to which is added the 4.5 percent charge the Fox Agency applies to receipts it handles. These are some of the principal foreign mechanical rights organizations that make collections for the Harry Fox Agency.

- Argentina: SADAIC
- Australia and New Zealand: AMCOS
- Bolivia, Colombia, and Peru: FONOPERU
- Former Soviet Union countries: RAO
- France, the former French colonies, Belgium, and Luxembourg: Société pour l'Administration du Droit de Reproduction Mécanique (SDRM)
- Germany, Austria, Bulgaria, Rumania, Hungary, Czechoslovakia, Poland, South Korea, Taiwan, Yugoslavia, Turkey, and the Philippines: GEMA

- Great Britain, Scotland, and Northern Ireland: Mechanical Copyright Protection Society (MCPS)
- Israel: ACUM
- Italy: SIAE
- Japan: JASRAC
- Netherlands: STEMRA
- Portugal: SPA
- Scandinavia (Denmark, Estonia, Finland, Iceland, Lithuania, Norway, Sweden): Nordisk Copyright Bureau (NCB)
- Spain: SGAE
- Switzerland: SUISA
- Trinidad and Tobago: COTT

Some of the societies handle performing rights licensing and collections as well as mechanical rights licensing and collections. American publishers can make direct arrangements for the collection of mechanical right fees in some foreign territories; among these are MCPS, SDRM, GEMA, and NCB. JASRAC and SIAE do not permit such arrangements. Through direct dealings with mechanical right societies, American publishers can eliminate the Harry Fox Agency charge of 4.5 percent, but they forgo the convenience of having different territories serviced through the one agency.

Each society operates under the customs and laws of its applicable home base. However, in the European Union, consolidated negotiations for all of the continental countries have resulted in a rate of 9.01 percent of published price to dealer (PPD) until June 30, 2000, at which date, a new negotiated rate will be applicable.

The Writer's Share of Mechanical Fees

In contracts between publishers and songwriters it is standard for the writer to receive 50 percent of the mechanical license fees collected by the contracting ("original") publisher. Where foreign subpublishers are entitled to retain 50 percent of the mechanical fees collected by them and they remit the balance to the original publisher, the writer in effect receives one-quarter of the amount collected at the source by the foreign subpublisher. In computing royalties due to the original publisher (and which the original publisher shares with the writer), it is common to disregard charges made by the local mechanical rights society that collected mechanical license fees from local record companies in the first instance, since the royalty to the original writer is customarily computed only on the balance remitted by the subpublisher to the original publisher (after the subpublisher has deducted its charges).

It should be noted that the writer share of public performance income is more favorable to the writer because it is computed at the source in each country and remitted through affiliated societies, whereas the writer share of mechanical income is filtered through the publisher and subpublisher.

Record Clubs

Historically, record clubs did not obtain their own mechanical licenses when they reissued products under club imprint. The record clubs aimed to be an extension of the original record manufacturer, and in most instances they relied on industry custom in paying 75 percent of either the compulsory license rate or the negotiated or controlled-composition rate for a composition re-released through a club.

The Harry Fox Agency has taken the position that clubs should no longer rely on industry custom and usage but should have specific mechanical licenses for each record club release, which sets forth the manner of computation of royalties and the basis of which an audit can be conducted. The agency noted that previous difficulties have become even greater now that many royalty statements are rendered electronically. The reason for this is the absence of an electronic database with separate licenses against which automatic tracking and verification could otherwise be done. The agency also noted that the recent *Sleepless in Seattle* decision set forth the rule that old recordings issued by a new licensee allows new licensing rates for that use and a club issuance can qualify for the new rates on which the 75 percent customary computation is made. (See page 386.) It is obviously in the best interest of publishers to update the basic mechanical royalty in view of the escalation over the years of compulsory license rates.

Title Use Restrictions

According to instructions from certain publishers, a Harry Fox Agency license may contain a restriction against the use of a licensed song as the title of a record album. Such uses may be the special concern of publishers affiliated with motion picture companies or with record companies that release soundtrack albums or original cast albums. Where the title song of a film is named after the film—for example, "Never on Sunday"—an album with the same title as the song may be confused by the public with the soundtrack album from the motion picture. The same would apply to a song from a show that has a title identical to that of the show, for example, "Oklahoma." The publishers that impose the restriction seek to avoid this confusion and regulate this type of usage.

Record Rentals

The Record Rental Act of 1984, an amendment to the Copyright Act of 1976, provides that no copies of sound recordings acquired on or after October 4, 1984, may be commercially rented, leased, or lent by the owner of the copies unless authorized by the copyright proprietors of the recordings and of the underlying musical works. This legislation represents a modification of the so-called *first-sale concept* of copyright law, according to which a purchaser of a phonorecord or an audiovisual recording, whether disc, tape, compact disc, or other configuration, had been permitted to rent, lease, or lend it without the consent of such copyright proprietors. The first-sale concept continues to apply to audiovisual recordings such as videocassettes. An unauthorized commercial rental, lease, or lending constitutes a copyright infringement subject to civil but not criminal infringement penalties under existing copyright laws.

A record company wishing to engage in the commercial rental, lease, or lending of records may negotiate a voluntary license from the music copyright owner or obtain a compulsory mechanical license. However, for the compulsory licensing of rentals, leasing, or lending, the statute requires the payment of a royalty over and above that applicable to sales of records. The compulsory licensee must share its rental, lease, or lending revenues with the music copyright proprietor in the same proportion as revenues from the sales of recordings are allocated between the copyright owners of the sound recording and the underlying music. At this writing, the royalty formula remains to be implemented by regulations to be issued by the Copyright Office.

Congressional hearings leading up to the passage of the Record Rental Act of 1984 suggested a direct link between rental, leasing, and lending activities and the making of copies of records without the permission of or compensation to the copyright owners, the recording artists, the musicians, and the composers. There was also a potential threat of a substantial loss in sales for manufacturers, distributors, and retail record stores. These factors were keys to the economic and policy concerns behind the legislation.

The Record Rental Act of 1984 provided that its provisions would become ineffective after 5 years. In 1988 the act was extended by Congress for an additional 8 years, until October 4, 1997. This "sunset provision" for the rental of records was totally removed in 1994, thus making a permanent extension. Accordingly, the commercial rental of recordings now requires the consent of both the music publisher and the record company.

16

Songwriter Contracts and Royalty Statements

An article in *Billboard* once remarked that the music business was similar to the meat-packing business in that it used everything on the animal but the squeal. (Some music critics might even include the squeal.) Yet there are songwriters who sign agreements that make specific provisions for their participation in print music receipts and receipts from the sale of phonograph records and film synchronization licenses but fail to provide for their participation in many other commercial uses, such as advertising jingles and new technologies. Many writers have found a solution to this problem by providing that they must share equally in all receipts from unspecified sources. Other writers, especially writers for theater, put the burden on the music publisher to specify sources of income in which the publisher shall have any participation.

Unfortunately, many novice songwriters sign whatever is placed before them fearing that otherwise they may jeopardize the music publisher's willingness to enter into an agreement. Unlike the typical book publishing or theatrical contract, all rights under copyright are customarily assigned to the publisher of popular music. Thus, if writers are not protected by contract, they have little hope of being safeguarded.

Duration of Copyright Protection

It is essential that both parties to a songwriter contract be fully aware that the relationship is likely to last a long time. How long a music publisher may continue to exploit and administer rights is determined both by the songwriter contract and by statute. As noted below, some contracts, such as the 1948 and 1969 Songwriters Guild contract forms, expressly limit the publisher's worldwide rights to 28 years, subject to certain notices applicable to foreign rights. With respect to songs first fixed before January 1, 1978, the Copyright Act of 1909 contained a concept of a 28-year term original of copyright and a 28-year renewal period; generally speaking, U.S. rights reverted to the author or the author's successors at the end of the initial term of copyright unless the author also expressly granted rights for the renewal term to the publisher.

However, rights would remain with the publisher in foreign territories for the full duration of copyright protection there. The Copyright Act of 1976 has added a 19-year extension to the renewal term, subject to a right of termination of the additional 19 years in favor of the author or the specified statutory heirs. It also created a right of termination of grants or licenses of U.S. rights made by the author for compositions first fixed on or after January 1, 1978. The termination becomes effective within a period of 5 years from the end of the 35th year following the date of the grant or license, provided that timely notice is given by the terminating writer or designated successors. If the grant or license covers publication, the 5-year period begins at the end of 35 years from the date of publication or 40 years from the execution of the grant, whichever is earlier. This right of termination takes precedence over contrary contractual provisions. However, the parties are free to contract for a term of rights that is less than 35 years.

Prior to passage of the Copyright Act of 1976, most songwriter contracts granted rights to the publisher for what was then the original term of U.S. copyright—28 years—and in many instances for the 28-year renewal period of U.S. copyright. This establishes a 35-year period as the minimum duration of the term of a publisher's rights, as compared to the 28-year term under the Copyright Act of 1909. In any event, whether 28 years, 35 years, or longer, the extensive length of the relationship between a songwriter and a publisher emphasizes the importance of a carefully written publishing agreement. (See Chapter 11, "Duration of Copyright and Limitation of Grants.")

Songwriters Guild Contracts

The Songwriters Guild of America (SGA), originally founded in 1931 as the Songwriters Protective Association, is an organization of songwriters with a present membership of over 5,000 writers. It is presently headquartered at 1500 Harbour Blvd., Weehawken, NJ 07087 and maintains branch offices in New York, Nashville, and Los Angeles. The organization recommends to its members that they use a standard songwriter contract form published by the SGA. The contract was originally issued in 1948, revised slightly in 1969, and amended substantially in 1978 in light of the Copyright Act of 1976.

Under the 1948 contract and the revised 1969 contract, the grant of world-wide rights to the publisher was for the original period of U.S. copyright, 28 years, or for 28 years from publication, whichever was shorter. However, writers would forfeit the right to recapture foreign copyrights, other than in Canada, if they did not give the original publisher at least 6 months' written notice of their intention to sell or assign to a third party their rights in U.S. renewal copyright or any of their rights in the United States or elsewhere for the period beyond the original grant.

The 1978 SGA contract form increased the 28-year period to a worldwide maximum of 40 years from the date of the agreement or 35 years from the first release of a commercial sound recording of a composition, whichever is earlier; however, the parties can specify a lesser period. At the expiration of this period, worldwide rights revert to the writer even though the term of copyright extends until 70 years from the death of the last surviving collaborator on a song in most major countries. Because of the contractual limitation on duration, there is no need for designated statutory notices to effectuate the right of termination under the Copyright Act of 1976. Termination is automatic and applies to worldwide rights, whereas the statutory right of termination covers only U.S. rights. (The accompanying CD-ROM includes the following SGA publications: "Ten Basic Points Your Contract Should Include," "Overview of the SGA Popular Songwriters Contract," and "Popular Songwriters Contract.")

Many music publishers argue that a recapture right on the part of the writer is wrong in principle because it fails to recognize the importance of the publisher's efforts and expenditures in establishing the popular acceptance of compositions. These music publishers attempt to obtain an assignment of copyright and full administration and publishing rights for the maximum possible period for any and all countries of the world. In negotiations between publishers and songwriters, a full understanding of the applicable statutory provisions concerning the duration and right of termination is essential.

While recognizing the merit of certain provisions in the SGA contract form, such as the right granted to the writer to participate in all possible revenue from a song, publishers contend that some clauses are outdated and tend to impede the proper administration of a publisher's functions. They assert, for instance, that a writer's consent should not be required for issuance of television or motion picture synchronization licenses. These are some of the issues discussed in this chapter.

Copyright Divisibility

Except in rare instances, the music industry customarily treats all aspects of music copyright as a single bundle of rights exclusively owned and administered by the music publisher. As owner and administrator, the music publisher handles the separate rights of mechanical reproduction, preparation of derivative works, reproduction in printed editions, and publication.

Before passage of the Copyright Act of 1976, copyright was generally considered indivisible. There could be only an inseparable ownership of the rights under copyright, although such rights might be the subject of exclusive or nonexclusive licenses. The 1976 Copyright Act expressly recognizes, for the first time, that copyright is divisible. There can therefore be a separate transfer and ownership of any of the exclusive rights that collectively comprise a copyright.

Thus, it is possible under the 1976 statute for a writer to assign to a publisher the ownership of certain rights under copyright while reserving the ownership of one or more other such rights. Conceivably, a writer could assign the ownership of some rights to one publisher and ownership of other rights to another publisher. In practice, however, a single publisher generally owns and administers all rights, except in the case of "split copyrights." (See Chapter X.)

Royalty Statements

Obtaining a satisfactory contract is only part of a songwriter's job. A writer must also know how to read the publisher's royalty statements. In the past songwriters would sometimes boast of their ignorance in this respect by saying that they filed royalty checks in the bank and royalty statements in the wastepaper basket. In an era of computerized royalty statements with code letters or numerals instead of clearly understandable designations, songwriters may be even more tempted to ignore such matters. However, machine-prepared royalty statements can contain mistakes because somewhere in the data chain there is a human operator and each operator works from a source document. Reading the royalty statement not only informs writers as to the source of their livelihood but also keeps them alert to possible areas of exploitation that may not have been tracked.

An alert writer should have in mind specific questions when reading royalty statements:

- Is a certain song's advance being charged against the writer's other songs handled by the same publisher?
- Is the 50 percent division of mechanical royalties being properly allocated among collaborators, as in the case of a song with two lyricists and only one composer, where contractual provision is made that the sole composer is entitled to half of the writer royalties?
- Is payment being made immediately in respect of a foreign advance obtained by the publisher? Or is it being withheld pending the publisher's receipt of foreign royalty statements showing actual earnings against that advance—usually a long time later?
- Is the Harry Fox Agency commission being deducted in full by the publisher from mechanical receipts?
- Are the public performance license fees collected from a motion picture producer for U.S. theater performances being distributed at the same time as the synchronization license fees?

These and other questions can be raised only if the contract contains appropriate provisions.

Recapture of Rights

Writers must try to ensure that a composition does not lie unnoticed on a publisher's shelf for an extended period of time. Under the 1978 SGA contract form, the writer is entitled to recapture rights from the publisher after 1 year from the date of the agreement, or such shorter period as may be specified, if the publisher has not made and distributed a commercial recording. However, if prior to the end of this period the publisher pays the writer a nonrecoupable bonus of $250 (or any larger amount that has been mutually agreed on), the period to obtain the release of a commercial recording is extended for up to 6 months (or such lesser period as may be specified by the parties).

Some non-SGA publishing agreements make no provision for the recapture of rights by the writer for a publisher's failure to exploit recordings. Other agreements may forestall recapture by one or more of the following acts on the part of the publisher: (1) printing sheet music copies, (2) obtaining a commercial recording of the composition, (3) licensing the music composition for inclusion in a television, motion picture, video, or dramatic production, or (4) paying a certain amount of money. The publisher may protect itself by a clause that requires the writer to give a 30-day (or longer) notice of intention to recapture, during which period the publisher may cure any default.

Printed Editions

In recent years, sales of single copies of sheet music of most songs have slowed to a mere trickle in the United States, although some hit songs can still sell in large quantities. A customary provision in a songwriter's contract is for the payment to the writer of 6 to 8 cents per copy of sheet music sold in the United States and Canada, plus 50 percent of the sheet music royalties received by the publisher for sales in other countries. (The publisher usually contracts to be paid 10 to 12.5 percent of the retail selling price of sheet music sold outside the United States and Canada.) In common practice, most printing is done under license, and 50 percent of net receipts is the basis of print music royalties, just as it is with mechanicals.

For compositions included in printed song folios, the SGA contract provides for the writer to be paid a royalty of 10 percent of the wholesale selling price (less trade discounts, if any) prorated downward by the ratio between the number of compositions written by the writer and the number of other copyrighted compositions in the folio. If the publication contains more than 25 compositions, the 10 percent royalty rate is increased by an additional 0.5 percent for each additional composition. It is not uncommon for publishers to issue deluxe higher-priced folios containing as many as 45 to 50 songs, and usually writers gladly consent to such editions and waive extra royalties.

With respect to folios, many songwriter contracts provide for the payment of a one-time fixed sum to a writer, ranging anywhere from $1 up to about $25, irrespective of the number sold. A reasonable fee should exceed 150 percent of standard royalties on first printing, whether it is of a mere 2,000 copies or more. If the lump-sum payment is reasonable no substantial harm results, since the sales of folios are often limited. There have been exceptional folios that sold in excess of 100,000 copies, such as those comprising the songs of

Paul Simon, Andrew Lloyd Webber, Michael Jackson, or Lennon-McCartney. That having been said, it is generally advisable to avoid fixed-fee buyouts.

In the exploitation of music, the publisher is called on to distribute promotional or professional copies of printed editions. These copies may be given to the A&R personnel of record companies whose function it is to acquire material that has the potential to be recorded by artists under contract to their companies. Other copies may be delivered to orchestras or vocalists in order to encourage their performance of the composition. Additional copies may be sent to managers, agents, and producers. The SGA contract and most songwriter agreements provide that the publisher is not obligated to pay royalties for promotional or professional copies.

Mechanical Rights

The songwriter grants a publisher the right to reproduce the music by mechanical means, including tapes, CDs, and records. The publisher then gives a *mechanical license* to a record company. As discussed in Chapter 15, the fee for mechanical licenses is usually based on the statutory rate. As of January 1, 1998, the royalty was 7.1 cents per composition for each phonorecord made and distributed up to 5 minutes' duration or 1.35 cents per minute or fraction thereof, whichever is greater. The rate is adjusted every 2 years according to changes in the Consumer Price Index. The rate as of January 1, 2000, is 7.55 cents per composition or 1.45 cents per minute.

In some instances the mechanical royalty for a composition included in an album will be less than for a single because of the number of compositions on the album. This is often the case where the artist is the writer and the recording agreement has a controlled-composition clause with a cap on the number of compositions. (See page 25.)

As discussed in Chapter 15, a great majority of the active publishers in the United States use the services of the Harry Fox Agency. In the agreement between a songwriter and a publisher, provision is made for the writer to share in mechanical license fees received by the publisher. The customary share is 50 percent of the publisher's receipts in the United States. This means 50 percent of 100 percent of license fee payments from U.S. record companies, after deducting the Harry Fox Agency collection charges: 4.5 percent on mechanicals, 5 percent (up to $2,200 maximum per item) on TV synchronization licenses, and 10 percent (up to $250) for motion picture synchronization licenses. For mechanical license earnings outside the United States, the writer is usually entitled to 50 percent of the net sums received domestically by the U.S. publisher.

A similar provision prevails with regard to a publisher's receipts from licensing the synchronization or reproduction of music on television, video, and motion picture soundtracks. Such licenses are referred to as *synchronization licenses.* Many publishers also use the Harry Fox Agency for the issuance of these licenses.

In promoting a new recording, a publisher may spend money in trade paper advertising and in the purchase and distribution of promotional records. These expenses are not normally chargeable either in whole or in part to the writer. Some publishers charge the writer's royalty account for one-half of these expenses by authorizing the record company to undertake the entire expense of the advertisements or promotional records and then deduct the portion of that expense that the publisher would usually bear from mechanical record royalties otherwise payable to the publisher. The publisher is obligated to pay the writer one-half of the receipts, but by allowing the record company to deduct the cost of advertising and promotion "off the top"—that is, from the mechanical royalties that it sends to the publisher—the publisher receives, and shares with the writer, reduced remittances. This practice is a violation of most songwriter agreements, including the SGA standard songwriter agreement. However, it is difficult to determine the extent of the practice without a detailed audit. The SGA recommends that all songwriter agreements include an audit provision with no time restriction.

Accountings and Audits

The SGA agreement stipulates that the publisher will account to writers either quarterly or semiannually, depending on what period is customary for the publisher, within 45 days after the end of the applicable period. Other agreements usually provide for semiannual accountings. Quarterly accountings are obviously more desirable for a writer than semiannual accountings. Naturally, a publisher seeks fewer accountings, which lessens administrative costs and overhead.

Songwriters should be alert to provisions by which they waive any objections to royalty accountings unless such objections are lodged within a given period, such as 1 year. These provisions are generally enforceable. Of course, a publisher is entitled to some protection against complaints received long after events transpire.

Frequently, a basis for complaint regarding an accounting can be found only on an audit of the books of the publisher. Many reputable publishers will cooperate with a request for an audit even in the absence of a contractual provision permitting the songwriter to audit. Other publishers require such contractual provisions before they are willing to allow an audit. A contractual provision has the advantage of fixing rights and obligations without requiring a court order, although such orders are generally granted, even in the absence of contractual provisions.

Under the SGA contract, any writer may demand a detailed breakdown of royalties on 60 days' written notice, showing the receipts attributable to each record label for each song as well as the details of other uses and the number of copies sold in each royalty category. The writer must pay the cost of the examination; but if the audit reveals that the writer is owed 5 percent or more of the amount shown on royalty statements the publisher must pay for the cost of the examination, up to 50 percent of the amount found to be due to the writer. When a record company and a publishing company are under common ownership and the publishing company does its own licensing of sound recordings, the writer may examine the books of the record company if royalty payments are questioned.

The SGA Collection Plan is a compulsory system of collection and auditing required of all members of SGA. It is designed to avoid the expense and delay involved for a songwriter in the auditing of publisher's books. The charge is 5.75 percent of the writer royalties collected from publishers, with a maximum charge of $2,170 a year. Under the system the writer directs publishers to send his or her checks and statements to the SGA office. Not all publisher accounts are audited, since the time and expense would be inordinate. SGA accountants make a random selection of publishers for the purpose of auditing the accounts for several years at the same time. Many responsible publishers welcome the opportunity to be audited in order to reassure their writers of their accounting integrity. Furthermore, by dealing with an accountant who represents many writers, the publisher avoids the loss of time required to make individual explanations to writers.

Many songwriters have requested that SGA charge only for collections and audits to particular publishers designated by the writers, rather than to all publishers audited by the SGA. This is not permitted on the ground that the 5.75 percent fee, in respect of publishers who pay regularly and honestly, is required to subsidize the expense of auditing and collecting with regard to the less scrupulous publishers. However, if a publisher is owned in whole or in part to the extent of at least 25 percent by an SGA writer, the songwriter can exclude the royalties from that publisher in the collection plan and still use the collection service for other publishers.

Default

Occasionally a songwriter complains that royalties are not paid when due and that statements are insufficient in detail. In the face of continued refusals to account, a claim can be made of a breach in the contract between the writer and the publisher. The writer can sue in the courts for an accounting, and under usual court procedure the writer will be able to examine the books and records of the publisher in support of the writer's action.

The writer may also take the position that the breach justifies termination of the contract and that on such a termination all rights in the copyright revert to the writer. It may be expected that the publisher will strongly oppose this position. A court has to decide whether the breach is material or immaterial—that is, whether or not it goes to the essence of the agreement and therefore permits the aggrieved party to cancel it. A refusal to account for one period may well be deemed immaterial, whereas failure to account for several periods, during which repeated requests for accountings were made by the writer, may be judged material.

The prospect of court litigation discourages many songwriters from moving to obtain accountings or to nullify their agreements with publishers. There are at least two practical approaches for a writer to avoid having to pay for litigation. Under one approach, the writer may assign all publication rights to another publisher, and the writer and publisher may join in notifying the performing rights organization that the original publisher's rights have been canceled and that the publication rights have been vested in a new publisher. On such notice BMI may hold up payments of the publisher's share of performance royalties to the original publisher with a doubtful credit standing. ASCAP will hold back payments of the publisher's share of performance monies but will resume payments within 6 months if a suit is not filed or within 1 year if a filed suit is not adjudicated, provided the original publisher files an agreement to indemnify ASCAP against claims by the other publisher and, in addition, in disputes over renewal rights, files documentary support of its position. The performing rights organization's action may by itself be sufficient to make the original publisher willing to negotiate an agreeable settlement of the controversy.

Using the second approach, the writer, as a condition of the assignment to the new publisher, may require it to finance all litigation to establish the new publisher's rights to the material.

Obviously, it is to the writer's advantage to insert a clear and appropriate default clause in the songwriter's agreement. It should be provided that certain specified events constitute grounds for requesting arbitration or for the termination of the agreement. Among these events would be the failure to supply royalty statements and remittances, and the publisher's refusal to allow an inspection of its books and records.

The publisher may strongly oppose the default clause and claim, arguing that the writer is protected by law in case of a material breach. While this may be true, it entails the potential expense of litigation to establish the materiality of a breach and does not meet the objective of the writer to avoid litigation. The writer can counter with an offer to give adequate notice to the publisher of a default and a sufficient opportunity to cure it. Another counteroffer may be one calling for alternate dispute resolution by mediation or arbitration in the event of a dispute.

Performance Fees

As discussed in Chapter 14, performance fees are collected by performing rights organizations—ASCAP, BMI, and SESAC in the United States—from radio and television stations and from other commercial users of music, such as nightclubs and hotels, for the right to publicly perform copyrighted music. Under the Copyright Act of 1909, the performance would ordinarily have to be for profit. The Copyright Act of 1976 deletes this requirement, but it substitutes certain specific and limited exemptions set forth in Section 110, such as noncommercial performances during religious services in places of worship or in face-to-face classroom instruction. The performing rights organizations make distributions separately to the writers and publishers of musical compositions. They will not pay the writer's share to the publisher. As a consequence, songwriter agreements with publishers do not provide for the payment of performance fees by the publisher to the writer. To clarify the matter, agreements often state that the publisher is not obligated to pay any public performance fees to the writer.

The SGA contract specifically denies the right of the writer or publisher to share in the revenues distributed to the other by the performing rights organization with which both are affiliated.

Assignments

Many songwriter agreements permit a publisher to assign its rights. Consequently, a songwriter who enters into an agreement relying on the personnel and integrity of a particular publisher may find that by virtue of an assignment the writer is dealing with a different entity. The SGA contract meets this problem by requiring the writer's consent to an assignment by the publisher, except if the song is included in a bona fide sale of the publisher's business or entire catalog, or in a merger, or as part of an assignment to a subsidiary or affiliate. However, in all cases a written assumption of obligations must be delivered to the author by the new assignee-publisher.

It is clear that over the long life of a copyright many situations may arise that can be handled more flexibly and expeditiously if a publisher can assign his or her rights. The principals of independent publishers die and estates may be forced to sell interests in a copyright, or they may retire and desire to dispose of their music publishing interests. There can be little cause for concern when the assignment is made to a large, established, reputable publisher, as is the tendency, since this type of purchaser is generally able to make higher offers.

Lyrics versus Music

A song may be written for instruments alone, without lyrics, but more frequently it consists of both music and lyrics. While there are writers who write both music and lyrics, it is more common for an artist to be either a composer or a lyricist. The wedding of lyrics and music is an integral part of the business of a music publisher. A good publisher must know the commercial potential of various types of lyrics as well as qualified lyricists who can write them.

Through the grant of all rights under copyright, the publisher obtains the right to set words to the music and to modify and adapt the music. These powers are usually necessary for the proper exploitation of a composition. A publisher must be careful to determine whether the writer has the right to approve changes in the music, including any new lyrics, as well as whether the writer has agreed to share royalties with the lyricist or other writer engaged by the publisher. Where the SGA contract has been used, it is prudent to draw a new agreement that includes all of the writers of the final version of the song and thus avoid any later problem of consent or sharing of royalties. Under the SGA agreement, unless specifically agreed otherwise, the royalties are shared equally among all the writers, regardless of the total number. Consequently, if there is only one lyric writer and there are three melody collaborators, each receives 25 percent. An agreement among the writers changing their participation may be required to avoid an injustice.

Earlier sections of this chapter deal with royalties payable to writers for printed editions and mechanical licenses. Normally, these royalties cover the writers as a collective unit rather than composer and lyricist separately. The total writer royalties are ordinarily shared equally between the composer and lyricist. Specifically, a royalty of 6 cents per copy of sheet music sold is remitted as follows: 3 cents to the composer and 3 cents to the lyricist. Similarly, mechanical license royalties, which are usually 50 percent of the publisher's collections, are paid half to the composer and the other half to the lyricist. If there are three or more collaborators on a song, they usually determine among themselves their respective shares of the total writer royalties.

It should be recognized that some songs never reach the public eye and the writers may wish to attempt to salvage their individual contributions of title, words, or music for future use.

Royalties Held in Trust Funds

A potent weapon to ensure that songwriters receive the monies they are due is to provide that these monies collected by the publisher are held in trust by the publisher. A fiduciary relationship between the publisher and the writer is thus created in place of a debtor-creditor relationship. Under the debtor-creditor status, the failure to account to the writer might entail only a simple claim against the publisher. This claim has the same standing as that for any other debt owed by the publisher. The bankruptcy of the publisher erases the debt to the writer in the same way that other debts are canceled.

However, under the trust concept the writer becomes the legal owner of the funds, and the publisher is the custodian on behalf of the writer. The claim of the writer is not then dischargeable in the bankruptcy of the publisher, and the writer achieves a preferred status in relation to other creditors. Furthermore, there is a basis for criminal prosecution if the publisher becomes insolvent and does not pay writer royalties, since there will have been a misappropriation of funds that belong to another, namely, the writer. A similar charge may be brought in case the publisher refuses to pay.

The trust concept is clearly established under the SGA contract. Publishers using other songwriter forms will oppose the insertion of trust clauses because of the drastic consequences that may ensue. They point out, and with merit, that they may be unjustly prosecuted criminally if an honest dispute develops, for example, concerning whether monies are actually owed to the writer. Publishers also contend that innocent officers in a publishing enterprise may become tarred with a criminal brush because of acts or defaults of other officers. They argue that, for full protection of personnel, there has to be established separate and burdensome trust accounts and other administrative procedures that the average publisher cannot afford in terms of either time or expense.

Arbitration

As may be expected, disputes arise between publishers and writers concerning their respective rights and obligations under their agreements. If they cannot compromise, the SGA contract relegates both parties to arbitration, before a sole arbitrator, under the prevailing rules of the American Arbitration Association. A decision by the arbitrator is enforceable by the courts. Some songwriter agreements follow the example of the SGA contract in providing for arbitration. Many do not.

From the writer's point of view, arbitration is desirable since it affords a relatively inexpensive and expeditious method for resolving conflicts. Many music publishers favor arbitration for the same reason. Due to the technical aspects of copyright law and the tendency of arbitrators to compromise differences rather than decide disputes on principle, other publishers prefer the courts. Moreover, publishers can often bear the expense of litigation more readily than writers and the expense may well force writers to settle for less than they might be entitled to under a court decision.

Exclusive-Writer Agreements

Publishers interested in a continuous supply of good material may attempt to negotiate an exclusive agreement with a desirable composer or lyricist. Most major exclusive-writer deals with large advance payments concern writers who are also producers or featured artists with recording commitments and therefore the possibility of significant publishing revenues. Under an exclusive-writer agreement the writer assigns all compositions written during its term solely to the publisher, which becomes the owner of all copyrights. Royalties payable to the writer are usually the same as those on compositions that are accepted for publication in the absence of an exclusive writer's agreement.

A songwriter is not likely to sign an exclusive contract unless he or she is to be paid a cash consideration in the form of a lump sum or weekly payments. Frequently, a payment beyond an initial advance is conditioned on the commercial U.S. release of an agreed number of recordings on a major label.

All the payments are deemed to be advances against, and recoupable from, royalties that otherwise become payable to the writer.

It is a customary provision in exclusive-writer agreements that the publisher has one or more options to extend the term of the agreement, either on the same terms or on modified terms. When the songwriter is not also a producer or featured artist, it may be that the publisher cannot exercise the option unless the publisher has passed certain performance tests indicating that it is actually working in the interest of the writer. One test may be that a certain number of the writer's compositions have been recorded commercially. Most agreements (especially those where there is a producer or featured major-label artist involved) provide for an escalation in the cash consideration to be paid in option periods. Some writers may be able to negotiate their right to copublish all works written in any option periods.

In recent years publishing affiliates of major label record companies offer to copublish, or to be the full publisher of, music of songwriter-artists on affili-ated labels by offering special inducements. A major inducement is to have the record label waive its normal controlled-composition 75 percent of statutory rate request and to allow the full statutory rate to be applied. However, if there is a copublishing relationship, the net to the writer-copublisher is usually somewhat less than 75 percent of the statutory rate after the deduction of a copublisher share and an administrative charge. A simple explanation will demonstrate this. The publisher usually takes 10 percent off the top as admin-istrative charges; 50 percent goes to the writer, leaving 40 percent of the statu-tory rate. The remaining balance of 40 percent is divided equally between the writer (copublisher) and publisher. The final outcome is that the writer receives 70 percent (50 percent plus 20 percent), which is less than the normal 75 percent statutory rate applicable if no copublishing deal had been made. (A sample "Songwriter Exclusive Copublishing Agreement" is included in the accompanying CD-ROM.)

A more conventional inducement is the payment of a substantial advance on signing plus additional advances during successive option periods, which usually run parallel to the record company option periods, extending for as many as seven albums. Such advances can be significant sums but are usually based on the assumption that all or substantially all of the compositions recorded by the songwriter-artist are subject to the agreement. If a lesser number are delivered, there is a proportionate reduction in the advance.

Further negotiations sometimes provide not only that the stated minimum advances be escalated as each successive album is delivered but also that such amount be a minimum, with a higher amount applicable if 66.67 percent of earnings on the preceding album justify this amount, provided that even with a blockbuster sale the formula payment can never exceed 200 percent of the negotiated minimum payment. A pro-rated schedule of minimum and maximum amounts per album is usually set out, together with the formula of a 6- to 9-month period after release of the prior record. For formula purposes, customary reserves are usually disregarded.

If a writer is working under an exclusive contract, the status of the works becomes a matter of debate: Are such works to be considered works-for-hire or independent-contractor works under the Copyright Act of 1976? This is a complex subject that will be discussed in Chapter 17. The decision affects the initial ownership of copyright, the duration of copyright, the owner's copyright renewal rights, and the copyright termination rights.

Since many minors become songwriters and are asked to sign exclusive-writer contracts, questions arise as to whether the minors can be legally bound and, if so, in what manner. A consideration of these questions appears in Chapter 3, on page 34.

17

Works for Hire

Section 101 of the Copyright Act of 1976 provides two mutually exclusive definitions of a work made for hire:

1. A work prepared by an employee within the scope of his or her employment
2. A work specially ordered or commissioned for use as a contribution to a collective work, as a part of a motion picture or other audiovisual work, as a translation, as a supplementary work, as a compilation, as an instructional text, as a test, as answer material for a test, or as an atlas, provided that the parties expressly agree in writing that the work shall be considered a work for hire.

In the first definition the work is that of a conventional employee, and in the second it is considered to be the work of a conventional employee although it is actually produced by an independent contractor who has consented in writing to such treatment. Whether or not a composition or a recording is a work for hire can have profound significance. It affects the initial ownership of copyright, the duration of copyright, copyright renewal rights (if created before 1978), and copyright termination rights.

The Copyright Act of 1976 provides that "copyright in a work protected under this title vests initially in the author or authors of the work." But if a work is "for hire," the act considers the hiring party (the employer or commissioning party) to be the author of the work and (absent any written agreement to the contrary) the owner of copyright in the work.

Copyright in works for hire written in 1978 or later last for 95 years from the year of first publication, or 100 years from creation, whichever is shorter. If the work is not a work for hire, copyright remains in effect for the author's life plus 70 years. An independent contractor who has not created a work for hire can usually terminate his or her grant of rights after 35 years, subject, however, to the right of the owner to continue to use derivative works prepared before the termination. (See Chapter 11.) There can be no such termination by the actual creator of the work in the case of a work for hire.

With regard to sound recordings created between February 15, 1972, and December 31, 1977, the conventional exclusive recording artist agreement frequently states that the recording artist is deemed to be an "employee for hire." However, given the absence of regular work hours, withholding of taxes and social security, and other indications of a normal employer-employee working relationship, the recording artist is likely to be considered an independent contractor. Furthermore, audio recordings were not included among the nine categories specified in the 1976 Copyright Act defining a work for hire by an independent contractor. Therefore, we can anticipate that there will be disputes concerning the ownership of rights in sound recordings made between February 14, 1972, and December 31, 1977, when the initial 28-year-terms of copyright end between the years 2000 and 2006.

On November 29, 1999, a special amendment was signed into law which added "sound recordings" as a tenth category of works otherwise created by an independent contractor but which are capable of being confirmed in writing, as intended to be employment for hire, along with audiovisual works, collective works, etc. This obviously allows the customary exclusive record artist relationship to be covered from and after the date of November 29, 1999.

However, there is a major issue as to whether this purported "clarification" of the earlier statute is retroactive to January 1, 1978, or not. Record Industry Association of America spokesmen claim that it is, whereas others have commented that in the absence of any legislative hearings before passage of the amendment, it is not clear. In fact, Marybeth Peters, the Register of Copyrights, immediately commented that the claim that the amendment is merely "technical" and that it "clarifies" what was intended in 1976 when the Copyright Act of that year was passed is unlikely. Contentions are likely to be asserted by artists who recorded before passage of the amendment that they have the same rights of renewal or of termination that are discussed in Chapter 16 and that a statute cannot take such property interests away on a retroactive basis. This contention will have to be resolved in future legal actions.

Factors Determining a Work-for-Hire Relationship

A written statement in a contract as to whether a work was prepared by an employee in the scope of his or her employment is not by itself decisive of this issue. In *Community for Creative Nonviolence et al. v. Reid,* 109 Sup. Ct. 2166 (1989), the Supreme Court stated that the standard for determining the existence of an employment relationship is the common law of agency. The Court rejected a test based simply on whether the hiring party controlled or had the right to control the production of the work and instead set forth various factors to be considered in deciding whether an employment-for-hire relationship exists. The Court further stated that each factor is one among other factors, with no one factor being determinative.

These are some of the factors identified by the Supreme Court as they apply to recording artists and songwriters.

- *The skill required.* This factor might weigh in favor of finding that a recording artist and an exclusive writer is an independent contractor, not an employee, since it requires great skill on the part of the artist and song writer to create these works.

- *The source of the instrumentalities and tools.* This factor favors both artists and writers because rarely do artists record at studios owned by the record company, and typically the company provides the artist with a recording fund, which the artist uses to create and deliver master recordings.

- *The location of the work.* This factor also favors both artists and writers because, as referred to above, rarely do artists and writers record or write on the premises of the company or publisher.

- *The duration of the relationship.* Since artist and writer exclusive agreements are usually for a period of years, this factor may favor the hiring party being defined as the "employer."

- *The hiring party's option to assign additional projects.* Many recording contracts call for additional recordings at the option of the record company. Exclusive writer agreements may not contain similar provisions.

- *The extent of the hiring party's discretion over when and how to work.* A record company's control is likely limited to choosing producers and material to record. Publishers do not control the manner in which their writers write music.

- *The method of payment.* While writer agreements often provide for periodic salary or other payments, the recording artist is more likely to receive union scale and stipulated advances. Both probably also rely on royalty compensation, which is contingent on success. Additionally, the companies rarely withhold income taxes or contribute to social security, as regular employers are required to do.

- *The hired party's role in hiring and paying assistants.* This is commonly not a factor in exclusive writer agreements, but it would ordinarily relate to hiring and paying musician sidemen for recording sessions.

- *Whether the hiring party is in business.* Both the record company and the music publisher are obviously in business.

- *Whether the work is part of the regular business of the hiring party.* This factor favors the record company and the music publisher.

Subsequent cases have attached greater weight to certain factors than to others. However, on balance it appears that recording artists and songwriters are not employees of either the record company or the music publisher. Furthermore, as determined by a federal court of appeals in the case of *Forward v. Thorogood*, 985 F.2d 604 (1st Cir. 1993), paying for a recording and possessing the master tapes do not create a work-for-hire relationship.

Commissioned Works for Hire

Since recording artists and songwriters are not likely to be considered employees of the record company or music publisher, a hiring party might, in appropriate circumstances, rely on the specific categories under the second part of the 1976 Copyright Act definition of works for hire.

One of these categories is contributions to a motion picture or other audio-visual work. This clearly covers music in motion pictures, television, films, videos, and films of live concerts, as well as the soundtrack recordings. However, most musical recordings would not fit in this category, except as specifically added by the amendment of November 29, 1999.

Another of the categories of commissioned works with possible relevance to the music industry is a compilation. A *compilation* is defined in the 1976 Copyright Act as "a work formed by the collection and assembling of preexisting materials or of data that are selected, coordinated, or arranged in such a way that the resulting work as a whole constitutes an original work of authorship." The issue of whether an album is a compilation and whether recordings are specially commissioned as part of the album is not clear. In order to be separately copyrightable as a compilation, sufficient original authorship must be involved in the selection and arrangement of the works. If an artist delivers 12 songs, and all are included in an album, there has been insufficient selectivity. It may also be argued that the recordings were not specially commissioned to be a part of the album, since record companies sell single recordings as well. On the other hand, it may be argued that single recordings are only sold for purposes of promoting the album. In the case of "greatest hits" albums, which would clearly be considered compilations, one cannot argue that the component songs (presumably pre-existing) were specially commissioned to be included in the compilation.

A third category of commissioned works that might relate to the music industry is supplementary work. A *supplementary work* is defined in the Copyright Act of 1976 as one "prepared for publication as a secondary adjunct to a work by another author for the purpose of introducing, concluding, illustrating, explaining, revising, commenting upon, or assisting in the use of the other work, such as forewords, afterwords, pictorial illustrations, maps, charts, tables, editorial notes, *musical arrangements,* answer material for tests, bibliographies, appendixes, and indexes" (emphasis added). This category seems applicable to printed editions of musical compositions.

Although it appears that it would be difficult for record companies to show that recordings were specially commissioned as part of one of the categories listed in the second part of the definition of a work for hire, the issue is not entirely clear.

Assignments of Copyright

In agreements that state that the work is deemed to be a work for hire, there is often a further provision assigning the copyright, including any renewal and extension rights, to the hiring party. This should not be necessary because technically a true employment contract makes the need for such assignment unnecessary. Some contracts may simply state that the parties intend that the results and proceeds of the services involved belong to the hiring party. In the absence of direct language of assignment to the hiring party, a court may decide that the contractual characterization of the work as one for hire indicates an intention to make an assignment to the hiring party. As a result, even though a court may declare the work not to be a work for hire, the court might also find that the hiring party (that is, the record company or music publisher) owns the copyright by assignment.

Works commissioned and created prior to January 1, 1978, the effective date of the Copyright Act of 1976, were generally presumed to be owned by the commissioning party. The 1976 Copyright Act changed this presumption by providing that only certain categories of commissioned works, created in conformity with an agreement in writing signed by the parties, would be eligible for work-for-hire status. For pre-1978 compositions, the right to renew for the 28-year renewal period and the right to extend for the extra 19-year period runs in favor of the independent contractor or his or her successors under certain circumstances, as previously indicated. For compositions created on or after 1978, the assignment to the hiring party can usually be terminated after 35 years. Although the issue of whether sound recordings are created as works for hire has not yet been determined and is not immediately pressing, a notice of termination for a recording delivered in 1978 could be sent as early as the year 2003.

Joint Work Status

In *Community for Creative Nonviolence et al. v. Reid,* the district court had to decide whether the product created was a joint work, with the hiring party and the independent contractor as joint authors. According to the Supreme Court, this depends on a determination that the parties prepared the work with the "intention that their contributions be merged into inseparable or interdependent parts of a unitary whole." The language quoted from the Court opinion is itself contained in the definition of a joint work in the Copyright Act of 1976.

Whether or not a joint work was created is an issue of fact. The intention at the time of creation is the touchstone. To qualify as a joint author, the commissioning party must materially contribute to the creation of the work. Each contribution must be more than minimal. It is not sufficient that the commissioning party merely furnish the financing for the work. It may be expected that the written expression of the parties' intention—that the work is one for hire—may influence whether a joint work is determined to exist.

What might the contributions of a record company or a music publisher be to the creation of a joint work? The record company's A&R personnel may suggest the compositions to be recorded, the appropriate commercial music arrangements, the special effects from synthesizers or other recordings, the proper makeup of the orchestra, and so on. The record producer may supervise in great detail the entire recording session and may have significant input into the editing of the recording sessions after their completion. In *Forward v. Thorogood* the court determined that in order for a producer to be considered a joint author, he or she must artistically contribute to the production. All contributions have to be weighed in deciding whether the finished product is a joint work.

The professional personnel of the music publisher may suggest the subject and titles of compositions to be written and may participate in changing the words and music or the arrangements in order to make the product more attractive. They may also supervise the production of demonstration records and initiate arrangements and make editing decisions that enhance the appeal of otherwise raw compositions. A court may consider such participation in deciding whether the music publisher should be considered a joint author.

If a work is determined to be a joint work, the commissioning party is assured of sharing in the work for the full duration of copyright. Although the independent contractor or his or her heirs is thus entitled to participate in the work, there is a joint sharing with the commissioning party, as in the case of multiple authors of other joint works. (For a further discussion of joint works, see Chapter 18.)

18

Co-Ownership and Joint Administration of Copyrights

Even a cursory review of recent chart hits reveals the practice of two or more publishers sharing the ownership of popular songs. This commonly exists where there are two writers of a joint work, with each being a co-owner of the entire copyright and entitled to assign his or her interest to a separate publisher.

To establish co-ownership of the work, both writers must contribute to it. In a case previously cited in Chapter 17, *Forward v. Thorogood,* Thorogood arranged and paid for two recording sessions for his band, but the plaintiff, Forward, retained the tapes of the session, claiming co-ownership. The court rejected Forward's claim, holding that he was not a joint author because he had not engineered or directed the recording sessions, nor had he made any other discernible musical or artistic contribution to the tapes. The plaintiff's claim was totally rejected and the band played the songs as it always had.

Sharing of copyright often occurs when the recording artist who introduces a new song owns his or her publishing firm. It may also occur when a record company's publishing affiliate has been granted a stake in the copyright in order to induce the record company to sign an artist-writer, or when an established song is in the renewal term of copyright and each of the two writers has granted his or her renewal rights to a different music publisher.

Joint ownership, or co-ownership, of copyright is sometimes called a "split copyright." In theory, this phrase is a misnomer because prior to the Copyright Act of 1976, the courts regarded a copyright as "indivisible." In practice, however, while there could be only one legal owner of a copyright, this was not regarded as barring joint ownership of undivided interests in the bundle of rights that constitute a copyright. Under the Copyright Act of 1976, there was a statutory recognition of the divisibility of copyright. Now, any of the exclusive rights under copyright, and any subdivision of them, can be transferred and owned separately. Most agreements between joint owners relate to the entire copyright and its undivided interests or shares, although under the Copyright

Act of 1976 there is no bar to joint ownership of a particular exclusive right, such as the right to reproduce printed copies of a musical work. (The accompanying CD-ROM contains an agreement "Joint Ownership of Copyright.")

Registration and Notice

The Copyright Office recognizes joint ownership of copyright as an appropriate matter to be registered. When there is joint ownership of copyright, the notice of copyright on copies should contain the names of all co-owners, and such names should be the same as the names of the copyright owners on the copyright registration form.

The General Rights of Co-Owners

A joint owner of a copyright is free to use or license the use of the work without the knowledge or consent of the other co-owners, provided that the use does not amount to a destruction of the work. Judges use the analogy to joint ownership of real estate. If two or more persons own a cabin on a wooded plot of land, any of the owners can make use of the property or may authorize third parties to use it. However, no joint owner may chop down the trees or authorize third parties to destroy the joint property without the consent of the other owners.

The courts have uniformly held that when any one of the co-owners of a copyright licenses the use of the work, he or she must account to the other co-owners for their share of the profits. Although there is a split of opinion among music publishers regarding the need to account to co-owners for profits from a music publisher's own printed editions as distinguished from usages licensed for exploitation by third parties, the better view favors a requirement to account.

Even the field of printing and distribution of printed sheet music and folios is adapted to co-ownership. Firms such as Warner Bros. Music and Hal Leonard Publishing Corporation serve as licensees to handle printing and distribution and to remit to the joint owners their respective shares of the net receipts.

The Problems of Co-Ownership

Limited problems do exist in the administration of a jointly owned copyright for purposes of licensing and collection. ASCAP, BMI, and SESAC have no difficulty in administering jointly owned performing rights, provided that all co-owners are affiliates or members of the same performing rights organization. Even where the performing rights are divided among several performing rights organizations, they will generally honor directions to divide publisher and writer credits as directed by the co-owners. Some dissatisfied publishers claim that they are forced to share copyrights with recording stars and record company publishing affiliates, and that this is akin to payola; however, the practice appears uncoerced from a legal point of view.

At times the co-owners may have a conflict of interests. For instance, a record company co-owner may wish to grant itself a favorable reduced mechanical licensing rate, despite the decrease in publisher receipts that will result. Record company and artist co-owners may want to discourage obtaining and exploiting cover records of the same song by other artists and record companies.

In making a deal with a record company to share in the copyright, the publisher or artist-writer should contractually provide for the minimum mechanical license rate that the record company must pay. Otherwise the label may be in a position to grant itself a favorable rate, despite the objections of the co-owner, subject to a possible claim for breach of trust.

With regard to cover records, neither joint owner can bar the other, except contractually, from seeking and exploiting those records. On the other hand, no joint owner can insist, in the absence of a contractual provision, on joint expenditures for advertising and exploitation of any nature, whether they be for a cover record or otherwise.

Synchronization Rights

Although it is simple to instruct the Harry Fox Agency to divide synchronization fees in the same manner as mechanical license royalties received from record companies, synchronization rights may require different treatment. Since synchronization rights apply worldwide, the joint administration agreement must provide for an allocation of the synchronization fee between the United States and elsewhere when the co-ownership involves only U.S. rights, as may occur in the case of joint ownership during the renewal term of the U.S. copyright of pre-1978 works.

Many publishers agree that 50 percent of the synchronization fee should be attributable to the United States and the balance to the rest of the world. Some knowledgeable industry accountants, however, state that the percentages should be 45 percent for the United States and 5 percent for Canada, with 50 percent for the remainder of the world.

In the case of motion pictures, synchronization license fees must be distinguished from fees for the license of U.S. performing rights. A motion picture producer or other user of music who seeks a synchronization license must also acquire a U.S. public performance license. In the United States, ASCAP is barred by a court decree based on antimonopoly laws from licensing on behalf of its members theaters to perform music contained in film soundtracks. Because of this, the specific licenses for the performance of the music in motion picture soundtracks are customarily issued to the producer by the publisher for a specific motion picture. The fee is customarily equal to the worldwide synchronization fee. Consequently, where the co-ownership includes only the United States, the agreement between the co-owners should provide for the division of the performance license fee in proportion to the writer interest controlled by the respective owners, whereas the worldwide synchronization fee should be divided only in respect of the 45 or 50 percent attributable to the United States.

Foreign Rights

Agreements for the co-ownership of new songs should provide for one or the other of the owners to have sole control of foreign rights or should set forth the basic terms for acceptable foreign licensing contracts. This provision is essential because in a number of foreign countries, including England, either joint owner may arbitrarily veto a license negotiated by the other. This is in contrast to the freedom to license accorded to each co-owner under U.S. law.

Where joint ownership pertains to pre-1978 songs for their U.S. renewal period, it may also involve foreign administration of the songs if the foreign rights were reacquired by the writers beginning with the renewal term of the U.S. copyright. This reacquisition is provided for in the Songwriters Guild of America standard agreement between publishers and writers relating to pre-1978 songs. Prior to the 1948 and 1969 forms of the American Guild of Authors and Composers (the SGA's predecessor organization), most agreements with writers did not limit the term of foreign rights.

Consent by Silence

Many joint ownership agreements provide for consultation and reasonable consent before either owner grants a license to a recording company at rates less than the compulsory license rate per composition (7.55 cents, or 1.45 cents per minute or fraction thereof, whichever is greater). Where the co-owner may be unavailable for consultation and consent, it is advisable to provide that, a reasonable amount of time after notification by registered or certified mail, consent shall be assumed in the absence of written objection.

Restrictions on Assignment

As in any partnership or joint venture, there may be a strong element of reliance on a specific individual or company in selecting the co-owner. If the joint owner is a top recording star or a respected publisher, it may be appropriate to have different provisions relating to assignment than if the co-owner is merely a financial speculator. Where the joint administration agreement is based on special personal factors, it may be desirable to provide that neither co-owner may assign his or her interest without the approval of, or rights of first refusal in, the other owner.

The Writer's Interest in Co-Ownership

Especially with regard to renewal copyrights of pre-1978 compositions, writers are often cautioned against allowing joint ownership of copyrights. In actuality, there is little practical effect on the writer's royalty computations, although there may be a more significant effect on the exploitation of the song involved. Critics of the practice of "splitting copyrights" point out that the incentive to promote a song may decrease when a publisher's share is decreased.

If there are two writers on a musical work and each grants publishing rights to a different publisher, the writers will normally look solely to their own publisher for their share of royalties unless both publishers agree that one of them will assume full writer royalty obligations with respect to the entire composition. Where two publishers share equally in the mechanical license fees payable for a song, each publisher pays its own contributing writer as if there were no collaborator on the song. Each publisher would pay its writer one-half of its mechanical license receipts (which is the usual total writer's rate), and since each publisher receives 50 percent of the total mechanical license fees, each writer will in effect receive 25 percent of the combined publishers' receipts. This is the same rate and amount that would be payable to each writer if there were only one publisher and two writers.

For sheet music and other printed uses, there is no difference to the writers if the publishers agree to account to each other and to the writers for their separate publications or if they use the same printer, such as Warner Bros. Publications, which is directed to render separate accountings to each publisher. Without such arrangements, writers obtain print royalties only from their own publisher and receive no accountings from the other publisher. This may prove inequitable if the other publisher is more energetic and capable and achieves greater sales of printed editions. This situation occurs rarely, however, and in view of the limited sales of printed editions, the harm to a writer is not likely to be serious.

It has been observed that publishers with less than a 100 percent interest in a song have sometimes used the split copyright as a loss leader in the form of reduced mechanical license fees in order to induce a record company to take other songs from the publisher's catalog at a higher rate. Obviously, in such cases the writer and the other publisher both lose. Flagrant abuses of this sort can lead to a claim by the writer of a breach of the obligation of the publisher to exploit the composition equitably and fairly, and may result in an enforced accounting by the publisher for additional royalties. Similarly, the other co-owner may contend that any discount must apply to all the licensed compositions rather than to the one composition alone. On the other hand, the participation of another publisher in the song proceeds may add an extra measure of exploitation, to the ultimate benefit of the song.

The Cut-In

As an alternative to the joint ownership of copyrights, some songwriters and publishers recommend that, wherever feasible, the record artist or the record company should receive a "cut-in," an authorized participation in publishing income instead of an interest in the copyright itself. In this instance the financial reward does not need to include management rights in the copyright. This leaves in the hands of the publisher the control of license rates, foreign deals, collection vigilance, and exploitation, subject only to money payments out of receipts to the person or firm that helps to launch, or "break," the song. In some instances the cut-in is limited to a share of the publisher's earnings derived from the particular recording.

It is important to make sure that the cut-in is nullified if the record is not released. The mere making of a recording is no guarantee that it will be released. Accordingly, many publishers insist that the actual general release of a single record on a specified label by a designated artist must occur before the cut-in takes effect. Others permit the agreement to become effective but provide for a right of recapture in the event that the specified recording is not released within a given period of time.

The cut-in is a practice that is often condemned. When given to record company personnel without the knowledge of the employer, it may constitute commercial bribery under state laws. It can be argued that when properly and openly made, a cut-in is acceptable as a reputable business device that preserves the integrity of management of a copyright and is an appropriate recognition that copyright laws give no benefit to the artist who establishes the popularity of the song or to the record company whose arrangers are responsible for its successful commercial presentation. Asking for a cut-in is not the same as demanding to be named a cowriter of the composition in order to obtain a share of the writer credits and payments from ASCAP or BMI. The latter practice may constitute a fraudulent registration in the Copyright Office.

When a songwriter regrets or renounces a cut-in deal it is important that he or she take action expeditiously. In a 1999 case concerning writer credits for the 1959 song "The Sea of Love," the writer threatened legal action unless he got 100 percent of writer royalties. The court ruled that any such action had to be taken within 3 years of discovery. In this case, 40 years had passed, the statute of limitations had been exceeded, and the case was rejected. However, when a song from before 1978 is still the subject of potential renewal in its 28th year, a timely action can still be taken to contest the claimed authorship of the cut-in "writer." This is especially desirable if the cut-in was not listed on the original copyright registration.

19

Copyright Infringement

Copyright infringement lawsuits are common in the music industry, and no song or artist is immune. Cases of infringement have involved such artists as Andrew Lloyd Webber, Michael Jackson, Michael Bolton, and the Rolling Stones. There are two basic types of copyright infringers: (1) those who use copyrighted material without obtaining the requisite permission, in the form of a license, and (2) those who claim to originate a work but, consciously or unconsciously, copy another's original work.

Not all infringements are willful acts of evil. For example, the great composer Jerome Kern was found to have infringed an earlier work, "Dardanella," in one of his compositions; a recognizable copy of the "Dardanella" bass line had somehow crept into his subconscious and erupted in Kern's allegedly original work, "Kalua." Even though it was unconscious, it was nonetheless a copyright infringement. George Harrison, the former Beatle, was found guilty of copyright infringement; the court found that Harrison's 1970 hit "My Sweet Lord" was plagiarized from the 1962 tune "He's So Fine."

Proof of Access to a Copyrighted Work

Whether conscious or subconscious infringement is involved, an indispensable prerequisite to a finding of infringement is the *access* of the second writer to the work of the first. No infringement occurs merely because the identical melody or lyric is reproduced in the second writer's song. The copyright owned by the first writer is protection against being copied, but it does not provide a basis for a claim against a second person who independently creates the same result. An obvious example would be a copyrighted photograph of the George Washington Bridge at sunset taken from a position that permitted the inclusion of the little red lighthouse in the same picture. A second photographer might independently take the same picture at the same time of day and at the same place, without access to the first photograph and thus without infringement of copyright. Similarly, the simple melodic lines of popular songs can be the subject of duplication by sheer coincidence.

Consequently, it is important for an infringement claimant to establish access to his other copyrighted work by showing the public dissemination of the song through the release of sheet music or recording and public performance, or by proving that the defendant had actual personal contact with the song. Clearly, the active wrongdoer will deny having any contact with the song, whether over the transom in a heavily frequented music industry office or otherwise, and this makes proving access difficult. However, the courts will recognize circumstantial evidence as establishing proof of access. The access of a linking third party, such as a record producer, can suffice to show the required access to the copyright material. Similar complexities in the original work and the copies are considered to demonstrate the presence of access. In music, extended duplication in more than isolated instances can also prove copying, defined by one court as "a striking similarity which passes the bounds of mere accident."

Even when access can be shown, there is no copyright remedy for minimal similarities. There must be substantial copying; this refers to quality and not necessarily quantity: There is no "four-bar exception." In 1993, Takeall, an unknown rap musician, brought suit against Pepsico, claiming that the song in a Pepsico commercial was a copy of the "hook" in the plaintiff's song. The hook involved the syncopated, quadruple repetition of the slang term "uh-oh." The court stated that "the repetition of the non-protectible word 'uh-oh' in a distinctive rhythm comprises a sufficiently original composition to render it protectible by the copyright laws." As further support for its finding, the court noted that Pepsico had licensed its version of the hook for use in a television commercial and had described it as "commercially marketable."

Another court held that common errors in a plaintiff's version of music in public domain and in the defendant's use of this music, such as the misspelling of an author's name and the failure to carry over a musical "slur" mark at the same exact place in the composition, although technically and musically required, "are unmistakable signs of copying."

The Use of Music in the Public Domain

A common defense of an individual who is charged with having infringed a copyrighted song is that the musical work is in the public domain. This can result from the abandonment of the copyright by the plaintiff through his or her failure to use proper notices of copyright when such notices were required by law, failure to renew the copyright when such renewals were required prior to 1992, as well as other actions or inactions. It can also result from the defendant's proving that the duplicated melody line or lyric originated from sources other than the plaintiff. In an infringement action against the producers of the children's TV show *Sesame Street*, the court found the original source to be an old Russian folktale and held that "the most that could be said is that [the defendant] read the plaintiff's work and retold the story in [his] own words. Such a finding will not, given the derivative nature of plaintiff's work, support a course of action for copyright infringement." See *Reyher v. Children's Television Workshop*, 533 F.2d 87 (2d Cir. 1976).

Copyright is not jeopardized by the acknowledgment that a composition in the public domain is the basis of the writer's song. In such a case, however, the copyright obtained is not on the work in the public domain but on the arrangement, revision, or other new material added. Consequently, a user could record the original Chopin *Polonaise* melody, which is in the public domain, but not the arrangement or adaptation of the melody contained in the song "'Til the End of Time." (See Chapter 12, "The Uses of Public Domain.")

Innocence as a Defense

When a music or record supplier is found guilty of infringement of copyright, retail stores or other intermediaries between the customer and the original infringer cannot hide behind their own ignorance. The H. L. Green chain store was held liable for infringement in connection with the sale of bootleg records by a concessionaire that operated its music department. Similarly, the advertising agency Batten, Barton, Durstine & Osborn was held liable for a commercial jingle supplied by an infringer. The various infringers are not only jointly liable, but also individually liable if the other parties are unable to bear the cost of the settlement. For this reason, suits may be aimed at the more financially responsible member or members of the infringing group—a pressing plant, a distributor, a record or music store, as well as the composer of the infringing work.

The Copyright Act of 1976 took a more liberal approach toward authors who had failed to register their copyright in a timely or correct manner. At the same time, the act tried to provide some protection to copyright infringers who had been misled by the absence of a copyright notice: The innocent infringer was granted a complete defense in cases of an incorrect name in a copyright notice as long as the infringer acted in good faith under the authority of the person in the notice and the Copyright Office records did not show the real owner in a copyright registration or in a document executed by the person named in the notice. The infringer was not liable for actual or statutory damages prior to receiving notice of a copyright registration. In that situation the court might (1) allow claims for the infringer's profits, (2) enjoin future infringement, or (3) require the infringer to pay the copyright owner a reasonable license fee fixed by the court in order to continue the venture.

Works published on or after March 1, 1989, the effective date of the Berne Convention Implementation Act of 1988, no longer require a copyright notice to receive copyright protection. The presence of a proper copyright notice defeats a defense of innocent infringement. If the defense is sustained, though, this may result in the limiting of the actual or statutory damages awarded the copyright holder. In allowing or disallowing injunctive relief, the discretion of a court is involved. The innocent intent of an infringer can be a factor in the exercise of a court's discretion.

Who May Sue for Infringement

Prior to the Copyright Act of 1976, generally only the holder of the copyright was considered to be entitled to bring an action for infringement. Exclusive licensees might sue for infringement on the condition that the copyright holder was joined as a party to the suit. This policy was aimed at avoiding a multiplicity of suits. A copyright was usually regarded as an indivisible bundle of rights as far as infringement actions were concerned.

The 1976 Copyright Act effected a major change in copyright law. All rights under copyright, including performance rights, printing rights, and mechanical reproduction rights, are now clearly divisible. As a result, the owner of an exclusive right can bring an action in his or her own name for infringement of the owner's right. For example, if a firm such as Hal Leonard Publishing Corporation is the exclusive licensee of the right to print a particular song, it can sue infringers of that right without the participation of the licensor.

The beneficial owner of an exclusive right, as distinct from the legal owner, is also entitled to sue for infringement. An example of a beneficial owner is an author who has assigned his or her legal title to a copyright in return for the right to receive percentage royalties computed on the basis of sales fees or license fees.

In recognition of the fact that an action for infringement can affect the rights of others who have an interest in the copyright, a court can require that the plaintiff provide written notice of the action to any interested parties. The court may also require or permit any persons whose rights may be affected to join in the action. A copyright action may be brought only by the legal or beneficial owner, and the ability to join in the suit is limited to those who have an interest in the copyright. Licensing agents such as ASCAP have neither ownership nor other interest in the copyright.

Civil Remedies for Infringement

There are various remedies available to a plaintiff who claims the infringement of a copyright. The plaintiff may seek a court-ordered injunction. The plaintiff may request that the infringing copies, as well as the plates, molds, matrices, tapes, and other means of reproduction, be impounded or destroyed. More commonly, the plaintiff will sue for his or her actual damages and any additional profits made by the infringer from the infringement that are not taken into account in computing the actual damages.

In suits for an infringer's profits, the burden of proof tends to be on the defendant. The Copyright Act of 1976 states that the copyright proprietor need prove only "the infringer's gross revenue, and the infringer is required to prove his or her deductible expenses and the elements of profits attributable to factors other than the copyrighted work." In the past, determining an infringer's gross revenue has been a difficult task for plaintiffs attempting to calculate damages. However, in current practice, judges can rely upon the sales figures compiled by SoundScan to determine the amount of damages to be paid. (SoundScan is a relatively new company which tracks sales of music at most retail outlets. It does this by scanning the record at the cash register as it is being sold. In only a few years, SoundScan has become the industry standard. However, critics of SoundScan say that it ignores the sales of mom-and-pop record stores and is thus not completely accurate.)

At any time before final judgment during a legal action, a plaintiff under the 1976 statute can elect to recover statutory damages in lieu of actual damages and the additional profits of the infringer. For such damages the court must generally award between $500 and $20,000 for all infringements of a single work. For that purpose, the components of a compilation or derivative work constitute one work. However, where there is a willful infringement, as in the case of a defendant who infringes a copyright after written notice, the court may award up to $100,000 for statutory damages. A reduction to a minimum of $200 can apply if the court finds that the defendant "was not aware and had no reason to believe" that the act was an infringement. The court may also omit any award against instructors, librarians, and archivists in nonprofit institutions who honestly but mistakenly relied on fair use where there were reasonable grounds for the belief that fair use was applicable to their reproductions.

A 1998 Supreme Court decision regarding a television station's copyright infringement in syndicated programs after the expiration of a negotiated license also applies to the music industry. The decision held that though the Copyright Act of 1976 does not specify or provide for a jury trial to determine damages, there is a constitutional right to a jury trial in such situations.

An example of the computation of statutory damages under the Copyright Act of 1909 is offered in a court decision in an action regarding the copyright infringement of songs from the musical play *Jesus Christ Superstar*. A series of 48 live performances in the United States resulted in a judgment for $48,000. The computation was based on a statutory minimum amount of $250 per copyright for each of four infringed copyrights, multiplied by the number of performances. As previously noted, under the Copyright Act of 1976, a court would generally make a single statutory damage award for all infringements as to an individual work.

In a 1994 infringement action, the Isley Brothers' copyrighted song "Love Is a Wonderful Thing" was infringed by a song of the same title by Michael Bolton and Andrew Goldmark. It was ruled that Bolton and Goldmark's song infringed upon 66 percent of the Isley Brothers' song and contributed to 28 percent of the profits from Bolton's multiplatinum album (10 million copies sold) *Time, Love and Tenderness.* The disputed song was only one of the many songs on the album. As a result, the Isley Brothers are entitled to 18 percent of the revenues earned by the album as well as 66 percent of the entire income of the song from music publishing.

In addition to infringements by performances, statutory damages are also applicable to other infringements, such as by printed copies, film synchronization, mechanical reproduction other than under a compulsory license, or transcriptions.

The reason for statutory minimum damages is that frequently proof of actual damages or profits is difficult or impossible to achieve, even though other elements of infringement, such as access to the plaintiff's original work and a substantial similarity, are shown. The availability of minimum damages to a successful plaintiff is an important deterrent against infringements. In fact, such a remedy is considered valuable, if not essential, to performing rights societies such as ASCAP, BMI, and SESAC, especially in dealing with smaller broadcasting stations that might otherwise be tempted to risk infringement on the chance of nondiscovery or the inability of a plaintiff to prove damages or the defendant's profits.

Court Costs and Attorney Fees

In 1990 Ray Repp, a relatively unknown composer, brought an infringement case against composer Andrew Lloyd Webber. Repp claimed that the central theme of *Phantom of the Opera* was taken from "Till You," a little-known song that Repp wrote in 1978. Although Repp's composition earned less than $100, he claimed that Webber had had access to the song. Ultimately, the jury found for Webber, but what was noteworthy about the case was the amount of legal fees incurred by Webber in his successful defense: $2.3 million.

When sued for copyright infringement, a defendant may request a summary judgment (i.e., a finding that the plaintiff's case has no merit and should be dismissed out of hand). If this request is denied, the defendant may seek a finding that there is a "likelihood" of the defendant's success at trial. This is a way of putting financial pressure on a plaintiff, because such a finding may lead the court to require that the plaintiff post a bond for "costs" in the event of the defendant's success. In copyright actions, costs can include sizable attorney's fees. However, in the case of *Selletti v. Mariah Carey*, 173 F.3d 104 (2d Cir. 1999), a court said that "the imposition of a security requirement may not be used as a means to dismiss suits of questionable merit filed by plaintiffs with few resources."

Many copyright actions involve long, expensive, and burdensome trials with verdicts of fairly small awards based on actual or statutory damages. In such instances, the plaintiff is faced with empty justice if he or she has to foot the bills for court costs and legal expenses. The court may award reasonable attorney's fees and court costs to the successful party in a copyright suit. This is a double-edged sword, however, since the successful defendant can also obtain such relief.

In the 1994 *Fogerty v. Fantasy Inc.* decision, the U.S. Supreme Court leveled the playing field for plaintiffs and defendants on the subject of lawyers' fees. The Court overturned a ruling that required successful copyright defendants to prove that the suit was frivolous or brought in bad faith in order to recoup their lawyers' fees. The case dealt with lawyers' fees of $1.35 million. Fantasy appealed the $1.35 million award, claiming that it had brought its action in "good faith" and was thus "blameless." The appellate court stated that "a court's discretion may be influenced by the plaintiff's culpability in bringing or pursuing the action, but blameworthiness is not a prerequisite to awarding fees to a prevailing defendant." The court also allowed John Fogarty to collect additional attorney's fees in his defense of Fantasy's unsuccessful appeal of the attorney's fees issue. This ruling will obviously make the prospective infringement claimant give more thought about settlement or dropping the suit.

Some copyright cases have proven to be so complex that attorneys' fees, based on the amount of work involved, the skill shown, the results obtained, and the responsibility indicated by the decision, have been awarded by the courts in the amounts of $7,500 to $10,000 in cases where the awards for infringement were less. However, the attorneys' fees awarded by courts are often not for the full amount of the fees incurred. Under federal as well as local court rules, there are procedures to order sanctions against the attorneys as well as the party who failed to make a reasonable investigation before bringing copyright actions.

As a result of these rules, the claimant as well as the attorney should compile and review all information for accuracy and investigate any discrepancies found, review any and all information publicly available concerning the factual issues, and interview any person with knowledge of any relevant information. These same sanction rules also apply to wrongfully continuing an action that might initially have been justified but subsequently was shown to lack a justifiable factual issue. Engaging a qualified musicologist before beginning the action and not merely "shooting from the hip" is an essential first step. Similarly, a defendant faced with what appears to be a meritorious claim should likewise get expert guidance as to melodic comparisons.

Criminal Remedies for Infringement

In a recent sampling case involving rap music, a judge who was sitting in a civil case found that the infringement was so blatant that he referred the case to the U.S. Attorney for possible criminal action. "Thou shalt not steal" stated the judge, quoting the ancient prescript as the criminal basis of copyright law. The Copyright Act of 1976 provides that a willful infringement for commercial advantage or private financial gain can result in a fine of not more than $25,000, or imprisonment for not more than 1 year, or both. The No Electronic

Theft Act (NET Act) changes the standard of financial gain and commercial gain to include anything of value, including the receipt of other copyrighted works. The act is aimed at hackers on the Internet who do not have the profit incentive of conventional counterfeiters and bootleggers.

Special penalties apply to infringements of a certain magnitude of sound recordings or motion pictures and other audiovisual works. A fine of not more than $250,000, or imprisonment for not more than 2 years, or both, may be imposed if in any 180-day period there was an unauthorized reproduction or distribution of more than 100 but fewer than 1,000 phonorecords, or more than 7 but fewer than 65 copies of one or more motion pictures or other audiovisual works. The same maximum fine of $250,000, or imprisonment of up to 5 years, or both may be the sentence if the offense involves (1) the production or distribution of at least 1,000 copies of phonorecords, or at least 65 copies of motion pictures or other audiovisual works, or (2) a subsequent offense in a case where the fine for any prior offense could have been up to $250,000.

Mechanical Right Infringement

The 1976 Copyright Act provides a special limitation on the exclusive right to record musical compositions. If the copyright owner has authorized a recording that has been distributed to the public in the United States, the compulsory mechanical license provisions of the act are applicable. Without the proper notice of intention to rely on those compulsory license provisions, these provisions do not pertain, and the making and distribution of records become actionable acts of infringement for which full civil and criminal remedies are available. In *Harris v. Emus Records*, 1984, a California court held that once a record has been distributed, it is too late to rely on this compulsory license provision. In that case, Emmy Lou Harris succeeded in having the court rule that the owner of an unlicensed master who had already issued the record without a license could thereafter "listen to the master in his own living room" but make no other use of it.

Under the compulsory license provisions, the copyright owner is entitled to receive monthly payments and statements of mechanical royalties as well as cumulative annual statements certified by a public accountant. If the monthly payments and the monthly and annual statements are not received when they are due and the default is not remedied within 30 days after written notice by the copyright owner, the compulsory license is automatically terminated. At this point, the making or distributing of all records for which royalties had not been paid become acts of infringement for which civil and criminal remedies apply.

Infringement by Importation

One of the rights of a copyright owner is to prevent the importation of copies or phonorecords of a work. Importation is an infringement of the owner's exclusive right to distribute copies or records; civil and criminal remedies for an infringement apply.

As provided by the 1976 Copyright Act, however, individuals arriving from abroad can include a single copy or record as a part of their personal baggage. In addition, a nonprofit organization that operates for scholarly, educational, or religious purposes may import not more than one copy of an audiovisual work, such as a motion picture, for its archives and not more than five copies or records of any other work for its archives or for library lending.

The Copyright Act of 1976 bars the importation of pirated copies or phonorecords, namely, those whose manufacture would be a copyright infringement if the Copyright Act had been applicable. While the manufacture may be lawful in the country where it was made because, perhaps, that country has no copyright relations with the United States, importation nevertheless is prohibited if the making would be illegal under the U.S. Copyright Act. In the 1991 case, *BMG Music v. Perez,* the court determined that the first-sale doctrine is not a valid defense where records lawfully made in the country of manufacture and first sale are thereafter imported in bulk into the United States without the copyright license from the American owners. Further, the payment of copyright fees abroad is not enough in itself, said the Circuit Court for the Ninth District, thereby endorsing a prior 1987 New Jersey decision of Jem Records importers. The U.S. Customs Service is authorized to prevent the importation of unlawful copies or records.

Whether the making is lawful or unlawful, the Secretary of the Treasury may publish procedures whereby an individual claiming an interest in a copyrighted work can, for a fee, become entitled to notice from the U.S. Customs Service of the importation of copies or phonorecords.

When finished goods have been manufactured in the United States and shipped abroad for a bounce-back into U.S. markets, the first-sale doctrine has been considered a sufficient defense. The *first-sale doctrine* refers to a rule of law that any right of distribution stops after the first authorized sale of a copyrighted item, and that a subsequent holder in due course can sell again, ad infinitum, provided that authorized first sale was by or authorized by the American copyright proprietor. However, when the overseas source is the place of manufacture, the import into the United States of any such finished record of other goods is not granted this defense because the Supreme Court has determined that the first-sale doctrine applies only to goods manufactured under license within the United States and not abroad.

The recent success of on-line book and CD distributors has complicated this issue. These on-line distributors have caused the long-standing concepts of territorial publishing rights to vanish. In 1999, amazon.com began selling copies of *Harry Potter and the Prisoner of Azkaban,* an immensely successful British children's book that had not yet been published in the United States, much to the dismay of the American publisher who paid for the rights to release the book in the United States. Current laws do not address the issue of individual copy importation such as by mail order or Internet. As a result, the Association of American Publishers (AAP) is considering lobbying for legislative change.

Copyright Registration

The 1976 Copyright Act, as modified by the Berne Convention Implementation Act of 1988, encourages copyright registration by making it a prerequisite to the start of an infringement action involving works of U.S. origin and foreign works not originating in a Berne nation. By virtue of the Berne Act, there is no requirement of registration for copyright of a Berne work of non-U.S. origin as a prerequisite to initiation of an infringement action with respect to such work.

The failure to register where required constitutes grounds for dismissal, but after registration the suit can proceed with regard to both past and future infringements. There is, however, a penalty imposed for failure to register those works where registration is a prerequisite to an infringement suit. Despite registration, the remedies of statutory damages and attorneys' fees are not available to prior acts of infringements with respect to an unpublished work. The same remedies are also unavailable concerning published works with respect to infringements between first publication and copyright registration, unless the registration was made within three months after initial publication.

The Recordation of Copyright Transfer

Under the law in effect before March 1, 1989, the owner of an allegedly infringed copyright or exclusive right who had obtained the rights by a transfer of copyright could not institute an infringement action until he or she had recorded the instrument of transfer in the Copyright Office. After recordation the owner could sue on past infringements. The above requirement was eliminated by the Berne Act.

Time Frame for Legal Actions

The Copyright Acts of 1909 and 1976 provide for a 3-year statute of limitations for the start of a court action or criminal proceedings for copyright infringement. This means that a lawsuit must begin within 3 years after the claim arises and a criminal proceeding must be instituted within 3 years after the cause of action occurs.

Infringements concerning phonograph records or printed editions may continue for longer than 3 years. Only those infringements that occurred before the latest 3-year period are barred by the statute of limitations.

For injunctive relief, as distinguished from claims for monetary damages or profits, a suit must be brought within a reasonably prompt period after the discovery of the infringement. The failure to institute the action within such a period, which is likely to be less than 3 years, may cause a court to deny the injunction on the ground of the plaintiff's "laches," or undue delay in seeking legal redress.

Sampling and Copyright Infringement

In recent years an entire industry has been created based on copyright infringements. In its early days, sampling was the double infringement—of sound as well as song. A segment of an earlier recording is incorporated into a new recording, either alone or together with other segments. A brief musical accompaniment may be created by "looping" a short segment of sound recording from a prior record and repeating it for extended periods as an accompaniment, often to rap lyrics. When it is without license, it is an infringement.

The customary practice in regard to sampling is to appropriate a brief segment of the original source and to loop it for continuous usage within the new recording, often of a duration much longer than the original segment itself. Thus, a segment of only 6 seconds can be used for as much as 90 seconds within, and often as background to, the new recording. Plus, the original brief segment can be digitally altered. In the case of *Jarvis v. A&M* 827 F. Supp. 282 (D.N.J. 1993), the court categorized the process as "the conversion of analog sound waves into a digital code [which] can then be reused, manipulated or combined with other digitized or recorded sounds using a machine with digital data processing capabilities, such as a computerized synthesizer."

Record companies have learned to discipline artists and producers by making them bear the full responsibility of unlicensed sampling. They have learned that to search out the two owners (record company for sound and publisher for song) is not only expensive in itself; it is a mere preliminary to the expense of a retroactive license after the record is already issued. Numerous research and negotiating service houses have arisen for handling these claims. When it is possible to clear in advance, the price is obviously cheaper, since there is the possibility of switching tracks to a more cooperative source if there is resistance from the first selection. When a retroactive license has proved impossible, records have been withdrawn from the market at great expense; this is in addition to payment of considerable damage claims for past sales. A frequent negotiation that avoids such consequence is to transfer all or part of the copyright in the new version to the owner of the sampled song.

In the 1999 case *Emergency Music v. Isbell*, involving the use of a sample of the song "I'm Ready" in the hit song "Whoomp! There It Is!" by the one-hit wonder Tag Team, a district court ordered the defendants to pay $707,766.47 in damages even though the defendants had obtained a license for the sample. Because the defendants had failed to pay at the appropriate payment periods, even after receiving written notice by the plaintiff, the court ruled that the license was terminated. This made use of the sample a copyright infringement.

Negotiations for the clearance of sampled material necessarily involve knowing the nature of the use. An analysis of the use should cover the following:

- Length of basic material sampled
- Whether the sampled material is extended in its actual intended use through looping or other repetitive devices
- Whether the sampled material is the primary focus of audience attention or just in the background
- Whether the other interested party—the record company or the music publisher—has already cleared the sample use as well as price or other form
- Whether this is the only instance of sampling in the resulting song or one of several, and if so, what deals were offered to the other parties
- The past sales history of the artist who did the sampling as an indication of likely volume of sales on the current recording
- The name of the publisher of the sampled song and the owner of the sampled sound recording

With this information in hand, it can be determined whether an outright fixed price for permission to sample is appropriate or whether a demand should be made for a share (or all) of the copyright in the resulting song. Since the law does not permit an unauthorized adaptation, it is possible to insist on a delivery of 100 percent of the copyright in the resulting song. Whether it is part or all of the song, the next question pertains to the mechanical royalty rate: Will it be a reduced rate consistent with any controlled-composition requirements of the artist's contract with the record label, or will the full statutory rate apply? Finally, should an advance be paid against the resulting royalties, thereby guaranteeing a certain sum that would normally be substantially less than if an outright sale were made?

Record company negotiations for clearances of sound recordings usually operate on a fixed sum, while the negotiations of music publishers more often involve a continuing royalty claim. Some observers note that a record company may be more leniently disposed toward clearing samples of a fellow record company in recognition that the next time around the negotiating sides will be reversed and a courtesy given may be reciprocated. Music publishers rarely feel that way.

Successful records are rarely limited to the United States. Consequently, a sample clearance should be worldwide. Nonetheless, some American music publishers who have granted foreign rights to subpublishers prefer to get a larger up-front payment and, in that event, have a confidentiality clause that gives limited protection to the infringing companies. The same applies if a copublisher pursues a sampling claim without confiding in the other partner or intending to share the results. This is not only unethical, but it is also illegal, as copublishers have a duty to account for profits to their partners.

Sampling clearances that do not get settled on outright sums usually refer to 100 percent or lesser shares of statutory compulsory mechanical royalty rates. However, a hard-hitting negotiator dealing with a sampled recording that has already been released has a hidden weapon for asking for even higher rates, since compulsory rates do not apply once a recording has been distributed without a license.

A note of caution: With the assignment of the offending copyright can come possible claims from other affronted sampled parties who might not have been disclosed by the assignor.

Is there a defense available to the sampler? The defense of fair use is not available because the use is invariably commercial, without claim of being socially constructive criticism, parody, or reference, and although it may not detract from sales or licenses of the original, it is a taking without compensation, and with the intention of saving recording costs. Frank Zappa sampled his own material, which, of course, is the most exemplary form of all. Other strategies are for the interested record company to invite licensed uses of its own recorded library. Many artists of earlier recordings would welcome recognition and payment resulting from an unauthorized sample.

If possible, the major defense in sampling is that the use is not "substantial." If the resulting sound is unrecognizable by the ordinary audience, it may escape the onus of copyright infringement even though it is an unlicensed and unfair appropriation of the work product of the original recording artist and production company. However, if it escapes detection and is as a result not "substantially similar," it also escapes the normal goal of sampling, which is often seen as a game of hide-and-seek and an appeal to subliminal or actual nostalgia for the sounds of yesteryear. There is no need to settle a case of noninfringing use, so the question arises: Why it was taken in the first instance if the purpose was to tease the listener with recognizable snatches of older recordings?

Record companies defending or negotiating sample clearances are usually fully aware that they can charge 100 percent of the costs against the artist's account. They also have the right to charge the producer's account under the usual warranty. Yet producers are not customarily charged unless the artist or artist's manager insists.

When a music publisher settles a sampling claim, it has a legal right to look to the sampling songwriter to indemnify against costs. A flat-sum settlement is easily charged against a songwriter's royalties, but whether a reduction or abandonment of publisher shares can result in such a charge against the songwriter raises major questions of publisher-writer relations and is usually avoided by taking the reduction "off the top," to be shared between publisher and songwriter.

Many record companies now recognize the complexity of obtaining appropriate sampling licenses. As a result, sampling "clearinghouses" have arisen in the 1990s. Duties performed by the clearinghouses include searching out the potential licensors and negotiating the terms and conditions of the licenses. The clearinghouses are usually compensated for their services on a fixed-fee basis, the rates for which are currently around $200 for finding the owner of the sound recording and $200 for finding the owner of the underlying musical composition. These fees normally include the clearinghouse's negotiating services, but if there are extended negotiations, additional charges may apply.

20

International Copyright Protection

Although the U.S. balance of trade since the mid-1980s has been character-ized by substantial deficits, the nation's copyright industries have consistently continued to produce a trade surplus. In recognition of the importance to the U.S. economy of safeguarding this area of trade, Congress voted in 1988 to ratify the international Berne Copyright Convention, the world's oldest, most comprehensive, and most protective reciprocal copyright treaty, as part of an effort to maximize copyright protection for American works in foreign coun-tries.

The Berne Convention

The Berne Convention for the Protection of Literary and Artistic Works is a century-old copyright treaty that has undergone several revisions, the most recent known as the Paris Act of July 24, 1971. Berne stipulates specific minimum levels of copyright protection that must be enacted by member nations for the benefit of eligible copyrighted works (except phonorecords), including a minimum term of protection for copyrighted works of the life of the author plus 50 years in most cases; protection of foreign copyrights without the requirements of notice, deposit, registration, and other formali-ties; and limited moral rights for authors.

Advocates of U.S. adherence to the Berne Convention argued long and hard in the intervening years between 1955—when the United States first joined the less stringent but popular international copyright treaty, the Universal Copyright Convention (UCC)—and 1988 that UCC membership alone was inadequate to protect U.S. copyrights abroad. Their argument centered on the fact that the United States, as the world's leading copyright nation, greatly diminished its influence in the international copyright commu-nity and invited retaliatory and discriminatory treatment of American works in foreign countries by continuing to rely on a "free ride" for U.S. works on Berne. By illustration, American works were often accorded Berne-level protection through the back door because many UCC countries were also Berne members whose national copyright laws had been made compatible to Berne. U.S. works benefited on a nonreciprocal basis, even as the United States steadfastly refused to join the Berne Union.

With the enactment of the revised 1976 U.S. Copyright Act, which raised the term of U.S. copyright protection to the minimum Berne level of author's life plus 50 years (which has now been extended to life plus 70) adherence became more of a possibility. It took 12 more years, however, for Congress to pass the U.S. Berne Convention Implementation Act, finally bringing the United States into Berne compliance. The official entrance into the Berne Union of the United States came in March 1989.

The Effects of Berne Adherence

Works of American authors are now protected automatically in all countries of the Berne Union. There is a minimum level of copyright protection agreed to by members of the Union, and each Berne country provides at least that guaranteed level to American authors. Since members of the Berne Union agree to treat nationals of other member countries like their own nationals for purposes of copyright, American authors frequently receive greater levels of protection than the guaranteed minimum.

Works of foreign authors who are nationals of a Berne Union country and works first or simultaneously published in a Berne country are automatically protected in the United States. This is especially important for material in the public domain. As was discussed in Chapter 12, a significant revision of U.S. copyright policy now allows retroactive copyright protection for certain foreign works that were in the public domain due to the frequent failure to follow U.S. copyright formalities.

The Berne Convention Implementation Act of 1988 amended the Copyright Act of 1976 in several significant ways: copyright notice was eliminated as a prerequisite for U.S. copyright protection; the necessity for recordation of copyright assignments and documents of transfer as a prerequisite to suit was abolished; and the necessity for copyright registration of foreign works originating in other Berne member countries as a prerequisite to suit was also eliminated.

However, various incentives were included in the Copyright Act amendments to encourage copyright owners to continue to register and deposit copyrighted works with the U.S. Copyright Office, to include copyright notices on all copies, and to register works prior to suit. For instance, statutory damages and attorneys' fees are available only for registered works, and a certificate of registration acts as prima facie evidence of the validity and ownership of a copyright. In addition, if an infringement suit is instituted and there has been a copyright notice, the defendant cannot successfully mitigate actual or statutory damages by the defense of innocent infringement.

Under the Berne Act, Congress has made clear its view that existing statutory and common law in the United States satisfies the Berne moral rights standard without the need to amend U.S. law. The Berne standard provides that an author "shall have the right to claim authorship of [his or her] work and to object to any distortion, mutilation, or other modification of, or other derogatory action in relation to [his or her] work, which would be prejudicial to his honor or reputation."

An immediate effect of the entry of the United States into the Berne Union was the establishment of copyright relations for the reciprocal protection of copyrighted works in at least 24 non-UCC nations with whom the United States had no prior copyright treaties, including Egypt, Turkey, and Romania. (Appendix C lists both the members of the Berne Union and the signatories to the UCC.)

As Senator Patrick Leahy stated in introducing his Berne adherence bill in the U.S. Senate, "Vital American interests can be fully represented in the international copyright system only if we get off the sidelines and onto the playing field, by joining the Berne Convention." Illustrative of Senator Leahy's point, revision of the Berne Convention requires a unanimous vote of Berne members. By joining the Berne Union, the United States immediately acquired the right to veto amendments to Berne that could injure American interests. In addition, in this age of rapid technological developments and increasing worldwide popularity and use of American music, the United States gained a voice in the administration and management of the most important international copyright treaty.

Trade Negotiations and GATT

The United States has recognized that its copyright industry of film, records, music, and books are major contributors to its strength as an exporting nation. This "invisible export" is, in fact, second in importance to the aeronautics industry. Berne membership has also strengthened the ability of the U.S. Trade Representative to lobby for tougher copyright protection and more active enforcement of existing laws in foreign countries. This is especially true in regard to "pirate-haven" nations, which often used the U.S. failure to join Berne as an excuse not to heed American demands for more active protection of U.S. works.

By joining Berne, the United States increased its ability to influence the initiative of the international General Agreement on Tariffs and Trade to develop a new international code of minimum copyright protection and enforcement. A report released in February 1988 by the U.S. International Trade Commission estimated worldwide losses to American industry from inadequate protection of intellectual property rights to be between $43 and $61 billion. These rights are broader than copyright rights alone and include such rights as patent protection, trade secret protection, and enforcement to stop the counterfeiting of trademarks. No longer ostracized for its failure to join Berne, the United States is in a better position to be a leader among the approximately 100 World Trade Organization nations in striving for maximum international protection of intellectual property rights. These safeguards will supplement those set forth in Berne and the UCC.

U.S. Trade Representative

The office of the U.S. Trade Representative (USTR) has an important function in the motivation of foreign nations to protect U.S. copyrights. Under the strengthened Section 301 provisions of a recent omnibus trade act, the USTR may place those foreign nations engaging in unfair or lackadaisical treatment of U.S. intellectual property rights on its Priority Watch List. Once added to the list, those nations have 6 months to demonstrate "a full commitment toward the resolution" of intellectual property protection problems or face the possibility of trade sanctions. In the late 1980s, Brazil, China, India, Mexico, Saudi Arabia, South Korea, Taiwan, and Thailand were named to such a Priority Watch List, although subsequently Saudi Arabia, South Korea, and Thailand were deleted. A crisis was reached with China, that resulted in a February 26, 1995, trade agreement in which the Chinese government shut down more than six pirate CD plants. (Some of these plants have been reopened, albeit under government supervision.) The 1999 report listed the Dominican Republic, Egypt, Greece, Guatemala, India, Indonesia, Israel, Italy, Kuwait, Macao, Peru, Russia, Turkey, and Ukraine and detailed how each country had impacted American entertainment companies.

The USTR may also recommend that countries receiving trade preferences from the United States be denied such privileges for failure to protect American intellectual property within their national borders.

The International Intellectual Property Alliance, a group of seven major U.S. copyright industry associations, is dedicated to assisting the USTR in evaluating the treatment of U.S. works abroad and advising the USTR as to which nations the U.S. private sector believes should be targeted for inclusion on the Super 301 priority watch list.

The Buenos Aires Convention

The United States is also a signatory to the Buenos Aires Convention of 1910, along with Argentina, Brazil, Chile, Colombia, Costa Rica, Dominican Republic, Ecuador, Guatemala, Haiti, Honduras, Nicaragua, Panama, Paraguay, Peru, and Uruguay. By this convention, compliance with the copyright law of the country of first publication qualifies the work for protection in the other signatories to the convention. However, to secure copyright in these countries, each work must carry a notice to the effect that property rights in the copyright are reserved. While the U.S. copyright notice would appear to satisfy this requirement, it is advisable to add to the notice "All Rights Reserved."

Geneva Phonogram Convention

The Geneva Convention of October 29, 1971, for the Protection of Producers of Phonograms against Unauthorized Duplication (Geneva Convention of 1971) is an international treaty to protect sound recordings against piracy. Under the treaty, ratified by the United States on March 10, 1974, the participating countries agree to protect the nationals of other states against the production or importation of unauthorized duplicate recordings if the purpose is to distribute them to the public. The method used to accomplish this result is determined by the domestic law of each participating country and includes one or more of the following:

▸ Protection by means of the grant of copyright or other specific right
▸ Protection by means of the law relating to unfair competition
▸ Protection by means of penal sanctions

The United States, which became a member on March 10, 1974, implements the treaty through the federal copyright in sound recordings. However, the Geneva Convention is considered an inadequate alternative to the Rome Convention of 1961, which the United States has never signed. (For a description of international copyright relations of the United States, see Appendix C.)

WIPO Treaties

In December 1996, the World Intellectual Property Organization (WIPO), an intergovernmental organization based in Geneva that has been in existence since 1967, concluded two important treaties designed to establish minimum standards of copyright protection within the digital environment: the WIPO Copyright Treaty and the WIPO Performances and Phonograms Treaty. According to WIPO:

> These treaties contain a general update of the legal principles underpinning international protection of copyright and the rights of performers and phonogram producers in cyberspace. They also clarify that national law must prevent unauthorized access to and use of creative works which, given the global reach of the Internet, may be distributed, accessed, and reproduced anywhere in the world at the push of a button.

The United States is one of 11 countries that have ratified the Performances and Phonograms Treaty and one of 10 that have ratified the Copyright Treaty. A minimum of 30 countries must become signatories before either of these treaties can be implemented by statute. The American film, book, and music industries have been in the forefront of the international effort to obtain support for both treaties and for enforcement provisions that would establish private rights of civil litigation as well as local criminal enforcement in each member country. Controls against electronic theft in the digital age include prohibition against deletion or alteration of copyright management encryption and watermarking and any other practice designed to circumvent protection and facilitate theft.

In 1998, WIPO set up a Standing Committee on Copyright and Related Rights, which, to date, has met three times. At the third session, held in November 1999 and attended by 80 member states, one important topic for discussion was the need to establish an international instrument for protection of audiovisual performances.

Appendix A consists of excerpts from the memorandum issued by WIPO in 1996 explaining the reasoning behind the wording of the treaties referred to above. Appendix B reproduces all articles in the Berne Convention referred to in the WIPO memorandum. Appendix C, U.S. Copyright Office Circular 38a: International Copyright Relations of the United States, sets forth U.S. copyright relations of current interest with the other independent nations of the world. Appendix D provides most of the text of the Digital Millennium Copyright Act of 1998, the passage of which made the United States a signatory to the WIPO treaties.

21

Foreign Publishing

In the past, American music publishers derived most of their income on a composition from its exploitation in the United States and Canada. Only a rare song, such as one from a motion picture or musical play, could pierce the barriers of foreign languages and different tastes abroad. Consequently, American publishers often negotiated foreign subpublishing deals that emphasized obtaining a locally originated foreign recording (in trade parlance, a "cover record") or an immediate advance of monies. There was a minimum of bargaining as to the amount of royalty, the extent of the territory licensed, the duration of the license, and the minimum exploitation to be guaranteed by the subpublisher.

Today the international aspects of the music industry are firmly established and foreign earnings have become a major factor in the profit-and-loss figures of American publishers. It is now possible for sales of an American recording in Europe to equal or even surpass sales in the United States. Language barriers are disappearing. Young people throughout the world have learned at least some English from listening to popular music. Despite the efforts of some countries, such as France, to preserve national culture by requiring that broadcasts contain a minimum content of local music, English is still the most important language for lyrics on a worldwide basis.

A number of factors contribute to the internationalization of popular music: airings on local stations, the influence of Armed Forces radio stations, international tours of recording and concert stars, promotional videos disseminated via the Internet, cheaper air freight charges for finished records, worldwide marketing of motion pictures and syndicated television shows, reduced trade barriers, and the increase in disposable income in many countries.

In the past, American jazz, film, and show music were particularly strong in the international market. More recently, American rhythm and blues, rock, and even country music have gained international acceptance. As a result, competition to acquire foreign rights to successful American songs is intense.

The World Market for Music

Based on statistics compiled by the International Federation of the Phonographic Industry (IFPI), worldwide sales of sound recordings in 1997 were $38.1 billion. These figures represent a worldwide decline of 4 percent from 1996, including a 7 percent decline in the United States and an 11 percent increase in Latin America. (See Table 21-1.)

According to the National Music Publishers Association (NMPA), total 1997 worldwide music publishing income from all sources was $6 billion. (See Table 21-2.) This included income from performance (radio, cable and satellite TV, and live performance), reproductions (phonomechanical, synchronization and transcription, and private copy), distribution (sale of printed music and rental and public lending), and miscellaneous sources (including interest and investment income).

Representation by Subpublishers

Foreign publishers who represent American music are called *subpublishers*, while the American publishers that own the music in the first instance are called *original publishers*. Agreements with subpublishers are commonly referred to as *subpublication agreements*. (See the accompanying CD-ROM for a sample of a "Foreign Subpublication Agreement.") Apart from differences in geographical scope, subpublication agreements may be limited to one or more compositions or may encompass all compositions owned or controlled by the original publisher. The latter agreement is called a *catalog subpublication contract*.

American music publishers have various options for achieving proper representation abroad. If the original publisher chooses to deal with a large international publisher such as Warner/Chappell or EMI Music Publishing, it enjoys the convenience of a single point of contact. The original publisher may also obtain a larger advance from a single entity than it can from making separate territorial deals, since the advance will be cross-collateralized out of earnings from multiple territories. On the other hand, through the wise selection of separate subpublishers in various foreign territories, a U.S. publisher may achieve better overall representation, including more aggressive promotion in each territory. The territory-by-territory approach necessarily assumes a much greater investment in time and effort on the part of the original publisher to investigate and become familiar with the music business and publishers in each territory and to correspond and enter into contractual relations with them.

Whether the subpublication agreement includes a single composition or an entire catalog, there are various provisions to be negotiated. Most important among these is the division of royalties between the original publisher and the subpublisher and whether the division of royalties is to be calculated "at the source" when more than one territory is involved. Also to be negotiated are the

Table 21-1
Distribution of Sound Recording Sales Worldwide, 1997 (%)

North America	33.8 %
Europe	33.3 %
Japan	16.4 %
Latin America	6.8 %
Rest of the world	9.7 %

subpublisher's ability to retain rights beyond the expiration of the term if a local recording or some other substantial level of exploitation is attained as a result of the subpublisher's efforts, and whether the royalty division changes in favor of the subpublisher if this occurs.

Foreign Performing Rights Societies

Performing rights societies exist in most countries of the world to license performing rights and collect fees for such licenses. In some instances the same society also licenses mechanical rights. In terms of collections, the largest societies outside the United States and Canada are GEMA in Germany, JASRAC in Japan, the PRS/MCPS alliance in the United Kingdom, and SACEM/SDRM in France. (The functions of these foreign societies are discussed in Chapters 14 and 15.)

There are two important aspects of foreign publishing contracts that need to be recognized. First, an original publisher may (but usually does not) require that its share of public performance income be routed back to its own performing rights society, in accordance with multilateral agreements between the various societies, rather than being collected by the subpublisher. Second, the writers' share of public performance income may in some instances be automatically reduced by the share payable to foreign translators and arrangers under the rules of the local performing rights society.

Table 21-2
Worldwide Music Publishing Income from All Sources, 1997 ($ billions)

United States	$1.473
Germany	.831
United Kingdom	.779
Japan	.656
France	.480
Italy	.357
Netherlands	.302

Foreign Mechanical Licensing

Many American publishers use the services of the Harry Fox Agency to license and collect mechanical royalties (discussed in Chapter 15). Although the agency has traditionally asserted jurisdiction only over phonorecords distributed within the United States and permitted records made domestically to be exported without payment of American mechanical royalties where it had reasonable assurance that mechanical royalties would be paid in the country of sale, it has taken the position that U.S. mechanical royalties must be paid even on exports, owing to alleged difficulties in obtaining verification of foreign mechanical royalty payment. This position has irritated foreign mechanical societies and thrown a new wrinkle into the negotiation of foreign subpublication agreements.

Outside the United States, and particularly in Europe, the usual method of collection of mechanical royalties is through national mechanical rights societies. With the exception of the United Kingdom, the national societies in Europe negotiate industrywide licenses for phonorecord reproduction rights through a confederation known as BIEM (Bureau International des Sociétés Gérants des Droits d'Enregistrement et de Reproduction Mécanique), which negotiates with IFPI, the record industry trade association. These negotiations are on two levels. On an international basis BIEM and IFPI negotiate the general licensing system and the standard rate. Then the national societies settle such things as the amount of deductions from the standard rate and the minimum royalty.

The structure of BIEM licensing is conceptually different than in the United States. In the United States the reproduction of each musical composition on each phonorecord is individually licensed, whereas the BIEM-IFPI agreement grants phonograph record manufacturers a blanket license, similar to the music licenses that performing rights organizations grant to broadcasters. In the United States the current statutory rate is 7.55 cents per song per phonorecord sold, whereas the net BIEM rate (after deductions for discounts and packaging) under the July 1, 1997, agreement (effective until June 30, 2000) was 9.009 percent of the published price to dealers (PPD) on full-price product before the implementation of the Cannes Accord (see below). Depending on the rate of exchange and relative prices, the BIEM rate generally works out to a higher amount (in dollars and cents) than the mechanical royalty rate in the United States.

The European scene has undergone substantial changes in recent years. Before the formation of the European Union, there was some dissension over which national society would handle collections on exported records, as well as which national licensing rate would apply. Since the formation of the EU, any member-country society can license reproduction rights, regardless of the place of ultimate sale. This initially led to intense competition between the various national mechanical rights societies to make "central licensing" deals with international record companies. PolyGram initially made a deal with STEMRA in the Netherlands and subsequently with MCPS in the United Kingdom; BMG and Warner dealt with GEMA in Germany; and Sony dealt with SDRM in France.

In order to deal with the issues such as the "social and cultural" deductions levied by various national societies (especially GEMA in Germany and SACEM in France) as well as high administration costs, the principal publishers and the European societies struck an agreement in Cannes in January 1997. Under this so-called Cannes Accord, the societies pledged to reduce their average administration charges from more than 8 percent to 7.1 percent as of December 1998, 6.27 percent as of June 2000, and 6 percent as of June 2001. The Cannes Accord also established an ultimate goal of distributions within 90 days of each calendar quarter. Whether these goals can be attained remains to be seen.

In 1999 a consortium of ASCAP, BUMA/STEMRA, and PRS/MCPS joined forces under the rubric of the International Music Joint Venture. The express purpose of the IMJV is to bring together the "back office" aspects of operations so as to eliminate duplication, increase efficiency, reduce operating costs, and thereby improve services to members. If the IMJV program goes as planned, a shared service center should be up and running in the Netherlands by 2002. Although the centralization of administrative aspects of the various national societies seems inevitable, there are powerful local interests, which suggests that the local societies will continue to be important.

Unauthorized reproduction of music has been a problem in several territories, most recently in Brazil, Bulgaria, China, Panama, Paraguay, Russia, and certain other countries in the Pacific Rim. This problem threatens to become even more serious as digital recording devices proliferate. Continuing vigilance, such as the Harry Fox Agency's 1993 agreement with more than 100 Pacific Rim record companies represented through the Audio Publishing Commercial Association of the Republic of China (APAROC) in Taiwan, will be required to combat this threat.

The Harry Fox Agency represents the mechanical rights controlled by most of the foreign mechanical rights societies (and through them their publisher affiliates) in the United States. Many of these foreign societies accept direct membership by U.S. publishers without the intercession of a local publisher. Through its relationship with foreign societies, the Harry Fox Agency can act as agent for those American publishers that have not directly affiliated with the foreign societies and have not authorized a local foreign publisher to subpublish their copyrights. (The Harry Fox Agency is discussed in detail in Chapter 15.)

As noted previously, mechanical license fees relate to a license to use copyrighted compositions on records. Mechanical license fees are customarily based on the number of copies of a record that are sold and are divided proportionately among the copyright owners of the music used on the record.

When subpublishers are granted subpublication rights in a composition, they customarily receive the power to collect mechanical license fees and the publisher's share of performance fees. (Only the remaining "publisher share" is remitted to the subpublisher when it has the right to collect performance fees; the U.S. writer's share of performance fees—usually 50 percent of total performance fees—is reserved for the writers by the local performing rights society and remitted directly to the writer's society.) The historical division of collections between the original (U.S.) publisher and the local subpublisher is 50-50. However, competitive forces have tended to increase the percentage paid to the U.S. publisher to 75 percent (and sometimes more) of the amounts collected by the subpublisher.

If a composition has been released on a commercial record in the United States and the same recording has been or is likely to be released in the foreign territory, the original publisher in the United States may insist on receiving more than the usual share of performance fees and mechanical fees. The argument for this is that the subpublisher is only a collecting agent, and therefore only a collection charge, from 10 to 15 percent, should be retained by the local subpublisher. Some subpublishers accede to such arguments.

Other subpublishers oppose any reduction in their fee. They contend that they may be the moving force in causing the local release of the original U.S. recording. They must spend time and money promoting the U.S. recording to make it successful. They also point out that performance fees are earned by live as well as record performances and that a reduced fee would unfairly compensate them for their efforts in printing, arranging, and distributing the composition so that it will be performed by orchestras and vocalists. Their position is reinforced if they obtain local cover recordings. They also argue that the performing rights societies' records do not adequately separate performances of the original U.S. recordings from other performances.

In the area of motion picture and television film performance fees, the subpublisher will generally agree to a fee of 10 to 15 percent because only a collection arrangement is involved. Music cue sheets that list the music in American films are received from the United States and are filed with the performing rights society. The society makes clear and separate accountings for each film, and the subpublisher can do little to affect the amounts collected. In Europe, motion picture performance fees for theatrical films are collected from theaters as a small percentage of box office receipts. Television film performance fees are received from the television stations.

Under some contractual arrangements a subpublisher retains from 10 to 25 percent of receipts in its territory on compositions for which there is no locally originated recording and a higher percentage after a local recording is obtained. The increased rate may be 30 to 50 percent of all receipts from the composition; or the higher rate may be limited to mechanical and synchronization income from the local version only. If the local version has a different title than the original song, it is possible to distinguish the performance earnings of the original and local versions and to accurately allocate to the subpublisher a lower percentage of income from nonlocal recordings and a higher percentage of income from the local version.

Synchronization Fees

A synchronization license fee is payable for a publisher's consent to the recording of a composition as a part of the soundtrack of a motion picture or television film. When a composition is subpublished, it is standard for the subpublisher to acquire the right to grant worldwide nonexclusive synchronization licenses for motion picture or television films originating in the local territory. Fifty percent or more of the synchronization fees are payable to the American publisher. However, for films originating outside the subpublisher's territory, the U.S. publisher usually reserves the right to issue worldwide synchronization licenses for fees in which the local subpublisher does not share, even though the film may be shown in the local territory. However, the subpublisher participates in local performance income from the music in the film.

Under the Songwriters Guild of America's standard songwriter agreement, the writer must approve vocal renditions, dramatic representations, or exclusive uses of a composition in films. As a consequence, American publishers may reserve all synchronization rights or may insist on the right to be notified and to approve synchronization licenses proposed for issuance by a subpublisher. Regardless of the SGA form, American publishers may desire this notice and right of approval in order to have control on the proposed price to be charged for the synchronization license.

The producers of audiovisual devices such as videocassettes or videodiscs customarily request worldwide licenses for synchronization and marketing rights. To facilitate such licenses, original publishers may deny subpublishers the right to license and collect fees on audiovisual recordings that originate outside the subpublisher's territory, even though the devices containing such recordings are distributed in the subpublisher's territory.

Printed Editions

The royalty customarily payable by the local subpublisher to the original publisher in the United States for printed editions is 10 to 12.5 percent of the suggested retail price of such editions. If folios or albums are printed, and the U.S. publisher's composition is included with other compositions, the American publisher receives a prorated share of 10 to 12.5 percent computed in the ratio that the composition bears to the total number of compositions in the edition. Many agreements provide that public domain compositions in the editions be excluded in calculating the publisher's prorated share.

Provision should be made for sample copies of printed editions to be supplied gratis to the original publisher. A reasonable number of copies—four, for example—may be required.

Local Lyrics and Versions

A subpublisher usually acquires the right to make translations, adaptations, and arrangements of a composition so that it may be exploited commercially in the local territory. This includes the right to provide new lyrics and a new title. For compositions other than instrumentals, the subpublisher will have difficulties marketing the composition if it cannot be adapted for use in the subpublisher's territory by the addition of lyrics in the local language, a new title, and appropriate musical arrangements. For instance, the popular song "Never on Sunday" is called "Les Enfants du Pire" (Children of Piraeus) in France and "Ein Schiff Wird Kommen" (A Ship Will Come) in Germany, and there are different lyrics in each language. The song would not have achieved its worldwide popularity without these local versions. In fact, one criterion in selecting a subpublisher is its ability to cause appropriate adaptations of a composition to be made and recorded by significant local talent.

Local Writer Royalties

Royalties payable to a sublyricist—the person who writes lyrics for the local version—are frequently 12.5 percent of the subpublisher's gross receipts for mechanical and synchronization uses, 25 percent of the total writer's share payable in the territory in respect of public performance income, and 50 percent of the usual lyric writer royalties for territorial printed edition sales. It is customary for the subpublisher to bear, out of its share, the royalty payable to the local lyric writer for mechanical and synchronization uses and for the sale of printed editions. The subpublisher can more easily afford this when provision is made for its royalties to increase when there are local cover records. The share of public performance fees due the local lyric writer is usually deducted by the local public performance society from the share of the original writer. If the music and lyrics of the original song were written jointly by two separate writers, the public performance fees payable to the local writer is deducted equally from the shares of the original writers.

Some public performance societies provide for local arrangers to receive a portion of the original music writer's share of public performance fees. For many years, local lyric adapters of successful English language songs participated even when the original version was played or sold. The argument given was that the local version helped to popularize the original version in the local territory, as well as the convenience of having a uniform royalty division for all versions of the song. The result was grossly unfair to original writers, and much money was diverted to local writers who had nothing to do with the work actually performed. Under the rules adopted by CISAC (the international association of performing rights societies), sublyricists participate only when their local version is actually used, at least on a prospective basis, but this may not affect some pre-existing situations where the local adapter had nothing to with the original recording. (See Chapter 14.)

Copyright and Term of Rights

Subpublishers once sought to have rights conveyed to them for the entire term of copyright in their territory rather than for a limited number of years. It is in the interest of the American publisher to limit the duration of the grant of rights, but not to the point of discouraging activity by the subpublisher. In recent years the trend has been to grant rights for shorter periods, usually not more than 3 years, with the possibility of an extension where cover records or use in a motion picture is obtained. Some foreign societies, such as GEMA in Germany, may not recognize a subpublication agreement unless it has a minimum duration, ordinarily 3 years, although they may accept a reversionary clause that is activated sooner by the subpublisher's failure to achieve certain performance tests.

Under the Copyright Act of 1976 as amended in 1998 by the Sonny Bono Term Extension Act, copyrights now last for the author's life plus 70 years, the same as the term of copyright in most European countries. Although the author may have the right to terminate grants after 35 years, the exercise of this termination right will not affect foreign subpublication rights. (Where publication is involved, the period is 35 years from publication or 40 years from execution of the grant, whichever is earlier. See Chapter 11.)

While all rights under copyright may be granted to a subpublisher, the original publisher normally reserves the ownership of the copyright. This is a necessity if the agreement with the writer is a Songwriters Guild of America contract. If the original publisher requests it, the subpublisher will agree that each copy of the composition published by the subpublisher will bear a notice of copyright in the name of the original publisher.

A problem may arise, however, regarding local arrangements, translations, and adaptations, as well as local lyrics and titles. The subpublisher may attempt to retain the copyright for these local modifications and versions insofar as they contain new material. An experienced American publisher will oppose this because, unless that publisher acquires the copyright in new material, it may be unable to exploit the composition fully in the local territory after the subpublisher's rights expire. In addition, the subpublisher who owns the copyright in new material would have to be asked to consent to its use by another subpublisher in a different territory and would presumably require a royalty payment as the price for such consent. The American publisher should insist upon acquiring all rights in new material outside the particular local territory.

In catalog deals it is common to provide that compositions revert to the original publisher at the end of the term. Exceptions are sometimes made for compositions that have been printed locally, or released on a locally originated record, or both printed and released on records. The subpublisher may contend that the local release of the original American recording should justify continuing rights in a composition, since the subpublisher may cause such release. The duration of the continuing rights is a matter of negotiation between the original publisher and the subpublisher. Provision is sometimes made for some extension of rights in compositions that are made available to the subpublisher only toward the end of the catalog deal and for which there has been printing or release on a local record, or both, before the close of the term; otherwise, the subpublisher would have little or no incentive to promote such songs.

Fees from All Usage, Accounting, and Audits

Subpublication contracts specify the royalties payable to the original publisher for various uses of a composition. In order to avoid being penalized for failing to set forth all conceivable uses, the American publisher must be careful to provide that it is entitled to a stipulated percentage of all monies collected by the subpublisher for any use other than those specified in the agreement, whether or not such use is presently known or subsequently invented. There should be no objection by the subpublisher to the inclusion of this provision.

Problems may develop regarding accountings and royalty payments due to the American publisher. The subpublication contract should clearly define the subpublisher's obligation to account for and make payment. A common provision requires the subpublisher to send the original publisher an itemized and detailed royalty statement every 6 months within 90 days of the end of each calendar half-year, and at the same time to remit all royalties shown to be due. It is advisable to specify the items to be included in the statement so that disputes about the completeness of the accounting may be avoided. For mechanical income these items may consist of a list of the individual records released in the territory, the names of the artists and record companies on the records, the number of records sold, and the total fees received. Accountings for printed editions should itemize separately the different editions, the retail price, and the number of copies sold.

Most countries have reciprocal tax treaties with the United States whereby copyright royalties are exempt from withholding taxes or subject to reduced withholding taxes. Japan is an example of the latter. Where there are foreign withholding taxes on remittances to the original publisher, the latter should be furnished with an appropriate certificate to enable the original publisher to obtain a U.S. tax credit for foreign taxes paid.

In certain instances the subpublisher may agree to furnish a photocopy of all statements received from the mechanical rights society and the performing rights society. It is more likely that this will apply to a single song than to a catalog since the societies account alphabetically, with many compositions on a page, and hundreds of pages may be involved in the latter instance. On the other hand, the subpublisher may so strongly desire the rights to a catalog that it will agree to the extra work involved in extrapolating the pertinent portions of its general statements or in organizing the separate registration of a catalog at the local societies.

In order to verify and facilitate the collection of royalties due, American publishers may wish to have royalties paid directly to their own performing rights society and mechanical rights collection agency. In these cases, the subpublisher may be required to instruct its local performing rights society to pay the original publisher's share to that publisher's own performing rights society. If the American publisher has entered into an affiliation agreement with a local mechanical rights society, that society may be instructed to pay the appropriate share of mechanical rights collections directly to the American publisher. Alternatively, the Harry Fox Agency may serve as the American publisher's representative abroad and receive the American publisher's share of mechanical rights collections on the American publisher's behalf. The Cannes Accord, discussed above, is one attempt to reduce delays in remittances from abroad as well as administrative charges by the foreign societies.

There are also risks of loss caused by commingling the accounts of many publishers or by the failure to identify foreign version song titles. These risks may be worthwhile if the appointment of a subpublisher results in the receipt of greater overall royalties, some of which might otherwise fail to be accounted for. A prudent American publisher will obtain the right to inspect and audit the account books of the subpublisher. It may be impracticable for the American publisher to exercise the right through its own employees or accountant because of the expense involved, but the publisher's audit rights may be exercised by a local accountant at a lower cost.

Subpublication for Diverse Territories

An American publisher may contract with a subpublisher for several countries under one agreement. However, within the 15 member states of the European Union, where free trade is mandated by EU directive, the traditional country breakdowns seem increasingly irrelevant. To the extent that the original American publisher considers it desirable to enter separate subpublishing agreements for various territories, the following are the traditional grouping (italicized names represent countries that may also be licensed alone):

- European Union, excluding the United Kingdom and Ireland
- *Germany*, Austria, and Switzerland
- Scandinavia, including Sweden, Norway, Denmark, Finland, and Iceland
- *Spain* and Portugal
- *United Kingdom and Northern Ireland*
- *France* and territories under the jurisdiction of SACEM
- *Japan*

- Far East, including China, Singapore, Malaysia, Taiwan, and Thailand
- *Belgium, the Netherlands,* and Luxembourg, often collectively referred to as Benelux. (Belgium is sometimes included with France, and Luxembourg is split between Germany and France on a language basis.)
- *Italy,* Vatican City, and San Marino
- *Australia* and New Zealand
- *South Africa*
- *Mexico,* Central America, Venezuela, Colombia, Ecuador, and Peru
- *Argentina,* Uruguay, Chile, Paraguay, and Bolivia
- *Brazil*
- *Greece*
- Poland, the Czech Republic, Slovak Republic, Romania, Hungary, and other former nations of the Soviet Union. (The effect of political and economic changes in the countries of the former Eastern Bloc makes it difficult to predict the future state of business relations with these countries.)

As indicated above, the original publisher in the United States receives royalties equivalent to negotiated percentages of various types of income collected by the subpublisher. Where the subpublisher's territory includes more than one country and the subpublisher uses the services of one or more secondary subpublishers in other countries, the latter will deduct a fee before remitting collections to the former, which can reduce the royalties paid to the original publisher. For example, if the secondary subpublisher's fee is 50 percent, the primary subpublisher will be paid only 50 percent of the funds earned "at the source." If the primary subpublication contract requires 50 percent of collections to be remitted to the American publisher, the American publisher would then be entitled to be paid only 25 percent of the earnings "at the source." As a result, nearly all subpublishing calculations are required to be made "at the source," thus requiring the primary subpublisher to absorb the cost of collection commissions deducted by the secondary subpublishers. Moreover, as the original American publisher must usually pay 50 percent of its own receipts to the writer, the writer is also vitally interested in not allowing the diminution of monies as they pass from one country to another.

It should be noted that 50 percent of performing rights society monies are invariably collected and paid at the source to the account of the writer's originating society so that only the publisher's share of performing rights monies are involved in the subpublishing collection and payments. The writer does not get paid again out of the publisher share of performing rights income remitted to the original publisher.

The European Union

At present there are 15 member states in the European Union: Austria, Belgium, Denmark, England, Finland, France, Germany, Greece, Ireland, Italy,

Luxembourg, the Netherlands, Portugal, Spain, and Sweden. Relations among members are governed by the Treaty of Rome, which provides for the abolition of tariff barriers and the free and unrestricted movement of goods across state borders. Territorial sales restrictions in license agreements among the EU countries are generally invalid. Similar restrictions apply to the four nations in the European Free Trade Association: Iceland, Liechtenstein, Norway, and Switzerland.

Questions arise as to the legality of exclusive subpublishing agreements with publishers in different EU states. For example, there may be one agreement with a subpublisher in England covering exclusive rights there and another with a subpublisher in France providing for exclusive rights in that country. Must each of these subpublishers respect and recognize the exclusive rights of the other? In practice, if a subpublishing agreement is for a limited term, the prospect of nonrenewal by the original American publisher may tend to keep each subpublisher within the bounds of its own territory. But third parties, such as companies that buy phonograph records lawfully licensed for manufacture in France are free, under the Treaty of Rome, to export the records into England and other EU countries. The same also applies to printed editions manufactured in one EU state and bought for export to another.

The Treaty of Rome has been said not to affect the exclusive rights of copyright proprietors with respect of such matters as rented sheet music or the licensing of the public performance of copyrighted works. To what extent the Treaty of Rome restricts exclusivity and territorial restraints in subpublishing agreements is not entirely clear, and consequently the advice of local counsel should be obtained. Infringements of the treaty may involve not only the negation of business deals but also, in certain cases, prosecution and fines by the European Commission, which is one of the five governing institutions within the European Union.

Frozen Funds

Because of government restrictions, funds may not always be readily transmittable to the United States in payment of royalties due to the American publisher. In such cases, a clause in the subpublication contract may provide that in the event that remittances are prohibited or delayed by governmental authority, the American publisher may direct the subpublisher to deposit the funds to the account of the American publisher in a designated depository. It is possible that the American publisher may be able to use the monies on deposit for local purchases, transportation, and living expenses; some American publishers affiliated with motion picture companies have been able to use portions of frozen funds for the production of motion pictures in the local country. In addition, the money may earn interest and be invested locally. It is also removed from the risk of insolvency or misuse of the funds by the subpublisher.

Default Clauses

It is difficult and often impossible to anticipate the legal effect, especially in a distant territory, of a default by a subpublisher in the performance of an obligation without a clear statement in the agreement of the effect intended by the parties. For example, if an accounting statement or a royalty payment is delayed, can this be a ground for canceling the agreement?

It is therefore advisable to include in the subpublication agreement a clause that defines the rights and obligations of the parties in case of default. From the American publisher's point of view, it can be provided that there will be a material default if the subpublisher fails to (1) make periodic accountings, (2) pay royalties when due, or (3) release local cover records if that has been promised. Such a failure may give the American publisher grounds to terminate the agreement and cause a reversion of all rights in the composition. The subpublisher can in turn guard against cancellation by a clause under which the subpublisher must receive written notice of any default and an opportunity for a certain period, perhaps 30 days, to cure the default.

The default clause may further state that the American publisher can cancel the subpublication agreement in the event an insolvency or bankruptcy proceeding is begun by or against the subpublisher and is not dismissed within a given period, such as 30 to 60 days. Such a provision may protect the American publisher from the possibility of its copyright being administered by a trustee or an assignee by reason of an insolvency or bankruptcy action. Should the subpublisher continue in control of the copyright, such a provision gives the American publisher the possibility of reassessing the financial and other capability of the subpublisher and of terminating the agreement in case the American publisher is dissatisfied.

Jurisdiction over Disputes

Despite careful draftsmanship, subpublication contracts may still result in disputes regarding their interpretation. Recognizing this fact and the expense involved in litigating a matter in a foreign country, American publishers strive to provide in subpublication agreements that the exclusive forum for the determination of controversies will be American courts or an American arbitration tribunal in a specified location (customarily where the original publisher's main office is located) and that the subpublisher consents to that jurisdiction. Even when such a clause exists in a subpublication agreement, there may be problems enforcing an award in a foreign jurisdiction if the due process standards of that jurisdiction are not complied with.

Catalog Agreements

It has been previously stated that if all the compositions of an American publisher are the subject of a publication agreement, the agreement may be considered as a *catalog subpublication contract* under which all compositions are subpublished by the subpublisher for the term of the agreement. A catalog subpublication agreement has the advantage of relieving the American publisher of the burden of negotiating separately for representation in the territory of each composition in the catalog. However, it also means that the American publisher cannot shop for the largest cash advance among the various foreign subpublishers that may be interested in a musical work.

On the other hand, an American publisher can require an overall cash advance for its catalog as the price for committing its entire catalog to a single subpublisher. It is possible, although unlikely, that the overall advance will exceed the separate advances that might be negotiated for individual compositions. In negotiating a catalog deal, an American publisher may be able to obtain other concessions, such as increased royalty rates and a shorter term for the subpublisher's interest in copyrights, which would not be granted if single compositions were involved.

Local Firms

Larger American publishers may eventually try to establish their own firms in a local territory. The attempt may prove to be unfeasible economically unless their catalog is suitable for and potentially strong in the locality. Otherwise the investment for office space, personnel, and overhead may be unwarranted.

Some foreign performing rights societies tend to discourage foreign-controlled publishing firms. As a condition of membership, a society may insist that a new firm control a stipulated amount of locally originated material. Generally, lower-rung memberships in societies may be permitted, which gives the right to be represented by the society and to receive publisher distributions. Becoming a full member with additional voting and other rights can be more difficult. For example, PRS, the British performing rights society, requires an associate member to earn a minimum of about £17,000 a year in at least 2 of 3 recent years before qualifying for full membership.

At times the problem of attaining full membership may be solved by the purchase of local publishing firms that have already qualified for such memberships. On the other hand, an American publisher may be satisfied with a lower-rung membership provided that, as is commonly observed by societies, the lesser members receive distributions on an equal basis with full members. The practices of each society should be investigated prior to the establishment of a local firm by an American publisher.

Joint Firms

Recognizing the perils and problems represented by a firm that is wholly owned locally, many American publishers have in the past embarked on joint publishing ventures with an established local publisher. Together the parties create a jointly owned firm. In this way the American publisher acquires local management and know-how at a minimum of cost. Advantageous arrangements can be made whereby the local partner manages the joint company and supplies the necessary office and other facilities for a fee, which is commonly a percentage of gross revenues of the joint company. The fee may be roughly 10 to 15 percent and is generally exclusive of direct expenses billed to the joint company for costs of demonstration records, advertising in trade publications, salaries of personnel who work solely for the joint company, and special legal and accounting services. In some instances the local partner may absorb all expenses in return for a negotiated fee.

Where a new joint firm is organized, the local partner arranges for its formation through territorial counsel. The local partner may advance the organization expenses as a charge against future net income of the joint company. Because the American publisher should be fully aware of the impact of territorial laws and practices, it should give serious consideration to being represented by its own local counsel, who, for adequate representation, should be familiar with the music business in the area, including the practices of the performing rights society.

If the local performing rights society will not qualify a new firm for membership unless it controls locally originated material, arrangements must be made with the territorial partner to supply this material. Otherwise the joint firm may never achieve membership in the society and may continue to be dependent on firms with membership for relations with the society.

The local performing rights society may not qualify a new firm for full membership unless certain standards are met. If the American publisher wants full membership for the proposed joint firm, the contract with the territorial partner may provide for the acquisition of a local publishing company that is a full member.

A problem in the operation of joint firms is that they may be administered by the local partner as if they were catalog deals. In other words, only the material from the American publisher goes into the joint firm, and nothing is done by the local partner to develop the firm's status as a local publisher that vigorously seeks to acquire and exploit territorial copyrights. This is easily understood, since the local partner must decide whether to place any new material with its own publishing enterprise or with the joint firm in which it has merely a 50 percent interest. In effect, the local partner tends to treat a joint firm as a catalog deal in which the American partner's 50 percent interest is equivalent to an increased royalty; in return for the increased royalty the territorial partner is assured of a flow of desirable product for a number of years.

Overcoming the inertia of the territorial partner is not easy. One approach may be to employ a professional manager who works solely for the joint firm. This can result in a large financial burden for the firm, which the American partner and the territorial partner may be unwilling to risk. The local partner is ordinarily the one who chooses the professional manager and may therefore be able to influence the manager to permit choice copyrights to remain with the local partner's publishing firm. The territorial partner may consciously choose an ineffective professional manager so that the joint firm is not built up as a strong competitor in local publishing.

Perhaps the answer lies in a formula, undoubtedly difficult to administer, whereby a certain proportion of local copyrights acquired by the territorial partner must rest with the joint firm. Of course, even with a formula, the American partner cannot be sure of receiving an interest in quality copyrights.

Joint firms have a number of advantages over catalog arrangements. For example, if the joint firm is a member of the local performing rights and mechanical rights societies, the accountings for copyrights controlled by the firm will be completely segregated, and losses due to improper accountings by the local partner will be avoided. Where the subpublisher's honesty and dependability are above reproach, this advantage may be of little importance. The American publisher may anticipate a greater overall return from a joint company than would otherwise be derived from a catalog deal, but if the publisher fails to assess all the factors adequately, this will ultimately affect the company's earnings.

Let us take a practical example. Assume that the joint firm grosses $50,000 during a given year, of which $25,000 (50 percent, per contract) is paid to the American partner as customary subpublication royalties. A balance of $25,000 remains. From the $25,000 the local partner deducts its management fee of 10 percent of the gross ($5,000), leaving $20,000. Direct expenses, such as demonstration records and advertising, are also deductible. Assuming direct expenses of $5,000, or about 10 percent of the gross, the balance is $15,000, which constitutes net profits. Taxes on profits in European countries range from about 30 to 55 percent. Assuming in this instance a 50 percent tax rate, the taxes on net profits are $7,500. The remaining profits, $7,500, are split equally between the partners, so that each receives $3,750.

In terms of the gross, $50,000, the profit share of each partner in the example given is about 7.5 percent. On the face of it, it would appear that the U.S. publisher is receiving the equivalent of a 57.5 percent royalty. In fact, the publisher is receiving more. The 7.5 percent increase should be doubled to 15 percent, bringing the total received to 65 percent, because under international tax conventions, the 50 percent (or other percentage) tax paid in the principal foreign countries can be offset against U.S. domestic taxes. Under catalog arrangements, on the other hand, royalties received are subject to U.S. domestic taxes, whereas the profit from a joint company would in a real sense be exempt from domestic taxes.

Even the 65 percent figure does not offer an absolutely true comparison with a catalog arrangement, since in the case of catalog royalties, 50 percent of monies received in the United States as foreign mechanical fees and foreign printed editions are payable to the writers. As a result, the American publisher would get only half of the extra 15 percent for mechanical fees and a printed editions royalty received under a catalog deal, whereas writers would not be likely to share in any part of an equivalent 15 percent received in the form of profits. Of course, the writers would not participate in any performance fees collected under a catalog deal, and such fees can be expected to account for a significant percentage of additional earnings from increased royalty rates.

It can be argued that an American publisher with a joint firm is better able to acquire from other American publishers foreign territorial rights in American copyrights. With a joint firm an American publisher may effectively represent that it is actually in business in a territory. It may actively engage in pursuing territorial rights in attractive U.S. copyrights. It may have the authority to execute subpublication agreements with and make cash advances to American publishers on behalf of the joint firm. Its representatives outside the United States may also seek to obtain rights in local copyrights for areas where there are joint firms.

In the absence of a joint firm, arrangements can be made with subpublishers for an American publisher to receive a commission or finder's fee for copyrights acquired for subpublication by the subpublishers; these commissions or fees may equal the compensation accruing through an interest in a joint firm. But such arrangements are unlikely to operate as flexibly and as well as those with a joint firm. In the one instance the American publisher is merely an agent for the subpublisher, with limited powers and authority; in the other the publisher is a partner striving to increase the profits and minimize the risks and losses for a jointly owned business.

Finally, it must be recognized that while a catalog deal is designed to exploit a catalog and result in a profit to the American publisher, the joint firm not only accomplishes the same purpose but can also act as a necessary prelude to a wholly locally owned publishing enterprise. It has been pointed out that many American publishers cannot afford the expense and overhead of a wholly owned local firm. This may be true only for the period of years during which the American publisher's catalog is becoming established in an area. At the end of the period, the American publisher may have both the earnings and the vehicle, namely the joint company, for its own publishing business. To convert the joint firm into one owned entirely by the American publisher means that it must acquire the interest of the local partner.

The Termination of Joint Ownership

Inherent in the formation of a joint company is the agreement on the part of the American partner to make a catalog deal with the company for a period of years. The number of years is subject to negotiations: 3 to 5 years is common. It is usual to provide for the manner in which the joint firm will continue after the period of years expires. The American partner will wish to have an option to buy out the local partner so that it has a wholly owned firm in the territory. This option may be exercised in many ways. An agreement may be struck that the purchase price for the half-interest of the local partner will be computed as a certain number times the average net income or the last year's net income of the company. Assuming it is reasonable to value a publishing company's net income in a range of 6 times such income, the parties might then fix the purchase price for a half-interest at 3 times the net income. To this might be added half the costs of organizing the company, which may come to only a few hundred dollars. For instance, if the company's net income is $10,000, the purchase price for the half-interest may be stipulated as $30,000.

A second method of obtaining an option to buy out a local partner is to provide for negotiations on the price and, if the parties are unable to agree, to have the price settled by designated arbitrators. A third method is to have a local partner divide the copyrights into two lists of equal quality and give the American partner the right to elect to take either list plus the stock interest of the territorial partner. Again the parties may agree to have half of the costs of organizing the company reimbursed to the local partner.

A different approach may be for the parties to offer successive bids, each a stipulated amount higher than the previous bid, until the highest bidder prevails. For example, bids might start at $500, with each counterbid being $500 greater. The problem here is that the local partner may prevail and the American partner will be defeated in its attempt to have a wholly owned firm.

The parties may also agree on a buy or sell clause whereby either party may make an initial bid to buy the other's interest on the understanding that the other party may instead buy out the bidder at the same price. Here once more, the local partner may be the final buyer and thus frustrate the purpose of the American partner.

To avoid the necessity for a complicated procedure for either party to acquire the other's interest, the American publisher may trade a long-term catalog deal—say, 10 years with the joint company—in return for an assignment to it gratis of the local partner's interest at the end of that period. An alternative approach, with practically the same economic results to the local partner, might be for the American partner to retain 100 percent ownership at all times but have the firm managed by the local publisher on a basis that would give the same net return to the local publisher that it would receive if it were a partner; this scenario may not be practicable where the joint firm must have some local ownership in order to qualify for membership in local societies.

The parties may not only provide a procedure by which one partner may acquire the interest of the other, but also set forth their rights and obligations in the event an acquisition is not made. The partners would own a company that is no longer receiving new copyrights from the American partner. It will be at that time largely a repository of the copyrights previously certified to it. It will require accounting, administrative, and legal services, but to a limited extent. In such circumstances the American partner will want to limit the management fee of the local partner, who may have been receiving 10 to 15 percent of the gross receipts of the joint firm for providing physical facilities and services. It may be provided that the management fee will drop to a lower percentage, such as 5 percent, when the catalog deal with the American partner expires. It may be further agreed that the direct expenses of the company will not exceed specific amounts for any one item, perhaps $100, without the consent of both partners.

American tax laws should be part of the equation in determining whether to buy out the local partner or have complete ownership from inception. Especially where the local firm will be largely a repository of copyrights without substantial operating activities, sole ownership by the American partner may be a factor in a potential decision by U.S. tax authorities that the American partner is a foreign personal holding company, subject to specified high taxes in the United States. If the local firm is to be run from the United States as though it were a branch operation, the local government may possibly declare that the American owner has a permanent establishment in the foreign territory and that the usual tax exemption on original publisher royalties is inapplicable under international tax conventions. This may be somewhat offset by the ability in certain cases to reduce U.S. domestic taxes by the additional foreign taxes that would be payable. (For a further discussion of tax aspects, see Chapter 33.)

22

The Writer as Publisher

Some, such as Warner/Chappell and the EMI group of publishers, have extensive administrative and promotional offices. Others share little rooms in the Brill Building in New York City, or in Nashville, or in Los Angeles. Some rarely have cash reserves equal to the next month's rent. Many are private firms owned and operated by the writer with the assistance of the writer's own attorney and accountant. These firms usually concern shares of songs written by the writer that have not been placed with conventional publishers or with such interests recaptured due to statutory provisions.

No license is required to become a music publisher. The Constitution of the United States provides for freedom of the press, which is not limited to newspaper, magazine, and book publications. Anyone can publish in the printed sense. However, in the music industry a publisher is more likely to be interested in other, more profitable aspects of music publishing, such as collecting broadcast and other performance fees through ASCAP, BMI, SESAC, and foreign performing rights societies and granting mechanical rights licenses for phonograph records.

Both ASCAP and BMI are under consent decrees that tend to encourage people to qualify as publishers. (See Chapter 14.) ASCAP is required to advertise in music trade journals that anyone can become a publisher member with proof of being actively engaged in the music publishing business, and with musical compositions that have been used or distributed for at least one year. The BMI consent decree requires the acceptance of any publisher engaged in the music publishing business whose musical publications have been commercially published or recorded and publicly promoted or distributed for at least one year. In fact, ASCAP and BMI move promptly to grant publisher membership to persons active as publishers without insisting on any set prerequisite time period of operations. Writer membership in ASCAP or BMI is available to any composer or lyricist who has had at least one work published or recorded.

Publisher membership in ASCAP involves a $50 annual fee. BMI publisher status does not call for a fee—only a one-time $150 application charge. Affiliation is generally available to all applicants, no matter how modest their publishing activities. SESAC, a for-profit corporation, does not charge an application or annual fee; however, affiliation is not available to all applicants, as SESAC grants membership only to those applicants they choose.

Writer-Publisher Joint Firms

Some successful writers such as Stevie Wonder, Henry Mancini, Richard Rodgers, and the Gershwins have founded publishing firms for their compositions in conjunction with and administered by established publishers. This type of writer-founded firm frequently involves common stock participation by the writer and the administering publisher in proportions commensurate with the bargaining power of the writer.

The supervising publisher usually requests an administration fee—a fixed percentage fee ranging from 7.5 to 25 percent of gross receipts—in lieu of charges for rent, local telephone services, management salaries, and other general overhead. In some instances, again dependent on the bargaining power of the composer or lyricist, the administration fee will be waived. In effect, the firm jointly owned by a writer and a publisher is a device for increasing the earnings of the writer as well as providing more control over his or her copyrights.

Writer Firms

Other successful writers such as Quincy Jones, Paul Simon, Bruce Springsteen, and Bob Dylan act as their own publishers, with limited administrative assistance supplemented by the services of regular accountants and attorneys.

Less successful writers may decide to act as their own publisher because no other publishing company is interested in their compositions. These writers have to make demonstration records and attempt to place their compositions with record companies and artists. Some composers are by nature very active in promoting the recording of their compositions and their performance on the air, and they can easily claim that they are performing as a publisher. Until such time as they find an alert publisher that will match or exceed their efforts, they see no reason to share publishing income with another entity. They keep 100 percent of the publishing income by forming one of the thousands of music companies in existence and by qualifying the firm for membership in ASCAP or affiliation with BMI, depending on their own writer status. However, they also have to assume all the advertising, promotion, accounting, and other expenses, which may sometimes prove to be high.

Songwriters who are their own publisher rarely print their songs; if they want printed copies, they can deal with independent sheet music printer-distributors. They may arrange for the Harry Fox Agency to license and collect mechanical license fees for recordings of their compositions. The Harry Fox

Agency will act on their behalf in the same manner as it does for larger publishers.

For some publisher services, writers may resort to the assistance of organizations such as the American Mechanical Rights Agency (AMRA) in Los Angeles; BUG Music, with offices in Hollywood, California, and Nashville, Tennessee; Copyright Management in Nashville, Tennessee; and the Publisher's Licensing Corporation in Englewood, New Jersey. (See Chapter 15, "Mechanical Rights.")

The Songwriters Guild of America in New Jersey has recognized that more and more of its songwriter members own the publishing rights as well, either through initial retention of rights or their recapture of rights in renewal periods. The SGA offers a limited catalog administration plan for the worldwide administration of the publishing rights of its members. The fee is 9 percent of the gross receipts, with a lesser charge of 3 percent of publisher small performance income. There is a one-time setup charge of $2 per song. A writer-publisher in the SGA is not required to pay the service fee of 5.75 percent otherwise payable under the SGA's collection plan; this is a compulsory system of collection and auditing applicable to all members and relates only to writer royalties collected from third-party publishers. The services offered by the SGA do not include the negotiation of contracts for printed publications or foreign subpublishing. Grand rights, or dramatic rights, are not administered under SGA or other customary administrative plans. However, firms such as Tams-Witmark Music Library, Music Theater International, Rodgers & Hammerstein Repertory, and Samuel French are available for such services; see Chapter 25. ("Small rights" and "grand rights" are discussed in Chapter 14 under the section "Dramatic Performance Rights.")

Under the Copyright Act of 1976, the period of copyright was extended by 19 years. A writer who has terminated a grant of rights may want assistance in evaluating the monetary value of the additional period and determining whether to keep the ownership of the publishing rights or reassign the composition to a publisher. The SGA, through its catalog evaluation plan, offers to provide the valuation for an hourly fee, which is lower for members than for nonmembers.

In certain instances, a writer will make a joint copyright ownership arrangement with a publisher and retain a portion of the publisher's share of income. If the writer is able to retain a part interest in the copyright of a composition, he or she can organize a publishing firm and register as an ASCAP or BMI publisher member. This procedure is often chosen by recording artists who write their own material. In fact, many record companies will negotiate with recording artists for a joint copyright ownership by the company and the artist of all original songs written or controlled by the artist and recorded during the term of the recording contract. Negotiations will determine who administers the copyrights and the extent of any administration fee.

Under a current BMI payment schedule, if there is no publisher writers are entitled to receive the performance fees ordinarily payable to both the publisher and the writer. It is possible for the writer's share of performance fees to exceed 50 percent of the combined writer-publisher total, although the publisher's share cannot exceed one-half. This practice eliminates the need for a writer to form a publishing firm for the purpose of collecting more than the usual BMI writer's share of performance fees. (For a further discussion, see Chapter 14, "Performing Rights Organizations.")

Copyright Renewal Notification

The Songwriters Guild of America offers the following as instructions to renewal copyright claimants:

> Once you have renewed a copyright in its 28th year, you generally have three options. You can assign the copyright back to the original publisher, or to a new publisher. In exchange for this you ought to receive better royalty rates, or a bonus, or both. The third option, which is increasingly popular, is to have the copyright held by you or your own publishing company. This enables you to act as publisher and receive both writer and publisher shares of royalties.

> You are reminded that to place the copyright in your own company, you must do more than just renew the copyright. You must notify the Harry Fox Agency and your performing rights organization (ASCAP, BMI, or SESAC) that you have renewed the copyright and now claim your rights by serving a notice under Paragraph 8 of the Guild's 1947 contract, then you should also notify all foreign subpublishers that you have reacquired 100% of your rights to the songs. The original publisher must tell you who these subpublishers are.

> Your songs are never automatically placed in your own company simply by renewing the copyright. You must notify the appropriate parties and claim your rights each time a song is renewed. If you fail to give these notices, the old publisher will continue to collect all royalties.

The Termination of Grants

Under the Copyright Act of 1976, there are additional times to recapture music publishing rights. Songs originating before January 1, 1978, are subject to recapture at the end of the 56th year, which occurs at the end of the first 28th-year renewal period, just before the extended copyright term. Thus, if a renewal period was previously transferred to a publisher, the right of termination covers the basic 19-year extension period under the 1976 Copyright Act as well as the further 20-year extension under the Sonny Bono Term Extension Act.

Songs written after January 1, 1978, have a different period for the termination of rights: either 35 years from earliest publication but not more than 40 years from the date of grant, depending on status of publication of the song. In all instances, rights of termination differ substantially from rights of renewal in that they involve only new licensing rights and do not change the rights of the prior publisher to collect, subject to royalty payments, on prior licenses with continuing flow of new royalties on old uses.

However, as discussed in Chapter 11, there are commercial licensing opportunities to acting as or appointing new administrative publishers or copublishers of the rights under termination. Some of these opportunities include advertising jingles, motion picture synchronization licenses, and new record licenses. All such rights are limited to the United States and do not affect foreign rights, which continue with the original publisher, except under foreign statutory reversionary rights.

Reversionary Rights

Songs written before 1956 are subject to the British Commonwealth reversion of rights back to the estate of the author. This occurs at the 25th anniversary date of death regardless of whether the author was British, American, or from any other country having copyright treaty status with countries of the British Commonwealth.

The computation is quite simple for instrumental works and other songs where there is no collaborator. The problem arises when the song is a joint work. Under British law, if the words are attributed exclusively to one writer, the song is treated as if there was no collaborator; the same is true if the music is attributed solely to one writer. But if words and music are jointly attributed to a team of writers, or if the words are attributed to two or more writers, or if the music is attributed to a team of composers, it is considered a collaboration. Under British rules, the date of reversion is 25 years from the date of the *first* to die, but not earlier than the date of death of the last to die. The Canadian rule, however, is 25 years from the date of death of the *last* to die, thus substantially delaying date of reversion. (This follows the general rule of international copyright, namely, that the local place of copyright enforcement is the applicable governing law even though the copyright originates from a foreign country.) Once reversion occurs, a new publisher or copublisher or administrator for an estate as self-publisher can be negotiated. The SGA does not handle such reversionary rights, but it will recommend independent British-affiliated publishers for such negotiations and administration.

As in the situation concerning U.S. renewal and termination rights, the incentive to assert reversionary rights is to participate in the performing rights royalties otherwise paid to publishers. A further incentive in dealing with overseas rights is to avoid "filtering" mechanical royalties through an extra process of subpublishers and to be able to compute songwriter royalties "at the source" by dealing directly with a British, Australian, or other Commonwealth publisher directly. Often the original publisher will seek to retain reversionary rights on improved negotiated terms of greater participation to the estate.

23

Music for Motion Pictures

Music is very important to the motion picture industry and, reciprocally, motion pictures are of prime importance to the music industry. A considerable amount of music appears in the average film. Films usually get broad exposure to the public, and there is commensurate exposure of the music in the picture.

It is indisputable that motion pictures are a prime source of music evergreens, which, in turn, help the box office appeal of motion pictures. For example, the theme songs and music for the films *Days of Wine and Roses, Never on Sunday,* and the *The Pink Panther* have contributed significantly to the success of the films themselves. Other songs from film scores are notable for the large number of cover records that have achieved *Billboard* chart status: for example, "Moon River" (55 covers), "More" (54 charted covers), and the venerable "White Christmas" (74 chart covers). The song "Unchained Melody" was first issued as the theme song of the film *Unchained* and some 30 years later was featured in *Ghost;* the result was two records on the *Billboard* chart at the same time.

The public distribution and promotion of the films have aided materially in popularizing the music. Similarly, film soundtracks can turn into best-selling albums, which serve to promote the films at the box office: for example, *Saturday Night Fever* and *Flashdance* in the 1970s; *Dirty Dancing* in the 1980s; and *Titanic, City of Angels,* and DreamWorks' *Prince of Egypt* in the 1990s.

Billboard's Top-Selling Albums Chart for the week ending January 30, 1999, shows 22 soundtrack albums reaching the pop charts, with notable successes for *Titanic* (listed for 58 weeks), *The Wedding Singer* (50 weeks), and *City of Angels* (42 weeks). Soundtracks have garnered such notable success in recent years that companies have occasionally released two soundtrack albums for a new film. Both *Back to Titanic* and *The Wedding Singer, Volume 2* spent over 20 weeks on the *Billboard* charts. In fact, motion picture soundtracks have been so successful that television has taken their cue and begun promoting new series through album releases such as *Touched by an Angel:*

The Album, which reached number 11 on the charts, and *Chief Aid: The South Park Album,* which peaked at number 8.

Rights Required for Films

In order to use music in a motion picture, the producer must acquire several fundamental rights. These include the *synchronization right,* the right to record the music in synchronized or timed relation to the pictures in a film, video, or laserdisc; the *performance right,* the right to perform publicly the music that is recorded under the synchronization right; and the right to make copies of the film, video, or laserdisc and to distribute them to the public by sales or rental. Ordinarily the right to make copies and distribute them, for the purpose of negotiations, is encompassed under the synchronization and performance rights.

In the discussion that follows, it may be assumed that when a producer applies for a synchronization and performance license for a film, the producer is seeking the fundamental rights required to make and exploit the film. The Harry Fox Agency checklist for film licensing now specifies fee quotations for world synchronization, U.S. theatric performance rights, videogram rights, as well as new media to cover DVD and other new technology. Included in the world synchronization package are subitems: so-called free broadcast television—whether network, syndicated, or local and whether commercial or public television—as well as cable in its formats of basic, subscription, pay-per-view, closed-circuit hotel television, and satellite.

Employee-for-Hire Agreements

If the producer wishes to have original music created for a motion picture, the producer customarily makes an employee-for-hire agreement with a composer, according to which fundamental rights are acquired from the composer. Under the contract the composer will create the music and in addition will usually arrange the music and select and conduct the orchestra. All rights under copyright in the music will reside with the producer as the so-called author under copyright law, including all rights of recording, performance, and music publishing. Motion pictures are, of course, audiovisual works and consequently fit into the 1976 Copyright Act definition of a work for hire: a work that is not only prepared by an employee in the scope of his or her employment but also specially ordered or commissioned, if the parties expressly agree in writing that the work shall be considered one made for hire.

Under the Copyright Act, the great body of motion picture music has been written on an employee-for-hire basis, and the copyright renewal rights for the 28-year renewal period are therefore controlled by the copyright proprietor, regardless of whether the composer survives to the renewal copyright period. In the rare instance where a song or score does not fit into the employment-for-hire status, the producer must exercise caution to have a composer as well as his or her potential statutory heirs confirm that renewal rights arising after the basic 28-year term are included in the original or revised license. No renewal rights arise with regard to works originating in and after 1978 and the statutory rights of termination under the 1978 Copyright Act do not allow a terminating party to renegotiate or terminate rights under a prior license.

Synchronization and Performance Licenses

A producer's alternative to contracting with a composer to create original music for a film is to use music not specifically composed for the picture. In that event, the producer will seek a synchronization and performance license from the copyright proprietor, who is likely to be a music publisher. (The accompanying CD-ROM lists a "Synchronization and U.S. Theatrical Performing Rights License.")

In negotiating a synchronization and performance license, the producer and publisher must come to terms on the nature of the license that the publisher is willing to grant. A producer will seek a broad license that permits the exploitation of the film in all conceivable media throughout the world. The publisher, on the other hand, may wish to limit the license to theatrical exhibition in theaters, thus reserving the right to further fees for exhibition over free television or pay-TV or in respect of exploitation via videocassettes, which can be sold or rented to the public. Prolonged negotiations may be necessary before a mutually agreeable license is arrived at.

It is essential for a producer to obtain a comprehensive synchronization license. Also, as a result of the decision in the 1948 case of *Alden-Rochelle v. ASCAP*, which held that under antimonopoly laws, performance licenses for ASCAP music in theatrical films cannot be required of theaters, it is also customary to acquire a performance license for the theatrical exhibition of the picture in the United States at the same time. However, in countries outside the United States that have substantial consumer markets, theaters are granted blanket licenses by the local performing rights society for the performance of music in conjunction with films; theaters usually pay a small percentage of their net box office receipts after taxes as consideration for the license. The local performing rights societies outside the United States operate under agreements with ASCAP and BMI, according to which the foreign societies are authorized to grant licenses for the performance of music controlled by ASCAP- or BMI-affiliated societies; most music in which the producer may be interested is controlled in this manner.

Because U.S. antimonopoly laws do not apply in foreign countries, the producer may rely on standard performance licenses granted by local societies to theaters outside the United States. Similarly, the producer may depend on the blanket or other licenses issued by the performing rights organizations to television stations throughout most of the world.

Prices charged by publishers for synchronization and performance licenses vary with the proposed use of the music in the film. For background instrumental use, the price is less than for a background vocal use, and visual performances command higher fees than background performances. The fee is usually structured on a one-time flat-fee basis that includes both types of licenses (U.S. performance plus world synchronization). The performance license is usually determined by simply taking half the U.S. portion of the worldwide synchronization fee. The U.S. portion is sometimes one-half of the world total and sometimes somewhat less—Canada may be considered up to one-tenth of the North American share, but the share may be subject to negotiation, especially where a different publisher controls Canadian rights.

Although limited to licensing performance rights in film music to television and not theaters, BMI recognizes the special value of film music in its repertoire by two special treatments. It pays two times a conventional performance royalty for feature performances on television or radio of music originating in films. It also sponsors a tuition-free workshop annually—the Earl Hagen Film Scoring Workshop—in its Los Angeles offices for qualifying students with orchestral composition background.

Licensing Agents and Research Firms

Many publishers license synchronization and performance rights for motion pictures through the Harry Fox Agency. That office will supply information regarding who controls music rights and will, after consultation with the publishers it represents, quote prices to be paid for synchronization and performance rights. If music is not administered for licensing purposes through the Harry Fox Agency, the producer has to deal directly with the music publisher. Among the larger publishers that license directly are EMI, the Opryland Music group, and the Goodman group. Certain publishers, such as Warner/Chappell, may license directly or through the Harry Fox Agency.

While the Harry Fox Agency is reliable in its information as to who controls music rights, the cautious motion picture producer will have a search made nevertheless. This is especially prudent because in issuing licenses, publishers commonly insist on limiting any liability for breach of their warranties concerning the ownership or control of the music to the fee paid for the license.

Extreme caution is advised in dealing with songs that are not yet in their renewal term. Under a 1990 Supreme Court decision concerning the film *Rear Window,* it was determined that a license validly granted at the time the film was made can be rejected after the renewal of a component part. As a result, a song originating in 1972 could have a valid synchronization license issued in 1995 that loses its validity in the United States as of 2001, requiring further negotiations at such time if the potential renewal claimant did not endorse the original license at or before the time of issuance. (This is discussed in more detail in Chapter 10, "Copyright Law in the United States.")

It is quite common for a producer to refer such a matter to a copyright search firm that specializes in rendering copyright reports. It frequently happens that the particular matter has been researched previously and a quick reply can be forwarded to the producer. Among copyright search organizations are Thomson & Thomson Copyright Research Group, a firm with offices in Boston and Washington, D.C., and Government Liaison Services of Washington, D.C. Of course, the Research Division of the Copyright Office can make a report at their rate of $65 per hour. If an interpretation of law is required to clarify a search, the producer has to refer the report to specialist copyright attorneys for an opinion.

Videos

Video rental and promotion looms large in the marketing of feature films. Although the release date of a video is usually delayed until the exhaustion of the original theatrical run, and further delayed during pay-cable showings, the eventual revenues from video marketing are an essential part of the film financial picture. For purposes of large-volume sales, a lower price, between $15 and $25, is applicable in what is called "sell-thru" marketing to the consumer, as distinguished from the original higher price, which is usually over $70 for rental shops.

Billboard's Top Video Sales for the week ending April 24, 1999, shows that 22 of the 40 top video sales are feature films, 13 are music videos or music concerts, 2 are physical fitness videos, and the remaining 3 are adult entertainment. On Billboard's Top Video Rentals, all of the top 40 video rentals are feature films.

As of 1994, the RIAA gold certificate required video sales of 50,000 units or $1 million in suggested retail sales, whereas platinum was double this figure. The International Recording Media Association (IRMA) also certifies different types of releases: theatrically released titles qualify for a gold certificate with 125,000 units or $9 million of retail sales; nontheatrically released programs qualify for the gold at the lower plateau of 50,000 units or $2 million in retail sales.

A 1998 nationwide survey revealed that as many as 85 percent of American homes had videocassette recorders, up from 54 percent in 1987. Analysts forecast further growth in forthcoming years. In the first 6 months of 1998, 502.5 million video units were shipped with a retail dollar value of $5.8 billion.

Producers of feature films generally insist on music licenses from publishers that permit the use of their product in the form of videos. Publishers, and through them the songwriters they represent, seek to share in the substantial revenues to be generated by videos. Negotiations between producers and publishers are initiated by a producer application for a synchronization license.

Where the use of music is limited, a music publisher may agree to a customary type of synchronization fee, with an extra payment for video rights. Or the producer may be granted an option to secure video rights, for a fixed sum within a given period. As of this writing, there has been a nearly uniform approach of the licensee to seek a flat-fee buyout of video rights. Publishers often seek to negotiate a "rolling advance" based on a figure roughly double the applicable royalty statutory rate (as of this writing, 7.55 cents) and payable in advance of each set of 30,000 to 50,000 units. However, in the overwhelming majority of negotiations for such uses, the film producers have succeeded in worldwide buyouts at prices ranging from $5,000 to $15,000, depending on the expected video sales and importance of the song to the film score. Negotiations for this type of use recognize that the normal expected collections from ASCAP or BMI of television and foreign theatrical payments are reduced by the growing popularity of home video rental or purchase and that the negotiated fixed flat or royalty payment is the only benefit to be obtained for video use.

Where recordings are licensed for inclusion in a film, producers have to clear the right to incorporate the recordings into videos. The bargaining with record companies is analogous to negotiations with music publishers. A special obstacle may be the need to obtain the approval of the recording artists. (See also Chapter 24, "Licensing Recordings for Motion Pictures." For a further consideration of the problems in acquiring video rights, see Chapter 35, "Music Videos.")

Music Publishing Rights

Contracts with composers constitute publishing agreements insofar as they indicate rights granted and royalties payable. If commercial records are made from the soundtrack, the agreement may also include terms for a mechanical license.

Music publishing rights are ordinarily covered by employee-for-hire language, by which all rights of every nature and description reside with the producer. The royalties paid to the composer fall into several categories, similar to those in agreements with composers who are submitting pop tunes to a publisher. For printed editions, the composer will be paid a specified amount, perhaps 6 to 9 cents, for piano copies sold in the United States and Canada, and 10 percent of the wholesale price (after trade discounts, if any) of other printed editions sold and paid for in those countries. For foreign printed editions, the standard royalty is 50 percent of the royalties received by the original publisher. The composer is usually paid 50 percent of the mechanical license receipts of the original publisher. Composer royalties are split evenly with the lyricists, if any.

Recording Artist Royalties

Motion picture producers are reluctant to provide contractually for a royalty to be paid to the composer-conductor on sales of soundtrack recordings. The reason for this is that such a payment, which is in the nature of a recording artist royalty, is ordinarily deducted from royalties otherwise payable to the producer. However, in the case of more prominent motion picture composers, some of whom are recording artists in their own right, the agreement provides for a special royalty to be paid on the sale of commercial phonograph records manufactured from any part of the soundtrack recorded by the orchestra conducted by the composer. This royalty may be 6 percent of the retail list price of records sold in the United States (less taxes and price of the album cover), frequently with the provision for lower royalties for foreign and record club sales.

In the case of composer-conductors who are recording artists in their own right, the royalties may exceed 6 percent. If the composer-conductor undertakes the obligation to prepare an edited soundtrack recording tape as a basis for the manufacture of phonograph records, the royalty otherwise payable is likely to increase by about 2 percent for such services. The royalties are generally subject to reduction to the extent that royalties are payable to other artists and are likely to be payable only after recoupment of all or a portion of union reuse fees that must be paid if records are manufactured from a soundtrack. (Under agreements that producers enter into with the American Federation of Musicians covering the studio orchestra, arrangers, and copyists used to make a picture score, the union must consent to the use of a soundtrack for the manufacture of records. Consent is usually given on the condition that the musicians, arrangers, and copyists involved in the original recording are paid full scale for the music that appears on the record. It is not unusual for union reuse fees to reach $12,000 or more for a soundtrack album. For expensive films with large orchestras, the reuse fees can easily exceed $100,000.)

Soundtrack Album Contracts with Record Companies

From time to time, the larger record companies have complained that soundtrack albums are preempted by the record companies affiliated with the motion picture companies. This was more true of the past than the present, since film companies such as MGM-UA, Paramount Pictures, and 20th Century Fox no longer have active record company firms. Even when a motion picture company has its affiliated operative record firm, the soundtrack album rights may go to an unaffiliated record label. The Disney film organization, together with its affiliate, Miramax Films, often issues its soundtrack records through its own record company, Hollywood Records. This is the affiliate that has released *Prince of Egypt* and *The Postman* soundtracks. RCA obtained rights to a number of soundtrack albums because of its exclusive recording contract with Henry Mancini, the late motion picture composer. On another occasion, CBS Records (now Sony) issued the soundtrack album of *West Side Story* because it had reserved the right to the soundtrack when it contracted for album rights to the Broadway show. There are also instances of soundtrack album rights being acquired by an unaffiliated record company for foreign motion pictures that are uncommitted to the record company subsidiaries of the film companies that are distributing the films.

In cases where soundtrack album rights are acquired by unaffiliated record companies, the agreement between the record company and the producer may represent the result of intensive bargaining on such matters as the royalty percentage; advances against royalties; promises of singles records by outstanding artists; and the use, exclusive or otherwise, of the art, logo, and stills from the picture. If the soundtrack was recorded by members of the American Federation of Musicians, the problem of reuse fees would have to be covered; usually there is a provision that the record company will pay such fees as an advance against royalties.

In recent years there has been a noticeable trend toward re-recording soundtrack scores for a soundtrack album rather than using the original soundtrack. This has several advantages. First, it is possible to use a smaller orchestra and thus avoid excessive union reuse fees. Second, a new recording with an album in mind, with arrangements and orchestrations appropriately modified, may result in a more listenable and commercial record.

The prospect of synergy in the music promoting the film and the film promoting the music comes to the forefront in the case of sales of soundtrack albums. There are film buffs and souvenir purchasers who will buy a sound-track of a film for its own sake. Recent trends in the R&B and hip-hop market have seen soundtrack sales as independent from the success of the film. *Dangerous Minds, Soul Food,* and *How Stella Got Her Groove Back* each reached the *Billboard* charts with a compilation of popular rap and R&B artists. However, the multiplatinum pot at the end of the rainbow looms large when a major film is accompanied by a significant score. The 1997 film *Titanic* sold nearly 4 million copies by February 1998 and continued on the *Billboard* charts over a year later with a 66-week run by March 1999.

Television is also quickly becoming a lucrative market for popular music. The soundtrack to the Fox series *Ally McBeal,* featuring vocalist Vonda Shepard, sold over 1 million copies. Sometimes, as part of negotiation for the basic synchronization, U.S. performance, and video buyout terms, the astute music publisher will insist on a guaranteed inclusion within the possible soundtrack album.

Component Parts of Films

Under the Berne Convention, the use of a copyright notice to protect films and music is optional. In the past, music publishers associated with film companies wanted to be named as the copyright owners in notices of copyright for the new music in films. This has been traditional and prestigious and has facilitated the administration and exploitation of the music.

For some years the Copyright Office, for purposes of deposit and registration, considered a copyrightable component part of a motion picture, such as the new music, an integral part of the film. If the film had been released prior to the publication or registration of a copyrightable component part, the Copyright Office refused separate registration for the component part unless a separate copyright notice for that part had been placed on the film: for example, an individual notice naming the music publisher as the copyright owner of the music. Based on the Copyright Act of 1976, which requires a copyright notice on only publicly distributed copies of works that could be "visually perceived," the position of the Copyright Office changed. Music in films is not visually perceptible, and the conclusion followed that a separate copyright notice was unnecessary. The Berne Act further removed formalities such as notice of copyright as essential to copyright claim or registration.

The Copyright Office now accepts the simultaneous registration of separate copyright claims for a film and for the new music in the motion picture. The multiple registrations can be made by different copyright claimants, with the deposit of only one "copy" of the film, which can be a videocassette. There is no need to make separate deposits of "lead sheets" or other copies of the music.

While a soundtrack recording is an integral part of a motion picture, record companies have not had the same problem with the Copyright Office as the music publishers. By editing, mixing, assembling, and altering the movie soundtrack for a soundtrack album, a record company becomes entitled to treat an album as a derivative work for which the notice of copyright can be in the name of the record company. (For a further discussion, see Chapter 7, "The Copyright in Sound Recordings.")

Performances in Europe

A great incentive arises from earnings in Europe based on the performance of the music in conjunction with the film. Under the system prevalent in Europe, performing rights societies license theaters on the condition that the theaters pay to the societies a percentage of the box office receipts. These payments, which are based on music cue sheets, are then divided between the publishers and writers of the film scores. (A "Cue Sheet Sample" for a television film is listed on the accompanying CD-ROM.) Payments are related to the success of a film, and it is not unusual for a successful film to earn thousands of dollars. The percentages collected generally range between 1 percent and slightly over 2 percent of the net box office receipts after taxes, with England, France, and Italy constituting the countries that generate the greatest film performance earnings. Composers can also expect performance compensation when the films are shown on television in the United States and elsewhere.

Foreign Productions of Motion Picture Music

This chapter has been mostly concerned with motion picture music composed in the United States and music licensed by U.S. publishers. However, motion pictures are also made and scored abroad, and special problems may arise as a consequence. In particular, it should be noted that in the case of British and French composers, their performing rights societies claim the exclusive right to license the performance of the music in U.S. theatrical exhibitions. This is in contrast to the practice in the United States, where composers hired to create motion picture scores offer producers the exhibition rights to the music; according to a court consent decree entered into by ASCAP and the Antitrust Division of the Department of Justice, members of ASCAP are prohibited from granting a synchronization right to any film producer unless the member, or ASCAP, grants corresponding motion picture performance rights.

Assuming that the scoring is done by a British or French composer, the producer may initiate negotiations to obtain a U.S. theatrical performance license from the Performing Right Society (PRS) in London for the British composer, or from the Société des Auteurs, Compositeurs, et Editeurs de Musique (SACEM) in Paris for the French composer. PRS applies fixed standards of compensation for licenses, namely, a flat rate plus an amount calculated on the duration of the PRS music in the film. The first 30 minutes of PRS music are charged at the rate of £120 per minute, and any subsequent minutes at the rate of £72 per minute. This applies to both music commissioned for the film and other PRS music inserted in the motion picture.

For non-French pictures there are several ways to obtain from SACEM's composer members the rights to perform a film theatrically in the United States and in other territories where performance fees are not collected from cinemas. In certain instances, particularly those involving a well-known composer, the contract may provide that the composer is responsible for acquiring the SACEM license for no additional fee and SACEM will comply. An alternative is for the producer to agree to pay SACEM a fee of 3 percent of the net producer's share from the film. Another approach is for the producer to pay SACEM a flat fee based on the budget of the picture.

24

Licensing Recordings for Motion Pictures

From time to time record companies with sizable catalogs or current hits receive requests for permission to use their recordings in films. There are usually four categories of films to which requests relate.

1. A full-length theatrical film, such as *Saturday Night Fever,* one of the earliest examples of the successful use of recordings, which featured hits by the Bee Gees; or the more recent *You've Got Mail,* which used old recordings such as Bobby Day's rendition of "Rockin' Robin," Louis Armstrong's version of "Dummy Song" and Stevie Wonder's "Signed, Sealed, Delivered, I'm Yours."
2. Nonprofit, educational, or religious films, such as a film on race relations, which might contain recorded recitals by black poets.
3. Television commercials, such as a Diamond Crystal Salt commercial that incorporated a recording of the song "Chitty, Chitty, Bang, Bang."
4. Television features or series that use actual source recordings for portions of their score.

Film producers favor certain recordings because they present in tangible form the exact flavor desired for particular scenes. A rendition of Aretha Franklin issued by Atlantic Records or a performance by Herb Alpert on an A&M release may present a background that a studio orchestra would be hard-pressed to duplicate. The actual recordings dispel the need to guess at how a future rendition, made especially for the film, will sound.

Film producers also consider the right to use recordings in films as a simple, inexpensive method for obtaining soundtrack music. This belief may be without merit. Multiple hurdles may have to be cleared before a recording becomes available for a motion picture. Appropriate consents or permissions may have to be acquired from artists, record companies, unions, and music publishers. (See the accompanying CD-ROM for a copy of a licensing agreement for film.)

The Protection of Recordings

Legitimate film producers always seek approvals before using recordings in motion pictures, recognizing the property rights of the record companies, the music publishers, the recording artists, and the affected unions. It is rare that recordings are used for publicly exhibited films without proper authorization.

The legal bases for the protection of property interests in recordings are multiple and complicated. As detailed in Chapter 7, the rights of the copyright proprietors in sound recordings that were fixed and published on or after February 15, 1972, and before January 1, 1978, are protected under the Copyright Act of 1909, as amended. Effective January 1, 1978, sound recordings fixed on or after that date, regardless of whether they are published or unpublished, are given copyright protection under the 1976 Copyright Act. The rights of the owners of the underlying compositions are protected under copyright statutes and also safeguarded under the motion picture copyright, regardless of the date the recordings are made or released. Pre-February 15, 1972, recordings are safeguarded state by state under case law and under state statutes against record piracy; pursuant to the 1976 Copyright Act, these recordings will enter the public domain on February 15, 2047.

As to pre-February 15, 1972, recordings, performers and record producers have depended largely upon several legal theories to secure the recognition of their rights in recordings, namely, unfair competition and common law copyright. These concepts are frequently confused in the decisions. To a lesser degree, plaintiffs have resorted to the performer's right of privacy in regard to the artist's name and likeness, and to the artist's right to control and profit from publicity values he or she has achieved.

Unfair Competition

Traditionally, the courts have held that for a case of unfair competition the following elements must be present: (1) competition between the plaintiff and defendant, (2) the misappropriation of a business asset, and (3) the defendant's fraudulent passing off the appropriated asset as the plaintiff's. However, courts in more recent decisions have tended to discard the elements of direct competition or passing off, relying instead on the "misappropriation" or "free-ride" theory, which has sometimes been paraphrased as "Man shall not earn his bread by the sweat of another person's brow" or, alternatively, as "unjustly taking the fruits of another's labor without consent."

Common Law Copyright

A maze of conflicting opinion exists regarding the question of common law copyright in sound recordings. Although it has been settled that the performances of recording artists in a pre-February 15, 1972, sound recording constitute an original artistic or intellectual creation eligible for common law copyright protection against unauthorized use, there has been a split of authority on whether sales or public distribution of records comprises a general publication of the work that throws it into the public domain. This issue arose because common law protection formerly expired immediately upon "publication," whereupon the work either went into public domain or required registration under the copyright laws. Before February 15, 1972, there simply was no copyright registration available for records and the argument was often presented that the public domain alternative was required. (See the discussion of *La Cienega Music Co. v. ZZ Top*, in Chapter 7, page 72.) In contrast, the concepts of unfair competition and property rights were not affected by publication through sales of records.

The Statutory Copyrighting of Recordings

While statutes in many states bar the unauthorized dubbing and sale of phonograph records, it appears that these laws are addressed to sales of dubbed records and do not relate to the unauthorized integration of records into films. Under U.S. copyright laws, a motion picture, including its soundtrack, is the subject of statutory copyright. Audiovisual works as such do not qualify for a copyright as sound recordings, but they are protected by the copyright as part of audiovisual works.

The exclusive right of a copyright owner of sound recordings fixed on or after February 15, 1972, to "reproduce the copyrighted works in copies or phonorecords" covers reproduction in visual media. There is, therefore, a statutory basis for requiring the consents of record companies for the use of their copyrighted recordings in motion pictures.

The Consent of the Music Publisher

Chapter 23, "Music for Motion Pictures," discusses the film synchronization and performance licenses that should be sought from music publishers. These ordinarily relate to existing music that is proposed to be recorded in the soundtrack of a film. The same types of licenses must be acquired for music embodied in existing recordings proposed to be integrated in a film.

Union Reuse Fees

Under union agreements with the American Federation of Musicians and the American Federation of Television and Radio Artists, the record company must pay reuse fees if domestic phonograph recordings are used in different media, such as theatrical films, television films, or film commercials. The record company is liable to the vocalists, musicians, conductors, arrangers, orchestrators, and copyists for reuse fees in an amount equal to applicable union scale for that medium for the services previously performed. The reuse fees may be substantial, depending upon the number of union members involved in the original recording and the extent of their services. In 1968, at a time when union-scale payments were much lower than today, the chief counsel for Capital Records observed: "When a record company says 'yes,' the record company would be obligated to pay all the musicians, all the AFTRA performers, the arranger, the copyist, everybody, a new additional scale payment. If you want to do that for a symphony, the cost to the record company may well be $50,000." Standard licensing agreements provide that the cost of union reuse fees are assumed by the licensee.

In certain instances, the unions on application may grant waivers of reuse fees if the film is of a nonprofit public service nature. Since the record company may be charging little or nothing for its consent, it may require the film producer to apply for the waiver. Otherwise, unremunerative staff time may have to be devoted to the application.

Artist Contract Restrictions

If the film producer is not discouraged by reuse fees and by the need for music publisher licenses, the record company must still examine its own files to determine whether permission may be granted and on what terms. The record company will turn first to the recording contract under which the recording was originally made. In many cases, the contract will not limit the type of usage of a recording. This is especially true for recordings by newer artists. For established artists, another situation may prevail; the artist may have negotiated a restriction on the sale or use of the recording to home phonograph records or tapes, or the contract may require the artist's consent for the synchronization of the recording in films.

In such situations, where there are restrictions or a consent is required, the record company must furnish the details to the film producer if it elects to require the film producer to obtain the necessary waivers. Then, the producer must proceed to obtain the appropriate consent of the artist. If a license fee is to be paid to the record company, the artist may request a portion of the fee as the price for consent.

Soundtrack Albums

The record manufacturer may be informed that the film producer plans to issue a soundtrack album that includes the recording. This poses additional problems. For instance, the record company may have granted exclusive foreign phonograph record rights in the recording to foreign record companies. Therefore, worldwide record rights may not be licensed to the film company unless the foreign record companies consent.

Assuming other problems have been solved, the record company may request a royalty based on sales of the proposed soundtrack album. This may be necessary in order to meet commitments to the artist, who is entitled to a royalty on all sales of the recording. Depending on what the traffic will bear, the royalty will vary. For example, if the artist must be paid a royalty of 7 percent of sales, prorated in relation to the number of selections in the album, the record company will seek a higher royalty to provide the company with a profit after the deduction of the artist royalty.

In many instances, the record company will reserve all singles rights to the recording. If the film becomes popular and the soundtrack album emerges as a good seller, the record manufacturer may benefit by a resurgence in singles sales. For example, when the 1965 Righteous Brothers recording of "Unchained Melody" was reissued for the motion picture *Ghost,* the single went to number 13 on the *Billboard* charts, and resulted in substantial additional sales on the reissue of the record.

In licensing the music publishing rights to a song originally issued for a former commercially released recording, the parties should bear in mind a case concerning singer Joe Cocker's recording of "Bye Bye Blackbird" in the film *Sleepless in the Seattle* (see page 128). The soundtrack album was issued on a new label and thus required a new license from the new publisher. The continuing sales of the original Joe Cocker version by its original record company required license payments to the former publisher. This complex situation, which concerns the right to terminate grants and licenses as of the 57th year of copyright, is discussed in detail in Chapter 11.

25

Music for the Theater

It is a rare popular songwriter who doesn't aspire to write show music for the theater. Yet it is a rare show music writer who writes popular music outside the framework of a show. For example, Ira Gershwin's "Fascinatin' Rhythm," "Embraceable You," and "It Ain't Necessarily So" are all strong contenders in any popular music category, yet each of these was written for a specific Broadway show; so was "Don't Cry for Me, Argentina," which Tim Rice and Andrew Lloyd Weber originally wrote for *Evita*. At the same time, ask such show writers for a popular song written independently of a show and it is a scarce song that they can mention. Even Stephen Sondheim, who wrote such shows as *Sweeney Todd* and *A Little Night Music,* would have difficulty pointing to a popular song written by him outside a show context.

On the other hand, Paul Simon, one of the world's most acclaimed popular songwriters, whose credits include "Mrs. Robinson," "Bridge Over Troubled Water," "Slip Slidin' Away," and "Cecelia," made an attempt at Broadway in 1998 with *Capeman*. Simon described the lavish production, which ran for only 20 performances after extended previews and major rewrites, as "one of the biggest beatings that I have ever taken. It hurt, it really hurt." Cy Coleman, who wrote the popular tunes "Witchcraft" and "The Best Is Yet to Come," later came to Broadway and enjoyed considerable success with such shows as *City of Angels, The Life,* and *Ziegfeld Follies* for which he was awarded two of his six Tony Awards.

Sometimes there is a successful crossover from film composing to show music. *A Chorus Line* represented the first Broadway credits for composer Marvin Hamlisch and lyricist Edward Kleban. The composer had won an Oscar for his earlier adaptation of Joplin's music for *The Sting* and awards for the score and song for the film *The Way We Were.* Kleban previously had written only for television and was known as a composer rather than a lyricist.

A popular song can be launched with only a few hundred dollars, a demonstration record or master, and a lot of effort. However, Broadway musicals historically involve rapidly escalating costs that may reach several million dollars. The Canadian-based company Livent went bankrupt in 1999 after investing some $40 million in *Ragtime, Fosse,* and *Showboat*—three highly successful shows with long runs that continued even past the date of bankruptcy. Apparently, the high costs of the successful productions, and the further costs of launching second companies running simultaneously, exceeded the available bank accounts. Even successful reviews and Tony Awards require additional funds to let the potential audience know of such success, and while full potential box office sales build up, high day-to-day expenses must still be paid. Disney did much better; it was able to convert the film *Lion King* into a lavish, Tony Award-winning Broadway musical. As of mid-1999, *Lion King* had sold over 100 percent of the available tickets with a top price of $85, had grossed nearly $900,000 weekly since its late 1997 opening, and was predicted to best *Beauty and the Beast,* which was successfully running for its fifth year.

   Ain't Nothin' but the Blues is an example of what is generally considered a low-budget musical. It was initially capitalized at $900,000, but it required an additional $700,000 for its first move to Lincoln Center's Vivian Beaumont Theater, where it lasted for 19 weeks, and an additional $300,000 for its move to the Ambassador Theater on Broadway, where it lasted another 18 weeks. By the time the show closed, it was running at an average weekly loss of $10,000. However, the show had received favorable Broadway reviews and the producer expressed optimism about its scheduled national tour.

The Rights of Producers and Writers

The Dramatists Guild is not a union. It is a voluntary association that is responsible in large part for the contractual strength of composers and lyric writers. Composers, lyric writers, and playwrights are accepted as full members of the Guild. The Approved Production Contract (APC) of the Dramatists Guild indicates acceptable terms regarding the rights of composers and lyricists in show music. The basic concept expressed throughout the contract is that legal title to the book music and lyrics is at all times reserved by the writers, subject only to limited rights licensed to the producer and to a limited financial participation accorded to the producer in certain "subsidiary rights." The latter include motion picture, television, and radio rights to the play; touring company rights (other than a first-class company); stock rights; amateur rights; concert tour rights; and grand opera versions. The producer is granted no interest in music publishing rights, which would include payments of mechanical license fees by record companies for cast albums sold, all ASCAP or BMI performance payments for the songs, and all other royalties or income from printed editions or from licensing to record companies, Muzak, commercial jingles, or other music uses.

   The producer's rights are confined to uses on the stage in the United States and Canada, and even these rights are dependent on the show reaching the stage in a specified reasonable time. These rights can be extended to the United Kingdom, Ireland, Australia, and New Zealand within 6 months from the closing of the play in New York City and can be further extended by payments of specified amounts. Even with regard to stage rights, the writers reserve the right to protect the integrity of their work. A song cannot be added without their approval, nor can deletions occur without their consent. Any deleted material belongs to the writers completely, and any corrections, additions, or changes made with or without their consent are nevertheless the property of the writers subject only to the limited rights licensed to the producer; consents are determined by the majority vote of the composer, lyricist, and author of the play. The writers have the right to approve the cast, director, conductor, and choreographer.

Under many of the older contracts, all writers receive fixed-option payments for the preproduction period of the show, and thereafter they are normally paid a royalty of 4.5 percent (going to 6 percent after recoupment of production costs) of the gross weekly box office receipts, shared among the book writer, lyricist, and composer. In a typical case, the book writer receives one-third, and remaining two-thirds is shared equally among composers and lyricists. During the weeks when the show is not operating at a profit, the book writer, lyricist, and composer forgo percentage royalties and each is paid a minimum weekly amount of $1,000.

An alternative to this is the profit pool. The profit pool is a relatively new concept whereby royalty recipients share in operating profits, not gross receipts, with a minimum guarantee. In almost all cases these recipients get less royalty money, but more money is available to the investors. Running expenses for this purpose include theater rental, cast, stagehands, insurance, legal and accounting, general and company managers, as well as any minimum weekly guarantees that are not covered by the pool. The goal of the profit pool is to give the investors a better chance to recoup and achieve profits. The incentive to royalty participants is not only the guaranteed weekly payments but the practical economics of the industry where the investors and producers insist on a pool.

Original-Cast Albums

By their very nature, original-cast albums require performances by the members of the cast as well as the use of the musical and literary material. Because of the cast participation and by custom, the producer preserves a strong role in bargaining for the cast album placement. Frequently the producer and the writers' representatives collaborate in the bargaining. In all instances the approval of the writers is required.

The royalty for the cast album is customarily 12 to 15 percent of retail; the writers ordinarily receive 60 percent of the total royalty and the producer is paid the balance. Royalties are commonly subject to the recoupment of the cost of production of the cast album. Depending on the agreement between the collaborators, the royalties payable to the writers are ordinarily divided two-thirds between the composer and lyricist and one-third to the book writer. The writers' music publisher, who is selected by the composer and lyricist without any voice, other than advisory, by the producer, is also paid mechanical license fees by the record company.

Compared to the sales of such older popular musicals as *My Fair Lady*, *South Pacific*, and *Sound of Music*, sales of recent cast albums have greatly diminished. The average Broadway cast album sales for recent shows are between 20,000 to 25,000 units—hardly an attractive number considering the high recording costs. The cast album for *Rent* is an exception; sales reached 700,000 copies by 1999, thanks in part to a million-dollar promotional budget.

Subsidiary Rights

Investors are increasingly aware that when a show is highly successful, the benefits in residual income such as performance and mechanical royalties of the composer and lyricist often are more attractive than those obtained by the investor. The producer and the investors receive from the writers the right to share in certain subsidiary rights; this is dependent on the producer's rights being vested in the territory on the basis of the play having been presented there for a specified number and type of performances. For a producer to be *vested*, the play has to have been presented in a territory for a specified number and type of performances. The share and the period of participation of the producer vary, depending on which of the alternatives in the APC the producer has chosen. Under all alternatives the producer shares perpetually in the proceeds from audiovisual productions, which include motion pictures, television productions, videocassettes, and soundtrack albums. Depending on the alternative chosen, the participation of the producer ranges from 30 percent to 50 percent.

As for stock and ancillary performances, the periods of participation under the different alternatives may be 10 years, 36 years, or 40 years, and the participation may be from 20 to 50 percent. In all these instances the writers have the sole bargaining power concerning subsidiary rights, except with respect to original-cast albums and the sale or lease of motion picture rights. Film rights are within the purview of the negotiator of the Dramatists Guild under special provisions.

The growing use of musicals in stock and amateur productions is an all-important revenue source after the show has closed its Broadway run; in some cases the revenue has exceeded the income generated on Broadway. Even 50 years after its opening, *Oklahoma* has been licensed to as many as 900 theaters a year in North America. *Variety* magazine reports that Broadway box office receipts reached $588,126,585 in the 1998–1999 season, whereas in the same season road box office receipts totaled $711,412,510. Amateur groups may pay between $75 and $125 a performance on average for the rights to an entire musical, while professional groups pay minimum weekly guarantees up to 10 percent of box office receipts. Both types of groups must also pay rental fees for the conductor's score and choral parts.

Licensing agents in the field include Tams-Witmark Music Library, Music Theater International, Rodgers & Hammerstein Repertory, and Samuel French, Inc. The in-house Rodgers & Hammerstein licensing company takes in more than $10 million in licensing revenues a year for such uses, which often include foreign productions as far away as Japan and Denmark as well as regular uses in Britain and Australia. Usually only successful plays are handled by the licensing agents.

American Productions Abroad

If a producer whose domestic production qualifies him or her under the APC provisions produces or, with the consent of the writers, arranges for the production of a show in the United Kingdom, Ireland, Australia, or New Zealand, royalties are payable to the writers based on gross weekly box office receipts. For shows in the United Kingdom and Ireland, the royalties are 4.5 percent of such receipts, rising to 6 percent after the recoupment of production costs; royalties with respect to performances in Australia or New Zealand are 6 percent of such receipts. If the producer fails to produce or arrange for the production of the show, the producer and the investors participate in 25 percent of the net proceeds received by the writers on contracts for such production in the United Kingdom and Ireland executed within 7 years from the date when the producer's rights vest in that territory. In Australia or New Zealand, the percentage is 35 percent on contracts executed within 7 years from the vesting of the producer's rights in the particular territory. In foreign areas other than the United Kingdom, Ireland, Australia, and New Zealand, the writers control the production of the show, and they pay the producer and the investors 25 percent of the writers' net proceeds received by virtue of contracts made within 7 years from (usually) the New York opening.

Writing a Show

On the practical side, the job of writing a show score is sometimes assigned by a producer who owns rights granted by the author of the book; usually the author assigns rights on options only, for a limited time. The Broadway show *The Life* by Cy Coleman and Ira Gasman is an example of the value of long-term dedication to a prospective show by the composer and lyricist. The collaborative team spent over 10 years developing and tightening the score with the book writer before a producer took on the role of required financing for its Broadway debut. Creative teams for Broadway shows such as *Grease, Jelly's Last Jam,* and *Cats* also had to search for a producer after completing the initial stages. Such a collaboration may begin prior to the solicitation of a producer.

If underlying rights to a film, a play, or a book are involved, they might negotiate for an option period that may expire unless a producer is obtained within the stated term, such as a year. The producer, in turn acquires a secondary option from the author for a given period, which under the APC is 1 year from the contract date or 1 year from delivery of the unfinished play, whichever is later, in which to produce a show.

There are hundreds of aborted show ventures, with the composer and lyricist investing the time, talent, and energy all for nothing. *Li'l Abner* went through three sets of writers before being produced. Even the great Alan Jay Lerner was in the also-ran category on this show. Similarly, it was announced that Richard Rodgers was working on many musical versions that failed to come to fruition.

Music in Dramatic Shows

Some shows use music only as background to dramatic action. In such instances, the composer usually is not covered by the Dramatists Guild contract, and his or her compensation and rights will be different from those of the author of the play. A common arrangement is for the composer to receive a single stipulated payment plus specified amounts for each week of the run, as distinguished from a royalty based on box office receipts. There is no fixed rule as to the amount or nature of payment; a top-rated composer may be able to obtain an initial fixed payment plus a percentage of gross weekly box office receipts, such as 0.5 percent. The agreement with the composer ordinarily covers the use of the music for stock and amateur rights or for a television production, with appropriate payment to the composer for such use.

Then, too, incidental music is often used in a straight drama. This is called an *interpolation* of a song. For example, the 1998 production of *Blue Room* starring Nicole Kidman used Elvis Presley's recording of "Love Me Tender." A dramatic script such as *Sisters Rosensweig* may call for putting on a specific record, for which the producer frequently pays a fee of $100 per week to the music publisher. Sometimes an authorized title song is written for a Broadway hit, although this is more common with regard to motion pictures. Such a tie-in helps promote the play or film by disc jockey use and may provide a promotional head start for the song based on public interest in the play.

Investment in Musical Theater

Analysis of the 1998–1999 Broadway season shows impressive attendance at 11,605,278 tickets sold and a monetary gross of $588,126,585. Further analysis shows that musicals contributed more than half of the Broadway revenues. However, the sad story is that only 1 of the 16 new and revival Broadway musicals introduced that recent season—*Peter Pan,* a revival—was able to repay investors in its first year; 9 of the musicals closed without recoupment, while 6 struggled on and may recoup in the 1999–2000 season. Notable among the many losers running during that season was *Titanic,* which survived nearly 2 years and achieved five Tony Awards and nevertheless failed to recoup its investment. The revival of the acclaimed *On the Town* had an investment of $6 million and also closed without recoupment. The lesson here is that musicals rarely get to Broadway without multimillion-dollar investments, and they need extended runs in big and expensive theaters to recoup. Thus, legendary hits like *Cats,* still running after 6,000 performances starting in 1982, and *Phantom of the Opera,* with about 5,000 performances starting in 1987, and the 1998 Disney-backed *Lion King,* with its weekly gross exceeding $900,000, are exceptions to the norm.

A further exception is achieved with shows like *Rent, Annie,* and *Ain't Nothing but the Blues,* where initial entry is not to the Broadway stage but regional, low-budget, or workshop stagings. A revival of Lerner and Loewe's *Paint Your Wagon* was achieved for under $150,000; this was possible because it first opened at the Goodspeed Opera House in East Haddam, Connecticut, with the help of state and other subsidies. However, despite indirect introductions of *Ain't Nothin' but the Blues* via New Jersey and Lincoln Center, conversion to the Broadway stage still required additional investments of hundreds of thousands of dollars.

Investors frequently include the Schubert Organization, Nederlander Organization, and Jujamcyn Theatres, a phenomenon of the past two decades. Previously, such theater owners would have merely leased the theater and personnel for about 30 percent of the box office receipts, without investing as a partner. The practice today is more complicated, with the producer's out-of-pocket costs such as box office personnel, stage crew, and utilities being covered first, then show costs, with 5 to 10 percent of gross weekly box office receipts being paid as rent.

Long recognized as a most vital part of the world of musical theatricals is the Schubert Foundation. Founded by the Schubert brothers and part of theater history, this organization owns 16 Broadway theaters and a half-interest in another, as well as theaters in Boston and Philadelphia. The Schubert Organization, a subsidiary of the foundation, manages the National Theater in Washington, D.C., and, through lease arrangements, a major Los Angeles theater. It is considered to be worth well over $100 million, and it generates enough profits to have paid out grants of $8.283 million in 1998. In one outstanding example, the Schubert Foundation bestowed money on Playwrights Horizons, a nonprofit Manhattan theater company. Its production of *Sunday in the Park with George,* by Stephen Sondheim and James Lapine, went on to play at the Schubert Theater in 1984.

In recent years record companies have generally had little interest in or incentive to finance musical plays in order to obtain cast album rights. The present tendency is for a record company to await the opening of a play in out-of-town tryouts or on Broadway before determining whether to invest in the play or in the large recording costs of a cast album, which often amount to over $100,000.

The lack of major-label interest in original-cast albums had created a vacuum that is being filled to some extent by a newcomer, TVT Records. The firm started with a novelty collection of television jingles and has evolved to include a show album line. They issued a cast album of the show *1776* and sold 25,000. In addition, TVT has issued copies of the 1998 version of *The Wizard of Oz*, featuring Mickey Rooney and Eartha Kitt, as well as a version of *Follies* made 27 years after the show originally opened on Broadway.

AFM Union Scale

The pit orchestra members and conductor are subject to AFM-scale minimum rates. The rates as of 1999 required that each musician be paid for eight weekly performances at a base rate of $1,231 per week, to which vacation and pension pay is added. Additional pay is required for doubling on more than one instrument, for instrument maintenance, for extra rehearsal calls; further sums are also paid if the musicians are required to appear on stage or in costume. The conductor's base pay starts at $2154.34 a week, with extras amounting to a gross weekly pay of about $2,500. Associate union scale for conductor and musicians appearing for a cast album amounts to additional pay equal to 1 week of regular performances.

26

Commercial Jingles

The early success of "Pepsi-Cola Hits the Spot" heralded an ever-growing reliance by the advertising industry upon commercial jingles. The production of jingles has developed into a specialized segment of the music industry, employing not only composers and arrangers but also many successful recording stars, such as the Spice Girls, Ray Charles, and Brandy.

Some of the standards of commercial jingles have been Coca-Cola's "I'd Like to Teach the World to Sing" and "It's the Real Thing," as well as Lowenbrau's "Here's to Good Friends." In addition, there have been such long-running successes as Ford Mercury Cougar's use of Steppenwolf's rendition of the song "Born to Be Wild" as part of a campaign aimed at a younger market, Nike's use of the Beatles song "Revolution," and Fruit of the Loom calling on Graham Nash of Crosby, Stills and Nash for his song "Teach Your Children." The practice of using songs as commercial jingles is becoming more and more popular. In 1999 Burger King used such classic soul tunes as Minnie Ripperton's "Loving You" and Chick's "Le Freak" to sell flame-broiled hamburgers, while Gap commercials featured Bill Wither's "Lovely Day" and "Dress You Up in My Love" by Madonna.

Uses of Music in Commercial Jingles

Music can be used in two ways in commercial jingles. Established songs can be used in either derivative or integral ways. A derivative use is a new version of a previously established song, such as R. Kelly's "I Believe I Can Fly," used in a McDonald's advertisement with revised lyrics. An integral use is when the original version of an established song is used, such as the use of Bob Seger's "Like a Rock" in the Chevrolet truck commercials.

Music can also be newly created for a specific purpose. Considered works for hire under copyright law, these songs are owned by the advertising agency that commissioned the work. Some of the more notable examples include the

Folger's coffee jingle "The Best Part of Waking Up" and Coca-Cola's "Always Coca-Cola."

ASCAP Payments for Music Used in Commercials

In payment formulas for the use of music in commercials, ASCAP distinguishes between well-established songs, called *qualifying works;* songs written specifically for advertising purposes; and lesser-known songs adopted for advertising purposes. The measurement of what is "qualified" requires a statistical review of prior ASCAP credits for radio or television feature performances: simply stated, 20,000 such credits accumulated since October 1959; or 5,000 feature credits with the last 5 years, of which not more than 1,500 can be counted in any one year. Such qualifying works get 12 percent of what a regular featured performance would earn whereas a nonqualifying work receives a mere 3 percent. The reason given for such a substantial difference is that a qualifying work offers the advertiser a well-established audience identification, which is a valuable factor in the ASCAP licensing negotiation for its blanket license. On the other hand, newly created or lesser-known works rely more heavily on being tailor-made for the advertisement and should be more reliant on the compensation paid for such creation.

In addition to the distinctions between qualifying and nonqualifying works, ASCAP also accords a sharply reduced performance credit to jingles. As ASCAP defines it, a commercial jingle is "an advertising, promotional or public service announcement containing musical material (with or without lyrics)" in which:

> (a) the musical material was originally written for advertising, promotional or public service announcement purposes, or (b) the performance is of a musical work, originally written for other purposes, with the lyrics changed for advertising, promotional or public service announcement purposes with the permission of the ASCAP member or members in interest, or (c) the performance is of a musical work, originally written for other purposes, which does not have at least one hundred and fifty feature performance credits recorded in the Society's radio and television surveys during the five preceding fiscal survey years.

Commercial music can also be used as background for a spoken message, such as a strain from "Rhapsody in Blue" for an international ad campaign of United Airlines. This category is defined by ASCAP as "a musical work (other than a jingle) used in conjunction with an advertising, promotional, or public service announcement." For such a use, ASCAP generally accords the credit as

> the greater of (i) the credit for use of the work in a single program computed on a durational basis ... or (ii) 50% of a use credit for the first

such performance on a single program, and only 5% of a use credit for each subsequent such performance on such program, provided, however, that in the event credit is computed as set forth in (ii) of this subparagraph ... no work shall receive more than one use credit for a single program.

ASCAP will not pay performance fees to a jingle composer who writes the music for an advertiser as a work for hire or under an agreement that prevents it from licensing the performing rights.

Payments for Music Used in Commercials

Since July 1981 BMI has been making payments for the use of music as jingles. These payments do not, however, include uses for "network or station promotional or public service announcements." This is because no revenue is earned by the station for such uses.

To qualify for payment, the music must be the sole focus of audience attention for at least 15 seconds during the commercial. There is also a payment schedule for background and underscore music for ABC, CBS, and NBC only, with a minimum of 7 seconds of original music. In addition, there is payment for feature performances on the ABC, CBS, and NBC network TV with a minimum of 15 seconds of sole focus of original music. There even is a bonus for works that have received a minimum of 25,000 feature perform- ances on American radio and local television as measured by BMI. This bonus is for ABC, CBS, and NBC network TV only.

In addition to sending the required notice of the commercial to the BMI Jingle Department on forms supplied and processed by that department, an audiotape of the commercial as broadcast must be submitted. In the case of a television commercial, the sender can supply a videotape if he or she desires. Another item that must be submitted is a list of the broadcast time bought on behalf of the sponsor. The music will not qualify if written for the advertiser as a work for hire or written according to any agreement whereby BMI is unable to license the performing rights.

Recent rates paid by BMI, to both the writer *and* the publisher are 1 cent for a local radio performance, 37.5 cents for a local television performance, and $30 for a television network performance on ABC, CBS, or NBC. The rates are subject to change by BMI.

In the world of the commercial jingle, BMI and ASCAP recognize that invariably their members receive significant license payments for the right to synchronize songs for advertising purposes. However, they remind members that synch licenses do not necessarily include the right of public performances. Customarily, ad agencies permit language in the agreement reserving the right of the applicable performing rights society to license nondramatic public performance.

Both BMI and ASCAP identify performances for radio, local television, and most cable television surveys by the product and the first line spoken or sung and request that their members provide them with this information. They also request the television commercial reports, which can be obtained from the advertising agency. On each report, ASCAP and BMI ask for the name of the network, the name of the program, the date of the performance and the industry standard coding identification number. (The ISCI number consists of four letters and four numbers; it is an identifying code used by the advertising industry and broadcast media for airing and billing purposes.) For existing works used in a commercial, ASCAP and BMI request that the member indicate if the work is being used as instrumental, with original lyrics, or if the lyrics have been changed for a commercial purpose.

Negotiations for Licensing Fees

Much money can be made from the licensing of well-known songs for jingles or from commissioning the creation of original jingle music and lyrics. (The accompanying CD-ROM contains a sample "Commercial Jingle License" form.) Jingle rights to well-recognized songs for use in commercial jingles have been known to command impressive fees, reaching above $500,000 in numerous instances. Such songs include "You'd Be So Nice to Come Home To," used by Chanel perfumes, "Stand by Me," used by Citibank, "It's Impossible," used by Polaroid and "Bye Bye Blackbird," used by Pontiac. Reportedly Microsoft paid several million dollars for the Rolling Stones song "Start Me Up" for use in its Windows 95 advertising campaign.

Although payments in excess of $150,000 are relatively rare for U.S. rights, fees approximating $75,000 are often negotiated. For regional ads, where full U.S. rights are not required, payment is proportionately reduced based on the share of the population that the region represents. Some regions are a group of states, whereas limited regions can be specific cities. These fees are significant when compared to annual earnings from conventional music sources, but the amounts are small in relation to the large amounts—even millions of dollars— that may be spent in the advertising campaign built on a jingle.

To put licensing fees in the context of an advertising agency budget, keep in mind that a single 30-second commercial on a popular network show such as "Friends" costs $310,000 in air time alone and that even less successful network shows charge an average price of almost $200,000 for each similar 30-second spot, whereas music license fees are for an unlimited number of spots within the negotiated time period. An agency may not wish to jeopardize a costly campaign by a nonexclusive license that might permit another competing advertiser to use the same tune. An advertiser usually requests category exclusivity, such as "soft drinks," "automotive supplies," or "air transportation," thus permitting the same song to be used to advertise a noncompeting product. The simultaneous use of one song for advertising different products is infrequent but it does sometimes happen, as in the case of "The

Pink Panther Theme," which was used in commercials advertising an insurer and a supplier of building products.

Negotiations for the appropriate license are sometimes initiated by the advertiser through the Harry Fox Agency, but they are ordinarily concluded by the advertising agency in consultation with the music publisher and often with the composer. It is not uncommon for an advertising agency to shop around for alternative tunes to test-market, and then, when they have settled on two or three choices, get bids for airing the various choices. Publishers have learned that in such a high-stakes competition it is best to agree to test-marketing for a portion of the licensing fees (usually 10 percent), with the balance of the fee to be paid if the test is successful.

Among items of negotiation in the licensing of songs for commercials are exclusivity, the extent of the licensed territory, and the duration of the license, including options to extend the term, usually at escalated fees. A relatively new aspect of negotiations is permission for cable TV usage as well as for radio and television. Many sponsors seek an extension of rights to cover trade shows and sales meetings. The most important factor is whether the song is widely known. If it is a current or recent hit, the advertiser will want the commercial to be released while the tune is fresh in the listener's memory. The publisher and writer usually prefer to wait until the song is declining on hit charts, so as not to detract from record sales and regular air play.

Some composers object to any use of their song in a commercial as an affront to artistic integrity and reputation or as detracting from normal use of the song. For a long time composer Bob Dylan refused to allow his songs to be used in jingles, but he finally relented. He allowed the international accounting firm of Coopers and Lybrand to use "The Times They Are A-Changin' " provided that they not identify it further by direct or indirect use of his name or likeness. Graham Nash, of Crosby, Stills and Nash, was less demanding. He allowed not only his song "Teach Your Children" to be used for Fruit of the Loom underwear ads, but his voice as well, noting modestly, "We're not talking Mozart, here."

Warranties and Indemnities

A further item for negotiation in the licensing of songs for jingles is the matter of warranties and indemnities sought by advertisers from the licensors of the music. Advertisers who plan to invest substantial sums in the production and use of a jingle are naturally concerned about obtaining clear and unimpeded rights to the music. They fear infringement claims that might result in an obligation to pay damages or a share of profits greatly in excess of the license fees or other costs paid to the supplier of the music. The potential liability, as well as the possibility of high attorney's fees involved in such litigation, impels advertisers to require appropriate warranties and indemnifications, even if they carry their own "errors and omissions" insurance.

The standard license form or other form submitted by or on behalf of the advertiser contains unlimited warranties and indemnities. At the same time, publishers, composers, and producers seek to limit their exposure, ordinarily to the amounts paid or payable for the rights to the jingle. The advertiser and its agency are commonly protected by any errors and omissions insurance policy, whereas such insurance may be unusual for the music licensors. The latter, for their protection, can attempt to negotiate being named as additional insured parties in the advertiser or agency's insurance policy.

Uses of music "in conjunction with" advertising messages, such as in background instrumental form, fall within the general ASCAP license and do not usually require a special performance license for the arrangement or adaptation. However, advertising campaigns are not founded on a live use of background music, and accordingly, a license is necessary for synchronizing the music with the taped television film or for mechanical reproduction on a transcribed announcement.

The Packaging of Jingles

Writers commissioned to create tailor-made jingles sometimes prepare the entire package of the musical composition, lyric, performance, and recording, thereby reaping a financial benefit in addition to the flat fee for composing and writing the jingle. While the advertiser receives rights free of writer royalty obligations, the writer may nevertheless attempt to retain the right to collect performance fees that may be payable by a performing rights organization. It is not uncommon, however, for writers to reserve no rights whatsoever.

Many commercial jingles are purchased in package deals from producers specializing in music for commercials. They frequently have their own staff of writers and composers who receive guaranteed earnings either as salary or as advances. Such packagers were one of a group studied by the 4-A (four big advertising agencies) in 1993, which determined that packagers charged a markup of about 28 percent over actual production costs, representing profits and overhead. Nonetheless, having the creative services of multiple professionals beyond the jingle composer, including director, editor, engineer, musicians, actors, and voice-over narrators as a team, can result in budget savings and competitive bidding advantages as well as economies of time on tightly scheduled assignments.

Participation in the creation and production of a jingle can carry with it the advantage of becoming one of the singers and musicians in the production sessions or choosing the personnel for the session. These performers receive union residual payments that often are substantially greater than the fixed fees paid to the creator or producer. Creators and producers sometimes successfully bargain that if they are not engaged for a follow-up to the initial campaign, they will receive the union rate payable to a singer on future versions of their original jingle.

Payments to Singers and Instrumentalists

Minimum payment rates to singers who perform in commercial jingles are governed by the applicable American Federation of Television and Radio Artists (AFTRA) or Screen Actors Guild (SAG) rate schedules. In general, jingles for radio are subject to AFTRA jurisdiction, and those for television are subject to SAG jurisdiction, although in a field such as video, where tape is employed instead of film, the user can opt for either AFTRA or SAG jurisdiction. Union scale under either jurisdiction is similar.

AFM rate schedules cover minimum rates of payment to instrumentalists, orchestrators, arrangers, and copyists. Payments under union agreements are usually geared to particular periods or cycles of use, and additional payments are commonly required for continued use beyond the original period. In 1993, amendments to the Television and Radio Announcements Agreement (Jingles) were ratified. The new agreement includes a wage increase of 7.5 percent (the 1-hour-minimum call session fee is now $86 per musician). The wage increase is applicable to sideline musician rates, music preparation scales, and foreign use payments. Use, reuse, dubbing fees, and so forth increased from $60 to $64.50. The rate category for two to four sidemen was eliminated. Also, the pension contribution for radio commercials increased to 10 percent, now equal to television commercials.

Singers can earn substantial monies by participating in commercial jingles for radio and television. As of this writing, under AFTRA minimum-rate session fees, singers receive the following:

	Radio	Television
Solo	$185.00	$333.30
Group 3–5	$136.40	$187.95

These fees are per spot recorded or for each 90 minutes in the studio, whichever is greater. The session fee generally covers the use in one small market for 13 weeks.

Additionally, substantial residual payments are involved when a commercial goes into a number of major markets and even more when it goes national or is broadcast on a major network. For example, for the New York market, together with Los Angeles, Chicago, and 100 other units (cities), the singer would be paid, for each 13 weeks of unlimited use:

	Radio	Television
Solo	$754.20	$1,959.00
Group 3–5	$311.20	$601.65

Simultaneous broadcast on a major network of a commercial for a national advertiser requires the payment of a fee for each individual use; over the period of a year, this can add up to very significant earnings.

The Simulation of an Artist's Style in Jingles

It is obviously more economical for an advertiser to use studio musicians and singers for commercials than to hire famous stars. When a synchronization license for a commercial jingle is obtained from a music publisher for a song made famous by a top star, it is quite tempting for the advertiser to simulate the star's arrangement and style in the jingle. Nancy Sinatra's rendition of "These Boots Were Made for Walking" was imitated for a Goodyear Tire and Rubber Company commercial, and the Fifth Dimension's style was used for TWA's "Up, Up, and Away" advertising campaign. In separate suits brought for each of these two cases, the courts held that the artists had no property right in their style of rendition or arrangement and that there was no unfair competition.

However, in a 1988 case involving the imitation of Bette Midler's voice in a Ford Motor commercial, the U.S. Circuit Court for the Ninth District held that, under California law, the imitation of a voice closely identified with that of the plaintiff gave rise to a cause of action against the imitator. One commentator noted:

> The Midler case signals a possible end to judicial resistance to the concept that a performer may be as readily identifiable by voice as by mere facial appearance.... As commercial exploitation of a persona expands to encompass name, likeness, voice, and style, judicial and legislative protection must expand as well. The common thread of this fascinating body of law is preventing one who has not expended the "sweat equity" in achieving distinction from reaping the commercial benefits that come with public recognition and success.

In 1992, Circuit Court for the Ninth District, building on the *Midler* decision, affirmed a $2.4 million award to artist Tom Waits against Frito-Lay for running an ad using a sound-alike singer to sing Waits's song "Step Right Up" and to imitate Waits's distinctive, raspy, gravelly singing voice. The court described the sound-alike as "near perfection" and ruled "when a distinctive voice of a professional singer is widely known and is deliberately imitated in order to sell a product, the sellers have appropriated what is not theirs and have committed a tort in California." The court went on to rule that "a voice is a sufficient indicia of a celebrity's identity and the right of publicity protects against its imitation for commercial purposes without the celebrity's consent."

In New York, in 1994, U.S. district court judge Charles S. Haight, Jr., ruled that the distinctive sound of the group the Fat Boys was available for copyright protection and denied summary judgment to Miller Brewing Company and others whom the Fat Boys sued in 1988 after a Miller Lite commercial aired featuring three Fat Boys look-alikes performing in the group's distinctive style.

It would appear that the risks of a successful lawsuit against them are likely to dampen any continued interest by advertisers and their agencies in simulating a star's arrangement and style for a proposed commercial jingle.

27

Buying and Selling Copyrights

Throughout the nineties, there was substantial competition in buying and selling large music catalogues. EMI claimed about 1 million song titles and Warner/Chappell claimed 800,000. As of this writing, their respective owners had announced plans to merge publishing operations throughout the world with a likely yearly combined gross of $1 billion and a market share of 25.3 percent. In 1999, Universal Music Group added the music publishing interests of Polygram Music to its MCA holdings and now controls more than 700,000 copyrights and over 26 percent of the market share. Other major publishers include BMG Music, which claims over 250,000 titles, and the Sony/ATV Music joint venture, discussed below.

However, songs are not interchangeable commodities like ears of corn or tons of steel. A hit song obviously generates substantially more income than an unrecorded song in manuscript or demo form. Consequently, sophisticated participants in the music publishing field look to earnings history, among other factors, for the valuation of a catalog.

The Buying and Selling of Large Catalogs

In 1985, Michael Jackson acquired the ATV catalog, which included the 251 Beatles titles as well as such other hits as "He's So Shy," "Lucille," "Long Tall Sally," "Ramblin' Rose," and "Girl's Night Out," for $47 million. EMI reportedly paid $70 million for the right to administer the catalog, which it did for a number of years under a form of lease that did not include full transfer of title. In 1995, Sony Music Entertainment and Michael Jackson announced that they had formed a new worldwide joint venture that would encompass all the present and future music publishing interests of both parties (except for Jackson's own compositions in his MIJAC catalog, which continue to be administered by Warner/Chappell). The Beatles catalog continued to be administered by EMI through February 1998 under the prior arrangement, although the revenues (after the deduction of EMI's administration fee) went into the joint venture. No financial terms were disclosed, but it may be surmised that the price was substantially higher than what Jackson paid in 1985 or EMI subsequently. With the addition of the ATV catalog to Sony's own catalog of songs recorded by Willie Nelson, Little Richard, Elvis Presley, Lloyd Price, the Pointer Sisters, Babyface, Cindi Lauper, and others, it may well be that Sony/ATV's claim to be number 3 among the majors is fully justified—at least prior to the combination of MCA and PolyGram within the Universal Music Group.

Chappell Music is another good example of how prices have escalated. The Warner group acquired the Chappell catalog, with its wealth of standards, for twice as much as was paid in 1985 when PolyGram, the former owner of the catalog, sold it for about $140 million to a consortium of various private banking and other investors organized and administered by Bienstock Enterprises, the owner of Carlin Music Ltd. of England as well as important American catalogs. Prior to this, the Bienstock organization had acquired the E. B. Marks Music Company in association with the estates of Richard Rodgers and Oscar Hammerstein. The Rodgers and Hammerstein catalogs were administered, though not owned, by Chappell; therefore, they were not a part of the Warner purchase.

In 1990, EMI acquired another major group of old-line music firms in Robbins Music, Feist Music, Miller Music, and later Mills Music. These firms had been assembled through the years by various transfers to and among United Artists, CBS Songs, Belwin Music, and Filmtrax. Just two years prior to the eventual EMI acquisition, a portion consisting only of Robbins, Feist, Miller, and CBS Songs was sold to SBK (eventually part of EMI) for $170 million and thereafter repackaged with the Filmtrax-Belwin-Mills copyrights and the relatively small catalog of Ivan Mogul for a considerably higher total sales price. In 1999, the Windswept Pacific catalog of approximately 40,000 songs was sold by its owner, Fujisankei Communications of Japan, to EMI for a reported $200 million.

It is interesting to note that Sony acquired CBS Records without its former portfolio of songs and embarked anew on a search for catalogs, buying Tree Music of Tennessee, just as PolyGram, having reviewed its retreat from the music scene after its sale of Chappell, re-entered the field and built up PolyGram Music Publishing to over 250,000 titles before this catalog was sold in 1999 to Seagram (the parent of MCA), along with PolyGram's record and film interests, as part of the multibillion-dollar transaction.

As has been noted, the number of songs is not as important as their earning power. However, the historic earnings of a former hit are not sufficient assurance of value. While it is desirable to have songs that will likely continue to be popular, it is also desirable to avoid putting all of one's eggs in one basket, with only a few major earners instead of the more desirable broad-based catalog with the same earnings being generated by a larger number of songs, each with its own following, history of past hit records, and likely recurrence of earnings in the future. How far into the future is important as well, and the formula for valuation must always consider the duration of copyright and contractual rights owned or controlled by the seller.

The sale of a catalog featuring "Happy Birthday to You" to Warner/Chappell for a reported $25 million was a newsworthy event in 1990. But it was a relatively high risk. Despite the song's prominence as one of the three songs listed in the *Guinness Book of World Records* as most played, as well as its assured repetition of earnings, it is a very old copyright, written originally in 1893 and surviving public domain merely by the revision of a "Good Morning" greeting for the famous birthday greeting. At the time of its purchase, the revised adapted version was threatened by public domain status as of the year 2010. However, the 1998 extension of copyright by 20 years has made the purchase (with the benefit of hindsight) less risky.

Foreign earnings and the status of subpublisher commitments is another factor to be considered. An important American catalog with long-term 50-50 deals throughout the world is obviously less desirable than a catalog available for worldwide exploitation and administration without extended prior commitments. On the other hand, when BMG acquired Italy's largest firm, G. Ricordi, it acquired the right to administer numerous songs that would otherwise have been in its competitors' catalogs, because Ricordi had previously made long-term deals on many important American songs. Another consideration is the ability to acquire or consolidate foreign operations, as shown by the PolyGram acquisition, which enabled MCA to take over PolyGram's existing offices in Latin America and southeast Asia, without incurring the expense and effort of setting up its own operations in these territories.

A windfall benefit to purchasers should be considered when reviewing historic buy-sell deals. First, almost all well-established catalogs seem to defeat inflation by a gradual increase in earnings. This may be due to an increase in mechanical royalty collections in most countries of the world. Another factor, no longer applicable, was the surge in earnings brought about by the re-release of many records in CD format. At the same time, industry observers are concerned about the possibilities of unlicensed duplication resulting from these new technological developments. Whether these can be averted by consortiums like the Secure Digital Music Initiative remains to be seen.

New financial growth may also result from increased commercial radio and television in foreign territories previously dominated by state-owned and low-royalty-paying public bodies, as well as Internet-generated revenues. The 1994 adoption of GATT, with its emphasis on intellectual property rights, is expected to give rise to legal and economic recognition of copyrights in countries previously the source of piratical uses. All these factors may help to sustain the historical rise in publishing earnings.

The Buying and Selling of Smaller Catalogs

There is little debate that the music publishing industry is becoming more centralized and that true independents, although numbering in the many thousands, are capturing less of the total cash flow of the industry. Outstanding independent music publishers at the time of this writings are Zomba, Peer, Almo Irving, Music Sales, and Carlin Music.

Certain smaller independent publishers and even some individuals have, like the majors, engaged in a deliberate course of investment in copyrights and interests in copyrights. This demonstrates that sophisticated professionals are convinced that copyrights represent excellent investments. Their principal interest, of course, lies in established musical compositions rather than untried, unproven ones. Some publishers have bought half-interests, and even quarter-interests, in musical copyrights and seem to have prospered.

There are various incentives for selling music publishing catalogs: for example, the death of a principal owner (and the possible need to raise cash to pay estate taxes); the retirement of a principal owner; a disagreement among joint owners; the fear of decreasing value as the catalogs mature without new promotion. In addition, tax benefits can be a powerful incentive in a stock-for-stock transaction where the catalog is transferred to a publicly traded entity. If the seller is not the original composer, author, or donee of the compositions, capital gains treatment may be applicable at a lower tax rate than the otherwise applicable income tax rate.

Public corporations may regard the acquisition of a broad-based, well-managed music publishing catalog as a sound way to enter or expand their presence in the "content" side of the entertainment market. It may also be seen as a way to enhance the earnings on their common stock, especially when the price paid for the acquisition compares favorably with the price of the purchaser's stock and its past earnings. For example, purchasing a music catalog at 10 times the amount of average expected annual net earnings would be particularly advantageous if the stock of the purchasing company is being valued at 20 times its average net earnings.

Sources of Individual Copyrights

The sources of individual copyrights are largely smaller publishers (including artists and writers who may have retained all or part of their ownership in works) and composers who have obtained control of their copyrights during the renewal term of copyrights, that is, after the initial 28-year period. Under the Songwriters Guild of America contract developed in 1948 and used before the 1978 effective date of the Copyright Act of 1976, worldwide ownership of copyrights in the renewal period can vest in the writer. The better copyrights in the 1930s and early 1940s, written by writers who insisted on earlier SGA terms under a pre-1948 contract, have come under the control of the writers for only the United States and Canada. (See "Songwriters Guild Contracts" in Chapter 16.)

Knowledgeable publishers interested in such copyrights study the Register of Copyright publications and ferret out the better copyrights that will shortly be up for renewal. They then initiate negotiations with the writers or their estates for the right to publish the copyrighted material in the renewal period.

Until the year 2005, such renewal opportunities still exist for songs originating prior to 1978. Subsequent compositions are governed by the Copyright Act of 1976 and are subject to return of U.S. rights either at the 35-year mark from date of publication in print or record form or 40 years from date of execution of grant, whichever is earlier. The prospective buyer must make a full and thorough examination of the con-tracts entered into by the writers and the prior publishers in order to determine what rights and territories have not previously been assigned to third parties.

Purchasers of older copyrights know that when a composition became popular in the years up to the 1980s and sometimes later, there was a flurry of interest by American-based international firms or overseas publishers who offered to subpublish the composition in a particular country. A single compo-sition may have been subpublished by many different subpublishers throughout the world under separate agreements, each with its own terms. In certain areas, the composition's subpublishing rights may have been assigned for 10 years, in others, for the original period of the U.S. copyright, and in the balance, for the entire period of copyright in the particular territory. In the major music territories, the latter period is often the life of the writer plus 70 years. Buyers must determine, on the basis of the subpublishing agreements, whether they are purchasing the full publishing rights for each country or only the right to receive royalties from a subpublisher already in place, and if the latter, for how long.

Renewal and Reversion Rights

In the case of purchases of compositions first fixed before 1978 that are in the original 28-year period of the U.S. copyright, the status of the right to renew the U.S. copyright is important, even though the formality of actual renewal registration is not required after the Copyright Renewal Act of 1992. (Of course, this does not include songs written on an employee-for-hire basis.)

The buyer who purchases a pre-1978 copyrighted composition from a publisher who does not control the renewal right must understand that the acquired rights for the U.S. market will cease at the end of the 28th year from the inception of the copyright. If the publisher is also selling the renewal right, the buyer must recognize that the seller can convey only a contingent interest in the renewal period and that the contingent interest will vest only if the writer who granted the renewal rights is alive in the 28th year. The same contingency is present if the seller is also the writer. Should the writer not live to the 28th year, the renewal right belongs to the surviving spouse and chil-dren; if there is no such immediate family and the writer left a will, the right goes to the executor of the writer's estate; if there is no will, the renewal right vests in the writer's next of kin. It should be noted that for compositions written on an employee-for-hire basis there is no reversion in the event of the writer's death before the 28th year.

For compositions written in and after 1978, except in an employment-for-hire situation, there is a right of termination between the 35th and 40th year from the date of the grant of copyright. This right cannot be waived any earlier than 10 years before the effective date of any such termination. (See Chapter 11.) Nevertheless, as the risk of termination is not automatic in the absence of affirmative action by the terminating party, some value may be attributed to the possibility of inertia when purchasing compositions otherwise subject to termination.

A buyer must take steps to protect the rights to the renewal period if renewal-term rights are a significant part of the purchase. In the case of a writer still in his or her forties or fifties, with the renewal period but a few years away, it may be regarded as a good business risk to assume that the writer will live to the 28th year of the copyright. A more practical approach is to require that the writer's spouse and children join in the sale agreement and convey to the buyer their contingent interest in the renewal period.

Locating the wife or husband and children may be a long and expensive task, sometimes further complicated by the status of illegitimate children. Under the Copyright Act of 1976, illegitimate children were recognized by statute as "children." Previously, the problem of illegitimacy was the subject of the 1956 case of *DeSylva v. Ballentine,* which involved a claim by the illegitimate son of the deceased George G. DeSylva that he was entitled to share in renewal rights under Section 24 of the Copyright Act of 1909. The U.S. Supreme Court held in favor of the son, declaring that if an illegitimate child is considered to be an heir of a writer under the laws of the applicable state (in this case, California), he or she is also in the class of children entitled to the benefits of copyright renewal rights. In a 1992 case concerning the songs of Hank Williams, a U.S. Court of Appeals held that an adopted illegitimate child was included within the state's definition of children entitled to inherit, and therefore the child was to share in copyright renewals under the Copyright Act of 1909, Section 24, and the Copyright Act of 1976, Section 304(a).

Even the joinder of the wife or husband and children as parties to the purchase agreement does not give full protection, because if the children are minors they may disaffirm the agreement and grant their proportionate share of the renewal copyright to another publisher. But it is possible to dissuade such disaffirmance by a provision in the sale agreement that the adults in the family guarantee performance by the children; the adults would be personally liable if the children disaffirm, and the buyer would also be secured by the rights of the adults to receive writer royalties from the buyer-publisher during the renewal period. (For the possible use of court approval of minor agreements to prevent minor disaffirmance and to sanction parental guarantees, see Chapter 3, "Contracts with Minors.")

For further protection against the loss of renewal rights, the buyer may take out insurance on the life of the writer, since the buyer has acquired an insurable interest. Should the buyer have such insurance in mind, the buyer should be careful to include in the sale agreement a provision that the writer will cooperate in the obtaining of such insurance, including appearing for medical examinations.

Because renewal rights may vest in the executor of the writer's estate if the writer dies and leaves no spouse or children, the contract may require the writer to agree to execute a new will or a codicil to an old will in which the executor is instructed to convey renewal rights to the buyer.

In the case of compositions already in the renewal term, consideration must be given to the author's right under the Copyright Act of 1976 to terminate after the 56th year. For compositions first fixed after 1977, the author's right, under the same statute, to terminate after the 35th year should be weighed. (For a further discussion, see Chapter 11.)

There may be a special problem in the case of copyrights created before 1957 in the United Kingdom, Canada, Australia, and other nations or territories that were in the British Commonwealth at that time. Under the applicable law concerning such compositions, the copyright will revert to the estate 25 years after the writer's death for the balance of the period of the copyright protection. Any prospective buyer of older copyrights must reckon with this right of "reversion" of copyright.

As for works originating in or before 1934, purchasers of such works should be aware of possible similar problems with regard to German rights. The issue concerns whether a publisher/assignee or the heirs of a composer benefit from a statutory extension of the life of a copyright. On December 13, 1934, the period was extended from 30 years to 50 years after the death of the composer. The duration for Germany was subsequently further extended to 70 years after death.

The Purchase of Copyrights or Stock

Where the entire catalog of a publisher is for sale, the buyer usually prefers to acquire the copyrights rather than the corporate stock of the publisher, in order to obtain the right to depreciate the cost of the acquisition for tax purposes. One advantage of purchasing assets instead of stock is the opportunity to amortize the assets over several years for tax purposes of sale, thereby establishing a new valuation basis as well as preserving a corporate shield against prior underpayment of taxes. It is possible that the corporate entity of the publisher may offer some tax-loss benefits, or that purchasing the corporate entity may have some advantage such as the avoidance of restrictions against the assignment of copyrights or writer contracts.

In some instances, the seller insists on the sale of the corporate stock. Acquiring the corporate entity may create complicated legal and accounting problems, since the buyer then inherits the corporate liabilities, including possible claims for back taxes, writer suits for royalties, etc. In the usual case, it is simpler for the buyer to purchase the assets of the publisher rather than its stock. If the individuals who are the principals in the publishing firm are financially responsible, it is possible for the buyer to achieve some measure of protection in buying the corporate stock by obtaining the individual guarantees of the corporation's warranties and indemnifications. Satisfactory protection may also be provided if the consideration for the sale is payable over a period of years, so that any adverse claims will likely appear while a significant portion of the consideration is still unpaid. It may also be specifically provided that a portion of the price will be held in escrow for a certain period, for satisfy tax and other claims. To ensure that tax claims are made promptly, the buyer may request a government tax audit of the returns for past years.

Whether the underlying copyrights or stock is purchased, it is wise for the buyer to insist on warranties and indemnities relating to the absence of litigation or threats of litigation and to the fact that the copyrights are original, do not infringe the rights of any third party, and are not subject to any liens or other encumbrances.

The Price of Purchasing a Copyright

In arriving at a price to be paid for a copyright, the buyer requires information about the past earnings of that copyright. These earnings generally fall into four categories: performance fees, mechanical and synchronization fees, and earnings from printed editions and foreign editions. The buyer requests that the owner of a copyright submit financial data for a period of years, including copies of statements rendered by ASCAP or BMI as well as by the Harry Fox Agency, if it represented the owner in the collection of mechanical and synchronization fees. If the printed editions were handled by independent organizations, the buyer wants access to the statements rendered by these organizations.

In the more distant past, a common rule of thumb in the music publishing industry was that the buyer would pay the seller a price equal to from 5 to 8 times the average yearly performance earnings paid by ASCAP or BMI for a musical composition over a representative period such as 5 years. This figure was without reference to mechanical and synchronization fees or foreign earnings of any kind.

The recent tendency is to increase the weight given to mechanical and synchronization fees and to foreign earnings, although banks continue to rely on ASCAP or BMI earnings history. A further reason is the possibility of periodic raises in the compulsory mechanical license rate. In January 2000, the mechanical rate was raised to 7.55 cents per song, or 1.45 cents per minute (previously, the rates were 7.1 cents per song or 1.35 cents per minute). Since 1992 the Copyright Arbitration Royalty Panel (CARP), an ad hoc panel appointed by the Register of Copyrights makes such decisions.

In recent years cable TV, home video, CD releases, and commercial jingles have been making greater use of favorite old films and film clips. As digital technology becomes established, new sources of music publishing revenues may appear.

The expansion of satellite broadcasting stations, as well as the replacement in Europe of state-supported stations by private commercial stations, may also generate new sources of income in the near future. Paralleling this is growth of commercial television programming in the American pattern; for example, in England, annual program output is expected to increase more than 300 percent in the next decade, with music in its customary participating role, thereby generating performing rights and synchronization payments.

Other new or enlarged music income sources are coming from developing countries. These substantially improved music earnings are the result of GATT negotiations and the American endorsement of the Berne Convention.

Les Bider, the president of Warner/Chappell, has said: "A lot of people are realizing publishing is a good investment. You're more cushioned from recession than in most businesses." This is because music users—including record companies, TV producers, and film studios—are themselves resistant to recession. Bider went on to say "music publishers benefit from new technology and new ways to use music."

As a consequence, the old rule of thumb of 5 to 8 times the average yearly performance earnings is now on the conservative side. A more likely figure is 5 to 8 times or more—sometime as high as 12 to 13 times or more—of the total of (1) the average performance earnings, (2) the average over the same period of the publisher's share of mechanical earnings, that is, the gross mechanical earnings less the writer's mechanical royalties, and (3) the average of the publisher's share of foreign performance income and foreign mechanical earnings remitted to the United States.

Under Internal Revenue Service tax law, a seller who receives all or part of the sale price after the year of sale can treat the transaction as an installment sale provided the sale is at a gain. The seller is thus entitled to file a return for each year showing only the payments received in that year. A portion of each payment will represent a part of the gain, with the profit percentage or ratio applied to each payment being computed by dividing the gross profit by the gross selling price. If the contract fails to charge interest at a minimum rate, the IRS will charge interest at that rate. Under this approach, a portion of each installment payment is considered to be a payment of interest rather than a capital gain. Like depreciation costs, interest payments are tax-deductible. Accountants or attorneys should be consulted as to the rules and regulations covering the computation of the minimum rate.

Table 27-1 shows what happens in the case of a $10,000 copyright purchase and sale with certain assumptions, listed in the table footnotes. It is assumed that the purchase price of the copyright is depreciated for tax purposes over a period of 10 years. Ordinarily, depreciation is over the term of copyright established in the Copyright Act, but in practice shorter periods have been permitted. Under the assumption of a 10-year period of depreciation, a 40 percent income tax rate, and yearly earnings of 20 percent of the purchase price, 80 percent of the earnings from the composition would be available for recoupment of the purchase price. Consequently, if the purchase price were $10,000, the yearly earnings before taxes $2,000, and the yearly depreciation $1,000 (i.e., one-tenth of $10,000), the net income before taxes would be $1,000 and the after-tax net income $600. The aggregate of the depreciation ($1,000) plus the net income after taxes ($600) would be $1,600, or 80 percent of the yearly earnings of $2,000.

Table 27-1 also assumes that the costs of administering the copyright are absorbed as a part of the present overhead of the purchaser, which may not be entirely true but is basically accurate for larger publisher-purchasers. There is a further assumption that interest on the investment is disregarded.

On the basis of the given assumptions, Table 27-1 indicates that for an investment averaging less than 20 percent of the purchase price for 7 years, the prospective buyer seeks to acquire the full available duration of copyright protection subject only to the possibility of statutory terminations and reversions by the authors or their heirs. Table 27-1 further shows that the pretax return on the average investment, after the sixth year, would tend to be 100 percent or more per year, although the principal of the investment would have been recouped in full. Obviously, if depreciation were to extend over a period longer than 10 years (e.g., 28 years) and costs of administration and interest on investment were to accrue, the average investment would be greater and the period of recoupment longer than demonstrated by the table, which is intended merely to illustrate the type of computations that may be made by a prospective buyer.

Table 27-1

Investment and Recoupment in a Copyright Purchase [a]

Year	Total less payments[b]	Average cumulative recoupment at 20% before taxes[c]
1	$2,900 (29%)	$2,000 (20%)
2	$4,700 (47%)	$4,000 (40%)
3	$6,500 (65%)	$6,000 (60%)
4	$8,300 (83%)	$8,000 (80%)
5	$10,000 (100%)	$10,000 (100%)
6	$10,000 (100%)	$12,000 (120%)
7	$10,000 (100%)	$14,000 (140%)

[a] Percentages shown are of $10,000 purchase price.
[b] Assumes 29% down payment and installment payments of 18% per year for 3 years and 17% for the last
[c] Assumes annual earnings of $2,000 per year before taxes.
[d] Ten-year depreciation assumes annual depreciation of $1,000 per year as a deduction from $2,000 annual earnings, leaving a taxable balance of $1,000 per year, which, after taxes at a 40% rate, amounts residual balance of $600 per year.

Users of Copyrights

Some purchasers of copyrights are in a special position because they are users of copyrights in addition to being music publishers. The five major label record companies are obviously users of copyrights. In addition, most of them (Universal Music Group, Warner/Chappell and Sony/ATV) have related motion picture companies. They are therefore capable of enhancing the value of a composition by planned exploitation, which results in increased earnings from mechanical fees, performance fees, and more frequent opportunities to earn synchronization fees.

The increased earnings from mechanical fees result from recordings by the record company, while the earnings from performance fees increase from performances of the records and of the television and motion pictures in which the composition appears. Synchronization fees are payable for use in television and motion pictures. It is obvious that the user-purchaser is frequently able to justify a higher purchase price for a composition than a purchaser who is not a user. With the judicious, planned use of a composition, user-purchasers may recoup their investment more quickly than other purchasers.

Capital Gains

A problem that confronts a seller of copyrights is whether to report the sum received as the proceeds from the sale of capital assets, which are taxable at capital gain rates, or whether to consider the income as royalties. Under the Internal Revenue code, the term *capital asset* does not include musical copyrights held by the writer or the writer's donee, and therefore if such individuals

Yearly cumulative taxes on assumption of 10-year duration and 40% tax rated[d]	After-tax cumulative recoupment (col. 2 less col. 3)	Net investment per year (col. 1 less col. 4)
$400 (4%)	$1,600 (16%)	$1,300 (13%)
$800 (8%)	$3,200 (32%)	$1,500 (15%)
$1,200 (12%)	$4,800 (48%)	$1,700 (17%)
$1,600 (16%)	$6,400 (64%)	$1,900 (19%)
$2,000 (20%)	$8,000 (80%)	$2,000 (20%)
$2,400 (24%)	$9,600 (96%)	$400 (4%)
$2,800 (28%)	$10,000 (100%)	$0 (0%)

are the seller, they must report the amount received, or the value of property acquired in exchange, as ordinary income, not as capital gain.

In contrast, other sellers, including the heirs of a writer, have the benefit of capital gains treatment. For this purpose, heirs include "statutory heirs" for U.S. renewal and termination rights, whereas British reversions are for the benefit of "heirs under will." With regard to assets obtained from a legatee under a will, a "stepped-up" tax basis valuation applies, and the heirs are not considered donees of the composer. For U.S. renewal and termination assignments, the statutory heirs use a capital gains basis of valuation at the effective date of acquisition of the copyright interest. Other sellers, including, as noted above, the heirs of a writer, have the benefit of capital gains treatment. (For a further discussion of capital gains, see Chapter 33, "Taxation in the Music Business.")

Due Diligence

A "due diligence" investigation is a detailed review of the chain of title and other aspects of what is being sold and the value of the catalog being purchased. It is usually conducted by qualified expert attorneys or accountants and is essential in any purchase transaction. This is especially true if the purchase price is financed in whole or in part by a bank or third-party loan, since the purchaser must usually warrant and represent to the lender that all third-party obligations, including all licenses, agency agreements, foreign subpublishing deals, outstanding advances, collaborator status, and related essential status reports have been fully disclosed. The following is a due diligence checklist that might be used in a typical purchase:

- ▸ Name, address, tax identification number, and legal status of owner of songs (i.e., the owner as shown in the Copyright Office registrations and performing rights society affiliations).
- ▸ Song-by-song list of those songs that together constitute 80% of the net publisher share (NPS) of the entire catalog, showing author and publisher splits, copyright registration data (date of filing and registration number), NPS, and recording information.
- ▸ List of songwriters currently under contract, including contract date, current period and options, ongoing advance obligations, as well as copies of the songwriter agreements.
- ▸ List of unrecouped advance balances to songwriters,
- ▸ List of subpublishing licenses, including date of license, territory, term, retention and collection period, advances and unrecouped balances, along with copies of the licenses.
- ▸ List of any other advances recoupable from earnings of the assets (e.g., BMI or ASCAP advances, to be cross-checked with the societies).
- ▸ List of print contracts, including term, advances and unrecouped balances,

sell-off rights, plus copies of the contracts.
- ▸ Copies of recording agreements, including controlled-composition provisions.
- ▸ Copies of all other pertinent contracts, other than Harry Fox Agency standard form mechanical licenses and other nonexclusive licenses.
- ▸ Copies of copyright documents, including registrations, assignments, etc.
- ▸ List of the names, addresses, and ages of all the songwriters and their spouses and children (natural or adopted), if any of the major compositions are pre-1978 and are not works for hire.
- ▸ Addresses for the last 5 years of each owner (as reflected in the Copyright Office records).
- ▸ If the seller is a corporation, a recently certified good-standing certificate and tax good-standing certificate; at closing, minutes of directors meeting approving the transaction certified by the secretary of the corporation. If the seller is "doing business as" (dba), a recently certified copy of the fictitious name filing.
- ▸ Copies of all source royalty statements received by company from record companies, the Harry Fox Agency, performance societies, subpublishers, etc. (5 years).
- ▸ Copies of all royalty statements issued to songwriters, copublishers, etc. (5 years).
- ▸ Cash receipts book (5 years).
- ▸ Cash disbursements book (5 years).
- ▸ Bank statements (5 years).
- ▸ All available financial summaries relating to the compositions.
- ▸ Seller's federal tax returns (5 years).
- ▸ Authorization executed by seller authorizing BMI, ASCAP, and the other societies to turn over complete song lists, statements, and account status.
- ▸ Documentation on any pending claims or litigations relating to the catalog, including audit claims.
- ▸ Documentation relating to any liens, pledges, or security agreements relating to the catalog.
- ▸ Copy of publisher's current society affiliation agreements.
- ▸ Copy of publisher's current Harry Fox Agency agreement.
- ▸ List of all mechanical licenses, including song title, artist, label, selection number, and release date.

For additional consideration of factors relevant to the buying and selling of copyrights, see Chapter 28, "Loans to Music Publishers." See also the accompanying CD-ROM for a sample "Sale of Copyright" form.

28

Loans to Music Publishers

There are many good reasons why a music publisher might require a business loan. These reasons may include catalog acquisitions, writer royalty advances, new physical studio or equipment costs, costs of preparing new demonstration records, costs of preparing or financing others to make master recordings, and selective advertising and promotion of songs or recordings.

Until relatively recently, however, it was difficult to conceive of anything more foreign to a conservative banker than the needs of thousands of music publishers in New York's Tin Pan Alley, in Nashville, and in Hollywood. Assets literally worth no more than a song and administered in a highly personalized manner that emphasizes promotion, contacts, and ever-changing market conditions would hardly seem reassuring to a potential lender.

But today banking relationships are no longer exceptional in the music industry. Knowledgeable lenders have noted that ASCAP, BMI, and SESAC pay out millions of dollars a year to music publishers. Many loans are made on the basis of certified ASCAP and BMI reports of past performance fee earnings. Low-cost collection agencies, such as the Harry Fox Agency, which collects mechanical license fees from record companies for a fee of 4.5 percent or less of gross receipts, help materially to bolster the credit rating of the music business.

Some lenders have made something of a specialty of music industry loans. These lenders recognize that music copyrights are as good a form of collateral as anything else. One informed banker commented that any major loan requires two areas of security: first, the asset and cash flow of the entity being acquired, and second, the backup assurance of the borrower's basic business. Many of the major acquisitions of recent years have been financed by private investment bankers, such as Boston Ventures, rather than commercial banks.

As the banking world has acquired a basic understanding of the peculiar needs and resources of the music industry, they have increased loans to industry members. A method of securing loans initially established in the film industry has recently also become part of the music business, namely, a lien against future earnings. The first person to successfully launch this concept in the music business was the Pullman Structured Asset Sales Group, which successfully organized a $50 million loan secured by David Bowie's future artist and songwriter royalties. Pullman followed this with other loans based on the securitization of the Holland-Dozier-Holland producer and artist royalty streams and on the Ashford and Simpson artist and songwriter royalty streams. Others followed Pullman's lead. Owing to the expense of organizing, evaluating, and selling securities, however, only large loans can be "securitized" in this way.

The Special Risks in Loans to Music Publishers

Annually, more than 120,000 new copyrighted songs compete fiercely for the few spots on the record charts. The fact is, most new songs make no impact whatsoever in the music marketplace. As a result, in evaluating a proposed loan, lenders generally focus only on income from established songs with a provable financial history. In considering the business expenses of a music publisher, lenders focus on writer's royalties, which is a publisher's most important cost of doing business. On mechanical license income, the writer's royalty is usually 50 percent of the receipts; rent, salaries, independent promotion, and travel and telephone costs are the other principal items of expense.

Lenders must be aware of the special risks involved in loans to music publishers. An unscrupulous borrower may apply for a bank loan after having exhausted all other methods of obtaining money by way of cash advances against future earnings. Such advances may have been obtained from print licensees or from foreign subpublishers. The lender may have relied on earnings from such sources, only to find that the advances must first be recouped before the earnings are available to repay the loan.

Another special risk involved in loans to music publishers is the duration of the borrower's rights. On copyrights originating before 1978, the borrower may not possess rights beyond the original 28-year term of copyright because he or she has failed to obtain renewal rights from the author or a deceased author's statutory successors. As with all copyrights, consideration should be given to statutory rights of termination granted under the Copyright Act of 1976. If the copyright is of foreign origin, the borrower may have acquired U.S. publishing rights for only a limited term (for example, 10 years from the original foreign publisher). It should be remembered that all copyrights go into the public domain after the expiration of the applicable statutory periods of copyright. (For a discussion of such periods of copyright and rights of termination, see Chapter 11.)

Other unusual risks are posed by the possible negligent administration of copyrights prior to the granting of a loan. Under the Copyright Act of 1909 (still applicable to compositions originating before 1978), a careless publisher could have invalidated the copyright by printing or authorizing the printing of a song without the appropriate copyright notice. The copyright on the song "The Caissons Go Rolling Along" was forfeited by permitting such a publication. Forfeiture is less likely to have happened under the Copyright Act of 1976, with its more liberal treatment of omissions or imperfections. Nevertheless, there are still circumstances under that act in which failure to comply with notice requirements would cause the loss of copyright protection.

On copyrights originating on or after March 1, 1989, the effective date of the Berne Convention Implementation Act of 1988, which made copyright notices optional, forfeitures for negligence by publishers regarding copyright notices no longer occur. The passage of the Copyright Renewal Act of 1992 provides further assurance against forfeiture for failure to renew older copyrights in their 28th year. However, for maximum security one must still refer to the act under which the original copyright was issued. (For a further discussion of copyright notice requirements, see Chapter 10.)

It is no longer necessary to file a Notice of Use under the 1976 Copyright Act, although it was previously required for the first mechanical reproduction license. The act provides that a copyright owner cannot collect mechanical royalties under a compulsory license for records made and distributed before the owner is identified as such in the records of the Copyright Office, although recovery can be made for records made and distributed after such identification. A lender might therefore wish to check the status of current registrations of copyrights.

A more basic threat to music copyrights is the failure to defend adequately against litigation that attacks the validity of the copyright. This can result from the frequent defense of nonoriginality in lawsuits brought by the borrower. In fact, one prominent music industry lawyer has ventured a guess that a majority of important songs could not withstand the scrutiny of experts involved in extended litigation. Many an action for copyright infringement is settled or never brought because of fear that the defendant will put a valuable copyright in jeopardy by an attack on its originality.

The Amount of a Loan

A simple protection available to lenders in the music field is the limitation of the amount of a loan to the anticipated receipts of the borrower from sources akin to "accounts receivable" in other fields. In simple language, this is a form of "pipeline" estimate of money coming through the lines but delayed in receipt. This alleviates the necessity for a full investigation of copyright ownership and duration. It does, however, require access to information concerning (1) recent uses of compositions in the borrower's catalog and (2) advances against earnings previously obtained by the borrower.

A typical anticipated payment is the quarterly accounting by ASCAP or BMI based on public performances logged from 6 to 9 months prior to the

accounting. Similar in regularity are the Harry Fox Agency quarterly distributions of mechanical royalties collected on a quarterly or semiannual basis from
record companies. More delayed payments, often as much as one or two years
behind domestic payments, may come from foreign agents or licensees, who
ordinarily remit 50 percent or more of their territorial earnings from all
sources except printed uses, which are usually accounted for at a minimum
rate of 10 to 12.5 percent of the retail selling price. These anticipated receipts,
subject to outstanding advances, can be considered an appropriate basis for a
short-term loan. A lender usually requires the added protection of a notification to the appropriate society or collecting agency to make payment directly to
the lender.

An estimate of uncollected mechanical royalties can sometimes be made
on the basis of public announcements of verified sales of hit records. The song
of a proposed borrower may be contained in an album or single certified by the
Recording Industry Association of America as a gold record or a platinum
record. (The former relates to a certified shipment by the manufacturer of
500,000 units, and the latter to 1 million units.) Caution, however, must be
exercised before anticipating royalty receipts computed on the basis of RIAA
certification. Actual royalties are generally less than the simple arithmetic
would indicate because of possible returns, reserves, and nonroyalty sales. As a
backup, a lender may look to sales reported by SoundScan. Subject to such
caution, however, a true net sale of 1 million units, if licensed by the publisher
at 7.5 cents per selection, would result in the publisher's collecting $75,000 per
selection, of which $37,500 would remain for the publisher after the usual 50
percent writer royalties. This computation makes no deduction for the Harry
Fox Agency commissions, which would reduce the amount collected by 4.5
percent.

Both ASCAP and BMI promptly respond to written requests from a
member for a statement of outstanding advances and of the amounts of the
most recent distributions. Both ASCAP and BMI permit such instructions for a
general assignment to be irrevocable, providing the lender with further assurance that the instructions will not be revoked at a later date. (Note: When an
"irrevocable" assignment is made, it is up to the *borrower* to make provision for
the lender to reassign all such rights once the load has been fully repaid.)

The Harry Fox Agency will accept an irrevocable direction, signed by the
publisher and the bank, for payment to the bank of monies otherwise due to
the publisher for mechanical license and synchronization fees.

Copyright Search Report

One advantage of the federal copyright system is the maintenance of a public
registration procedure that makes available essential title information,
including the history of recorded assignments. The original copyright registrations of published and unpublished musical works are listed in the *Catalog of*

Copyright Entries issued by the Copyright Office and available at many libraries throughout the country as well as over the Internet.

However, the prospective lender should not rely on this listing alone because no reference is made to assignments or other recorded documents relating to the work. Complete reports are obtainable only by actual inspection of the copyright records maintained by the Copyright Office in Washington, D.C. The Thomson & Thomson Copyright Research Group makes private reports based upon actual inspection of Copyright Office records. The Copyright Office itself also offers search reports. Some lenders may prefer to use two or more of these services to cross-check for accuracy before making a substantial loan. (See Chapter 12 for a list of search services.)

All search reports should be examined closely to discern the effective date of the information contained as well as to determine whether the report includes the inspection of pending files. Because of the tremendous volume of recordations and the intricacies of Copyright Office filings, there is some delay between the date of receipt of assignments or related documents and their actual recordation.

It is also important to be aware of the hiatus permitted under the Copyright Act of 1976 whereby a prior assignee or mortgagee can delay recordation of a document for up to 1 month from execution in the United States and up to 2 months from execution abroad without losing his or her right to priority over a subsequent purchaser or mortgagee.

The Recordation of Loans in the Copyright Office

In music copyright matters the preferred form of security for a loan is referred to in the Copyright Act of 1909 as a mortgage, although the Copyright Act of 1976 lumps mortgages with other assignments of copyright interests under the phrase "transfer of copyright ownership." As noted in the *Peregrine Entertainment* decision, discussed on page 312, lenders gain a major advantage by recording their mortgages under federal law. For a single fee and by a single act of filing with the Copyright Office in Washington, D.C., the lender can obtain a nationwide protection against conflicting mortgages or assignments.

The procedure for recordation of a mortgage is the same as the recordation of a regular assignment of copyright. Recordation of a transfer of copyright ownership is provided for in Section 205 of the 1976 Copyright Act. No specific form of mortgage is indicated in the Copyright Acts of 1909 or 1976. Section 204 of the 1976 Copyright Act simply provides that there may be a transfer of copyright ownership (which includes a mortgage) by an instrument in writing signed by the owner of the rights conveyed or by his or her authorized agent.

As stated above, the period within which a mortgage must be recorded for protection against subsequent assignees or mortgagees who obtained their interest for value without notice is set by the Copyright Act of 1976 as 1 month from execution in the United States and 2 months from execution abroad. This permissible delay represents a convenience to a mortgagee. However, it creates a period of hiatus during which a lender cannot be certain that it is not a subsequent mortgagee lender being defrauded by the borrower. The only assurance possible is to make the mortgage commitment for payment effective 2 months after execution, provided there is a clear title report; of course, it will be a rare borrower who is willing to wait that long. The study made by the Copyright Office, in preparation for copyright act revision, is somewhat reassuring to the prospective bona fide lender in indicating that a significant majority of recordations of assignments or mortgages are made within 1 month of execution.

The procedure for recordation is to send the original mortgage document to the Copyright Office, preferably by registered or certified mail, along with the recordation fee of $50. For additional titles, the fee is $15 for each group of not more than 10 titles. The document should be submitted for recordation along with the required fee and the required cover page as furnished by the Copyright Office. The document, once recorded, will be returned to the sender with a certificate of recordation. A copy of the original document can be submitted instead of the original if accompanied by a sworn or official certification that the copy is a true copy of the original.

Certificates of acknowledgment are not required under the Copyright Act of 1976 to sustain the validity of a mortgage of copyright or other transfer of copyright ownership, whether executed in the United States or in a foreign country. This is in contrast to the 1909 Copyright Act, which called for all such documents executed in a foreign country to be acknowledged before a consular officer or secretary of legation of the United States authorized to administer oaths or perform notarial acts. Under the 1976 Copyright Act, certificates of acknowledgment of transfers of copyright ownership (which includes mortgages) executed in the United States or elsewhere are considered prima facie evidence of the transfer.

The Recordation of Loans in Local Jurisdictions

One federal court has held that federal recordation is necessary to preserve a security interest in copyright mortgages and preempts state recordation systems. In the 1990 decision of *Peregrine Entertainment v. Capitol Federal Savings and Loan Association of Denver*, a district court of California held that a creditor bank's security interest in a film company's copyrights were unperfected because the bank failed to record its mortgage in the Copyright Office. Therefore, it is still generally considered desirable for maximum security that the mortgagee comply with state as well as federal recordation law.

In a 1992 submission to Congress, the American Bar Association and the Copyright Office pointed out that it is unclear as to what extent the federal Copyright Act of 1976 preempts the field in order to make state recordation unnecessary (although a persuasive argument can be made that there is such preemption). This concern was in connection with the then-pending Copyright

Reform Act of 1993, which was never passed. One reason for compliance with state law is that the foreclosure of a copyright mortgage under court decisions is currently recognized as a matter for state law. When foreclosure of a copyright mortgage is sought and an independent ground of federal jurisdiction is available, such as diversity of citizenship of the parties, a federal court may accept jurisdiction over the controversy and apply state law to the foreclosure of a federally recorded mortgage.

State filing procedures are simplified in the music-centered states of New York, California, and Tennessee. Each state applies the Uniform Commercial Code, which recognizes mortgages on intangible property, such as copyrights. The UCC specifies that where national registration is available, as in copyrights, a state filing of a financial statement is not necessary or effective to perfect security interest.

In 1990, a federal district court ruling confirmed this status as a preemption of the Uniform Commercial Code, citing the need for national uniformity and value of eliminating the expense involved in carrying out searches in numerous state jurisdictions, and the risk of missing something along the way. However, in a 1992 bankruptcy decision concerning patents, also a federally protected intangible property, the court made a contrary ruling, although specifying that it was not intended to affect copyrights. The purpose of the proposed Copyright Reform Act of 1993 was clarification with regard to registration requirements and priorities between purchasers, mortgagees, and lien creditors. The proposed act was also designed to eliminate or shorten what is called the "look-back" provision of allowing a 1-month grace period for U.S. registrations and a 2-month period for foreign registrations, during which the lender has uncertainty as to whether it can safely rely upon the Copyright Office report on title clearance. Until clarified, compliance with the UCC by recordation of a mortgage in applicable county offices is still recommended, in addition to the clearly required Copyright Office procedure.

In the 1997 case of *Broadcast Music, Inc. v. Hirsch*, 104 F.3d 1163, the Ninth Circuit, applying New York law, recognized the priority of a writer's assignment of his BMI royalties to his creditors over an IRS lien for unpaid taxes in respect of periods after the assignment to creditors was made. The assignment of royalties was never recorded in the Copyright Office. The copyrights were owned by a music publisher, not by the debtor. The court declined to follow *Peregrine* because the assignment of the right to receive royalties was not a security interest in a copyright and therefore did not have to be filed or recorded anywhere in order to be binding and thus perfected. As a result, the creditors prevailed over the IRS.

Sale of Property upon Default

In rare instances it may become necessary to sell the copyright in order to repay a loan. In such a case, consideration must be given to whether there should be a public or a private sale. In some security agreements, it is expressly provided that in the event of a breach or default by the mortgagor, at the mortgagee's option the copyrights can be sold at either a private or a public sale after a reasonable notice to the mortgagor. The usual practice is to advertise the sale in trade papers such as *Billboard,* with the mortgagee reserving the right to bid at the sale. In bidding, the mortgagee may take credit for all or part of the indebtedness against the purchase price.

In the mid-1970s the Union Planters Bank of Memphis, Tennessee, tried to auction off the mortgage it held on the East Memphis music catalog, whose owner, Stax Records, had defaulted. Before the auction a number of potential buyers made inquiries, but none made the required minimum bid to match the bank's upset price (the minimum price at which bids would be accepted in the auction). Accordingly, the bank became the owner and administrator of the catalog, pending exploration of other sale possibilities. The upset price reported was about $2 million, representing at least that amount loaned upon such security.

Some modern mortgage agreements, instead of specifying the various remedies of the mortgagee in the event of a default, merely adopt by reference the "remedies of a secured party under the Uniform Commercial Code." The code sets forth in detail rights of sale and so forth.

Exclusive State Recordation for Certain Rights

Part of a music publisher's general assets given as security for a loan may include certain assets that relate to copyright and yet are not statutory copyrights. One of these assets is incomplete compositions—compositions that have not been fixed in any form, such as demo or other recording or appropriate manuscript form, for which no copyright registration has been obtained. Another asset is compositions to be written in the future under exclusive songwriter agreements. These common law copyrights and rights to future works are not protected under federal law; the only recordation procedure available for such rights is under state law.

Identification of these assets is obviously difficult. They do not bear the simple, official Copyright Office–assigned registration numbers that are convenient for identification. Identification for state recordation can be by composer and author names and, in the case of partially written compositions, by title or tentative title. Before granting a loan that relies in any part on such work, a careful lender will insist that unpublished works be registered under federal registration procedures, wherever possible. As previously discussed in Chapter 10, under the 1976 Copyright Act, even unpublished works are subject to automatic federal protection once they are fixed in some form.

Exclusive Writer Contracts

In evaluating an exclusive writer contract as an asset to secure payment of a loan, inspection of the contract must be made to determine whether there is any restriction on assignment in the event of foreclosure. Since the relationship between an exclusive writer and his or her publisher may be deemed highly personal, the contract should be expressly assignable if a lender is to be protected. In some instances, if the exclusive writer has a good relationship with his or her publisher, the writer may consent to a limited assignability in order to qualify the publisher for a loan that may also accrue to the writer's benefit.

The lender must also determine whether, as is frequently the case, there are unrecouped advances by the publisher to the writer. Such unrecouped advances constitute a valuable and well-defined asset if the writer's royalty statements show a consistent earnings history, since it is then clear that the advances can be charged against future earnings of the writer. On the other hand, without an earnings history, the advances should be largely disregarded because advances to writers are not ordinarily considered to be personal loans and are customarily recoupable only out of royalties otherwise due from the publisher to the writer.

Conditions on the Administration of a Loan

It would be a foolish business practice for a lender to forbid, out of a sense of extreme caution, any use of copyrights that are security for the loan, during the term of a loan. Such a prohibition might lead to the deterioration in value over an extended period of nonexploitation.

Just as in most business loans the trade reputation and skill of the borrower must be considered along with an analysis of his or her assets, so also the business skill of a music business borrower must be duly weighed. Even if the borrower is regarded as reputable and skillful, the lender is likely to condition the loan on compliance with certain conditions in the conduct of the music business while the loan is unpaid. These are some conditions that may be imposed.

- ▶ There shall be no publication (including but not limited to sheet music, folios, and orchestrations) of any of the mortgaged copyrights, by or with the consent of the mortgagor, unless an appropriate copyright notice is imprinted on such copy in the appropriate location. Even though the Berne Act of 1988 makes copyright notices optional, the use of copyright notices retains certain advantages that should not be disregarded.
- ▶ No license shall be granted that extends beyond the term of the security agreement unless the specific written consent of the mortgagee is first obtained, except with respect to the continued clearance of public perform-ance rights through ASCAP or BMI and except for nonexclusive phono-graph record mechanical reproduction licenses.
- ▶ Any phonograph record mechanical reproduction license that is to extend beyond the term of the mortgage shall be issued at not less than the statu-tory rate for compulsory licenses, subject only to customary record club and budget record discounts.
- ▶ No license shall be granted or agency relationship created that involves the

payment of money advances recoupable from earnings unless the full advance is applied upon receipt against the loan.

- No new version or arrangement can be made during the term of the mortgage unless the copyright is obtained by the mortgagor at its expense and the copyright is expressly made subject to the terms and provisions of the mortgage.
- No new lyric writer, composer, or arranger may be given any participation or claim of participation in rights or earnings of any of the mortgaged property, except on customary terms in the ordinary course of business, without the specific written consent of the mortgagee.
- All songwriter and composer royalties that may become due during the term of the security agreement shall be promptly segregated in a special bank account when collected, and shall be promptly remitted, together with required royalty statements, when contractually due. In the event that the borrower receives a claim of nonpayment or other breach in respect of such obligations or payment, written notice shall be promptly served upon the mortgagee.
- The provisions of the paragraph above shall also apply to royalties due under other agreements such as with a foreign original publisher whose composition is subpublished by the mortgagor.
- The mortgagee shall be promptly notified in writing of any claim by a third party that any of the mortgaged property infringes another work or lacks the required originality for a valid copyright.
- No infringement action shall be brought by or with the consent of the mortgagor without the written consent of the mortgagee.
- The services of a particular individual as general manager of the mortgagor shall continue during the term of the security agreement unless the mortgagee in writing shall approve his or her replacement.

If any of the above conditions is breached, the mortgagee may declare the loan to be in default and thereby become entitled to all available remedies under the security agreement.

Outstanding Advances at the Time of a Loan

The prospective lender should bear in mind that it is a well-established custom in the music industry for a music publisher to seek advances against future royalties. Advances not only finance the business but also assure proper exploitation by the party that makes the advances. These advances also ease the problem of delay in the collection of income, especially in fields such as foreign subpublishing.

In the past, advances from foreign subpublishers were less important than advances from the performing rights organizations. Both ASCAP and BMI have, however, as a general policy, discontinued making advances, except in emergency situations, although SESAC continues to make them. (For further discussion of advances by performing rights organizations, see Chapter 14.) The Harry Fox Agency, which functions as a collection agent for mechanical royalties payable by record companies, does not make advances to music publishers either. By the same token, record companies do not make advances against mechanical income that arise from the sale of regular retail product, although guarantees are not unknown to induce mechanical licenses to be given at a discount rate for so-called special-markets exploitation.

There are two types of advances—specific and general. A specific advance is recoupable only from the earnings of specified musical works or a single work. A general advance is usually recoupable from the earnings of the entire catalog of the publisher. Even a general advance is not a general obligation of the music publisher. It bears no interest, it is a debit against a specific earnings account, and it does not ordinarily continue in effect beyond the term of the applicable agreement.

If advances exist at the time a loan is applied for, prudent business practice of the lender dictates that they be given due weight in determining the size of the loan as well as whether the borrower should be required to repay the advances out of the loan proceeds. At the same time, some credit rating value should be given to a publisher regarding the publisher's right to recover advances made out of future writer or publisher royalty earnings.

The Appraiser's Report and Representations of the Borrower

Most major music business loans require expert business and legal analysis from accountants and attorneys who specialize in the field. However, even the experts must be given an accurate description of the property to be reviewed. The primary source of this information is the borrower. This information is subject to verification through various sources, such as the performing rights organizations, the Harry Fox Agency, and the Copyright Office. Here is a basic list of items or representations that a music publisher may be required to supply to a potential lender.

- ▸ Identification of the copyrights by title, author, composer, copyright registration number, and date of registration. Footnote details should be given if the balance of the current copyright term is not owned by the publisher or if the publisher has less than full ownership.
- ▸ A typical songwriter agreement and a footnote designation of any songwriter agreement with terms less favorable to the publisher.
- ▸ A representation that all songwriter royalty accounts are current unless otherwise stated.
- ▸ In the case of songs originating with a foreign or other third-party publisher, a representative subpublishing agreement and a specification of less favorable agreements and noncurrent royalty accounts.

- For any song where the borrower owns less than 100 percent of the U.S. rights, a designation of who has administrative rights and the responsibility to pay songwriter royalties, etc.
- Copies of royalty statements from the performing rights societies of which the publisher is a member and from the Harry Fox Agency (last 5 years).
- A summary of all advances currently outstanding against the publisher's account.
- A summary of each unrecouped advance given by the publisher against songwriters, other publishers, or other third-party accounts and a designation of whether the advance is general or specific.
- A summary of miscellaneous income (i.e., from commercial jingles, printed music users, foreign licensees) (last 5 years).
- A summary of all music deriving from or used in motion picture scores or musical plays.
- A list of exclusive writer contracts, showing the names of writers, the duration of exclusivity, and obligations for future salary payments or advances.
- For copyrights originating before 1978, a list of renewal copyright rights obtained from authors or their statutory successors (i.e., widows and children) as to both copyrights presently in the renewal term and copyrights in their original term, showing the grantor, the title of the song, the effective date of the renewal copyright period, whether any obligations were incurred over and above standard writer royalties, and whether life insurance has been obtained or is obtainable on the grantor's life; also whether a notice of termination has been received for the 19-year extended period after the 56 years of copyright or the 20-year extension after the 75th year of the copyright.
- The cost of acquisition of any portion of the catalog acquired from other publishers and the amortization of such acquisition cost.
- A schedule of major physical assets such as recording equipment, studio, and real estate, together with the date and cost of acquisition.
- A schedule of master recordings owned or controlled by the publisher and the royalty arrangements involved.
- An inventory of printed goods on hand.
- A salary schedule of the publisher's personnel.
- A schedule of all rents and the duration of all leases.
- A schedule of the publisher's stockholders and outstanding stock as well as any pension or profit-sharing plans.

Using this information, an expert appraiser can advise the prospective mortgagee regarding the potential future earnings and the resale value of the catalog involved. The appraiser should be selected by the lender, but the appraiser's fee should be paid by the loan applicant, whether the loan is granted or denied. An appraisal may involve substantial work, and the fee therefore would be a bar to many small loans.

The Bankruptcy of the Borrower

Music is traditionally a business of optimism. The low-salaried promotion person, expecting early wealth from a sure-fire series of hits, may be spurred to quit his or her job and open a publishing firm. Many of the applicants for the more than 120,000 copyright registrations each year expect that their composition will be among the few hundred titles that appear in the charts annually. This enthusiasm and optimism are evidence of the music industry's individuality and free enterprise. However, business failures and possible bankruptcy must be considered.

The voluntary or involuntary bankruptcy of a publisher has far-reaching consequences for potential creditors. Under the SGA contract, and under many other writer or subpublication agreements as well, the contract terminates and the copyright is subject to recapture in the event of bankruptcy. Thus the songs could become worthless to the potential creditor of a bankrupt publisher, if such a provision is enforceable.

However, to the extent that such agreements are executory (which is the case when both parties have not performed their obligations), these termination provisions are likely to be invalid. Under Section 541(c) of the Bankruptcy Code, any provision in a contract expressly prohibiting any assignment is invalid with respect to an assignment that benefits the estate. Therefore, if the value of the bankrupt's estate is increased owing to the continued ownership of compositions subject to these termination provisions, the compositions remain a part of the bankrupt's estate.

Under copyright law, exclusive licenses and assignments of copyrights are transfers of ownership and therefore, under bankruptcy law, fully executed rather than executory, even though the assignee (the publisher) may have ongoing future royalty obligations. By contrast, nonexclusive licenses are likely to be executory. As a result, a debtor must assume a nonexclusive license in order to continue deriving its benefits.

It has been held judicially in the case of *Waterson, Berlin & Snyder Co.*, 48 F.2d 704 (2d Cir. 1931) that the sale of copyrights by a trustee in bankruptcy does not destroy a contractual obligation to pay future royalties to writers. This continuing obligation means that the purchaser at a bankruptcy sale, including the lender, cannot acquire copyrights free of future royalty obligations.

Finally, whether it is a trustee or a debtor in possession, the bankruptcy filing exposes any security given to secure a loan to examination as an unlawful preference. If a security interest has been given within the 90-day period prior to filing, it may be set aside if a reasonably equivalent value has not been given. Thus, if there is a sale 100 days before a filing and a perfection of security interest only within the 90-day period, it is in jeopardy of being treated as preferential.

Part Four

Other Aspects of the Music Business

29

Privacy and Publicity Rights

The music and record industries thrive on publicity. Sales of records are stimulated by the use of a top artist's name or portrait on an album jacket. The use of an artist's name and likeness on sheet music and song folios is a valuable marketing device. In addition, television and radio commercials often use an artist's name or voice in advertising products. Hotels, resorts, and amusement parks frequently announce, by name and photograph, the personal appearance of top artists or make other similar associations between artists and merchandise. Items such as T-shirts, buttons, and posters featuring the recording artist's likeness are a valuable tie-in with record sales. Although most of these uses are eagerly sought by the artist and the industry and may be permissible by virtue of the operative contractual provisions, careful consideration must be given in each instance to the individual's right to control and benefit from the so-called right of publicity.

The Right of Privacy

The right of privacy, or the personal right "to be let alone," is a relatively new Anglo-American legal concept. Impetus to the development of this right is largely attributed to a *Harvard Law Review* article by Samuel D. Warren and Louis D. Brandeis, published in 1890. They wrote:

> The press is overstepping in every direction the obvious bounds of propriety and of decency. Gossip is no longer the resource of the idle and of the vicious, but has become a trade, which is pursued with industry as well as effrontery. To satisfy a prurient taste the details of sexual relations are spread broadcast in the columns of the daily papers. To occupy the indolent, column upon column is filled with idle gossip, which can only be procured by intrusion upon the domestic circle. The intensity and complexity of life, attendant upon advancing civilization, have rendered necessary some retreat from the world, and man, under the refining influ-

ence of culture, has become more sensitive to publicity, so that solitude and privacy have become more essential to the individual; but modern enterprises and inventions have, through invasions upon his privacy, subjected him to mental pain and distress, far greater than could be inflicted by mere bodily injury.

Warren and Brandeis sought recognition of a separate right distinct from defamation, contract, or property rights. At first there was some hesitation in legal circles to endorse this right of privacy. The highest court of the first state to directly confront the concept, New York, rejected the notion that there existed a separate legal right of privacy in that state. Reacting to this decision, the New York legislature enacted a statute that today is found in Sections 50 and 51 of the Civil Rights Law. This statute makes it a misdemeanor for a person, firm, or corporation to use for "advertising purposes, or for the purpose of trade, the name, portrait or picture of any living person" without first obtaining written consent. The statute also permits suit for injunctive relief as well as damages, including, in some cases, punitive damages.

As time went by, other states—including Oklahoma, Utah, Virginia, and California—also adopted acts similar to New York's. Today the right of privacy is recognized either by statute or through judicial decision in all but a few jurisdictions in the United States. Furthermore, the U.S. Supreme Court has said that an independent right of privacy is guaranteed by the Constitution against certain governmental interference.

The constitutional guarantees of freedom of speech and the press may be raised in opposition to a claim for invasion of privacy. Under the Supreme Court's holdings, the right of privacy cannot be asserted to prohibit the publication of matters that are "newsworthy." In other words, matters of public interest are allowed, even if the report is false, unless there is proof that the defendant published the report with knowledge of its falsity or in reckless disregard of its truth. This doctrine applies to an individual who is a "public figure" as well as an individual who may have been thrust into an event of public interest. A performing artist may well be viewed as a "public figure" in connection with his or her public activities. In addition, news functions or informative presentations are not considered to be limited to newspapers; magazines, newsreels, radio, television, and books have received this privilege as well.

Generally, the defense of freedom of speech or press would not apply to certain types of commercial speech, for example, an advertisement using the endorsement of a public figure, such as a celebrity. A defense of *express waiver* may be asserted—in other words, that the individual consented to the use. Under certain statutes, this consent must be in writing. Other defenses may stress that the use was incidental or insignificant, such as the mere mention of a celebrity's name in a film or book, or that the use was not for purposes of "advertising" or "trade" in jurisdictions where this type of use is prohibited by statute.

The Right of Publicity

The music and record industries' concern in their daily operations is how the exploitation of a personality is affected by the individual's right to privacy and publicity. In most instances, the primary concern of an artist is to obtain publicity and have his or her name and vocal or visual likeness recognized by the public. The artist does not seek privacy as much as control over and benefit from the commercial use of his or her name, photograph, and likeness. Some jurisdictions have recognized the legitimacy of this right of publicity and have granted it recognition either by statute or by case law. This right, which protects the ability of an individual to control and profit from the publicity values that the artist has achieved, is similar in theory to the exclusive right of a commercial enterprise to the benefits that goodwill and secondary meaning of its name produce. In those cases in which pure privacy theory might be unsuccessfully invoked, such as when the artist with a celebrity status may be considered a public figure, the right of publicity may nevertheless be successfully asserted.

This concept is generally credited as having grown from the 1986 case of *Original Appalachian Artworks, Inc. v. Topps Chewing Gum, Inc.*, 642 F. Supp. 1031, which dealt with baseball cards. In that case, a chewing gum manufacturer had entered into agreements with ballplayers for the exclusive right, for a limited time, to use the ballplayers' likenesses on baseball cards. Subsequently, another gum manufacturer obtained similar rights from the same ballplayers. The first gum manufacturer sued the second to protect its exclusive rights in the photographs. The defendant argued that the action was in privacy, that privacy actions were personal and not assignable, and that only the ballplayers had standing to sue. The late Judge Jerome Frank said:

> In addition to and independent of that right of privacy ... a man has a right in the publicity value of his photograph, i.e., the right to grant the exclusive privilege of publishing his picture. ... This right might be called a "right of publicity." For it is common knowledge that many prominent persons (especially actors and ballplayers) far from having their feelings bruised through public exposure of their likenesses would feel sorely deprived if they no longer received money for authorizing advertisements.

Thus, the court recognized the right of publicity and distinguished this right from the pure privacy theory. This was also significant because, without a contrary statute, the right of privacy is a personal right that terminates on the death of the individual. In New York, any right of publicity also terminates on death of the individual. Therefore, the right of publicity cannot be transferred to heirs. However, the majority of states (such as California) hold that the right survives death; as a precondition in such cases, though, the courts generally require that the right must have been exploited during the lifetime of the celebrity, for example, by the licensing of merchandising rights.

In right of publicity cases, the unauthorized use of a celebrity's name or likeness in connection with the dissemination of news or information of public interest is usually held to be privileged under the constitutional guarantees of the freedom of speech and of the press. This treatment is similar to that accorded in right of privacy cases. The constitutional privilege would not ordinarily apply where the unauthorized "use" is for commercial exploitation.

The Use of Name or Likeness for Trade or Advertising

In those jurisdictions that recognize that the individual has the right to control the use of his or her name or likeness, whether under a right of publicity or a right of privacy, the individual is protected against the unauthorized commercial use of his or her name or likeness, such as in an advertisement on T-shirts or in posters endorsing a commercial product.

As noted above, under a New York statute it is a criminal misdemeanor and the basis for an action for injunction and damages to use the name, portrait, or picture, for advertising or trade purposes, of any living person without written consent or, if a minor, the consent of the minor's parent or guardian. At the same time, this statute indicates that it shall not be construed to prevent the use of the "name, portrait or picture of any author, composer or artist in connection with his literary, musical or artistic productions which he has sold or disposed of with such name, portrait, or picture used in connection therewith." Consequently, the name of a composer can be used without written consent in connection with an authorized record of the author's composition.

Although California courts have recognized a right of privacy under the common law, the California legislature has enacted a statute dealing with the use of a person's name, photograph, or likeness for purposes of advertising products or services or for purposes of solicitation of purchases of products or services. Under this statute, any person who knowingly makes such use without the injured person's prior consent or, if a minor, the prior consent of a parent or guardian is liable for any damages sustained by the injured person. In addition, the person violating this law is liable to the injured party for no less than $300. The statute provides, however, that the "use of a name, photograph, or likeness in connection with any news, public affairs or sports broadcast or account, or political campaign shall not constitute a use for purposes of advertising or solicitation."

In *White v. Samsung Electronics America*, 971 F.2d 1395 (9th Cir. 1992), a federal court of appeals applying California case law ruled that TV star Vanna White could protect herself even when there was no use of name, voice, signature, or likeness. The case involved a robot dressed in White's style with hair in her style and standing before a Wheel of Fortune, which further tied the robot to Vanna White. This evocation of the star's image was held to be a violation of rights without reliance on the California statute itself. Many other jurisdictions, as well as a strong dissenting opinion in the California federal appeals court, consider this to be an extreme holding. Moreover, this case is significant because Vanna White resides in California, as do many other stars, and the ruling further stated that the star's place of domicile determines the applicable law, regardless of where the advertising is shown.

California and Tennessee have both passed special legislation affecting unauthorized posthumous exercise of rights of publicity for commercial purposes for periods of 50 years and 10 years, respectively, after death. However, with respect to California decedents, it is essential to note that there are specific registration requirements and statutory filing fees if recovery is to be sought from such uses.

In contrast to New York practice, most states that recognize the individual's right to control the use of his or her name or likeness do not require written consent to the use of such name or picture. Such consent may be oral or may be established by the custom of the business involved.

Privacy Contract Clauses

Contracts in the fields of music and records, in many instances, prevent problems with the right of privacy or the right of publicity by specific provisions regarding the use of name, image, or biographical material. Exclusive recording contracts between an artist and a record company usually state that the record company has the sole right to use and authorize others to use the artist's name, signature, likeness, and biographical material in connection with the artist's services under the agreement. This not only grants the required consent to the record company but may also serve as the basis for prohibiting another record company from similar use. Some record contracts also provide for the record company to handle "merchandising rights" in an artist's name and likeness. This covers such situations as the licensing of posters, T-shirts, buttons, and similar items, frequently on a basis that the artist will receive 50 percent of the company's net receipts.

Under the form of agreement developed by the American Federation of Musicians between a musician and a booking agent, the agent is granted rights to use the musician's name and likeness, and the right to authorize others to make such use, for advertising and publicity.

Careful drafting is necessary to properly delineate the rights that are to be transferred from the artist to the contracting company. In cases involving merchandising rights to the character of Count Dracula as portrayed by Bela Lugosi, and the commercial rights to the names and likenesses of Laurel and Hardy, the courts were called on to decide whether, under certain types of grant clauses, the performers had transferred their entire exclusive merchandising rights. In both instances the courts held that they had not and that the film companies had acquired only the right to use their name and likenesses in connection with specific films for which the performers had rendered their services. Where the contract is silent with respect to these rights, the courts may find that the rights remain with the artist.

Similarly, a divergence between the use authorized by the artist and the actual use made of his or her name, likeness, or biographical material may lead to a privacy suit. A slight variation in use may be insufficient to be actionable.

Works in the Public Domain

Reliance on the right of privacy was unsuccessful in preventing the publication of uncopyrighted works of Mark Twain under his name. The same theory was also rejected in the use of uncopyrighted Russian music with accurate composer credits given to Khatchaturian, Prokofiev, and Shostakovich. When a work is unprotected by copyright, there is no obligation to drop author credit; in fact, failing to give credit would appear to be more objectionable.

False attribution of a writer as author of a work not written entirely by that person may itself be held to be an invasion of the right of privacy. Such a writer would justifiably complain against an unfair appropriation of his or her reputation and possible damage to the reputation by a false author's credit. This frequently occurs in stage works where the writer wants to avoid unfavorable reviews by critics.

When a name or likeness is considered part of the public domain, such as the face of George Washington or a recording of Alexander Graham Bell's voice, it is considered a valuable part of cultural history. One judge said of attempts to extend rights of publicity into what should be public domain "as harmful as underprotecting [intellectual property]. Creativity is impossible without a rich public domain."

Remedies for the Invasion of Privacy

There are three types of relief granted by courts in cases where the right of privacy has been found to have been invaded. Courts may grant damages, issue injunctions prohibiting such conduct, and impose criminal penalties against the defendant.

Criminal penalties, where available, are rarely imposed. In New York, Virginia, Utah, and Oklahoma, a violation of the privacy statute is a misdemeanor. Yet the vast majority of cases brought under a statute such as New York's are civil actions.

Generally, a plaintiff in a privacy action is seeking redress in compensatory damages and, for certain abuses where malice is shown, punitive damages. There may be a damage award for mental pain and suffering, without proof by the plaintiff of actual monetary losses. In right-of-publicity cases, the measure of damages may be what the misappropriated right is worth rather than actual damages.

30

The Protection of Ideas and Titles

The originators of the hustle and the twist dance steps receive no royalties from other individuals who have profited from their ideas. Chubby Checker, who became synonymous with the twist in the public eye, with resultant financial rewards, owed no financial obligations to the inventor of the dance. Similarly, a rival network was able to copy the idea of the superstrong *Six Million Dollar Man* in a counterpart program entitled *The Bionic Woman* without fear of penalty.

Ideas themselves are not copyrightable and are ordinarily free for the taking due to the belief that society benefits from their free dissemination. Courts protect the manner in which ideas are expressed. For example, while a song lyric about aliens from Mars cannot be copied, another writer is free to pen a new lyric concerning such aliens. To the extent that the original lyric cannot be copied there is an indirect protection of the idea.

One copyright concept that affects ideas is the exclusive right to develop copyrighted material for further exploitation. For instance, a song such as "Frosty, the Snow Man" can be developed into a storybook only with the consent of the copyright owner, and a novel can be dramatized only with the permission of its copyright owner (usually the author). The reproduction of a doll or other three-dimensional form based on a character in story or song is also an exclusive right stemming from copyright. Comic strip heroes such as Superman help to demonstrate the concept of continuing rights in characters from copyrighted stories, separate and apart from the dialogue of the characters in the story. A comparable example from the world of popular music is Alvin and his brother chipmunks.

The legal bases for the protection of the development of such characters are a mixture of copyright law (for artistic, written, or three-dimensional reproduction of a fictional character) and unfair competition. The latter principle has been applied to prevent the misappropriation by one person of the results of another individual's labors.

Compensation for Ideas

Ideas themselves are safeguarded when disclosed privately under circumstances indicating a mutual understanding, express or implied, that there will be remuneration if they are used. In one case, the plaintiff had submitted to the secretary of a movie producer, orally and by a short outline in writing, the idea for a motion picture on the life of Floyd Collins, who had been trapped and had died in a cave after extensive rescue efforts. The plaintiff alleged that he had made it clear he was to be paid if the idea was used and the secretary had agreed. The defendant film producer subsequently made a motion picture on the life of Collins. The appellate court in California found, on the basis of the plaintiff's allegations, a claimed implied contract to pay for the plaintiff's services that would result in liability if, after a full trial, it was proven that there actually was such an understanding between the parties and that the synopsis as delivered by the plaintiff, in reliance on such an agreement, was the basis of the resulting film. This ruling was made despite the fact that the story was in the public domain, having been fully explored in the press.

In another breach of contract case, a California court held that the movie *Coming to America* was based on a two-page treatment by columnist Art Buchwald entitled "It's a Crude, Crude World," and that Buchwald and his producer, Alain Bernheim, were entitled to $150,000 and $750,000, respectively, for their contributions.

In the absence of an express or implied contract to pay, the courts have sometimes held a defendant liable for the use of a plaintiff's idea on the theory that otherwise the defendant would be unjustly enriched. This can result when the situation is similar to a contract relationship but essential elements of contractual agreement are lacking. For example, if an agent promises to pay, without authorization, for an idea accepted on behalf of a defendant, the defendant may be held liable if he or she uses the idea.

Some courts protect ideas on the ground of a breach of a confidential relationship. This may occur, for example, with regard to secret ideas disclosed in an employer-employee relationship. A court has held that where there was a confidential relationship and the plaintiff disclosed to the defendant a little-known song in the public domain discovered by the plaintiff, the defendant could not exploit the song.

Issues of Concreteness and Originality

While it is sometimes stated that a plaintiff must prove that his or her idea was novel and original and that it was reduced to concrete form, the facts necessary for such proof may vary widely. For example, the combination of three old ideas has been held to constitute a novel and original idea.

For an idea to be concrete, it is generally accepted that it need not be reduced to writing. To some courts, a concrete idea is one that has been developed to the point of availability for use. A concrete idea is sometimes explained as being different from an abstract idea and as having the status of property. If an idea is reduced to writing it may be protected by copyright on the basis of being considered an "original work...of authorship fixed in [a] tangible medium of expression" under the standards of Section 102 of the Copyright Act of 1976. This protection extends from fixation. The written expression can be submitted for registration as an unpublished work in the Copyright Office. Similarly, the recording of an idea can also be regarded as fixed and protected by copyright and may be registered as an unpublished work.

A further method employed by songwriters or record producers to establish the creation and date of origin of a work is to enclose their material in carefully sealed envelopes and to mail the material to themselves by registered mail, which, when received, remains unopened. This approach may be more effective than registration in maintaining the privacy of the idea, but is less reliable than an official registration.

In all cases, for their protection, the informed songwriter, music publisher, or record producer should keep business-like reference material such as index cards or files of letters accompanying enclosures indicating when and to whom proposals were submitted.

The Consideration of Unsolicited Ideas

Bearing in mind the potential litigation that may result from the disclosure of ideas, some companies, including music publishers and record companies, have adopted a policy of not considering unsolicited ideas. In this way lawsuits and attorneys' fees can clearly be avoided. If possible, the incoming material should be routed to persons, such as the comptroller, who have no responsibility for creative endeavors. The material should be handled by form replies and returned. While it can be argued that valuable ideas may be lost through this practice, professionals in the field can be trusted to supply most market requirements of ideas.

Other companies insist that they will not review an idea unless the submitter signs a release. One form of release makes the company and its officers the sole arbiter of the novelty, usability, and value of the idea. Since the obligation on the part of the company may be considered illusory, there is some doubt as to the legal enforceability of this type of release.

Another form of release provides that the parties will mutually agree on the value of an idea that is used, but if they disagree, the maximum value of the idea is fixed at a certain sum, such as $500 or $1,000. Or the release may provide initially that the value is a sum fixed at, say, $500. This type of release seems more enforceable than the release under which the company and its officers have complete discretion.

As a word of caution, however, it should be recognized that even a release form may prove to be inadequate protection against a bad faith appropriation of an idea without adequate consideration.

The Use of Titles

Titles are not subject to copyright protection. For example, the title "Stardust" is not protected by the Copyright Act. Titles have long been protected by the doctrine of unfair competition, which will be applied to titles that have achieved a secondary meaning in the eyes of the public as being associated with particular works. Most titles do not have a secondary meaning. A casual check of the ASCAP or BMI indexes or of the Copyright Office records will reveal numerous instances of title duplications. Indirectly, some copyright protection of titles can be accomplished by their insertion in the body of the song lyric.

To achieve a secondary meaning more readily, a title should be fanciful and use arbitrarily selected word groupings rather than generally descriptive or frequently used phrases. For example, "My Only Love" or "Yours Sincerely" are general phrases that probably could not be preempted. On the other hand, "Begin the Beguine" is a fanciful, unique title. It is possible that even a geographic description or other general title such as "Oklahoma!" or "South Pacific" can, over the years or other period required to establish a solid public acceptance, establish a secondary meaning of commercial value that cannot be usurped.

A secondary meaning is not necessarily permanent, though. Since unfair competition is not a copyright concept, there is no fixed period of exclusive protection and no easily determined date when the protection ceases and the title is in the public domain. The determinant is the matter of abandonment by failure to use or exploit. "Information Please" was a valuable title during its use on radio, but if not for the almanac using the title *Information Please,* it might be considered abandoned today and therefore available for anyone. Public identification does not necessarily mean that the title is associated with public success. *Slightly Scandalous* had a short life and was a failure as a play, but it nevertheless had sufficient secondary meaning to serve as the basis for an injunction against a motion picture of the same name.

Music is an essential ingredient of, and sister field to, motion pictures. It is common for a major motion picture to popularize a theme song from the movie with the same title. Many a film trades on the established goodwill of a well-known song title. Irving Berlin's "White Christmas," first sung by Bing Crosby in the film *Holiday Inn,* went on to be a great song success and was even used in another film entitled *White Christmas.* Likewise, the film originally identified with the biography *The Jane Froman Story* was released, finally, under the title *With a Song in My Heart.* The publisher of the relatively new success at the time, "Young at Heart," was paid $15,000 for a synchronization license and title use for a Warner Bros. picture of the same name. In addition, a popular song known as "Ode to Billy Joe" was featured in the music and story line of a film with that title.

Song titles are frequently used as the titles of record albums, as a natural identification of the type of music in the album, although the title song is often only one-tenth of the contents of the record. "Love Story," a composition from the popular film of the same title, was the title of a number of albums issued by different record companies. Rarely is the publisher paid a premium for such title use, but in one case, where the song was omitted from the record, a special royalty was paid. It is arguable that, on the same theory that a motion picture producer pays for the use of a song title for a motion picture, a record company should make a special payment for the right to use a song title as the title of an album.

31

Names and Trademarks

One cannot overemphasize the value of names in the music industry. The tremendous variety in names of artists, record companies, and music publishers ranges from names that simply identify, such as the Harry Connick, Jr. Orchestra, Sony Records, and the Famous Music Corporation, to such fanciful names as the Backstreet Boys, Pearl Jam, the Spice Girls, and the Dixie Chicks. While the names of record companies and music publishers are relatively insignificant in terms of their influence on consumer purchases in popular music—rarely does an individual go to a music store and request a "Dwarf Music song" or an "Acuff-Rose Music song"—consumers do purchase recordings by artist name. The consumer will ask for Rage Against the Machine (on Sony) or Sheryl Crow (on Universal/A&M).

The goodwill attached to names in the music business is more important in music industry circles. A dealer or jobber is more likely to stock and feature a new record released by a successful and established record label or artist than a record by a new firm or artist. An artist may favor a recording agreement with Sony Records over one with a lesser label. A writer may prefer to enter a contract with Warner/Chappell Music than with a less well-known publisher.

In the field of classical (sometimes called "serious") and educational music publishing, the names of established publishers tend to have greater value than the names of those in popular music. Purchasers of classical music rely on and respect the editorial selection and quality standards of well-known classical music publishers, whereas in the popular music field, printed sales usually depend on prior popular music recordings to stimulate consumer interest. Similarly, the consumer seeking a classical music recording may be influenced by the reputation of the record company on whose label the recording is released; certain labels have achieved a reputation for both technical and artistic quality.

The selection, protection, and development of names and trademarks are complex matters. The names and trademarks must be distinctive enough that property rights accrue to the proper persons or firms. For product identification they should not infringe on other persons' or firms' rights in names or trademarks previously used. Close similarity can lead to confusion concerning product, credit problems, misdirection of mail and telephone calls, and legal entanglements.

Copyrightability

There is no protection for brand names, trademarks, slogans, and other short phrases or expressions under the Copyright Act. Nor may familiar symbols or designs qualify for copyright registration in and of themselves. Legal protection of a name, slogan, phrase, or symbol must generally come from common law, the law of unfair competition, and registration under federal trademark law or the trademark laws of the individual states.

The Copyright Act of 1976 does provide that copyright can be obtained in "pictorial, graphic and sculptural works." In order to be copyrightable, a work must include an appreciable amount of original text or pictorial materials. Consequently, copyright may apply to qualifying prints, advertisements, and labels used in connection with the sale or advertisement of articles of merchandise. For example, a record label named Mountainview in conjunction with a photograph of Mount Vesuvius might seek copyright protection, in addition to protection under trademark law. The copyright protection would, however, not extend to the name separate and apart from the pictorial matter.

Trademarks and Service Marks

There are two types of marks that can be registered in the U.S. Patent and Trademark Office in Washington, D.C. The *trademark* distinguishes a product and identifies its origins: for example, the RCA Victor name and the logo of a dog with a phonograph. The *service mark* is used in the sale or advertising of services to identify the services of one person and distinguish them from the services of others: for example, the Bryan Setzer Orchestra. In some cases the identical mark may be used as both a trademark and a service mark by the same business, such as one selling musical instruments and rendering repair services under the same mark.

While service marks are often incorrectly referred to as trademarks, there are usually no important legal consequences resulting from the use of the incorrect terminology. Unless indicated otherwise, the word "trademark" as used in this chapter should be considered to include "service mark."

A recent development similar to trademark is the registration for Internet address "domain names." The two most significant categories have the name followed by ".com" for commercial organizations and ".org" for noncommercial organizations. Exclusivity of domain names is allocated by Network Solutions, Inc., a private company under contract with the National Science Foundation of the United States. However, the U.S. Department of Commerce is in the process of internationalizing and privatizing domain name registration, rendering Network Solutions nonexclusive. While the registration of a domain name is an efficient protection against competitive Internet use of a name, it is important to use conventional trademark registration procedures for legal protection.

Differentiating Between Copyrights and Trademarks

There is a tendency among people in the music business to refer to "copyright" when they mean exclusive rights that are available only through trademark protection or through rules of law relating to unfair competition. A simple distinction between copyright and trademarks is that copyright protects the *expression* of literary, artistic, and musical ideas, whereas trademarks and service marks serve as *badges of identification* that protect the goodwill attached to a particular product or service and safeguard the public from confusion as to the source or identity of the products or services involved. Other differences between copyright and trademarks are outlined in Table 31-1.

The Selection of a Name

Finding the right name for a record label or band can often be a time-consuming and fruitless task. All too frequently the selected name has already been taken. (The means of avoiding conflicting names are discussed later in this chapter.) Within the music industry, the stories are numerous and legendary regarding the sources of inspiration for new names. For instance, the historic record label OKEH, which was revived by CBS Records, originated with the initials of the owner. Laura Nyro's firm, Tuna Fish Music, memorializes her favorite sandwich. Certain names represent an attempt to present a consolidated trade image. For example, Screen-Gems-EMI Music indicates an identification with its original parent company, Capitol-EMI. MCA Music shows a relation to MCA, Inc. Warner Bros. Music was a change of name from the former Music Publishers Holding Company, purchased by Warner Bros. Pictures in 1929. Then in the late 1980s Warner Bros. Music acquired Chappell Music and became Warner/Chappell Music. Before their sale in 1986, CBS had two publishing firms, April Music and Blackwood Music; the initial letters of their names provided an easy identification as to which was the ASCAP-affiliated firm and which was the BMI-affiliated firm.

Varying devices are employed to suggest names for corporations or trademarks. A choice may be made from different categories, just as the U.S. Weather Bureau uses male and female names in alphabetical order to denote successive hurricanes, and the U.S. Navy uses the names of fish to differentiate among submarines. Music publishers may be named after fruits (Apple Music), birds (Thrush Music), or geographic locations (Broadway Music). Dictionaries, atlases, maps, and even telephone books are other sources of inspiration. Some fairly common devices that have been used include spelling a name backward (Patti Page's EGAP Music), using a child's name (Alice, Marie), combining the names of a husband and wife (Marydan), joining the syllables of partners' names (Franstan), or using the founder's name (Johnny Cash's House of Cash).

Many record companies are identified with parent firms such as Warner and MCA. Others, such as Elektra and Epic, are unique to themselves. Some common names, such as London, Capitol, and King, have their own special history and position. In general, however, a common name is less desirable for new companies for several reasons. A common name may be confused with the names of other companies in related or unrelated fields and consequently

Table 31-1

Differences Between Copyrights and Trademarks

Copyright	Trademark
• The duration is ordinarily limited to the life of the author plus 70 years.	• There is an unlimited number of successive 10-year terms.
• The certificate is issued by the government without prior search for conflicting claims or prior notice to the public.	• The certificate is issued by the government only after a search for conflicting marks, notice to the public of the pending application, and an opportunity for objections to be filed.
• Notice of copyright may be used from the first publication.	• Notice indicating registered federal trademark is not permitted until after registration.
• Statutory protection begins at fixation in a copy.	• Notice indicating registered federal trademark is not permitted until after registration.
• Registration of copyright is permitted for unpublished or published music at any time during the term of copyright protection.	• Common law protection begins at use.
• Originality is required for a valid copyright.	• The registration of trademark is not achieved (even if application has been previously filed) until after proven use in interstate commerce or in commerce between a state and a foreign country.
• Copyright is fully assignable.	• Originality or novelty is not essential for a valid trademark. Identification with product or service is significant.
• The licensee of a copyright need not be supervised by the owner of copyright.	• Trademark is assignable only with the goodwill of the business in which the mark is used.
• Under the Copyright Act of 1909, duration was limited to the original 28-year term plus one 28-year renewal, since extended for works fixed before 1978 to a total of 95 years.	• The licensee of the trademark must be under the owner's supervision and control to ensure that the product's identity, quality, and character are preserved.
• Under the 1909 Act, the statutory protection of unpublished compositions was conditioned on registration; prior to registration there was common law protection.	• Prior to the Trademark Law Revision Act of 1988, successive 20-year terms were applicable.

may subject the new company to a possible lawsuit on the grounds of trademark infringement or unfair competition. In addition, different rules of trademark registration apply to common names. And finally, the previous use of a common name may present a bar to the incorporation of a new firm.

The selection of an artist's name can be an art. There are many simple names. Janet Jackson, Garth Brooks, Whitney Houston, and Barbra Streisand have not suffered from the use of their own names. However, popular music abounds with highly imaginative names. A review of *Billboard's* charts reveals such names as LL Kool J, Eminem, Goo Goo Dolls, Foxy Brown, 'N Sync, Madonna, Blondie, and Silkk the Shocker.

Prior and Conflicting Company Names and Marks

In the initial enthusiasm of starting a new business, a music publisher or record company will frequently be annoyed when its chosen name is rejected by the nameless bureaucrat who passes on proposed incorporation documents for a new company. Each of the 50 states has its own corporate registration procedures. In the music-oriented states of New York, California, and Tennessee, it is usually the Department of State that refuses to accept a name it regards as too similar to other existing corporate names. Although such a rejection may be frustrating, it should be appreciated as an early warning of a possible conflict.

In music publishing, all major performing rights organizations—ASCAP, BMI, and SESAC—should be consulted before a new publisher name is adopted. The many thousands of names already on file should not be duplicated because important performance credits may be lost due to confusion of names. ASCAP and BMI issue alphabetical lists of current publisher affiliate names. These lists are available by request from either organization. In response to telephone or letter inquiry, both ASCAP and BMI also provide specific advice as to the availability of a name. In fact, it is the practice to reserve on request, for a limited period, a name determined to be available, in order to allow time to organize the new company.

Record company names and labels can be conveniently checked in the publication *Phonolog*, where all current records are listed and where label abbreviations are identified. If it is not readily available in libraries or music business offices, this service is often found in retail record outlets. The annual editions issued by music trade papers, such as the *Billboard International Buyer's Guide* and sourcebooks such as the *Recording Industry Sourcebook*, also list publishers and record company labels and names.

The Harry Fox Agency is another source of information as to possible conflicting names. Because it represents the majority of substantial music publishers in the United States and collects, on their behalf, mechanical royalties from nearly every existing record company, the Harry Fox Agency has on file information of vital importance to the selection of names. On its own behalf, it wants to do whatever possible to avoid duplicate and confusing names. In some instances its information as to publisher and record company names may be more complete than *Phonolog* or the *Billboard International Buyer's Guide* or the *Recording Industry Sourcebook* lists. However, because of the pressure of its normal services, it can only respond to queries concerning conflicting music publisher names for potential new members or affiliates.

In the age of the Internet and the need for domain names, a new name and trademark service is available. The firm of Thomson & Thomson, a global information company, offers NameStake, a commercial search service (www.namestake.com). This free service searches domain names, and provides a count of similar domain names.

Search Organizations and Services

Listings in trade publications, telephone books, the Internet, and other information sources noted previously are not necessarily complete, and in some cases a new company may want to hire professional help rather than making its own search. Of course, a trademark attorney has expertise in arranging for a search and interpreting the results, and this expertise is significant in giving assurance to a proposed trademark user. Trademark search organizations are listed in the Yellow Pages of telephone directories. Two of the better-known ones are

▸ Thomson & Thomson, which has offices throughout the United States, as well as in Canada, Japan, and several European countries. Its corporate headquarters are 500 Victory Road, North Quincy, MA 02171; telephone: 800-692-8833.

▸ Trademark Research Corporation, a division of Commerce Clearing House, located at 300 Park Avenue South, New York, NY 10010.

Both companies issue prompt reports on trademarks registered with the U.S. Patent and Trademark Office in Washington, D.C. On request, they also report on trademarks registered with the office of the state secretary's office in one or more designated states. Such reports may also be expanded to include similar names in telephone directories. Affiliates and associates of these firms in Washington, D.C. conduct similar research in the trademark records and the Copyright Office records to supplement their own music industry trade directories and their own files and resource material. Such a report can sometimes be used in a defensive stage rather than in searching for a new name. Thus, if an investment has already been made in a name and a claim is asserted by a third party that the name is unduly similar to its prior name, a search may reveal many other uses of the name, indicating that it should be regarded as public property available for further use.

Requests for a search should not be made to the U.S. Patent and Trademark Office since it does not offer a search service. On the other hand, its files are available for a personal search in the public search library of the Patent and Trademark Office, located on the second floor of the South Tower Building,

2900 Crystal Drive, Arlington, VA 22202, or at the Patent Office's Web site, www.uspto.gov. There are also approximately 75 patent and trademark depository libraries throughout the United States in which a search can also be conducted. These libraries have CD-ROMs containing the trademark database of registered and pending trademarks.

Primary sources of information used by trademark attorneys and available to the public are the *Trademark Register of the United States* and the *Compu-Mark Directory of U.S. Trademarks,* both of which appear annually. Both are convenient listings of all registered names and marks.

The trademark classes of interest to the music industry are International Class 15 (musical instruments), International Class 16 (paper goods and printed matter), and International Class 9 (records, tapes, CDs, etc.). A complete list of all classes may be found at the Trademark Office Web site.

A word of caution regarding the researching of conflicting names and marks: Because it is frequently difficult to decide whether names or marks are confusingly similar under legal principles, it is prudent to consult attorneys whenever problems arise that cannot be readily solved.

Prior and Conflicting Names of Artists

Although unique names for artists abound in the music field, some artists may be surprised to find that their flight of imagination in coining a name is not unique. Especially in situations where the artist wants to use his or her given name, which is not an unusual one, caution should be exercised. Undoubtedly, there are many women named Amy Grant and Anita Baker and many men named Barry White and Michael Jackson. In many cases it is advisable to change even a given name in order to avoid confusing the public and the music trade.

Before launching a public career, it is prudent to check with artist unions regarding the name desired. The American Federation of Television and Radio Artists, the union for performers on radio, television, and records, can provide information about similar names of performers on its roster. AFTRA's headquarters are located at 260 Madison Avenue, New York, NY 10016; telephone: 212-532-0800. The American Guild of Variety Artists (AGVA), the union for performers in night clubs and cabarets, will search its roster and report on possible conflicts in the use of a name as well. AGVA's office is located at 184 Fifth Avenue, New York, NY 10010; telephone: 212-675-1003; e-mail: agvany@aol.com.

The Registration of Names

ASCAP, BMI, and SESAC should each be consulted concerning prior uses of a name by their affiliated music publishers. If a proposed name is confusingly similar to other names, they may refuse to accept a new member or affiliate. In the area of records, the American Federation of Musicians enters into written union agreements with any record company using union musicians. The AFM maintains extensive lists of and data concerning record companies and record labels for use in union negotiations and for contract enforcement regarding pay and working conditions. Record producers or companies may file with the union a proposed record company or record label name; in response to inquiries, the union advises as to possible conflicting usage. All communications should be directed to the national office of the American Federation of Musicians, 1501 Broadway, New York, NY 10036; telephone: 212-869-1330.

A corporate name must have government approval before a company can be incorporated under that name. As indicated above, a proposed name must be cleared by the particular state in which incorporation is desired. One state does not require a search of the names incorporated in other states. But each state does cross-check proposed corporate names, no matter what the business. As a result, the Whiz Bang Music Corporation may fail to get clearance in a state that has previously granted such name clearance for, say, a hat company. If the party is still interested in that particular name, despite the rejection by the state secretary's office, clearance may be granted in some instances by obtaining waivers from prior users in the state.

Here is the procedure for obtaining corporate name clearance procedure in one state, New York. The first step is to send a letter to the state secretary's office at Albany, New York, requesting information as to the availability of one or more corporate names. The reply will list the available names. In effect, this constitutes a free search service by the state as to its corporation division files and a free evaluation of possible conflict with corporate names already in existence. The applicant can reserve an available name for 60 days by sending in a written request, together with a $20 fee; the reservation, based on good cause, may be extended for an additional 60 days. Up to two extensions may be granted by the Department of State. During these periods the registration of incorporation documents can be completed. Reservation-of-name procedures are also in effect in Delaware and California, and such procedures may apply in other states as well.

The Registration of Marks

Under the U.S. trademark law, provision is made for the registration of a trademark, which distinguishes a product and identifies its origins. Provision is also made for the registration of a service mark, which is used in the sale or advertising of services to identify the services of one person and distinguish them from the services of others. There is no statutory basis for the registration of trade or commercial names used merely to identify a business entity, but the name may be registered as a mark if it is also used as a trademark or service mark.

No time limit exists within which an application for registration should be filed. An application may be filed in three situations:

1. When the mark has already been used in interstate commerce or in commerce between a state and a foreign country
2. When there is a bona fide intention to use the mark in interstate commerce or in commerce between a state and a foreign country, but registration will not be issued until use is made and proved
3. Under certain international treaties, whereby an applicant may file based on an application or registration in a qualifying foreign country.

This last use in relation to goods or products means that the mark has been affixed to goods or their tags, labels, displays, or containers, and the product has been sold or shipped in such commerce. When the mark is used in relation to a service, it denotes the sale or advertising of services rendered in such commerce.

Once a mark has been registered, a registrant should give public notice of the registration by using, in conjunction with the mark, the words "Registered in U.S. Patent and Trademark Office" or "Reg. U.S. Pat. and TM. Off.," or the letter R enclosed in a circle: ®. In suits for infringement under Trademark Act of 1946, commonly known as the Lanham Act, failure to give such notice of registration prevents the registrant from recovering profits or damages unless the defendant had actual notice of the registration. It is legally improper to use this notice before the issuance of a registration and certificate. The impropriety may be a cause for refusal of registration and may result in fraud sanctions under the Lanham Act.

A complete application for the registration of a trademark or service mark consists of (1) a written application, (2) a drawing of the mark, (3) three specimens or facsimiles of the mark as used in commerce, which for service marks would include copies of advertisements, and (4) the filing fee of $325 per class. Forms for the registration of trademarks or service marks can be obtained online from the U.S. Patent and Trademark Office (www.uspto.gov) or by calling the Trademark Assistance Center at 703-308-9000. An applicant may file his or her own application, but in most instances it is wise to appoint an attorney for that purpose.

Before the Patent and Trademark Office issues a certificate of registration, the mark is published in the *Official Gazette*, a weekly PTO publication, which is also available on-line. The purpose of this publication is to allow anyone to object to the registration of the mark by filing an opposition to registration with the PTO within 30 days of publication. In an opposition proceeding, the prevailing party is the one that can prove prior use of the mark. If the mark is not opposed, the PTO generally issues a certificate of registration about 12 weeks after publication in the *Official Gazette*.

Anyone who claims rights in a mark may use the ™ or ˢ designation (for trademark or service mark) with the mark to alert the public to the claim. No registration or pending registration is necessary. The claim may or may not be valid. When a registration has been issued, the ™ or ˢ can be replaced by the symbol ® or words denoting registration.

A registration issued by the Patent and Trademark Office on or after November 16, 1989, the effective date of the Trademark Law Revision Act of 1988, remains in force for 10 years from the date of registration and may be renewed by filing a renewal application for additional 10-year periods, provided the mark is in use in commerce when the renewal application is filed. Registrations that were issued before November 16, 1989, have a 20-year original term and may be renewed for additional 10-year periods.

Trademark and service mark registrants must avoid official cancellation for nonuse of the mark. This requires the filing of an affidavit of use of the mark during the sixth year following the date of registration and again during the ninth year following the date of registration. The latter may be combined with a renewal application.

The Advantages of Registration

Under the Lanham Act, there is provision for registration on either of two registers, the *Principal Register* and the *Supplemental Register*. To qualify for registration on the *Principal Register,* a mark must be arbitrary, fanciful, or in any event "distinctive," as opposed to a descriptive or common name. Other marks that are capable of distinguishing the applicant's products can be registered on the *Supplemental Register.*

It is not necessary for the owner of a trademark to register the mark; the common law protects trademark rights. However, registration results in certain advantages. Registration on the *Principal Register* places the public on constructive notice of the registrant's claim to ownership. Registration also creates certain presumptions of ownership, of validity of the trademark, and of the exclusive right to use the mark on the goods or for the services for which the mark is registered. Registrants are given the right to sue in federal court, the right in certain cases to prevent importation of goods bearing an infringing mark, and also the benefit of incontestability on filing an affidavit showing continuous use of the mark for a 5-year period as indicated above.

Registration on the *Supplemental Register* does not give constructive notice to the public or presumptive evidence of ownership, validity, the exclusive right to the mark, or the right to prevent importation of goods carrying an infringing mark. Nor does it confer the benefit of incontestability. However, it does give the right to sue in federal court and the lawful right to use the notice of registration, which may be helpful in preventing infringement.

Trademark Registration at Home and Abroad

The registration of trademarks can be made under state laws as well as under the federal law. Usually a federal registration is considered to give sufficient protection to the trademark without the need for additional registrations under state laws. Of course, registration only under state laws is not as strong as federal registration. Registration under federal law will suffice as a holding pattern covering all states until use commences within a given state, whereas a state registration is strictly limited to its own borders.

The diverse nature of trademark laws in foreign countries makes it essential that those who wish to protect their marks abroad seek the advice of experts. In virtually all foreign countries a trademark need not have been used before it may be registered, and a registration may be used to bar the importation into the country of products to which the mark is affixed. In certain instances, individuals have been known to register the names and marks of world-renowned corporations and have blocked the efforts of those companies to register their marks until financial settlements are made.

In the case of the music industry, if a record company proposes to license its product to be released in a foreign country on its own label, it is important that trademark registrations for the label be obtained in the licensed territory. The terms of certificates of registration in foreign countries differ in accordance with the laws of each country. In the absence of registration, the legal protection of the label (trademark) license may be jeopardized. It is also prudent to have proper trademark license agreements, which must be recorded in many countries and, in many cases, approved by governmental authorities.

The advice of trademark experts should be obtained in the complicated and technical field of foreign trademarks and licenses. Certain law firms in the United States and foreign countries specialize in foreign trademark registrations. Generally, their services are obtained through other attorneys, but they may also be contacted directly.

The Ownership of Rights in an Artist's Name

In the field of music, numerous parties may claim the right to use and participate in the benefits from the use of an artist's name. These may include record companies, managers, and, the comembers of a group.

A record company usually has the exclusive right, by contract, to use and exploit an artist's name in connection with recordings made during the term of the exclusive recording contract. In addition, the company, after the expiration of the contract, has the continued right under the original contract to use the artist's name to identify, advertise, and promote the product previously made.

When popular group names such as the Ink Spots, Buffalo Springfield, Pink Floyd, and the Byrds become the subject of disputes among former members of the group, concepts of partnership property law become applicable to resolve the dispute.

Sometimes a performer changes names along the way, and questions arise as to whether the right to use the former name also encompasses the new name. For example, Tiny Tim was formerly known as Darry Dover. A record company was barred by a court from attempting to use Tiny Tim's current name and "unique style, appearance, and personality" to identify, advertise, and promote records made when he was identified as Darry Dover. However, some artist contracts specifically provide for the right to use names by which the artist may be known either now or in the future. Such a clause might have led to a different result in the Tiny Tim controversy.

The unauthorized use of a name may cause the intercession of the Federal Trade Commission or local criminal authorities interested in protecting the consumer from the fraudulent or deceptive use of popular artist names. A record company may confuse the public or subject itself to a possible lawsuit by use of record titles such as "A Tribute to Dylan" or "The Best of Sinatra" when the record contains performances by artists other than those named in the title. The public may buy the record on the supposition that only performances by the artist whose name appears in the title are contained in the record. To avoid confusion, the cover of the record should be clear as to whether only the artist's performances are included or whether the record contains performances by other artists, either in the style of the named artist or of repertoire made popular by the named artist.

A Record Company's Rights in a Name

As indicated above, in order for the record company to protect its investment in recordings and promotion, the typical artist's contract specifies that the record company has the exclusive right to use the artist's name on and in connection with the recordings made under the agreement, for the duration of the agreement. Sometimes this right is limited to use in connection with the recordings of the particular artist. More often the record company obtains the right to exploit the name for its own institutional advertising purposes, even without reference to specific recordings of the artist.

The typical contract forbids the artist from using his or her name during its term to advertise or promote records made by other persons or firms. This restriction seems natural and justified. However, if the artist is likely to produce records of other artists, he or she may seek to exclude such activities from the restriction. A typical clause submitted by a company to artists is as follows:

> We shall have the worldwide right in perpetuity to use and to permit others to use your name (both legal and professional) and likeness and biographical material concerning you for advertising and purposes of trade, and otherwise without restriction, in connection with our business and products. We shall have the further right to refer to you, by your legal or professional name, as our exclusive artist, and you shall, in your activities in the entertainment field, use your best efforts to be billed and advertised as our exclusive artist. During the term of this contract you shall not authorize your legal or professional name or your likeness to be used in connection with the advertising or sale of phonograph records other than those manufactured and sold by us.

Group Members' Rights in a Name

Most popular music groups have a highly informal arrangement among the individual members. The groups are often born in a spirit of great mutual enthusiasm and optimism, and rarely do they have the business acumen or exercise the caution to require the drafting and execution of a formal partnership agreement. Yet the typical popular music group is a partnership, no matter how informal the arrangement. When the group splits up, dissolves, or looks for substitutions, it must cope with principles of partnership law with regard to the asset of the group name.

In the case of the original Mills Brothers, there was a profusion of groups resulting from the diverse paths of the original members. When Buffalo Springfield broke up, the drummer formed a new group under that name. The other original members objected to the new group, labeling it "phony" in a statement to the public. The drummer then obtained a temporary restraining order by a court against such statements, asserting his right as a partner to use the group name. However, another court later dissolved the temporary restraining order on the ground that the other partners, even though no longer active, had the right to protect the name as a partnership asset by insisting on its use as identification of only the original group.

In their early days as a band, the Beatles had a drummer other than Ringo Starr. Although the Beatles were reorganized with the approval of the various members, the original drummer was not barred from referring to his "original" Beatles membership in connection with his new recordings.

One of the better transitions from a group to a solo name can be found in the divorce of soloist Diana Ross from the group known as the Supremes. For a considerable period of time before she left the group, with the cooperation of the Supremes' record company, Ross's name preceded the group name so that the public came to associate her as a solo artist. After the separation, both Diana Ross and the remainder of the group continued to enjoy popular success.

Doing Business Under an Assumed Name

It is not always essential to form a corporation to do business under an assumed name. In the early stages, and continuing indefinitely in many cases, a person or a group of persons may choose to do business under an assumed company name. Thus, the Ace Music Company, or the Jeff Tracy Music Associates, or the Gladstone-Black Company may be a convenient name selected for a business made up of one or more individuals. When this is done, however, a practical problem arises in cashing checks or opening bank accounts under the assumed name. The solution is compliance with state requirements for doing business under an assumed name. In New York, for example, this requires the filing of a sworn statement of identification of the true persons behind the new name.

An advantage of registering under the state statutes relating to doing business under an assumed name is that it may help to establish a priority of use in the event that groups with conflicting names are formed later.

The Protection of Names or Marks

The courts protect trade names against use or imitation under the doctrine of unfair competition. This form of unlawful business injury consists of the passing off or the attempt to pass off on the public the goods or business of one person as the goods or business of another, or the conduct of a trade or business in such a manner that there is an express or implied representation to that effect. There may also be unfair competition by misappropriation as well as by misrepresentation where there was no fraud on the public but where the defendant, for his or her advantage, has misappropriated the benefit or property right of another.

The test of a claim of trademark infringement depends on the likelihood of confusion regarding the source of origin of a product or service—in other words, whether the public would be misled into believing the product or service of the infringer was manufactured, sold, or rendered by the original trademark proprietor.

A remedy ordinarily available to redress or prevent infringement of trademarks or unfair competition is a suit for an injunction against the continuation of the wrong. If the wrongdoer did not act innocently, there may also be an action for an accounting and recovery of damages and profits based on the past infringement.

The Lanham Act permits federal district courts to grant injunctions to prevent the violation of the rights of the owner of a registered mark. Under the Lanham Act, the court may also order the destruction of the infringing labels, signs, prints, packages, plates, molds, matrices, and other reproductions or imitations of the mark or the means of making the same.

Under certain circumstances, when a registered mark has been infringed, the Lanham Act entitles the successful plaintiff to recover (1) the defendant's profits, (2) any damages suffered by the plaintiff, and (3) the costs of the action. With respect to the defendant's profits, the plaintiff need prove only sales by the defendant, who then must prove all elements of cost or claimed deductions. With regard to damages, the court may enter judgment for up to 3 times the actual damages. Should the court find the amount of recovery based on profits to be either inadequate or excessive, the court in its discretion may enter judgment for such sum as it shall deem just. The court may also award reasonable attorney's fees in exceptional cases.

In a number of states, as well as under federal law (18 USC Section 2321) it is a criminal offense to infringe, imitate, or counterfeit trademarks or to sell goods under such marks. Under the terms of some statutes, the offender is also subject to a penalty recoverable in a civil or quasi-criminal action.

Offenders must be found guilty of a fraudulent or criminal intent in order for the offense to constitute a violation of the statutes.

Generally, trademarks are not infringed if used for news purposes. In a 1992 case brought on behalf of New Kids on the Block, a federal court of appeals ruled that a fan magazine was not barred from using the picture and name of the group for news purposes. The magazine charged 50 cents for fans to call in and vote for their favorite member of the group and 95 cents to vote for "the sexiest." The court ruled that this was a news-gathering use of the names and likenesses and not an infringement of trademark because there was no indication of endorsement or sponsorship of the event by the group. The court made an analogy of the use to that of an unauthorized biography.

32

Agents and Managers

Agents and managers in the music business generally represent performing artists rather than composers and lyricists. Except in the case of songwriters involved in writing music for the stage, screen, or television, songwriters generally feel no need for a representative. On the other hand, songwriters usually have a music publisher (sometimes their own company) whose function is to promote and exploit their works by endeavoring to secure performances, recordings, and synchronization uses, as well as to administer foreign subpublishing. When a recording artist is also a songwriter, as is often the case, or when publishing rights are linked with dramatic rights, as in the case of show and film music, the artist may use a manager.

The Roles of Agents and Managers

The term *personal representative* is used to encompass both agents and managers, but the two play quite different roles. An *agent* finds or receives offers of employment and usually negotiates the terms of the contract. An agent works on a commission basis, normally 10 to 15 percent of the artist's earnings for a given engagement. The rate depends on state regulation, the particular talent union involved, and the duration of the engagement negotiated.

The leading general talent agencies are the William Morris Agency, International Creative Management (ICM) and Creative Artists Associates (CAA). Each has numerous clients in various entertainment fields and extensive staffs to represent them, with offices in the leading entertainment centers in the United States and abroad. Agents are constantly breaking away from the larger agencies and setting up their own agencies, usually of a "boutique" nature to accommodate the special interests of a particular clientele. Examples of specialized agencies in the music field are Premier Talent (rock); Famous Artists Agency (R&B, rap, dance); Associated Booking Corp. (ABC) (jazz, big band); and Jim Halsey Company (country).

In contrast to the agents, with their specialized function, *personal managers* are responsible for day-to-day career development, personal advice and guidance, and planning the long-range direction of the artist's career. Because of the broader nature of their responsibilities, managers usually have a much smaller number of clients than agents. Their responsibilities include:

- Choosing literary, artistic, and musical materials
- Handling matters relating to publicity, public relations, and advertising
- Adopting the proper format for the best presentation of the artist's talents
- Selecting booking agents to secure engagements for the artist
- Determining (in conjunction with the booking agent) the types of employment most beneficial to the artist's career
- Selecting and supervising the artist's accountants and attorneys

Personal managers generally do not travel with the artists they represent. Instead, road managers are engaged at the artists' expense; their job is to handle, under the manager's supervision, the numerous day-to-day business matters on the road, such as transportation, hotels, and collections, as well as stage, sound, and lighting needs. Personal managers may also serve as buffers to insulate the artist from requests for endorsements and appearances, as well as for charitable gifts, appearances, and the like. In addition, managers play important roles in the artist's relationships with the record label. Some are involved in the selection of songs and accompanists for the artist. They supervise relations with the talent agency to obtain the maximum benefits for the artist, and sometimes they assist in the selection of music publishers to administer songs the artist has written or has acquired an interest in.

Some artists rely so heavily on their managers for repertoire and creative guidance, as well as for business decisions, that there is sometimes as much truth as humor in the saying that the artist is a mere figment of his or her manager's imagination. Certain managers assume such control over the artist's career, business, and even personal relationships that they function as the artist's alter ego.

Managers receive commissions of between 15 and 25 percent of the artist's gross earnings, plus reimbursement for travel and other out-of-pocket expenses. Commissions payable to the manager are usually in addition to booking agent's commissions. In some instances, the manager has a large commission, but it is reduced by the amount of booking agency's commissions. Many management agreements, especially those with new artists, provide for escalating commissions, depending upon the artist's monthly or yearly gross earnings.

A new trend in artist management is to offer artists and their fans Internet exposure never before seen in traditional artist-manager relationships. For example, Left Bank, which represents such international recording artists as the Cranberries, Clint Black, and Richard Marx, was responsible for providing the music for the Backstreet section of Pepsi's Web site, which offers interactive e-mail between fans and the artists, including video and audio clips along with artist bios and interviews. Such exposure on the Web not only promotes an artist but also allows managers to accumulate e-mail addresses of fans and target potential audiences.

Although many personal managers undertake financial guidance and investment advice as a part of their functions, successful artists usually engage a business manager for these functions. This person will often be an accountant or a tax attorney. The business manager customarily collects the artist's earnings, pays the manager and other people working for the artist, manages the artist's investments, and keeps watch over the tax consequences of the artist's activities. Business managers' fees range from 2 to 6 percent of the artist's gross income, although sometimes a monthly or annual flat fee is arranged.

Exclusive Representation

Agents and managers almost invariably function as exclusive representatives of their clients in their respective fields of endeavor. This enables them to develop the artist's career without being concerned with conflicting or overlapping engagements. Because of this exclusivity, they are entitled to commissions even on earnings that do not result from their direct efforts, such as an opportunity presented by a friend or colleague of the artist. This is justified by the fact that their efforts serve to generate visibility for the artist that may lead to these other opportunities. In some instances, exclusivity is a necessary assurance to the personal representatives that they will be adequately compensated for their time and effort in building an artist's career.

However, some agents and managers have no interest or ability in fields outside of their particular area of expertise. In these situations, the artist may limit the representative's commissions to the areas in which they can be effective. Although a recording artist is normally represented for personal appearances, television shows, films, stage, and recording contracts by the same manager or agent, it is conceivable that one or more of these fields would be excluded, especially by a more successful artist who wants to retain control and avoid commissions. For example, some artists negotiate the exclusion of booking agent commissions in particular high-pay venues such as Atlantic City and Las Vegas and work solely through their managers or in-house staff in these excluded areas.

In the field of classical music, concert artists are frequently represented by personal managers who also serve as booking agents for combined fees. Firms active in this area include ICM Artists, which represents cellist Yo-Yo Ma; International Management Group (IMG), which represents violinist Itzhak Perlman; and, largest of all, Columbia Artists Management, Inc. (CAMI), which represents soprano Kathleen Battle. Some concert agents will act as the employer, as for a community concert touring series, in which event commissions are waived.

The Management Contract

A standard management contract provides for an initial term between 1 and 3 years, plus options (which the manager can exercise) to extend the term to a total of 5 years or the duration of a recording agreement secured during the term, whichever is longer. (A sample "Personal Management Agreement" is shown on the accompanying CD-ROM.)

Upon the termination of a management agreement, the manager's obligation to give advice and counsel terminates. However, almost every management agreement provides that management commissions continue after the end of the term on the artist's earnings under contracts or engagements entered into or performed during the term as well as all "substitutions, modifications and extensions by options or otherwise" of those contracts. For example, a recording artist with a former manager who participated in an early career decision to select a record company may be obliged to pay that manager commissions as long as royalties still flow from that record contract. In addition, if there is no hiatus (for example, an interim contract with another label before resuming relations with the first record company), the manager may have a claim that recordings made after the end of the manager's term are under an extension of, or substitution for, the original contract.

Managers' continuing commissions may seem unfair to an artist, who may end up paying commissions to a manager for years after their relationship has terminated. To remedy this situation, a so-called phase-out clause is frequently negotiated as part of the management contract. Under this type of clause, the manager may receive, for example, full commissions for the first 2 years after the expiration or termination of the management contract, half-commissions for the next 2 years, and no commissions thereafter. The phase-out can occur over any negotiated length of time and percentage increments.

Other important clauses and issues in the management contract include the following, all of which are negotiable:

A management contract may be terminated early if an achievement plateau is not reached, in either earnings or some other accomplishment, such as obtaining a major label record contract or booking a significant promotional tour. This clause is often referred to as a "kick-out clause." Generally, a manager will have 6 months to 1 year to obtain an offer from a major record label or label with national distribution, with a 1- to 3-month extension if the manager is engaged in bona fide negotiations with one of these labels.

The manager may not exercise an option to extend the term unless a minimum earnings level has been achieved. Generally, the plateaus increase for later options.

The term *commissionable income* in a management agreement includes the artist's gross income in whatever form (royalties, bonuses, and stock) earned by the artist as a result of the artist's activities in the entertainment field. As a result, both *gross income* and *entertainment field* should be defined in the contract.

There are certain items that should be excluded from gross income, including recording costs, video production costs, tour support from the record company, and sound and lights during touring. The theory behind these exclusions is that these moneys merely pass through the artist's hands to third parties and thus should not be commissionable. The exclusion of recording costs can make a big difference. For example, if the artist has a $200,000 recording fund and $150,000 is spent on recording costs, this leaves $50,000 for the artist. However, if the manager were to take a 20 percent commission on the whole fund ($200,000), the commission would be $40,000, leaving only $10,000 for the artist. If recording costs are excluded from gross income, the manager may only commission the remaining $50,000 and will receive $10,000, leaving $40,000 for the artist. Managers generally will agree to exclude recording costs from gross income, as well as the other exclusions mentioned above.

Managers may also waive or defer commissions for the weeks that the artist has not achieved a certain level of income. This is sometimes referred to as a "bread-and-butter clause": the manager will not earn commissions while the artist is simply trying to put food on the table.

Generally, managers will be reimbursed for out-of-pocket expenses incurred on behalf of the artist, such as long-distance phone calls, faxes, postage, messengers, and travel expenses. The artist should limit the manager's authority to incur excessive expenses. For example, the manager may not incur a single expense of $500 or $1,000 in total expenses during a single month without the artist's prior written approval.

Most managers seek a broad power of attorney to sign all contracts on the artist's behalf, endorse checks payable to the artist, and engage third parties (such as agents, accountants, and public relations firms) to work for the artist. However, such powers are sometimes too broad and can be exploited by an unscrupulous manager. The artist should limit the manager's power of attorney to signing engagement contracts for periods not in excess of 14 days. This much authority is necessary because offers of engagement by promoters do not stay open long, and the artist may not be available to sign the agreement. The manager should at least be required to consult with the artist regarding the engagement before exercising a power of attorney. However, consultation is considerably weaker than the right of approval. As a compromise, the artist retains a right of approval that is not to be withheld unreasonably.

In most cases, if a member of an artist group leaves, he or she is still bound to the manager as a performing artist, whether as a solo or with another group. The artist group should make sure that a departing member will not be bound to the manager for longer than the term of the management contract. In other words, the term of the management contract should not start running anew. Additionally, if new members join the group, they are likely to be required to enter into the same management contract as the existing one between the artist group and the manager.

The manager's ability to assign the management contract should be limited to assignments to an entity in which the original manager has an ownership or a controlling interest. In addition, a "key man clause" may be added to the contract, providing, for example, that if the manager is not involved in the day-to-day management of the artist for a period of 60 consecutive days, then the artist may terminate the management contract. (See Chapter 2 for a further discussion of the key man clause.)

The close and often trying relationship between artists and managers during the years of active management makes it desirable that the parties involved be sure of their compatibility before entering into binding contracts. The negotiation of a complete management agreement—one that deals with most of the areas mentioned above, with the assistance of attorneys experienced in the field—is perhaps one way to ascertain whether this compatibility exists. Simply stated, if the prospective manager and the artist cannot reach a working agreement in their initial negotiation, it is best for both concerned to avoid entering into a long-term contract.

Abuses by Agents and Managers

Although most agents and managers are ethical, the relationship with the artist does open the possibility of certain forms of abuse, each of which should be specifically recited in the management contract as a cause for termination. For example, the manager may

- Withhold monies from the artist through theft, embezzlement, misappropriation, forgery, fraud, or other dishonest conduct
- Enter into an arrangement with a third party for the services of an artist whereby compensation is paid directly to the agent, under terms not disclosed to the artist, with the intent to provide additional compensation to the manager
- Improperly represent the artist without the artist's authorization
- Commingle monies belonging to different artists

Regulation of Agents and Managers

While all states regulate employment agencies by statute, managers generally will not admit that they merely find jobs for their clients. Managers generally take the position that their services are outside the scope of state laws that govern employment agencies, and indeed most management agreements specifically disclaim any obligation to seek or obtain employment, even though this is exactly what many managers do and this provision is of questionable enforceability.

Among states that regulate agents and managers, California, with its obvious ties to the entertainment industry, is probably the leader. California statutes specifically govern talent and literary agents and control fees and the duration of the contracts with such agents.

Under California's Talent Agencies Act (California Labor Code section 1700), agents and managers who are in the "occupation of procuring employment" for artists must obtain a license. There has been considerable debate as to what amount of "procurement" is necessary to violate the act. In the 1996 case of *Anita Baker v. Sherwin Bush,* the California labor commissioner upheld the hearing officer's finding of fact that the unlicensed manager was not merely a "conduit" for employment offers that came to him, but was actively engaged in promoting employment opportunities, and that therefore his management agreement was unenforceable even though it contained the usual exculpatory language about not being required to seek employment. The act, which is under the jurisdiction of the California Labor Commission, attempts to protect artists from unscrupulous managers. Its licensing process involves, among other things, the submission of affidavits by "at least two reputable residents who have known or been associated with, the applicant for two years" which state "that the applicant is a person of good moral character" as well as the posting of a $10,000 bond, which is intended to confirm the manager's credit worthiness. After the application has been submitted, the labor commissioner may "cause an investigation to be made as to the character and responsibility of the applicant" (Sections 1700.6(d), 1700.15, 1700.7).

All disputes between artists and managers are decided by the California labor commissioner. An unlicensed manager who is found guilty of violating its provisions can face both the termination of the contract and the restitution to the artist of all commissions paid. There are no criminal penalties.

New York State regulates theatrical employment agencies by statute under its General Business Law. In New York, agents who seek engagements for performing artists can charge a maximum commission of 10 percent. A personal manager does not have to obtain a license under the statute if seeking employment is merely "incidental" to the manager's functions. In the case of *PPX Enterprises v. A Tribe Called Quest,* 1991, PPX, had contracted with the well-known rap group A Tribe Called Quest to obtain a recording agreement for them. PPX was not the group's manager, nor was it a licensed employment agent. Although PPX secured a recording agreement, the group refused to pay PPX its 15 percent fee. The court held the PPX contract unenforceable, and the group did not have to pay PPX because it was neither an agent nor a manager. (See also Chapter 36.)

Some states fail to give full protection to the artist in their regulation of agents and managers and their licensing requirements. In 1987 a Minnesota court held that no refund could be sought in civil action, notwithstanding the collection of some $80,000 in commissions while lacking a license to represent the band leader, because the statute only provided a criminal remedy.

(*O'Brien Entertainment Agency v. Wolfgramm*, 407 N.W.2d 463 [Minn. 1987]).

Unions such as the American Federation of Musicians, the American Federation of Television and Radio Artists, and the American Guild of Variety Artists (AGVA) also regulate agents. Only AGVA attempts to regulate managers, whereas all three unions supervise agents by granting them franchise certificates; union members are barred from dealing with agents who lack such certificates. Subjects of regulation include maximum commission rates, duration of the contract, and conflicts of interest. AFTRA and AFM disseminate approved forms of agreements between artists and representatives under which an artist is afforded an opportunity to terminate if the agency has not offered a designated number of engagements.

Similarly, AGVA, which operates in the area of musical performance in nightclubs, cabarets, theaters, and other areas of live entertainment, limits its members' contracts with agents to those agents who are franchised by AGVA. The representative of the authorized agents is the Artists' Representatives Association (ARA).

Trade Organizations for Personal Managers

Two major professional organizations exist for personal managers: the National Conference of Personal Managers (NCOPM), formerly the Conference of Personal Managers, and the International Managers Forum (IMF). Many leading managers belong to NCOPM, which operates an eastern division and a western division in addition to the national office. The NCOPM is actively involved in lobbying Congress on issues affecting managers and the artists they represent. Members of this organization adhere to its code of ethics and business practices. Benefits of membership include newsletters, an information library, publicity, and the right to use the NCOPM standard management contract. (For more information, write to the NCOPM, 1650 Broadway, New York, NY 10019.)

The IMF was formed in 1993 in New York to provide monthly forums for managers to discuss the various issues that affect them as well as to further their interests and those of the artists they represent in all aspects of the music industry. The organization has approximately 60 members, all in New York, and is associated with two sister organizations, IMF-UK and IMF-Canada. The IMF publishes a quarterly newsletter featuring information on the organization's activities. (For more information, write to the IMF at PO Box 444, Village Station, New York, NY 10014-0444.)

Competition for Personal Managers

For years personal managers have viewed with alarm the increasing number of attorneys, accountants, business managers, and even publicists undertaking functions formerly performed by personal managers. For example, it has been recognized that the complexities of negotiating a complicated agreement between a record company and an artist require the services of skilled attorneys. At times an experienced music attorney may be regarded as essential to making a recording deal for an artist. If the attorney is a strong negotiator and commands substantial fees, often on a contingent basis, the more sophisticated artist may question the rationale of having a manager as well. Similar problems occur where the functions of skilled accountants, business managers, or publicists tend to overlap with those of a manager.

When another professional replaces a personal manager, the artist should beware of potential conflicts of interest. The artist should be especially cautious when the artist's attorney is also a stockholder or officer in the manager's company or an employee of the artist's manager. In such an instance the artist should seek separate counsel. Although opportunities and temptations are ever-present, a lawyer should not simultaneously negotiate contracts for an artist while serving as that artist's manager. Nevertheless, a growing number of attorneys are assuming the role of personal manager and charging for their services on the same commission basis. While this scenario sometimes works, attorneys are often ill-suited to fill these dual roles. While they may be better at negotiating the record deal once it is achieved, finding such a deal often requires skills not taught in law school.

Because record companies routinely reject unsolicited materials, including demo tapes of unknown artists seeking record deals, many attorneys in the entertainment industry have undertaken the practice known as "shopping." Attorneys who "shop" record deals for artists often have varying fee arrangements for such activities. Some attorneys favor an hourly wage ranging from $150 to $300. Often the attorney will request a nonreturnable advance retainer, which can range from $1,500 to $5,000 and which is applied against a contingency fee. Other attorneys either opt for prepayment of expenses or for a percentage of a record deal (usually 10 to 15 percent of net advances and royalties). Fee arrangements between the attorney and artist may include any combination or all of the preceding elements. (Shopper arrangements are also discussed in Chapter 36.)

The attorney's role as a shopper primarily involves contacts with key record company personnel. In agreeing to pay advance retainers and contingency fees, the artist is essentially purchasing the attorney's access to those who may be in a position to offer a record deal. Consequently, shopping is inherently prone to ethical abuses. Unscrupulous attorneys may even offer shopping services in return for front money, even though they do not believe their efforts will be successful. Such attorneys may not even make sincere efforts to shop the artist for fear of damaging their own credibility with record company personnel. Accordingly, shopping for record deals may be a more appropriate activity for personal managers.

Relationships Between Artists and Personal Representatives

From time to time, there are changes in agency personnel. Two agencies will merge; or a well-known agent who has handled a particular motion picture or recording star will move from one agency to another or will establish a new agency; or a recognized personal manager will join a larger talent organization.

The artist who appreciates the greater attention and facilities that may accompany such a change may be happy with the new arrangements. On the other hand, an artist who enjoys being the stellar attraction of a small organization may be dissatisfied with being a small fish in a big pond. Artists who have developed close personal relations with an individual representative who has moved on to another agency or firm or formed his or her own business may be disgruntled unless they can follow their representative to their new connection. This is understandable because the manager-artist relationship is by nature extremely close.

Courts appreciate the significance of a personal relationship, and as a result they sometimes stretch in favor of the artist who is objecting to a material change in the basic relationship with his or her manager and wants to terminate the management agreement. Nevertheless, the courts must respect the intentions of the parties as revealed by their agreement. Thus, in the case of the contract with a large talent agency, where the relationship is not necessarily very personal, the court may be unwilling to relieve the artist of his or her contractual obligations if no specific provision has been made in the agreement. It is up to the artist to have provided in the agreement for such contingencies.

Some union agreements protect the artist in this area by requiring the talent agency to name several key individuals who will actually service the artist. Some artists will designate their own particular key person with whom they anticipate a close working relationship. Other union agreements permit termination of an agency agreement in the event of a merger of the agency with another agency.

The termination of an artist's relationship with an agency will apply only to new contracts not previously handled by the agency. There is a continuing right to commissions on earnings under contracts and engagements secured by the agency. In a 1992 case, *Watts v. Columbia Artists Management Inc.*, a New York county court held that Columbia Artists Management was due commissions from pianist Andre Watts for engagements scheduled before termination of the contract.

Notices and Payments

Most agreements negotiated by managers or agents provide that all notices and payments shall be made through the office of the manager or agent. This protects both the artist and the personal representative. Representatives can spot-check the artist's royalty receipts in order to ensure that royalty accountings are rendered in a timely fashion and are generally in order. They can also calculate and receive their appropriate commissions. Insofar as the record company is concerned, it may confer with the representative rather than with the artist on such matters, especially where the artist is frequently on tour or not known to attend to business.

Music Contractors

Music contractors select and assemble musicians for recording dates. Instead of charging the musicians an agent's commission in connection with the session based on union agreements with the American Federation of Musicians, the contractor charges a fee that is paid by the record company or record producer. The fee is generally fixed at a percentage of the minimum union scale for one participating musician. When one of the playing musicians arranges to assemble the others and thus assumes the duties of a contractor, he or she is paid both the union scale of a musician and the union scale of a contractor. (This is discussed in Chapter 6, "Labor Agreements.")

33

Taxation in the Music Business

Many a motion picture star or executive with unusually high current income is envious of a built-in factor in the music industry, namely, the spread of royalty payments over many years. Many accountants and attorneys in other areas of the entertainment field try to achieve for their clients the spread-forward of earnings that is provided naturally by the time it takes to collect performance payments through ASCAP and BMI, record royalties, foreign royalties, and other revenue. Even with popular hits that do not become standards, it takes years before all earnings from the initial success have been received. This natural spread-forward of earnings can sometimes be arranged contractually for high-earning artists by providing for a series of annual installments in specified amounts. Alternatively, earnings may be paid though the device of a loan that is "forgiven" at some future time based on success (which then becomes a taxable bonus).

Accountants and attorneys in the tax field often advise clients of the truism that "tax avoidance is not tax evasion." The U.S. Supreme Court has expressed its approval of tax avoidance as the act of an informed taxpayer who takes advantage by legal means of the right to decrease the amount of taxes he or she would otherwise have to pay. Tax savings may be achieved through depreciation allowances, certain charitable contributions, the transfer of rights in copyrights to a child or other person in a lower tax bracket, and the deduction of permissible business and professional expenses.

Capital Gains

The tax laws treat long-term capital gains more favorably than ordinary income. At this time, a favorable 20 percent rate applies to long-term gains and a rate of 28 percent applies to short-term capital gains. In general, an asset must be held for at least 18 months for gain to be long-term. For those in the 15 percent tax bracket, the capital gains rate is 10 percent. For assets acquired after December 31, 2000, and held for at least 5 years, the top rate drops to 18 percent. Obviously, this compares favorably with ordinary income tax brackets, which can be over 30 percent. In addition, capital losses may be used to offset capital gains plus $3,000 of ordinary income. Moreover, unused capital losses can be carried over to later years.

A musical composition or similar property is not considered a "capital asset" if it is held by a taxpayer whose personal efforts created such property. This applies not only to authors and composers but also to persons who receive rights in copyrighted works as donees by virtue of gifts or trusts. It does not include purchasers or heirs, and under the present tax laws, sales by them can qualify as capital gains if there are gains after depreciation recapture. By an amendment to the Internal Revenue Code, Congress provided that if there was a sale of property for a consideration in excess of its depreciated value, the amount of depreciation taken after 1961 must first be recognized as ordinary income. For example, if a spouse inherited a copyright at a value of $20,000, depreciated it by $4,000 so that its basis was $16,000, and then sold it for $25,000, the first $4,000 of gain would be considered ordinary income (to offset the ordinary deduction from ordinary income for depreciation taken in prior years); the remaining gain of $5,000 would qualify as capital gain.

Note the word "gain" in the term *capital gain*. There is no tax whatsoever on the basic cost recouped by the sale. For instance, disregarding the factor of allowable depreciation (which is discussed later), a music publisher that acquires a copyright for $15,000 and resells it a year later for $20,000 is not taxed on the $15,000 cost and pays tax at capital gain rates only on the $5,000 profit. In general, the cost basis allowed to be recovered, in the case of a sale by the author, is the sum of the costs incurred in obtaining the copyright, less any depreciation he or she may have taken on such costs; any excess over such depreciated cost is treated as ordinary income. For sales by purchasers of copyrights, the basis is the consideration paid by the purchaser, less any depreciation taken; any excess above this depreciated cost is treated as ordinary income to the extent of the depreciation already taken and any additional gain is treated as capital gain.

With regard to deceased authors, if a copyright is sold by the estate or a person deriving rights through the estate, a capital gain may generally be claimed using a higher cost basis. For inherited property the basis is usually the fair market value at the date of death. If a federal tax return has to be filed, the basis will be the fair market value at the date of death, or if elected by the estate, a date 6 months later. In the event that a federal tax return need not be filed, the basis will be the value at the date of death used for the payment of state inheritance taxes. This basis is used for both capital gain and depreciation purposes.

For situations involving an inheritance from an heir of the author, or the formula for increasing the cost basis for estate taxes paid on any appreciation in value, it is suggested that attorneys or accountants be consulted for appropriate advice.

Generally, in the case of gifts of property, the donee retains the donor's basis. If the donee sells for an amount less than his or her basis, resulting in a loss, then the donee is required to adopt the fair market value of the property at the date of the gift, which may reduce the loss for tax purposes. If the donee sells for an amount in excess of his or her basis, the excess is subject to capital gain treatment if otherwise qualified; but where the donor was the author, capital gain treatment would not be available.

Considerable difficulty was encountered in the past in determining the type of sale that qualifies for capital gain treatment. This difficulty existed because copyright was regarded as an indivisible entity for copyright purposes despite its various component elements such as motion picture rights, performance rights, mechanical rights, and publication rights, all of which make up what has been called a "bundle of rights." It was questionable whether the sale of particular rights would qualify for capital gain treatment for tax purposes. However, in *Hedwig et al. v. United States,* a 1952 case involving the film rights to *Forever Amber,* the court determined that for capital gain tax purposes there is nothing inherent in the nature of a copyright that prevents separate sales of each of the parts comprising the whole. This position is reinforced by the Copyright Act of 1976, which explicitly recognizes the divisibility of the various exclusive rights that comprise a copyright and provides that any of such exclusive rights may be transferred and owned separately.

Where the purchase price is a percentage of future earnings (akin to a royalty), the sale of rights by one music publisher to another is sufficient for capital gain treatment if the sale is full and final and the purchase price is not merely an anticipation of future income, such as an advance against future royalties. If the transaction qualifies as a so-called installment sale, the seller will report gains only as payments are actually received.

No capital gain advantages are available to persons or firms that hold properties "primarily for sale to customers in the ordinary course of ... business." Music publishers are normally licensors, not sellers, of copyrights and thus are excluded from the category of taxpayers who are required to pay taxes at ordinary income rates on amounts received from the sale of their catalog. It is a rare instance when the heirs of authors seek capital gain treatment. This situation may be in large part the result of a tradition against outright sale by authors' surviving spouses and children; they honor the authors' decision to keep a continuing royalty interest and forgo the attraction of an outright sale that may prove to be improvident. An author's heirs must bear in mind that the right to receive a substantial sum yearly in royalties over the remaining life of a copyright carries with it the obligation to pay income tax at ordinary rates, except as the copyright may be depreciated. The effect of depreciation is discussed below.

Depreciation and Amortization

A Treasury Department publication that specifies that copyrights are subject to depreciation states, "The purpose of depreciation is to let you recover your investment over the useful life of the property." Because a copyright is recognized to be an intangible asset of diminishing value, a portion of receipts from licenses or other uses of the copyright may be considered to be not ordinary income but a payment to replace lost value.

Unlike capital gain, depreciation is available to authors and composers as well as to music publishers. However, in practical effect, the depreciation allowance for original authors and the original publisher is small since normally only the copyright registration fees and attorney's fees involved in establishing the copyright can be depreciated. In addition, there is no value attributable to the services of the author or composer in creating the work unless the author was an employee-for-hire, in which case the compensation could be an element of cost for the publisher. Freelance, self-employed composers, lyricists, and recording artists are entitled to current tax-year deductions for qualifying business expenses. This avoids the limitation on depreciation write-offs. However, such expenses cannot exceed income related to the expense and are not available to the nonprofessional. Video and film expenses are not considered qualifying items.

The right to depreciate is applicable not only to purchasers of copyrights but also to estates, heirs, and trusts. This right is substantial in respect to purchases and can be substantial for heirs of writers as well. The depreciable value is generally "stepped up" to the fair market value of the copyright at the date of death of the last owner, or 6 months later if the estate was subject to federal estate tax, providing that there was a valid election by the executor or administrator to value the estate at the later date.

When a donee takes over a predecessor's asset valuation basis, the donee assumes both the basis and the accumulated depreciation of the former owner. Thus, in determining the amount of depreciation to be recaptured as ordinary income in the event of a sale, depreciation taken by both the seller and the prior owners (whose basis was assumed) must be considered.

As an example of the application of depreciation, let's assume a purchase by a music publisher of a copyright for $10,000. The music publisher would determine, after consultation with an accountant and attorney, the period over which the cost would be depreciated for tax purposes. If the period is 10 years, the $10,000 cost would normally be depreciated on a straight-line basis in 10 equal installments of $1,000 each so that the publisher would have an allowance of $1,000 per year against taxable earnings. In effect, at the end of 10 years, the publisher would have recaptured the basic investment and would be in a position to replenish the catalog by the purchase of another song. A record company is in a similar position with regard to the depreciation of the costs of its master recordings.

Until recently, the tax laws as interpreted by the Internal Revenue Service singled out copyrights and other intangibles by requiring that depreciation must be computed on a straight-line basis and disallowing the use of alternative methods available to other property owners. This meant that the cost for tax purposes (less projected salvage value at the end of the depreciation period) could only be depreciated in equal installments over the depreciation period. In the event that a copyright became valueless in any year before the end of the depreciation period, the unrecovered cost (or other basis for depreciation) might be deducted in that year.

In 1994, an Internal Revenue Service training manual for music industry audits stated that the flow-of-income approach can be used to amortize record masters unless the 3-year safe-harbor alternative is used. ("Safe harbor" is discussed on the next page.) Under the flow-of-income approach, an estimate is made of the total amount of income that is to be received over the economic life of the asset. The depreciable basis of the assets is written down each year in the same proportion that the receipts for a particular year bear to the total anticipated receipts. In this manner the years with the greatest proportion of receipts will bear the greatest proportion of depreciation, and there is a closer match between expenses and income. The IRS manual states that demo records can be treated either as current expense fully deductible in the year of expenditure or as research and development expense to be amortized over 60 or more months.

Where the safe-harbor approach is not applicable, it is probable that a flow-of-income method is now required for noncorporate producers, including S corporations and personal holding companies (described on pages 375 and 377, respectively). For these taxpayers, expenses for the production of a film, sound recording, book, or similar property that are otherwise eligible are deductible on a prorated basis over the years in which the income is received. The law defines the terms *film* and *sound recording* but does not define either *book* or *similar property*. Nevertheless, the Senate Committee Report on the Tax Reform Act of 1976 mandates the use of the flow-of-income method for a musical copyright on the theory that it is "similar property." Thus noncorporate producers are definitely required to use the flow-of-income method to depreciate record master costs and would appear to be required to use this method for musical copyrights as well. Corporate producers seem to have the option of depreciating on either a straight-line basis or a flow-of-income basis.

Depreciation of high-cost items used in a taxpayer's music business activities is increasingly important because of the high cost of electronic equipment such as synthesizers and studio equipment. Although there used to be an investment tax credit for purchases of new depreciable tangible property, this credit is no longer available, and costs must be spread out on a depreciation schedule based on the allowable useful life of the property. On the other hand, the cost of qualifying business equipment can be deducted in the year the equipment is purchased and first used, up to a limit of $20,000 in the year 2000, increasing to $24,000 in 2001 and to $25,000 in 2003.

Tax Treatment of Record Masters

It is well recognized in the record industry that the overwhelming majority of new recordings have a useful commercial life of less than 1 year from the date of release. This is primarily due to the fact that most popular recordings do not reach the break-even point of recovering their cost and are discontinued for lack of popularity. However, there are evergreens in the record field just as there are standards in the music publishing field. Vintage recordings of Duke Ellington, Hank Williams, the Rolling Stones, and the Beatles continue to have regular sales long after their original cost was recouped. These vintage recordings would have been fully depreciated many years ago, but when they are transferred to a new owner, the valuation of the sale creates a new basis for depreciation. In certain cases, there is no longer a question whether to treat recording costs as current expenses to be deducted from current income before computing taxable income or to capitalize them and depreciate them over time, because it was mandated that the flow-of-income approach is to be observed. The flow-of-income basis is mandated for noncorporate taxpayers only; corporate taxpayers have an option of using either a straight-line method or a flow-of-income basis.

The flow-of-income approach has caused major problems. It may require complicated estimates and calculations and can result in long delays in recovering expenses. To alleviate this inequity, the Internal Revenue Service has adopted a 3-year safe-harbor rule that can be elected by any individual creator (or by any corporation or partnership owned at least 95 percent by an individual alone or together with close family members). This safe harbor allows a rapid depreciation and amortization of costs, at the rate of 50 percent in the first year and 25 percent in each of the two successive years, provided that it applies to all creative costs incurred in the tax year in question. While some tax filers who are eligible for the flow-of-income or the safe-harbor approach may still attempt to deduct all expenses against current income, they risk the possibility that this will be rejected by the Internal Revenue Service.

In some instances it may actually suit the tax-planning needs of a record company to depreciate recording costs over time rather than deduct them as a current expense. This occurs typically when there are considerable startup costs and little current income but there are expectations of greater income in the future. Increased current profits can thereby be shown because there are fewer current expenses to be deducted, and the deductions are preserved for later years when they are able to offset greater income. Even a depreciation basis does not prejudice the right of the company to take a write-off of the undepreciated costs in the year when the record itself is discontinued from the company catalog and its inventory of such discontinued records is sold as scrap. However, most smaller companies seek maximum current deductions in order to decrease their taxes immediately and conserve their cash.

It should be remembered that the treatment of recording costs will affect the tax results applicable to gain on the sales of masters. When depreciation has been taken, the gains equal to the depreciation are considered as ordinary income and the remaining balance as capital gain if the master is a capital asset in the hands of the seller. The tax benefit rule is equally applicable when an expense other than depreciation is deducted. If, for example, the cost of producing a master recording is written off in the year of production and the master is later sold, to the extent of the original write-off, the gain is considered ordinary income and the remaining balance is considered capital gain, provided that the master is a capital asset of the seller.

Research and Experimental Expenses

Demonstration records often involve substantial outlays for studio costs and artist fees. This outlay would seem to be a capital expenditure to develop a new copyright just as much as both copyright registration and attorney's fees, which are considered a basis for depreciation. However, such expenses are not allowed for depreciation purposes. Instead, the taxpayer can choose either an immediate full deduction in the year of outlay or a special allowance permitted for "research and experimental expenses," which is so similar to depreciation that it is difficult to see the reason for a distinction. Under the special allowance, which applies only to costs of assets that have no determinable useful life, the expense is spread over a period of 60 or more months. For instance, if a music publisher with limited activity and earnings for any one year makes a substantial outlay for research and experimental purposes, the special-allowance procedure may be preferable to the full deduction in the year of outlay.

Musical arrangements for various possible uses of a song may also be regarded as being in the area of research and experimental expenses. If a composer makes an arrangement while he or she owns the copyright, the composer cannot charge for his or her own services as an expense; but if the composer engages outside arrangers, orchestrators, or copyists, he or she has the privilege of charging the expense against current income or resorting to the special allowance by which the expense is spread over 60 or more months.

Some writers or estates of writers assemble folios of songs or publish descriptive promotional material for distribution to potential users. These do not constitute research or experimental expenditures and are considered either as a current promotional expense or allocable as an item of cost against gross receipts from the sales of printed copies.

Charitable Contributions

Charitable gifts of appreciated property—such as a library of unreleased masters or a valuable copyright—given to a qualifying charitable organization can sometimes provide tax benefits to the donor. In certain cases, a donor can deduct the fair market value of a gift, as determined by an expert appraiser, from his or her taxable income. In contrast to a sale, a donor need not worry about finding a purchaser willing and able to pay the appraised value of the property.

The tax laws impose several limitations on the tax benefits of gifts of appreciated property. The benefits are largely unavailable to the taxpayer, such as a composer or lyricist who created the subject of the gift or to the donee of the composer or lyricist. In this case, the taxpayer can only deduct the original cost of creation, which is usually negligible. This limitation, however, is not ordinarily applicable to publishers or heirs. There is also a limitation if the donee's use of the gift is unrelated to the donee's charitable function.

Income tax deductions for the charitable contributions of individuals are restricted to 50 percent of adjusted gross income, subject, however, to a ceiling of 30 percent with certain carryover rights on the excess if a sale of a property would have resulted in a long-term capital gain. For corporations, the percentage restriction is 10 percent of taxable income, subject to certain adjustments. There may be a further limitation on the benefits of a charitable contribution with respect to the calculation of the alternative minimum tax. In calculating such tax, a taxpayer who is subject to such tax and who has made a charitable contribution of appreciated property must reduce the amount of the contribution by the amount of the untaxed appreciation.

At one time, for certain taxpayers in high-income tax brackets, the tax savings of charitable contributions of appreciated property could have been greater than the after-tax proceeds of a sale of the property. However, recent tax legislation has largely eliminated this situation, although possible tax advantages still exist.

Deductions for Home Used as Office or Studio

Many freelance vocalists and musicians require extensive rehearsals, coaching, and practice to maintain their income-producing skills. They often carry on these activities in their home. The Internal Revenue Service has strict limitations concerning the deduction of operating and depreciation expenses allocable to the portion of a home used for business purposes where the use is on an exclusive and regular basis as a principal place of business, as a place for seeing business clients, or as a separate business structure.

In 1997, the Congress reacted to a 1993 Supreme Court ruling that had tightened the meaning of "principal place of business." The new law relaxed the requirements for a deductible home office as of December 31, 1998, so that it would qualify if used for administrative or management activities of any trade or business if there was no other fixed location to perform such duties. In other respects it continued the two basic tests: (1) the importance of activities performed at each place of business and (2) the time spent at each place.

Several steps can be taken to protect the home office deduction.

- ▶ Perform most work activities at home and document them.
- ▶ Document all business meetings at home.
- ▶ Move the home office into a separate structure, such as a garage, and do not mix business and personal matters in same space.
- ▶ Prove that the employer requires a home office, for example, by a letter. If

the taxpayer is an employee, he or she must also show that the home office is being used for the "convenience" of the taxpayer's employer.

Items such as heat, electricity, insurance, and rent, or in the case of home ownership, taxes, mortgage interest, and depreciation, may be deducted on an allocated basis. If all rooms at home are approximately the same size, the business portion of office or studio-in-home expenses can be computed by the ratio of the number of rooms used for business purposes to the total number of rooms. Thus, in a 10-room dwelling of roughly equal size where one room is set aside for business purposes, 10 percent of the dwelling expenses are for business purposes. In other instances, the ratio is the number of square feet in the business space to the total square feet: for example, 330 square feet divided by 3,300 square feet, or 10 percent.

The home office deduction cannot be more than the total gross income from the business use of the home, after deduction of business expenses other than home expenses. Only household expenses and repairs that benefit the business space are deductible. The cost of painting another room would, for instance, not be deductible, although the cost of painting the outside of the house may be deductible. Lawn care and landscaping costs are not deductible. Small businesses can also deduct up to $20,000 of the cost of new qualifying business equipment.

Shifting Taxable Income to Persons in Lower Tax Brackets

Many a successful parent would like to avoid additional income at his or her current high tax rate by shifting the income to a child or other dependent in a lower tax bracket. Although this cannot be done with ordinary personal service income, it is perfectly legal in the case of music royalties. While the mere reallocation of actual or anticipated income within a family group is not permissible, it is considered proper to make a bona fide gift or transfer of copyright, since the conveyance is then not of income but of property capable of producing income.

An IRS ruling makes it attractive for a company owner to grant minority interests to children or other relatives while still living instead of through a will. This can reduce eventual estate taxes as well as the current income tax of the original parent owner. Such exemptions for gifts are currently $10,000 a year per recipient for each donor, but for community property of husband and wife a joint annual gift of $20,000 per child is allowed.

Where there is a direct transfer to a beneficiary, there can be no strings attached, such as a right of recapture after college graduation. The assignment cannot be hazy; it is best to document it fully by written notice to the publisher, by registration of copyright assignment, if any, and perhaps even by the appointment of a bank or other institution to collect and distribute the monies. Properly accomplished, it is clear that the income tax is chargeable to the new owner of the income-producing property and not to the assignor, although the assignor may be liable for gift taxes if the gift does not come within the statutory exemptions to which the donor may be entitled.

Some successful songwriters have established trust funds for their children without including ASCAP or BMI performance monies. The divisibility of copyright is accepted for tax purposes. No capital gain on resale can eventually be claimed by the child or trustee who received the gift from the songwriter because, under tax law, a donee of an author or composer is treated the same as the donor and is therefore barred from the benefit of capital gains.

When an aged person, such as a parent, is dependent on a successful songwriter for support, consideration may be given to shifting income by a transfer of copyright or of the property right to a royalty contract. There can be a direct conveyance to the parent, provided that there is no obligation to return the property in the future; it is reasonable to expect that the parent will express appreciation by a bequest back to the assignor. By virtue of the trust or conveyance, the assignor is relieved of taxes on the income. Taxes paid by the dependent are likely to be lower than those that would be payable by the assignor if the income were attributable to him or her.

In determining whether to shift income to the dependent, the grantor must consider the possible loss of a dependency deduction on his or her own tax return if the dependent's income increases beyond certain limits. For example, assigning property that produces sufficient income to a widowed parent over 65 to cover 50 percent or more of his or her living expenses may cause the grantor to lose the deduction for the dependent. Nevertheless, the assignment can result in a tax saving at the donor's top tax bracket.

Shifting Income from One Year to Other Years

On either a fiscal or calendar year, benefit may be obtained by deferring the receipt and reporting of income to a future date, despite the loss of use of the money until its receipt. One reason for this is the continued availability of monies that would otherwise have to be paid as taxes. Another reason may be the expectation that there will be lower earnings in future years and therefore the deferred income will be reported at a lower tax rate. Some writers, publishers, and record artists contract for delays in payments of royalties until a subsequent year.

In each case of income deferral, the question of "constructive receipt" arises. This problem is present if the taxpayer waives receipt of monies to which he or she is entitled in the tax year or delays cashing a check that is in his or her hands before the end of the current tax year. The element of subterfuge involved can be avoided by a forthright provision in a royalty agreement designed to accomplish the same benefit.

A typical acceptable provision, in the instance of a recording artist, provides that the royalties payable in any one year may not exceed a stated maximum, and that any excess is accumulated for disbursement in future years when the current earnings do not reach the earnings ceiling. Other contracts, such as that between a show music writer and a music publisher, or an exclusive service contract between a songwriter and publisher for the services of the writer, may call for an annual minimum guaranteed payment to the writer on the understanding that the publisher can withhold earnings in excess of a ceiling figure fixed in the agreement. At the end of the term of the agreement, the accumulated amount withheld, if any, is disbursed over a stated number of years at an annual figure set forth in the contract.

When this method of income deferral is used, it is required that the funds being held by the publisher or the recording company remain in the business and be subject to the risk of the business. A contractual provision whereby the person liable for the payment of the deferred amount places the funds in escrow or in trust, or in some other manner earmarks the funds and removes them from the possible claims of creditors, destroys the advantage sought and results in a constructive receipt of the funds by the person entitled to them.

Deferral of Income Through Retirement Plans

The Internal Revenue Code permits the deferral of a limited amount of such income without the previously described risk by the device of a retirement plan. For self-employed individuals, this can be a Keogh plan, an individual retirement account (IRA), a simplified pension plan (SEP), a deferred salary plan, or a Roth IRA.

There are two general types of Keogh plans: defined-benefit plans and defined-contribution plans. Most persons have a defined-contribution plan, the two main types of which are a money-purchase plan and a profit-sharing plan. Under a money-purchase plan, the participant agrees to put a certain minimum percentage of self-employed income into the account each year. Most Keogh plan holders who receive income from freelancing and who do not have employees, such as self-employed songwriters, have a money-purchase plan. Where the holder has employees, it is likely that a profit-sharing plan will be used.

Under either type of defined-contribution plan contributions can equal up to 25 percent of earned income, or $30,000, whichever is lower. For this purpose, earned income consists of net earnings from self-employment less the Keogh contribution; this, in effect, limits the contribution to 20 percent of the net earnings from self-employment before the Keogh contribution to a money-purchase plan. Under a money-purchase plan, the full amount of the contribution is deductible for tax purposes from gross income in the computation of adjusted gross income. Under a profit-sharing plan, the deduction from gross income for tax purposes is technically limited to 15 percent of the net earnings from self-employment, less the Keogh contribution, thus restricting the deduction to 13.0435 percent.

The effect of the use of the Keogh plan is virtually the same as if the writer had arranged for the deferment of the payment of the amount contributed to the plan. However, by using the plan, the writer removes the funds from the risk of the publisher's or recording company's business. The writer effectively pays no current tax on the contribution, earns interest on the contribution (no interest is earned when funds are left with the publisher), and pays no tax on the interest until it is withdrawn.

In a situation where income is deferred by contractual arrangements, the contract has to provide in advance how much is to be paid (or deferred) each year. Under the Keogh plan, annual determinations may be made as to how much to "defer" by making the contribution, so long as the limitations are observed. Contracts providing for deferments stipulate the time and amount of payout. Payouts under the Keogh plan are generally not permitted to begin before age 59 without penalty (except in case of total disability), and in any event must begin no later than April 1 of the year when the participant reaches the age of 70 years and 6 months. If not fully withdrawn by that year, the plan must provide for ultimate payout over a period that does not extend beyond the life expectancy of the participant, or the joint lives of the participant and his or her beneficiary, as computed in accordance with Internal Revenue Service regulations. Since, by virtue of having taken the deduction at the time of contribution, the self-employed individual has not paid tax in the earlier year, the entire amount drawn later, including the interest earned, is subject to tax.

A word of caution is required with respect to employees. In all probability, a self-employed composer or recording artist does not have employees, but if he or she does, and then adopts a Keogh plan, the plan usually must provide benefits for all full-time employees whose period of employment extends to 1 year or more and who are at least 21 years old.

Employed workers, as well as self-employed workers, may establish an individual retirement account (IRA), which, as in the case of a Keogh plan, permits the deferral, for income tax purposes, of a certain amount of income and the future earnings, such as interest, on such deferred income. To be eligible, neither the individual nor the spouse can be covered by an employer retirement plan unless the adjusted gross income is under $50,000 if married or under $35,000 if single. Only a partial tax deduction is permitted if the adjusted gross income is between $40,000 and $50,000 if married or between $25,000 and $35,000 if single. Where there is ineligibility for all or partial deductions for IRAs, nondeductible contributions are still allowed.

Under an IRA plan a worker can make deductible contributions of up to $2,000 of earned income annually, which amount might rise to $2,250 if the worker had an unemployed spouse. If earnings were less than $2,000, the contribution can be made for up to the full amount earned. A self-employed person may contribute to both an IRA and a Keogh plan, but after the age of 70 years and 6 months he or she may no longer contribute to the IRA plan.

In the instance where an individual is both employed, being, for instance, a member of a band, and self-employed, operating as a songwriter who receives royalties from ASCAP and a music publisher, that individual may establish and contribute to both an IRA and a Keogh plan. If both the participant and spouse work, each may establish an IRA and contribute up to $2,000 annually; the couple's total IRA annual contribution might thus total $4,000.

Under an IRA, as in the case of a Keogh plan, distributions to the participant may begin at the age of 59 years and 6 months without penalty but need not begin before the age of 70 years and 6 months. If the amount in the plan is not fully withdrawn in that year, the withdrawal must extend over a period not longer than the life expectancy of the participant or the joint lives of the participant and the participant's beneficiary, as computed in accordance with Internal Revenue Service regulations. All amounts withdrawn from IRAs are subject to income tax at the time of withdrawal, with the exception of amounts contributed where no deduction was previously claimed.

Keogh plan distributions are treated in the same manner as IRA distributions for income tax purposes, except that certain favorable tax provisions apply to lump-sum Keogh distributions.

Where an individual is employed, there are other retirement plans that might be considered. One is the simplified employee pension plan (SEP), set up by an employer, which is designed to give employers an easy way to make payments toward their employees' pension plans.

Another retirement plan is the Section 401(k), or deferred-salary plan, established by an employer, which permits employees to make contributions on a pretax basis.

Finally, the Taxpayer Relief Act of 1997 established the Roth IRA for contributions up to $2,000 a year, or $4,000 for a couple, for qualifying taxpayers whose adjusted gross income is within certain limits. This is known as a "backloaded IRA" because the contribution when initially made is not deductible and must use after-tax earnings, although certain of the distributions can be tax-free and all the earnings are tax-deferred. This means that funds can grow tax-deferred and, for example, be withdrawn up to $10,000 tax-free for the purchase of a first home or can be used for individual or family college expenses with taxation when withdrawn at ordinary income rates for the earnings accumulation portion. Otherwise, Roth IRA withdrawals must be deferred until the age of 59 years and 6 months unless a 10 percent penalty is paid.

Tax Benefits Through Business Organization

Tax benefits may be derived from the way in which a business is organized. Such business organization may include being an S corporation, a limited liability company (LLC), or a family-owned business.

An *S corporation* is one whose income and losses are allocable to its stockholders as if they were the stockholders' direct income or loss. For tax purposes, it is as if the corporation were a partnership or a sole proprietorship. Through use of an S corporation, a stockholder can achieve the limited liability afforded by a corporation and also avoid the double taxation of corporate profits and stockholder dividends.

The tax treatment is particularly beneficial in the case of new businesses expected to lose money at their beginning. A shareholder is entitled to take tax losses that may be offset against income from other sources.

An S corporation must have one class of stock with no more than 35 shareholders, and all of its shareholders must agree to the S status. Shareholders who work for the corporation are treated as employees for Social Security tax payments. They do not pay self-employment tax on their salary income or other receipts from the corporation.

There is a distinction between independent contractors and employees for purposes of tax treatment. The status is decided by three simple tests dealing with control, risk of loss, and continuity. If a person has no control over his or her work activities (how, where, when), has no risk of loss or chance for profits, and enjoys stable and continuous employment, then that person is an employee and not an independent contractor.

Limited liability companies are another business organization option now available in many states, including New York and California. They combine many of the features of both limited partnerships and corporations. Unlike a limited partnership, which prohibits a limited partner from actively participating in the business, the LLC allows its members to participate in management without jeopardizing limited liability. LLCs offer flow through taxation of its members much like an S corporation. However, LLCs may also create potential federal and state security law issues.

In the case of producers or musical recording or performance groups, such security issues may arise if there is a change in the relative ownership of the LLC. To prevent these problems, members should establish in their original operating agreement a warning initialed by all members stating that each member's ownership interest can be altered by decisions beyond the member's control. Members should recognize that although they may structure the original ownership to be exempt from public securities laws, if there is a change which triggers application of securities laws, it ensures that members do not violate the law, because of a stated declaration in the first instance that the securities were for the member's own account and not intended for resale.

Many songwriters and some independent publishers operate as a family-owned business. As such, there is a possible estate tax benefit under the Taxpayer Relief Act of 1997. Federal estate taxes normally apply to bequests other than to a surviving spouse at escalating rates. There is a basic exclusion of $650,000 for the year 1999, $675,000 for the years 2000 and 2001, $700,000 for the next two years, with further escalations up to $1 million in the year 2006 and thereafter.

A *family business* can qualify for more favorable treatment. Recognizing that it is undesirable to force a sale of all or part of a family business in order to pay estate taxes, the 1997 Taxpayer Relief Act excludes such businesses from estate tax if the value of the business exceeds 50 percent of the entire estate value (with certain adjustments). A further requirement is that the decedent be a U.S. citizen or legal resident and that the executor of the estate enter into an agreement that the exclusion will be waived if the family heirs to the business do not materially participate for at least 10 years or otherwise dispose of the business. A qualifying family business must have been owned by the decedent or members of the family for at least 5 of the 8 years preceding death and those members must have materially participated in the business operation. It is a further condition that not over 35 percent of the income of the business was in the category of personal holding company income. This determination involves careful analysis of what portion of the income came from, for example, concert income of a popular artist or producer or a composer-songwriter's current income. In some instances, careful management can reduce such percentages by spreading the source of such funds among members of a band, guest artists, etc.

Contractual Formats

Despite the right of the tax authorities to review documentation for the purpose of distinguishing substance from form, it is clear that a taxpayer's right to qualify for certain tax treatment may depend on the contractual format that has been chosen for a particular transaction. For example, if services are rendered to produce a master recording, the proceeds from the services might qualify as earned income; if there is a "lease" of the master recording, the proceeds might be regarded as ordinary income, whereas the proceeds from its "sale" might qualify for capital gains treatment. In each case, qualified attorneys and accountants should be consulted to consider alternative contractual formats.

The corporation approach to lower taxes can be treacherous. Even if the corporation is not classified as a personal holding company, the accumulated income, to the extent that it exceeds $250,000 ($150,000 if it is a service corporation in the field of performing arts) and is not required for the reasonable needs of the business, may be subject to certain surtaxes.

The income of a personal holding company is subject to regular corporate tax rates, and its undistributed income is taxed at 39.6 percent. A *personal holding company* is defined as a corporation a majority of whose stock is held, directly or indirectly, during the last half of the year, by not more than five persons and at least 60 percent of whose gross income is within the definition of personal holding company income. The latter income includes, among other types of receipts, the income from copyright and other royalties.

The extent of the activities needed to exclude personal holding company surtaxes and other techniques for using corporations to reduce taxes should be explored carefully with attorneys and accountants before action is taken.

Royalties as Income

Before an author or composer undertakes any of the aforementioned tax-saving devices, he or she should bear in mind that royalties are taxed on the same basis as ordinary income. Consequently, comparative calculations are advisable to determine whether there is a sufficient tax advantage to warrant the use of one of the tax-saving devices discussed.

Foreign Royalties Subject Only to U.S. Tax

By reciprocal treaties with many countries, American taxpayers are exempt from foreign income tax on royalties earned abroad. For example, the treaty between the United States and the United Kingdom provides for a tax exemption in the country of source of income, and taxation in the country of residence, with respect to royalties from copyrights and like property. This exemption, however, does not apply if the taxpayer has a permanent establishment in the country that is the source of income and the royalties are directly associated with the business operations carried on by the permanent establishment.

Most publishers and record companies are aware of the necessity of filing nonresident tax exemption claims with foreign governments, either directly or through foreign subpublishers or agents. Authors and composers encounter this necessity only when they deal directly with foreign music or record companies, instead of in the customary manner through an American firm. Reciprocal treaties are designed to avoid double taxation and the inconvenience of having to file for refunds of moneys withheld at the source. (Treaties are not uniform; specific reference should be made to the particular treaty when a question arises. Treaties are supplied by the Superintendent of Documents, U.S. Government Printing Office, Washington, DC 20005.) The National Music Publishers Association has maintained a list of foreign countries from which copyright royalties may be paid free of withholding taxes or at reduced withholding taxes. Notable among such countries are Australia, Belgium, Canada, France, Germany, Italy, the Netherlands, and the U.K.

Regarding royalties earned in a foreign country in which the recipient maintains a permanent establishment (so that the tax treaty would not be applicable) or earned in a country with which the United States does not have a tax treaty, it is probable that the source country will impose a tax on the income there derived and that the United States will also tax that income. Some or all of the adverse effects of that double taxation can be ameliorated by the appropriate use of the foreign tax credit in the U.S. tax return.

Tax Installment Agreement

An option available to those people who are unable to pay the tax shown on their tax return is an agreement that allows payment through monthly installments, up to 36 months. Applicants must fill out IRS Form 9465, Installment

Agreement Request, and staple it to the front of their tax return. The IRS is required to respond to the request within 30 days.

Retention of Tax-Related Documents

It is generally recommended that supporting records be retained for possible audit for at least 6 years, despite the fact that the IRS can only assess tax for a particular year for 3 years after a return for the applicable year was filed or due to be filed. However, this period is extended to 6 years if there is a 25 percent or more deficiency in gross income reports, and in the absence of a filing, there is no time limit. For purposes of capital gain or depreciation, the period of retaining basic historic accounting information is necessarily extended to the period for which the basic cost is established.

Audit Procedures

In 1994, the Internal Revenue Service prepared a training manual concerning music business audits. This manual, which is available to the public under the Freedom of Information Act, describes the functions of various participants in the industry, such as record and video producers, managers, performing artists (live performers), publishers, and songwriters, and cautions the IRS auditor in practical terms. For example, it states:

> There is extensive bartering activity in the industry. It occurs in the form of swap-outs (advertising for cars, advertising for tickets, etc.). ...There are many checks and balances in the industry on income reporting, but some activities, such as playing small clubs for the door receipts, love offerings at concerts and churches, and concession sales at small locations, present situations where income may go unreported.

The manual offers instructions for specific industry participants. For *songwriter* it states:

- A review is required of office-in-home expenses where the premises are not exclusively used for business.
- A vacation home or other such place claimed as a required "place to think" is not allowable.
- Travel expenses "in many cases, include personal expenses."
- With regard to related returns, partnerships and corporations may be formed to seek to shift income between entities for beneficial tax treatment, which, although allowable, must be cross-checked to get a true income picture.

For *music publishers,* the manual instructs that:

- Related returns may include separate publishing entities to conform to the requirements of performing rights societies. If the songwriter is a shareholder, issues with regard to royalty advances may warrant examination.

For *live performers,* it notes that:

- "The single most common audit adjustment is disallowance of personal expenses being claimed as business deductions. 'Stars' frequently take the position that since they are in the limelight all the time, virtually everything they do is 'business' and is part of the image-making and maintaining process." (Examples given are home improvements, vacation homes, and boats, as well as failure to distinguish stage clothes from street clothes. The position taken by the IRS is that peripheral business benefits from an activity do not convert personal expenses to business expenses.)
- With regard to the support personnel for a star, two deductions are not allowed, one for the reimbursement of "away-from-home" expenses paid by the featured artist and the other by the support personnel who has already been reimbursed.

For *video and record producers,* the manual says:

- "Determine if the producer has the opportunity for other types of income, such as studio rental, talent scouting, writing, etc. Question the producer about any label deals, pressing and distribution deals, agreements with other producers on joint production arrangements."
- "Watch for reimbursements to producers from record companies for out-of-pocket expenses."
- With regard to "custom sessions," described as vanity deals where a prospective artist pays cash for the studio and production services involved, unreported income should be sought out.
- "Past examinations have shown that some producers will purchase expensive gifts, such as autos, for artists as incentives ... without form 1099 being issued to the recipient."
- The cost of record masters should be amortized unless the 3-year safe-harbor alternative is used. This is defined as allowing depreciation and amortization of costs at 50 percent in the first year and 25 percent in each of the next two years.
- Payment of employment taxes for engineers, musicians, arrangers, backup vocalists, etc., whether freelancers or staff members should be checked. Avoidance of self-employment taxes on producer royalties by placement on Schedule E or on face of 1040 forms should also be checked.
- Related income sources such as songwriting, publishing, and performing should be compared. Some producers use a corporate form for one function and Schedule C for other business activities, and for a general audit all should be reviewed at once.

For *managers,* it asks that the auditor:

- ▸ Make sure that expenses claimed are not refunded by the artist. Some expenses may be capital in nature, requiring safe harbor or amortization and depreciation.
- ▸ Compare the related returns of the manager in other functions, such as music publisher or for merchandising and souvenir sales.

34

Record Clubs and Premiums

Approximately 17 million Americans belong to record clubs. Total club and mail-order sales in 1997 were about $1.5 billion, with close to 80 percent attributable to sales by record clubs. It is estimated that of the total record consumer group, those who rely exclusively on club sources are only 3 percent of the total consumer group and those who buy from club as well as retail outlets constitute 14 percent of all record-buying consumers.

In the field of general record club activity, there are two major record clubs. The first is Columbia House, with 8.5 million members. It is jointly owned by CBS Records (a subsidiary of Sony) and Time Warner (the parent of Warner Bros. Records). The Columbia Record and Tape Club, the CBS Compact Disc Club, and the CBS Classical Club are under the aegis of Columbia House.

The second major record club is BMG Direct Marketing, with 8 million members. BMG, which was formerly the RCA Record Club and is now an affiliate of the German firm Bertelsmann A.G., also operates the BMG Music Service, the BMG Compact Disc Club, and the International Preview Society, which handles classical recordings.

The major record clubs handle the catalogs of various record companies, as well as the basic catalogs of their mother companies. Under the terms of a Federal Trade Commission consent order issued in 1971, Columbia House is prohibited from acting as the exclusive record club for the labels of other record manufacturers. It is now the common practice of both major record clubs to obtain their product from manufacturers on a nonexclusive basis.

Membership Plans

Record clubs offer various purchasing plans to attract prospective members. For example, new members are usually offered a certain number of records free or for a nominal charge, subject to handling costs. Members then must purchase a given number of records at the regular price within a given number of years, such as six selections within 2 years. One recent BMG Web site offer was for 12 free introductory membership CDs with an obligation to buy 1 CD at the regular price within 2 years; if the purchase was made within 1 year, there would be a bonus of three CDs with free delivery.

It should be noted, however, that all CDs, whether free or at club price, are subject to shipping and handling charges. As of 1999, the minimum regular club price was $16.98. Mailing and handling charges were $2.59 for the first CD with a 10-cent reduction for the second and a further 10-cent reduction for all subsequent CDs in any one order.

Both BMG and Columbia House have relied on a negative option under which record club members receive a monthly featured selection unless they have declined such receipt by a specific date. However, Columbia House Record Club has recently established a new, alternative plan that eliminates the negative option of automatic shipment. This plan requires a commitment to buy six selections at regular club prices over a 2-year period and offers the member the right to cancel membership at any time after meeting his or her obligations. Further, no unrequested selections are sent to members.

With the advent of e-mail offers, members now not only have the opportunity to listen to samples of selected items but, in the case of BMG, also have the benefit of chat rooms for discussions among members. Record club members are also given access to CD samplers in order to audition new recordings. Further, Internet access offers both the customary array of informative magazines targeted by music category and Web sites with over 16,000 music selections.

Record clubs aim for buyers 30 years old and over, approximately 10 years older than the median age of record store buyers. According to the Recording Industry Association of America, a large percent of music consumers are older than 25, with the fastest-growing segment over the age of 45. However, record stores still cater to teenage buyers by blaring new releases, scaring off adult buyers. Record clubs allow adult buyers to avoid all the hassles of record stores, malls, and parking lots by purchasing music in the convenience of their own homes. In 1999, Columbia House's two co-owners, Time Warner and Sony, negotiated to each acquire a 37.5 percent stock interest in CDNow in exchange for a long-term agreement allowing Columbia House's members to download single selections and make custom CDs using CDNow's facilities.

Outside-Label Agreements

In their contractual agreements with outside labels, both BMG and Columbia House normally provide that the licensed product will bear the original label and jacket when sold through the club. All record club product, however, bears the club's bar code and is not subject to returns through conventional stores.

Royalties payable by Columbia House to the outside labels are about 9.5 percent of the regular club price (less a charge allocated to the record container), based on 85 percent of the records sold and not returned; the royalty for soundtrack, original-cast, and classical albums is typically about 12 percent. Other clubs may pay a similar royalty. It is common that no royalty is payable by clubs on "bonus" or "free" records distributed to members. However, clubs will sometimes accept a limitation on the number of bonus or free records approved for distribution. Limitations require that free records will not exceed a set percentage of the records sold; the clubs will pay royalties on any bonus CDs that exceed such limitations. In some contracts, such royalties will be at a lower rate than that applicable to regular club sales.

Ordinarily the Columbia House and BMG clubs take master tapes from outside labels on a nonexclusive basis and press records based on the tapes. Advances against royalties to become due to the label are customarily negotiated upon commencement of the term, and the duration of the term is for a limited number of years. The operation is thus similar to that of a foreign licensee of an outside label. The clubs pay, as in the case of foreign licensees, mechanical copyright license fees and payments on sales that become due to the Music Performance Trust Fund and the Special Payments Fund established through the American Federation of Musicians.

Artist Royalties

A fairly standard agreement with American artists provides that the artist receives one-half of his or her standard royalty rate on sales through clubs and that no royalties are payable on bonus or free records. The bonus and free-record clauses tend to match similar provisions in agreements between clubs and record companies.

Reduced artist royalties further serve to attract record clubs operating outside of the United States. It is common for foreign licensees to place American records in clubs on the basis of lower royalties payable to the U.S. licensors, as compared to the royalty rates on traditional sales.

Foreign Record Clubs

Foreign record club and direct marketing activity has been the scene of dramatic growth in recent years. Record clubs now exist in Australia, Austria, Belgium, Canada, Denmark, England, Finland, France, Germany, Japan, the Netherlands, Sweden, and Switzerland. In 1996 club sales in the United Kingdom were 10 percent of total record turnover, compared to 9 percent in 1989 and 12 percent in 1993. Germany's direct-mail market was at 16.5 percent in 1997 and was slightly more in 1994. Prior to its acquisition by Universal, PolyGram formed a direct-marketing division, consolidating its Dial Record Club (France), its 2-million-member Britannia Music (United Kingdom), and its Italian, Dutch, and German companies, giving it a base membership of well over 3 million members.

Mechanical License Fees

Throughout their history of operations in the United States, the major record clubs have relied on an industry-accepted practice of reduced mechanical license royalty rates. The assumed rate (payable quarterly) was placed at 75 percent of the standard rate paid by the originating record label. In 1990, music publishers unsuccessfully challenged this practice, claiming that club sales in the absence of written confirmation of such reduced rate constituted an infringement. The court dismissed the action on the grounds that acceptance and negotiation of royalty payments at the assumed rate, without restrictive endorsement or other effective notice of protest, ratified an implied license for use of copyrighted songs and created an implied license for future periods. (The case in question, *Wixen Music Publishing, Inc. et al. v. CBS Records dba Columbia House Records,* is unpublished.) Furthermore, even if a rare publisher were to object, any co-owner of the song in question could be the source of a binding, nonexclusive license if the co-owner did not join in a rejection of such rate.

The Harry Fox Agency, which represents many publishers, has balked at waiving royalties on free or bonus records and normally collects such royalties from record clubs. The Harry Fox Agency will accept the 75 percent rate provided that it does not reduce the royalty below 75 percent of the statutory compulsory mechanical license rate, regardless of lesser negotiated licenses with originating labels. A 1999 dispute arose as to whether this 75 percent rate should continue as an industrywide custom without formal regulation beyond merely incorporating the issuing label's terms of license minus 25 percent. The Harry Fox Agency claims that in a digital age, auditing and accounting procedures are more efficiently handled with specific licensees, whereas the clubs counter that a changeover is costly and unnecessary in the face of established cooperation between accounting staffs.

Premiums

A premium offer may arise when a business such as a supermarket or a tire company sells records at an unusually low price in order to encourage patronage for its regular products. This is a promotional plan that frequently involves a guarantee to the record company of a substantial number of sales.

Since the price paid to the record company is low, it must keep its costs at a reduced level. The margin of profit on each record is small, but a premium transaction entails large volume and low distribution expenses. In connection with a premium offer, the record company will seek low mechanical license rates from the music publishers and will have to evaluate the royalty rates that must be paid to the performing artists. Some agreements with artists provide for no royalties in the case of premium sales; others may establish reduced royalty rates. Where the artist agreement does not provide for low royalty rates, the record company may have to negotiate with the artist, stressing the promotional exposure and publicity value as well as the volume of sales, which may result in sizable royalty payments even at a lower royalty rate.

35

Music Videos

The creation, distribution, and broadcast of a music video is now considered an essential aspect of the promotion of a new record. The release of most major popular records is accompanied by a music video, usually a 3- to 5-minute visualization of a song featuring visual and audio performances by the artist who recorded it. Videos aired on MTV, the 24-hour cable music channel, or its sister channel, VH-1, as well as on other cable and regular TV music channels, clearly produce increased CD and cassette sales. One study shows that videos played in music retail stores are even more influential marketing tools than MTV.

Although music videos were initially seen primarily as promotional tools rather than as forms of commercial entertainment, the record company policy of granting free licenses to networks and programs is no longer necessarily the case. In recent years, for instance, MTV has had to negotiate multimillion-dollar payments with a number of major record companies for exclusive rights to selected video clips for periods ranging from 1 week to 30 days.

MTV and VH-1, both owned by Viacom's MTV Networks, continue to be the dominant video programmers. MTV, the first 24-hour music channel, now reaches between 65 to 73 million homes. In an attempt to maintain the interest of its target audience of 12- to 34-year-olds, executives have chosen to cut back on the number of nonmusic programs that had begun to dominate MTV's format. The 16-year-old channel has recently added such shows as *The Cut, BIOrhythm,* and *Fanatic,* all of which focus on music and recording artists. These recent changes have seen a substantial increase in ratings and profit for the MTV Networks.

VH-1 began as the stepchild of MTV when it began airing in 1985 in an effort by MTV to ward off competition. The programming began with little or no direction and a sparse audience. But since 1994 format changes similar to those of its parent company have made VH-1 a viable alternative to MTV, reaching over 68 million homes by the end of 1999. VH-1 has focused on the 18- to 49-year-old audience, a slightly older demographic than MTV targets.

With a mix of adult-oriented video rotations and shows such as *Pop-Up-Video* and *Behind the Music,* VH-1 has become the preferred channel for this coveted consumer group.

However, a number of channels serving specialized markets, both musically and geographically, now provide viable options to both the consumer and the industry. CMT (Country Music Television) and BET (Black Entertainment Television) focus on specific musical genres, while The Box, the only all-request video channel, allows the viewer to choose from up to 200 current videos of all genres. Such competitive programming has forced MTV Networks to adapt format and content in order to maintain its majority audience share.

However, the dominant strength of the two MTV services was such that the Justice Department commenced an investigation in late 1999 of possible antitrust violations in their dealings with music companies. In connection with this investigation, an MTV executive stated, "We took exclusive rights to only 4 of the more than 1,000 videos used this year." (See also Chapter 38, "Trade Practice Regulations.")

Today, music videos are also a part of a growing commercial market. The exploitation of music videos has resulted in revenues derived from exhibition on network, cable, and local television, viewings in commercial clubs, plays on video jukeboxes, and the sale of videocassettes and videodiscs for home use. All major record companies now deliver long-form music videos (such as concert films) and short-form music video compilations of their artists directly to music retailers and video distributors for home sale.

New Video Technology

The technology for storing and replaying video images continues to achieve great advances. Nonetheless, some familiar problems still exist. When consumer video was first introduced, consumers were faced with the dilemma of investing in one or another of two incompatible systems, Betamax or VHS. Similarly, software producers were required to invest in one or both of these technologies, resulting in general market resistance and delay. Today, new competitive clashes exist, as between the laser disc (LD) and digital versatile disc (DVD). Sales for the laser disc, a 12-inch video disc with a 120-minute capacity (60 minutes per side) are steadily declining as the market for DVD expands. Only one company, Pioneer, offers a dual DVD/LD player that continues to be popular on the market. However, trends clearly suggest that the laser disc will soon be outdated; major retail chains such as Tower and Virgin favor DVD and have ceased offering laser discs.

Introduced on the market in 1997, DVD has quickly become a format of choice for home video viewers. One year after their release into the market-place, nearly 600,000 DVD players had been sold. When compared to compact disc players, which sold only 320,000 after one year, and VCRs, which sold 515,000 in the same time span, the future for DVD seems bright.

Why has this format enjoyed such instant popularity among consumers? Much like the superior status of CDs over LPs, DVD promises to raise audiovisuals to a higher level with increased storage capacity and clearer sound and picture. The DVD, a 5 1/2-inch disc (the size of a standard CD), holds a capacity of 128 minutes of video capacity. In addition, the majority of DVD releases feature surround-sound capabilities.

The superior sound quality is especially appealing for music video buyers. The recent release *Tina Turner: Live in Amsterdam* features state-of-the-art digital surround sound (DTS) and requires a specific DVD player with DTS capability. Another 1999 DVD release, Mickey Hart's *Planet Drum*, featuring such world-renowned percussionists as Babatunde Olatunji, can be heard in stereo, Dolby, or DTS and includes interviews and other special features. Similar DVD projects are in development.

Also in development are DVD-ROM and DVD audio. The former, already available on the market, holds nearly seven times the capacity of a CD-ROM. The latter is in development and expected to be available to consumers in the near future. DVD audio releases will be recorded specifically for six-channel surround-sound systems, anticipating a shift in audio technology among consumers and within the recording industry.

Video Licensing

New video technology presents new licensing opportunities and challenges, requiring a combination of past licensing practices. For instance, conventional CDs use mechanical reproduction licensing, which in the United States is on a statutory base not exceeding 7.55 cents per song per unit (or 1.45 cents per minute or fraction thereof). However, visual materials require fully negotiated synchronization licenses; where lyrics or music are presented on screen in place of printed materials, a special form of synchronization license is required.

In addition, a "fixing fee" is evolving for video use; this is a fixed, nonre-coupable initial payment, which is often supplemented by an advance against royalties. The royalty structure itself can sometimes be analogized to "double statutory," which is a shorthand device used for requesting just over 14 cents, or simply negotiated fresh from a standpoint of between 8 cents and 15 cents per song per unit.

Meanwhile, for major-budget feature films, video uses are usually negoti-ated at significant fixed sums of as much as $7,500 to $12,500 worldwide. Whether this buyout includes foreign sales, for which different collection procedures apply, has not yet been tested. A rare alternative is a rollover advance in which the fixed sum constitutes an advance for the first 50,000 or other stated number of units upon either manufacture or sale, as negotiable, with additional advances for each successive plateau.

Advances in technology have led to "future-technology clauses" because some firms are concerned about broad licenses for all potential new technology and refuse to license or issue short-term licenses without options other than to negotiate in good faith consistent with then-existing industry standards to secure their rights as advanced technology becomes available. These clauses, however, cannot be limited to any medium or they will be strictly limited to the designated medium. For example, in *Subfilms, Ltd. v. MGM/UA Home Video, Inc.*, 988 F.2d 122 (9th Cir. 1993), the court held that a future-technology clause limited to theatrical and television rights did not encompass the right to distribute in videocassettes.

Audiovisual Rights

Music videos directly involve contractual rights and obligations among record companies, artists, producers, music publishers, and others. Perhaps to a lesser extent, other software programming may be concerned with all or some of the same entities, persons, or factors as well. Insofar as music videos and other software programming are audiovisual motion picture productions, the legal and contractual principles and standards involved in such technology are similar to those discussed in Chapter 23, "Music for Motion Pictures," and in Chapter 24, "Licensing Recordings for Motion Pictures."

Record manufacturers engaged in video programming, whether in the form of music videos or other software, have enlarged the scope of their operations to include filmmaking and its attendant problems. The increasing length of record company–artist contracts bears witness to this phenomenon, as record companies, artists, and producers attempt to cover contractually the multiplying complexities of the record and film business.

The music video's success in promotional and commercial markets has impelled record companies to strive vigorously to obtain video rights from artists. These rights have become key issues in contractual negotiations. In support of their claims to video rights, record companies contend that audiovisual products offer strong competition to traditional audio sound carriers—records, tapes, and CDs—for the future consumer home market.

For years record companies included language in their artist contracts permitting them to use recordings in audiovisual form and restricting artists from appearing in audiovisual media for other companies. One agreement provided that the artist's recording might be used exclusively "in any medium and by any means whatsoever, including but not limited to audiovisual records, motion pictures, television or any medium or devices now or hereafter known, and to utilize photographs, drawings, and pictorial animation in connection therewith." Another agreement defined a record or phonograph record as a "film, video tape, or similar device which embodies the artist's audio performance with a visual rendition of the artist's performance, i.e., a sight and sound device."

Today, recording agreements contain separate definitions for videos and their uses. One form defines video recordings to include "videocassettes, videodiscs, and new media video recordings that enable a program to be perceived visually ... when used in combination or as a part of a piece of electronic, mechanical or other apparatus." The same agreement also defines the terms videocassette, videodisc, and home video use.

While music videos are primarily 3- to 5-minute clips, like those used by MTV, the typical definitions of records or phonograph records or video recordings contain no time or length limitations. As defined, an artist would be disqualified from performing for third persons in films or videotapes of live concerts, full-length feature films or documentaries, or film television programs in which an artist visually performs only a single song. For example, a record company could require consent for an artist's participation in the Woodstock concert film or in a feature-length film such as *Detroit Rock City*. The record company could refuse consent or, theoretically, might even condition approval on its being granted the right to distribute the film theatrically, on television, and in videocassettes for home use. This can be intolerable to an artist who seeks and treasures film appearances.

Artists may therefore try to limit the definition of a record or video recording to audiovisual productions of a short duration, to audiovisual productions of one or two songs, or to copies to be marketed to the public for home use only. A common issue is whether there can be any commercial exploitation of audiovisual products without the express consent of the artist. While artists may agree to promotional uses of music videos, they may refuse to allow commercial exploitation without their prior written approval. Some companies may accept this restriction, but others will resist strongly. A new artist may find it very difficult to obtain the right to approve commercial uses of music videos.

Some record companies have acquiesced to limiting their rights to audiovisual performances of sound recordings produced under the recording artist agreement. Even in these cases, though, the record company would probably retain exclusive control over the video exploitation rights for promotional purposes and for home video sales.

Although it is common for a record company to have the exclusive right to make music videos for their artists, more often than not the record company will not be obligated to finance and produce such videos. This is similar to the record company's lack of specific obligations to carry out and finance promotional activities in support of phonograph records. However, unlike most new artists, established artists do obtain commitments from record companies to produce music videos, typically on a per-record basis. Because of the substantial costs of producing a music video, a record company will generally agree to create one for a new or less-established artist only after a record appears to be a commercial success. Some independent record companies are even starting to direct funds that were formerly devoted to independent promotion into video production.

Artists ordinarily have no rights to produce and finance a music video independently in the absence of the record company's consent, despite the record company's lack of any obligation to grant such approval or to produce a music video itself. But artists may attempt to protect themselves by reserving video rights, subject to granting the record company a right of first refusal, for a limited period of time, to produce and exploit the music video. Under the right of first refusal, the record company would have the prerogative of matching offers of third parties. The record company might also be granted the right of first negotiation, which would entitle it to be approached first and negotiated with before any third parties.

It is not uncommon for the artist and record company to agree that neither party shall have the exclusive right to produce and exploit a music video, prohibiting them from making a music video without mutual approval. This serves to delay their negotiations for control of music video rights until a future time when it may be easier to assess the appropriateness of any particular course of action.

The record company ordinarily acquires the entire ownership interest in the videotapes and other physical materials, as well as the copyright in the audiovisual work itself, including the visual images and the accompanying sounds. A motion picture or other audiovisual work such as a music video is generally deemed eligible for the © copyright notice. It is not qualified for the ℗ copyright notice applicable to sound recordings.

In the case of most artists, the agreement between a record company and the artist is an employment contract. The copyright in the audiovisual work, at least to the extent of an artist's contributions, thus belongs to the record company as a work for hire under the 1976 Copyright Act. The act grants work-for-hire status to one "specially ordered or commissioned for use ... as a part of a motion picture or other audiovisual work," where the parties have expressly agreed in writing "that the work shall be considered a work made for hire." In the case of a work for hire, the record company is the "author" for copyright purposes, as well as the owner of the video. The 1976 Copyright Act provides that for works made for hire the copyright will endure for a term of 75 years from the year of its first publication, or a term of 100 years from the year of its creation, whichever expires first. The record company, as "author," could not have its rights terminated by others under the termination provisions of the act. In any event there would be protection against termination under such provisions accorded to a music video as a derivative work. (See Chapter 11.)

Whether or not a record company owns the audiovisual work, as a work for hire or otherwise, a record company will demand that the artist grant it all exploitation rights in a music video. This will include not only promotional uses and home video sales but also licensing to third parties for broadcast or exhibition over free, pay, or cable television and in nightclubs.

While the main emphasis of record labels is on promoting their product, the major labels are increasingly requesting fees for the broadcast of their music videos on television and for their showings in nightclubs. For television usage, fees usually range up to $100, with some instances of larger payments for exclusive broadcast rights for a certain period of time. Some major labels have entered into license agreements with music video library agencies, such as Rockamerica. These agencies license music videos to nightclubs and may also license to colleges, restaurants, and retail stores. Typically, license fees paid by nightclubs range from about $3 to $9 per video clip per month.

Production Costs and Their Recoupment

Under most artist agreements, a record company advances production costs of music videos produced under the contracts. These costs may range anywhere from $25,000 to over $1 million, with the amounts usually below $100,000. Only artists who guarantee multiplatinum success will warrant costs near or exceeding the $1 million mark; rapper-actor Will Smith released the most expensive video to date, with production costs nearing $2 million.

Whether the music video is considered a promotional or a commercial vehicle largely influences the method for recoupment of production costs by the record company. Unlike most other record promotion expenses, which are borne entirely by the record company, the companies commonly insist on a form of recoupment that involves the artist. Under most label contracts, the record company becomes entitled to recoup a certain percentage of the video production costs out of the artist's record royalties, or out of the artist's share of the video income, or both. In most cases income derived by record companies from the exploitation of music videos is still insignificant in today's market. Accordingly, record companies look to the artist's record royalties for the recoupment of from 50 to 75 percent, and sometimes more, of the video production costs. At times the percentages are reduced if the underlying album achieves a high plateau of sales.

Typically, video production costs are also recoupable from the artist's share of net video receipts from the commercial exploitation of the music video. The usual artist participation is 50 percent of such net video receipts. These net receipts are defined as the gross receipts from commercial exploitation, less video production costs, distribution fees and expenses, and payments to third parties. In lieu of payment to the artist of a portion of the net video receipts, a less common approach is to pay a royalty to the artist on units of videocassettes and videodiscs sold. This royalty is from 10 to 25 percent of the wholesale selling price.

Under recoupment from the combination of record royalties and the artist's share of net video receipts or video royalties, the artist may bear at least 75 percent, and as much as 100 percent, of the video costs. However, an established artist may be successful in breaking the recoupment mold described above, causing the creation of separate royalty accounts for videos and for phonograph records, with no earnings from one source being used to recoup the production costs attendant on the other source. At least one major record company has been amenable to providing for such separate royalty accounts for most of its artists, whether new or established. There is as yet no indication of how royalties and recoupments will be handled in regard to CD videos, a hybrid format that contains several sound recordings and one or more short-form video.

One creative way employed by popular artists to subsidize the production costs of music videos has been corporate sponsorship. This may include the subsidization of the artist's music videos in exchange for featuring the product subtly in the video itself (e.g., the sponsor's beer bottle on the star's keyboard), with the cooperation and participation of the record company.

Musical Composition Licenses

Ownership interests in musical compositions contained in a music video are generally held by the music publisher of those compositions. In many cases the music publisher is the publishing affiliate of the record company. Among the essential rights for a music video controlled by the publisher or other copyright proprietor are the right to couple the music in timed relation to the visual images (often called the *synchronization right*), the right to publicly perform the compositions as a part of the video, the right to make copies of the compositions as included in the video, and the right to distribute to the public copies of the compositions as integrated into the music video.

There are also compositions written, owned, or controlled by the recording artist and embodied in music videos (known as *controlled compositions*). (See Chapter 2.) In this instance, record companies will demand the issuance of free synchronization licenses as well as free licenses for the other essential rights referred to above.

Publishers and artists ordinarily agree on the promotional uses of music videos because they stand to benefit from the performance royalties resulting from the exhibition of the music video as well as from the added exposure the video provides for the song. When music videos are shown, provisions for payment will vary. In justification of free licenses, the record company may contend that the songwriting artist does not lose a fee entirely since license fees are deductible in calculating the artist's share of net video receipts, and the artist's share is thereby increased if there is no deduction of license fees. Some record companies will provide for a fee, royalty, or other payment for the use of a controlled composition. This fixing fee may initially be set forth in the contract or may be deferred until industry standards have further evolved. At issue is the form of payment: Should there be a flat one-time fee, a per-copy remuneration, or a combination of both? Record companies usually choose to waive such fees for promotional videos.

Where compositions are not controlled, there are differing approaches to their licensing by the copyright proprietors or their representatives. Independent publishers may be willing to give free synchronization and other licenses for strictly promotional usages, although there is no uniformity. With regard to commercial use, compensation is a certain requirement. While record companies favor a complete flat-fee buyout of rights, many publishers demand a flat fee plus per-copy payment.

Trade Paper Coverage of Music Videos

In addition to *Billboard*, with its regular coverage of music videos, there are specialized publications that focus on the video field. *CVC Report: The Music Video Programming Guide,* issued twice monthly except in January and August, focuses on chart action and station play lists. Its charts are based on more than 100 reporting outlets and are presented as a general Top 50 list combining all music formats, and a Top 20 list for each specific genre of pop, R&B/rap, rock/alternative, and "club land" videos. *CVC* backs up the charts with individual play lists of TV and cable stations along with valuable personnel identification, such as program managers, producers, and music coordinators. In addition, its "Contact Update" column furnishes addresses, telephone and fax numbers, and suggested contact times for promotional reviews of new music videos as well as previews of videos in production.

The Urban Network, an industry magazine that focuses on R&B, hip-hop, rap, and gospel features an "Urban Video" column and Top 30 list. The list is based on national video stations and programs geared specifically to urban music fans. In addition to video charts and reviews, *The Urban Network* provides extensive information for radio programmers, industry news and events, and record sales reports.

36

Demonstration Records

The demonstration record, or demo, is the key means of showcasing a new song or artist. A songwriter may play a demo for a record company or music publisher to generate interest in a recording contract or in the possibility of publishing a tune; a publisher may use a demo to convince a record company's artist and repertoire personnel to record a song. In addition, demos are often presented directly to recording artists and producers who are seeking new material. And finally, demos bypass the problem of working with individuals who are unable to read music by presenting the product involved in a more easily accessible form.

While a songwriter or singer may produce a rough home-recorded demo, the tendency is to favor more elaborate demos recorded in studios. A publisher is likely to want to hear studio-produced demos recorded under the supervision of the publisher's professional manager or, on occasion, supervised for the publisher by the writer. Professionally executed demos usually use written arrangements, rather than impromptu or "head" arrangements, as well as a meticulous choice of musicians and instrumentation.

Although economy is an important factor in the preparation of a demo, quality is significant as well. The better the quality, the easier it may be to place an artist, group, or song. Contemporary technology has tended to make the completion of the home-recorded demo recordings of yesteryear more economical. It has also enhanced the possibility of achieving such quality that the demo may be acquired by a record company as a master recording for the production of phonograph records and tapes. (For a further discussion of this issue, see "Subsidized Demos," page 402, as well as Chapter 4, "Independent Record Producers.")

The Costs of Making a Demo

Smaller studios specializing in the production of demos often charge from $30 to $35 per hour for their facilities, which include a skilled studio engineer. The original recording is made on conventional or digital audio tape (DAT), from which cassette or CD demos are produced. There is likely to be a basic tape charge of about $30 for each 30 minutes of recording time. For the duplication of a cassette copy, the charge by a studio is around $6 for a single song, $7 for a cassette containing two songs, and $10 for a cassette with four songs. Studios used for making demos have singers and musicians on call for such work at rates averaging $50 to $75 dollars per song for each individual. The making of demos is in the nature of bread-and-butter work, and there are fine singers and musicians who are available for demo sessions when they are not otherwise employed. Some of the vocalists and musicians are under exclusive recording contracts with record companies, but their contracts are not usually construed as prohibiting performance on demos.

An economical alternative is "direct to DAT." This involves a one-time recording to DAT, where mix is achieved in the process, and thus it is not possible to make any changes or to equalize sound after selections are down on tape. The cost may be as low as $50 per hour where, of course, no additional funds are required for mix. Raw digital audio tapes are more expensive than conventional tapes (around $20).

An alternative to renting time in an expensive studio is home recording. To record a high-quality, three-song demo in an old analog studio might range between $5,000 and $10,000 in rental fees, whereas today artists can *purchase* comparable digital equipment for less. The number of home studios in the United States has dramatically increased in recent years. Companies such as Tascam, with the DA-98, and Alesis, with the A-DAT (two competing brands of DAT), have set the standards for the industry with their 8-track digital home studios. A digital home studio gives the artist greater flexibility in recording without the time pressures of hourly recording studio rates.

Important components of contemporary music technology are drum machines and synthesizers. Drum machines, which feature superb sound clarity, have commonly replaced live drummers for demo purposes, except perhaps for heavy metal, "roots" rock and roll, and acoustic music. The availability of music synthesizers and MIDI (musical instrument digital interface) computer technology has permitted even economically produced demos to sound sophisticated and complex. Using the great flexibility of synthesizers, many musicians with good musical ideas are able to construct elaborate arrangements. The resultant product can sound as if it was recorded at a multi-track studio session lasting many hours. Synthesizers and MIDI equipment are readily available and may be rented from studios or obtained through the collaboration of cowriters or friends. However, the technical sophistication of each machine and the user charges can vary greatly.

Recording studios were once rated by the number of tracks available and the width of the tape used. Tape width ranged from 1/2-inch to 2-inch tape and the number of tracks from 4 to 48. The greater the number of tracks and width of the tape, the higher the quality and the greater the cost of recording time. However, because digital reproduction is so clear, an 8-track digital recorder is equal to or better than a studio using a 24-track analog tape recorder, and a fraction of the cost. The reasonable cost of digital products has given many artists who would not normally have access to such high-priced equipment the opportunity to purchase their own equipment. The digital storage and reproduction of music has enhanced the artist's ability to record, through clearer, cheaper, and more accessible innovations. With the advent of digital recording technologies, old ideas of tape recording have disappeared nearly as fast as vinyl records.

The costs of a final demo vary considerably, depending on a number of factors: the number of musicians involved, whether the arrangements are impromptu or prepared, whether a home studio or a professional studio is used, and so on. For a better-quality demo made at a studio, the cost could be as low as several hundred dollars for a song that includes four or five musicians and a professional singer. Expenses can range as high as $1,000 per song for a more luxurious demo.

Payment to musicians and vocalists for demos is customarily at a lower rate than the regular union scale for commercial recordings, and the AFM differentiated between a demo session and a commercial session. However, the union requires that the full differential be paid if a demo is used as a final master for release by a record company. Vocalists on demo dates are subject to AFTRA regulation, which relies on the local chapter to decide on demo scale and whether subsequent use as a commercial record requires only the difference or a full commercial scale.

A demo may have sufficient quality to be released by a record company as a finished record, and many publishers that invest in better demos are hopeful that they will achieve such a quality. In that instance, the exclusive recording commitments of performers on the demo may bar its use as a master recording for a released record.

The Assumption of Demo Expenses

If a music publisher makes or authorizes the making of an ordinary, inexpensive demo, the publisher usually assumes the entire cost. Sometimes the cost of making a demo is paid for by the songwriter prior to placing his or her song with a publisher; and as a condition of the assignment of the copyright by the songwriter to the publisher, the latter is required to repay the cost. In either instance, the monies paid by the publisher for demos are treated as publisher expenses, as in the case of advertising or promoting a recording. Some publishers require songwriters to agree that anywhere from half to all of the cost of making a demo shall be considered an advance against writer royalties, although only partial recoupment by the publisher is common. If agreed to by the writer, it is in his or her interest to limit the recoupment of the cost to royalties on the song in the demo, rather than allowing the cost to be charged generally against the writer's royalties from all songs placed with the publisher.

Writers will contend that the cost of making a demo is in the nature of promotional expenses, since it is an essential first step in promoting a song, and that no promotional expenses should be charged to the writer. On the other hand, publishers may point out that the writer's performance fees are untouched and may argue that the recoupment of only one-half or more of the cost of making a demo from mechanical royalties is fair and equitable.

Subsidized Demos

A record company, music publisher, or producer can become sufficiently attracted by a rough demo to be willing to finance a better-quality, more expensive recording. As a result, the company or producer may enter into an exclusive demonstration recording artist agreement, which provides for limited funding for the express purpose of financing a quality demo. The record company, publisher, or producer may believe in the potential of the song or the artist enough to underwrite the expense of that recording but be unwilling to extend such financing without a written agreement granting specific rights.

The subsidizing party may request the right of first refusal to acquire the subsidized demo, including the song and the artist. It will then have a certain period of time after the completion of the demo to sign the artist or songwriter on the basis of terms already negotiated or to be negotiated in good faith during the first-refusal period. No other entity will be able to negotiate for the product until the first-refusal period has expired. The subsidizing party may also request a right of last refusal, which gives it a further option, for a period stated, to match any offer obtained from another record company. In defense against such impediment to free negotiations, it would be desirable if, prior to submission to any third party, the artist be given the right to purchase the demo at full cost and be released from such other obligation of last refusal.

The subsidizing party may also require that the demo cost be recouped from the first proceeds of a deal made with the completed subsidized demo, whether the deal is with a record company (including possibly the subsidizing party) or otherwise. The recoupment may be drawn from any advances or royalties earned by the music or artist, in the form of music publisher, producer, songwriter, or recording artist receipts. The subsidizing party, as part of the negotiations, may seek the right to participate in producer, writer, publisher, and artist earnings over and above recoupment.

A demo subsidy deal should be prepared in writing with clearly defined terms. (See accompanying CD-ROM for a sample "Demo Shopping Agreement.") It should include such items as a budget detailing all authorized expenditures for studio, musicians, and equipment. Many subsidized demos involve previously approved recording budgets of as much as $15,000 covering a basic two or three selections. The right of restricted ownership of the sound recording copyright in the demo should be expressed in the document, as should the description of the restriction (usually not for any unauthorized use other than for audition). Rights of first and last refusal as well as rights of recoupment should be expressed as well, including how long a demo will be "shopped" and whether the subsidizing party has a further right to recoup its investment if a later deal is made with a third party involving the subsidized demo.

A cautious investor will insist on the submission of invoices before each installment is paid, whereas a sophisticated demo producer may insist on a demo fund with retention of any saved amounts as a producer or artist fee for the demo itself. All participants in the demo session should be required to sign their consents to allow the conversion of the demo to a record master that can be commercially released, subject only to appropriate union scale, pension, and welfare payments; however, most demo deals tend to disregard or neglect such consents until the actual conversion is made.

Occasionally a record studio will subsidize the production of a demo by providing studio time and facilities. It will expect recoupment of its investment and possible participation in the earnings of the producer, writer, publisher, and artist involved, as will other subsidizing parties.

A demonstration recording agreement gives the artist an opportunity to submit a quality demo for maximum showcasing of talent and also gives the record company a chance to hear a product under conditions similar to what would be delivered under a full-budget deal. The disadvantage to the artist is restricted bargaining power, but the advantage often outweighs this inasmuch as the artist is guaranteed an interested audition from the financing party that has put money into the project and is obviously interested in further review.

The Submission of Demos

Aspiring recording artists often face the dilemma of how to get their demo records considered by A&R people. The simple answer is to find a manager or producer who is respected in the industry to make the submission for them. This is easier said than done because it is often like putting the cart before the horse: managers and producers with a track record of success are usually available only after the artist has surmounted substantial initial hurdles. One effective way for artists to distribute their demos to these often-elusive industry professionals is to showcase themselves at one of the many annual trade shows. (See Chapter 40.) In addition to offering the artist the opportunity to perform live for industry personnel, the trade shows are an excellent place for artists to hand out demos to any interested individuals. Even artists who do not earn a showcase slot can benefit from attending these conferences. Often the record companies have booths where A&R staff will listen to demos on the spot and offer comments and criticisms.

Because of the difficulty that artists experience in reaching A&R, a new breed of music industry representative has emerged—the shopper. These individuals are often attorneys willing to make the submission on a personal presentation basis or producers seeking to make an early tie-in with potential talent for a combined package. (See Chapter 32, "Agents and Managers.")

On rare occasions, the artist or his or her sponsor may agree to pay both costs and a flat fee or hourly rate for services rendered. Sometimes an attorney will get a contractual understanding that his or her legal services will also be used in the event that a contract results. More often, a shopper's contract, whether with an attorney or another party, is a contingent-fee percentage deal. The applicable percentage can vary from 10 to 20 percent; the higher rate is justified as replacing what a personal manager would have received for the same services. The base on which this negotiated percentage is applied varies from:

- Any and all advances and earned royalties exceeding such advances for the full contract life and for so long as royalties are paid
- Any and all initial recording costs and net cash advances for the first album
- Only the initial net cash advance without reference to the recording costs paid by the label but not retained by the artist
- A combination of any of the above together with "best efforts" to use the shopper as producer or as executive producer of all songs recorded on first album or first two albums
- A combination of the above but with escalated percentages based on the amount of initial or otherwise qualifying advance payment, such as 10 percent on an amount of $10,000 or less, 15 percent on $15,000 or more, and 2 percent for amounts of $25,000 or more
- If the shopper is an attorney, agreement to engage the attorney's services for further legal services in negotiation of contract

There is also a major issue to be settled as to the length of time the exclusive shopper's status applies. A nonexclusive shopper's deal is less desirable since possible disputes may result as to who obtained the deal. Most term contracts further provide that for a reasonable period, such as 6 months after expiration of the allowed period, any resulting contract with a label that had entered into negotiations during the allowed term shall be considered still under the contract. A fair provision is to give up to a 90-day extension at the normal end of term if negotiations are then in progress with a qualifying label and full details of such party and offer are disclosed.

In any instance, the parties should be alert to a court ruling that a shopper's deal is possibly an illegal employment agency relationship, due to the lack of an employment agency license. In the 1991 case of *PPX Enterprises v. A Tribe Called Quest,* discussed in Chapter 32, a New York court held that shopper's services should be stated in terms similar to that of a personal manager who advises, guides, and consults rather than seeks employment. Whether this is realistic and can be upheld in a contested proceeding is in doubt. However, nearly every professional management contract has a provision that states (usually in bold type) that the artist confirms that he or she fully understands that the manager is not an employment agency and has not represented that he will seek employment opportunities for the artist.

When referring to a "record deal" as a qualification for the shopper's fee, caution should be exercised to define what qualifies: one of the five major labels (Universal, WEA, EMI, BMG, Sony); any independent label distributed by one of the five major labels; an independent label with other national distribution; an independent label with regional distribution; any label capable of undertaking a "commercial release"; or any label that will finance two or more record sides. In considering the above, the artist should realize that when it comes to distribution, not all record deals are created equal.

Artists should keep in mind that a shopper is often the only way to directly submit a demo to a major label. According to *Arista Records Submission Guidelines,* unsolicited materials are not accepted directly from artist-writers. In order to submit unsolicited material the artist-writer must be represented by a lawyer, manager, or music publisher. The demo must not be more than four songs in length and must be accompanied by a letter to a specific A&R person. It is critical that the demo be submitted to the proper A&R person for the particular style of music.

The Independent Demo

In today's market, making an independent demo of master quality is still done. If the goal is to make a demo master that is a salable product for use in retail stores, it pays to get a bar code. Distributors and retailers do not want to carry a product that cannot be processed through bar code procedure for inventory and other purposes. Bar code numbers are assigned through the Uniform Code Council, which can be reached at 800-543-8137 or 937-435-3870. A processing fee is required that is based on annual sales. If the company's annual sales are under $2 million, the fee is $500.

In addition, a record release number is necessary. It can be based on any letters or numbers and gets printed on inserts, inscribed on stampers, marked for identification on master tapes, and is often used in computer entries of inventory where bar codes do not operate. An example of such a release number picked at random would be MWK-0005.

Pressing and packaging services are often advertised in *Billboard* and other trade journals. An example of a leading supplier of such services is Disc Makers, which claims to be "America's Number 1 Manufacturer for the Independent Music Industry." Disc Makers can be reached at 800-468-9353 or 212-645-0312 and will supply a free package of valuable information materials, including a list of names and addresses of available distributors, suggestions for independent music publicity, and a useful *Guide to Master Tape Preparation.* In addition, they will send their own illustrated catalog of available services and packages for production of CDs and cassettes.

37

Payola

As commonly used in the music industry, *payola* is the unauthorized payment of money, services, or other valuable considerations to broadcasting station personnel (usually disc jockeys, record librarians, or program directors) in return for their broadcast use of a particular record or song. Under the federal Communications Act of 1934, as amended, since 1960 payola has been a federal crime carrying a sentence of up to $10,000 in fines, or imprisonment of up to 1 year, or both. It is not an offense, however, if the payment is disclosed to the station as well as to the independent or other program producer or person for whom the program is produced or supplied.

Where the station licensee has knowledge of the payment, it must inform the public by means of an announcement on the program involved. The station cannot willingly remain in ignorance of such payment while its employees supplement their income by payola. Section 317 of the Communications Act of 1934 provides that radio executives must exercise "reasonable diligence" in supervising their employees.

The Incentive to Engage in Payola

The obvious incentive for engaging in payola is to promote the sale of records and the performance and other use of a song by creating the public illusion of its spontaneous and genuine promotion. Payola is a crutch on which a promotion man with a second-rate product or insufficient contacts or ability may be tempted to lean. Unfortunately, even meritorious material can fall prey to this practice when, in the absence of payola, a record may be bottled up and kept from the public ear by a bribe-taking disc jockey or other station employee.

Contacts and promotion are recognized as essential and legitimate factors in the success of a recording in the popular music industry. An excellent song or record is worthless without public exposure. One witness in the first congressional hearings on payola said, "Until the public actually hears your product, you can't tell whether you have a hit or not." The editorial work of a music publisher must be supplemented by the vital work of joining with the record company in convincing disc jockeys and video programmers to play a particular record and song. This is a function of music publishers' and record companies' promotion departments.

It is not unusual for personnel in the broadcasting and music industries to have mutual interests and good rapport. Music and record company promotion people often achieve a "friend of the family" status with one another and with broadcasting personnel that may be expressed by tips on employment opportunities and other favors. Disc jockeys sometimes help music promoters by calling attention to new songs and master recordings from their local area or an up-and-coming "regional breakout" of records or songs. There are other areas of constructive cooperation as well, like promoting charities sponsored by the record industry, such as the T. J. Martell Foundation for Leukemia, Cancer and AIDS Research, and attending industry functions. In addition, many radio and video programmers are invited to record company staff conventions at which the talents of their artists are displayed and the artists personally meet the programmers.

It becomes a matter of degree as to when gifts and entertainment at theaters, restaurants, nightclubs, and other arenas leave the realm of normal business socializing and enter the area of payola through implication of a promise of airplay.

Commercial Bribery

Although the relationships of music publishers and songwriters to record company personnel are not subject to the federal payola statute, they may constitute another type of payola. Such relations, as well as those in broadcasting station payola situations, are subject to the commercial bribery laws in effect in many states when they involve the payment of money or other valuable consideration to an employee behind the back of his or her employer.

Payola in the sense of pay-for-play, or "plugging," has been with the music industry for many years. In 1916, the Music Publishers Protective Association noted that publishers were paying as much as $400,000 a year to artists to plug their songs. The publishers agreed to levy a fine of $5,000 on any member who continued the practice. However, the agreement was unenforced and ineffective. In the late 1930s, a group of publishers retained the late Joseph V. McKee, attorney and one-time acting mayor of New York City, to work with the Federal Trade Commission in obtaining a code outlawing payola. This move also failed.

Publishing Interests and Payola

In the early 1970s, it was reported that an important recording star, who was often his own composer and publisher, saw fit to pay $250,000 for the U.S.

and Canadian rights to publish about 100 songs written and recorded by himself in the years prior to the formation of his own publishing firm. While he was creating a greater incentive to record his own songs, this action did not constitute payola. Nor does it constitute payola when a recording star who is not a writer acquires a financial publishing interest in a song that may be suitable for his or her recording. This situation is similar to the ownership of music publishing firms by record companies that may be motivated to record songs in their publishing catalog. In fact, some record firms make special incentive payments to their A&R people who obtain publishing rights to material recorded.

Payola and Trade Papers

Payola has also been offered with respect to record charts in trade papers. A prominent trade paper research director once reported that he personally turned down a bribe of $3,000 to put a song on the charts, and that he had to discharge two employees in his department who received valuable gifts from record manufacturers. Former *Billboard* publisher Hal B. Cook has advocated an independent audit of industry rating systems, stating: "If charts are unduly influenced by economic considerations, a false market condition is created."

At one time there was a suspicion that record retailers were taking bribes in order to report falsely inflated sales figures in order to influence record charts. However, with *Billboard*'s adoption of data processing through Broadcast Data System and SoundScan, this practice appears to have been alleviated.

Practices of Payola

The 1959 report of the congressional subcommittee investigating payola stated:

> The subcommittee held 19 days of hearings on "payola" and related unfair and deceptive practices. ...Fifty-seven witnesses were heard; they included disc jockeys and other programming personnel, network and licensee executive personnel, phonograph record manufacturers and distributors, independent data processors, trade paper representatives, songwriters and publishers, and members of the subcommittee staff. Testimony appears to indicate that the selection of much of the music heard on the air may have been influenced by payments of money, gifts, etc., to programming personnel. In some instances, these payments were rationalized as licensing fees and consultation fees.

The practices of payola revealed by the testimony were varied. Automobiles were purchased for disc jockeys. Television sets were given as gifts. Weekly or monthly checks were remitted. Stipulated payments based on the number of records sold in an area were made. "Cut-ins" (a portion of revenues) on publishing rights were arranged. The ways were many, but the motivation was the same.

After its extensive study of payola in the music broadcasting business, the congressional committee successfully introduced a number of amendments to the law in 1960, making payola a federal crime. In recommending these amendments, the committee offered numerous examples of situations that would be affected by the amendments.

- A record distributor supplies copies of records to a radio station or disc jockey for broadcast purposes. No announcement is required unless the supplier furnishes more copies of a particular recording than are necessary. Thus, should the record supplier furnish 50 or 100 copies of the same release, with an agreement by the station, express or implied, that the record will be used on a broadcast, an announcement is required because consideration beyond the matter used on the broadcast has been received.
- An announcement is required for the same reason if the payment to the station or disc jockey is in the form of cash or other property, including stock.
- Several distributors supply a new station, or a station that has changed its program format (e.g., from rock and roll to popular music), with a substantial number of different record releases. No announcement is required under Section 317 of the U.S. Criminal Code where the records are furnished for broadcast purposes only; nor does the public interest require an announcement in these circumstances. The station would have received the same material over a period of time had it previously been on the air or followed this program format.
- Records are furnished to a radio station or disc jockey in consideration of the special plugging of the record supplier or performing talent beyond an identification reasonably related to the use of the record on the program. If the disc jockey states, "This is my favorite new record, and is sure to become a hit; so don't overlook it," and it is understood that some such statement is made in return for the record and would not otherwise have been made, an announcement is required. It does not appear that in those circumstances, the identification is reasonably related to the use of the record on that program. On the other hand, no announcement is required if a disc jockey states: "Listen to this latest release of performer 'X,' a new singing sensation," and such an advertisement is customarily part of the disc jockey's program format regardless of whether or not the particular record had been purchased by the station or furnished free of charge. It would appear that the identification by the disc jockey is reasonably related to the use of the record on that particular program.
- Free books or theater tickets are furnished to a book or drama critic of a station. When the books or plays are reviewed on the air, no announce-

ment is required. On the other hand, if 40 tickets are given to the station with the understanding, express or implied, that the play will be reviewed on the air, an announcement is required. There has been a payment beyond the furnishing of a property or service for use on or in connection with a broadcast.

▸ A well-known performer appears as a guest artist on a program at union scale because the performer likes the show, although the performer normally commands a much higher fee. No announcement is required.

Despite the widespread publicity that the federal payola law of 1960 received, payola has continued. In 1986, Senator Al Gore launched a Senate investigation of the record business, stating that the practice of giving gifts in exchange for air time "has again reared its ugly head" and noting that a great deal of money, as well as drugs and prostitution, was involved. It was indicated that indirect payola had become a common occurrence because of the record companies' having hired some 200 "independent promoters" who were to use their own devices when promoting records, without direct instructions or control by the record companies that hired them. According to *The Wall Street Journal,* some $80 million a year was being spent for this function. The cost of the individual record promotion necessary for Top 20 chart status was quoted at somewhere between $150,000 and $250,000. As a result of the investigation and Senate hearings, the use of independent promoters was largely discontinued in the record industry.

Because payola is a federal crime, it may someday be used as a basis for civil or criminal RICO litigation. The Racketeer-Influenced and Corrupt Organizations statute was used in the 1990 federal prosecution of record promoter Joe Isgro; the government indictment elevated the payola misdemeanor charge into mail fraud to qualify for RICO status. The case, which alleged the use of multiple independent promoters engaged by Isgro on behalf of client record labels to buy airplay on key stations, was ultimately dismissed owing to procedural defects. However, a 1995 court of appeals decision overturned the procedural dismissal and authorized reinstatement of the case for trial. The charges involved defrauding record companies, making undisclosed payments of cash and cocaine to radio station personnel, and racketeering. (Procedural complications resulted in a final dismissal.)

The pattern established in the Isgro case will likely be repeated in other similar situations. Likewise, in civil actions under RICO, a station owner who can claim that an employee received illegal payments could sue for triple damages under this statute.

Payola also concerns the Federal Trade Commission, which is charged with regulation of competition in supplying of goods in interstate commerce under Section 5 of the Federal Trade Commission Act. Under that section, unfair or deceptive acts or practices, as well as unfair competition, are declared unlawful. The FTC construed payola as a violation of Section 5 and investigated numerous record manufacturers and distributors. As a result, many such companies entered into consent decrees under which they agree to cease and desist from payola practices. Violations of the decree will usually subject the companies to penalties, in contrast to the warnings likely to be meted out to companies not parties to a decree.

Yet another blow to the practice of payola was administered by the Internal Revenue Service, which initiated its own investigation after having been apprised of evidence indicating the possibility that disc jockeys and other persons were understating taxable income. As a result, firms making payola payments were not allowed to deduct such bribery expenses from their income, and they also became subject to audit by the tax authorities.

38

Trade Practice Regulations

The Federal Trade Commission and the Department of Justice enforce statutes designed to foster and promote the maintenance of fair competitive conditions in interstate commerce in the interest of protecting industry, trade, and the public. For example, MTV plays a dominant role in the presentation of music videos to cable viewers through MTV, VHS, and The Box. In late 1999 the Department of Justice began looking into possible antitrust violations on the part of MTV in their dealings with the music companies that supply the videos. The FTC has intervened to bar the practice of giving payola to broadcasting station personnel in order to achieve a preferred position in the exposure of records and musical compositions over the air to the public.

Payola is only one of the many abuses that have been called to the attention of the FTC. A substantial number of complaints relate to discrimination between retail outlets and chain stores regarding prices, services, and facilities. Other complaints deal with misrepresentation and deception by various members of the music industry engaged in the manufacture, distribution, and sale of recordings.

The FTC has adopted a procedure to clarify and define practices that violate the statutes it enforces in order to encourage voluntary compliance with the laws on the part of the industry. This procedure includes trade practice hearings at which all members of the industry and other interested parties are offered an opportunity to present views, information, and suggestions regarding the establishment of rules designed to furnish guidance in the requirements of the applicable laws. Following the consideration of these comments and suggestions, the FTC publishes trade practice rules for the industry.

In 1964, the FTC scheduled a trade practice hearing for the phonograph record industry in Washington, D.C.; all important segments of the industry were represented. A set of proposed rules consisting of industry proposals that FTC staff felt should be considered were made available for review, and written comment was invited prior to the hearing. After the hearing, the FTC published Trade Practice Rules for the Phonograph Record Industry, which became operative on November 9, 1964. These rules were rescinded on December 3, 1979, but they are still helpful in indicating practices that violate the statutes administered by the FTC.

Discriminatory Price Differential Practices

Under the Trade Practice Rules of 1964, Rule 1 prohibited discriminatory price differential practices where the effect may substantially lessen competition, or create a monopoly, or injure, destroy, or prevent competition with a competitor or its customers. The rule bars both secret and open direct and indirect rebates, refunds, discounts, credits, or other forms of price differential to purchasers of goods of similar grade and quality.

Various examples of such discriminatory practices are presented under Rule 1. For instance, it would be a violation of the code if freight were paid on shipments to one customer and not to others, if a higher price were charged one customer than another, if some customers and not others were permitted to take discounts above the usual discounts, if one customer but not others were allowed a discount based on a percentage of total purchases in a given period, and if "free" records were supplied to some but not to all customers. The rule was not intended to prohibit differentials that make only due allowance for differences in the cost of manufacture, sale, or delivery resulting from differing methods or quantities in which products are sold or delivered.

Neither did Rule 1 bar the granting of different prices to customers in different functional categories. For example, a seller could grant a lower price to wholesalers than to retailers, to the extent that such wholesalers resell to retailers. On the other hand, if the wholesalers also sell at retail in competition with their customers, the prices charged to the wholesalers could not be lower on that portion of the goods they sell at retail than the prices charged to competing retailers.

While there appears to be no contention about the right to fix different prices for customers in varying functional categories, there can be factual disputes regarding whether a purchaser qualifies for the classification of distributor, rack jobber, one-stop, or retailer. Although there is little argument about the functions of a distributor, the first link in the chain of distribution headed by manufacturers, some distributors simultaneously operate as rack jobbers on the side and service locations that undersell their regular dealer customers. There are even distributors who own one-stops. The rack jobber, as commonly understood, services supermarkets, variety stores, drug stores, and other busy retail outlets, whereas the one-stop stocks the records of many manufacturers so that jukebox operators and small dealers can purchase their requirements at one location instead of having to contact a number of distributors.

Retailers who are affected adversely by rack jobbers have contended that a rack jobber should be classified as a retailer and therefore should not be entitled to a lower price than that charged to retailers. Rack jobbers argue that they operate as a subdistributor in furnishing racks and record stocks to retailers who actually own the operation; some rack jobbers have even claimed the status and privileges of a distributor. Retailers in competition with the rack locations assert that in reality the entire risk and control are vested in the rack jobbers and that they should therefore be regarded as retailers. These contentions present a factual problem underlying proper functional classification on which differing prices depend.

In 1994, the FTC conducted hearings regarding opposition to the resale of used CDs. This developed into a general inquiry into the fixing of CD price levels and whether there was any concerted activity among otherwise competing labels. The descriptive legal phrase for this is *conscious parallelism* where, although not an active conspiracy involving face-to-face meetings or correspondence, memoranda, and agreements between competitors, there is an effort to match price levels other than for purely competitive purposes. Good-faith business judgment of matching prices is still allowed, whereas intended parallel pricing that is against the self-interest of the party concerned is proof of conscious parallelism.

On the matter of used CDs, the FTC investigated whether there was illegal refusal to allow retailers their normal co-op advertising allowances when the retailer was offering used CDs in their stores. The argument of the record labels was that they did not feel obliged to help pay for the cost of attracting customers to stores that would compete with new merchandise by selling the customer a used CD instead. The resulting reaction of the retailers was to confirm the simple fact that co-op advertising monies were only used to advertise new merchandise. A similar investigation occurred in England, where CD price levels were generally much higher than in the United States and the question was whether concerted price maintenance was shown.

A variation on illegal conspiracy to fix uniform prices occurs when otherwise competitive labels agree among themselves on a uniform credit discount for prompt cash payment of outstanding invoices. That would be almost the same as uniform price fixing. On the other hand, a trade association, or even an informal agreement between otherwise competing labels, to exchange credit quality information as to prospective or actual customers is allowed. This exchange of good or bad or intermediate credit history is a valuable self-protection in furtherance of honest competition. A poor credit history of a customer might appropriately be dealt with by a decision to require cash on delivery.

Proportional Equality in Advertising, Promotional Allowances, or Facilities

The Trade Practice Rules required proportional equality in the treatment of competing customers in the supplying of advertising or promotional allowances, marketing services, or facilities. Where the allowance, service, or facility offered to certain customers was not suitable to others, an equivalent alternative allowance, service, or facility was to be offered.

Under the rules, it was considered a violation if racks, browsers, bins, displays, special packaging, and other similar services and facilities were supplied to certain customers but not made known and available on proportionally equal terms to all competing customers. A similar conclusion applied to preferential treatment in cooperative advertising allowances, to the furnishing of free merchandise with the proviso that it be used for advertising or that the proceeds of its sale be used for advertising purposes, or to the granting of allowances for advertising based on a fixed percentage of a customer's purchases.

Price Fixing, Tie-in Sales, and Other Deceptive Practices

Under the rules, a planned common course of action to fix or maintain prices was forbidden. For example, it would be a violation if record company members of the RIAA agreed not to compete on cash discounts to stores or on advertising allowances or agreed to refuse to service stores or chains that gave loss-leader discounts.

Also prohibited were tie-in sales that involved the coerced purchase of one product as a prerequisite to the purchase of other products. A tie-in would occur if a store were required to order 100 singles for every 20 albums of a particular artist or to purchase a minimum of 10 new releases of a designated new artist in order to get a standard discount on established charted album artists.

Under another rule, companies may not sell products or fix prices on condition that the purchaser not deal in the products of competitors. For example, a record company cannot put a particular store on its black list if that store seeks to handle the product of a competitor label. Similarly, a record label may not refuse to sell the work of a particular artist who refuses to extend his or her contract with that record label.

A number of the Trade Practice Rules addressed misleading and deceptive practices. The misuse of the labels "stereo" and "stereophonic" was attacked by a prohibition against referring to a record as stereo that does not have two distinctly separate modulations derived from an original live recording for which a minimum of two separate channels were employed. However, the words may be used with a monaural recording having two separate modulations provided there is clear disclosure that the recording was originally monaural and was altered to simulate stereophonic reproduction.

The rules also attempted to control deception regarding performing artists, misrepresentation of the contents of recordings, and deception involving reissues, new titles, and date or origination.

In addition, the use of the terms *close-outs, discontinued lines, special bargains,* and similar phrases was barred by a rule that applied when the terms are false or lead the public to believe wrongly that products are being offered at bargain prices.

In 1999 the Federal Trade Commission was continuing a 2 $^{1}/_{2}$-year investigation into music industry advertising practices. The probe concerned minimum advertised price policies of major labels and whether setting such levels constitutes price fixing. Complaints had been made to the FTC that the major labels were enforcing such policies by denying advertising allowances to noncooperating outlets. For example, a label that followed a practice of donating CDs to a retail outlet to defray the cost of an joint advertisement might withold the donation unless the outlet agreed not to advertise any releases at less than the minimum cost, or as loss leaders to entice customers into the store. At the same time, on-line music outlets, which are growing in popularity, have been able to offer substantial discounts. As of this writing, the FTC had not reached any conclusions. However, the fact that the inquiry is ongoing is, in and of itself, of concern to the music industry and focuses attention on the role of the FTC.

Sound-Alike Recordings

With the crackdown on record piracy (discussed in Chapter 8), there was an accompanying growth in what have been called *sound-alike recordings,* recordings of hit songs by artists other than the original artist where the expectation is that the recording features the original artist.

Although it is established that sound recording copyright does not protect against a sound-alike imitation by another artist, the Federal Trade Commission is alert to unfair trade practices that might otherwise occur in sound-alike situations. The FTC has issued warnings and taken action when names and likenesses of the original performers are used to deceive consumers into the belief that the record offered for sale was the actual original version by the original artist. It often occurs in situations when "A Tribute to Frank Sinatra" or to Tommy Dorsey or to Elvis Presley is printed in large letters with a picture of the original artist. The FTC requires a disclaimer in such instances stating that "This is not an original artist recording" as well as a disclosure of the actual name of the performer.

In 1980, the FTC issued a special guide concerning the use of endorsements and testimonials in advertising. The guide outlines the requirements for accuracy in advertising and promotion. For example, if a critic says that a recording is "technically great, but artistically inadequate" and the promotional quotation merely reads that the recording is "great," the promoter has violated FTC requirements. Similarly, if a superstar records as a sideman early in his or her career and is then advertised as a "featured artist," promoters have violated FTC requirements. Even consumer endorsements used in promotion are subject to the commission guidelines. A consumer cannot be paid for a favorable endorsement unless full disclosure of such a paid testimonial is made.

39

Work Permits for Foreign Artists

American artists such as Pearl Jam and R.E.M. have conducted successful tours of Europe or Africa, and European artists such as the Rolling Stones and U2 have achieved tremendous acceptance in the United States. Underlying the exchange of artists and their performance in foreign countries is a world of red tape and procedures involving international policy issues of safeguarding native artists from job insecurity and protecting local balances of trade.

For a foreign artist who wants to perform or record in the United States, there is a complicated process that often involves alien employment certification preliminary to the issuance of a temporary work visa. An understanding of the procedures, rules, and overlapping authority of the U.S. State Department, the Immigration and Naturalization Service of the Department of Justice, and in some circumstances the U.S. Department of Labor is essential to any concert producer, booking agent, record company, and television or film producer who wants to import musical talent from other countries.

Types of Work Visas

There are three categories of temporary work visas available to foreign artists. The preferred O status is available to those artists who can support a claim of "extraordinary ability." The P status covers those artists who do not qualify under the extraordinary ability standard, but who perform individually or as part of a group that has received international recognition as outstanding. The claim of O or P status can be evidenced by supporting documentation of the petitioner's achievements. The third category is H-2B status; to qualify for this category, the entertainer must get a certification from the Department of Labor that there are no comparably qualified persons available for the employment, and that the pay and other facets of such employment satisfy prevailing standards.

The Proper Petitioner and Petitions

Although vitally interested, the foreign musician or musical group is only the beneficiary of the alien employment certification and the immigration petition, and not the proper party to act as the official petitioner. The petitioner must be in the category of the "importing employer" or an agent. The petitioner need not be a U.S. resident or citizen.

Petitions are commonly filed by booking agencies, concert promoters, and the like, who are deemed to have the proper status for such filings. Caution must be exercised to assure that the petitioner's status and relationship to the beneficiaries should be continued throughout the U.S. engagement for which application is made. If there is a switch in persons holding the particular petitioner status, an application by the new party is necessary. Thus, a Boston concert promoter may be an appropriate petitioner for a single appearance in that city. But if a six-city tour is planned, the booking agency handling the entire tour should be the single petitioner, eliminating the need for six individual petitions, one for each city. If a tour is part of a record promotion, the record company as employer, though only indirectly involved in specific concert appearances, can be the petitioner for the entire tour, including employment at a record studio. More normally, a general agency (e.g., William Morris Agency, Associated Booking Corporation) serves as petitioner representing an interested party in all facets of U.S. employment.

The services of foreign entertainers are restricted to the activity, area, and employer specified in the petition. A new petition is required for further engagements, or if there is a change of employer or area of performance. An exception, where the performer is already in the United States, is an appearance without compensation on a charity show, for which no musician or other performer receives any compensation or reimbursement of expenses. When there are changes in the itinerary of an O, P, or H-2B entertainer beneficiary within the time period of the original itinerary, it is common simply to notify the Immigration and Naturalization Service office that handled the original petitions by submitting a letter of notification, preferably either in person or by certified mail, return receipt requested. Any new or separate engagement on other media, such as television or radio, requires a new petition.

An O or P status petitioner may petition directly to the Immigration and Naturalization Service and need not obtain an application from the Department of Labor. The H-2B petitioner, however, must first file with the Department of Labor for certification before petitioning the INS. Some cautious petitioners who seek the O or P status also apply at the same time (without advising the other agency) to the Department of Labor. The latter's certification may be used for obtaining an H-2B or other status in the event of rejection of the claim of extraordinary ability or outstanding international recognition by the adjudicating officer of the INS.

Even if the artist is as well established as Elton John, Cecile Bartoli, or the

Vienna Philharmonic, it is important to buttress the claim of extraordinary ability or of outstanding international recognition (the basis for an O or P petition, respectively) with all the supporting proof available. The following extract from the applicable INS regulations indicates the criteria involved in the determination of extraordinary ability:

> Whether the alien has been nominated for or has been the recipient of significant national or international awards in the particular field, such as an Academy Award, an Emmy, a Grammy, or a Director's Guild Award, or at least three of the following forms of documentation that the alien: (1) has or will perform a lead or starring role in productions or events that have a distinguished reputation; (2) has achieved national or international recognition for achievements; (3) has performed a lead, starring, or critical role for organizations and establishments that have a distinguished reputation; (4) has a record of major commercial or critically acclaimed successes; (5) has received significant recognition for achievements from organizations, critics, government agencies, or other recognized experts in the field in which the alien is engaged; (6) has commanded or now commands a high salary or other substantial remuneration for services in relation to others in the field; (7) other comparable evidence.

This extract below indicates the criteria involved in the determination of outstanding international recognition:

> Whether the alien group has been nominated or has received significant international awards or prizes for outstanding achievement in its field, or by three of the following types of documentation that establish that the entertainment group has: (1) performed or will perform as a starring or leading entertainment group in productions or events that have a distinguished reputation; (2) achieved international recognition and acclaim for outstanding achievements in its field as evidenced by reviews in major newspapers, trade journals, magazines, or other published material; (3) performed and will perform services as a leading or starring group for organizations and establishments that have a distinguished reputation; (4) acquired a record of major commercial or critically acclaimed successes; (5) achieved significant recognition for achievements from organizations, critics, government agencies, or other recognized experts in the field; or (6) commanded or now commands a high salary or other substantial remuneration for services compared to others similarly situated in the field.

The foregoing standards are designed to show whether the foreign entertainer is clearly preeminent in his or her specialty.

Types of Petitions and Accompanying Documents

Most visiting musicians and singers do not choose to apply as regular immigrants from their native lands; such applications involve lengthy procedures described under the section "Immigrant Status." They instead seek to qualify as nonimmigrants for temporary work visas. If they are applying for H-2B status, they must first get a certification from the Department of Labor, on Form ETA 750, Part A, that their employment will not take jobs from American artists. This is preliminary to petitioning the Immigration and Naturalization Service on Form I-129 and the H supplement to the form.

When an entire orchestra, band, or other group with a single itinerary requests a temporary work visa, it is desirable to file petitions in group form rather than individually. One reason for this is that the $50 filing fee covers all members of the group. A more important reason is that it avoids duplicative adjudication and the risk that one group member may hold up others whose petitions have already been approved. If there is a change in group personnel and group qualification before the commencement of a tour, the original petition may be amended. However, a change in personnel after initial entry into the United States usually requires a new petition and new filing fee. The new petition should be sent to the same INS processing center as the previous petition with a copy of the original petition, approval notice, and all supporting documentation, and should make reference to the file number and the date of the earlier approval.

It is to be assumed that a group known and regularly appearing under a group name is an entity and that the qualifications are the group's rather than the individuals'. In fact, the petition should use the group name in the space for "name of beneficiary"; individual member names can be attached on an accompanying schedule showing names, citizenships, birth dates, places of birth, and current addresses.

If the artists are already in the United States, forms must be filed to allow them to change status, for example, from visitor to temporary worker, or to extend their stay. To change status, the artist or artists must file Form I-506, along with the entry permit he or she was given on arrival, known as the I-94 form. Artists wishing to extend their stay within the same visa status must each file Form I-539 with their I-94 form. H-2B artists must file with the Department of Labor seeking certification, then file Form I-797, the approval notice of the initial petition, along with the I-94 form. All material to be filed should be submitted together with the O, P, or H-2B petitions to the Immigration and Naturalization Service.

Whether for an O, P, or H-2B petition, the petition should be accompanied by documentary proof of professional standing. This may be in the form of record or concert reviews or hit charts. It is also advisable to have letters of endorsement from recognized experts in the applicant's field of music, such as critics, concert promoters, recognized artists, publishers, or record company personnel (when the record company is not acting as petitioner), or a certificate of membership in a select professional society. Such endorsements should be in the English language or accompanied by an English translation made by a translator who submits a certificate of competency to translate and a notarized statement of the accuracy of the translation.

Before a foreign artist can be approved for a work permit with an O or P petition, a consultation requirement must be met. This consultation requirement can be met by the petitioner if he or she either submits, with the petition, an advisory opinion from a peer group with expertise in the specific entertainment field involved or provides evidence that such a peer group does not exist. However, if no advisory opinion is submitted and a peer group exists, the Immigration and Naturalization Service must give the appropriate labor organization an opportunity to submit an advisory opinion on the application. The labor organization has 15 days to submit a written advisory opinion. After this 15-day period is over and the petitioner has had an opportunity to submit rebuttal evidence, the Immigration and Naturalization Service has 14 days to make a decision on the application.

In cases in which the INS has determined that expedited consultation procedures are required to accommodate a production or an event, it contacts the appropriate organization by telephone and requests an advisory opinion if one is not submitted by the petitioner. The organization has 24 hours to respond by telephone to the request. If it fails to respond, the Immigration and Naturalization Service will make a decision without an advisory opinion. All documents accompanying a petition for a work permit must be submitted in duplicate. If the return of documents is desired, this must be explicitly requested, and two photocopies must accompany the originals when submitted.

Where to File Petitions

There are three governmental departments normally concerned with the foreign artist's entry into the United States for employment purposes. They are the Department of Labor, the Immigration and Naturalization Service of the Department of Justice, and the Department of State. The Departments of Labor and of Justice are the primary agencies concerned with the foreign artist's employment petitions in the United States.

Department of Labor filings for certification (required only in an H-2B case) are handled initially by the applicable state employment service local office where the employment is to take place. After a period ranging from 45 days to 6 months, the state office then forwards the papers to the regional office of the U.S. Department of Labor, without the further intervention of the petitioner. In some areas of greater noncitizen employment (e.g., Los Angeles, Chicago, and New York), the applicable state office may set up a special division to handle requests for certification.

The Immigration and Naturalization Service of the Department of Justice maintains 37 district offices spread throughout the United States, plus four district offices in foreign countries (Italy, Mexico, the Philippines, and Germany). There are also a number of remote adjudication centers, called regional service centers, where most applications and petitions are processed. While forms can be obtained from the INS district offices, they should be submitted to the appropriate remote adjudication center by mail. In the New York area, for example, petitions and applications are sent to the Eastern Regional Service Center, 1A Lemnah Drive, St. Albans, VT 05479-0001 (802-527-4913). Any regional center can handle all territorial employment included in the itinerary of an artist, so long as the petition at least partially involves employment in the territory of the district office.

It is neither necessary nor desirable to send multiple petitions to a number of regional service centers. In fact, it is sometimes better to select one regional service center in preference to another. Factors to consider include the possibility of faster service and familiarity with entertainment industry problems. Since all dealings with these remote adjudication centers are required to be by mail or telephone only, geographical proximity to the parties or their attorney is not crucial.

A matter of convenience to all parties concerned is the use of telegrams by the regional adjudication centers to confirm to petitioners located in other cities entry approval for a foreign artist. This is also available to notify U.S. consular offices abroad of the petition approval so that they may process the visa applications of the artist beneficiaries. Such telegraphic notification is offered without fee or special request when the petitioner simply notes "Cable Requested" on the top of the forms. Often, when time is of the essence and any delay may be costly, a cable request can be extremely valuable.

Personal appearance by the petitioner is strongly discouraged, and all requests for expedited consideration must now be made by overnight or same-day mail with a request for cable notification and documentation of the urgency of the case. Attorneys may not be given information about the status of a pending case unless they have filed a special notice of appearance on INS Form G-28, signed by the petitioner.

When requested by a petitioner residing abroad, the Department of State is primarily involved with handling requests for information, forms, the processing of papers in foreign countries through the various U.S. consular offices, and the issuance of visas where approved. The actual approval is handled by the Department of Labor and INS, as noted above.

Artist's or Group's Accompanying Personnel

Performing artists attract ticket buyers and high fees on the basis of their individual reputations and talent. However, few major artists are truly a solo entity. They usually depend on backup musicians, accompanists, road managers, publicity agents, sound technicians, and in some instances, even special hairdressers, valets, or maids. When applying for work visas in the United States, the unique and special talent of the major artist often cannot envelop all of his or her entourage. The hairdresser, so essential to an artist in London, might be replaced in the United States by an equally qualified American. A bass player or pianist who accompanies the artist overseas may be regarded by an AFM union representative as merely a competitor of an equally competent American musician.

In one petition application for a foreign orchestra that used electronic instruments and equipment, a sound technician was recognized as a uniquely qualified member of the group despite having talents generally no greater than those of available American technicians. His special status arose from the fact that the orchestra itself was using special sound equipment designed by this individual. The equipment was subject to constant repair and rearrangement to fit different concert halls, for which functions the equipment designer had special training and experience that was not interchangeable with that of other technicians who did not have such familiarity with the orchestra or equipment. However, the road manager familiar with the personal whims and needs of the orchestra personnel as to dining, accommodations, and travel was held not so exceptional that his duties could not be similarly performed by an American citizen without special and extensive training and thus his work visa was not approved.

In the end, decisions regarding the issuance of work permits are highly subjective, and supporting affidavits and explanations must clearly delineate the unique qualities of accompanying personnel.

Immigrant Status

Discussion in this chapter thus far has focused on the nonimmigrant status of the foreign artist. However, those artists who have gained immigrant status must be discussed as well. Immigrant status, sometimes referred to as permanent resident status, is reflected by issuance of a "green card," which is actually now issued in other colors. Because of the unlimited duration of the right under such card to work in the United States, it is in many instances more desirable to the foreign artist than O, P, or H-2B nonimmigrant status.

In the past, immigrant quotas were set for each national group, beyond which no more applicants could be accepted. Since 1968, national origin quotas have been abolished and replaced with a worldwide quota, with a maximum of 20,000 citizens from any one country. Spouses and parents of children over 21 years of age who are U.S. citizens are exempt from this quota, and if the alien fits into this group, known as "immediate relatives," he or she should consider applying for permanent resident status by this route rather than through his or her profession. (It is to be noted that immigrants do not automatically lose foreign citizenship or commit themselves to accepting U.S.

citizenship, which may be available upon application after 5 years of permanent residence, or 3 years if living with one's U.S. citizen spouse.)

Except for immediate relatives, green cards are reserved for people in categories known as "preferences." For those without family ties here, there is a
category known as "first preference," which applies to persons "of extraordinary ability in the arts and sciences." A fixed percent, subject to congressional
revision, is allotted annually to these immigrants and their families. Green
cards granted to individuals of "extraordinary ability" are reserved for those at
the top of their respective field. To obtain the preference, a petition by a
sponsor offering full-time employment must be filed with and approved by the
Immigration and Naturalization Service. Foreign artists in this category must
obtain a certification from the Department of Labor stating that their coming
to the United States will not adversely affect American labor. However, where
the department determines that the individual is of extraordinary ability, the
certification is routinely issued. Once the first preference is approved, the artist
must apply for an immigrant visa, either at the U.S. consulate in his or her
home country or in the United States if he or she is already in this country and
has never been employed here without government permission.

Because there are waiting lists for immigrant visas, the process can be a
lengthy one, lasting two or more years. After the process to procure an immigrant visa has begun, it is inadvisable for the performer to travel in and out of
the United States on any temporary visa, such as a tourist or visitor visa. This is
because the intent to reside in the United States permanently is inconsistent
with the intent to return abroad, which is required for a temporary visa. To use
a temporary visa while taking steps to obtain a green card may therefore be
regarded as possible visa fraud. Visitors who are admitted to the United States
under temporary visas and who plan to leave for short trips abroad should
apply for permission to reenter *before* leaving the United States; otherwise,
such visitors risk losing their previous visa status. A touring artist whose itinerary includes Canada or Mexico as part of a North American tour may obtain
a multiple entry form of visa.

There are also other classes of aliens permitted to work in the United
States without an employer filing any petition. One group consists of those
who have qualified under the legalization program and have cards issued by
the Immigration and Naturalization Service showing them to be temporary
residents. A second group is composed of those who have applied for or been
granted political asylum or refugee status and who carry cards showing
"employment authorized," stamped by the Immigration and Naturalization
Service.

Rejection and the Right of Appeal

In the fast-moving world of musical entertainment, a frequent concern in the
employment of foreign artists is undue delay in clearing the artist for an

engagement. Delay may force a prospective employer to find substitute artists to fill a concert hall or other place of engagement. Rarely will the employer be able to wait for the extended time involved in new applications or appeals.

In the event of a refusal to admit, the petitioning artist has the possibility of curing the refusal through appeal or a subsequent application. The beneficiary will be interested in the reasons for the denial. The regulations of the Immigration and Naturalization Service require that if a petition is denied, the petitioner must be notified of the reasons for such denial of his or her right to appeal. With regard to the O and P petitions, the regulations further require that if an adverse decision is proposed, based upon any evidence not submitted by the petitioner, then the petitioner must be so notified and invited to rebut such third-party evidence. The third-party evidence may have been submitted by parties such as unions, other organizations, critics, or experts in the related entertainment field who are frequently consulted by the adjudicating officer of the Immigration and Naturalization Service in order to obtain an advisory opinion regarding the qualifications of the alien and the nature of the services to be performed. Advisory opinions are sometimes given orally in the interest of expeditious handling of applications. For purposes of appeal from a rejected petition, even an oral opinion is subject to review by a petitioner because the opinion must be confirmed in writing within 15 days from the date when it was requested.

With respect to H-2B petitions, the Secretary of Labor must certify that (1) qualified persons are not available in the United States and (2) the employment will not adversely affect the wages and working conditions of workers in the United States similarly employed. If a notice is attached to the petition by an official that such certification cannot be made, the petitioner can produce countervailing evidence.

Under statutory standards, O, P, and H-2B petitions are denied for such items as insanity, chronic alcoholism, narcotics addiction, conviction of trafficking in narcotics, and evasion of the U.S. military draft, unless service is waived by the government.

Union Comity

Although not required by law or regulation, it is advisable for foreign artists on a U.S. tour to consult the applicable American union as to its requirements. For example, the AFM for the United States and Canada have reciprocally agreed to assist musicians in obtaining work permits in either country. Canadian musicians, who are members of the AFM for the United States and Canada jointly, must pay a "work dues equivalent" to certain AFM locals where the artist's services are performed, which charge its U.S. members similarly. These dues may run as high as 5 percent of wage scale in some instances. (These dues are not charged to foreign musicians who are not from Canada.)

The AFM Canadian office (416-391-5161) services all work permits of Canadian or American AFM members for cross-border North American engagements. Its administrative fee for this service is $15 (Canadian) for regular services and $25 (Canadian) if given less then a 35-day advance notice before engagement. The Canadian work permit is called a Temporary Employment Authorization (IMM-1120); the U.S. customary form for similar engagements is called a Class P-2. The cost of a work permit for American musicians to work in Canada is $110 (U.S.) per petition, plus a $5 "user fee" if the group is driving a commercial vehicle across the border or is importing merchandise for sale; for Canadian musicians to work in the United States, the fee is $150 (Canadian) for single musicians and $450 for multiple entry of 2 to 14 musicians traveling and entering United States as a unit.

In another example, foreign artists seeking employment abroad under continuing union review, members of the British Musicians Union are expected to abide by the category and hours of employment of American musicians for whom reciprocal employment in the British territory was obtained. Although such a "trade" of work is sometimes arranged through a booking agency, the international unions themselves may at times informally facilitate such an exchange and thereby clear the way for the American union to advise the applicable government office of no objection to the permit. International union arrangements with the union in a foreign artist's home country often cover membership status in the United States as well. Nonunion members can be required to join the American union after 30 days from the commencement of employment in a "union shop."

Multiple Entries into the United States plus Extensions

Performing artists may interrupt a U.S. tour to perform in other countries before returning to the United States. This interruption does not require duplicate work clearances because multiple-entry permission is available. In such cases, the foreign musician should ask the U.S. consul for a multiple-entry visa. On the artist's arrival in the United States, the Immigration and Naturalization Service will determine the length of that particular stay on the Form I-94 issued to that performer. Artists with O visas can receive a stay of up to 3 years initially and may be granted extensions, in 1-year increments, in order to permit that individual to continue to complete the same event or activity. Artists with P visas may be granted a stay of up to 5 years, with extensions up to another 5 years in 1-year increments in order to permit the artist to complete the same event. Artists with H-2B visas may be granted stays of up to 1 year, with three possible 1-year extensions. However, each extension requires a new labor certification.

Applications for extensions are made to the Immigration Service on Form I-539. In addition, the petitioner must request an extension of the validity of the initial petition on Form I-129B. The two are considered separately although filed together. A denial of an extension of a stay is not appealable; a denial of extension of the petition is. If the petition is extended but the stay is not, the artist may go to another country, such as Canada, and ask the U.S. consul there for a new visa based on the extended petition. If new engagements are involved, a new I-129B petition must also be filed with the Immigration Service.

Taxation

Compensation for professional appearances in the United States is subject to the income taxes of either the United States, the country of origin of the artist, or both countries. Artists from some countries—Canada, France, Germany, Sweden, and the United Kingdom—can avoid U.S. federal income tax on American earnings because of the existence of treaties between the United States and those countries called Conventions for the Avoidance of Double Taxation. Artists from nontreaty countries are subject to a U.S. tax on their earnings from appearances in the United States. Artists are required to obtain tax clearance or an exemption certificate from the IRS district director before departure from the United States.

Eligibility under double-taxation treaties requires the filing of proof with the IRS district director that the artist qualifies as a taxpayer in the artist's country of origin. For instance, British taxpayers obtain such a certificate from Financial Intermediaries and Claims Office, Fitz Roy House, PO Box 46, Nottingham, England NG2 1BD.

Artists with resident (immigrant) status are considered the same as U.S. citizens for income tax purposes regardless of where the income originates. In recent years the United States and Canada have initiated a fixed percentage of withholding tax on foreign artists present on a temporary basis unless qualification under a tax treaty is first established. Where not so established, applications for refunds are later required.

40

Sources of Information

It is important for people in the music business to keep informed of news and developments in the industry. A prime source of information is the trade press. In addition, there exists a large network of publications, archives, organizations, research services, and reference materials that provide information on all aspects of the music industry. The Internet now serves to link these sources and to provide an unprecedented range of news and information to both interested browsers and industry professionals.

Trade Press

Two of the leading weekly trade publications that concentrate on the music industry are *Billboard,* and *College Music Journal New Music Report (CMJ)*. To keep abreast of developments in the business, songwriters, performers, publishers, and record companies read at least one of these magazines.

Billboard is probably the most widely read trade publication in the industry, covering domestic and international artists, sales, radio programming, marketing and industry news. *Billboard* includes weekly reviews of new singles and albums. Singles are subdivided into pop, R&B, country, adult contemporary (AC), rap, dance, gospel, and jazz. Each subclassification is further divided into "picks" and "recommended." The picks are new releases that, in the opinion of reviewers, have the greatest chart potential in the particular format. The "recommended" have the "potential for significant chart action." There is a separate category of "new and noteworthy" that highlights new and developing acts worthy of attention.

Billboard's album reviews classify the better albums as pop, R&B, country, jazz, new age, dance, Latin, contemporary Christian, and classical. Those albums named as "picks" in one of these formats are predicted to hit the top half of the chart for that format. The most outstanding of the week's releases is given the *Billboard* "Spotlight" attribution and is thereby forecast to reach the top 10 on *Billboard*'s Top Pop Albums chart or to earn a platinum sales certification from RIAA. There are also "recommended" albums that include other releases expected to reach the chart in the respective format, as well as other albums of superior quality.

CMJ focuses primarily on independent artists and labels and is often used by many new artists to identify alternative outlets, such as college, noncommercial, and alternative radio stations. *CMJ* contains album and video reviews next to the various charts. The captions of these reviews reflect the format being covered. For example, the Beat Box chart review, which lists rap music, is titled "Dope," and the Jazz chart review is titled "Brass Tracks." Other reviews are also presented in the magazine's section "JackPot."

The range of musical formats and genres in contemporary music is indicated by the many charts in a typical issue of *Billboard* or *CMJ*. For example, in one week in 2000 there were separate *Billboard* charts for the following:

- *Top albums:* The Billboard 200 (top-selling albums); Classical; Classical Crossover; Country; Heatseekers (new and developing artists); Jazz/Contemporary; New Age; Pop Catalog; R&B
- *Top singles:* Hot 100; Adult Contemporary; Adult Top 40; Country; Dance/Club Play; Dance/Maxi Singles Sales; Hot Latin Tracks; R&B; Rap; Rock/Mainstream Rock Tracks; Rock/Modern Rock Tracks; Top 40 Tracks

There were also charts headed Top Video Sales, Top DVD Sales, Top Rentals, and Top Kid Video. In any given week, *Billboard* may also include charts for reggae, world music, Latin, contemporary Christian, blues, and kid audio, and music video sales.

Billboard's best-selling pop singles chart, called the Hot 100, lists records by title, name of the artist, name of the producer, and record label name and number. Also indicated are the number of weeks a record has been on the chart, its standing in each of the two previous weeks, the availability of video clips, the names of its writers, publisher, and sheet music supplier, and the publisher's affiliation with ASCAP or BMI. Songs registering the greatest airplay and sales gains for the past week are marked by a red circle around the number of their standing on the chart. Each song certified as a 500,000 -unit shipment (gold) by the Recording Industry Association of America (RIAA) is accompanied by a black bullet; songs with shipments of 1 million (platinum) are marked with a black triangle.

Billboard ranks albums in a separate chart entitled Top Pop Albums, which sets forth the 200 best-selling albums in the United States. Those that register the greatest sales gains in the latest week are noted by a circle around the number of their status on the chart. Those certified by the RIAA for net shipment of 500,000 units (gold) are marked by a black bullet; net shipment of 1 million units (platinum) are marked by a small black triangle; songs with net shipment of 10 million (diamond) are marked with a black diamond.

Sales reports underwent a major change in the early 1990s when *Billboard* scrapped its reliance on telephone or other manually entered sales reports and substituted its electronic SoundScan reports. Such point-of-sale reports rely on bar-coded entries of actual cash register sales. The immediate accuracy of such reports and reduced temptation to manipulate the figures was welcomed by the industry. However, glitches arose when numbers for country and western and R&B music sales were not recorded when sold outside of the major chains, in outlets that did not have the expensive SoundScan equipment. As a result, the SoundScan base was augmented by the addition of independents to the panel of reporters.

While *Billboard* charts are influenced by record sales, *CMJ* weekly charts focus on record airplay on college, commercial, and noncommercial radio. *CMJ* charts include Top 20, Beat Box (hip-hop and urban), Triple A (adult album alternative), Loud Rock, Jazz, New World, RPM (electronic music), and Internet Broadcast. *CMJ* does not chart pop singles, but its Core College Radio and Commercial Alternative Cuts charts list singles in the alternative music category. Each chart lists in green print the records that received a "significant increase in airplay." Additionally, a green triangle indicates the records that have experienced the "greatest chart movement" and a heart indicates the "most requested titles." Table 40-1 illustrates the difference in focus between *Billboard* and *CMJ*.

In addition to reviews and charts, *Billboard* contains coverage of international news and lists the best international sellers in designated markets. A typical issue of *Billboard* also reports changes in artist affiliations with record companies, shifts in record company personnel, special sales promotions, news of governmental laws and investigations, meetings of distributors, discussions of publishing and record company business developments, and acquisitions and mergers of publishing and record companies.

Billboard also issues annual directories that include valuable information about record manufacturers, music publishers, record wholesalers, and firms engaged in services and supplies for the music industry. The *Billboard* directories are international in scope, and are a great aid to American record companies and publishers who want to familiarize themselves with their counterparts in foreign countries. For example, the *Billboard International Buyer's Guide* lists record and video companies, music publishers, music industry distributors and suppliers, equipment manufacturers, and sources of music industry services. Other directories include the *Billboard International Talent & Touring Directory,* the *Billboard Record Retailing Directory, The Radio Power Book, The Nashville 615/Country Music Sourcebook,* and the *International Latin Music Buyer's Guide.*

CMJ provides a listing of new releases from various alternative record companies. Further, *CMJ* convenes its annual CMJ Music Marathon &

Musicfest, an alternative music convention that showcases new artists and provides industry information to executives and to fans.

In addition to *Billboard* and *CMJ*, there are a number of other trade publications that provide valuable information to industry professionals. *Radio & Records* (*R&R*) is a weekly in-depth trade paper targeted to radio programmers and executives, but with significant coverage of the music industry. *R&R* furnishes extensive and detailed information on the current music programming of leading radio stations throughout the United States, subdivided by

Table 40-1
Top Albums Listed by *Billboard* and *CMJ*, March 8, 1999

Chart Position	Billboard	CMJ
1	Baby One More Time Britney Spears Jive	Keep It Like a Secret Built to Spill Warner Bros.
2	The Miseducation of Lauryn Hill Lauryn Hill Ruffhouse/Columbia	The Sebadoh Sebadoh Sub Pop/Sire
3	Americana The Offspring Columbia	Up, Up, Up, Up, Up, Up Ani DiFranco Righteous Babe
4	Wide Open Spaces Dixie Chicks Monument	Can You Still Feel? Jason Falkner Elektra/EEG
5	'N Synch 'N Synch RCA	What Is Not to Love Imperial Teen Slash/London
6	Greatest Hits 2Pac Amaru/Death Row	Cloudy Cloud Calculator Takako Minekawa Emperor Norton
7	Believe Cher Warner Bros.	Chrominance Decoder April March Ideal/Mammoth
8	Flesh of My Flesh Blood of My Blood DMX Ruff Ryders/Def Jam/Mercury	Songs for the Jet Set, Vol. 2 Various Artists Jetset

region and by music format. Unlike the *Billboard* charts, which give weight to both store sales and airplay information, or *CMJ*, which gives some consideration to sales, *R&R* does not use sales information. Its top singles chart is titled CHR, an abbreviation for Contemporary Hit Radio. It includes the top 40 songs in the country based on national airplay and also shows the standing of each song in the previous two weeks. The chart identifies a rising chart status by a black circle around the number on the chart. A song that has concurrent airplay on 60 percent of the reporting stations is highlighted by the word "Breaker." It designates songs as "Most Added" to station playlists and "Hottest" to indicate those receiving the heaviest airplay reports. *R&R* also lists a limited number of top-played records in Australia, Canada, and the United Kingdom, based on foreign sources.

Gavin Report, a part of the Miller Freeman Entertainment group, is a weekly radio and music trade magazine featuring charts, industry news, and artist profiles. *Gavin* charts are based on playlists from over 1,300 American radio stations and are presented in 14 formats: Top 40, Rhythm-Crossover, Hot Adult Contemporary, Adult Contemporary, Urban, Rap, Alternative, College, Active, A3, Country, Americana, Jazz, and Smooth Jazz. *Gavin* also stages a yearly convention for radio executives.

Urban Network is a trade magazine focusing on urban music, including such genres as rap, hip-hop, R&B, and gospel. All aspects of the industry are covered, including extensive radio playlists and charts, record reviews, industry news, video charts, and "clip of the week," as well as artist profiles and album sales distinguished by American region.

Music Business International, a London-based monthly, issues an exclusive World Chart bringing together current data from 19 music trade journals in leading countries around the world. There is an appropriate weighting by market strength of the country involved; for example, a hit in Spain is one-sixtieth the strength of a similar spot for a hit in the larger market of the United States. Accompanying specific record information is an overall graphic report showing the relative strength of top record companies in the albums and singles categories.

Subscription Services

The underlying data for the *Billboard* charts are available to those who subscribe to the *Billboard Information Network,* operated as a division of Billboard Publications, Inc. This service is another important source of information for those working in the music industry.

The *Billboard Information Network* provides an analysis of individual station playlists, regional airplay, and individual and regional store activity. Professional promotion people employed by music publishers and record companies find the service useful in pinpointing activity and making prompt evaluations of results.

New on the Charts is a monthly information service sold by subscription only to professionals in the music industry. Sometimes called "the tip sheet," it supplies the names, addresses, and telephone numbers of producers, publishers, booking agents, record labels, and personal managers associated with the chart entries in *Billboard* magazine.

The *A&R Registry* is another information magazine published every 2 months by the Music Business Registry. The *A&R Registry* is a nearly complete list of U.S.-based record labels along with the relevant executives and A&R support staffs. Contact information including the addresses, phone numbers, fax numbers, and e-mail is also available.

Amusement Business, the "international newsweekly for sports and mass entertainment," covers musical and theatrical entertainment, carnivals, circuses, and variety and specialty acts. It reports on all aspects of live musical entertainment, from jazz to symphony and from country to ragtime. It includes valuable directory and chart materials as well.

Pollstar is a weekly guide for music industry professionals in the field of concert, club, theater, and other live entertainment venues. It furnishes tour itineraries, box office results, contact directories, news items, and profiles of artists, agencies, and managements.

Government Institutions

The U.S. Copyright Office became particularly valuable as a result of the physical destruction of buildings in Europe during World War II and the resulting loss of important copyright records. News came from Finland that its great composer Jan Sibelius had insufficient data to furnish his advisers and was thus unable to keep abreast of the uses of his extensive catalog in the United States. The Copyright Office, as a gesture of goodwill, made a complete analysis of his approximately 800 works registered at any time in the United States, setting forth the dates of original and renewal registrations, the history of any assignments, and the original recordings indicated by Notices of Use on file. This gift required 200 hours of work. The Copyright Office made a similar study of about 3,000 musical compositions of German origin, replacing catalog information that had been destroyed in wartime.

Today, the facilities of the Copyright Office are available for such research services at a service charge of $65 per hour. When a search is requested, all known basic facts should be sent to the office. These should be assembled on a search request form furnished by the Copyright Office. An estimate of the hours and charges will be furnished upon receipt of the request form.

In addition to its search services, the Copyright Office can be of value in furnishing copies of missing songs that have been filed with a copyright registration. A copy of unpublished manuscripts and published songs will be supplied, provided that the copy request is authorized in writing by the copyright owner or the owner's agent, the request is made by an attorney for use in a court proceeding, or there is a court order requiring such a copy.

All pre-1978 registrations are recorded on index cards. Entries from January 1, 1978, to the present are recorded electronically and published on the Internet (lcweb.loc.gov/copyright). Entries are published in the *Catalog of Copyright Entries,* which is on file in larger public libraries, available for inspection on microfiche in the Search Room of the Copyright Office and in the Library of Congress, and available for sale to the public. The catalog will continue to be published in eight parts, among which are separate parts for performing arts (which includes musical works), sound recordings, and renewals. Unpublished as well as published materials are included in all parts except renewals. The catalog is indexed by copyright registration number, title of the work, claimant's name, and in the case of sound recordings, the names of principal performers. The appropriate use of the catalog can satisfy simply and inexpensively many requests for information regarding copyrighted material.

Orders for subscriptions to one or more parts of the catalog may be sent to the Superintendent of Documents, U.S. Government Printing Office, Washington, DC 20402. The music and sound recording data are available for viewing on-line from 1978 on. Earlier entries still require printed copies or microfiche.

The Copyright Office assembles important federal and state court decisions regarding copyrights and related subjects in the field of intellectual property; these are published in a series of bulletins entitled *Decisions of the United States Courts Involving Copyright.* Orders for these bulletins should be sent to the Superintendent of Documents. The Copyright Office also issues gratis a series of individual circulars explaining various aspects of domestic and international copyright protection.

Although copyright reports are available for a modest charge from the Copyright Office research department as well as from the Copyright Office Web site, many searches are obtained from private firms. A prominent firm such as Thomson & Thomson charges varying rates depending on type of report and time of requested report:

1. *Full U.S. copyright search:* Search for the copyright ownership of a specified property, such as a motion picture, literary work, television program, screenplay, or song. The search is based on a search of U.S. Copyright Office records, on-line databases, and Thomson & Thomson's propriety sources and includes:
    Information revealing underlying and derivative works
    Copyright registration and renewal data
    A summary of assignments and other recorded instruments
    Biographical information on the authors
2. *Original or unexploited work search:* Full U.S. copyright search coverage for original screenplays or unexploited works that do not involve a derivative or underlying work.

3. *U.S. copyright screening search:* A search of the U.S. Copyright Office records for registration and renewal data and a listing of recorded documents for a particular work.

Another excellent government source of information is the Archive of Folk Culture. In 1928, the Library of Congress Music Division established a national repository for documentary manuscripts and sound recordings of American folk music. In 1981, its official name was changed from the Archive of Folk Song to the Archive of Folk Culture. Since its establishment, over 30,000 hours of recordings containing more than 300,000 items of folk song, folk music, folk tale, oral history, and other types of folklore have been sent to the Library of Congress, primarily from the United States. Through gift, exchange, and field-collecting projects, the archive has also acquired folk song material from Canada, Latin America, the British Isles, Europe, Africa, and some areas of Asia and the Pacific Rim. From this extensive collection, the Library of Congress has, over a period of years, issued a number of selected recordings for use by universities, libraries, students, and other interested parties. These records include traditional sea chanteys, authentic cowboy songs, songs of the Mormons, ballads of the Civil War, Anglo-American songs and ballads, Negro work songs and spirituals, fiddle and banjo tunes, songs of many Indian tribes, as well as folk songs and music from Brazil, Mexico, Morocco, Puerto Rico, and Venezuela.

A catalog listing the entire series of recordings available from the Library of Congress may be obtained from the Archive of Folk Culture, Library of Congress, Washington, DC 20540; Web site: http://lcweb.loc.gov/folklife/archive.html. The archive has available extensive field notes, many textual transcriptions, and some musical transcriptions, in folders and bound volumes, for supplementary information about the recordings. It has also compiled about 200 bibliographies and other reference lists covering many areas and subjects in the field of folklore and folk music; an inventory of the bibliographies and lists is available upon request.

The Smithsonian Institution, a nonprofit organization, is in the unique position not only to record but also to keep in print valuable archival music. Its mission as a curator is to keep alive a record of music from around the world that reflects our varied history and culture. Among its collections is the historic Folkways label, acquired in 1987, and the additional labels of Cook, Dyer-Bennett, Fast Folk, Monitor, and Paredon. Folkways has approximately 30,000 musical performances, ranging from folk, jazz, blues, classical, the spoken word, and native oral traditions to sounds from nature and children's recordings. Its music comes from around the world, from the Americas, Africa, Asia, Europe, and the Caribbean.

The Smithsonian provides a full description of its musical operations at its Web site (http://www.si.eda/folkways/start.htm). Folkways also distributes its music via Liquid Audio on the Internet and Nordic Records sites, avoiding the typical mail-order process. These sites include music, video clips, liner notes, and, for special releases, educational audiotapes, musical instructional videos, video anthologies, and books.

Yet another program that disseminates music is Smithsonian Productions, which has produced many radio and television programs. These include the radio series *Jazz Smithsonian,* a multiyear series on public radio, featuring performances by the Smithsonian Jazz Masterworks Orchestra, and *Folk Masters,* another public radio series that aired for several years and showcased performances by top artists in traditional music. The Peabody Award–winning radio series, *Black Radio: Telling It Like It Was,* included many examples of African-American music from the middle and latter parts of the 20th century. In 1998, Smithsonian Productions coproduced the public radio series *Remembering Slavery,* with a companion book and audiotape set. In 1999, it joined forces with PBS and the Filmmakers Collaborative of Boston to present a four-part television series entitled *The Mississippi River Song.* The project also included a seven-part public radio series, a companion book, and a two-CD set from Folkways Recordings.

Information can also be obtained from the Center for Black Music Library and Archives, a research facility dedicated to the collection and preservation of all genres of African-American music—popular, jazz, and classical—from all regions. Located at Columbia College in Chicago, CBM subscribes to OCLC, a nationwide library network, and has an Internet link. The center has also developed the CBM Database, an in-house database designed primarily to record the African-American music holdings of six Chicago-area libraries, to serve as a union catalog for Chicago, and to index the holdings of the CBM. The database currently focuses on entering data that are not generally included in most national library databases: music scores, books and dissertations, sound recording singles (45s and 78s), and ephemera and clippings.

Music Organizations

Because the music business is based on vast catalogs of millions of titles, each with its own history of legal title and licensing history, it is ideally suited to the modern database operation that these organizations have adopted. ASCAP, BMI, and the Harry Fox Agency are important sources of information regarding the history, ownership, and rights under copyright of musical works. ASCAP and BMI maintain index departments that supply information to the industry and to the public concerning millions of old and more recent compositions. All new copyright registrations in the U.S. Copyright Office are entered into their indexes. ASCAP offers its song index information through the ASCAP Clearance Express (ACE) on-line service.

The Harry Fox Agency also has a great volume of data on file that is made available to publisher participants and to record companies, motion picture producers, and other users of music. As of 1998 there were approximately

600,000 compositions in the Harry Fox Agency catalog, with an annual revision of ownership by assignment, renewals, etc., of about 49,000. New works are added at the rate of about 25,000 a year. Annual record licenses run about 150,000 a year, and synchronization licenses about 7,000 annually. (A single license includes any combined CD and cassette and any combined co-owner joint licensing.) The agency's audit program brings in $15 million to $29 million a year. This complex operation is greatly assisted by current and planned computer technology. The Harry Fox Agency reports that more than 15 record manufacturers, including all of the top five major labels, are electronically connected to the agency's Song Information Request (SIR) database for convenient identification of required licensors. There is no charge for this service to authorized users.

Harry Fox also offers publisher-member access to the Publisher Online Inquiry System (POLI). This service allows members to access information on their own catalogs by using a personal identification number (PIN). As of 1995, the agency began accepting license requests on-line via modem or by electronic data on diskette.

The performing rights societies throughout the world cooperate in the collection of performing rights royalties and in their distribution to appropriate writers and publishers. These activities require extensive identification facilities and services. Two reference lists used by the societies are the CAE list, made up of composers, authors, and publishers who belong to any society, and the WWL list, which is a worldwide list of all works. The various societies all contribute information regarding their respective registered repertoire to these lists. Because of such lists and other materials and services, the problem of unidentified works and claimants has been dramatically reduced in recent years. As of 1999, ASCAP, PRS, and BUMA undertook the most significant centralized data bank with a projected budget of over $20 million. (See Chapter 14.)

The many performing rights societies, through their membership with CISAC, have organized a central information center through Switzerland's SUISA for general cross-checking of all repertoires. Similarly, Norway's Nordisk Copyright Bureau has accepted the role of central research source for various societies involved in mechanical licensing. This is a major step toward erasing the infamous "black box" problem of unallocated monies due to absence of identification of the owner. In addition, individual members of the Harry Fox Agency, ASCAP, BMI, or SESAC are able to request access to their respective private economic data.

Professional Research Services

When it is necessary to locate the owners of musical copyrights in connection with prospective motion picture, television, stage, and record productions,

ASCAP, BMI, the Harry Fox Agency, and unions and trade organizations may be helpful. The U.S. Copyright Office can be helpful. Where an initial request for information produces unsatisfactory results, or where the inquirer does not have the staff, time, or expertise to make his or her own inquiries, professional services may be employed. The same services may also be sought where expertise is needed for the neinvestigation of outstanding licenses.

In addition to Thomson & Thomson, investigative and negotiating services are available through Arlene Fishback Enterprises, 420 California Avenue, Santa Monica, CA 90403. Similar functions are performed by Evan M. Greenspan/EMG, the Winogradsky Company, and the Copyright Clearing-house, all found in California. Susie Vaughan Associates, of Van Nuys, California, furnishes one-stop music and related entertainment clearance for commercial jingles, film, television, and video clips, and rights of publicity. Finally, research services such as BZ/Rights and Permissions, Diamond Time, and Modern World Music (all based in New York) represent other such clearance houses for uses of music in commercials, television and movies.

Reference Materials

There are a number of reference books and manuals that can be used to supplement the aforementioned sources of information.

For more than 40 years, Schwann has published important reference guides to available recordings. Three Schwann publications currently address the American music scene: *Spectrum,* a quarterly guide to nonclassical recordings (rock, pop, jazz, world, gospel, etc.) in all formats; *Opus,* a quarterly guide to more than 40,000 classical recordings; and the *Artist Issue* (organized by performer's name), an annual cross-reference to *Opus* (which is organized by composer's name). Further, both quarterlies feature articles, interviews, and reviews of new releases. The Schwann guides are available for sale in major American record stores as well as by subscription.

Joel Whitburn's Record Research releases a series of books prepared under license from *Billboard* magazine detailing the history of all *Billboard* chart action for singles and albums. Organized alphabetically by artist name and also by song title, Whitburn's publications furnish research and programming material as well as incidental facts concerning both the recordings and the artists.

Billboard Books publishes a number of useful sources that provide record charts, reference materials, and how-to guides. Books such as *Top Pop Singles, Top Pop Albums, Billboard's Top 10 Charts,* and *The Billboard Book of Number One Hits* are chart-based books that span 40 years of popular music. Billboard's reference titles include *This Business of Artist Management, This Business of Music Marketing and Promotion,* and *The Encyclopedia of Record Producers.* Finally, such sources as *How to Be a Working Musician, The Real*

Deal: How to Get Signed to a Record Label from A to Z, and *Start and Run Your Own Record Label* are guides for both amateurs and professionals in the music industry.

Other important print sources are the massive 20-volume 1980 edition of *The New Grove Dictionary of Music and Musicians* (with a new edition to be issued in December 2000), the 8-volume *Encyclopedia of Popular Music* (3rd ed.), and the *Encyclopedia of Popular Music in the World. The New Grove Dictionary* is an extremely thorough reference to all genres of music, including classical, popular and jazz. Entries include information on musical forms, citations and institutions, terms and definitions, instruments, composers and performers, as well as musical history. *The Encyclopedia of Popular Music* is the successor to the 6-volume *Guinness Encyclopedia of Popular Music* and provides over 18,500 profiles of performers, albums, musicals, movies, instruments, and events in the popular music business. The *Encyclopedia* focuses on the genres of rock, country, soul, jazz, rap, folk, new age, blues, R&B, and show music, primarily as the music developed in the United States and the United Kingdom. The *Encyclopedia of Popular Music in the World* is a three-volume source covering the music industry, social and cultural contexts, various musical genres, and the music of various countries and world regions. While it is considerably less thorough than the *Encyclopedia of Popular Music,* its global focus makes it a valuable resource.

In addition, there is a tremendous amount of information available on the Internet. A simple search on the word "music" will return in excess of 30,000 links.

International Trade Shows and Associations

A number of domestic and international trade shows, associations and societies offer a wealth of information as well as prime networking opportunities for those in the record industry.

Since 1967, the International Music and Publishing Market, commonly known as MIDEM, has held an annual international trade show for music business participants including publishers, record companies, artists, managers, performance rights societies, and equipment manufacturers and suppliers. Held in Cannes, France, at the end of January, the 5-day networking event features conferences and concerts showcasing new and established international artists. In 1997, MIDEM launched the annual Latin America and Caribbean Music Market in Miami Beach, Florida. Renamed MIDEM Americana in 1999, this market focuses on music of the Americas and the Caribbean.

Throughout the year, *Billboard* magazine organizes and sponsors trade meetings in the United States as well as abroad. The subject matter ranges from such diverse topics as music videos at the annual Billboard Music Video Conference, to music programming and international music business trade at

Billboard's annual Dance Music Summit. Other *Billboard*-sponsored events include the Music and Marketing Seminar, and the Latin Music Conference.

The International Association for the Study of Popular Music is a nonprofit organization headquartered in Bay City, Michigan. Started in 1981 by musicians, music teachers, researchers, and journalists, its aim was to pool information about popular music otherwise neglected in academic circles and cultural administration. The association continues to organize conferences, symposia, and meetings to exchange information and ideas on various topics at regional and international levels. In addition, it publishes two newsletters, *The Review of Popular Music* and *Popular Music Perspectives,* the latter covering its biannual international conferences.

41

Technology and Music

The music business finds itself in a world of often confusing but always challenging acronyms: DAT, CD-ROM, CD, DVD, Super Audio CD, MP3, SDMI, MIDI. How comforting were the old days when we could wonder at the beneficence of technology and its many gifts to the copyright industries. Recall the statement of Zechariah Chafee Jr. in 1939:

> Copyright is the Cinderella of the law. Her rich older sisters Franchises and Patents, long crowded her into the chimney corner. Suddenly the fairy godmother, Invention, endowed her with mechanical and electrical devices as magical as the pumpkin coach and the mice footmen. Now she whirls through the mad mazes of a glamorous ball.

Indeed, thanks to such technological innovations as radio, television, video, satellite broadcasting, LPs, and CDs, the music industry has danced all the way to the bank with its profits. The worldwide impact of technology rewarded many music industry participants with profit growth figures for many years. When technology raised the specter of new unauthorized uses, such as record rental shops or home copying, legislative changes were enacted to protect the flow of royalties.

Today, technological advances revolve around the Internet. The relationship between the Internet and the music industry promises (or threatens) to bring about a revolution in music marketing and distribution. As the on-line consumer base expands, so too do the capabilities of computer programming. By the dawn of 1999, there were over 1 million music-related Web sites. Internet users can receive music without leaving the home, send music to others, communicate with others who are listening to the same music, make customized compilations, and access information about music that they are listening to.

As digital transmission grows in capacity and popularity, major corporations are forced to take heed. Similarly, music business establishments such as ASCAP, BMI, SESAC, NMPA, and RIAA have expanded their watch on technology in order to both maintain and expand their profit base. Cinderella may be at the ball, but she needs a bodyguard.

The New Technology

Internet music distribution has operated in two ways. The user may make selections from an on-line music catalog—with the completed order being delivered by mail—or the consumer may download music directly from the Web. While some consumers enjoy the ease of on-line purchasing, it still takes a while for products to arrive. Given our society's growing demand for immediate gratification, this method is viewed by some as only a small improvement over traditional retail stores or record clubs. Downloading is rapidly becoming the favored alternative not only for buyers, but also for pirates.

At the time of this writing, there are several technological formats for compressing music so that it can be easily downloaded from the Internet. Most prominent are MP3 (which is not proprietary and therefore available to all), Liquid Audio's Liquid Music System (which encrypts music so that it cannot be illegally copied), and AT&T's a2b format. In addition, Microsoft has its own MS Audio format, which creates files half the size of MP3, and VQF has announced a program that is said to compress files three times as much as MP3 with higher quality. The list will undoubtedly have expanded by the time this book is published; indeed, MP3 already has its own successor, MP4.

The most controversial and best-known compression format is MP3. Originally intended for digital video, it didn't catch on for music until the early 1990s. This technology allows audio files to be squeezed into a much smaller storage space without sacrificing quality, so that what formerly took a user hours to download can now be transmitted in minutes. Compression is accomplished by discarding data which the computer thinks the ear will not hear.

Once the music has been converted into a digital format and compressed into an MP3 file, it can be posted on a Web site for downloading. To play back MP3 files, the user must have special decoding software, most of which is widely available for downloading free of charge. Winamp and Musicmatch are popular for Windows users; Macintosh users can try Macamp. The Real Player Plus G2 from RealNetworks supports MP3, as well as streaming RealAudio and RealVideo. In addition to playing MP3 files on computers, there is now special hardware that allows listeners to enjoy music away from the computer, the most prominent of which is Diamond's palm-sized Rio player.

Any selection of recorded music can be transformed into an MP3 file with the use of an encoder, sometimes called a "ripper," which can also be downloaded from several Web sites. A user can also purchase software that records an MP3 file onto a CD, a process that is called "burning." Once music has been converted to an MP3 file, it can be distributed as an e-mail attachment, posted on the Internet, or "burned" onto a CD.

Furthermore, there is no limit to the number of copies that can be made. It therefore becomes clear why MP3 is the preferred format for pirates. Most legitimate companies that have attempted to discourage such Internet piracy use Liquid Audio, a2b, or some other new secured software. These downloading formats employ security devices to discourage unauthorized copying. While a2b prevents a sound file from being copied, Liquid Audio allows one copy only to be made onto a CD-Recorder. (See "Security on the Internet," page 452.)

Music can also be performed over the Internet through audio streaming. *Audio streaming*, which is likened to an Internet radio, involves transmitting music in a noncompressed, digitized audio file. The music is available for listening purposes only; it can only be stored in the computer's temporary memory, and cannot be downloaded. Streaming has gained popularity among Internet music providers who have begun to recognize the vast marketing and promotional possibilities of "webcasting."

Audio broadband streaming allows webcast programmers to operate without either FCC licenses or territorial limitations. Traditionally, licensed radio stations have limited reception range and high startup costs and must target a broad audience in order to remain competitive. Because a webcast can aim at a niche audience throughout the world at extremely modest startup and running costs, streaming is especially attractive to students, artists, and new entrepreneurs trying to compete in the music business.

The Market

Just how popular has Internet distribution and streaming become? While some observers believe that the industry will gradually but inevitably change over to direct distribution, others believe that there will be a rapid, radical shift. They point to the almost overnight switch from vinyl LPs to CDs as an indicator of how fast a technological development can sweep through the industry. They believe that digital distribution will level the playing field between independent and major record labels, since on-line distribution affords even the smallest record labels the opportunity to reach as wide an audience as a major record label. The prospect of direct foreign sales makes on-line retail particularly attractive to smaller labels that cannot afford their own international setup.

An early example of the power of the Internet is the David Bowie single "Telling Lies," which was made available in September 1996 for download, free of charge, for one week. In that week the single was downloaded 450,000 times to users in 87 countries. In 1999, Bowie, a committed Internet advocate, arranged with 50 participating U.S. retail Web sites for a two-week advance to have 10 songs of his forthcoming Virgin album available for digital downloading in to the North American market. The media barrage sent his new album to the Top 5 charts in several European markets within a week of its official release. Artists such as the Beastie Boys, Soul Coughing, and Public Enemy have recently followed this trend. In May 1999, through the multimedia project atomicpop.com, Public Enemy became the first major recording artist to sell an entire album through direct download, before the product was available in record stores.

In 1998, the International Federation of the Phonographic Industry (IFPI) reported that approximately 90 million MP3 tracks were downloaded each month. MP3.com, the fourth largest music site at that time, reported that in September 1998, 1.5 million separate users downloaded 2 million tracks. Free single downloads have also proven extremely effective promotion tools for new CD releases. Pop band Sugar Ray offered a 30-day download promotion of an exclusive live track to promote their new release. Orders for their CD increased by 70 percent while the download was available. Todd Rundgren, Jethro Tull, and Tori Amos all witnessed similar success in offering free single downloads prior to new releases.

As of 1998, over 5 million players capable of accepting MP3 files were in existence. MP3 software was included by Microsoft as part of its Netshow multimedia package on Windows 98. Winamp, the most popular software used to listen to MP3 format over the Internet, had been downloaded roughly 5 million times by mid-1999.

In 1996, three Internet-only radio stations were in operation. By 1999, there were at least 185 radio stations operating only on the World Wide Web. In June 1999, one radio site, spinner.com, reported 1.5 million listeners monthly. They broadcast over 2 million songs per day and maintained a library of 175,000 selections.

The critics point to the modest start of on-line distribution and seem to feel that until the major labels fully embrace this technology, it will not become the norm. Although a 1998 study by Jupiter Communications entitled "Music Industry and the Internet: Usage, Retail & Digital Distribution" recommended that labels should "proactively adopt digital distribution as a means of delivering music," the major labels have responded cautiously to Internet distribution. They are not willing either to relinquish copyright control of their biggest artists to potential on-line piracy or to upset relationships with traditional retail middlemen. However, despite their initial reluctance, most major labels have become increasingly involved in on-line distribution as the number of on-line buyers continues to grow. In 1997, only 0.3 percent of music buyers purchased on-line. A year later, the number had tripled to 1.1 percent.

The Players

The first company to use the powerful MP3 technology and offer downloadable titles was Internet Underground Music Archive (IUMA). IUMA was started in 1993 by two college students who offered users free access to songs from unknown bands who had paid IUMA to promote their music. By 1998 the company was grossing approximately $1 million per year, receiving approximately 250,000 hits per day, and offering titles from over 1,000 artists.

A California-based record company, Good Noise, entered the world of direct on-line distribution using MP3 technology. Good Noise also encouraged purchasers to distribute the music to others via e-mail. While the music files were encoded with the customers' identity, nothing was added to prevent further distribution. Good Noise took the position that encouraging users to trade music via e-mail could have a positive effect on sales. As Good Noise president and CEO Gene Hoffman stated, "The upside is that one song might become so popular it gets e-mailed back and forth amongst friends ... and they end up saying, 'Let's see what the rest of the album sounds like' " (*Billboard* 11 July, 1998). Others in the industry fear that the approach taken by Good Noise could dramatically reduce CD sales.

Companies in the forefront of music technology such as CDNow, a2b, and Liquid Audio have been consistently developing innovative methods of getting music to people in faster, clearer, and more convenient ways, while endeavoring to ensure that the rights of copyright owners of copyright are safeguarded.

N2K, one of the first on-line music retailers, reported revenues of $13.6 million in the third quarter of 1998. Its retail site, Music Boulevard, carried 260,000 titles and provided 350,000 audio clips in addition to offering music fans access to information about its artists through cybercast concerts and on-line reviews. This company was subsequently acquired by CDNow.

In 1997, CDNow reported $16 million in revenues from sales over the Internet and claimed 33 percent of the market for Internet music sales. Targeted toward young audiences, CDNow focused on rock and pop genres and became the exclusive music retailer for MTV. Having absorbed N2K in a 1998 merger, CDNow became on of the largest on-line music retailer, with over 1 million customers. As of the third quarter of 1998 their music-related revenues were $15.1 million. As of the fourth quarter of 1998, CDNow reportedly sold approximately 2,000 titles per day, comparable to the sales of one or two large Tower Records stores. They offered 250,000 titles and 315,000 audio clips and had developed Audio Advisor, a system whereby customers can e-mail questions about certain selections. However, by midyear 1999, their sales, though quite substantial, were still not enough to constitute a profit. In 1998, they generated $98.5 million in revenue and suffered a net loss of $120.8 million.

In June 1998, amazon.com, the largest retailer of books on-line, added music to its repertoire. With only 125,000 titles and 225,000 clips as of 1999, amazon.com is not as large as CDNow. However, only 6 months after introducing music to their customers, amazon.com's sales were higher than those of its primary competitor. Their substantial profits made them the leading music retailer by midyear 1999. Amazon also offers a free digital download area, which has included such superstars as Sheryl Crow and David Byrne. In

October 1999 *Billboard* reported that amazon.com led the on-line music retailers with over 12 million consumer visits that month. Barnesandnoble.com placed second, with nearly 5 million hits, while CDNow.com was in third place for the month, with 3.5 hits.

By midyear 1999, corporations including Barnes and Noble, Time Warner, Sony, Universal Music Group, and the Virgin Entertainment Group announced plans to aggressively enter the world of on-line sales. Barnesandnoble.com promoted their new site with a previously unreleased live track from the popular recording artist Jewel. The company also hired expert music critics, including jazz critic Gary Giddens, to review new releases, and featured a "listening wall" with 30-second sound bites of music offered at the site.

In midyear 1999, Time Warner began a test project offering new music for digital download. The company offered free bonus tracks from their artists as an incentive to purchase a new album from participating on-line merchants, including CDNow, Tower Records Online, barnesandnoble.com, and Wherehouse Entertainment. Warner used Liquid Audio for established acts and a time-sensitive technology for new and developing acts. This latter method offered tracks that could only be played within a designated time period, or a specific number of times. Reflecting the company's evolving attitude toward new technology, one Time Warner executive stated: "There is not [just] one way to sell music; there is a whole lot of ways to sell music. Retail will sell from brick-and-mortar [conventional stores], through on-line, through download, and through third party downloads. We are just trying to make the pipe bigger. At the end of the day we are going to sell more music through the same people."

In 1999, Time Warner and Sony merged their mail-order operation, Columbia House, with CDNow and planned to offer music for direct download. (As of this writing, The Columbia House–CDNow relationship is uncertain, following the Time Warner–AOL merger.) Similarly, Seagram's Universal Music Group launched a joint venture with BMG known as getmusic.com. In order to secure the music rights, Seagram forged a partnership with Inter-Trust Technologies to protect all music and information transmitted through the site. The Virgin Entertainment Group announced plans to launch an on-line retail site by the end of 1999, offering 1 million items to consumers in the United States, the United Kingdom, Europe, and Japan. The site was designed to feature Radio Free Virgin, a webcast of the songs played in stores across the world.

And not just the major labels are entering the expanding digital market—major computer companies are taking heed as well. In early 1999, the music industry observed the entry-level efforts of two computer-Internet giants: IBM and Microsoft. IBM, with the support of the five major labels, announced that it would be testing its newest direct downloading technology, Electronic Music Management System (EMMS). According to *Replication News* (now *Media Line*), this technology would offer customers full-length CD-quality albums that could be downloaded within 3 minutes. IBM et al. share the RIAA's concern about piracy, so the EMMS uses encryption, watermarking, and the Serial Copy Management System (SCMS) technology, which is designed to prevent additional copying. (See "Security Devices.")

In a parallel operation, Microsoft announced in early 1999 that it would be entering the business of downloading and streaming music using Windows Media Technologies 4.0. This technology promised greater sound quality than the MP3 format, with only half the memory space. Some industry analysts believed that because of its obvious dominance and entrenchment in the computer market, Microsoft would have a considerable advantage. Some have expressed concern that Microsoft may exert the same control over the music industry as it does over current operating systems. However, as of spring 1999, the major labels had not openly embraced the new system from Microsoft.

Such media giants as Sony Entertainment and Intel have also made multi-million-dollar investments in streaming technology. Similarly, established music companies such as Rolling Stone and MTV Networks run their own on-line stations, offering a variety of unique listening formats. And many radio stations now offer their programs over the Internet in addition to conventional broadcasting.

America Online (AOL), the largest Internet service provider, purchased two companies: Spinner Networks, which operates the Internet radio site spinner.com, and Nullsoft, the company that makes Winamp and Shoutcast, which allows users to broadcast MP3-coded audio over the Web. In 1999, AOL announced an agreement with emusic.com that would enable users to down-load from AOL's spinner.com, ICQ, and Winamp sites, thereby positioning itself to be a major on-line distributor. Early in 2000, America Online merged with Time Warner, a source of vast music and recorded music catalogs and significant cable facilities. This merger brought together the leading Internet service provider with one of the foremost content providers. Immediately after this announcement, the record and music publishing divisions of Time Warner and EMI entered into a joint venture, making the available content for the AOL operations even more important.

Yahoo!, a leading search service, bought broadcast.com, an Internet site that delivers music, sports events, and book readings among other audio programming. In 1999, in partnership with Emusic, Yahoo! began selling digital downloads through its digital Web site, both in the Liquid Audio secure-compression format and the open MP3 format. The site provides a means for users to remix selected tracks on-line, to view videos on demand, to interact with artists via live programs, to receive streaming audio content from Yahoo! Broadcast Services, and to browse a licensed music directory.

Also in 1999, RealNetworks developed the PC Jukebox, which allows a user to load CDs into the computer and organize songs by artist, genre, and title. Users can then customize a playlist from thousands of songs and stream the songs from the Internet. RealNetworks claims an 85 percent share of the market for streaming software and has about 60 million registered users. Early in the year 2000 MPS.com introduced a "digital storage locker" called "Da Bomb." Customers could establish an account number for streaming CDs of even big-name stars upon proof of purchase of the CD. Ten labels brought suit, which is now pending. However, the threat of piracy looms large and Microsoft is developing competitive software that protects copyrighted works. (See also "CD Kiosks," below.)

In contrast to the low-budget, niche marketing of audio-only transmission is the high-stakes phenomenon of converging interactive TV. Time Warner test-marketed this product without success in the early 1990s in Orlando, Florida. In the 1970s, there were aborted experiments with videotext, video on demand, and more recently, Internet via TV. Of current interest are the multi-billion-dollar investments being made by telecommunications giants in inter-active cable companies that hold out the prospect of fully integrated telephone service, video on demand, stereo audio, video games, and Internet access.

Security on the Internet

As Internet technology has developed, so has the demand for more advanced security systems. The protection of literary and artistic rights through technical devices is not a recent concept. For years, pay-TV channels have had limited access through scrambled channels. Because on-line retail activity is on the rise, the success of the Internet as a profitable business vehicle hinges upon the security of payment and the protection of exclusive rights. The two primary forms of security are watermarking and encryption.

Watermarking involves embedding data into a digital file that cannot be removed without damaging the file. Watermarked files are likened to a digital fingerprint and can contain copyright ownership information, customer identi-fication, and royalty tracking information. One form of watermarking is *data authentication,* which prohibits the work from being modified and ensures that the information received is authentic.

Given the increased use of the Internet as a source of retail, the impor-tance of effective watermarking has become a global agenda. In June 1997, the Digital Media Management in the European Music Sector (Muse), along with the six major record labels, the RIAA, and IFPI, challenged technology compa-nies to come up with an industry-standard watermarking system. The water-marking system finally chosen must be effective for monitoring artist performance rights, piracy, copy management, as well as keeping track of copy-right information in downloaded material.

Encryption is the process of encoding data or communications in a form that only the intended recipient can understand. Encryption can be put in the software file or the device that receives the file. The receiving device recognizes the recipient's formula, or key, and allows the user to decode the encrypted data. Encryption devices are often used to limit access to certain persons or portions of the work or for specific amounts or periods of time. Liquid Audio has created an encryption device through which the customer's credit card number is encoded in the digital music file. Each time a copy is made, it is charged to the customer's account.

With the advent of digital versatile discs (DVD), encryption technology has become all the more important. The potential risk of home copying is far greater for DVD than for videotape because of its digital format. The advent and release of material on both DVD video and DVD audio have been hindered by the lack of an effective security technology. Although sound and video quality is superior to compact discs and videotapes, major record labels and film production companies have been apprehensive about releasing material in this format.

Critics feel that these security devices may never be fully effective against computer hackers, who seem to always be one step ahead. According to David Leibowitz of Aris Technologies, "Encryption is like building a better mouse-trap: what you often get is better-educated mice." This argument may have merit given some recent developments. According to *Replication News* (now *Media Line*), Internet hackers have organized to develop ways to defeat the anticopying protection in DVD players and have set up a number of Web sites that offer the information to users. There are a number of software programs available on the Internet that allow users to disable copy protection. In addition, there are hardware options that can be used to defeat security devices.

In early 1999, IBM, Intel, Toshiba, and Matsushita Electric Industrial developed a way to prevent the illegal copying of DVD audio discs. The new technology "marked" and "coded" the discs so that a signal is sent to the potential recorder (whether personal computer or DVD player) and limits the number of copies that can be made. This latest security is superior to watermarking in that the record companies will be able to control exactly how many copies of a particular disc can be made, thus minimizing copyright infringement. IBM has also been working with other companies on developing a similar system for DVD video.

Policing the Internet

Internet piracy—downloading and recording music for free—has become rampant in recent years, particularly as the required file space has become compressed and as the speed of transmission and accessibility to the Internet has increased. Additionally, on-line violations are extremely difficult and tedious to track. Web site creators often encourage downloaders to take music for free and merely ask them to upload new music in exchange. Their argument is that no money is exchanged. Nonetheless, piracy displaces retail sales.

The development of portable MP3 players is of major concern for groups such as the RIAA and IFPI, who are committed to stamping out Internet piracy. These groups feel that since the MP3 format is the overwhelming choice of Internet pirates, hardware such as the MPMan and the palm-sized Rio, developed by Diamond Multimedia Systems, are simply fueling the flames of Internet piracy.

In *RIAA v. Diamond Multimedia Systems, Inc.*, 180 F.3d 1072 (9th Cir. 1998), the RIAA sought an injunction against the sale of the Rio, claiming that this device encouraged users to download pirated music and would thus replace the sale of CDs. The case turned on whether or not the Audio Home Recording Act of 1992, which was passed to protect artists from copyright infringement involving digital recording devices, included the MP3 player. Under that act, all digital recording devices must include a serial copy management system (SCMS). However, the act provided for an exemption for computer equipment. The court of appeals determined that since MP3 players are primarily used for playback purposes, they fall within the exemption.

In December 1998, the RIAA took further action along with the five major labels, other recording industry associations, and technology companies such as Liquid Audio, America Online, Lucent Technologies, AT&T, RealNetworks, Toshiba, and Matsushita and instituted the Secure Digital Music Initiative (SDMI). The SDMI is an attempt to create a universal security standard for distributing music via the Internet, one that will protect the rights of copyright holders and replace the MP3, which offers no such protection. In fact, the creator of the MP3 format, Leonardo Chiariglione, was chosen to head the SDMI. Chiariglione predicted that a format would be developed and approved in time for the major labels to sell on-line music for Christmas 1999. Many involved with the SDMI predicted that a final digital downloading system would not be operating before mid-2000.

Because of the courts' refusal to grant an injunction against Diamond Multimedia, many companies developing similar products were unsure whether to wait for the SDMI standard or to begin selling players that use the MP3 format. If a new standard is developed, there is much debate as to whether these players should use both the new format and MP3. A sunset compromise has been proposed whereby the MP3 format will be accepted until a certain date. Some companies, such as Creative Labs, which developed its own player, the Nomad, are undecided about embracing the new technology. According to Hock Leow, vice president of Creative Labs, "We're definitely interested, but it depends on how difficult it is to implement their specification. If it's very hard for consumers to use or cost-prohibitive, I don't think we'll manufacture it."

In 1997, RIAA joined 12 record companies in copyright infringement lawsuits against three Internet music archive sites that offered MP3 compressed titles, seeking restraining orders and temporary injunctions. The cases were settled on January 21, 1998; the defendants were required to pay $100,000 for each infringed sound recording, but the RIAA agreed to forgo payment provided that the defendants not repeat the offense.

RIAA admits that there is no way to stop the problem completely. According to RIAA vice president and associate director of antipiracy Frank Creighton, "the real goal is to minimize the problem ... we're not so naive as to be sitting here telling you it will all go away."

The RIAA has begun experimenting with software that automatically searches the Internet for sites offering downloaded music. Intersect, a company designed to scan the Internet for sites that use audio and video download, offers a service called MusicReport. In 1998, MusicReport stated that there were over 2,600 sites offering illegal or "pirated" audio downloads and CDs over the Internet.

The RIAA has also attacked the problem at what it perceives as its source: college campuses. Students often have access to their colleges' powerful computer systems and a great deal of Internet piracy activity takes place on campus. The RIAA has implemented an educational program called Sound-byting. According to Mark Mooradian, senior analyst at Jupiter Communications, "There is a real educational initiative that needs to be taken by the music industry to teach people that music has value that needs to be paid for." Numerous universities and other institutions are working with the RIAA to identify and curtail the activities of students who are using the institutional Internet to post records on MP3. According to the RIAA, piracy creates a loss of $300 million per year to the American recording industry.

Internet Effect on Performance Rights Organizations

As with all other digital technologies, streaming can rob the copyright holder of performance rights. All three of the U.S. performance rights organizations (ASCAP, BMI, and SESAC) believe that artists deserve performance royalties for audio streaming. The Digital Millennium Copyright Act, passed in 1998, required performance fees be paid to artists and labels for recordings played on digital radio. However, various issues revolving around licensing and monetary rates remain to be settled.

In a 1998 speech, John Hutchinson, CEO of the MCPS/PRS Music Alliance, expressed the view that performance rights societies could be threatened by the advent of the Internet. "Even though they have survived and largely thrived in a span of time since before broadcasting and commercial sound recordings began," he stated, "can this creaking and groaning gang of old timers—societies, that is—really survive the onslaught of the digital age?" Hutchinson went on to give some survival tips to the performance rights societies. He began by stating that proper electronic copyright management systems must be implemented to facilitate and expedite royalty information and payments to the societies. He believed that the societies must realize that the Internet will bring competition, and that they will no longer possess a monopoly in the industry. As a result, ASCAP and BMI have to be vigilant in collecting from Internet music users in order to offset conventional broadcast uses that have been their mainstay.

ASCAP introduced EZ-Eagle (formerly EZ-Seeker) software technology, the result of a joint effort between ASCAP and Online Monitoring Service (OMS); EZ-Eagle offers a potential solution to the problem of finding, licensing, and tracking music performed on the Internet. It locates Internet sites using commonly available audio and video file formats and assesses the relative value of the site by monitoring the size and amount of advertising on the site. The EZ-Eagle automatically issues license forms where appropriate and monitors compliance with these licenses. According to John LoFrumento of *Playback* magazine, "this remarkable software identifies the highest value music sites, captures song title information, decodes any watermarking technology, identifies the user, and automatically sends licensing materials." ASCAP states that it will make EZ-Eagle available to foreign performance and mechanical rights societies.

In 1998, ASCAP developed RateCalc to solve the difficult problem of licensing music over the Internet. RateCalc allows Internet music users to determine their ASCAP licensing fees while on-line. The Web site licensee must answer four simple questions and is then allowed to view a quick calculation of a basic license. The licensee can then choose which rate schedule is most suited to his or her needs. As of this writing, ASCAP is the only performance rights organization to distribute royalties to songwriters for on-line performances of their songs.

ASCAP has also introduced ACE, an on-line service that provides information about a particular song. The user simply enters the title of the song and is then given the writers and publisher of the song. Each song in the ASCAP directory is given a title code (T-code), which allows the user to differentiate between two songs with the same title.

SESAC, in agreement with Aris Technologies, was the first performance rights organization to employ MusiCode watermark technology for the identification and tracking of musical performances. MusiCode delivers information to allow proof of ownership, proof of copyright violation, and unauthorized copying of music.

Hoping to protect copyright owners' performance rights over the Internet, SESAC has made an agreement with Liquid Audio. The agreement is intended to "simplify music rights licensing and reporting via the World Wide Web." The agreement calls for Liquid Audio to promote SESAC's Internet/New Media License to Web sites that use Liquid Audio's music downloading technology by distributing license agreements and supporting material to Web site operators. Liquid Audio has also provided SESAC with information about sites that engage in the downloading of music. According to John Stone, manager of business development at Liquid Audio, "By partnering with SESAC, we are enabling our customers who offer music on the Internet to handle rights reporting seamlessly so that SESAC affiliates receive payment without hassle."

In April 1995, BMI contracted with On Ramp, a music Web site that allows its users to browse or direct-download songs. The agreement was a blanket song performance license giving On Ramp unlimited access to BMI's entire list of more than 3 million titles recorded by over 160,000 artists. BMI offers assistance to both members and nonmembers on its own Web site. One noteworthy feature of the BMI site is the HyperRepertoire service, which is a song database in which the user can search for information on writers or publishers. The database allows the user to search by song title or by writer's name. (See Chapter 14.)

Copyright Legislation

As discussed in Chapter 7, the first federal statute to expressly address the digital music revolution was the Audio Home Recording Act of 1992. It was followed in 1995 by a second statute, the misnamed Digital Performance Right in Sound Recordings Act (DPRSR Act). This legislation was intended to assure hardware manufacturers as well as tape and blank CD suppliers that they would be immune from copyright infringement lawsuits if they honored statutory license fees based on their gross receipts. The legislation was endorsed by the copyright and record industries, including the RIAA, AFM, AFTRA, ASCAP, BMI, and the Songwriters Guild of America.

Although attention has been directed to statutory protection and judicial enforcement (or, in the case of Rio and MP3, the refusal of the court to interpret statutory language as sufficient), another aspect must be considered: international treaty. Article 11 of the WIPO treaty requires that the parties "provide adequate legal protection and effective legal remedies against the circumvention of effective technological measures." The article also provides for protection against "acts ... which are not authorized by the authors concerned or permitted by law." It is conceivable that once the SDMI system is generally approved and in place, the circumvention will be considered a violation of the treaty and any statute that is insufficient to fulfill treaty obligations will be amended.

When it comes to the other aspect of DAT record distribution, including downloading via CDNow, MusicMaker, etc., the DPRSR Act uses the same "voluntary" or arbitration procedures as set out for performances but at the special reproduction rates so negotiated or set, calculated on each song and each unit of reproduction. The act calls it "digital phonograph delivery" as distinguished from subscription or other performance without downloading capacity. Of special note is the recognition that a controlled-composition rate is inapplicable except for an artist contract wherein the artist was contractually obligated before June 22, 1995, and where the controlled-composition rate contract was entered into by an artist who retained administrative or ownership rights after the songs in question were recorded.

It is obvious that these exceptions recognize a need not to detract from contractual rights previously owned by a record company and contractual negotiations freely entered into by an artist/owner of music publishing rights. It is a limited victory for the music publisher group.

Under the Copyright Act of 1976, an individual cannot be convicted of criminal copyright infringement unless he or she willfully infringes a copyright "for purposes of commercial advantage or private financial gain." In

United States v. LaMacchia, 871 F. Supp. 535 (D. Mass. 1994), the defendant, a graduate student attending MIT, solicited users of a bulletin board system to submit copies of copyrighted computer software programs for posting on the system and then encouraged users to download the copies illegally. Because there was no evidence that LaMacchia had profited in any way from the act, the district court dismissed the charges. Congress attempted to address this problem in the No Electronic Theft Act (NET Act), signed by President Clinton on December 16, 1997 (Public Law 105-147), which added a definition for the term *financial gain* to include the receipt (or expectation of receipt) of anything of value, including other copyrighted works. Further, this act also criminalizes the electronic reproduction or distribution of copyrighted works by electronic means, if more than $1,000 in total retail value during any 180-day period is involved.

On October 28, 1998, President Clinton signed the Digital Millennium Copyright Act (DMCA) so that the United States would be in compliance with two treaties: the WIPO Copyright Treaty and the WIPO Performances and Phonograms Treaty. The treaties are intended to make digital networks safe places to disseminate and exploit copyrighted works and to assist the copyright owner in controlling access to his or her copyrighted work. The treaties address the possible circumvention of technologies such as encryption, used to protect copyrighted works in the digital environment. One way to prevent unauthorized access to music on the Internet is to prohibit the manufacturing of technologies or products used to defeat such security devices as watermarking and encryption. Such preventive measures stop illegal circumvention at the source and result in wide results as opposed to measures which target only isolated illegal acts. The treaties further target the deliberate alteration or deletion of copyright management information, which identifies a work, its owners, and its permissible use.

Some believe that on-line service providers should be held liable for the illegal distribution of copyrighted works, whether they had any knowledge of the illegal distribution or not. Under Title 2 of the Digital Millennium Copyright Act of 1998, a service provider that falls within one of the "safe harbors" created by the act will be subject only to carefully proscribed injunctive remedies and will be exempt from any monetary damages. These safe harbors are set forth by the act.

- Where the service provider acts as a "mere conduit" for an infringing transmission
- For system caching
- For unknowingly storing infringing material, where the on-line service provider receives no financial benefit and responds "expeditiously" to remove the infringing material
- For unknowingly linking users to sites containing infringing material, and the on-line service provider responds "expeditiously" to remove the infringing material

Thus service providers are now cleared from any contributory liability if their activities fall within one of the above categories. Also the key to safety seems to hinge on the level of cooperative activity the on-line service provider exhibits after it becomes aware of the infringing material. In order to qualify for these safe harbors, the service provider must inform its users that it will terminate the services of repeat infringers. Also the service provider must accept and accommodate any "standard" technological security devices used by the copyright owners to identify and protect the copyright owner's rights. Appendix D reproduces excerpts from Titles I and II of the DMCA.

Other Areas of Technology

CD KIOSKS

In 1998, CD World initiated Music Point kiosks at some 400 locations, including airports and music stores, designed to deliver custom-made CDs to consumers in just 4 minutes. The tracks were stored in a digital format on a central IBM computer database in New York. As of late 1998, CD World had licensed 339,000 tracks and was negotiating an additional 214,000. Each kiosk also offered video screens to attract customers with music promotions and sponsor's ads. The kiosks offered CDs that contain 45 minutes of music and charged approximately $18 for a complete CD or $4.20 for a CD single containing two recordings. The kiosk actually "burned" the CD as the consumer waited, with the retailer responsible for supplying blank discs.

CD World's kiosks keep track of royalty distribution through a copyright management system that pays a royalty of 40 cents per track. CD World obtained mechanical licensing agreements from the Harry Fox Agency, the Swiss collection society SUISA, and the French organization SACEM.

AUDIOPHILE

Companies involved in developing the latest technologies in music are constantly searching for ways to improve sound quality. Just as the CD virtually replaced the vinyl record, it is hoped that DVD audio will raise the level of fidelity even higher and enable users to have surround sound with up to six speakers.

Prior to the release of DVD audio, some companies used the technology of DVD video. These new "advanced audio" discs—called digital audio discs (DADs)—were available from Classic Records and Chesky Records and could be played on DVD players. Classic Records used this new technology to improve vintage recordings of jazz and blues artists such as Johnny Lee Hooker and Red Rodney; as of December 1998, Classic had released four titles on this new format. Chesky Records chose to release new performances by more modern artists.

In the fall of 1999, two formats of DVD audio were finally made available to the public. The first is called DVD Audio and has the backing of major corporations such as Hitachi, JVC, Matsushita, Mitsubishi, Pioneer, Seagram, Thomson, Time Warner, and Toshiba. The other format is called Super Audio CD and has the backing of Sony and Phillips, the same companies that created the CD. The DVD Audio is targeted at the mass market and is considerably cheaper than the Super Audio CD, which targets audiophiles. In addition, the DVD Audio is compatible with DVD video disc players, which are already in many homes. Although there may be some competition between the two formats, spokespeople for each format say that they do not believe that a war will ensue, such as the one between the early video formats, VHS and Betamax.

CD-ROMs

The popularity of CD-ROMs has created a new realm for the licensing of music. Music has become an integral part of most types of CD-ROMs, which range from educational to entertainment. Video games often use popular songs to enhance the effect on the player. An example might be the use of the "Star Wars" theme song for a space game. In the past, most video arcades obtained performance licenses from ASCAP or BMI.

Another growing use of music on CD-ROMs has been music software for the aspiring musician. Many of these allow the user to compose music on a five-line musical staff. Most have music programmed into the software that allows the user to play along. More advanced home studios, such as those offered by Cakewalk, can convert a home PC into a digital multitrack home studio through musical instrument digital interface (MIDI). These types of programs usually have sequenced music, which the user can pick from when creating a composition.

The use of music on CD-ROMs has created new issues for licensing. There are three basic ways of licensing music on CD-ROMs, depending on the circumstances.

1. A flat fee is usually charged for works where relatively few copies will be made and none will be sold. This method is often used for promotional CD-ROMs or for corporate training videos.
2. For CD-ROMs that are for sale or that will be mass-produced, a royalty system is most often employed. The copyright owner will charge a royalty based upon the sales of the work containing the music.
3. In instances where there is more than one song involved in the work (some CD-ROMs can have thousands of songs), music copyright owners will typically request a royalty that is prorated among the number of copyrighted musical selections in the work.

MIDI

Musical instrument digital interface (MIDI) is another recent technological development. It has become the most common way of storing and transferring musical instrument data and has allowed for the direct digital linkup of musical instruments. MIDI products give the musician tremendous flexibility. Given the right equipment, any instrument or sound can be converted to and stored in MIDI—guitars, drums, and vocals. There are, however, copyright implications for licensing the manufacture and distribution of MIDI files. The Copyright Office states that MIDI files are indistinguishable from other sound or phonogram recordings. Thus an audio-only MIDI license would be subject to the statutory rate, which is 7.55 cents for each song, or 1.45 cents for each fraction thereof, as of January 1, 2000.

DIGITAL HOME RECORDING

Not only have technological advances affected music for the consumer, but with the advent of digital recording technologies, old methods of tape recording have disappeared nearly as fast as vinyl records. Digital products are now financially within the reach of many artists, and the number of home studios in the United States has dramatically increased. Owning a digital home studio gives the artist greater flexibility in recording without the time pressures of hourly recording studio rates. (See Chapter 36, section entitled "The Costs of Making a Demo.")

MINI DISC

When Sony Music first introduced the MiniDisc in 1992, they hoped it would replace the CD as the preferred consumer format. Their expectations were not realized, owing in part to a recession and in part to competing formats such as the digital cassette. However, in 1998 sales of MiniDisc players rose dramatically to 10.5 million units sold internationally; they are expected to rise to 22.9 million in 2000 and 65.7 by 2005. The MiniDisc offers the consumer the same digital quality and compact size as a CD, but also allows the consumer to record to blank discs. While Sony has increased its investment in the MiniDisc based on the recent sales growth, many industry experts believe that the growth will be stifled as the price of CD-Recorders continue to drop to more affordable ranges.

The Future

As technology continues to advance, bringing music to people in ways never dreamed of, it will bring with it new issues and problems that even the keenest imagination cannot predict. Some technology issues that were only posited in the last edition of this book have now come to the fore.

If legislation is passed requiring encoding of the music owner's identity and royalty provisions, this will detract from traditional rights of bargaining for individual uses. This may indeed lead to music being treated as a public utility with standardized rates. The encoding of CDs will allow cheaper and more efficient logging of broadcast uses and will compete with the logging techniques of ASCAP and BMI.

Expired copyrights, once in the public domain, will be easily identified through the use of new data banks and encoding devices, making users better aware of the economic benefits of using public domain music at the expense of copyrighted music. Artist and record company performance rights, once long delayed, will be hastened by the easier identification of broadcast uses through encoding devices. Satellite broadcast technique has transcended historic national boundaries, making obsolete the licenses issued on an exclusive territorial basis. Sampling of earlier recordings will now be easily identified through encoding.

The dramatic growth of the Internet and digital technology creates some interesting scenarios for the future. Given the latest downloading capabilities over the Internet, what will be the fate of traditional retailers? If anyone can simply download a favorite song (after sampling the song for free), will the need for music stores be eliminated? As the price of CD-Recorders and blank discs drops, most people will be able to "burn" their own CDs directly off of the Internet in the near future. Where do traditional record stores and CD replicators fit in?

This downloading and uploading technology, coupled with the availability and low cost of high-quality recording equipment, seems to minimize the need for record companies. An artist who owns a high-quality digital recording studio may be able to do his or her own recording and then offer the song to millions of consumers over the Internet without the aid of a record company. Of course, the artist would still need promotion and marketing. However, with the increased use of the Internet, one wonders how these processes will evolve as well.

The arrival of such power in such a short time span may seem to have complicated the music industry, but this is not actually the case. Since music is available to the consumer in faster, clearer, and more flexible formats, the consumer becomes interested in staying abreast of these latest technologies; that is what happened when CDs replaced LPs. Consumers can now sample the latest release of an artist before making a purchase, thus creating greater consumer satisfaction. Technological advances are now helping songwriters who would normally not collect royalties to finally collect the money they deserve. Other advances allow for storage directly onto the hard drive of a computer, eliminating the need for packaging. These and other advances will no doubt have a positive effect on the music industry as a whole. As the consumer becomes more sophisticated, the music industry will simply have to adapt.

It is easy to sympathize with Chicken Little, who cried in absolute dismay, "The sky is falling." The music industry views the challenges and opportunities of the digital age with fascination and dismay. The sky is not falling. The prospect of unlicensed digital bootlegging or free offerings from unsigned acts is no more difficult a challenge to the music industry now than home taping, rental shops, photocopying, and other music reprography was in the past.

Where there is a challenge there are creative minds working to meet the challenge. If absolutely free music is offered, there will be advertising revenues in all likelihood. If valuable archive recordings are slipped onto Web sites by illegal hackers, investigators and enforcement agencies will likely use some new form of technology to find and punish the interlopers. If consumers demand do-it-yourself compilations, licensed middlemen will be available for a fair redistribution of revenues.

The sky can only fall on an industry that is sleeping, and that is not the case with the music industry. The concerned industry members who generate millions of words of comments in *Billboard* and other trade papers and in convention gatherings and lectures clearly recognize the problem, see the opportunities, and accept the challenge.

At the end of the first calendar quarter of the year 2000, industry leaders quoted in *The Wall Street Journal* expressed cautious optimism.

Edgar Bronfman, Jr., Chief Executive of the Universal Music Group parent corporation, Seagram Co., made the following prediction: "Over the next 10 years, these new music-delivery systems will grow the industry to approximately $100 billion in global sales, up from the current $38 billion. ... You'll be able to program bundles or song packages, compilations, video singles and video compilations. You'll be able to buy or program songs by genre, by era, by the hour or half-hour or minute or day." Aram Sinnreich, an analyst for Jupiter Communications, said that on-line music sales should reach $2.6 billion by the year 2003, or 14 percent of all U.S. music sales. He also predicted, however, that the bulk of those sales will be through mail order, with digital downloading limited to an estimated $150 million by 2003.

Other analysts looked forward to the benefits of the Digital Millennium Copyright Act of 1998 and the various means it provides of licensing music performance in the digital environment. Referring to the Act, Paul Vidich, Executive Vice-President of Time-Warner's Music Group, said, "In the Net, for the first time we actually have the legal basis on which to license for a fee."

At the same time, the companies that have invested in promotional ventures that offer downloading from their Web sites, such as BMG/Universal's getmusic.com, will have to keep an active eye on MP3.com, which is offering $200,000 a month in prizes for best activity to unsigned artists that use MP3.com facilities to avoid the middleman services of the major labels.

Obviously, the music world is changing rapidly and continues to be a fascinating game to watch.

Appendixes

A

WIPO Memorandum of August 1996

In Geneva from December 2 to 20, 1996, several committees that had been formed under the auspices of the World Intellectual Property Organization (WIPO) convened for the purpose of discussing a possible protocol to the Berne Convention for the Protection of Literary and Artistic Rights. According to the WIPO program for the 1990–91 biennium: "[T]he protocol would be mainly destined to clarify the existing, or establish new, international norms where, under the present text of the Berne Convention, doubts may exist as to the extent to which that Convention applies." The following document has been excerpted from a memorandum issued on August 30, 1996 by the Chairman of the WIPO Committees of Experts. There were two committees: One dealt with the question of Berne Convention protocol; a second addressed the issue of a possible new international instrument on the protection of the rights of performers and producers of phonograms.

[*Note:* Appendix B consists of selected articles from the Berne Convention of 1971, including all those mentioned in the WIPO memorandum.]

...2. The Committee of Experts was convened in two sessions, the first in November 1991 and the second in February 1992. The sessions were started on the basis of working documents covering a broad range of topic areas including the subject matter of copyright, certain particular rights, the applicability of minima, and the obligation of granting national treatment. Among the questions concerning subject matter was the desirability of covering the rights of producers of sound recordings in the protocol. ...
4. The Committee of Experts on a Possible Protocol to the Berne Convention was charged with the responsibility of considering ten specific items: (1) computer programs, (2) databases, (3) rental rights, (4) non-voluntary licences for sound recordings of musical works, (5) non-voluntary licences for primary broadcasting and satellite communication, (6) distribution rights, including an importation right, (7) duration of the protection of photographic works, (8)

communication to the public by satellite broadcasting, (9) enforcement of rights, and (10) national treatment.

The Committee of Experts on a Possible Instrument for the Protection of the Rights of Performers and Producers of Phonograms was charged with the responsibility of discussing all questions concerning the effective international protection of the rights of performers and producers of phonograms. This broad charge left unresolved whether the Committee should consider the rights of performers to extend exclusively to the fixation of their performances in phonograms or also to audiovisual fixations...

The work of the Committees of Experts was based on memoranda prepared by the International Bureau of WIPO until December 1994. Following the recommendation of the Committees of Experts, the Director General of WIPO invited Government members of the Committees and the European Commission to submit proposals for discussion at the September 1995 and February 1996 sessions.

10. As a result of this invitation from the Director General, the International Bureau received written proposals and comments from Argentina, Australia, Brazil, Canada, the European Community and its Member States, Japan, the People's Republic of China, the Republic of Korea, South Africa, the Sudan, the United States of America, and Uruguay. ...

[Editor's Note: The Committees of Experts also received input from the following countries: Africa: Burkina Faso, Cameroon, Côte d'Ivoire, Egypt, Ghana, Kenya, Malawi, Namibia, Nigeria, Rwanda, Senegal, Togo, Tunisia, and Zambia. South America: Argentina, Bolivia, Brazil, Chile, Colombia, Cuba, Ecuador, El Salvador, Honduras, Jamaica, Mexico, Panama, Paraguay, Peru, Trinidad and Tobago, and Venezuela.]

15. Basic Proposals for the substantive provisions of three treaties are proposed by the Chairman of the Committees of Experts:
1. "Treaty on Certain Questions Concerning the Protection of Literary and Artistic Works",
2. "Treaty for the Protection of the Rights of Performers and Producers of Phonograms",
3. "Treaty on Intellectual Property in Respect of Databases."

[Editor's Note: The articles presented in the memorandum are relatively brief, and these have been quoted in their entirety. In the original document, preceding each Article and the Preamble were numerous explanatory notes drafted to offer guidelines for interpreting specific paragraphs and to explain the reasoning behind the proposals. Only some of these have been included. They have been placed *after* the paragraphs they pertain to, and are preceded by the word *Note:*.]

Preamble

The Contracting Parties,

Desiring to develop and maintain the protection of the rights of authors in their literary and artistic works in a manner as effective and uniform as possible,

Recognizing the need to introduce new international rules and clarify the interpretation of certain existing rules in order to provide adequate solutions to the questions raised by new economic, social, cultural and technological developments,

Recognizing the profound impact of the development and convergence of information and communication technologies on the creation and use of literary and artistic works,

> *Note:* The third paragraph acknowledges the connection of the proposed Treaty to the evolution of the overall environment of the intellectual property system: the accelerating development and convergence of information and communication technologies. This evolution extends its effects even to the convergence of the structures of industries and the content they produce, i.e. protected works and performances, and it has a profound impact on the production and distribution of the results of creative work by authors. While introducing certain provisions on "traditional issues", the proposed Treaty also includes solutions to urgent questions raised by the technological developments referred to above. The proposed Treaty is therefore part of a series of simultaneously published draft Treaties which could be characterized as "Global Information Infrastructure Treaties" in the field of copyright and rights related to copyright.

Have agreed as follows:

Article 1: Relation to the Berne Convention

(1) This Treaty is a special agreement within the meaning of Article 20 of the Berne Convention for the Protection of Literary and Artistic Works, as regards Contracting Parties that are countries of the Union established by that Convention.

> *Note:* ... Article 20 of the Berne Convention ... provides that "[t]he Governments of the countries of the Union reserve the right to enter into special agreements among themselves, in so far as such agreements grant to authors more extensive rights than those granted by the Convention, or contain other provisions not contrary to this Convention." Thus, the proposed Treaty could not contain provisions that would diminish the existing rights of authors under the Berne Convention.

(2) Nothing in this Treaty shall derogate from existing obligations that

Contracting Parties have to each other under the Berne Convention for the Protection of Literary and Artistic Works.

(3) Hereinafter, "Berne Convention" shall refer to the Paris Act of July 24, 1971 of the Berne Convention for the Protection of Literary and Artistic Works.

(4) Contracting Parties that are not countries of the Union established by the Berne Convention shall comply with Articles 1 to 21 and the Appendix of the Berne Convention.

Article 2: Application of Articles 3 to 6 of the Berne Convention

Contracting Parties shall apply the provisions of Articles 3 to 6 of the Berne Convention in respect of the protection provided for in this Treaty.

> *Note:* Paragraph (1) of Article 3 of the Berne Convention includes provisions on the main points of attachment: the nationality of the author and the place of publication of the work. Paragraph (2) assimilates habitual residence of an author to nationality. Paragraph (3) defines the expression "published works". Paragraph (4) defines simultaneous publication. Article 4 of the Berne Convention extends the protection of the Convention to authors of cinematographic works, works of architecture and certain other artistic works, even where the conditions of Article 3 are not met. Article 5 of the Berne Convention confirms in its paragraph (1) the principle of national treatment and the obligation to grant the rights specially granted in the Convention and in paragraph (2) the principles of formality-free or automatic protection and independence of protection. Paragraph (3) specifies that national law governs protection in the country of origin. Paragraph (4) lays down the rules that determine the country of origin of a work. In addition, a reference to Article 6 of the Berne Convention has been made in order to provide for the possibility of restricting in certain cases the protection given to works of non-nationals of other Contracting Parties.

Article 3: Notion and Place of Publication

(1) When literary or artistic works are made available to the public by wire or wireless means in such a way that members of the public may access these works from a place and at a time individually chosen by them, so that copies of these works are available, Contracting Parties shall, under the conditions specified in Article 3(3) of the Berne Convention, consider such works to be published works.

(2) When applying Article 5(4) of the Berne Convention, Contracting Parties shall consider works referred to in paragraph (1) of the present Article to be published in the Contracting Party where the necessary arrangements have been made for availability of these works to members of the public.

> *Note:* One of the objectives of the proposed Treaty is to offer solutions to certain questions concerning the impact of new technologies on authors'

rights. Numerous questions are posed, for example, by the interactive, on-demand transmission of works to the public directly into their homes or offices. New forms of electronic publishing have already replaced some forms of traditional dissemination of works. As far as the public is concerned, these new forms of publishing are functionally no different than the traditional forms: the works are available. ...

[T]he provisions of Article 3(3) of the Berne Convention may be applied quite satisfactorily to new forms of electronic publication. The key requirement of Article 3(3) is the availability of copies sufficient to satisfy the reasonable requirements of the public. Electronic publishing over a computer network may easily satisfy this requirement. In an open network environment, any member of the public may have access to copies that can be downloaded into the memory of his computer.

Article 4: Computer Programs

Computer programs are protected as literary works within the meaning of Article 2 of the Berne Convention. Such protection applies to the expression of a computer program in any form.

Article 5: Collections of Data (Databases)

Collections of data or other material, in any form, which by reason of the selection or arrangement of their contents constitute intellectual creations, are protected as such. This protection does not extend to the data or the material itself and is without prejudice to any rights subsisting in the data or material contained in the collection.

Note: This provision is of a declaratory nature. It confirms what is already covered by the Berne Convention.

Article 6: Abolition of Certain Non-Voluntary Licenses

(1) Within three years of ratifying or acceding to this Treaty, Contracting Parties shall no longer provide for non-voluntary licenses under Article 11bis(2) of the Berne Convention in respect of the broadcasting of a work.

(2) Within three years of ratifying or acceding to this Treaty, Contracting Parties shall no longer apply the provisions of Article 13 of the Berne Convention.

Article 7: Scope of the Right of Reproduction

(1) The exclusive right accorded to authors of literary and artistic works in Article 9(1) of the Berne Convention of authorizing the reproduction of their works shall include direct and indirect reproduction of their works, whether permanent or temporary, in any manner or form.

(2) Subject to the provisions of Article 9(2) of the Berne Convention, it shall be

a matter for legislation in Contracting Parties to limit the right of reproduction in cases where a temporary reproduction has the sole purpose of making the work perceptible or where the reproduction is of a transient or incidental nature, provided that such reproduction takes place in the course of use of the work that is authorized by the author or permitted by law.

Note: The author's right of reproduction in literary and artistic works has been laid down in Article 9 of the Berne Convention. According to paragraph (1) of that Article, "[a]uthors of literary and artistic works protected by this Convention shall have the exclusive right of authorizing the reproduction of these works, in any manner or form". The scope of the right of reproduction is already broad. The expression "in any manner or form" could not be more expansive in scope. It clearly includes the storage of a work in any electronic medium; it likewise includes such acts as uploading and downloading a work to or from the memory of a computer. Digitization, i.e. the transfer of a work embodied in an analog medium to a digital one constitutes always an act of reproduction. ...

The first element in this provision is the explicit inclusion of direct and indirect reproduction. ...

The second element in the proposal is intended to clarify the widely held understanding that both permanent and temporary reproduction constitute reproduction within the meaning of Article 9(1) of the Berne Convention. The result of reproduction may be a tangible, permanent copy like a book, a recording or a CD-ROM. It may as well be a copy of the work on the hard disk of a PC, or in the working memory of a computer. A work that is stored for a very short time may be reproduced or communicated further, or it may be made perceptible by an appropriate device. ...

Technological developments have had a great impact on the means that may be used for reproduction. Complete and accurate reproductions may be made quickly and in such a way that the material reproduced resides only a short while in the memory of a computer. In some cases, a certain work or piece of data may never be reproduced as a whole in the memory of a computer; only those parts of the material that are necessary to achieve a certain result may be reproduced, for instance in order to make a work perceptible. In such cases, successive reproduction of portions of a work may, over a period of time, cover the whole work. Some relevant uses may, now or in the future, become totally based on a temporary reproduction.

Today, the countries of the Berne Union may interpret the right of reproduction in different ways. Some countries may consider that temporary reproduction, at least some acts of reproduction the results of which live only a very short time, does not fall under the right of reproduction, whereas other countries may take a contrary interpretation.

The interpretation of a right of such importance as the right of reproduction should be in fair and reasonable harmony all over the world. A uniform interpretation is necessary. Already, the need for legal certainty and predictability has been felt and found lacking in concrete cases. The need for a uniform interpretation is dictated by the need to secure the functioning of the copyright system in a digital future.

Article 8

ALTERNATIVE A: RIGHT OF DISTRIBUTION AND RIGHT OF IMPORTATION

(1) Authors of literary and artistic works shall enjoy the exclusive right of authorizing:
- (i) the making available to the public of the original and copies of their works through sale or other transfer of ownership;
- (ii) the importation of the original and copies of their works, even following any sale or other transfer of ownership of the original or copies by or pursuant to authorization.

(2) National legislation of a Contracting Party may provide that the right provided for in paragraph (1)(i) does not apply to distribution of the original or any copy of any work that has been sold or the ownership of which has been otherwise transferred in that Contracting Party's territory by or pursuant to authorization.

(3) The right of importation in paragraph (1)(ii) does not apply where the importation is effected by a person solely for his personal and non-commercial use as part of his personal luggage.

ALTERNATIVE B: RIGHT OF DISTRIBUTION

(1) Authors of literary and artistic works shall enjoy the exclusive right of authorizing the making available to the public of the original and copies of their works through sale or other transfer of ownership.

(2) A Contracting Party may provide that the right provided for in paragraph (1) does not apply to distribution after the first sale or other transfer of ownership of the original or copies of works by or pursuant to authorization.

Note: The two Alternatives presented in Article 8 reflect the genuine diverging views of many nations in this matter. On the level of an international agreement the Alternatives seem to exclude each other, are apparently contradictory and impossible to reconcile. As an intermediate solution the introduction of agreed conditional limitations of the right of distribution and right of importation, based on Alternative A in Article 8(1), could be explored. National legislation of a Contracting Party could for example provide that these rights do not apply to the distribution or importation of copies of works that have been sold with the consent of the author anywhere in the world, if copies of that work have not been made available in a Contracting Party in a quantity sufficient to satisfy the reasonable needs of the public, within an agreed period of time, e.g. one year, calculated from the publication of that work outside that Contracting Party. An alternative along these lines has not, however, been presented. Any third alternative would have required extensive international consultations which it would not have been possible to organize during the preparation of the proposed Treaty.

The rights provided for in the proposed Treaty, including the right of distribution, are minimum rights. Contracting Parties may provide a higher level of protection. A more restricted concept of exhaustion than international exhaustion represents a higher level of protection. Thus, the solution in Alternative B would not preclude any Contracting Party from applying any conditions or restrictions to the circumstances giving rise to exhaustion. National or regional exhaustion is in full conformity with this provision for those Contracting Parties that take this approach to the distribution right. Introduction of a right of importation is not excluded either.

The main contents of Alternative A follow the proposal made by the United States of America for the February 1996 session of the Committees of Experts. As far as the basic right is concerned, Argentina and Uruguay presented proposals with the same effect but without offering a proposal concerning exhaustion. Alternative B is based on the main approach taken in the proposals made by Australia, Brazil, Canada, Japan, and the Republic of Korea. The group of African countries favoured the international exhaustion of the right of distribution and supported the proposal made by Australia.

Article 9: Right of Rental

(1) Authors of literary and artistic works shall enjoy the exclusive right of authorizing the rental of the original and copies of their works even after distribution of them by or pursuant to authorization by the author.
(2) Except in the case of computer programs, collections of data or other material in machine-readable form, and musical works embodied in phonograms, specific types of works may be excepted from the provisions of paragraph (1) unless the rental of such works has led to widespread copying that materially impairs the exclusive right of reproduction.
(3) Contracting Parties may provide in their national legislation that the provisions of paragraph (1) and paragraph (2) do not apply in respect of architectural works or in respect of works of applied art.

Note: The Berne Convention does not contain any provisions on the rental of copies of literary and artistic works. ...

Paragraph (1) of Article 9 provides authors of literary and artistic works with the exclusive right of authorizing the rental of the original and copies of their works. The right of rental differs from the right of distribution as laid down in Article 8. Paragraph (1) explicitly provides that the right of rental survives distribution, i.e. the first sale or other transfer of ownership. In principle, this right could cover all categories of works. However, in order to design a proposal that would be acceptable to as many Contracting Parties as possible, such a far-reaching solution has not been proposed. ...

Paragraph (2) would maintain the exclusive right of rental for three specific types of works: computer programs, collections of data or other material, within the meaning of Article 5, in machine-readable form, and musical works embodied in phonograms. Contracting Parties could exempt other categories of works from this right, but they would not have this option if such rental led to widespread copying that materially impaired the exclusive right of reproduction....

[C]omputer programs have been excluded from the scope of the right of rental where the program is not the essential object of the rental.... The question of the essentiality of the object of rental may also concern other categories of works, such as databases. The proposed Treaty takes the position that this matter may most feasibly be settled at the national level.

Article 10: **Right of Communication**

Without prejudice to the rights provided for in Articles 11(1)(ii), 11*bis*(1)(i), 11*ter*(1)(ii), 14(1)(i) and 14*bis*(1) of the Berne Convention, authors of literary and artistic works shall enjoy the exclusive right of authorizing any communication to the public of their works, including the making available to the public of their works, by wire or wireless means, in such a way that members of the public may access these works from a place and at a time individually chosen by them.

Note: In the Berne Convention the exclusive right of communication to the public of works has been regulated in a fragmented manner. ...

Technological developments have made it possible to make protected works available in many ways that differ from traditional methods. This is a source of concern in connection with the categories of works that are not covered by the provisions on the right of communication in the Berne Convention. In addition, the interpretation of these provisions may differ. It has become evident that the relevant obligations need to be clarified and that the rights currently provided under the Berne Convention need to be supplemented by extending the field of application of the right of communication to the public to cover all categories of works. ...

The right of communication does not presently extend to literary works, except in the case of recitations thereof. Literary works, including computer programs, are presently one of the main objects communicated over networks. Other affected categories of works are also not covered by the right of communication, significant examples being photographic works, works of pictorial art and graphic works....

The provisions of Article 10 consist of two parts. The first part extends the exclusive right of communication to the public to all categories of works, including any communication by wire or wireless means. It leaves the provisions of Articles 11(1)(ii), 11*bis*(1)(i), 11*ter*(1)(ii), 14(1)(i) and 14*bis*(1) applicable as they are in the Berne Convention.

The second part of Article 10 explicitly states that communication to the public includes the making available to the public of works, by wire or wireless means, in such a way that members of the public may access these works from a place and at a time individually chosen by them. The relevant act is the making available of the work by providing access to it. What counts is the initial act of making the work available, not the mere provision of server space, communication connections, or facilities for the carriage and routing of signals. It is irrelevant whether copies are available for the user or whether the work is simply made perceptible to, and thus usable by, the user.

One of the main objectives of the second part of Article 10 is to make it clear that interactive on-demand acts of communication are within the scope of the provision. This is done by confirming that the relevant acts of communication include cases where members of the public may have access to the works from different places and at different times. The element of individual choice implies the interactive nature of the access.

The features described in the preceding Note entail important delimitations of the relevant acts. The provision excludes mere private communication by using the term "public". Furthermore, the requirement of individual choice excludes broadcasting from the scope of the provision.

Article 10 leaves intact the rights provided for in the listed Berne Convention provisions. The proposal supplements existing Berne Convention protection by adding a right of communication to the public for all categories of works, including literary works, to which the existing right of communication does not apply. These elements in the proposal constitute new rights or an additional dimension to the right of communication. However, the features that have been confirmed in the second half, the "making available" part of the provision, could fall within a fair interpretation of the right of communication in the existing provisions of the Berne Convention. Nevertheless, other interpretations may also exist concerning obligations under the Convention. The objective of the proposal is to harmonize the obligations and to avoid any discrepancies that may be caused by different interpretations.

The expression "communication to the public" of a work means making a work available to the public by any means or process other than by distributing copies. This includes communication by wire or wireless means. The technology used may be analog or digital, and it may be based on electromagnetic waves or guided optical beams. The use of the nonrestrictive term "any" in front of the word "communication" in Article 10, and in certain provisions of the Berne Convention, emphasizes the breadth of the act of communication. "Communication" implies transmission to a public not present in the place where the communication originates.

Communication of a work can involve a series of acts of transmission and temporary storage, such incidental storage being a necessary feature of the communication process. If, at any point, the stored work is made available to the public, such making available constitutes a further act of communication which requires authorization. It should be noted that storage falls within the scope of the right of reproduction (see Notes on Article 7).

As communication always involves transmission, the term "transmission" could have been chosen as the key term to describe the relevant act. The term "communication" has been maintained, however, because it is the term used in all relevant Articles of the Berne Convention in its English text. It deserves to be mentioned that in the French text the expression "la transmission publique" has been used in Articles 11 and 11ter, and the expression "la transmission par fil au public" has been used in Article 14 while "communication to the public" and "communication to the public by wire" are the English expressions. In Article 11bis of the French text of the Convention, the corresponding expression is "la communication publique."

It seems clear that, at the treaty level, the term "communication" can be used as a bridging term to ensure the international interoperability and mutual recognition of exclusive rights that have been or will be provided in national legislations using either the term "transmission" or the term "communication". The former refers to a technical transfer while the latter implies, in addition to the technical transfer, that something is communicated. For the purposes of the proposed Treaty, this slight difference between the terms is irrelevant. What is transferred or communicated is the work.

The term "public" has been used in Article 10 as it has been used in the present provisions of the Berne Convention. It is a matter for national legislation and case law to define what is "public". However, the aspects dealt with in Note 10.10 should be taken into account. The "public" consists of individual "members of the public" who may access the works from different places and at different times.

It is stated [above] ... that one of the purposes of Article 10 is to "complete" the right of communication, extending it to all works. One may note that the proposed language of Article 10 does not explicitly include the limiting terms "performance" or "recitation" of a work as included in Article 11(1)(ii) and Article 11ter(1)(ii) of the Berne Convention. This is not an omission but a more modern formulation of the provision.

The wording "communication ... of their works" also covers the communication of performances and recitations of works. It may be recalled, for example, that when Article 9 and Article 11bis were introduced into the Berne Convention, no corresponding clauses were considered to be necessary. ...

It is strongly emphasized that Article 10 does not attempt to define the nature or extent of liability on a national level. This proposed international agreement determines only the scope of the exclusive rights that shall be granted to authors in respect of their works. Who is liable for the violation of these rights and what the extent of liability shall be for such violations is a matter for national legislation and case law according to the legal traditions of each Contracting Party.

In respect of rights provided for in Article 10, Contracting Parties may apply certain limitations and exceptions traditionally considered acceptable under the Berne Convention. The proposal is not intended to impair the ability of Contracting Parties to maintain in their national laws exceptions that have traditionally been viewed as "minor reservations".

Article 11: Duration of the Protection of Photographic Works

In respect of photographic works, the Contracting Parties shall apply the provisions of Articles 7(1), 7(3), 7(5), 7(6), 7(7) and 7(8) of the Berne Convention and shall not apply the provisions of Article 7(4).

Article 12: Limitations and Exceptions

(1) Contracting Parties may, in their national legislation, provide for limitations of or exceptions to the rights granted to authors of literary and artistic works under this Treaty only in certain special cases that do not conflict with the normal exploitation of the work and do not unreasonably prejudice the legitimate interests of the author.

(2) Contracting Parties shall, when applying the Berne Convention, confine any limitations of or exceptions to rights provided for therein to certain special cases which do not conflict with the normal exploitation of the work and do not unreasonably prejudice the legitimate interests of the author.

Note: ... It bears mention that this Article is not intended to prevent Contracting Parties from applying limitations and exceptions traditionally considered acceptable under the Berne Convention. It is, however, clear that not all limitations currently included in the various national legislations would correspond to the conditions now being proposed. In the digital environment, formally "minor reservations" may in reality undermine important aspects of protection. Even minor reservations must be considered using sense and reason. The purpose of the protection must be kept in mind.

When a high level of protection is proposed, there is reason to balance such protection against other important values in society. Among these values are the interests of education, scientific research, the need of the general public for information to be available in libraries and the interests of persons with a handicap that prevents them from using ordinary sources of information.

Article 13: Obligations concerning Technological Measures

(1) Contracting Parties shall make unlawful the importation, manufacture or distribution of protection-defeating devices, or the offer or performance of any service having the same effect, by any person knowing or having reasonable grounds to know that the device or service will be used for, or in the course of, the exercise of rights provided under this Treaty that is not authorized by the rightholder or the law.

(2) Contracting Parties shall provide for appropriate and effective remedies against the unlawful acts referred to in paragraph (1).

(3) As used in this Article, "protection-defeating device" means any device, product or component incorporated into a device or product, the primary purpose or primary effect of which is to circumvent any process, treatment, mechanism or system that prevents or inhibits any of the acts covered by the rights under this Treaty.

> *Note:* ... Contracting Parties are free to choose appropriate remedies according to their own legal traditions. The main requirement is that the remedies provided are effective and thus constitute a deterrent and a sufficient sanction against the prohibited acts.
>
> Contracting Parties may design the exact field of application of the provisions envisaged in this Article taking into consideration the need to avoid legislation that would impede lawful practices and the lawful use of subject matter that is in the public domain. Having regard to differences in legal traditions, Contracting Parties may, in their national legislation, also define the coverage and extent of the liability for violation of the prohibition enacted according to paragraph (1).

Article 14: Obligations concerning Rights Management Information

(1) Contracting Parties shall make it unlawful for any person knowingly to perform any of the following acts:

- (i) to remove or alter any electronic rights management information without authority;
- (ii) to distribute, import for distribution or communicate to the public, without authority, copies of works from which electronic rights management information has been removed or altered without authority.

(2) As used in this Article, "rights management information" means informa-

tion which identifies the work, the author of the work, the owner of any right in the work, and any numbers or codes that represent such information, when any of these items of information are attached to a copy of a work or appear in connection with the communication of a work to the public.

Note: ... Contracting Parties may, when implementing the obligations established by this Article, specifically limit the scope of the provisions in their national law in such a way that technically non-feasible requirements are not imposed on broadcasting organizations and other users engaged in the duly authorized communication of works or retransmission of broadcasts.

It should be pointed out that the use of electronic rights management information is voluntary. The obligations of Contracting Parties concerning rights management information only apply in cases where such information has been given.

It should be observed that the willful removal or alteration of rights management information in order to achieve financial gain is a matter which falls within the scope of the provisions of the penal codes in most countries. This may be taken into account when the obligations of the Contracting Parties are considered by the Diplomatic Conference.

Article 15: Application in Time

Contracting Parties shall apply the provisions of Article 18 of the Berne Convention to all protection provided for in this Treaty.

Article 16: Special Provisions on Enforcement of Rights

ALTERNATIVE A

(1) Special provisions regarding the enforcement of rights are included in the Annex to the Treaty.
(2) The Annex forms an integral part of this Treaty.

ALTERNATIVE B

Contracting Parties shall ensure that the enforcement procedures specified in Part III, Articles 41 to 61, of the Agreement on Trade-Related Aspects of Intellectual Property Rights, Including Trade in Counterfeit Goods, Annex 1C, of the Marrakesh Agreement Establishing the World Trade Organization, concluded on April 15, 1994 (the "TRIPS Agreement"), are available under their national laws so as to permit effective action against any act of infringement of the rights provided under this Treaty, including expeditious remedies to prevent infringements, and remedies that constitute a deterrent to further infringements. To this end, Contracting Parties shall apply mutatis mutandis the provisions of Articles 41 to 61 of the TRIPS Agreement.

Note: Two alternatives on enforcement are presented in Article 16. The choice between them has been left to the Diplomatic Conference. This is because the issue of enforcement is a horizontal one that must be considered in connection with the two other proposed Treaties published simultaneously with the present proposed Treaty. Each of the two alternatives is based on the enforcement provisions of Part III, Articles 41 to 61, of the TRIPS Agreement.

Alternative A consists of the text of Article 16 and an Annex. Paragraph (1) introduces the Annex which contains the substantive provisions on enforcement. Paragraph (2) states that the Annex forms an integral part of the proposed Treaty. The provisions of the Annex have the same status as the provisions of the proposed Treaty.

Alternative B incorporates the enforcement provisions in the TRIPS Agreement by reference. The provisions of Alternative B obligate Contracting Parties to ensure that proper enforcement procedures, as specified in Part III, are available. To this end, Contracting Parties shall apply the relevant provisions of the TRIPS Agreement mutatis mutandis.

ARTICLE 16, ALTERNATIVE A, ANNEX: ENFORCEMENT OF RIGHTS

SECTION 1: GENERAL OBLIGATIONS

Article 1

1. Contracting Parties shall ensure that enforcement procedures as specified in this Annex are available under their law so as to permit effective action against any act of infringement of rights covered by this Treaty, including expeditious remedies to prevent infringements and remedies which constitute a deterrent to further infringements. These procedures shall be applied in such a manner as to avoid the creation of barriers to legitimate trade and to provide for safeguards against their abuse.

2. Procedures concerning the enforcement of rights covered by this Treaty shall be fair and equitable. They shall not be unnecessarily complicated or costly, or entail unreasonable time-limits or unwarranted delays.

3. Decisions on the merits of a case shall preferably be in writing and reasoned. They shall be made available at least to the parties to the proceeding without undue delay. Decisions on the merits of a case shall be based only on evidence in respect of which parties were offered the opportunity to be heard.

4. Parties to a proceeding shall have an opportunity for review by a judicial authority of final administrative decisions and, subject to jurisdictional provisions in a Contracting Party's law concerning the importance of a case, of at least the legal aspects of initial judicial decisions on the merits of a case. However, there shall be no obligation to provide an opportunity for review of acquittals in criminal cases.

5. It is understood that this Annex does not create any obligation to put in place a judicial system for the enforcement of rights covered by this Treaty distinct

from that for the enforcement of law in general, nor does it affect the capacity of Contracting Parties to enforce their law in general. Nothing in this Annex creates any obligation with respect to the distribution of resources as between enforcement of rights covered by this Treaty and the enforcement of law in general.

SECTION 2: CIVIL AND ADMINISTRATIVE PROCEDURES AND REMEDIES

Article 2: Fair and Equitable Procedures

Contracting Parties shall make available to the right holders civil judicial procedures concerning the enforcement of any right covered by this Treaty. Defendants shall have the right to written notice which is timely and contains sufficient detail, including the basis of the claims. Parties shall be allowed to be represented by independent legal counsel, and procedures shall not impose overly burdensome requirements concerning mandatory personal appearances. All parties to such procedures shall be duly entitled to substantiate their claims and to present all relevant evidence. The procedure shall provide a means to identify and protect confidential information, unless this would be contrary to existing constitutional requirements.

Article 3: Evidence

1. The judicial authorities shall have the authority, where a party has presented reasonably available evidence sufficient to support its claims and has specified evidence relevant to substantiation of its claims which lies in the control of the opposing party, to order that this evidence be produced by the opposing party, subject in appropriate cases to conditions which ensure the protection of confidential information.

2. In cases in which a party to a proceeding voluntarily and without good reason refuses access to, or otherwise does not provide necessary information within a reasonable period, or significantly impedes a procedure relating to an enforcement action, a Contracting Party may accord judicial authorities the authority to make preliminary and final determinations, affirmative or negative, on the basis of the information presented to them, including the complaint or the allegation presented by the party adversely affected by the denial of access to information, subject to providing the parties an opportunity to be heard on the allegations or evidence.

Article 4: Injunctions

1. The judicial authorities shall have the authority to order a party to desist from an infringement, inter alia to prevent the entry into the channels of commerce in their jurisdiction of imported goods that involve the infringement of a right covered by this Treaty, immediately after customs clearance of such goods. Contracting Parties are not obliged to accord such authority in respect of protected subject matter acquired or ordered by a person prior to knowing or having reasonable grounds to know that dealing in such subject matter would entail the infringement of a right covered by this Treaty. [Paragraph 2 of Article 44 of the TRIPS Agreement is not reproduced here.]

Article 5: Damages

1. The judicial authorities shall have the authority to order the infringer to pay the right holder damages adequate to compensate for the injury the right holder has suffered because of an infringement of that person's right covered by this Treaty by an infringer who knowingly, or with reasonable grounds to know, engaged in infringing activity.

2. The judicial authorities shall also have the authority to order the infringer to pay the right holder expenses, which may include appropriate attorney's fees. In appropriate cases, Contracting Parties may authorize the judicial authorities to order recovery of profits and/or payment of pre-established damages even where the infringer did not knowingly, or with reasonable grounds to know, engage in infringing activity.

Article 6: Other Remedies

In order to create an effective deterrent to infringement, the judicial authorities shall have the authority to order that goods that they have found to be infringing be, without compensation of any sort, disposed of outside the channels of commerce in such a manner as to avoid any harm caused to the right holder, or, unless this would be contrary to existing constitutional requirements, destroyed. The judicial authorities shall also have the authority to order that materials and implements the predominant use of which has been in the creation of the infringing goods be, without compensation of any sort, disposed of outside the channels of commerce in such a manner as to minimize the risks of further infringements. In considering such requests, the need for proportionality between the seriousness of the infringement and the remedies ordered as well as the interests of third parties shall be taken into account. [A clause not reproduced here.]

Article 7: Right of Information

Contracting Parties may provide that the judicial authorities shall have the authority, unless this would be out of proportion to the seriousness of the infringement, to order the infringer to inform the right holder of the identity of third persons involved in the production and distribution of the infringing goods or services and of their channels of distribution.

Article 8: Indemnification of the Defendant

1. The judicial authorities shall have the authority to order a party at whose request measures were taken and who has abused enforcement procedures to provide to a party wrongfully enjoined or restrained adequate compensation for the injury suffered because of such abuse. The judicial authorities shall also have the authority to order the applicant to pay the defendant expenses, which may include appropriate attorney's fees.

2. In respect of the administration of any law pertaining to the protection or enforcement of rights covered by this Treaty, Contracting Parties shall only exempt both public authorities and officials from liability to appropriate remedial measures where actions are taken or intended in good faith in the course of the administration of that law.

Article 9: Administrative Procedures

To the extent that any civil remedy can be ordered as a result of administrative procedures on the merits of a case, such procedures shall conform to principles equivalent in substance to those set forth in this Section.

SECTION 3: PROVISIONAL MEASURES

Article 10

1. The judicial authorities shall have the authority to order prompt and effective provisional measures:

   (a) to prevent an infringement of any right covered by this Treaty from occurring, and in particular to prevent the entry into the channels of commerce in their jurisdiction of goods, including imported goods immediately after customs clearance;

   (b) to preserve relevant evidence in regard to the alleged infringement.

2. The judicial authorities shall have the authority to adopt provisional measures inaudita altera parte where appropriate, in particular where any delay is likely to cause irreparable harm to the right holder, or where there is a demonstrable risk of evidence being destroyed.

3. The judicial authorities shall have the authority to require the applicant to provide any reasonably available evidence in order to satisfy themselves with a sufficient degree of certainty that the applicant is the right holder and that the applicant's right is being infringed or that such infringement is imminent, and to order the applicant to provide a security or equivalent assurance sufficient to protect the defendant and to prevent abuse.

4. Where provisional measures have been adopted inaudita altera parte, the parties affected shall be given notice, without delay after the execution of the measures at the latest. A review, including a right to be heard, shall take place upon request of the defendant with a view to deciding, within a reasonable period after the notification of the measures, whether these measures shall be modified, revoked or confirmed.

5. The applicant may be required to supply other information necessary for the identification of the goods concerned by the authority that will execute the provisional measures.

6. Without prejudice to paragraph 4, provisional measures taken on the basis of paragraphs 1 and 2 shall, upon request by the defendant, be revoked or otherwise cease to have effect, if proceedings leading to a decision on the merits of the case are not initiated within a reasonable period, to be determined by the judicial authority ordering the measures where a Contracting Party's law so permit or, in the absence of such a determination, not to exceed 20 working days or 31 calendar days, whichever is the longer.

7. Where the provisional measures are revoked or where they lapse due to any act or omission by the applicant, or where it is subsequently found that there has been no infringement or threat of infringement of a right covered by this

Treaty, the judicial authorities shall have the authority to order the applicant, upon request of the defendant, to provide the defendant appropriate compensation for any injury caused by these measures.

8. To the extent that any provisional measure can be ordered as a result of administrative procedures, such procedures shall conform to principles equivalent in substance to those set forth in this Section.

SECTION 4: SPECIAL REQUIREMENTS RELATED TO BORDER MEASURES

Article 11: Suspension of Release by Customs Authorities

Contracting Parties shall, in conformity with the provisions set out below, adopt procedures to enable a right holder, who has valid grounds for suspecting that the importation of [words omitted] pirated goods may take place, to lodge an application in writing with competent authorities, administrative or judicial, for the suspension by the customs authorities of the release into free circulation of such goods. [A clause omitted]. Contracting Parties may also provide for corresponding procedures concerning the suspension by the customs authorities of the release of infringing goods destined for exportation from their territories.

Article 12: Application

Any right holder initiating the procedures under Article 11 shall be required to provide adequate evidence to satisfy the competent authorities that, under the laws of the country of importation, there is prima facie an infringement of the right holder's right covered by this Treaty and to supply a sufficiently detailed description of the goods to make them readily recognisable by the customs authorities. The competent authorities shall inform the applicant within a reasonable period whether they have accepted the application and, where determined by the competent authorities, the period for which the customs authorities will take action.

Article 13: Security or Equivalent Assurance

1. The competent authorities shall have the authority to require an applicant to provide a security or equivalent assurance sufficient to protect the defendant and the competent authorities and to prevent abuse. Such security or equivalent assurance shall not unreasonably deter recourse to these procedures. [Paragraph 2 of Article 53 of the TRIPS Agreement is not reproduced here.]

Article 14: Notice of Suspension

The importer and the applicant shall be promptly notified of the suspension of the release of goods according to Article 11.

Article 15: Duration of Suspension

If, within a period not exceeding 10 working days after the applicant has been served notice of the suspension, the customs authorities have not been informed that proceedings leading to a decision on the merits of the case have been initiated by a party other than the defendant, or that the duly empowered authority has taken provisional measures prolonging the suspension of the release of the goods, the goods shall be released, provided that all other conditions for importation or exportation have been complied with; in appropriate cases, this time-limit may be extended by another 10 working days. If proceedings leading to a decision on the merits of the case have been initiated, a review, including a right to be heard, shall take place upon request of the defendant with a view to deciding, within a reasonable period, whether these measures shall be modified, revoked or confirmed. Notwithstanding the above, where the suspension of the release of goods is carried out or continued in accordance with a provisional judicial measure, the provisions of paragraph 6 of Article 10 shall apply.

Article 16: Indemnification of the Importer and of the Owner of the Goods

Relevant authorities shall have the authority to order the applicant to pay the importer, the consignee and the owner of the goods appropriate compensation for any injury caused to them through the wrongful detention of goods or through the detention of goods released pursuant to Article 15.

Article 17: Right of Inspection and Information

Without prejudice to the protection of confidential information, Contracting Parties shall provide the competent authorities the authority to give the right holder sufficient opportunity to have any goods detained by the customs authorities inspected in order to substantiate the right holder's claims. The competent authorities shall also have authority to give the importer an equivalent opportunity to have any such goods inspected. Where a positive determination has been made on the merits of a case, Contracting Parties may provide the competent authorities the authority to inform the right holder of the names and addresses of the consignor, the importer and the consignee and of the quantity of goods in question.

Article 18: Ex Officio Action

Where Contracting Parties require competent authorities to act upon their own initiative and to suspend the release of goods in respect of which they have acquired prima facie evidence that a right covered by this Treaty is being infringed:

(a) the competent authorities may at any time seek from the right holder any information that may assist them to exercise these powers;

(b) the importer and the right holder shall be promptly notified of the suspension. Where the importer has lodged an appeal against the suspension with the competent authorities, the suspension shall be subject to the conditions, mutatis mutandis, set out at Article 15;

(c) Contracting Parties shall only exempt both public authorities and officials from liability to appropriate remedial measures where actions are taken or intended in good faith.

Article 19: Remedies

Without prejudice to other rights of action open to the right holder and subject to the right of the defendant to seek review by a judicial authority, competent authorities shall have the authority to order the destruction or disposal of infringing goods in accordance with the principles set out in Article 6. [A clause not reproduced here.]

Article 20: De Minimis Imports

Contracting Parties may exclude from the application of above provisions small quantities of goods of a non-commercial nature contained in travellers' personal luggage or sent in small consignments.

SECTION 5: CRIMINAL PROCEDURES

Article 21

Contracting Parties shall provide for criminal procedures and penalties to be applied at least in cases of wilful [words omitted] piracy on a commercial scale. Remedies available shall include imprisonment and/or monetary fines sufficient to provide a deterrent, consistently with the level of penalties applied for crimes of a corresponding gravity. In appropriate cases, remedies available shall also include the seizure, forfeiture and destruction of the infringing goods and of any materials and implements the predominant use of which has been in the commission of the offence. [A clause not reproduced here.]

Selected Excerpts from the Berne Convention, 1971

Article 1

The countries to which this Convention applies constitute a Union for the protection of the rights of authors in their literary and artistic works.

Article 2

1. The expression "literary and artistic works" shall include every production in the literary, scientific and artistic domain, whatever may be the mode or form of its expression, such as books, pamphlets and other writings; lectures, addresses, sermons and other works of the same nature; dramatic or dramatico-musical works; choreographic works and entertainments in dumb show; musical compositions with or without words; cinematographic works to which are assimilated works expressed by a process analogous to cinematography; works of drawing, painting, architecture, sculpture, engraving and lithography; photographic works to which are assimilated works expressed by a process analogous to photography; works of applied art; illustrations, maps, plans, sketches and three-dimensional works relative to geography, topography, architecture or science.
2. It shall, however, be a matter for legislation in the countries of the Union to prescribe that works in general or any specified categories of works shall not be protected unless they have been fixed in some material form.
3. Translations, adaptations, arrangements of music and other alterations of a literary or artistic work shall be protected as original works without prejudice to the copyright in the original work.
4. It shall be a matter for legislation in the countries of the Union to determine the protection to he granted to official texts of a legislative, administrative and legal nature, and to official translations of such texts.
5. Collections of literary or artistic works such as encyclopaedias and anthologies which, by reason of the selection and arrangement of their contents,

constitute intellectual creations shall be protected as such, without prejudice to the copyright in each of the works forming part of such collections.

6. The works mentioned in this article shall enjoy protection in all countries of the Union. This protection shall operate for the benefit of the author and his successors in title.

7. Subject to the provisions of Article 7(4) of this Convention, it shall be a matter for legislation in the countries of the Union to determine the extent of the application of their laws to works of applied art and industrial designs and models, as well as the conditions under which such works, designs and models shall be protected. Works protected in the country of origin solely as designs and models shall be entitled in another country of the Union only to such special protection as is granted in that country to designs and models; however, if no such special protection is granted in that country, such works shall be protected as artistic works.

8. The protection of this Convention shall not apply to news of the day or to miscellaneous facts having the character of mere items of press information.

Article 2*bis*

1. It shall be a matter for legislation in the countries of the Union to exclude, wholly or in part, from the protection provided by the preceding Article political speeches and speeches delivered in the course of legal proceedings.

2. It shall also be a matter for legislation in the countries of the Union to determine the conditions under which lectures, addresses and other works of the same nature which are delivered in public may be reproduced by the press, broadcast, communicated to the public by wire and made the subject of public communication as envisaged in Article 11bis (1) of this Convention, when such use is justified by the informatory purpose.

3. Nevertheless, the author shall enjoy the exclusive right of making a collection of his works mentioned in the preceding paragraphs.

Article 3

1. The protection of this Convention shall apply to:

   (a) authors who are nationals of one of the countries of the Union, for their works, whether published or not;

   (b) authors who are not nationals of one of the countries of the Union, for their works first published in one of those countries, or simultaneously in a country outside the Union and in a country of the Union.

2. Authors who are not nationals of one of the countries of the Union but who have their habitual residence in one of them shall, for the purposes of this Convention, be assimilated to nationals of that country.

3. The expression "published works" means works published with the consent of their authors, whatever may be the means of manufacture of the copies, provided that the availability of such copies has been such as to satisfy the

reasonable requirements of the public, having regard to the nature of the work. The performance of a dramatic, dramatico-musical cinematographic or musical work, the public recitation of a literary work, the communication by wire or the broadcasting of literary or artistic works, the exhibition of a work of art and the construction of a work of architecture shall not constitute publication.

4. A work shall be considered as having been published simultaneously in several countries if it has been published in two or more countries within thirty days of its first publication.

Article 4

The protection of this Convention shall apply, even if the conditions of Article 3 are not fulfilled, to:

(a)   authors of cinematographic works the maker of which has his headquarters or habitual residence in one of the countries of the Union;

(b)   authors of works of architecture, erected in a country of the Union or of other artistic works incorporated in a building or other structure located in a country of the Union.

Article 5

1. Authors shall enjoy, in respect of works for which they are protected under this Convention, in countries of the Union other than the country of origin, the rights which their respective laws do now or may hereafter grant to their nationals, as well as the rights specially granted by this Convention.

2. The enjoyment and the exercise of these rights shall not be subject to any formality; such enjoyment and such exercise shall be independent of the existence of protection in the country of origin of the work. Consequently, apart from the provisions of this Convention, the extent of protection, as well as the means of redress afforded to the author to protect his rights, shall be governed exclusively by the laws of the country where protection is claimed.

3. Protection in the country of origin is governed by domestic law. However, when the author is not a national of the country of origin of the work for which he is protected under this Convention, he shall enjoy in that country the same rights as national authors.

4. The country of origin shall be considered to be

(a)   in the case of works first published in a country of the Union, that country; in the case of works published simultaneously in several countries of the Union which grant different terms of protection, the country whose legislation grants the shortest term of protection;

(b)   in the case of works published simultaneously in a country outside the Union and in a country of the Union, the latter country;

(c)   in the case of unpublished works or of works first published in a country outside the Union, without simultaneous publication in a country of the

Union, the country of the Union of which the author is a national, provided that:

   (i)   when these are cinematographic works the maker of which has his headquarters or his habitual residence in a country of the Union, the country of origin shall be that country, and

   (ii) when these are works of architecture erected in a country of the Union or other artistic works incorporated in a building or other structure located in a country of the Union, the country of origin shall be that country.

Article 6

1. Where any country outside the Union fails to protect in an adequate manner the works of authors who are nationals of one of the countries of the Union, the latter country may restrict the protection given to the works of authors who are, at the date of the first publication thereof, nationals of the other country and are not habitually resident in one of the countries of the Union. If the country of first publication avails itself of this right, the other countries of the Union shall not be required to grant to works thus subjected to special treatment a wider protection than that granted to them in the country of first publication.

2. No restrictions introduced by virtue of the preceding paragraph shall affect the rights which an author may have acquired in respect of a work published in a country of the Union before such restrictions were put into force.

3. The countries of the Union which restrict the grant of copyright in accordance with this Article shall give notice thereof to the Director General of the World Intellectual Property Organization (hereinafter designated as "the Director General") by a written declaration specifying the countries in regard to which protection is restricted, and the restrictions to which rights of authors who are nationals of those countries are subjected. The Director General shall immediately communicate this declaration to all the countries of the Union.

Article 6*bis*

1. Independently of the author's economic rights, and even after the transfer of the said rights, the author shall have the right to claim authorship of the work and to object to any distortion, mutilation or other modification of, or other derogatory action in relation to, the said work, which would he prejudicial to his honor or reputation.

2. The rights granted to the author in accordance with the preceding paragraph shall, after his death, be maintained, at least until the expiry of the economic rights, and shall be exercisable by the persons or institutions authorized by the legislation of the country where protection is claimed. However, those countries whose legislation, at the moment of their ratification of or accession to this Act, does not provide for the protection after the death of the author of all the rights set out in the preceding paragraph may provide that some of these

rights may, after his death, cease to be maintained.

3. The means of redress for safeguarding the rights granted by this Article shall be governed by the legislation of the country where protection is claimed.

Article 7

1. The term of protection granted by this Convention shall be the life of the author and fifty years after his death.

2. However, in the case of cinematographic works, the countries of the Union may provide that the term of protection shall expire fifty years after the work has been made available to the public with the consent of the author, or, failing such an event within fifty years from the making of such a work, fifty years after the making.

3. In the case of anonymous or pseudonymous works, the term of protection granted by this Convention shall expire fifty years after the work has been lawfully made available to the public. However, when the pseudonym adopted by the author leaves no doubt as to his identity, the term of protection shall be that provided in paragraph (1). If the author of an anonymous or pseudonymous work discloses his identity during the above-mentioned period, the term of protection applicable shall be that provided in paragraph (1). The countries of the Union shall not be required to protect anonymous or pseudonymous works in respect of which it is reasonable to presume that their author has been dead for fifty years.

4. It shall be a matter for legislation in the countries of the Union to determine the term of protection of photographic works and that of works of applied art in so far as they are protected as artistic works; however, this term shall last at least until the end of a period of twenty-five years from the making of such a work.

5. The term of protection subsequent to the death of the author and the terms provided by paragraphs (2), (3) and (4), shall run from the date of death or of the event referred to in those paragraphs, but such terms shall always be deemed to begin on the 1st of January of the year following the death or such event.

6. The countries of the Union may grant a term of protection in excess of those provided by the preceding paragraphs.

7. Those countries of the Union bound by the Rome Act of this Convention, which grant, in their national legislation in force at the time of signature of the present Act, shorter terms of protection than those provided for in the preceding paragraphs, shall have the right to maintain such terms when ratifying or acceding to the present Act.

8. In any case, the term shall be governed by the legislation of the country where protection is claimed; however, unless the legislation of that country otherwise provides, the term shall not exceed the term fixed in the country of origin of the work.

Article 7bis

The provisions of the preceding Article shall also apply in the case of a work of joint authorship, provided that the terms measured from the death of the author shall be calculated from the death of the last surviving author.

Article 8

Authors of literary and artistic works protected by this Convention shall enjoy the exclusive right of making and of authorizing the translation of their works throughout the term of protection of their rights in the original works.

Article 9

1. Authors of literary and artistic works protected by this Convention shall enjoy the exclusive right of making and of authorizing the translation of their works throughout the term of protection of their rights in the original works.
2. It shall be a matter for legislation in the countries of the Union to permit the reproduction of such works in certain special cases, provided that such reproduction does not conflict with a normal exploitation of the work and does not unreasonably prejudice the legitimate interest of the author.
3. Any sound or visual recording shall be considered as a reproduction for the purposes of this Convention.

Article 10

1. It shall be permissible to make quotations from a work which has already been lawfully made available to the public, provided that their making is compatible with fair practice, and their extent does not exceed that justified by the purpose, including quotations from newspaper articles and periodicals in the form of press summaries.
2. It shall be a matter for legislation in the countries of the Union, and for special agreements existing or to be concluded between them, to permit the utilization, to the extent justified by the purpose, of literary or artistic works by way of illustration in publications, broadcasts or sound or visual recordings for teaching, provided such utilization is compatible with fair practice.
3. Where use is made of works in accordance with the preceding paragraphs of this Article, mention shall be made of the source, and of the name of the author, if it appears thereon.

Article 10bis

1. It shall be a matter for legislation in the countries of the Union to permit the reproduction by the press, the broadcasting or the communication to the public by wire, of articles published in newspapers or periodicals on current

economic, political or religious topics, and of broadcast works of the same character, in cases in which the reproduction, broadcasting or such communication thereof is not expressly reserved. Nevertheless, the source must always be clearly indicated; the legal consequences of a breach of this obligation shall be determined by the legislation of the country where protection is claimed.

2. It shall also be a matter for legislation in the countries of the Union to determine the conditions under which, for the purpose of reporting current events by means of photography, cinematography, broadcasting or communication to the public by wire, literary or artistic works seen or heard in the course of the event may, to the extent justified by the informatory purpose, be reproduced and made available to the public.

Article 11

1. Authors of dramatic, dramatico-musical and musical works shall enjoy the exclusive right of authorizing:

(i)   the public performance of their works, including such public performance by any means or process;

(ii) any communication to the public of the performance of their works.

2. Authors of dramatic or dramatico-musical works shall enjoy, during the full term of their rights in the original works, the same rights with respect to translations thereof.

Article 11*bis*

1. Authors of literary and artistic works shall enjoy the exclusive right of authorizing;

(i)   the broadcasting of their works or the communication thereof to the public by any other means of wireless diffusion of signs, sounds or images;

(ii) any communication to the public by wire or by re-broadcasting of the broadcast of the work, when this communication is made by an organization other than the original one;

(iii) the public communication by loudspeaker or any other analogous instrument transmitting, by signs, sounds or images, the broadcast of the work.

2. It shall be a matter for legislation in the countries of the Union to determine the conditions under which the rights mentioned in the preceding paragraph may be exercised, but these conditions shall apply only in the countries where they have been prescribed. They shall not in any circumstances be prejudicial to the moral rights of the author, nor to his right to obtain equitable remuneration which, in the absence of agreement, shall be fixed by competent authority.

3. In the absence of any contrary stipulation, permission granted in accordance with paragraph (1) of this Article shall not imply permission to record, by means of instruments recording sounds or images, the work broadcast. It shall, however, be a matter for legislation in the countries of the Union to

determine the regulations for ephemeral recordings made by a broadcasting organization by means of its own facilities and used for its own broadcasts. The preservation of these recordings in official archives may, on the ground of their exceptional documentary character, be authorized by such legislation.

Article 11*ter*

1. Authors of literary works shall enjoy the exclusive right of authorizing:
    (i)   the public recitation of their works, including such public recitation by any means or process;
    (ii) any communication to the public of the recitation of their works.
2. Authors of literary works shall enjoy, during the full term of their rights in the original works, the same rights with respect to translations thereof.

Article 12

Authors of literary or artistic works shall enjoy the exclusive right of authorizing adaptations, arrangements and other alterations of their works.

Article 13

1. Each country of the Union may impose for itself reservations and conditions on the exclusive right granted to the author of a musical work and to the author of any words, the recording of which together with the musical work has already been authorized by the latter, to authorize the sound recording of that musical work, together with such words, if any; but all such reservations and conditions shall apply only in the countries which have imposed them and shall not, in any circumstances, be prejudicial to the rights of these authors to obtain equitable remuneration which, in the absence of agreement, shall be fixed by competent authority.
2. Recordings of musical works made in a country of the Union in accordance with Article 13 (3) of the Convention signed at Rome on June 2, 1928, and at Brussels on June 26, 1948, may be reproduced in that country without the permission of the author of the musical work until a date two years after that country becomes bound by this Act.
3. Recordings made in accordance with paragraphs (1) and (2) of this Article and imported without permission from the patties concerned into a country where they are treated as infringing recordings shall be liable to seizure.

Article 14

1. Authors of literary or artistic works shall have the exclusive right of authorizing:
    (i)   the cinematographic adaptation and reproduction of these works, and the distribution of the works thus adapted or reproduced;

(ii) the public performance and communication to the public by wire of the works thus adapted or reproduced.

2. The adaptation into any other artistic form of a cinematographic production derived from literary or artistic works shall, without prejudice to the authorization of the author of the cinematographic production, remain subject to the authorization of the authors of the original works.

3. The provisions of Article 13 (1) shall not apply.

Article 14*bis*

1. Without prejudice to the copyright in any work which may have been adapted or reproduced, a cinematographic work shall be protected as an original work. The owner of copyright in a cinematographic work shall enjoy the same rights as the author of an original work, including the rights referred to in the preceding Article.

2.

(a) Ownership of copyright in a cinematographic work shall be a matter for legislation in the country where protection is claimed.

(b) However, in the countries of the Union which, by legislation include among the owners of copyright in a cinematographic work authors who have brought contributions to the making of the work, such authors, if they have undertaken to bring such contributions, may not, in the absence of any contrary or special stipulation, object to the reproduction, distribution, public performance, communication to the public by wire, broadcasting or any other communication to the public, or to the subtitling or dubbing of texts, of the work.

(c) The question whether or not the form of the undertaking referred to above should, for the application of the preceding subparagraph (b), be in a written agreement or a written act of the same effect shall be a matter for the legislation of the country where the maker of the cinematographic work has his headquarters or habitual residence. However, it shall be a matter for the legislation of the country of the Union where protection is claimed to provide that the said undertaking shall be in a written agreement or a written act of the same effect. The countries whose legislation so provides shall notify the Director General by means of a written declaration, which will be immediately communicated by him to all the other countries of the Union.

(d) By "contrary or special stipulation" is meant any restrictive condition which is relevant to the aforesaid undertaking.

3. Unless the national legislation provides to the contrary, the provisions of paragraph (2) (b) above shall not be applicable to authors of scenarios, dialogues and musical works created for the making of the cinematographic work, nor to the principal director thereof. However, those countries of the Union whose legislation does not contain rules providing for the application of the said paragraph (2) (b) to such director shall notify the Director General by

means of a written declaration, which will be immediately communicated by him to all the other countries of the Union.

Article 18

1. This Convention shall apply to all works which, at the moment of its coming into force, have not yet fallen into the public domain in the country of origin through the expiry of the term of protection.

2. If, however, through the expiry of the term of protection which was previously granted, a work has fallen into the public domain of the country where protection is claimed, that work shall not be protected anew.

3. The application of this principle shall be subject to any provisions contained in special conventions to that effect existing or to be concluded between countries of the Union. In the absence of such provisions, the respective countries shall determine, each in so far as it is concerned, the conditions of application of this principle.

4. The preceding provisions shall also apply in the case of new accessions to the Union and to cases in which protection is extended by the application of Article 7 or by the abandonment of reservations.

United States Copyright Office Circular 38a: International Copyright Relations of the United States

General Information

This sets forth U.S. copyright relations of current interest with the other independent nations of the world. Each entry gives country name (and alternate name) and a statement of copyright relations. The following code is used:

Berne Party to the Berne Convention for the Protection of Literary and Artistic Works as of the date given. Appearing within parentheses is the latest Act [1] of the Convention to which the country is party. The effective date for the United States is March 1, 1989. The latest Act of the Convention, to which the United States is party, is the revision done at Paris on July 24, 1971.

Bilateral Bilateral copyright relations with the United States by virtue of a proclamation or treaty, as of the date given. Where there is more than one proclamation or treaty, only the date of the first one is given.

BAC Party to the Buenos Aires Convention of 1910, as of the date given. U.S. ratification deposited with the Government of Argentina, May 1, 1911; proclaimed by the President of the United States, July 13, 1914.

None No copyright relations with the United States.

Phonogram Party to the Convention for the Protection of Producers of Phonograms Against Unauthorized Duplication of Their Phonograms, Geneva, 1971, as of the date given. The effective date for the United States is March 10, 1974.

SAT Party to the Convention Relating to the Distribution of Programme-Carrying Signals Transmitted by Satellite, Brussels, 1974, as of the date given. The effective date for the United States is March 7, 1985.

UCC Geneva Party to the Universal Copyright Convention, Geneva, 1952, as of the date given. Effective date for U.S. is September 16, 1955.

UCC Paris Party to the Universal Copyright Convention as revised at Paris 1971, as of the date given. Effective date for U.S. is July 10, 1974.

Unclear Became independent since 1943. Has not established copyright relations with U.S., but may be honoring obligations incurred under former political status.

WTO Member of the World Trade Organization, effective as of the date indicated, established pursuant to the Marrakesh Agreement of April 15, 1994, to implement the Uruguay Round Agreements. Effective date for U.S. membership in the WTO is January 1, 1995.

Note: The Numbers in brackets refer to footnotes at the end of the article.

Brazil
BAC Aug. 31, 1915
Berne Feb. 9, 1922 (Paris) [2]
Bilateral Apr. 2, 1957
UCC Geneva Jan. 13, 1960
Phonogram Nov. 28, 1975
UCC Paris Dec. 11, 1975
WTO Jan. 1, 1995

Brunei Darussalam
WTO Jan. 1, 1995

Bulgaria
Berne Dec. 5, 1921 (Paris) [2]
UCC Geneva June 7, 1975
UCC Paris June 7, 1975
Phonogram Sept. 6, 1995
WTO Dec. 1, 1996

Burkina Faso (formerly Upper Volta)
Berne Aug. 19, 1963 (Paris) [2]
Phonogram Jan. 30, 1988
WTO June 3, 1995

Burma
(See Myanmar, Union of)

Burundi
WTO July 23, 199

Cambodia
UCC Geneva Sept. 16, 1955

Cameroon
Berne Sept. 21, 1964 (Paris) [2]
UCC Geneva May 1, 1973
UCC Paris July 10, 1974
WTO Dec. 13, 1995

Canada
Bilateral Jan. 1, 1924
Berne Apr. 10, 1928 (Paris) [2]
UCC Geneva Aug. 10, 1962
WTO Jan. 1, 1995

Cape Verde
Berne July 7, 1997 (Paris)

Central African Republic
Berne Sept. 3, 1977 (Paris) [2]
WTO May 31, 1995

Chad
Berne Nov. 25, 1971 (Brussels) [2]
WTO Oct. 19, 1996

Chile
Bilateral May 25, 1896
BAC June 14, 1955
UCC Geneva Sept. 16, 1955
Berne June 5, 1970 (Paris) [2]
Phonogram Mar. 24, 1977
WTO Jan. 1, 1995

China

Bilateral Jan. 13, 1904 [5]
Bilateral Mar. 17, 1992 [9]
Berne Oct. 15, 1992 (Paris)
UCC Geneva Oct. 30, 1992
UCC Paris Oct. 30, 1992
Phonogram Apr. 30, 1993

Colombia

BAC Dec. 23, 1936
UCC Geneva June 18, 1976
UCC Paris June 18, 1976
Berne Mar. 7, 1988 (Paris) [2]
Phonogram May 16, 1994
WTO Apr. 30, 1995

Comoros

Unclear

Congo

Berne May 8, 1962 (Paris) [2]
WTO Mar. 27, 1997

Costa Rica [6]

Bilateral Oct. 19, 1899
BAC Nov. 30, 1916
UCC Geneva Sept. 16, 1955
Berne June 10, 1978 (Paris) [2]
UCC Paris Mar. 7, 1980
Phonoginam June 17, 1982
WTO Jan. 1, 1995

Cote d'Ivoire (Ivory Coast)

Berne Jan. 1, 1962 (Paris) [2]
WTO Jan. 1, 1995

Croatia

UCC Geneva May 11, 1966
UCC Paris July 10, 1974
Berne Oct. 8, 1991 (Paris) [2]
SAT Oct. 8, 1991

Cuba

Bilateral Nov. 17, 1903
UCC Geneva June 18, 1957
WTO Apr. 20, 1995
Berne Feb. 20, 1997 (Paris)

Cyprus

Berne Feb. 24, 1964 (Paris) [2]
UCC Geneva Dec. 19, 1990
UCC Paris Dec. 19, 1990
Phonogram Sept. 30, 1993
WTO July 30, 1995

Czech Republic

UCC Geneva Jan. 6, 1960
UCC Paris Apr. 17, 1980
Berne Jan. 1, 1993 (Paris)
Phonogram Jan. 1, 1993
WTO Jan. 1, 1995

Czechoslovakia [11]

Bilateral Mar. 1, 1927

Democratic Republic of Congo (formerly Zaire)

Berne Oct. 8, 1963 (Paris) [2]
Phonogram Nov. 29, 1977
WTO Jan. 1, 1997

Denmark

Bilateral May 8, 1893
Berne July 1, 1903 (Paris) [2]
UCC Geneva Feb. 9, 1962
Phonogram Mar. 24, 1977
UCC Paris July 11, 1979
WTO Jan. 1, 1995

Djibouti

WTO May 31, 1995

Dominica

WTO Jan. 1, 1995

Dominican Republic [6]

BAC Oct. 31, 1912
UCC Geneva May 8, 1983
UCC Paris May 8, 1983
WTO Mar. 9, 1995
Berne Dec. 24, 1997 (Paris)

Ecuador

BAC Aug. 31, 1914
UCC Geneva June 5, 1957
Phonogram Sept. 14, 1974
UCC Paris Sept. 6, 1991
Berne Oct. 9, 1991 (Paris)
WTO Jan. 21, 1996

Egypt

Berne June 7, 1977 (Paris) [2]
Phonogram Apr. 23, 1978
WTO June 30, 1995

El Salvador

Bilateral June 30, 1908 by virtue of
  Mexico City Convention, 1902
Phonogram Feb. 9, 1979
UCC Geneva Mar. 29, 1979
UCC Paris Mar. 29, 1979
Berne Feb. 19, 1994 (Paris)
WTO May 7, 1995

Equatorial Guinea

Berne Jun. 26, 1997 (Paris)

Estonia

Berne Oct. 26, 1994 (Paris)

Ethiopia

None

European Community

WTO Jan. 1, 1995

Fiji

Berne Dec. 1, 1971 (Brussels) [2]
UCC Geneva Mar. 13, 1972
Phonogram Apr. 18, 1973 [3]
WTO Jan. 14, 1996

Finland

Berne Apr. 1, 1928 (Paris) [2]
Bilateral Jan. 1, 1929
UCC Geneva Apr. 16, 1963
Phonogram Apr. 18, 1973 [3]
UCC Paris Nov. 1, 1986
WTO Jan. 1, 1995

France

Berne Dec. 5, 1887 (Paris) [2]
Bilateral July 1, 1891
UCC Geneva Jan. 14, 1956
Phonogram Apr. 18, 1973 [3]
UCC Paris July 10, 1974
WTO Jan. 1, 1995

Gabon

Berne Mar. 26, 1962 (Paris) [2]
WTO Jan. 1, 1995

Gambia, The

Berne Mar. 7, 1993 (Paris)
WTO Oct. 23, 1996

Georgia

Berne May 16, 1995 (Paris)

Germany [10]

Berne Dec. 5, 1887 (Paris) [2, 7]
Bilateral Apr. 15, 1892
UCC Geneva Sept. 16, 1955
Phonogram May 18, 1974
UCC Paris July 10, 1974
SAT Aug. 25, 1979 [4]
WTO Jan. 1, 1995

Ghana

UCC Geneva Aug. 22, 1962
Berne Oct. 11, 1991 (Paris)
WTO Jan. 1, 1995

Greece

Berne Nov. 9, 1920 (Paris) [2]
Bilateral Mar. 1, 1932
UCC Geneva Aug. 24, 1963
SAT Oct. 22, 1991
Phonogram Feb. 9, 1994
WTO Jan. 1, 1995

Grenada

WTO Feb. 22, 1996
Berne Sept. 22, 1998 (Paris)

Guatemala [6]
BAC Mar. 28, 1913
UCC Geneva Oct. 28, 1964
Phonogram Feb. 1, 1977
WTO July 21, 1995
Berne Jul. 28, 1997 (Paris)

Guinea
Berne Nov. 20, 1980 (Paris) [2]
UCC Geneva Nov. 13, 1981
UCC Paris Nov. 13, 1981
WTO Oct. 25, 1995

Guinea-Bissau
Berne July 22, 1991 (Paris)
WTO May 31, 1995

Guyana
Berne Oct. 25, 1994 (Paris)
WTO Jan. 1, 1995

Haiti
BAC Nov. 27, 1919
UCC Geneva Sept. 16, 1955
Berne Jan. 11, 1996 (Paris)
WTO Jan. 30, 1996

Holy See
(See entry under Vatican City)

Honduras [6]
BAC Apr. 27, 1914
Berne Jan. 25, 1990 (Paris)
Phonogram Mar. 6, 1990
WTO Jan. 1, 1995

Hong Kong [12]
WTO Jan. 1, 1995

Hungary
Bilateral Oct. 16, 1912
Berne Feb. 14, 1922 (Paris) [2]
UCC Geneva Jan. 23, 1971
UCC Paris July 10, 1974
Phonogram May 28, 1975
WTO Jan. 1, 1995

Iceland
Berne Sept. 7, 1947 (Rome) [2]
UCC Geneva Dec. 18, 1956
WTO Jan. 1, 1995

India
Berne Apr. 1, 1928 (Paris) [2]
Bilateral Aug. 15, 1947
UCC Geneva Jan. 21, 1958
Phonogram Feb. 12, 1975
UCC Paris Apr. 7, 1988
WTO Jan. 1, 1995

Indonesia
Bilateral Aug. 1, 1989
WTO Jan. 1, 1995
Berne Sept. 5, 1997 (Paris)

Iran
None

Iraq
None

Ireland
Berne Oct. 5, 1927 (Brussels) [2]
Bilateral Oct. 1, 1929
UCC Geneva Jan. 20, 1959
WTO Jan. 1, 1995

Israel
Bilateral May 15, 1948
Berne Mar. 24, 1950 (Brussels) [2]
UCC Geneva Sept. 16, 1955
Phonogram May 1, 1978
WTO Apr. 21, 1995

Italy
Berne Dec. 5, 1887 (Paris) [2]
Bilateral Oct. 31, 1892
UCC Geneva Jan. 24, 1957
Phonogram Mar. 24, 1977
UCC Paris Jan. 25, 1980
SAT July 7, 1981 [4]
WTO Jan. 1, 1995

Ivory Coast
(See entry under Cote d'Ivoire)

Jamaica
Berne Jan. 1, 1994 (Paris)
Phonogram Jan. 11, 1994
WTO Mar. 9, 1995

Japan [8]
Berne July 15, 1899 (Paris) [2]
UCC Geneva Apr. 28, 1956
UCC Paris Oct. 21, 1977
Phonogram Oct. 14, 1978
WTO Jan. 1, 1995

Jordan
Unclear

Kazakhstan
UCC Geneva May 27, 1973
Berne Apr. 12, 1999 (Paris)

Kenya
UCC Geneva Sept. 7, 1966
UCC Paris July 10, 1914
Phonogram Apr. 21, 1976
SAT Aug. 25, 1979 [4]
Berne June 11, 1993 (Paris)
WTO Jan. 1, 1995

Kiribati
Unclear

Korea (Democratic People's Republic of Korea)
Unclear

Korea (Republic of Korea)
UCC Geneva Oct. 1, 1987
UCC Paris Oct. 1, 1987
Phonogram Oct. 10, 1987
WTO Jan. 1, 1995
Berne Aug. 21, 1996 (Paris)

Kuwait
WTO Jan. 1, 1995

Kyrgyz Republic
WTO Dec. 20, 1998

Laos
UCC Geneva Sept. 16, 1955

Latvia
Berne Aug. 11, 1995 (Paris)
Phonogram Aug. 23, 1997
WTO Feb. 10, 1999

Lebanon
Berne Sept. 30, 1947 (Rome) [2]
UCC Geneva Oct. 17, 1959

Lesotho
Berne Sept. 28, 1989 (Paris)
WTO May 31, 1995

Liberia
UCC Geneva July 27, 1956
Berne Mar. 8, 1989 (Paris)

Libya
Berne Sept. 28, 1976 (Paris) [2]

Liechtenstein
Berne July 30, 1931 (Brussels) [2]
UCC Geneva Jan. 22, 1959
WTO Sept. 1, 1995

Lithuania
Berne Dec. 14, 1994 (Paris)

Luxembourg
Berne June 20, 1888 (Paris) [2]
Bilateral June 29, 1910
UCC Geneva Oct. 15, 1955
Phonogram Mar. 8, 1976
WTO Jan. 1, 1995

Macau
WTO Jan. 1, 1995

Macedonia (former Yugoslav Republic of)
Berne Sept. 8, 1991 (Paris)
SAT Nov. 17, 1991
UCC Geneva July 30, 1997
UCC Paris July 30, 1997
Phonogram Mar. 2, 1998

Madagascar (Malagasy Republic)
Berne Jan. 1, 1966 (Brussels) [2]
WTO Nov. 17, 1995

Malawi
UCC Geneva Oct. 26, 1965
Berne Oct. 12, 1991 (Paris)
WTO May 31, 1995

Malaysia
Berne Oct. 1, 1990 (Paris)
WTO Jan. 1, 1995

Maldives
WTO May 31, 1995

Mali
Berne Mar. 19, 1962 (Paris) [2]
WTO May 31, 1995

Malta
Berne Sept. 21, 1964 (Rome) [2]
UCC Geneva Nov. 19, 1968
WTO Jan. 1, 1995

Mauritania
Berne Fob. 6, 1973 (Paris) [2]
WTO May 31, 1995

Mauritius
UCC Geneva Mar. 12, 1968
Berne May 10, 1989 (Paris)
WTO Jan. 1, 1995

Mexico
Bilateral Feb. 27, 1896
UCC Geneva May 12, 1957
BAC Apr. 24, 1964
Berne June 11, 1967 (Paris) [2]
Phonogram Dec. 21, 1973 [3]
UCC Paris Oct. 31, 1975
SAT Aug. 25, 1979 [4]
WTO Jan. 1, 1995

Moldova
Berne Nov. 2, 1995 (Paris) UCC
Geneva July 18, 1997

Monaco
Berne May 30, 1889 (Paris) [2]
Bilateral Oct. 15, 1952
UCC Geneva Sept. 16, 1955
Phonogram Dec. 2, 1974
UCC Paris Dec. 13, 1974

Mongolia
WTO Jan. 29, 1997
Berne Mar. 12, 1998 (Paris)

Morocco
Berne June 16, 1917 (Paris) [2]
UCC Geneva May 8, 1972
UCC Paris Jan. 28, 1976
SAT June 30, 1983 [4]
WTO Jan. 1, 1995

Mozambique
WTO Aug. 26, 1995

Myanmar, Union of (formerly Burma)
WTO Jan. 1, 1995

Namibia
Berne Mar. 21, 1990 (Paris)
WTO Jan. 1, 1995

Nauru
Unclear

Nepal
None

Netherlands
Bilateral Nov. 20, 1899
Berne Nov. 1, 1912 (Paris) [2]
UCC Geneva June 22, 1967
UCC Paris Nov. 30, 1985
Phonogram Oct. 12, 1993
WTO Jan. 1, 1995

New Zealand
Bilateral Dec. 1, 1916
Berne Apr. 24, 1928 (Rome) [2]
UCC Geneva Sept. 11, 1964
Phonogram Aug. 13, 1976
WTO Jan. 1, 1995

Nicaragua [6]
BAC Dec. 15, 1913
UCC Geneva Aug. 16, 1961
SAT Aug. 25, 1979 [4]
WTO Sept. 3, 1995

Niger
Berne May 2, 1962 (Paris) [2]
UCC Geneva May 15, 1989
UCC Paris May 15, 1989
WTO Dec. 13, 1996

Nigeria
UCC Geneva Feb. 14, 1962
Berne Sept. 14, 1993 (Paris)
WTO Jan. 1, 1995

Norway
Berne Apr. 13, 1896 (Paris) [2]
Bilateral July 1, 1905
UCC Geneva Jan. 23, 1963
UCC Paris Aug. 7, 1974
Phonogram Aug. 1, 1978
WTO Jan. 1, 1995

Oman
None

Pakistan
Berne July 5, 1948 (Rome) [2]
UCC Geneva Sept. 16, 1955
WTO Jan. 1, 1995

Palau
Unclear

Panama
BAC Nov. 25, 1913
UCC Geneva Oct. 17, 1962
Phonogram June 29, 1974
UCC Paris Sept. 3, 1980
SAT Sept. 25, 1985
Berne June 8, 1996 (Paris)

Papua New Guinea
WTO June 9, 1996

Paraguay
BAC Sept. 20, 1917
UCC Geneva Mar. 11, 1962
Phonogram Feb. 13, 1979
Berne Jan. 2, 1992 (Paris)
WTO Jan. 1, 1995

Peru
BAC Apr. 30, 1920
UCC Geneva Oct. 16, 1963
UCC Paris July 22, 1985
SAT Aug. 7, 1985
Phonogram Aug. 24, 1985
Berne Aug. 20, 1988 (Paris) [2]
WTO Jan. 1, 1995

Philippines
Bilateral Oct. 21, 1948
Berne Aug. 1, 1951 (Paris) [2]
UCC status undetermined by
UNESCO (Copyright Office
  considers that UCC relations
  do not exist.)
WTO Jan. 1, 1995

Poland
Berne Jan. 28, 1920 (Paris) [2]
Bilateral Feb. 16, 1927
UCC Geneva Mar. 9, 1977
UCC Paris Mar. 9, 1977
WTO July 1, 1995

Portugal
Bilateral July 20, 1893
Berne Mar. 29, 1911 (Paris) [2]
UCC Geneva Dec. 25, 1956
UCC Paris July 30, 1981
WTO Jan. 1, 1995
SAT Mar. 11, 1996

Qatar
WTO Jan. 13, 1996

Romania
Berne Jan. 1, 1927 (Paris) [2]
Bilateral May 14, 1928
WTO Jan. 1, 1995
Phonogram Oct. 1, 1998

Russian Federation
UCC Geneva May 27, 1973
SAT Dec. 25, 1991
UCC Paris Mar. 9, 1995
Berne Mar. 13, 1995 (Paris)
Phonogram Mar. 13, 1995

Rwanda
Berne Mar. 1, 1984 (Paris) [2]
UCC Geneva Nov. 10, 1989
UCC Paris Nov. 10, 1989
WTO May 22, 1996

St. Christopher (St. Kitts) and Nevis
Berne Apr. 9, 1995 (Paris) [2]
WTO Feb. 21, 1996

Saint Lucia
Berne Aug. 24, 1993 (Paris) [2]
WTO Jan. 1, 1995

Saint Vincent and the Grenadines
UCC Geneva Apr. 22, 1985
UCC Paris Apr. 22, 1985
WTO Jan. 1, 1995
Berne Aug. 29, 1995 (Paris)

San Marino
None

São Tomé and Principe
Unclear

Saudi Arabia
UCC Geneva July 13, 1994
UCC Paris July 13, 1994

Senegal
Berne Aug. 25, 1962 (Paris) [2]
UCC Geneva July 9, 1974
UCC Paris July 10, 1974
WTO Jan. 1, 1995

Seychelles
Unclear

Sierra Leone
WTO July 23, 1995

Singapore
Bilateral May 18, 1987
WTO Jan. 1, 1995
Berne Dec. 21, 1998 (Paris)

Slovakia
UCC Geneva Jan. 6, 1960
UCC Paris Apr. 17, 1980
Berne Jan. 1, 1993 (Paris) [2]
Phonogram Jan. 1, 1993
WTO Jan. 1, 1995

Slovenia
UCC Geneva May 11, 1966
UCC Paris July 10, 1974
Berne June 25, 1991 (Paris) [2]
SAT June 25, 1991
WTO July 30, 1995
Phonogram Oct. 15, 1996

Solomon Islands
WTO July 26, 1996

Somalia
Unclear

South Africa
Bilateral July 1, 1924
Berne Oct. 3, 1928 (Brussels) [2]
WTO Jan. 1, 1995

Soviet Union
(See entry under Russian Federation)

Spain
Berne Dec. 5, 1887 (Paris) [2]
Bilateral July 10, 1895
UCC Geneva Sept. 16, 1955
UCC Paris July 10, 1974
Phonogram Aug. 24, 1974
WTO Jan. 1, 1995

Sri Lanka (formerly Ceylon)
Berne July 20, 1959 (Rome) [2]
UCC Geneva Jan. 25, 1984
UCC Paris Jan. 25, 1984
WTO Jan. 1, 1995

Sudan
Unclear

Suriname
Berne Feb. 23, 1977 (Paris) [2]
WTO Jan. 1, 1995

Swaziland
WTO Jan. 1, 1995
Berne Dec. 14, 1998 (Paris)

Sweden
Berne Aug. 1, 1904 (Paris) [2]
Bilateral June 1, 1911
UCC Geneva July 1, 1961
Phonogram Apr. 18, 1973 [3]
UCC Paris July 10, 1974
WTO Jan. 1, 1995

Switzerland
Berne Dec. 5, 1887 (Paris) [2]
Bilateral July 1, 1891
UCC Geneva Mar. 30, 1956
UCC Paris Sept. 21, 1993
SAT Sept. 24, 1993
Phonogram Sept. 30, 1993
WTO July 1, 1995

Syria
Unclear

Tajikistan
UCC Geneva May 27, 1973

Tanzania
Berne July 25, 1994 (Paris)
WTO Jan. 1, 1995

Thailand
Bilateral Sept. 1, 1921
Berne July 17, 1931 (Paris) [2]
WTO Jan. 1, 1995

Togo
Berne Apr. 30, 1975 (Paris) [2]
WTO May 31, 1995

Tonga
None

Trinidad and Tobago
Berne Aug 16, 1988 (Paris) [2]
UCC Geneva Aug. 19, 1988
UCC Paris Aug. 19, 1988
Phonogram Oct. 1, 1988
WTO Mar. 1, 1995
SAT Nov. 1, 1996

Tunisia
Berne Dec. 5, 1887 (Paris) [2]
UCC Geneva June 19, 1969
UCC Paris June 10, 1975
WTO Mar. 29, 1995

Turkey
Berne Jan. 1, 1952 (Paris) [2]
WTO Mar. 26, 1995

Tuvalu
Unclear

Uganda
WTO Jan. 1, 1995

Ukraine
UCC Geneva May 27, 1973
Berne Oct. 25, 1995 (Paris)

United Arab Emirates
WTO Apr. 10, 1996

United Kingdom
Berne Dec. 5, 1887 (Paris) [2]
Bilateral July 1, 1891
UCC Geneva Sept. 27, 1957
Phonogram Apr. 18, 1973 [3]
UCC Paris July 10, 1974
WTO Jan. 1, 1995

Upper Volta
(See entry under Burkina Faso)

Uruguay
BAC Dec. 17, 1919
Berne July 10, 1967 (Paris) [2]
Phonogram Jan. 18, 1983
UCC Geneva Apr. 12, 1993
UCC Paris Apr. 12, 1993
WTO Jan. 1, 1995

Vanuatu
Unclear

Vatican City (Holy See)
Berne Sept. 12, 1935 (Paris) [2]
UCC Geneva Oct. 5, 1955
Phonogram July 18, 1977
UCC Paris May 6, 1980

Venezuela
UCC Geneva Sept. 30, 1966
Phonogram Nov. 18, 1982
Berne Dec. 30, 1982 (Paris) [2]
WTO Jan. 1, 1995
UCC Paris Fob. 11, 1997

Vietnam
Bilateral Dec. 23, 1998 [13]

Western Samoa
Unclear

Yemen (Aden)
Unclear

Yemen (San'a)
None

Yugoslavia
Berne June 17, 1930 (Paris) [2]
UCC Geneva May 11, 1966
UCC Paris July 10, 1974
SAT Aug. 25, 19794

Zaire
(See entry under Democratic
  Republic of Congo)

Zambia
UCC Geneva June 1, 1965
Berne Jan. 2, 1992 (Paris) [2]
WTO Jan. 1, 1995

Zimbabwe
Berne Apr. 18, 1980 (Rome) [2]
WTO Mar. 3, 1995

Statutory Provisions

The copyright law embodied in title 17 of the United States Code was
completely revised by the Act of October 19, 1976 (Public Law 94-553, 90 Stat.
2541), which became fully effective on January 1, 1978. Reprinted below is
section 104 of that Act, as amended by the Act of October 31, 1988 (Public Law
100-568, 102 Stat. 2853, 2855).

§104. Subject Matter of Copyright: National Origin

(a) UNPUBLISHED WORKS. The works specified by sections 102 and
108, while unpublished, are subject to protection under this title without
regard to the nationality or domicile of the author.

(b) PUBLISHED WORKS. The works specified by sections 102 and 103,
when published, are subject to protection under this title if—

(1) on the date of first publication, one or more of the authors is a
national or domiciliary of the United States, or is a national, domiciliary, or
sovereign authority of a foreign nation that is a party to a copyright treaty to
which the United States is also a party, or is a stateless person, wherever that
person may be domiciled; or

(2) the work is first published in the United States or in a foreign
nation that, on the date of first publication, is a party to the Universal Copyright Convention; or

(3) the work is first published by the United Nations or any of its
specialized agencies, or by the Organization of American States; or

(4) the work is a Berne Convention work; or

(5) the work comes within the scope of a Presidential proclamation.

Whenever the President finds that a particular foreign nation extends, to works by authors who are nationals or domiciliaries of the United States or to works that are first published in the United States, copyright protection on substantially the same basis as that on which the foreign nation extends protection to works of its own nationals and domiciliaries and works first published in that nation, the President may by proclamation extend protection under this title to works of which one or more of the authors is, on the date of first publication, a national, domiciliary, or sovereign authority of that nation, or which was first published in that nation. The President may revise, suspend, or revoke any such proclamation or impose any conditions or limitations on protection under a proclamation.

(c) EFFECT OF BERNE CONVENTION. No right or interest in a work eligible for protection under this title may be claimed by virtue of, or in reliance upon, the provisions of the Berne Convention, or the adherence of the United States thereto. Any rights in a work eligible for protection under this title that derive from this title, other Federal or State statutes, or the common law, shall not be expanded or reduced by virtue of, or in reliance upon, the provisions of the Berne Convention, or the adherence of the United States thereto.

NOTE:

Subsequent amendments to the Copyright Act of October 19, 1976, included the North American Free Trade Agreement Implementation Act of December 8, 1993, Pub. L. 103-182, 107 Stat. 2057, and the Uruguay Round Agreements Act of December 8, 1994, Pub. L. 103-465, 108 Stat. 4809. The latter Act amended section 104A of the Copyright Act in its entirety so as to provide for the automatic restoration of copyright in certain foreign works that were in the public domain in the United States but are protected by copyright or neighboring rights in their country of origin. The effective date for restoration of copyright in such foreign works is January 1, 1996

SOME POINTS TO REMEMBER REGARDING THE INTERNATIONAL PROTECTION OF LITERARY AND ARTISTIC WORKS

There is no such thing as an "international copyright" that will automatically protect an author's writings throughout the world. Protection against unauthorized use in a particular country basically depends on the national laws of that country. However, most countries offer protection to foreign works under certain conditions that have been greatly simplified by international copyright treaties and Conventions. There are two principal international copyright conventions, the Berne Union for the Protection of Literary and Artistic Property (Berne Convention) and the Universal Copyright Convention (UCC).

An author who wishes copyright protection for his or her work in a particular country should first determine the extent of the protection available to works of foreign authors in that country. If possible, this should be done before the work is published anywhere, because protection may depend on the facts existing at the time of first publication.

If the country in which protection is sought is a party to one of the international copyright conventions, the work generally may be protected by complying with the conditions of that convention. Even if the work cannot be brought under an international convention, protection under the specific provisions of the country's national laws may still be possible. There are, however, some countries that offer little or no copyright protection to any foreign works. For current information on the requirement and protection provided by other countries, it may be advisable to consult an expert familiar with foreign copyright laws. The U.S. Copyright Office is not permitted to recommend agents or attorneys or to give legal advice on foreign laws.

Notes

[1] "Paris" means the Berne Convention for the Protection of Literary and Artistic Works as revised at Paris on July 24, 1971 (Paris Act); "Stockholm" means the said Convention as revised at Stockholm on July 14, 1967 (Stockholm Act); "Brussels" means the said Convention as revised at Brussels on June 26, 1948 (Brussels Act); "Rome" means the said Convention as revised at Rome on June 2, 1928 (Rome Act); "Berlin" means the said Convention as revised at Berlin on November 13, 1908 (Berlin Act). NOTE: In each case the reference to Act signifies adherence to the substantive provision of such Act only, e.g., Articles 1 to 21 and the Appendix of the Paris Act. Articles 22 to 38 deal with administration and structure.

[2] The Berne Convention for the Protection of Literary and Artistic Works of September 9, 1886, as revised at Paris on July 24, 1971, did not enter into force with respect to the United States until March 1, 1989.

[3] The Convention for the Protection of Producers of Phonograms Against Unauthorized Duplication of Their Phonograms done at Geneva on October 29, 1971, did not enter into force with respect to the United States until March 10, 1974.

[4] The Convention Relating to the Distribution of Programme-Carrying Signals Transmitted by Satellite done at Brussels on May 21, 1974, did not enter into force with respect to the United States until March 7, 1985.

[5] The government of the People's of China views this treaty as not binding on the PRC. In the Territory administered by the authorities on Taiwan the treaty is considered to be in force.

[6] This country became a party to the Mexico City Convention, 1902, effective June 30, 1908, to which the United States also became a party, effective on the same date. As regards copyright relations with the United States, this Convention is considered to have been superseded by adherence of this country and the United States to the Buenos Aires Convention of 1910.

[7] Date on which the accession by the German Empire became effective.

[8] Bilateral copyright relations between Japan and the United States, which were formulated effective May 10, 1906, are considered to have been abrogated and superseded by the adherence of Japan to the UCC Geneva, effective April 28, 1956.

[9] Bilateral copyright relations between the People's Republic of China and the United States of America were established, effective March 17, 1992, by a Presidential Proclamation of the same date, under the authority of section 104 of title 17 of the United States Code, as amended by the Act of October 31, 1988 (Public Law 100-568, 102 Stat. 2853, 2855).

[10] The dates of adherence by Germany to multilateral treaties include adherence by the Federal Republic of Germany when that country was divided into the Federal Republic of Germany and the German Democratic Republic. However, through the accession, effective October 3, 1990, of the German Democratic Republic to the Federal Republic of Germany, in accordance with the German Unification Treaty of August 31, 1990, the German Democratic Republic ceased, on the said date, to be a sovereign state. Previously, the German Democratic Republic had become party to the Paris Act of the Berne Convention for the Protection of Literary and Artistic Works on February 18, 1978, but ceased to be a party to the said Convention on October 3, 1990. The German Democratic Republic had also been a member of the Universal Copyright Convention, having become party to the Geneva text of the said Convention on October 5, 1973, and party to the revised Paris text of the same Convention on December 10, 1980.

[11] See also Czech Republic and Slovakia.

[12] Prior to the return of Hong Kong to China, bilateral copyright relations existed with Hong Kong through the United Kingdom (from August 1, 1973), and Phonogram Convention Membership existed through the United Kingdom (from March 4, 1975).

[13] Bilateral copyright relations between the Socialist Republic of Vietnam and the United States were established effective December 23, 1998, by Presidential Proclamation No. 7161 of that same date, at 63 Fed. Reg. 71571 (1998), under the authority of sections 104(b)(5) and 104A(g) of title 17 of the United States Code, as amended.

D

The Digital Millennium Copyright Act of 1998

By passing the Digital Millennium Copyright Act of 1998 The United States became a signatory to the WIPO Copyright Treaty and the WIPO Performances and Phonograms Treaty (see Appendix A). The following pages reproduce some of the key parts of Titles I and II of that Act: WIPO Treaties Implementation, Online Copyright Infringement Liability Limitation.

Title I: WIPO Treaties Implementation

SECTION 103. COPYRIGHT PROTECTION SYSTEMS AND COPYRIGHT MANAGE-MENT INFORMATION.

...IN GENERAL—Title 17, United States Code, is amended by adding at the end the following new chapter:

CHAPTER 12—COPYRIGHT PROTECTION AND MANAGEMENT SYSTEMS

Sec. 1201. Circumvention of copyright protection systems.

Sec. 1202. Integrity of copyright management information.

Sec. 1203. Civil remedies.

Sec. 1204. Criminal offenses and penalties.

Sec. 1205. Savings clause.

SEC. 1201. CIRCUMVENTION OF COPYRIGHT PROTECTION SYSTEMS
(a) VIOLATIONS REGARDING CIRCUMVENTION OF TECHNOLOG-

ICAL MEASURES—(1)(A) No person shall circumvent a technological measure that effectively controls access to a work protected under this title. The prohibition contained in the preceding sentence shall take effect at the end of the 2-year period beginning on the date of the enactment of this chapter.

(B) The prohibition contained in subparagraph (A) shall not apply to persons who are users of a copyrighted work which is in a particular class of works, if such persons are, or are likely to be in the succeeding 3-year period, adversely affected by virtue of such prohibition in their ability to make noninfringing uses of that particular class of works under this title, as determined under subparagraph (C).

(C) During the 2-year period described in subparagraph (A), and during each succeeding 3-year period, the Librarian of Congress, upon the recommendation of the Register of Copyrights, who shall consult with the Assistant Secretary for Communications and Information of the Department of Commerce and report and comment on his or her views in making such recommendation, shall make the determination in a rulemaking proceeding on the record for purposes of subparagraph (B) of whether persons who are users of a copyrighted work are, or are likely to be in the succeeding 3-year period, adversely affected by the prohibition under subparagraph (A) in their ability to make noninfringing uses under this title of a particular class of copyrighted works. In conducting such rulemaking, the Librarian shall examine—

(i) the availability for use of copyrighted works;

(ii) the availability for use of works for nonprofit archival, preservation, and educational purposes;

(iii) the impact that the prohibition on the circumvention of technological measures applied to copyrighted works has on criticism, comment, news reporting, teaching, scholarship, or research;

(iv) the effect of circumvention of technological measures on the market for or value of copyrighted works; and

(v) such other factors as the Librarian considers appropriate.

(D) The Librarian shall publish any class of copyrighted works for which the Librarian has determined, pursuant to the rulemaking conducted under subparagraph (C), that noninfringing uses by persons who are users of a copyrighted work are, or are likely to be, adversely affected, and the prohibition contained in subparagraph (A) shall not apply to such users with respect to such class of works for the ensuing 3-year period.

(E) Neither the exception under subparagraph (B) from the applicability of the prohibition contained in subparagraph (A), nor any determination made in a rulemaking conducted under subparagraph (C), may be used as a defense in any action to enforce any provision of this title other than this paragraph.

(2) No person shall manufacture, import, offer to the public, provide, or otherwise traffic in any technology, product, service, device, component, or part thereof, that—

(A) is primarily designed or produced for the purpose of circumventing a technological measure that effectively controls access to a work protected under this title;

(B) has only limited commercially significant purpose or use other than to circumvent a technological measure that effectively controls access to a work protected under this title; or

(C) is marketed by that person or another acting in concert with that person with that person's knowledge for use in circumventing a technological measure that effectively controls access to a work protected under this title.

(3) As used in this subsection—

(A) to "circumvent a technological measure" means to descramble a scrambled work, to decrypt an encrypted work, or otherwise to avoid, bypass, remove, deactivate, or impair a technological measure, without the authority of the copyright owner; and

(B) a technological measure "effectively controls access to a work" if the measure, in the ordinary course of its operation, requires the application of information, or a process or a treatment, with the authority of the copyright owner, to gain access to the work.

(b) ADDITIONAL VIOLATIONS—(1) No person shall manufacture, import, offer to the public, provide, or otherwise traffic in any technology, product, service, device, component, or part thereof, that—

(A) is primarily designed or produced for the purpose of circumventing protection afforded by a technological measure that effectively protects a right of a copyright owner under this title in a work or a portion thereof;

(B) has only limited commercially significant purpose or use other than to circumvent protection afforded by a technological measure that effectively protects a right of a copyright owner under this title in a work or a portion thereof; or

(C) is marketed by that person or another acting in concert with that person with that person's knowledge for use in circumventing protection afforded by a technological measure that effectively protects a right of a copyright owner under this title in a work or a portion thereof.

(2) As used in this subsection—

(A) to "circumvent protection afforded by a technological measure" means avoiding, bypassing, removing, deactivating, or otherwise impairing a technological measure; and

(B) a technological measure "effectively protects a right of a copyright owner under this title" if the measure, in the ordinary course of its operation, prevents, restricts, or otherwise limits the exercise of a right of a copyright owner under this title.

(c) OTHER RIGHTS, ETC., NOT AFFECTED—(1) Nothing in this section shall affect rights, remedies, limitations, or defenses to copyright infringement, including fair use, under this title.

(2) Nothing in this section shall enlarge or diminish vicarious or contributory liability for copyright infringement in connection with any technology, product, service, device, component, or part thereof.

(3) Nothing in this section shall require that the design of, or design and selection of parts and components for, a consumer electronics, telecommunications, or computing product provide for a response to any particular technological measure, so long as such part or component, or the product in which such part or component is integrated, does not otherwise fall within the prohibitions of subsection (a)(2) or (b)(1).

(4) Nothing in this section shall enlarge or diminish any rights of free speech or the press for activities using consumer electronics, telecommunications, or computing products.

(d) EXEMPTION FOR NONPROFIT LIBRARIES, ARCHIVES, AND EDUCATIONAL INSTITUTIONS—(1) A nonprofit library, archives, or educational institution which gains access to a commercially exploited copyrighted work solely in order to make a good faith determination of whether to acquire a copy of that work for the sole purpose of engaging in conduct permitted under this title shall not be in violation of subsection (a)(1)(A). A copy of a work to which access has been gained under this paragraph—

(A) may not be retained longer than necessary to make such good faith determination; and

(B) may not be used for any other purpose.

(2) The exemption made available under paragraph (1) shall only apply with respect to a work when an identical copy of that work is not reasonably available in another form.

(3) A nonprofit library that willfully for the purpose of commercial advantage or financial gain violates paragraph (1)—

(A) shall, for the first offense, be subject to the civil remedies under section 1203; and

(B) shall, for repeated or subsequent offenses, in addition to the civil remedies under section 1203, forfeit the exemption provided under paragraph (1).

(4) This subsection may not be used as a defense to a claim under subsection (a)(2) or (b), nor may this subsection permit a nonprofit library, archives, or educational institution to manufacture, import, offer to the public, provide, or otherwise traffic in any technology, product, service, component, or part thereof, which circumvents a technological measure.

(5) In order for a library or archives to qualify for the exemption under this subsection, the collections of that library or archives shall be—

(A) open to the public; or

(B) available not only to researchers affiliated with the library or archives or with the institution of which it is a part, but also to other persons doing research in a specialized field.

(e) LAW ENFORCEMENT, INTELLIGENCE, AND OTHER GOVERN-

MENT ACTIVITIES—This section does not prohibit any lawfully authorized investigative, protective, information security, or intelligence activity of an officer, agent, or employee of the United States, a State, or a political subdivision of a State, or a person acting pursuant to a contract with the United States, a State, or a political subdivision of a State. For purposes of this subsection, the term "information security" means activities carried out in order to identify and address the vulnerabilities of a government computer, computer system, or computer network.

(f) REVERSE ENGINEERING—(1) Notwithstanding the provisions of subsection (a)(1)(A), a person who has lawfully obtained the right to use a copy of a computer program may circumvent a technological measure that effectively controls access to a particular portion of that program for the sole purpose of identifying and analyzing those elements of the program that are necessary to achieve interoperability of an independently created computer program with other programs, and that have not previously been readily available to the person engaging in the circumvention, to the extent any such acts of identification and analysis do not constitute infringement under this title.

(2) Notwithstanding the provisions of subsections (a)(2) and (b), a person may develop and employ technological means to circumvent a technological measure, or to circumvent protection afforded by a technological measure, in order to enable the identification and analysis under paragraph (1), or for the purpose of enabling interoperability of an independently created computer program with other programs, if such means are necessary to achieve such interoperability, to the extent that doing so does not constitute infringement under this title.

(3) The information acquired through the acts permitted under paragraph (1), and the means permitted under paragraph (2), may be made available to others if the person referred to in paragraph (1) or (2), as the case may be, provides such information or means solely for the purpose of enabling interoperability of an independently created computer program with other programs, and to the extent that doing so does not constitute infringement under this title or violate applicable law other than this section.

(4) For purposes of this subsection, the term "interoperability" means the ability of computer programs to exchange information, and of such programs mutually to use the information which has been exchanged.

(g) ENCRYPTION RESEARCH—

(1) DEFINITIONS—For purposes of this subsection—

(A) the term "encryption research" means activities necessary to identify and analyze flaws and vulnerabilities of encryption technologies applied to copyrighted works, if these activities are conducted to advance the state of knowledge in the field of encryption technology or to assist in the development of encryption products; and

(B) the term "encryption technology" means the scrambling and descrambling of information using mathematical formulas or algorithms.

(2) PERMISSIBLE ACTS OF ENCRYPTION RESEARCH—Notwithstanding the provisions of subsection (a)(1)(A), it is not a violation of that subsection for a person to circumvent a technological measure as applied to a copy, phonorecord, performance, or display of a published work in the course of an act of good faith encryption research if—

(A) the person lawfully obtained the encrypted copy, phonorecord, performance, or display of the published work;

(B) such act is necessary to conduct such encryption research;

(C) the person made a good faith effort to obtain authorization before the circumvention; and

(D) such act does not constitute infringement under this title or a violation of applicable law other than this section, including section 1030 of title 18 and those provisions of title 18 amended by the Computer Fraud and Abuse Act of 1986.

(3) FACTORS IN DETERMINING EXEMPTION—In determining whether a person qualifies for the exemption under paragraph (2), the factors to be considered shall include—

(A) whether the information derived from the encryption research was disseminated, and if so, whether it was disseminated in a manner reasonably calculated to advance the state of knowledge or development of encryption technology, versus whether it was disseminated in a manner that facilitates infringement under this title or a violation of applicable law other than this section, including a violation of privacy or breach of security;

(B) whether the person is engaged in a legitimate course of study, is employed, or is appropriately trained or experienced, in the field of encryption technology; and

(C) whether the person provides the copyright owner of the work to which the technological measure is applied with notice of the findings and documentation of the research, and the time when such notice is provided.

(4) USE OF TECHNOLOGICAL MEANS FOR RESEARCH ACTIVITIES—Notwithstanding the provisions of subsection (a)(2), it is not a violation of that subsection for a person to—

(A) develop and employ technological means to circumvent a technological measure for the sole purpose of that person performing the acts of good faith encryption research described in paragraph (2); and

(B) provide the technological means to another person with whom he or she is working collaboratively for the purpose of conducting the acts of good faith encryption research described in paragraph (2) or for the purpose of having that other person verify his or her acts of good faith encryption research described in paragraph (2).

(5) REPORT TO CONGRESS—Not later than 1 year after the date of the enactment of this chapter, the Register of Copyrights and the Assistant Secretary for Communications and Information of the Department of Commerce shall jointly report to the Congress on the effect this subsection has

had on—

    (A) encryption research and the development of encryption technology;

    (B) the adequacy and effectiveness of technological measures designed to protect copyrighted works; and

    (C) protection of copyright owners against the unauthorized access to their encrypted copyrighted works. The report shall include legislative recommendations, if any.

(h) EXCEPTIONS REGARDING MINORS—In applying subsection (a) to a component or part, the court may consider the necessity for its intended and actual incorporation in a technology, product, service, or device, which—

    (1) does not itself violate the provisions of this title; and

    (2) has the sole purpose to prevent the access of minors to material on the Internet.

(i) PROTECTION OF PERSONALLY IDENTIFYING INFORMATION-

    (1) CIRCUMVENTION PERMITTED—Notwithstanding the provisions of subsection (a)(1)(A), it is not a violation of that subsection for a person to circumvent a technological measure that effectively controls access to a work protected under this title, if—

    (A) the technological measure, or the work it protects, contains the capability of collecting or disseminating personally identifying information reflecting the online activities of a natural person who seeks to gain access to the work protected;

    (B) in the normal course of its operation, the technological measure, or the work it protects, collects or disseminates personally identifying information about the person who seeks to gain access to the work protected, without providing conspicuous notice of such collection or dissemination to such person, and without providing such person with the capability to prevent or restrict such collection or dissemination;

    (C) the act of circumvention has the sole effect of identifying and disabling the capability described in subparagraph (A), and has no other effect on the ability of any person to gain access to any work; and

    (D) the act of circumvention is carried out solely for the purpose of preventing the collection or dissemination of personally identifying information about a natural person who seeks to gain access to the work protected, and is not in violation of any other law.

    (2) INAPPLICABILITY TO CERTAIN TECHNOLOGICAL MEASURES—This subsection does not apply to a technological measure, or a work it protects, that does not collect or disseminate personally identifying information and that is disclosed to a user as not having or using such capability.

(j) SECURITY TESTING—

    (1) DEFINITION—For purposes of this subsection, the term "security testing" means accessing a computer, computer system, or computer network, solely for the purpose of good faith testing, investigating, or

correcting, a security flaw or vulnerability, with the authorization of the owner or operator of such computer, computer system, or computer network.

(2) PERMISSIBLE ACTS OF SECURITY TESTING— Notwithstanding the provisions of subsection (a)(1)(A), it is not a violation of that subsection for a person to engage in an act of security testing, if such act does not constitute infringement under this title or a violation of applicable law other than this section, including section 1030 of title 18 and those provisions of title 18 amended by the Computer Fraud and Abuse Act of 1986.

(3) FACTORS IN DETERMINING EXEMPTION—In determining whether a person qualifies for the exemption under paragraph (2), the factors to be considered shall include—

(A) whether the information derived from the security testing was used solely to promote the security of the owner or operator of such computer, computer system or computer network, or shared directly with the developer of such computer, computer system, or computer network; and

(B) whether the information derived from the security testing was used or maintained in a manner that does not facilitate infringement under this title or a violation of applicable law other than this section, including a violation of privacy or breach of security.

(4) USE OF TECHNOLOGICAL MEANS FOR SECURITY TESTING—Notwithstanding the provisions of subsection (a)(2), it is not a violation of that subsection for a person to develop, produce, distribute or employ technological means for the sole purpose of performing the acts of security testing described in subsection (2), provided such technological means does not otherwise violate section (a)(2).

(k) CERTAIN ANALOG DEVICES AND CERTAIN TECHNOLOGICAL MEASURES—

(1) CERTAIN ANALOG DEVICES—

(A) Effective 18 months after the date of the enactment of this chapter, no person shall manufacture, import, offer to the public, provide or otherwise traffic in any—

(i) VHS format analog video cassette recorder unless such recorder conforms to the automatic gain control copy control technology;

(ii) 8mm format analog video cassette camcorder unless such camcorder conforms to the automatic gain control technology;

(iii) Beta format analog video cassette recorder, unless such recorder conforms to the automatic gain control copy control technology, except that this requirement shall not apply until there are 1,000 Beta format analog video cassette recorders sold in the United States in any one calendar year after the date of the enactment of this chapter;

(iv) 8mm format analog video cassette recorder that is not an analog video cassette camcorder, unless such recorder conforms to the automatic gain control copy control technology, except that this requirement shall not apply until there are 20,000 such recorders sold in the United States in any one calendar year after the date of the enactment of this chapter; or

(v) analog video cassette recorder that records using an NTSC format video input and that is not otherwise covered under clauses (i) through (iv), unless such device conforms to the automatic gain control copy control technology.

(B) Effective on the date of the enactment of this chapter, no person shall manufacture, import, offer to the public, provide or otherwise traffic in—

(i) any VHS format analog video cassette recorder or any 8mm format analog video cassette recorder if the design of the model of such recorder has been modified after such date of enactment so that a model of recorder that previously conformed to the automatic gain control copy control technology no longer conforms to such technology; or

(ii) any VHS format analog video cassette recorder, or any 8mm format analog video cassette recorder that is not an 8mm analog video cassette camcorder, if the design of the model of such recorder has been modified after such date of enactment so that a model of recorder that previously conformed to the four-line colorstripe copy control technology no longer conforms to such technology.

Manufacturers that have not previously manufactured or sold a VHS format analog video cassette recorder, or an 8mm format analog cassette recorder, shall be required to conform to the four-line colorstripe copy control technology in the initial model of any such recorder manufactured after the date of the enactment of this chapter, and thereafter to continue conforming to the four-line colorstripe copy control technology. For purposes of this subparagraph, an analog video cassette recorder "conforms to" the four-line colorstripe copy control technology if it records a signal that, when played back by the playback function of that recorder in the normal viewing mode, exhibits, on a reference display device, a display containing distracting visible lines through portions of the viewable picture.

(2) CERTAIN ENCODING RESTRICTIONS—No person shall apply the automatic gain control copy control technology or colorstripe copy control technology to prevent or limit consumer copying except such copying—

(A) of a single transmission, or specified group of transmissions, of live events or of audiovisual works for which a member of the public has exercised choice in selecting the transmissions, including the content of the transmissions or the time of receipt of such transmissions, or both, and as to which such member is charged a separate fee for each such transmission or specified group of transmissions;

(B) from a copy of a transmission of a live event or an audiovisual work if such transmission is provided by a channel or service where payment is made by a member of the public for such channel or service in the form of a subscription fee that entitles the member of the public to receive all of the programming contained in such channel or service;

(C) from a physical medium containing one or more prerecorded audiovisual works; or

(D) from a copy of a transmission described in subparagraph (A) or from a copy made from a physical medium described in subparagraph (C). In the event that a transmission meets both the conditions set forth in subparagraph (A) and those set forth in subparagraph (B), the transmission shall be treated as a transmission described in subparagraph (A).

(3) INAPPLICABILITY—This subsection shall not—

(A) require any analog video cassette camcorder to conform to the automatic gain control copy control technology with respect to any video signal received through a camera lens;

(B) apply to the manufacture, importation, offer for sale, provision of, or other trafficking in, any professional analog video cassette recorder; or

(C) apply to the offer for sale or provision of, or other trafficking in, any previously owned analog video cassette recorder, if such recorder was legally manufactured and sold when new and not subsequently modified in violation of paragraph (1)(B).

(4) DEFINITIONS—For purposes of this subsection:

(A) An "analog video cassette recorder" means a device that records, or a device that includes a function that records, on electromagnetic tape in an analog format the electronic impulses produced by the video and audio portions of a television program, motion picture, or other form of audiovisual work.

(B) An "analog video cassette camcorder" means an analog video cassette recorder that contains a recording function that operates through a camera lens and through a video input that may be connected with a television or other video playback device.

(C) An analog video cassette recorder "conforms" to the automatic gain control copy control technology if it—

(i) detects one or more of the elements of such technology and does not record the motion picture or transmission protected by such technology; or

(ii) records a signal that, when played back, exhibits a meaningfully distorted or degraded display.

(D) The term "professional analog video cassette recorder" means an analog video cassette recorder that is designed, manufactured, marketed, and intended for use by a person who regularly employs such a device for a lawful business or industrial use, including making, performing, displaying, distributing, or transmitting copies of motion pictures on a commercial scale.

(E) The terms "VHS format", "8mm format", "Beta format", "automatic gain control copy control technology", "colorstripe copy control technology", "four-line version of the colorstripe copy control technology", and

"NTSC" have the meanings that are commonly understood in the consumer electronics and motion picture industries as of the date of the enactment of this chapter.

(5) VIOLATIONS—Any violation of paragraph (1) of this subsection shall be treated as a violation of subsection (b)(1) of this section. Any violation of paragraph (2) of this subsection shall be deemed an "act of circumvention" for the purposes of section 1203(c)(3)(A) of this chapter.

SEC. 1202. INTEGRITY OF COPYRIGHT MANAGEMENT INFORMATION

(a) FALSE COPYRIGHT MANAGEMENT INFORMATION—No person shall knowingly and with the intent to induce, enable, facilitate, or conceal infringement—

(1) provide copyright management information that is false, or

(2) distribute or import for distribution copyright management information that is false.

(b) REMOVAL OR ALTERATION OF COPYRIGHT MANAGEMENT INFORMATION—No person shall, without the authority of the copyright owner or the law—

(1) intentionally remove or alter any copyright management information,

(2) distribute or import for distribution copyright management information knowing that the copyright management information has been removed or altered without authority of the copyright owner or the law, or

(3) distribute, import for distribution, or publicly perform works, copies of works, or phonorecords, knowing that copyright management information has been removed or altered without authority of the copyright owner or the law, knowing, or, with respect to civil remedies under section 1203, having reasonable grounds to know, that it will induce, enable, facilitate, or conceal an infringement of any right under this title.

(c) DEFINITION—As used in this section, the term "copyright management information" means any of the following information conveyed in connection with copies or phonorecords of a work or performances or displays of a work, including in digital form, except that such term does not include any personally identifying information about a user of a work or of a copy, phonorecord, performance, or display of a work:

(1) The title and other information identifying the work, including the information set forth on a notice of copyright.

(2) The name of, and other identifying information about, the author of a work.

(3) The name of, and other identifying information about, the copyright owner of the work, including the information set forth in a notice of copyright.

(4) With the exception of public performances of works by radio and television broadcast stations, the name of, and other identifying information

about, a performer whose performance is fixed in a work other than an audio-visual work.

(5) With the exception of public performances of works by radio and television broadcast stations, in the case of an audiovisual work, the name of, and other identifying information about, a writer, performer, or director who is credited in the audiovisual work.

(6) Terms and conditions for use of the work.

(7) Identifying numbers or symbols referring to such information or links to such information.

(8) Such other information as the Register of Copyrights may prescribe by regulation, except that the Register of Copyrights may not require the provision of any information concerning the user of a copyrighted work.

(d) LAW ENFORCEMENT, INTELLIGENCE, AND OTHER GOVERN-MENT ACTIVITIES—This section does not prohibit any lawfully authorized investigative, protective, information security, or intelligence activity of an officer, agent, or employee of the United States, a State, or a political subdivision of a State, or a person acting pursuant to a contract with the United States, a State, or a political subdivision of a State. For purposes of this subsection, the term "information security" means activities carried out in order to identify and address the vulnerabilities of a government computer, computer system, or computer network.

(e) LIMITATIONS ON LIABILITY—

(1) ANALOG TRANSMISSIONS—In the case of an analog transmission, a person who is making transmissions in its capacity as a broadcast station, or as a cable system, or someone who provides programming to such station or system, shall not be liable for a violation of subsection (b) if—

(A) avoiding the activity that constitutes such violation is not technically feasible or would create an undue financial hardship on such person; and

(B) such person did not intend, by engaging in such activity, to induce, enable, facilitate, or conceal infringement of a right under this title.

(2) DIGITAL TRANSMISSIONS—

(A) If a digital transmission standard for the placement of copy-right management information for a category of works is set in a voluntary, consensus standard-setting process involving a representative cross-section of broadcast stations or cable systems and copyright owners of a category of works that are intended for public performance by such stations or systems, a person identified in paragraph (1) shall not be liable for a violation of subsection (b) with respect to the particular copyright management information addressed by such standard if—

(i) the placement of such information by someone other than such person is not in accordance with such standard; and

(ii) the activity that constitutes such violation is not intended to induce, enable, facilitate, or conceal infringement of a right under this title.

(B) Until a digital transmission standard has been set pursuant to subparagraph (A) with respect to the placement of copyright management information for a category of works, a person identified in paragraph (1) shall not be liable for a violation of subsection (b) with respect to such copyright management information, if the activity that constitutes such violation is not intended to induce, enable, facilitate, or conceal infringement of a right under this title, and if—

(i) the transmission of such information by such person would result in a perceptible visual or aural degradation of the digital signal; or

(ii) the transmission of such information by such person would conflict with—*(I)* an applicable government regulation relating to transmission of information in a digital signal; *(II)* an applicable industry-wide standard relating to the transmission of information in a digital signal that was adopted by a voluntary consensus standards body prior to the effective date of this chapter; or *(III)* an applicable industry-wide standard relating to the transmission of information in a digital signal that was adopted in a voluntary, consensus standards-setting process open to participation by a representative cross-section of broadcast stations or cable systems and copyright owners of a category of works that are intended for public performance by such stations or systems.

(3) DEFINITIONS—As used in this subsection—

(A) the term "broadcast station" has the meaning given that term in section 3 of the Communications Act of 1934 (47 U.S.C. 153); and

(B) the term "cable system" has the meaning given that term in section 602 of the Communications Act of 1934 (47 U.S.C. 522).

SEC. 1203. CIVIL REMEDIES

(a) CIVIL ACTIONS—Any person injured by a violation of section 1201 or 1202 may bring a civil action in an appropriate United States district court for such violation.

(b) POWERS OF THE COURT—In an action brought under subsection (a), the court—

(1) may grant temporary and permanent injunctions on such terms as it deems reasonable to prevent or restrain a violation, but in no event shall impose a prior restraint on free speech or the press protected under the 1st amendment to the Constitution;

(2) at any time while an action is pending, may order the impounding, on such terms as it deems reasonable, of any device or product that is in the custody or control of the alleged violator and that the court has reasonable cause to believe was involved in a violation;

(3) may award damages under subsection (c);

(4) in its discretion may allow the recovery of costs by or against any party other than the United States or an officer thereof;

(5) in its discretion may award reasonable attorney's fees to the prevailing party; and

(6) may, as part of a final judgment or decree finding a violation, order the remedial modification or the destruction of any device or product involved in the violation that is in the custody or control of the violator or has been impounded under paragraph (2).

(c) AWARD OF DAMAGES—

(1) IN GENERAL—Except as otherwise provided in this title, a person committing a violation of section 1201 or 1202 is liable for either—

(A) the actual damages and any additional profits of the violator, as provided in paragraph (2), or

(B) statutory damages, as provided in paragraph (3).

(2) ACTUAL DAMAGES—The court shall award to the complaining party the actual damages suffered by the party as a result of the violation, and any profits of the violator that are attributable to the violation and are not taken into account in computing the actual damages, if the complaining party elects such damages at any time before final judgment is entered.

(3) STATUTORY DAMAGES—(A) At any time before final judgment is entered, a complaining party may elect to recover an award of statutory damages for each violation of section 1201 in the sum of not less than $200 or more than $2,500 per act of circumvention, device, product, component, offer, or performance of service, as the court considers just.

(B) At any time before final judgment is entered, a complaining party may elect to recover an award of statutory damages for each violation of section 1202 in the sum of not less than $2,500 or more than $25,000.

(4) REPEATED VIOLATIONS—In any case in which the injured party sustains the burden of proving, and the court finds, that a person has violated section 1201 or 1202 within 3 years after a final judgment was entered against the person for another such violation, the court may increase the award of damages up to triple the amount that would otherwise be awarded, as the court considers just.

(5) INNOCENT VIOLATIONS—

(A) IN GENERAL—The court in its discretion may reduce or remit the total award of damages in any case in which the violator sustains the burden of proving, and the court finds, that the violator was not aware and had no reason to believe that its acts constituted a violation.

(B) NONPROFIT LIBRARY, ARCHIVES, OR EDUCATIONAL INSTITUTIONS—In the case of a nonprofit library, archives, or educational institution, the court shall remit damages in any case in which the library, archives, or educational institution sustains the burden of proving, and the court finds, that the library, archives, or educational institution was not aware and had no reason to believe that its acts constituted a violation.

SEC. 1204. CRIMINAL OFFENSES AND PENALTIES

(a) IN GENERAL—Any person who violates section 1201 or 1202 willfully and for purposes of commercial advantage or private financial gain—

(1) shall be fined not more than $500,000 or imprisoned for not more than 5 years, or both, for the first offense; and

(2) shall be fined not more than $1,000,000 or imprisoned for not more than 10 years, or both, for any subsequent offense.

(b) LIMITATION FOR NONPROFIT LIBRARY, ARCHIVES, OR EDUCATIONAL INSTITUTION—Subsection (a) shall not apply to a nonprofit library, archives, or educational institution.

(c) STATUTE OF LIMITATIONS—No criminal proceeding shall be brought under this section unless such proceeding is commenced within 5 years after the cause of action arose. ...

Title II—Online Copyright Infringement Liability Limitation

SECTION 202. LIMITATIONS ON LIABILITY FOR COPYRIGHT INFRINGEMENT

...IN GENERAL, Chapter 5 of Title 17, United States Code, is amended by adding after section 511 the following new material:

SEC. 512. LIMITATIONS ON LIABILITY RELATING TO MATERIAL ONLINE

(a) TRANSITORY DIGITAL NETWORK COMMUNICATIONS—A service provider shall not be liable for monetary relief, or, except as provided in subsection (j), for injunctive or other equitable relief, for infringement of copyright by reason of the provider's transmitting, routing, or providing connections for, material through a system or network controlled or operated by or for the service provider, or by reason of the intermediate and transient storage of that material in the course of such transmitting, routing, or providing connections, if—

(1) the transmission of the material was initiated by or at the direction of a person other than the service provider;

(2) the transmission, routing, provision of connections, or storage is carried out through an automatic technical process without selection of the material by the service provider;

(3) the service provider does not select the recipients of the material except as an automatic response to the request of another person;

(4) no copy of the material made by the service provider in the course of such intermediate or transient storage is maintained on the system or network in a manner ordinarily accessible to anyone other than anticipated recipients, and no such copy is maintained on the system or network in a manner ordinarily accessible to such anticipated recipients for a longer period than is reasonably necessary for the transmission, routing, or provision of connections; and

(5) the material is transmitted through the system or network without modification of its content.

(b) SYSTEM CACHING—

(1) LIMITATION ON LIABILITY—A service provider shall not be liable for monetary relief, or, except as provided in subsection (j), for injunctive or other equitable relief, for infringement of copyright by reason of the intermediate and temporary storage of material on a system or network controlled or operated by or for the service provider in a case in which—

(A) the material is made available online by a person other than the service provider;

(B) the material is transmitted from the person described in subparagraph (A) through the system or network to a person other than the person described in subparagraph (A) at the direction of that other person; and

(C) the storage is carried out through an automatic technical process for the purpose of making the material available to users of the system or network who, after the material is transmitted as described in subparagraph (B), request access to the material from the person described in subparagraph (A), if the conditions set forth in paragraph (2) are met.

(2) CONDITIONS—The conditions referred to in paragraph (1) are that—

(A) the material described in paragraph (1) is transmitted to the subsequent users described in paragraph (1)(C) without modification to its content from the manner in which the material was transmitted from the person described in paragraph (1)(A);

(B) the service provider described in paragraph (1) complies with rules concerning the refreshing, reloading, or other updating of the material when specified by the person making the material available online in accordance with a generally accepted industry standard data communications protocol for the system or network through which that person makes the material available, except that this subparagraph applies only if those rules are not used by the person described in paragraph (1)(A) to prevent or unreasonably impair the intermediate storage to which this subsection applies;

(C) the service provider does not interfere with the ability of technology associated with the material to return to the person described in paragraph (1) (A) the information that would have been available to that person if the material had been obtained by the subsequent users described in paragraph (1)(C) directly from that person, except that this subparagraph applies only if that technology—

(i) does not significantly interfere with the performance of the provider's system or network or with the intermediate storage of the material;

(ii) is consistent with generally accepted industry standard communications protocols; and

(iii) does not extract information from the provider's system or network other than the information that would have been available to the person described in paragraph (1)(A) if the subsequent users had gained access to the material directly from that person;

(D) if the person described in paragraph (1)(A) has in effect a condition that a person must meet prior to having access to the material, such as a condition based on payment of a fee or provision of a password or other information, the service provider permits access to the stored material in significant part only to users of its system or network that have met those conditions and only in accordance with those conditions; and

(E) if the person described in paragraph (1)(A) makes that material available online without the authorization of the copyright owner of the material, the service provider responds expeditiously to remove, or disable access to, the material that is claimed to be infringing upon notification of claimed infringement as described in subsection (c)(3), except that this subparagraph applies only if—

(i) the material has previously been removed from the originating site or access to it has been disabled, or a court has ordered that the material be removed from the originating site or that access to the material on the originating site be disabled; and

(ii) the party giving the notification includes in the notification a statement confirming that the material has been removed from the originating site or access to it has been disabled or that a court has ordered that the material be removed from the originating site or that access to the material on the originating site be disabled.

(c) INFORMATION RESIDING ON SYSTEMS OR NETWORKS AT DIRECTION OF USERS—

(1)   IN GENERAL—A service provider shall not be liable for monetary relief, or, except as provided in subsection (j), for injunctive or other equitable relief, for infringement of copyright by reason of the storage at the direction of a user of material that resides on a system or network controlled or operated by or for the service provider, if the service provider—

(A) (i) does not have actual knowledge that the material or an activity using the material on the system or network is infringing;

(ii) in the absence of such actual knowledge, is not aware of facts or circumstances from which infringing activity is apparent; or

(iii) upon obtaining such knowledge or awareness, acts expeditiously to remove, or disable access to, the material;

(B) does not receive a financial benefit directly attributable to the infringing activity, in a case in which the service provider has the right and ability to control such activity; and

(C) upon notification of claimed infringement as described in paragraph (3), responds expeditiously to remove, or disable access to, the material that is claimed to be infringing or to be the subject of infringing activity.

(2) DESIGNATED AGENT—The limitations on liability established in this subsection apply to a service provider only if the service provider has

designated an agent to receive notifications of claimed infringement described in paragraph (3), by making available through its service, including on its website in a location accessible to the public, and by providing to the Copyright Office, substantially the following information:

(A) the name, address, phone number, and electronic mail address of the agent.

(B) other contact information which the Register of Copyrights may deem appropriate.

The Register of Copyrights shall maintain a current directory of agents available to the public for inspection, including through the Internet, in both electronic and hard copy formats, and may require payment of a fee by service providers to cover the costs of maintaining the directory.

(3) ELEMENTS OF NOTIFICATION—

(A) To be effective under this subsection, a notification of claimed infringement must be a written communication provided to the designated agent of a service provider that includes substantially the following:

(i) A physical or electronic signature of a person authorized to act on behalf of the owner of an exclusive right that is allegedly infringed.

(ii) Identification of the copyrighted work claimed to have been infringed, or, if multiple copyrighted works at a single online site are covered by a single notification, a representative list of such works at that site.

(iii) Identification of the material that is claimed to be infringing or to be the subject of infringing activity and that is to be removed or access to which is to be disabled, and information reasonably sufficient to permit the service provider to locate the material.

(iv) Information reasonably sufficient to permit the service provider to contact the complaining party, such as an address, telephone number, and, if available, an electronic mail address at which the complaining party may be contacted.

(v) A statement that the complaining party has a good faith belief that use of the material in the manner complained of is not authorized by the copyright owner, its agent, or the law.

(vi) A statement that the information in the notification is accurate, and under penalty of perjury, that the complaining party is authorized to act on behalf of the owner of an exclusive right that is allegedly infringed.

(B) (i) Subject to clause (ii), a notification from a copyright owner or from a person authorized to act on behalf of the copyright owner that fails to comply substantially with the provisions of subparagraph (A) shall not be considered under paragraph (1)(A) in determining whether a service provider has actual knowledge or is aware of facts or circumstances from which infringing activity is apparent.

(ii) In a case in which the notification that is provided to the service provider's designated agent fails to comply substantially with all the provisions of subparagraph (A) but substantially complies with clauses (ii), (iii), and (iv) of subparagraph (A), clause (i) of this subparagraph applies only if the service provider promptly attempts to contact the person making the notification or takes other reasonable steps to assist in the receipt of notification that substantially complies with all the provisions of subparagraph (A).

(d) INFORMATION LOCATION TOOLS—A service provider shall not be liable for monetary relief, or, except as provided in subsection (j), for injunctive or other equitable relief, for infringement of copyright by reason of the provider referring or linking users to an online location containing infringing material or infringing activity, by using information location tools, including a directory, index, reference, pointer, or hypertext link, if the service provider—

(1) (A) does not have actual knowledge that the material or activity is infringing;

(B) in the absence of such actual knowledge, is not aware of facts or circumstances from which infringing activity is apparent; or

(C) upon obtaining such knowledge or awareness, acts expeditiously to remove, or disable access to, the material;

(2) does not receive a financial benefit directly attributable to the infringing activity, in a case in which the service provider has the right and ability to control such activity; and

(3) upon notification of claimed infringement as described in subsection (c)(3), responds expeditiously to remove, or disable access to, the material that is claimed to be infringing or to be the subject of infringing activity, except that, for purposes of this paragraph, the information described in subsection (c)(3)(A)(iii) shall be identification of the reference or link, to material or activity claimed to be infringing, that is to be removed or access to which is to be disabled, and information reasonably sufficient to permit the service provider to locate that reference or link.

(e) LIMITATION ON LIABILITY OF NONPROFIT EDUCATIONAL INSTITUTIONS—(1) When a public or other nonprofit institution of higher education is a service provider, and when a faculty member or graduate student who is an employee of such institution is performing a teaching or research function, for the purposes of subsections (A) and (B) such faculty member or graduate student shall be considered to be a person other than the institution, and for the purposes of subsections (C) and (D) such faculty member's or graduate student's knowledge or awareness of his or her infringing activities shall not be attributed to the institution, if—

(A) such faculty member's or graduate student's infringing activities do not involve the provision of online access to instructional materials that are or were required or recommended, within the preceding 3-year period, for a course taught at the institution by such faculty member or graduate student;

(B) the institution has not, within the preceding 3-year period, received more than two notifications described in subsection (c)(3) of claimed infringement by such faculty member or graduate student, and such notifications of claimed infringement were not actionable under subsection (f); and

(C) the institution provides to all users of its system or network informational materials that accurately describe, and promote compliance with, the laws of the United States relating to copyright.

(2) INJUNCTIONS—For the purposes of this subsection, the limitations on injunctive relief contained in subsections (j)(2) and (j)(3), but not those in (j)(1), shall apply.

(f) MISREPRESENTATIONS—Any person who knowingly materially misrepresents under this section—

(1) that material or activity is infringing, or

(2) that material or activity was removed or disabled by mistake or misidentification, shall be liable for any damages, including costs and attorneys' fees, incurred by the alleged infringer, by any copyright owner or copyright owner's authorized licensee, or by a service provider, who is injured by such misrepresentation, as the result of the service provider relying upon such misrepresentation in removing or disabling access to the material or activity claimed to be infringing, or in replacing the removed material or ceasing to disable access to it.

(g) REPLACEMENT OF REMOVED OR DISABLED MATERIAL AND LIMITATION ON OTHER LIABILITY—

(1) NO LIABILITY FOR TAKING DOWN GENERALLY—Subject to paragraph (2), a service provider shall not be liable to any person for any claim based on the service provider's good faith disabling of access to, or removal of, material or activity claimed to be infringing or based on facts or circumstances from which infringing activity is apparent, regardless of whether the material or activity is ultimately determined to be infringing.

(2) EXCEPTION—Paragraph (1) shall not apply with respect to material residing at the direction of a subscriber of the service provider on a system or network controlled or operated by or for the service provider that is removed, or to which access is disabled by the service provider, pursuant to a notice provided under subsection (c)(1)(C), unless the service provider—

(A) takes reasonable steps promptly to notify the subscriber that it has removed or disabled access to the material;

(B) upon receipt of a counter notification described in paragraph (3), promptly provides the person who provided the notification under subsection (c)(1) (C) with a copy of the counter notification, and informs that person that it will replace the removed material or cease disabling access to it in 10 business days; and

(C) replaces the removed material and ceases disabling access to it not less than 10, nor more than 14, business days following receipt of the counter notice, unless its designated agent first receives notice from the person who submitted the notification under subsection (c)(1) (C) that such person has filed an action seeking a court order to restrain the subscriber from engaging in infringing activity relating to the material on the service provider's system or network.

(3) CONTENTS OF COUNTER NOTIFICATION—To be effective under this subsection, a counter notification must be a written communication provided to the service provider's designated agent that includes substantially the following:

(A) A physical or electronic signature of the subscriber.

(B) Identification of the material that has been removed or to which access has been disabled and the location at which the material appeared before it was removed or access to it was disabled.

(C) A statement under penalty of perjury that the subscriber has a good faith belief that the material was removed or disabled as a result of mistake or misidentification of the material to be removed or disabled.

(D) The subscriber's name, address, and telephone number, and a statement that the subscriber consents to the jurisdiction of Federal District Court for the judicial district in which the address is located, or if the subscriber's address is outside of the United States, for any judicial district in which the service provider may be found, and that the subscriber will accept service of process from the person who provided notification under subsection (c)(1)(C) or an agent of such person.

(4) LIMITATION ON OTHER LIABILITY—A service provider's compliance with paragraph (2) shall not subject the service provider to liability for copyright infringement with respect to the material identified in the notice provided under subsection (c)(1)(C).

(h) SUBPOENA TO IDENTIFY INFRINGER—

(1) REQUEST—A copyright owner or a person authorized to act on the owner's behalf may request the clerk of any United States district court to issue a subpoena to a service provider for identification of an alleged infringer in accordance with this subsection.

(2) CONTENTS OF REQUEST—The request may be made by filing with the clerk—

(A) a copy of a notification described in subsection (c)(3)(A);

(B) a proposed subpoena; and

(C) a sworn declaration to the effect that the purpose for which the subpoena is sought is to obtain the identity of an alleged infringer and that such information will only be used for the purpose of protecting rights under this title.

(3) CONTENTS OF SUBPOENA—The subpoena shall authorize and order the service provider receiving the notification and the subpoena to expeditiously disclose to the copyright owner or person authorized by the copyright owner information sufficient to identify the alleged infringer of the material described in the notification to the extent such information is available to the service provider.

(4) BASIS FOR GRANTING SUBPOENA—If the notification filed

satisfies the provisions of subsection (c)(3)(A), the proposed subpoena is in proper form, and the accompanying declaration is properly executed, the clerk shall expeditiously issue and sign the proposed subpoena and return it to the requester for delivery to the service provider.

(5) ACTIONS OF SERVICE PROVIDER RECEIVING SUBPOENA— Upon receipt of the issued subpoena, either accompanying or subsequent to the receipt of a notification described in subsection (c)(3)(A), the service provider shall expeditiously disclose to the copyright owner or person authorized by the copyright owner the information required by the subpoena, notwithstanding any other provision of law and regardless of whether the service provider responds to the notification.

(6) RULES APPLICABLE TO SUBPOENA—Unless otherwise provided by this section or by applicable rules of the court, the procedure for issuance and delivery of the subpoena, and the remedies for noncompliance with the subpoena, shall be governed to the greatest extent practicable by those provisions of the Federal Rules of Civil Procedure governing the issuance, service, and enforcement of a subpoena duces tecum.

(i) CONDITIONS FOR ELIGIBILITY—

(1) ACCOMMODATION OF TECHNOLOGY—The limitations on liability established by this section shall apply to a service provider only if the service provider—

(A) has adopted and reasonably implemented, and informs subscribers and account holders of the service provider's system or network of, a policy that provides for the termination in appropriate circumstances of subscribers and account holders of the service provider's system or network who are repeat infringers; and

(B) accommodates and does not interfere with standard technical measures.

(2) DEFINITION—As used in this subsection, the term "standard technical measures" means technical measures that are used by copyright owners to identify or protect copyrighted works and—

(A) have been developed pursuant to a broad consensus of copyright owners and service providers in an open, fair, voluntary, multi-industry standards process;

(B) are available to any person on reasonable and nondiscriminatory terms; and

(C) do not impose substantial costs on service providers or substantial burdens on their systems or networks.

(j) INJUNCTIONS—The following rules shall apply in the case of any application for an injunction under section 502 against a service provider that is not subject to monetary remedies under this section:

(1) SCOPE OF RELIEF—(A) With respect to conduct other than that which qualifies for the limitation on remedies set forth in subsection (a), the court may grant injunctive relief with respect to a service provider only in one

or more of the following forms:

(i) An order restraining the service provider from providing access to infringing material or activity residing at a particular online site on the provider's system or network.

(ii) An order restraining the service provider from providing access to a subscriber or account holder of the service provider's system or network who is engaging in infringing activity and is identified in the order, by terminating the accounts of the subscriber or account holder that are specified in the order.

(iii) Such other injunctive relief as the court may consider necessary to prevent or restrain infringement of copyrighted material specified in the order of the court at a particular online location, if such relief is the least burdensome to the service provider among the forms of relief comparably effective for that purpose.

(B) If the service provider qualifies for the limitation on remedies described in subsection (a), the court may only grant injunctive relief in one or both of the following forms:

(i) An order restraining the service provider from providing access to a subscriber or account holder of the service provider's system or network who is using the provider's service to engage in infringing activity and is identified in the order, by terminating the accounts of the subscriber or account holder that are specified in the order.

(ii) An order restraining the service provider from providing access, by taking reasonable steps specified in the order to block access, to a specific, identified, online location outside the United States.

(2) CONSIDERATIONS—The court, in considering the relevant criteria for injunctive relief under applicable law, shall consider—

(A) whether such an injunction, either alone or in combination with other such injunctions issued against the same service provider under this subsection, would significantly burden either the provider or the operation of the provider's system or network;

(B) the magnitude of the harm likely to be suffered by the copyright owner in the digital network environment if steps are not taken to prevent or restrain the infringement;

(C) whether implementation of such an injunction would be technically feasible and effective, and would not interfere with access to noninfringing material at other online locations; and

(D) whether other less burdensome and comparably effective means of preventing or restraining access to the infringing material are available.

(3) NOTICE AND EX PARTE ORDERS—Injunctive relief under this subsection shall be available only after notice to the service provider and an opportunity for the service provider to appear are provided, except for orders ensuring the preservation of evidence or other orders having no material

adverse effect on the operation of the service provider's communications network.

(k) DEFINITIONS—

(1) SERVICE PROVIDER—(A) As used in subsection (a), the term "service provider" means an entity offering the transmission, routing, or providing of connections for digital online communications, between or among points specified by a user, of material of the user's choosing, without modification to the content of the material as sent or received.

(B) As used in this section, other than subsection (a), the term "service provider" means a provider of online services or network access, or the operator of facilities therefor, and includes an entity described in subparagraph (A).

(2) MONETARY RELIEF—As used in this section, the term "monetary relief" means damages, costs, attorneys' fees, and any other form of monetary payment.

(l) OTHER DEFENSES NOT AFFECTED—The failure of a service provider's conduct to qualify for limitation of liability under this section shall not bear adversely upon the consideration of a defense by the service provider that the service provider's conduct is not infringing under this title or any other defense.

(m) PROTECTION OF PRIVACY—Nothing in this section shall be construed to condition the applicability of subsections (a) through (d) on (1) a service provider monitoring its service or affirmatively seeking facts indicating infringing activity, except to the extent consistent with a standard technical measure complying with the provisions of subsection (i); or (2) a service provider gaining access to, removing, or disabling access to material in cases in which such conduct is prohibited by law.

(n) CONSTRUCTION—Subsections (a), (b), (c), and (d) describe separate and distinct functions for purposes of applying this section. Whether a service provider qualifies for the limitation on liability in any one of those subsections shall be based solely on the criteria in that subsection, and shall not affect a determination of whether that service provider qualifies for the limitations on liability under any other such subsection.

E

American Federation of Musicians Interactive/New Media Projects [Non-Symphonic]

Editor's Note: Appendix E consists of substantially abridged excerpts from the American Federation of Musicians Interactive/New Media Projects. It is intended to provide a basic idea of the wages and conditions addressed in this agreement. However, interactive/new media agreements are complicated and subject to change. It is important for you to contact the AFM directly if you have specific questions.

The following is informational and to be used as a guideline only. It is essential to contact the AFM for a Special Agreement for each project. Each of these rates will continue to be subject to negotiation within the context of each individual project. For commercials call 323-461-3441 x206. All other requests call 323-461-3441 x202. You may also visit our Web site at: www.afm.org. For information on symphonic projects call 212-869-1330 x225

Term:

One year experimental rates (as of 3/25/2000). These are subject to change in the future.

Benefits (for Categories I, II & III):

1. Pension Fund Contribution—10%
2. Health & Welfare Fund Contribution—$15 per 12-hour day per musician to the Local Health & Welfare Fund in whose jurisdiction the work is performed.

Additional Session Information (for Categories I, II & III):

1. Leader/Contractor to receive double scale.

2. Doubling—1st double—30% of basic rate, 2nd double 15% of basic rate and each subsequent double.
3. Music Preparation—Copyists, Orchestrators and Arrangers are to be paid in accordance with the applicable rates set forth in the now current Basic Theatrical Motion Picture Agreement scale wages, with the same benefits as the playing musicians. (See Plateau payment, Category I, Option 1, for music preparation payment upon sale of 25,000 units.)
4. Motion Picture/TV Film premium pay provisions, including time span, etc., shall apply throughout.

Report Forms:

All sessions must be reported on a B-7 Report Form (with the exception of commercials, which must be reported on a B-6 Report Form). In the memo field, note type of project i.e., Interactive CD-Rom, DVD or Menu Music for the Internet/WWW, etc., per Special Agreement with AFM. Be sure to attach a copy of the Special Agreement to all payments, including Wages, Pension, H&W. Pension and Health and Welfare benefits will not be applied to any project not under an AFM Special Agreement.

CATEGORY I—CD-ROM, DVD & Dedicated Console Platforms.
Final product to include games, entertainment, promotional and educational areas:

Option 1—Plateau Payment:

a. Regular Session (plus benefits)

	3-Hour Minimum	Overtime (OT) ½ Hour
	15 mins recorded music max	2 ½ minutes recorded music
Per musician	$250	$41.67

Upon the sale of 25,000 units, an additional fee of $250, plus 10% pension will be due each side musician & copyist (double scale for leader, contractor, musician performing alone, arranger & orchestrator). No further payment will be due.

b. Multi-Tracking Rates[1] (plus benefits)

	3-Hour Minimum	OT ¼ Hour
Per musician	$230/hour	19.17

[1]Option to use these rates must be exercised prior to session call and with prior notification to musician(s), this will allow unlimited multiple parts and doubles, with a maximum of ten hours worked at straight time.

Upon the sale of 25,000 units, an additional fee equal to the Electronic Multi-Tracking wages earned at the time of original session, plus 10% pension will be due. No further payment will apply.

Option 2—One Time Payment Only (Musicians must be informed prior to session):

a. Regular Session (plus benefits)

	3-Hour Minimum	OT ½ Hour
	15 mins recorded music max	2½ minutes recorded music
Per musician	$400	$66.67

No further payment due.

b. Multi-Tracking Rates[1] (plus benefits)

	3-Hour Minimum	OT ¼ Hour
Per musician	$368/hour	30.67

[1]Option to use these rates must be exercised prior to session call and with prior notification to musician(s), this will allow unlimited multiple parts and doubles, with a maximum of ten hours worked at straight time.

No further payment will be due.

CATEGORY II—Theme & menu Music, Web Site and Web Link music for the Internet & WWW, Online Services (AOL, etc.), Interactive Cable Stations, Virtual Reality Rides and Kiosks.

LENGTH OF SESSION TO BE ANNOUNCED AT TIME OF CALL

a. Regular Session (plus benefits)

	1-Hour Minimum	OT ¼ Hour
	5 mins recorded music max*	1¼ mins recorded music*
Per musician	$100	$25

*In long or short formats.

b. Multi-Tracking Rates[1] (plus benefits)

	1-Hour Minimum	OT ¼ Hour
Per musician	$275/hour	$68.75

[1] Option to use these rates must be exercised prior to session call and with prior notification to musician(s), this will allow unlimited multiple parts and doubles, with a maximum of ten hours worked at straight time.

After one year's use, re-use fees based on original session fee, will be prorated and due in quarterly segments.

CATEGORY III—Live Performances on the Internet/WWW

> **The use of these live performances on the Internet/WWW requires advance notice to the Federation and the signing of a Special Agreement.**

Note: There will be no scale rate distinction between the use of audio/video, audio only or video only.

Option I: Live Performance for exclusive Internet/WWW use only (plus benefits)

	1-Hour Minimum	OT ¼ Hour
Per musician	$165/hour	$41.25

After initial use period of 6 months, a payment of $65 to each musician for every 6 month period will apply.

Option II: Live Performance for Internet/WWW/combined with other live performance or electronic media service (plus pension)

	1-Hour Minimum	OT ¼ Hour
Per musician	$65*/hour	$16.25

*This is in addition to the applicable live performance scale, established through a collective bargaining agreement or through a general/casual wage scale book.

After initial use period of 6 months, a payment of $65 to each musician for every 6 month period will apply.

CATEGORY IV—Commercials on the Internet/WWW

A Special Agreement must be drafted for each project. Contact the administrator at the AFM West Coast office—323-461-3441 ext. 206.

CATEGORY V—Commercials on Kiosks

A Special Agreement must be drafted for each project. Contact the administrator at the AFM West Coast office—323-461-3441 ext. 206.

CATEGORY VI—Re-use of existing Recorded and/or Recorded and Filmed or Taped Performances

Each of these varies according to the amount of music or length of clips utilized and the source(s) of these clips or tracks. Each project is being individually negotiated with the producer. A Special Agreement is then drafted and signed covering such use. Contact the administrator at the AFM West Coast Office—323-461-3441 x202

CATEGORY VII—Use on Enhanced CDs and CD-Plus:

These vary according to the amount of music or length of clips utilized, the source(s) of these clips or tracks, and whether they involve a self-contained or royalty group and/or studio musicians. Each project is negotiated individually. A Special Agreement is then drafted and signed covering such use. Contact our administrator at the AFM West Coast Office—323-461-3441 x202

F

Music Industry Resources on the Internet

Alliance of Artists and Recording Companies (AARC)
www.riaa.com/aarc.htm
1330 Connecticut Ave., NW
Suite 300
Washington, DC 20036
tel: 202-775-0101

American Federation of Musicians
www.afm.org
1501 Broadway, Suite 600
New York, NY 10036
tel: 212-869-1330
fax: 212-764-6134

American Federation of Television and Radio Artists
www.aftra.com/home/html
260 Madison Avenue
New York, NY 10016-2402
tel: 212-532-0800
fax: 212-532-2242

American Mechanical Rights Agency (AMRA)
www.amermechrights.com
1818 Century Park E., Suite 222
Los Angeles, CA 90067
tel: 310-785-1600
fax: 310-785-1800

American Society of Composers, Authors, and Publishers (ASCAP)
www.ascap.com
1 Lincoln Plaza
New York, NY 10023
tel: 212-621-6000

Australasian Performing Right Association (APMRA)
www.apra.com.au/FrameSet.htm
6-12 Atchison St.
St. Leaonard's NSW 2065
tel: 02-9935-7900
fax: 02-00-35-7999

Broadcast Music Incorporated (BMI)
www.bmi.com
320 West 57th Street
New York, NY 10019
tel: 212-586-2000

Canadian Music Reproduction Rights Agency (CMRRA)
www.cmrra.ca/home4/home4.html
50 Eellesley St. West #320
Toronto, Ontario M5S 2S3
Canada
tel: 416-926-1966
fax: 416-926-7521

Copyright Agency Limited (CAL)
www.copyright.com/au
Level 19, 157 Liverpool Street
Sydney NSW 2000
Australia
tel: 61-2-9394-7600
fax: 61-2-9394-7601

Dutch Performing and Mechanical Rights Society (BUMA)
www.buma.nl
Prof. E.M. Meijerslaan 3
1180 AS Amstelveen
Holland
tel:020-34-70-911

Gesellshaft für Musikalishe Aufführungs (GEMA)
www.gema.de
Bayreuther
Strasse 37
1087 Berlin
Germany
tel: 030-21-245-00
fax: 030-21-245-950

Harry Fox Agency (HFA)
www.nmpa.org/hfa.html
711 3rd Avenue
New York, NY 10017
tel: 212-370-5330
fax: 212-953-2384

International Confederation of Societies of Authors and Composers (CISAC)
www.cmrra.ca/home4.html
11, rue kepler
75116 Paris
France
tel: 33-2-53-57-34-00
fax: 33-1-53-57-34-10

International Federation of the Phonographic Industry (IFPI)
www.ifpi.org
54 Regent St.
London W1R 5PJ
England
tel: 171-878-7900

Latin American Federation of Phonographic Industry (ISPI)
www.ispi.org
804 Douglas Rd. Suite 373
Coral Gables, FL 33134
tel: 305-567-0861

Mechanical Copyright Protection Society (MCPS)
www.mcps.co.uk/
Elgar House
41 Streatham High Rd.
London SW16 1ER
England
tel: 020-8769-4400
fax: 020-8378-7300

Motion Picture Association of America (MPAA)
www.mpaa.org
1600 Eye Street
Washington, D.C. 20006
tel: 202-293-1966

National Academy of Recording Arts & Sciences, Inc.
www.grammy.com/academy
3402 Pico Boulevard
Santa Monica, CA 90405
tel: 310-392-3777

National Music Publishers Association (NMPA)
www.nmpa.org
711 3rd Ave.
New York, NY 10017
tel: 212-370-5330
fax: 212-953-2384

Recording Industries Music Performance Trust Funds
www.mptf.org
1501 Broadway
Suite 401
Washngton, DC 20036
tel: 212-391-3950

Recording Industry Association of America (RIAA)
www.riaa.com
1330 Connecticut Avenue, NW
Suite 300
Washington, DC 20036
tel: 202-775-0101

Société du Droit de Reproduction des Auteurs (SODRAC)
www.sodrac.com/anglais/index.html
759 Victoria Square
Suite 420
Montreal PQ H2Y 2J7
Canada
tel: 514-845-3268
fax: 514-845-3401

Society of European Authors and Composers (SESAC)
www.sesac.com
421 W. 54th St.
New York, NY 10019
tel: 212-586-3450

Songwriter's Guild of America
www.songwriters.org
1500 Harbor Boulevard
Weehawken, NJ 07087
tel: 201-867-7603
fax: 201-867-7535

U.S. Copyright Office
lcweb.loc.gov/copyright
101 Independence Avenue, SE
Washington, DC 20559-6000
tel: 202-707-6737

Index

A&R (artists and repertoire)
executives, 13, 16, 19, 34, 37
See also Contract(s)
ABC, 285
Accountings
artist, 29
compulsory license, 178–179
foreign distribution, 55
independent producer, 45–46
performing rights organization,
309–310
songwriter, 193–194
subpublishing, 242–243
Account stated clause, 29
ACUM, 183
Adaptations. *See* Arrangements and
adaptations
ADD (analog to digital), 89
Adelphia, 79
Ad Hoc Committee on Copyright
Law Revision, 109
Advances
foreign distribution, 48–49, 53
loans to music publishers and,
316–317
payments from, 42, 43
performing rights organization,
152–153, 168, 316–317
producer, 43
recording funds as, 23–24,
40–41
songwriter, 168, 198–200,
316–317
union scale and, 14
Advertising
commercial jingles, 215, 283–291
costs of, 193
endorsements in, 417
promotional equality in, 415–416
scale payments for commercials,
60–61
testimonials in, 417
use of name or likeness for,
326–327, 349
Aeolian Company, 175
AFM. *See* American Federation of
Musicians
AFTRA. *See* American Federation
of Television and Radio Artists
Agent(s), 351–361
general talent agencies, 351, 420
licensing, 174, 255, 279
merchandising rights, 327–328
minors and, 34–35
shoppers, 359, 402–405
See also Contract(s)
Ain't Nothin' but the Blues, 276,
281
Almo Irving, 296
Album(s)
categories, 431–432
compilation. *See* Compilation
albums
contingent-scale payments, 61
as copyrightable works, 74–75
cover records, 54, 148, 150,
176–177, 209, 238,
290–291
covers, 55

increasing emphasis on, 38
packaging. *See* Packaging
recording costs, 23
royalty rate, 20
sound-alikes, 417
titles, 87–88
See also Motion-picture
soundtracks; Original-cast
albums; Singles
Alden-Rochelle v. *ASCAP*, 261
Allen and Company, 155
Alliance of Artists and Recording
Companies (AARC), 69, 78
All-in-one royalty agreements,
21–22, 39
All Platinum, 30
Ally McBeal, 266
Alternative minimum tax, 370
Amalfi resolution, 150
amazon.com, 6, 221, 449–450
AMCOS, 182
American Arbitration Association
(AAA), 60, 198
American Association of
Publishers (AAP), 221–222
American Bar Association, 312–313
American Civil Liberties Union
(ACLU), 91
American Federation of Musicians
(AFM)
agent regulation, 358
contractors, 65, 361
contracts with instrumentalists,
15, 45, 282
demo records, 401
dubbing, 65–66
dues, 59
Electronic and Media Services
Division, 66
illicit practices, protection
against, 66–67
as information source, 341–342
labor agreements with, 59–70
membership, 59, 64, 254
merchandising rights, 327–328
Motion Picture Special
Payments Fund, 62
Music Performance Trust Fund,
48, 385
new rights for performing
artists, 69
Phonograph Record Labor
Agreement, 60, 62–63
Phonograph Record Trust Fund,
60, 62, 63
promotional videotapes, 69–70
recording territory, 68–69
reuse fees, 64, 265, 266, 271
royalty performers, 64–65
scale payments, 14, 45, 60,
61–62, 64, 282, 401,
427–428, 535–539
Special Payments Funds, 48, 60,
62–63, 385
work permits for foreign artists,
427–428
American Federation of Television
and Radio Artists (AFTRA)
agent regulation, 358
Code of Fair Practice for
Phonograph Recordings,
60, 67–68

commercial jingle singles,
289–290
contractors, 65
demo records, 401
dubbing, 66
dues and initiation fee, 59
Health Fund, 60, 61, 64, 67
illicit practices, protection
against, 66–68
labor agreements with, 59–70
membership, 59
names of members, 341
new rights for performing
artists, 69
nonroyalty performers, 61
promotional videotapes, 69–70
recording territory, 68
Retirement Fund, 60, 61, 64, 67
reuse fees, 265, 266, 271–272
royalty performers, 64–65
scale payments, 14, 45, 60–61,
64–65, 67, 289–290, 401
Sound Recording Code, 69–70
American Guild of Authors and
Composers, 210
American Guild of Variety Artists
(AGVA), 341, 358
American Mechanical Rights
Agency (AMRA), 181, 255
American Society of Composers,
Authors, and Publishers
(ASCAP), 153–154
ACE, 154, 456
advances, 152–153, 168, 316–317
ASCAP Hit Songs, 139
awards to writers, 170
blanket license, 153, 261
catalog of songs in repertoire,
137–138, 153–154, 439
clearing function, 152–153
collections for members, 5,
151–153, 158, 159, 170–172
commercial jingles, 284–286,
288
consent decree, 161–163, 253,
268
copyright issues, 78, 127, 149,
208–209, 212
credits, 165–166, 284–285
dramatic performance rights,
172–173
dues, 163
EZ-Eagle, 154, 455–456
Fairness in Music Licensing Act
(1999), 9, 164
grievance procedures, 161–162,
195
as information source, 300, 332,
341–342, 439–440
insurance plans, 169
international information
collection, 157, 170–172
Internet effect on, 455–456
loan assistance, 169, 307,
309–310
membership, 162–164, 253–254
payments for music used in
commercials, 284–285
payment system, 164–166,
285–286
qualified work designation, 166
RateCalc, 154, 456